Celebrating
What Is Important to Me

East
Grades 4-6
Spring 2006

Creative Communication, Inc.

Celebrating What Is Important to Me
East
Grades 4-6
Spring 2006

An anthology compiled by Creative Communication, Inc.

Published by:

CREATIVE COMMUNICATION, INC.
1488 NORTH 200 WEST
LOGAN, UT   84341

Copyright © 2006 by Creative Communication, Inc.
Printed in the United States of America

ISBN 1-60050-017-X

Foreword

Welcome! This anthology is filled with the words of our youth. We are proud to provide this outlet for young writers. These essays would have been lost in a backpack or discarded when a school assignment was completed. By preserving the essays in this anthology we have recorded a slice of our youths' history. Thank you for participating in this project.

As we work with teachers and students across the United States and Canada, we have learned several things. Our youth are hard working, caring and bright. The youth today have challenges placed before them, but they are rising to the occasion. The essays included in this anthology reflect youth who care about their world; youth who care about their future; youth who want to succeed. We hope that by recognizing the young writers in this anthology, we have provided an extra motivation that moves them toward a future of success.

In our Fall 2005 edition we experimented with a new format for the anthology. In that anthology we did not provide an individual page for the winners of the essay contest. After receiving feedback from many students and teachers, we have gone back to the original layout. The Top Ten Winners receive their own page in this anthology. They have earned it. We also congratulate the other writers who did not make the Top Ten, but were accepted to be published. By being included between these pages, they have proven themselves to be better writers than most of the other students in this region. Congratulations.

The Top Ten Essays were chosen by students and teachers across the United States and Canada. Through online voting we were able to use Creative Communication's judges and peer review to choose the Top Ten.

We hope you enjoy this anthology. By reading the fears, hopes and dreams of these young writers, we have provided an insight into each of their lives. We are pleased to present the essays in this anthology.

Gaylen Worthen, President
Creative Communication

WRITING CONTESTS!

Enter our next POETRY contest!
Enter our next ESSAY contest!

Why should I enter?

Win prizes and get published! Each year thousands of dollars in prizes are awarded in each region and tens of thousands of dollars in prizes are awarded throughout North America. The top writers in each division receive a monetary award and a free book that includes their published poem or essay. Entries of merit are also selected to be published in our anthology.

Who may enter?

There are five divisions in the poetry contest. The poetry divisions are grades K-3, 4-6, 7-9, 10-12, and adult. There are three divisions in the essay contest. The essay division are grades 4-6, 7-9, and 10-12.

What is needed to enter the contest?

To enter the poetry contest send in one original poem, 21 lines or less. To enter the essay contest send in one original essay, 250 words or less, on any topic. Each entry must include the writer's name, address, city, state and zip code. Student entries need to include the student's grade, school name and school address. Students who include their teacher's name may help the teacher qualify for a free copy of the anthology.

How do I enter?

Enter a poem online at:
www.poeticpower.com
or

Mail your poem to:
    Poetry Contest
    1488 North 200 West
    Logan, UT 84341

Enter an essay online at:
www.studentessaycontest.com
or

Mail your essay to:
    Essay Contest
    1488 North 200 West
    Logan, UT 84341

If you are mailing your poetry entry, please write "Student Contest" at the top of your poem if you are in grades K-12. Please write "Adult Contest" at the top of your poem if you are entering the adult division.

When is the deadline?

Poetry contest deadlines are August 15th, December 5th, and April 5th. Essay contest deadlines are October 17th, February 15th, and July 18th. You can enter each contest, however, send only one poem or essay for each contest deadline.

Are there benefits for my school?

Yes. We award $15,000 each year in grants to help with Language Arts programs. Schools qualify to apply for a grant by having a large number of entries of which over fifty percent are accepted for publication. This typically tends to be about 15 accepted entries.

Are there benefits for my teacher?

Yes. Teachers with five or more students accepted to be published receive a free anthology that includes their students' writing.

For more information please go to our website at **www.poeticpower.com**, email us at editor@poeticpower.com or call 435-713-4411.

Table of Contents

States included in this edition:

Connecticut
Delaware
District of Columbia
Maryland
Maine
Massachusetts
New Hampshire
New Jersey
New York
Pennsylvania
Rhode Island
Vermont
Virginia

Spring 2006 Writing Achievement Honor Schools

* Teachers who had fifteen or more students accepted to be published

The following schools are recognized as receiving a "Writing Achievement Award." This award is given to schools who have a large number of entries of which over fifty percent are accepted for publication. With hundreds of schools entering our contest, only a small percent of these schools are honored with this award. The purpose of this award is to recognize schools with excellent Language Arts programs. This award qualifies these schools to receive a complimentary copy of this anthology. In addition, these schools are eligible to apply for a Creative Communication Language Arts Grant. Grants of two hundred and fifty dollars each are awarded to further develop writing in our schools.

Al-Rahmah School
Baltimore, MD
Taihisa Abdul-Aziz*

Assumption School
Atco, NJ
Karen Gulla*

Bellport Middle School
Bellport, NY
Christine Napolitano*

Burgettstown Elementary Center
Burgettstown, PA
Lorraine MacFarlane*

Christian Brothers Academy
Albany, NY
Diane Babble
Eileen Loomis

East Lake Elementary School
Massapequa Park, NY
Kim Cawley*

Edmond P Talbot Middle School
Fall River, MA
Susan Makuch*

Edmunds Consolidated School
Edmunds, ME
Sally Fitzsimmons*

Eugene A Tighe Middle School
Margate City, NJ
Roseann Cahill*
Amie E. Sykes*

Fairview Middle School
Fairview, PA
Pamela Hurt*

George L Hess Educational Complex
Mays Landing, NJ
Maria Sarno
Jennifer Schairer

George Staley Middle School
Rome, NY
Anthony D. Lanzi*

Gilmore J Fisher Middle School
Ewing, NJ
Regina Wachter*

Hillside Elementary School
Montclair, NJ
Lisa Frankle
Dr. Saundra Woody*

Huber Street School
Secaucus, NJ
Kelly Waters*

Hudson Falls Intermediate School
Hudson Falls, NY
Suzanne Buell
Chris Kugler
Heather McLaughlin
Tim Paris
Kyle Porter

John J Flynn Elementary School
Burlington, VT
Karen R. Paquette
Dave Weissenstein

Marlton Christian Academy
Marlton, NJ
Nancy Kaluka*

Mother Seton Parochial School
Union City, NJ
Adrian Cortes
Lorraine DePinto
Alex Pino
Catherine Rivera

Our Lady of Assumption School
Lynnfield, MA
B. Monagle*

Our Lady of Grace Elementary School
Pittsburgh, PA
Kirstina Popey*

Parkville Middle School and Center of
Technology
Baltimore, MD
Scott Bayne
Linda Posten*

Roselle Park Middle School
Roselle Park, NJ
Joanne Carbotti
Giuliana Melo

Sacred Heart of Jesus School
Dupont, PA
James Renfer*

Saints Mary and Elizabeth Academy
Linden, NJ
Nellie Cummins*

Shelter Rock Elementary School
Manhasset, NY
Mr. Collyer
Mrs. Lawrence
Mrs. Mitchell
Joyce Rappaport
Mr. Sirof

Southwest Academy
Baltimore, MD
Mrs. Mitchell*

St Alexis School
Wexford, PA
Sandra Ross*

St Hilary of Poitiers School
Rydal, PA
Mary Ann Powell
Patricia Sermarini*

St John School
Goshen, NY
Arlene Melillo*

St John the Baptist School
Silver Spring, MD
Mrs. Jenkins*
Amy Ruggles

St Mary School
Milford, CT
Paula J. Eisenhandler*

St Stephen's School
Grand Island, NY
Sarah Lazewski
Jennifer O'Laughlin*

Stafford Elementary School
Bristol, CT
Susan Nichols
Neil O'Rourke
Michael Tartarelli

Thomas R Grover Middle School
Princeton Junction, NJ
Ginny McNeil
Pam Twiggs*

Victor Intermediate School
Victor, NY
Beth McKee*

Waverly Yowell Elementary School
Madison, VA
Mr. Kubricki
Michele Reuss*

West Allegheny Middle School
Imperial, PA
Deana Mack*

Language Arts
Grant Recipients
2005-2006

After receiving a "Writing Achievement Award" schools are encouraged to apply for a Creative Communication Language Arts Grant. The following is a list of schools who received a two hundred and fifty dollar grant for the 2005-2006 school year.

Acushnet Elementary School – Acushnet, MA
Admiral Thomas H. Moorer Middle School – Eufaula, AL
Alta High School – Sandy, UT
Alton R-IV Elementary School – Alton, MO
Archbishop McNicholas High School – Cincinnati, OH
Barbara Bush Elementary School – Mesa, AZ
Bellmar Middle School – Belle Vernon, PA
Bonham High School – Bonham, TX
Cool Spring Elementary School – Cleveland, NC
Douglas Elementary School – Liberty, KY
Dumbarton Middle School – Baltimore, MD
Edward Bleeker Jr High School – Flushing, NY
Emmanuel/St. Michael Lutheran School – Fort Wayne, IN
Floyds Knobs Elementary School – Floyds Knobs, IN
Fox Creek High School – North Augusta, SC
Friendship Jr High School – Des Plaines, IL
Gibson City-Melvin-Sibley High School – Gibson City, IL
Hamilton Jr High School – Hamilton, TX
John F. Kennedy Middle School – Cupertino, CA
John Ross Elementary School – Edmond, OK
MacLeod Public School – Sudbury, ON
McKinley Elementary School – Livonia, MI
Monte Cassino School – Tulsa, OK
New Germany Elementary School – New Germany, NS
North Beach Elementary School – Miami Beach, FL
Paradise Valley High School – Phoenix, AZ
Parkview Christian School – Lincoln, NE
Picayune Jr High School – Picayune, MS
Red Bank Charter School – Red Bank, NJ
Sebastian River Middle School – Sebastian, FL
Siegrist Elementary School – Platte City, MO

Language Arts Grant Winners cont.

Southwest Academy – Baltimore, MD
St. Anthony School – Winsted, CT
St. John Vianney Catholic School – Flint, MI
St. Paul the Apostle School – Davenport, IA
St. Rose School – Roseville, CA
St. Sebastian School – Pittsburgh, PA
Sundance Elementary School – Sundance, WY
Thorp Middle School – Thorp, WI
Townsend Harris High School – Flushing, NY
Warren Elementary School – Warren, OR
Washington High School – Washington Court House, OH
Wasilla Lake Christian School – Wasilla, AK
Woodland Elementary School – Radcliff, KY
Worthington High School – Worthington, MN

Grades 4-5-6

Top Essay Grades 4-5-6

Winter

The most anticipated season of the year for me is winter. As the leaves turn crisp and dry they gently fall to the ground. To many people this is a given sign of the upcoming season of winter. I know that winter is coming when the temperature gradually drops making way for the intricately designed pieces of Mother Nature's artwork to come down to the ground as frosty snow.

For many hours or sometimes even days, I watch and wait for the last snowflake to fall. I wait patiently in the warmth of my house before coming out and meeting the blistering snow and wind hitting my face like flying prickly quills. With my many layers of clothing to keep me warm, I begin my adventure trying to keep my balance as I step carefully on the deep snow. Although this snow seems like the ultimate plaything to me and others like me who share the same love for snow, it is dreaded by most adults. Shoveling snow entails back-breaking work that many people try to avoid.

The most common snow creation of all is the "snow ball." Its size may vary from inches to a few feet wide in diameter and it can be used from making snow sculptures to projectiles for paltering. I particularly enjoy making snow forts. It takes skill, determination, and judgment to make the best snow fort. You have to pick out the perfect sized block of snow to fit like a puzzle, making sure to keep it balanced and sturdy.

Winter is one of the most loved seasons. The natural beauty and purity of a snowy winter makes me think of all the different wonders that have come to me at that moment. Surely this proves it is the best season of them all.

Matthew Bernardo
Grade 5

Top Essay Grades 4-5-6

Remembering New Orleans

Hurricane Katrina struck the Gulf Coast over five months ago, but people are still recovering from it. When I think of New Orleans, I remember the people, the food, and the wonderful places. I try to imagine how the city will look the next time I visit my grandparents there. I desperately hope this city will be somewhat the same!

Most importantly, I hope the people of New Orleans can return. New Orleans has always been a culturally diverse city, but most of the people left after the hurricane. All of the New Orleanians were very friendly as well. Many inspiring street musicians left, too.

After I think about the people of New Orleans, I start imagining the food. Some people will miss the red beans and rice, but if I were from New Orleans, I would miss the beignets, or French doughnuts. During Mardi Gras (meaning Fat Tuesday) the people serve delicious king cakes!

Last but not least, I remember the parks and buildings in New Orleans. Many of the buildings were beautiful, unique homes. The city's parks have huge old oak trees with low hanging Spanish moss in them. I also remember the Audubon Zoo and all its animals. Hurricane Katrina affected all these places.

Even though I have only visited New Orleans, I have many special memories of the people, the food, and the wonderful places. I hope the New Orleanians are able to experience these things again.

Mollie Donohue-Meyer
Grade 4

Top Essay Grades 4-5-6

Heroes of Today

Heroes are not just found in story books; they are found in the real world, too. Heroes are a necessity in our life because they are people who protect us and serve our country. Selflessly, they demonstrate sacrifice, are looked up to, and inspire us. They are regular people performing extraordinary things.

An example of someone who demonstrates sacrifice is my dad. He sacrifices his safety every day at work in the Pentagon. His office is on the same side of the building the terrorists hit on 9/11. Serving our country at work, each day he knows the danger of it happening again.

Heroes are looked up to by others because they show us how to live and are respectable examples. People look up to firefighters for their good deeds, because they risk their lives to save people from flames. These great men and women are models for everyone to follow their lead in helping others.

These popular figures inspire us as a nation and as individuals. They urge us to help those in need and try new things. There are many people in this world who are looked up to as heroes but do not think themselves heroes. They are noble people who do their best in their jobs and encourage us to do our best.

To conclude, heroes sacrifice their lives that we might be safe. We look up to them. They inspire us to assist our country. Without heroes, our country would not be the same.

Ashley Fancher
Grade 6

Top Essay Grades 4-5-6

Friendship

The dictionary meanings of friendship are "the state of being friends," and "a liking between friends." When I think of friendship I think of acceptance. A good friend always accepts another for who they are. Friendship is dwelling on the common interests of one another, not the differences. Friendship is finding the good in another, when others can't see the good. Friendship is hanging around and doing nothing, yet still having a great time together.

A toy or a present are both easy objects to give to someone. They are usually temporary and do not last long. However, friendship is something one can give to another. It is not always easily given, yet can last a lifetime.

Friendship can be given to any living thing. There are friendships between people and there are friendships between people and animals. Friendships teach individuals how to love and respect others. A good friendship teaches patience and compassion for others. Friendships are something that every living thing needs to survive. It is just as important as food and water. Friendships help a person's emotional and mental growth. It makes an individual have good self-esteem and confidence. Friendship is a very important tool to a healthy life.

Each person will hopefully have many friendships in their lifetime. Friendships will come and go. Strong and solid friendships will last forever. Friendships help to create a happy life. I hope I always find good friends and in turn am a good friend to another.

Connor Fitzpatrick
Grade 6

Top Essay Grades 4-5-6

What Is Small, Green, and Deadly

It was a sunny day in peaceful Hillsborough. My benevolent father was baking the worst food in the world. This food is feared by all kids. Little did I know that I was in for a disaster! It was like a lethal tornado attacking a vulnerable town. I was the vulnerable town.

My father hollered to my brother and me, "Time to wash up, it's dinner time." We slowly walked to the bathroom. I washed my hands thoroughly. I sat down in my comfortable chair. My cantankerous brother was still washing his grubby hands. He eventually sat down at our waiting table. Once I saw the contemptuous entrée I was petrified. It was like the food was a terrorist attacking me with full strength. It was the horrible *Brussels sprouts!*

I thought my life would be at an end once I ate that disgusting trash adults call food. My dad encouraged me to gobble it all down. I was miserable at that point. So I finally gave up. I ate the cadaverous Brussels sprouts. Once my tongue touched that revolting food I thought that second was my last. Then, I opened my eyes and I was alive. I dodged a bullet. My magnanimous dad said that was all I had to eat. I wanted to give a jubilant cheer, but it was dinner and I was silent. That was the worst dinner in the history of dinners.

Grant Jurkowich
Grade 4

Top Essay Grades 4-5-6

Those Tough Times

My mother was diagnosed with breast cancer in 2004. It has been an extremely scary experience for the whole family. When she told us the news, she said "It is what it is." I feel this way too. You can't change what happened, it can't be undone now, so what's the use of imagining that whatever happened didn't?

Whether it's school, work or cancer, challenges take place. In my opinion, the key to getting through tough times in life are friends, family, and being strong. Have hope! If you give up, the results will be worse. My mother had a great attitude and, of course, had a tough time accepting the fact she had cancer, but got over it. She was strong! "Better me than someone else who can't handle it as well," she thought. With a good attitude, she survived!

Sometimes we think that we are going through a tougher time than anyone else in the world! Think of it this way, some people have it worse. I think that in life, the saddest experience you will ever go through is the death of a loved one. It is hard knowing that they won't ever be on Earth again, but you'll see them again in Heaven.

In those tough times of life, just be strong, have faith and talk to friends and family. You can get through this! Remember, everything happens for a reason, although you may not figure it out immediately.

Jessica Ladd
Grade 6

Top Essay Grades 4-5-6

I Wonder Why…Such a Long Life Seems too Short

This weekend my loving, helpful person I look up to, Great Grandma Tina, passed away. I thought about how astounding her life was. When my dad spoke at her funeral I learned things I never knew about her life. I knew she lived in New York, but I did not know she was the champion of the Sunday Times Crossword Puzzle. In honor of that, my dad did the puzzle for her with my aunt and grandpa. After all, it was Sunday, the day of her funeral, and she was my loving, helpful person I look up to, Great Grandma Tina.

I also learned she ate so many eggs. I did not know the extravagant number. 33,945! At her funeral my dad jokingly said if you want to be as old as Grandma Tina, start eating eggs today. She liked them a little raw and runny. Over easy. We did not eat those on Sunday. (That would have been yucky.) After all, she was my loving, helpful person I look up to, Great Grandma Tina.

My dad said she used to make mud cookies. He said they were yummy but they just looked like little mud puddles. I don't doubt they were yummy. I am sure they were scrumptious. After all, the chef was my loving, helpful person I look up to, Great Grandma Tina.

My eyes are getting teary now, ready to cry, because my loving, helpful person I look up to, Great Grandma Tina, passed away.

Jennifer Silver
Grade 4

Top Essay Grades 4-5-6

Popularity

We go to school to learn, talk with friends, and, it seems, to get criticized by the popular kids. The fact that we care about popularity is sad. The fact that we judge ourselves by it is sadder. The fact that we change ourselves to be popular is saddest. So, let's look at popularity.

Why would you change yourself to hang out with people who didn't like you? Popular girls (and boys) are usually mean. They treat people nastily and hurtfully. It's sad. If someone is nice and popular, we must try to be friends, but not change ourselves.

In the novel *Stargirl* by Jerry Spinelli, the main idea is don't be afraid to be different. It matters how you look at yourself, not how other people look at you. All people are created equal.

I don't know why people judge themselves by how many friends they have, or the way they act or dress. For example, a kid who has glasses, reads all the time, and has no "fashionable" clothes would be considered either a geek, a nerd, or a bookworm. A guy who plays lots of sports and has lots of friends would be a jock. A person who has lots of friends and has "fashionable" clothes would be popular.

We must stop labeling ourselves. If you have friends, you're popular in your own special way. If we try, we can stop this "labeling." Everybody would be equal and happy.

Morgan Simpson
Grade 6

Top Essay Grades 4-5-6

Good Friends

I think having good friends is very important. Friends help you in school, encourage you, and play with you. Think about it, how could you survive school without friends there to back you up? At recess you would be bored, right?

Good friends should be honest. They should be honest because if they hide things from you then you don't really know much about them. You should also be honest towards them. Also, if you share your feelings you will feel a lot better.

Friends should also care about your feelings. Imagine you are on the playground and someone pushes you down. Your friend has three choices: A, laugh at you; B, stick up for you; and C, help you up. B or C is what a true friend would do.

Generosity is a great thing in a friend. A friend could be generous and lend you a pencil. They could also be generous and let you read one of their books. If someone were not generous, I would not want to be their friend.

Something I like in a friend is sharing. If you forget your lunch, your friend should give you something to eat. They should also share other things like books, toys, pencils, and a lot of things.

A good friend should be a great person.

Lukas Stock
Grade 4

Top Essay Grades 4-5-6

My Friends, My Belief, My Story

My name is Amber. I was named after the golden color of the sunset. I am ten years old and I am an individual with lots of dreams. I believe in myself and I usually have A's in all my classes. Recently, for the past three months I have been sad, for I am having difficulties with my female classmates.

The girls in my class are beautiful and intelligent. They have lots of fun. I was part of their group until they suddenly started calling me names and teasing me. I told my mom that I wanted to be transferred to another school and she said no. She told me that I have to believe in myself. She said that with believing in myself I can defeat anything in my life.

Today, we all had a meeting with the principal of the school about name-calling and forgiveness. She said that we have to respect each other. All of us were crying. I cried because they were not my friends, but I also cried for I suddenly realized that they may never be my friends again and that was ok. I know that friends are nice and not mean. Friends do not hurt each other, they help each other.

I am no longer sad. I am Amber, the believer in myself. I am named after the sunset. I am special, gifted and unique. I have other friends at dance school and piano class. I will continue to make new friends.

Amber Watson
Grade 5

No More Pollution

I think pollution is really bad. People should think more about the world. Fish are dying because of water pollution. People are dying because of air pollution. Also, animals are dying from land pollution.

People can avoid water pollution by not throwing cans into the oceans. I think that the President should make water officers who make sure that people stop littering our waterways.

People can avoid air pollution by building electric airplanes, cars, and trains. Use less factories and things that cause smoke. This is bad for people and also birds, bats, and other flying animals.

Motor vehicles produce most of the air pollution in the United States. The engines of these vehicles pour over 100 million tons of pollutants into the air every year.

Factories release fluoride dust, sulfur oxides, ammonia, and organic acids into the air each year. The burning of wastes creates a very visible air pollution: this black smoke. This adds another 4 and one half million tons of pollutants into the air.

Land pollution is caused by people. People can volunteer to clean up their neighborhoods. Trash should be picked up and disposed, not ignored. Animals die from eating trash on the street.

These are only three main pollutants. There are others. Pollution needs to stop!

Andre Proctor
Grade 5

My First Softball Game

It was my first softball game. I felt nervous. My family was cheering me on, then I was called up to bat. They finally pitched the ball. I hit the ball, and it flew into the outfield. I ran to first base, and then the coach told me to keep going. I made it to second base as they threw the ball to infield. Another girl was up to bat, and she hit a single. I ran to third base, and she ran to first. Then my sister hit a single. I was the first on my team to make it home.

About ten minutes passed, and then it was the other team's turn to bat. I was third baseman, and then I heard the girls on the other team say, "Third baseman better watch out." I looked at home plate, and there stood a very big girl. I said to myself "only one out to go." She hit the ball towards me; I caught it. I did not know she was out, so I threw the ball towards first base. The person at first did not catch it. Then everyone walked off the field, telling me I had done a great job.

The next thing I knew, I was batting again. I hit a triple, and ended up making it home. I was really happy after that game. I was not only happy that we won, but because I had helped my team.

Alaina Warner
Grade 6

The Feeling

Going to school one day I saw my mom crying, I heard that the towers had just collapsed and I knew my dad worked there, I go into school, my belly hurting and my head spinning, my family is now missing a very special man. When you lose something valuable you feel sad, that's the way my family is feeling. People do nice things but that won't stop the tears from coming down my face. We will always have lots of things to remember him by. He will always be in my heart, when my mom goes on to meet someone special we will treat him with respect. When we all meet in heaven the chain that has been broken since he died will be fixed and until that moment we will live every day of our life. I wish the best for everyone who had a loss that day or even if your parent just died, I just wish you the best because I know how you feel when you lose a parent. It hurts inside but you will go on to live without them, but always remember them not the bad things but only the good. God bless everyone over the seas. We hope you come home safe because you dedicated your life to fight for our country.

Frankie D'Amadeo
Grade 6

Home

I appreciate my home. I have a nice home. I have a good sized home and a good neighborhood. Some people do not have as nice a house like I do. My house is really nice.

My house is a nice size. I have a backyard. It is also a good size. I have a front yard too. It has a big tree on it. I have my own room. My house is pretty big.

I have a good neighborhood. I have nice neighbors that invite people to parties. They invite me over a lot. They help clean up messes like garbage. My neighbors are really kind.

People do not have as nice of houses as I do. People live on the streets. People also live in boxes. People live in shopping carts. I have a good home.

I have a decent home. I have a nice sized home, nice neighbors, and some people do not have as nice of homes as me. I appreciate my home.

Adam Trosko
Grade 6

Mali

Mali is in a region of Africa that has many Muslims. The religions of Mali include Islam, Africa religion and Christianity. Islamic has 90%, Africa religion has 9% and Christianity has 5%. Mali has the same holidays as America. It has Christmas and a holiday called Armed Forces Day, which is like our Memorial Day. People that live in Mali speak French because it is their official language. Mali is near other countries that are Muslim.

The word Mali means where the king lives. Where people live can be affected because the Sahara desert is getting closer to Mali. The country Mali is a desert so it is always hot and it is hard to grow anything unless it rains.

Tom Graham
Grade 6

My Dog, Jasmine

There are a lot of reasons why my dog Jasmine is important to me. She is a black Scottish terrier. She is funny and cute and very energetic.

She is also very weird. When she sees a squirrel, she goes CRAZY! I love her. I would take off my socks and she would go and put my socks in her mouth. She loves licking people.

She likes people food more than dog food, like turkey, salad, spaghetti and meatballs, and last of all, but not least, chicken. She also eats wet cat food and likes smelling my cat's butt.

We all love her. She always sleeps with my sister. Those were a few reasons why my dog is important to me.

Kayla Rosenkranz
Grade 4

My Trip to Germany

In December, 2001 my family and I went to Münich, Germany to visit my great-grandmother. I was only five years old, and I only knew a little bit of German. That December we spent 12 days and Christmas at my great-grandmother's apartment.

My mother, father, sister, and I had a great time roaming the city. We visited fabulous restaurants with frankfurters, waffle fries, and great pretzels.

The experience of walking through German streets and looking at different people speaking a different language felt like I was in a different world and someone who just didn't belong. I spoke to my parents in English, but I didn't say a word to my great-grandmother — not one.

Unfortunately, my great-grandmother's apartment building was knocked down and she died peacefully. Even though she died, I love her still because she named me as a baby, and I will never forget that.

Julia Bamburg
Grade 4

Miracle

The locker room was as quiet as ever. We were all getting our pep-talk like we do before all our games. The RMU Island Sports Center Arctic Foxes were playing the Wheeling Nailers in the Nutcracker Tournament Championship. They announced our names while we warmed up. The crowd was cheering and screaming as the puck dropped and the game began.

At six forty-eight in the second period, center Brendan Brown notched in a goal. Then Aaron Yeomans. Then, in what seemed like a split second, the Nailers were on the move and put it in behind goaltender Mike Heraty. Then they did it again. It was tied now. Then it was my turn. I got on the ice and caught up to the loose puck, pulled it back and shot. Then I saw the light come on and heard the buzzer. I had scored. Then the team poured off the bench and we congratulated the other team (the game was over). Then we all got our trophies.

Tiernan McGrath
Grade 4

The Gift of Hope

If I could give one gift from my heart to anyone I would give hope to the hurricane Katrina victims. When the hurricane hit New Orleans millions of towns and homes were destroyed and many lives were lost. This hurricane left thousands of people homeless and many families separated. Many survivors have moved to nearby places until New Orleans is safe again. Luckily the U.S. has rescued many, and citizens have been donating food, money, and other supplies to help rebuild the city and its people. One reason I would give survivors hope is so that they believe things will get better and soon they can move back to Louisiana. I would also give survivors hope for that some day they will be able to live a normal life like they did before the hurricane. Survivors need to have faith that they will soon be united with their families and be able to enjoy life. The people need to believe that with the help from other countries and states that their homes and cities will be rebuilt. Many people have lost faith, but with the gift of hope their lives and communities will be put back together. Survivors will soon be able to live in a civilized town like they did before the hurricane. In conclusion, hurricane Katrina was devastating to the U.S. Many people have lost hope that their lives will ever be the same. I would give them hope to overcome that fear.

Victoria DeVivo
Grade 6

NBA History

Do you know what it feels like to be a step under on fire? Well, Kobe Bryant did after he lit up the Toronto Raptors with 81 points. Read about how he made history in these next paragraphs.

Last Sunday Kobe had a historic night. He scored the second largest margin of points in NBA history behind Wilt Chamberlain, but when Wilt scored his 100 points it was against a very weak New York Knicks team. They only had 27 wins the whole season. Also, there wasn't as much competition as there is in the NBA today. So people are saying that Kobe's 81 points could be better then Wilt's 100 points.

The Lakers were down by a large margin before Kobe decided to kick it on. Kobe had 55 of his 81 in the second half. He outscored the whole Raptor team in the second half 55 to 42, and that led the Lakers to a comeback, and they beat the Toronto Raptor's 122 to 104.

At the end of the game Kobe's childhood idol, Magic Johnson, came up to him to congratulate him on his fantastic night. This meant a lot to him.

Bryant is so often unstoppable so people are saying that 81 points is pretty close; he might be able to break 100. But for now, we'll just have to watch and find out if he has it in him.

Daniel McGuckin
Grade 6

My Service Project

I did a fun service project at the Pregnancy Resource Clinic of North Penn. I cleaned, sorted and organized. I like doing it because it's not hard and doesn't take long, but does a lot. I think everyone that works there will benefit from what I do. I think I am doing a wonderful job.

I cleaned many things! The past times I was there I washed things, cleaned tables, washed all of the windows, and lots of other things. I think my favorite part of doing these things was shredding the papers. It takes a long time to shred because you can only shred three papers at a time. There are so many papers to shred; I bet you could make five books out of them!

I sorted tons of papers two different times. It took me a long time to do. It was actually hard! After I sorted them, I would hole punch them and put them into a binder.

I think a lot of people will benefit from what I am doing. I think that the people that work there will benefit by being able to find what they need. I also think that the company will benefit by me helping because the customers might think, "Wow, this is a nice place, I should tell my friends," or something like that. It really makes me feel good in what I am doing. I hope it will help others too.

Allegra Patkos
Grade 5

All About Me

Hi! My name is Douglas White, but everyone calls me D.J. I was born in Boston at the Beth Israel Hospital on February 3, 1996 at 8:45 PM. I weighed 9 lb. 4 oz. and was 23 1/2 inches long. When I was 1 year 3 months old, my sister Kaytie was born. When I was 3 years old I started preschool at the Adams School. I have played soccer, basketball, baseball and football. Last year I hit the winning ball for my baseball team the Everett Little League PADRES. I won 2nd place for the hitting tournament, for which I won two tickets for the movies. We won the Championship too. We had a banquet and they gave us the 1st place trophy. We traveled to Florida to see my cousin and uncle. In December of 1997 and 2002 we had Christmas in Florida. We have been in Disney World. We go camping every summer. I have been to Friendly Beaver in Manchester, NH, Yogi Bear in Ashland, NH, to Dan Forth Bay in NH, Niagara Falls in Canada, and to Hershey Park in PA.

When I was 4 years old my little sister Britney was born. I went to Devens School for first and second grade. My parents have always taken my sisters and me to Wakefield NH, where my grandparents have a camp at Pine River Pond. I have learned to wake board, swim, fish, tube, canoe, ride my dirt bike, and ATV. In wintertime we ride snowmobiles. When the lake is frozen, we skate and play hockey. We go to King Pine Resort to ski and snowboard. I have been in Sunday River, Cranmore, and Sunnape to snowboard. I have a turtle named Winky and a dog named Buffy.

I have an exciting life.

Douglas (DJ) White
Grade 4

Zips Chocolate Chip

One of my favorite horses is Zips Chocolate Chip or "Chip." He is a 1985 Bay Quarter Horse Stallion.

Zips Chocolate Chip's owner is Anne Myers. Zips Chocolate Chip lives in Valley View, Texas. He is famous among horse people. He was the first horse to be inducted into the National Snaffle Bit Association in two divisions: Show horse and sire. He is also famous for many other qualities. He was retired from showing at age four. His father recently passed away on January 12, 1998. He is such a good and well known horse that he even has his own website www.zipschocolatechip.com. You can also buy a Zips Chocolate Chip stuffed animal toy or a Breyer horse model of him signed by Anne Myers. He has excellent conformation. Anne Myers said that she never expected him to become such a big and well known horse. If you wanted to buy one of his babies you would have to pay ten thousand dollars or more. Most of his babies are a variety of colors but most are bays. Most of his babies are able to do what he does. For example he is extremely good at western pleasure, and one of his babies just won World Champion at Western Pleasure.

All these reasons are why Zips Chocolate Chip is one of my favorite horses!!

Rachael Harrington
Grade 6

A Day at the Flower Show

Every March my family and I go to The Philadelphia Flower Show in Philadelphia. My uncle's tree company puts on a display there. One year the company constructed a tree house surrounded by plants and trees. Another year they built a big tree stump. Inside the stump they told you about how to preserve trees and what you should do when one dies. One of my favorite displays was a glass office built among trees and plants. The office was a replica of their science lab in North Carolina where they do research on trees and the bugs that can kill the trees.

Some other landscape designers design and construct displays completely made out of plants and flowers. Last year a company built a huge lemonade stand with yellow flowers and lemons. It was built in honor of Alex the nine-year-old girl who encouraged people to sell lemonade to raise money for cancer research. Unfortunately Alex died from cancer.

At the show there are wedding displays made out of flowers. Last year my favorite display was a Harley Davidson wedding theme. The wedding site was decorated with black and orange flowers. Also at the show there is a display called miniatures. The miniatures are little flowers and mini appliances that are in a box. It takes people months to design and arrange them in the box. There are about twenty of them, and together they make a story. I can't wait until next year to see what the displays will look like.

Ryan Kacenski
Grade 6

Sisters Are Heaven Sent

"Sisters touch your heart in ways no other could. Sisters share…their hopes, their fears, their love, everything they have. Real friendship springs from their special bonds." Having two sisters has to be the best thing that has ever happened to me. They are very important in my life. No one could possibly understand all that we have been through together. Even though we are still young, we have formed a bond of trust and everlasting friendship. Without them, there would be no one to fight with about the littlest things, no one to share clothes with, no one to comfort me after I had the worst day of my life, and no one to share the joys of the happy times.

My younger sister Jamie is the person that always keeps me laughing. She has a great imagination and keeps my mind open to when I was her age. My older sister Marissa is someone who I can look up to for advice and style tips. She is always honest and always lets me know when I need to change my outfit. My wonderful sisters help me in everyday life whether it's with dance, soccer, or even my guitar homework. They are always there when I need them the most. My two sisters are the most important people to me. I love them with all my heart. Friends may come and go, but sisters will always be at your side.

Tara Bottino
Grade 6

Japan

Did you know Mt. Fuji is located in Japan? Well if you want to find out more interesting facts read my report!

Here are some general facts about Japan! Did you know the population of Japan is 126,320,000! The capital of Japan is Tokyo. The prime minister of Japan or as we say here president, is Junichiro Koizumi. Did you know Japan is on the continent of Asia and is surrounded by the North Pacific Ocean, the Sea of Japan, and the East China Sea. Those are some general facts about Japan!

Now you are going to learn about Japan's people and Japan's land. Some ethnic groups in Japan are Japanese, Korean, Chinese, Brazilian, and Filipino. People in Japan go to restaurants and eat Japanese food which includes fish, rice, and sushi. In Japan mountains claim 71% and plains claim about 29%. Also Japan is 377,818 square kilometers. I hope you learned some new facts about Japan's land and people.

If you ever visit Japan here are some places to visit. Mt. Fuji attracts many guests as well as the Japanese museum of arts. Check the newspaper for festivals too because they are very fun to see.

You have now learned about Japan's people, the land, where to go and general facts about Japan. I hope you learned and enjoyed my report!

Rachel Molloy
Grade 4

Amazing Species Are Scorpions!

Do you know all about scorpions? A scorpion is a small animal with a dangerous poison sting in its tail. A scorpion is not an insect. It is the class of arachnids. Most scorpions are black or yellowish and from one half to eight inches long. Their breathing pores are located on the abdomen.

As a result, a scorpion's body has two parts. Its forward part is called the cephalothorax. The second part is the long abdomen. Their characteristics are aggressive, intense, passionate, secretive and quick tempered. They have six to twelve eyes according to what kind of scorpion.

In fact, the scorpion sting doesn't always cause death, but it's very painful. The scorpion's sting is a curved organ in the end of its tail. The scorpion's symbol is a capital M with a tail. It has six to twelve eyes and it is in the class of arachnids.

Michael Bouloubasis
Grade 4

My Dirt Bike

For Christmas I got a dirt bike. It's a green Kawasaki. I love to ride it! I can never get off only when it's dark. I have never fallen off. I think it is hard to start. I need my dad to help me with that. I'm going to take the governor off soon that makes it go a lot faster. I have a jump in the backyard. I have to make it first. I have to find a lot of hard dirt. I have a lot of dirt in my backyard. My property is one acre. In the spring my dad is going to plant grass in the backyard because I tore it up with my dirt bike. But me and my uncle are going to take me to tracks in Peconic and up the island. I can't wait, some of the tracks have huge jumps. When I go to the tracks I will probably have butterflies in my tummy. I have never been on a big jump in my whole entire life, I will have now. I am not nervous at all. I'm just going to go fast and let the good times roll. Once I learn how to do tricks, I will be doing a lot of them. I really don't want to fall off, that will really hurt.

Jeffrey Laymon
Grade 4

The Blizzard of '05

In 2005 a major blizzard hit Massachusetts. 2 1/2 feet of snow fell and snow banks were about 10-20 feet. The snow was so deep that I could barely walk. The schools were closed for a week. People couldn't drive because of the condition of the road.

I was sleeping over at my friend, Eric's, house at the time. I went sledding on a hill near my house. I also used my bushes as a hill too. It took over a month for all the snow to melt. The blizzard was almost as big as the blizzard of 1978.

This memory was special to me because I saw with my own eyes what nature's fury can throw at you. I felt scared and frightened because it would not stop. I looked out my window and it looked like someone made the Earth into one big glacier.

Cory Leonardo
Grade 6

No Allowance, Sigh

Kids seriously should get at least a decent amount of money weekly or monthly. We do many things not for us but for our *parents*. We take out the trash, do the dreaded dishes, and clean *our* "abominable" room, when, in fact, we should be deciding when *we* want to clean *our* room. What do you give us in return, an excuse that the roof on our heads and the food on the table is our allowance? If you didn't give us *those*, we'd be dead. I want some *wants* every once in a while, not only *needs*. We get out of your face for *six hours and forty-five minutes*, five days a *week*; all you can give us is a lame excuse? Does *your* boss make you do work without any pay at *all*? I seriously doubt he/she does. If the chores cancel out with the needs, at least give us something for putting up with that excuse. You believe it was right for slavery to be abolished, so instead of practically being a hypocrite, give us an allowance. Work without pay involuntarily is similar to slavery, right?

Kevin Hazlett
Grade 6

European Sites

European countries have many historical sites. For instance, France has the Eiffel Tower, which was built on March 31, 1889 by Gustave Eiffel. In Italy, a famous historical site is the Coliseum which was used as an amphitheater between A.D. 72 and A.D. 81. Also Barcelona, Spain boasts its Grand Cathedral, the Sacred Heart. In Holland, there is Anne Frank's house where 12 year old Anne Frank and her family hid for two years from the Nazis. England has some memorable sites too, like the Tower of London, Big Ben, or the Eye. From the Eye (a huge ferris wheel,) you can see all of London. When you visit Europe, you will find many interesting sites!

Makayla Mercier
Grade 6

My Sax Attracts

Do you know what has a neck, a reed, a mouthpiece, and a ligature? It's an Alto Sax. A saxophone is a woodwind instrument. It is also my favorite instrument! Many children and adults love to hear the beautiful music of the sax. I've been encouraged to play an instrument by many people. The saxophone is what I picked. The reason I picked it is simple; many people have become famous from playing it. Students at BAEC say I'm very good. They especially love the "Mickey Mouse March" and the "Yellow Submarine." In May we will have our second, fifth grade concert. The members of the band are so excited. It takes a lot of talent, time, and practice to play any instrument. Mr. Cugini, my band instructor, told me to never give up on my dreams. I never am going to give up on my dreams!

Scott Ward
Grade 5

How I Love Sports

I love sports because sports are great and fun. My favorite sports are soccer and football. My most favorite sport is tennis. They can be fun activities. Sports are great.

Like I was saying in the other paragraph, tennis is my favorite sport because I am really good at it. I beat most people at it. I am really competitive. I put in a lot of effort. If it was sunny every day I would play tennis every day. Tennis is the best sport ever.

Two sports I like are soccer and football. I'm not really that good at soccer, but I still like it. I try to practice but I just can't get it. I like tackle football. I am a good tackler. I like these two sports. One day I would like to be a professional at these sports. I think that soccer and football are great.

Sabrina Guillaume
Grade 6

A Swim Year I Will Never Forget

One summer morning at swim practice everyone was all excited for the big swim meet. The swim team was making pep-posters and just playing in the pool. At the end of practice this is where it all began. We had to swim a lap without breathing, something terrible happened.

My friend, Cate, was before me she was very upset because she took a breath. Next her head was not moving under the water, which startled me. As I tried to lift her out of the pool, her face was turning a purplish blue. My mom saw me and questioned if anything was wrong and certainly there was. Mrs. Woltemate, a nurse, gave her CPR and there was no response. My heart was pounding harder and harder as the medical team arrived at Bustleton Swim Club to take her to Frankford Hospital. That is where she passed away form an unknown heart defect. Needless to say my swim team and I were very upset.

The next week we had a meet against Hatboro-Horsham Swim Club, where a boy named Sam died of the same thing Cate did. This surely is a swim year I will never forget.

Megan Moffett
Grade 6

Olympians vs Animals

Did you ever wonder if Olympic champions went against animals in their habitat who would win? If you read on you can find that out by reading this article!

I researched the sprint. It is the cheetah against Olympic record holder Michael Johnson of the USA. While both hold a record in running, the cheetah can run up to 70 mph in its environment. Michael can only run up to 23 mph. As you can see in the grassy plains the cheetah would win this race. Although they both hold a record in speed, the cheetah is much faster than the human.

The cheetah is much faster than the human in sprinting when the cheetah is in its environment, but we never know what it would be like if the cheetah was on a track!

Emily Murn
Grade 6

The Creator of All Things

God is so important to me. He is the creator of all things. He gives us all we need and He sent His son to die for our sins.

I love God so much, and if I didn't have Him I wouldn't have anything and I wouldn't be anything. The whole universe wouldn't exist. Everything I have is from God, like my family, my home, food, and everything and everyone I love. God blesses me with all this.

God gives us many gifts. He gives us the ability to create things and learn and make decisions. He gives us a heart to love. He also gives us the choice to do what we want, although God wants us to do what's right.

The most precious gifts God gives us are the Bible and His only son Jesus Christ. His son Jesus came to Earth and died on the cross for our sins. Then Jesus rose rose from the dead. Imagine seeing an innocent man killed for us and then in three days He is alive! This and all God's miracles are in the Bible. God had men write it with the help of the Holy Spirit. God wants us to follow His word and believe in it and His son, Jesus. If we do, we will go to heaven.

It is so great that we have God. God loves us each individually. I love God for all these things and more. I know God loves me too.

Mia Dina Screnci
Grade 6

My Lucky Day — 7-11

Elwyn Brooks White was born on July 11, 1899 — a day he considered an indicator of lifelong good luck. Referring to July being the seventh month and the day being the eleventh, hence seven-eleven.

Despite having a first name he could not stand, E.B. had a happy childhood. He lived in Mount Vernon, New York with his parents. Elwyn was the youngest of six children. His father, Samuel White, worked for the Waters Piano Company. His mother, Jessie White, had a passion for nature. The Whites were not educated, but were good writers.

Elwyn enjoyed writing and published stories in children magazines. One of his fears was failing, but he feared public speaking the most. At the age of 18 he attended Cornell University. After graduation in 1921, he worked for *The New Yorker* magazine. White married Katharine Angell and they had a child named Joel White. The Whites lived on a farm in Allen Cove, Maine that they bought in 1933.

In 1945, White published *Stuart Little*, a story of an adventurous mouse, a story he dreamed about back in 1926. In 1952, *Charlotte's Web* was released, his own back yard provided the inspiration for this story.

Several years later, Katharine's health was rapidly declining and on July 20, 1977 she was rushed to the hospital and died a few hours later. On October 1, 1985 White died at home of Alzheimer's disease. Even today, White is remembered for his essays, poems, and his guide to style of writing.

Steven Kilawattie
Grade 5

Babe Ruth

Babe Ruth was born on February 6, 1895, in Baltimore, Maryland. His real name was George Herman Ruth. He went to Saint Mary's High School, and never went to college.

In 1914, when Babe Ruth was only nineteen years old he was signed by the Baltimore Orioles (a Boston Red Sox minor league team at the time) and became a professional baseball player. In his rookie debut, he hit his first home run. He helped the Orioles win a lot of games, but his contract with them only lasted six months. It was one of the smallest contracts in baseball history.

When Ruth was young, he got into a log of fights, but he was actually a very nice person. Once he promised an ill child that he would hit a home run for him and ended up hitting three in that one game.

Babe Ruth helped the Boston Red Sox win a World Series in 1918. Then Ruth, nicknamed "the Bambino," was traded by the Red Sox to the New York Yankees in 1920. The Red Sox did not win another World Series for 86 years. Many believed this was the "Curse of the Bambino."

Babe Ruth set many records as a baseball player. He was the first person to have a batting average over 400. He has the record for most games pitched at the World Series. He is often considered one of the greatest athletes in American history.

Babe Ruth died in 1948, at age 53.

Luke Tetrault
Grade 5

Kid Stress

Have you ever asked yourself "Do kids have too much stress?" If you have, you might find the answer is yes. Where do you think it all comes from? I wanted to find out where all the "kid stress" comes from. (I think I found it)

Most of the stress comes from grades and tests. I asked some of my friends. They said that they get stressed out before a test and right before the test is passed out. I agree because there is always a surprise.

Are you curious about how you can help the stress level go down? Well I think you could do your homework during recess. This gets it done and out of the way. So when you get home you can do the stuff you love and relax.

Another way is to study for the test the night before. This will boost your confidence so you will have a better chance of getting a good grade. Studying will allow you to understand the material better.

One more way you can deal with stress is exercise. Exercising will relax you, and have fun, for you're getting rid of your stress. So exercise!

We all have it. Actually, some of us need it. Now I hope you kids can deal with it by doing homework during recess, studying, and exercising.

Olivia Ragan
Grade 5

A Late Night Treat

Last month my stomach ached for a treat. So I tiptoed downstairs, and went to the fridge. There it was, a sweet, juicy, chocolate, fudge brownie. I couldn't wait to eat it. Then, I chomped on it until it was all gone. While I was chomping, my taste buds were spinning. I felt so full. I couldn't believe how much I ate. My dad came downstairs, so I hid under the table. My dad wanted the fudge brownie too! I couldn't believe it because he was dancing. He screamed when he saw it was gone and I laughed quietly. Then, he went back grumbling to his room. I snuck to my room giggling and fell asleep quietly. That night, I dreamt about my dad dancing. I had the funniest night ever. Tomorrow I might do it again. Tomorrow will I have ice cream? I won't tell anyone but the world. So they can have a good laugh too.

Randy Piacentini
Grade 4

The Glide

I started putting on my skates. I felt like I was going to burst from fear. My throat felt like it was going down my stomach. I told myself, I was going to be fine.

I stepped on the ice. I glided across the frozen ice like I was going down a hill with my sled. My heart was beating me. My legs were shaking.

I watched myself glide across the ice like I was a professional ice skater. I kept on gliding and then I thought to myself, "I did it. I really did it."

Rochelle Hamlin
Grade 4

Sports

Sports get everyone active in a certain way. Do you like sports? It's fun to watch different sports. Playing sports makes you run and exercise. Playing lets you have fun with your team.

Watching sports is a lot of fun. In football there are two types of games. There is a one sided game where one team is so much better then the other. You have a good game where the teams are as good as each other. Basketball is a fast-paced game. Soccer is the same but more like football. It is always fun to watch sports.

Playing sports makes you run and exercise. Soccer helps you build stamina. Playing baseball gives you strong arms when you throw and hit the ball. Playing football you work out every single muscle in your body.

Playing sports also teaches you teamwork. You have fun because you don't work alone. You always have someone to play with. In some of the sports like soccer, hockey and basketball you get tired so other people on your team can help you out when you need a rest.

All sports have three things in common. They are fun to watch and play. They keep you active and fit, and they teach you teamwork. Being on a team is fun.

Anthony Capozzi
Grade 6

Mustang Sally

Until I was ten, I had a dog named Sadie. Sadie got very old and weak, so we had to put her to sleep. I asked my dad if we could get a new dog that looked just like Sadie and he said we would try. One day my dad and I put a warm blanket and a doll pillow in a small cardboard box: we were going to get a puppy! My family and I put the box in the car and left.

That day we were invited to my grandparents' house. The man who was selling puppies lived just a few miles away from my grandparents. What luck! After spending the day at my grandparents', listening to all the wonderful names they suggested for our new family member we left! We did not know what we were going to name the puppy, so we were getting suggestions from my grandparents.

I was nervous. I knew that if the puppies were not what we were looking for, my dad would not buy any of them. We looked at all of the puppies, and found the one we wanted. We looked at the puppy's registration forms; we saw that her grandmothers' name was Long Tall Sally. My mom really wanted the dog to be named Sally, and my sister really liked MUSTANG cars, so our choice was final: our new puppy's name would be Long Tall Mustang Sally. My new Puppy!

Kelley Foyle
Grade 6

There Is No One Like Me

There is no one like me, because everyone is different. I'm a kind, loving, helpful person. When someone needs help I usually always try to help. I am kind to animals, my friends, my family, and even strangers. Sometimes I wake up in a bad mood, but as soon as I get out the door my bad mood goes away. On my way to school I always make sure to say good morning to the crossing guards. When my grandmother comes home with groceries, I always help her with the bags. When my mom needs help around the house I always try to help her with the chores. If my brother or my friends need help I am always there with a helping hand.

Being loving to all my loved ones and my friends is a good way to describe me. I always have a good attitude with everyone and express my love by hugging them and telling them how much I love them and care for them. I also show love to my pets by taking good care of them and playing with them.

Kindness is also a good way to describe me. When homeless people pass me by I always make sure to give them some money. By doing this I feel that I have helped them get a bite to eat. If I could I would place all homeless people in a big warm mansion with a lot of food and give them the home they deserve.

These are the reasons why I think I'm kind, loving, and helpful. If everyone in the world would have these traits the world would be a better place.

Lauren Brooke Cornejo
Grade 5

The Super Man

I'm going to die!!! I am here at Six Flags on the biggest ride here, Super Man! It was scary! The first drop was high! People that work there say the ride is 208 feet in the air and goes 77 mph.

When the first drop hits it feels like your stomach is in your mouth. Then it shoots up in the air. Then your stomach goes to your feet and it tickles. All the people at the park look like ants running around looking for food and stuff to do. My favorite part is when it drops into the dark tunnel it gets all quiet, then it shoots out then there's up and downs. Finally it was over I was shaking like a little baby.

Todd Peixinho
Grade 6

Music Can Move the World

Music is more important than people realize. It unifies us and helps us spread our wings. It teaches us how to be ourselves.

Music is the key to our individuality. Whatever type you listen to, it will say something about you. If you like hip hop, you probably like to have fun and dance. If you like pop, you are always in on the latest things. You might be a wild beast if you listen to rock. Your personality is your music.

Music is the folder that holds our emotions. If you are down in the dumps, music will lift you to the sky. If might change your point of view too. You could think something stupid might mess up your life, but then you listen to those lyrics and you understand what those motivational speakers were talking about. Music can move the world.

Amusing, relaxing, booming, music is us. Music is our interest. Nobody can tell us what we like or what kind to listen to. All music is different than others. All music has a purpose, and we are our own music.

Ciara Windsor
Grade 5

My Inspiration

My grandma is my inspiration in life because she taught me to never give up and if you want to do something, set your mind to it and do it.

Grandmas should be everyone's inspiration. They are the ones with the best cookies. Grandmas also are the ones who give you the most hugs and kisses. Most importantly, they can teach you something in life.

My grandma passed away when I was six years old. During those six years she taught me more than I can ever imagine. She made the best angel food cake, which gave me an interest in cooking. I also learned to braid hair from her. Now that she is gone, I use what she taught me and use it in everyday life. That is how all grandmas are.

She may be gone, but she is still with me in my heart and my memories. She still teaches me things today. If everyone took time to understand what their grandma can teach them, then maybe someday they would be their inspiration, too.

Nicole Vecchio
Grade 6

Coach

Bill Enos, where do I begin? There are so many interesting things about him it would take a book as big as the fifth Harry Potter story to write about him.

Bill Enos is my snowboard coach. This is my first year in his program, Black and Blue Trail Smashers (B.B.T.S). I was in another program before, Seasonal, but Seasonal didn't involve competing in races, slopestyle, and boardercross events. Bill makes snowboarding that much better, he makes everyone laugh a lot, and encourages his team to achieve great things. At 8:00 in the morning, he has an amazing way to get you pumped up for your race. He'll ask, "Are you ready for this?!" or say "Knock'em dead!"

Olympics, when most people hear the word they might think of swimming and Michael Phelps or ice skating and Sasha Cohen. Not me, I think of snowboarding and Bill Enos.

On the first day of training with B.B.T.S. Bill taught me and the other few people in that lesson to do lots of tricks. For example Bill taught us how to do butters. Butters are when you do a 360 spin when you are moving down the mountain with just the tail of your board touching the snow. By the end of the day I was doing four of them in a row!

Bill is a "beyond great" snowboarding coach. I've learned so much from him and it hasn't even been three months of me being in his program. I'm looking forward to achieving more goals and trying my hardest to make it to the World Cup just like Bill did.

Carly Robb
Grade 6

Plié, Relevé…My Career

I will never forget my amazement as I watched a ballet for the first time. After the program was over, I knew that ballet was what I wanted to do. Thus, my main interest is dance. Currently, I'm enrolled in ballet, tap, jazz, hip-hop, and acrobats. My favorite style of dance is ballet, although hip-hop and jazz are enjoyable as well. Sometimes my ballet teachers decide to do conditioning, which is a class focusing on stretching physically to your limit.

I plan to work in the field of dance in some way because my dream is to dance professionally either for a ballet company or on Broadway. Teaching dance at a private studio or at my church is an option also. I plan to accomplish my goal by continuing dance classes, seeking the advice of professional dancers, and lastly, investigating colleges and other programs that offer dance.

I think I'll be successful because I have a passion for dance and I will have had proper training. Even though dancers don't earn a very high income, I could have two jobs. A few possibilities are a dance teacher, a birthday ballerina, or a piano teacher. After completing my training, that's what I'll be doing.

Diana Stancy
Grade 6

The Marbled Salamander

I'm doing a report on the Marbled Salamander. Did you know that the Marbled Salamander is an endangered species? We may discover in the future it is a cure for cancer. So please help save the Marbled Salamander. They help by keeping the insect population at a minimum. Please help to save this creature. Not only would you be doing something good, but you may also help many people. They eat zoo plankton and underwater leaf litter. Also, when they get older they eat insects, tadpoles, and small salamander larvae. They live in plains and swamps. The Marbled Salamander's scientific name is Ambystoma Opacum. The Marbled Salamander lives right here in Massachusetts. Please help to save the Marbled Salamander. You can help by doing a fundraiser, in which you can sell anything that has something to do with the Marbled Salamander, such as T-shirts, coffee cups and more. You just need to give the money to a captive breeding center for the Marbled Salamander. Also, you can do captive breeding yourself, you just need to get permission from the captive breeding center and capture a salamander. All you will do is go to the captive breeding center daily and check up on it with a person that works there and you can help that person take care of the salamander. Please help to save the Marbled Salamander. If you look to do the captive breeding you need to look both on dry land and wetland.

Ryan Marcyoniak
Grade 5

Time

What do you think passes and never stops? It's time. Time is something that deals with math and is very complicated. Without it, nothing would exist.

If you look at a clock, you see a "hand" that ticks each second. Comparing that second to a day would be 1/86,400 of one "set" of 24 hours! Now think about a second compared to a year. One second would be 1/31,536,000 of an entire year if the calculations were accurate or correct.

Light is the fastest "object" in the world. Nothing can travel faster or in the same precise speed. We have not yet found the technology to travel as fast. Einstein said if we want to travel in time, we must first travel at the speed of light. Of course, we cannot, but because there is such thing as a wormhole that can allow us to travel to another timeline, we might have a chance of experiencing it. The only thing about that is the fact that wormholes cannot be created unless the universe folds onto itself which of course, is highly unlikely.

There is something known as the fabric of time and space. Tampering with time and messing around with it can cause the universe to collapse onto itself or known as a paradox. However, no one is very sure of that because we have no evidence. We may not be able to figure the answers now but we might in the future. We just don't know.

Wenyu Deng
Grade 5

Mazeroski's Miracle

It was the 1960 World Series. The Pittsburgh Pirates were playing the New York Yankees. The Yankees had been heavily favored to win every game of the series, but the Pirates had made it to the seventh and final game. The game was played at Forbes Field on Forbes Avenue, home of the Pittsburgh Pirates.

After a grueling game, it was the bottom of the ninth, and possibly last, inning. The game was tied. Pirate second baseman Bill Mazeroski came up for his turn at bat. The ball was pitched and it was hit. The ball went all the way out of the park for a homerun.

Everyone in Pittsburgh rushed to downtown for a full night of partying. They talked about Mazeroski's hit for the rest of their lives. Mazeroski became a Pittsburgh legend.

Forty-six years later, the part of the outfield wall that the homerun soared over is still in the same spot. Home plate is also exactly where it used to be, but now it is under glass, inside of a building at the University of Pittsburgh. People can visit and remember where they were and what they felt when that famous run was scored!

Tony Satryan
Grade 5

The Effect of Drugs

The most important goal in my life is to always be drug free. It is very bad to sell or do drugs. It is bad because you can go to jail. Here is a story that I will never forget.

Drugs can kill you. One sunny day my friends and I went to the park. While we were at the park a man named Carl came up to my friend and offered her some drugs. Milaqua told Carl, "No." Milaqua also told what drugs can do, such as it can get you addicted. Then you can eventually die. After that day Carl went to sign up for a job to be a policeman. When he became a sheriff he left for the army. Carl has changed his ways.

Drugs can give you lung cancer. About ten thousand people died and have lung cancer each year. People should never suffer with lung cancer. You too still can save yourself from drugs, just like Carl.

Jamira DeJesus
Grade 6

A Hit Heard Around the World

Baseball can be a very exciting sport. The most exciting game I know of happened in 1960. It was the Pirates versus the Yankees in the World Series. The Yankees were winning nine to six, and the bases were loaded. It was the bottom of the ninth inning with two strikes and two outs. Bill Mazoroski from the Pirates was up at bat. He had gotten the Golden Glove award many times, but he had only hit about two homeruns that season. No one expected him to hit the game-winning, out-of-the-park grand slam that he did. That was one of the many games which proves that baseball can be a very exciting sport.

Michael Coyne
Grade 6

Do You Know My Family?

Do you have a big family? There are many benefits of being a member of a big family. Some of these benefits are one never gets lonely or bored, and you can count on others to help you. Even though sometimes everyone doesn't agree, I still love my family. My sisters, Cathy and Mary are really nice. Cathy is eighteen and Mary is fourteen. My brothers are Pat, a sixteen year old and Mike, who is twenty-one. I can't forget my mom, a stay at home mom, and my dad, a lawyer and district judge.

I can't get bored because there are a lot of people. I can always talk to and laugh with my dad. He is the funny one in the family and he always makes me laugh.

I can count on my family to help me through things. If I am mad or sad, they cheer me up. If I get in fights with my brothers or sisters, I try to forgive them and I always do. It is important to always forgive your family.

The things that I love about my sisters are we get along better than my brothers and me. My brothers and I get along too. You should love your family always. Having a lot of sisters is beneficial for many reasons. One benefit is that you can talk to them when you want or need to talk to someone. You should always love your family.

Colleen Zyra
Grade 6

Family Fun!

Have you ever been away from your family and realized how much you really need them? Your family is very important to you because they are fun, caring, and reliable.

Your family can be entertaining. One day three years ago my cousins Colton, Nick, and I built a bridge out of sticks and moss. The bridge lasted until my dad ran it over with a truck two years later.

Two years ago, my aunt, uncle, cousins, parents and I went to Grand Cayman. That was one of the best vacations ever. We went to the beach, snorkeled, jet skied, and swam in the pool that had a built in bar so you could swim up to it and get a Coke.

Your family is caring and will always be a comfort to you when you have a broken heart or are sad. When my grandmother died it was one day after Thanksgiving and two weeks before my fifth birthday. I didn't know what was happening. It was really scary because my mom, aunt, uncle, and father were all crying. I was very confused because of my birthday but also thought I should be sad. My family was there to comfort me and will be there to comfort me in the future.

I think that if I didn't have my family that I would die without them. My family is the most important thing to me in the whole world. They are the best thing that you will ever have.

Malayna Rogers
Grade 6

Basketballs

Have you ever stood up to a 16-year-old by yourself? I have.

I was at the pool about to meet my cousins in the park. I left the pool and went to the camper and got dressed. Then I got my bike and headed out. I had a few extra minutes, so I headed into the woods. I went to the ramps hidden there. Then I followed the path to the park.

When I arrived they weren't there, so I played a little basketball. Then these two teens came towards me. I had a basketball and ran to the slide but one followed me, and he stood waiting at the bottom.

He said to give him the ball, so I did. He didn't catch it, and it hit him on the head. I saw he was angry. Then I thought I could escape from this guy, and I hurried down the slide. Still he was standing at the bottom waiting for me. I slammed into him, and ran away. Then, I grabbed my bike and rode to the camper. When I told my cousins they said, "You got away. That kid is always looking for kids to tease and taunt." The next year we only saw him once, and thankfully that was all.

Ashleigh Fedei
Grade 5

The Best Place to Visit

What do you think is the best place to visit and explore? If you would ask me, I would say New York City because there are a lot of places to go. It is not just for fun but something that is educational!

The Empire State Building, is a nice place to explore and get a good view of New York City. During the night, you can see its colored lights. The lights change depending on the season. It has a big pointy top.

The Statue of Liberty and the Ellis Island are nice attractions, too. You can go there by a ferry. As you sail, you can see the nice open sea, New York's skyscrapers, and the horizon. You could also hear flying birds, excited people, rushing water and could feel the cold blowing wind. You haven't gone to New York City if you haven't gone to the Statue of Liberty. It's a very important landmark symbolizing democracy and freedom. Ellis Island shows how immigration started. It gives you an understanding of New York City being a mixture of different races.

Rockefeller Center is spectacular during the Christmas season. The huge Christmas tree, the different colorful lights and the skating rink give the season a wonderful spirit.

Central Park is a nice place to go and stroll. You can boat ride here; even rent a small boat which has a remote control.

There are a lot of Broadway shows to enjoy and museums to learn from. Restaurants and fast food chains are all over the city. Transportation is not something to worry about. The MTA transits and subways are very efficient.

With all these, I would say New York City is the best place to visit and explore! So, what else are you waiting for…let's go!

Augustine Jerard Caoile
Grade 5

Football

Football is a very exciting sport, it is an honor to represent your school, it keeps you physically fit, and you have a lot of equipment so you do not get hurt.

It is very exciting because you have supporting fans, there are always big hits that are exciting, also it is just exciting to watch. When you play football it is an honor to represent your school whether it is grade school, high school or even college. Playing for college is especially exciting because you have a very big student section where all your friends are cheering you on!

Playing football keeps you physically fit because you stretch before every practice, you run during practice, and you also do push ups and other physical workouts.

There is a lot of football equipment. There are shoulder pads that cost thirty to forty dollars, a helmet that costs eighty to one hundred twenty dollars, there are also pants and pant pads that cost fifteen to twenty dollars.

Football is the best sport because you keep physically fit, it is an honor to represent your school, you have a lot of equipment so you do not get hurt, and finally it is the most exciting sport in America!

Anthony Mazzarini
Grade 6

Alaska

Alaska became a state on June 30, 1958. It was the 49th state to make up the 50 United States. Juneau was the capital of Alaska then and it still is the capital today.

Alaska has also had a lot of disasters. Here is an example of a disaster Alaska has had. On March 27, 1964 Alaska was hit with a major earthquake, the greatest earthquake ever recorded in North America. An effect of the earthquake is that it created tidal waves in the ocean, which flooded nearby towns. Also, the tidal waves were so powerful that California people got washed out from the beach and drowned.

Alaska also had a huge field of oil discovered in Prudhoe Bay. This oil field was the biggest in North America. Everyone thought that the oil was so valuable that they called it 'black gold.'

The state of Alaska also has four major cities: Anchorage, Fairbanks, Ketchikan, and Juneau. The populations of these major cities are also big. Anchorage's population is 173,017, Fairbanks 22,645, Ketchikan 7,198, and Juneau 19,528.

Alaska has seven large principal rivers. They are the Yukon, Kuskokwim, Tanana, Matanuska, Porcupine, and Koyukuk. These rivers are very big and stretch for about 1,400 miles across the state.

The state bird is the Willow Ptarmigan, state fish the King Salmon, state tree the Sitka Spruce, state flower the Forget-me-not, and the state nicknames are 'The Last Frontier' and 'The Land of the Midnight Sun.' Alaska has many symbols to represent the state.

Alaska's flag was created by Benny Benson, a thirteen year old. Wow, Alaska is an amazing state!

Kristine Sass
Grade 4

Being Thankful

Being thankful simply means that you are glad or well-pleased with what you have. When you receive something you are thankful for, you become cheerful, happy and very joyful. Being so, I am very much thankful for life.

In my opinion, I believe that life is the most important thing to be thankful for because it is the heart of the world. Without my life, I wouldn't have the many choices I have like school, having fun, chatting with my friends and family and other necessities like going shopping and attending church.

Without my life, I would not be able to learn, which is my most favorite thing. I love learning because it is like a puzzle that I can take apart and put together again. I can make mistakes and can correct them and start over on a fresh page. Finally, having fun with my family and friends is a very important and required part of my life. This would not happen without my life. I leave you here to think about "What would life be without life?"

In conclusion, to be thankful means that you are happy or well-pleased with what you have. It could be anything you want from toys or books to school or family, which are two of my main things that I am thankful for.

Aaliyah McPherson
Grade 5

The Snow Day

On February 12, 2006, it snowed. It stopped snowing on February 13, 2006, at 2:30 p.m. We got 14.2 inches of snow. I went outside with my brother and we had a snowball fight. We also built a snowman and made snow angels. It was so much fun.

It snowed so much that the next day, on Monday, we didn't have school. So my brother and I went outside and had another snowball fight. After that his friend came over, so I went inside because I was cold. My mom made me hot cocoa with tiny marshmallows. It was yummy. After I drank my hot cocoa I went to my room and sang on my karaoke machine.

On my karaoke machine I sang older songs. I sang "Sugarpie Honey Bunch," "What a Feeling," and so much more. After I sang I watched television. I watched *Wild 'n out* and *Mad TV* I like *Wild 'n Out* better. I think it is funnier. The only thing I like about *Mad TV* is the character Stuart, played by Micheal MacDonald.

After watching TV I helped my mom cook dinner. We were having bacon, lettuce, and tomato sandwiches (BLT's for short). After we ate dinner we watched *Guess Who*. Then at 8:00 we watched *7th Heaven*. My mom and I love *7th Heaven*. This episode was very exciting because Annie is going through stress because she doesn't want Simon and Rose to get married. After that I went to bed thinking about all the fun I had.

Jessica Rivera
Grade 6

The Gift of Love

The best gift of all is love. Sure you're not able to touch it, but you certainly can feel it. Feeling loved is probably one of the best feelings too. When you know you're loved, it makes you feel all warm and fuzzy inside. Not only that, but you also know that someone cares a lot about you. Therefore, I'd give the gift of love to my family and friends because they mean a lot to me and they always return the gift of love back to me. Another great thing about love is that it can always put a smile on your face, even on the worst day ever. This is because the gift of love can warm the heart (no matter what). Something else that is special about love is that it's just as good for the giver as it is for the receiver. For example, the result of loving someone is that you know that you probably made someone else's day. Also it's a great gift and it doesn't even cost anything but affection, kindness and care. One more great thing about the gift of love is that it's very precious and that you can give it to someone anytime, anywhere. As a result, love is one of the best gifts of all (even if you can't touch it).

Lisa Cannistra
Grade 6

Be Safe! Be Smart!

Following fire safety rules is smart. On November 28, 2005 I was lighting a candle when a Kleenex caught on fire. I grabbed the Kleenex out of the box and ran into another room so nothing else would catch on fire. I put the fire out and then went to tell my brother. He called my mom. My mom came and took me to a doctor who said that it was a second degree burn on my thumb, and a first degree burn on my wrist. He also said not to burst the blister on my thumb and that I could not play drums or sports for two weeks. Then on December 5, 2005 my kitty popped my blister, but it did not get infected. How thankful I was! I learned the hard way that obeying fire safety rules is smart.

Andrew Niederlander
Grade 6

Cumulonimbus Cloud

I am a Cumulonimbus cloud. I am very big and tall. I look fuzzy and grey. I am a big, big, cloud too. I am very dangerous. I can hurt and bring heavy storms. I can make houses catch on fire.

I am a dark cloud. Cause I bring heavy storms and bring thunder storms. I make lightning and strike people. I am a thunder machine.

When I look down I see wet land, a little bit of colorful cars, I see wet people from the rain, no kids outside.

That's why I am very very dangerous cause I can do a lot of bad things. I can make your happy days miserable by doing a lot of things like, make your house on fire. I can bring heavy rain and thunder storms. I can make lightning, I can make big puddles. That's why nobody likes me as a cloud.

Kenneth Giles
Grade 4

Today's Patriots

In this essay I am going to tell you about today's patriots. One of the patriots from the past is George Washington. If you don't know what a patriot is I will tell you. A patriot is someone who takes care of their country and obeys all the laws. In my essay I will tell you about some patriots from the past and the present. Now that you know what a patriot is listen to my essay about some of today's patriots.

One example of a patriot is all presidents. The president of our time now is George W. Bush. He is a patriot because he runs our country, makes all the right choices for us and leads us in war. That's why George W. Bush is a patriot.

The soldiers in the army are good patriots. They are because they fight in wars so we can be safe. They also risk their lives for us.

One more example of a good patriot is firemen and policemen. Firemen are a good example because they go in to fires and risk their lives to save people from getting killed. Policemen are an example because they arrest criminals and don't hurt anyone. One disaster the police and firemen had to do their job on was the knocking down of the twin towers.

When I was writing this essay I learned that a patriot is a good person. I hope you learned something too.

Christina Crish
Grade 5

The Power of Pen Pals

This is how I became pen pals with a stranger. My mother found an organization where you sponsor a child. We read an article telling how the organization fed the starving and clothed the homeless. We filled out the application and I selected a girl my age. Later we received a response stating we were sponsors and it was our duty to write letters to show we care.

I sponsor Shangita, who is from the Philippines. In her first letter Shangita wrote, "I like to read your letter." Later on, she said it was very exciting getting letters from me. I wonder how some pen pals feel when every day they wait to get a letter and nothing arrives. I am comforted knowing my friend, who is thousands of miles away, looks forward to getting my letters.

I, too, wait excitedly for her letters. I am happy to know that Shangita wants to be friends, and we can do that without ever meeting. Letters are an invisible chain link connecting you to friends and family. Due to Shangita's resources, I might have to wait 2 or 3 months for a letter, so I write as I wait. That does not lessen my eagerness for Shangita's letters.

The first letter I wrote her it was difficult because I worried about offending her or knowing what to say, but the next letter was much easier. It is both our responsibilities to be faithful pen pals and friends.

Gabrielle Young
Grade 5

Cancer

Cancer. A horrible thought isn't it? Do you know anyone who has it? If you do I know how you feel. My Aunt Maryanne had it and survived it. My Aunt Maryanne, a high school science teacher, lives in South Carolina. My family would go down for Thanksgiving. Sometimes they would come up.

One night I went downstairs to get a drink. I stopped dead in my tracks at the sound of my parents' voice. They were talking about my Aunt Maryanne. She had breast cancer. My mom and dad did not know how to tell my brother and me.

The next day my brother Derek and I were going to go outside to shoot hoops, when my dad said "Hold on you two just a second. Come here, I need to talk to you. Your Aunt Maryanne has breast cancer!"

One day my Aunt Maryanne called and said that she would be coming up a little bit earlier. The day my aunt came I had a very good time with her but then she left. We got a call that said my aunt had finished her fourth operation.

While shopping one afternoon with my mom, we saw in front of us a rack of shirts for breast cancer. I had the idea to get one for my two aunts, my grandma, and me. That is why my Aunt Maryanne is so special to me.

Alexandra Yanosick
Grade 6

Egypt

In Egypt, the main language is Arabic. The main food is rice and vegetables. This is because people who live in Egypt are mostly poor, and meat is very expensive.

The clothing in Egypt is made out of cotton because it can get very hot there and cotton is very light.

Egypt has four land regions, the Eastern and Western Deserts; the Sinai Peninsula with the Rugged Mountains which rises 8,600 feet above sea level. The last region in Egypt is the Nile Valley. The Nile is the longest river in the world. About 99% of Egyptians live along the Nile.

A long time ago, Egyptians invented the first writing system. This system used pictures called hieroglyphics. They also built the pyramids. These structures held the Egyptian rulers called pharaohs. The Great Pyramids are one of the Seven Wonders of the World!

Cairo has become an important industrial centre. For example, cotton is now made into clothing there, instead of being sent to Britain to manufacture. There are many places to visit when you go to Egypt. One place you can visit is The Great Pyramids of Egypt. Another places you can visit is the Valley of the Kings. It is where all the kings of Egypt are buried!

I enjoyed writing about Egypt, and I hope you learned something new about Egypt!

Jessica Doss
Grade 4

Dolphins

Did you know one dolphin lived to be up to 100 years old? Can you believe he lived to be that old? Well it's true a dolphin can live almost as long as an average human.

There are many different breeds of dolphins. One of them is a bottlenose dolphin. It can weight up to 400-600 pounds and can live between 30-50 years old. Also a bottlenose dolphin doesn't have any taste buds. Another type is an hourglass dolphin. It can only get to be 220 pounds. Last but not least there is a striped dolphin, which can weigh between 200 to 330 pounds.

Did you ever wonder if dolphins sleep? Unlike humans dolphins only sleep for eight hours each day. If dolphins go into a deep sleep they will suffocate and die. Another interesting fact is that they sleep with one eye open and one eye shut so they can see predators.

It took many years for scientists to understand a dolphin's language. Did you know dolphins can make 300 sounds per second? A fin slapping against the water means that they are annoyed. Dolphins can also make many other different sounds such as whistling, meowing, barking, different clicks, and many others.

Dolphins can swim up to 24 miles per hour. They travel in pods up to 15 dolphins. Dolphins can also dive between 101-150 feet deep and can stay under the water for 8 to 10 minutes and then have to come up for air. When they need to get air they can jump up 90 feet into the air.

In conclusion, dolphins are a lot like humans. Dolphins are a lot like people because they have their own language, they can swim, they are all different. That's what a dolphin's day is like.

Erin McConnaghy
Grade 5

What It Means to Be an American

I am happy to be a United States citizen, where I am free to do whatever I want. I can grow up to be whatever I want. In the United States there are laws to protect people and schools to educate people. In the United States, people are equal under the law. In the United States, I am free to make my own future. In the United States, there are laws to protect all the people. The police make sure people can have a safe place to live. I don't have to be a slave because I am a free American and my dream is to work at NASA exploring space. In the United States, everyone gets to go to school. In other countries, a little girl like me could not go to school. I am free to go to school and learn as much as possible so I can grow up to get a good job, raise a family and have a good life. The best thing about being American is that everyone in America can vote. Voting is a special responsibility. Voting is how we pick our leaders. Our leaders make laws that protect our rights and freedoms and keep us safe. I'm glad to be an American. I am free to be a happy little kid. I can enjoy days and dream about my future. I can't imagine living my life any other way.

Savannah Cluster
Grade 4

Under the Lights

I never thought that the Boston Cannons were that great. Then one remarkable experience completely changed my perspective on them. It all happened on one night in June at a Boston Cannons game. I'd been playing lacrosse for only one year, and I was not too familiar with the sport. Of course, that wouldn't matter if I was there just to watch the Cannons play. Actually, I wasn't. My entire team was there, and we were all waiting to play at halftime in front of six thousand people. I couldn't have been more anxious. All through the first half I was on the edge of my seat. It was impossible to concentrate on the game with all this anxiety building up inside of me.

When the buzzer sounded for halftime, I had my pads on and my stick in hand. Halftime was going to be short, so we started as quick as we could. I sprinted onto the field, and I'm not sure if it was the beaming lights, the giant turf field, or the stares of six thousand people around me, but all my anxiety and nervousness vanished. By the time the whistle blew, I was ready to play. It was the most fun I've ever had playing sports in my life. The game was only five minutes with running time, and we lost 1-0, but the sound of the crowd gasping when the ball hit the crossbar, or cheering when we left the field, made it all worth it.

Matt Doyle
Grade 6

How to Be Drug Free...

Many people get pressured into drugs. Most are teens, many questions are about drugs, and many people wonder why drugs are so addictive.

When teens get older they still are getting pressured. Many people start and then they can't quit. Kids all around the world get pressured into drugs. Many of these kids want to know how to break the pressure. All you have to do is say no. It would be hard, but you have to stand up to your friends or whoever is giving you the drugs and say that's not cool, drugs are bad for you. Many kids think that if they don't smoke then they won't be cool. Just say no for yourself.

Friends are a huge part of drugs, especially cigarettes. Friends have something to do with drugs most of the time. When, this happens, you should just ignore it. You never want to start drugs; they are horrible for you and your body. Once you start, you probably won't be able to stop.

You shouldn't get other people to start drugs. Many people lose 20 years off of their life just because of smoking. This happens because teens start and they can't stop. By smoking you don't just hurt yourself, you hurt other people as well, like secondhand smoke.

Smoking is bad in all ways and if you start you can't stop. If your friends pressure you, then just say "NO," and walk away.

Tayler Haas
Grade 6

Dancing Is for Me

I dance three times a week, and I take ballet, jazz, and character. There are many reasons why I dance. I started dancing in kindergarten, when I took classes after school. I did it because my friend was also taking the class, and the teacher was her mother. Now I am eleven, and I have different reasons for dancing.

Two years ago, I saw the North Carolina Dance Company perform in Chautauqua, New York. When I saw the way they moved, I was transfixed. I wanted so badly to be like them, to move like they did, with expression and grace. Usually you hear four-year-olds say "I wanna be a ballerina when I grow up," but that is what I told my mother after that performance. It was then I enrolled in more classes.

I worked hard, and I still do. Not because I know the teacher, or because my friend is in the class, but because I want to amaze audiences, move with expression, and inspire children as I was inspired two years ago. Now, I have been dancing for six years, and I am about to get my pointe shoes, a sign that my feet are strong enough to go on toe. This is a big step in my ballet career, and I hope to take many more in order to eventually become a ballerina.

Rosalie Daniels
Grade 5

How Great Is Art!

Art is great because it is fun. I draw every day.

Art is fun because I do it in my free time. I would rather do art than anything else.

You can draw with everyday items. Some things are pencils, pens, markers, colored pencils, crayons, chalk, and paint. You can make art out of anything. A line can turn into a picture of a book.

That's why I think art is great!

Danielle Tabin
Grade 4

Stinky TV

Adults are always concerned with what their kids watch on TV. A lot of people wonder why. Well, I think it is because there are a lot of bad shows out there, and they don't want their kids to watch any of those shows. That is why they are coming out with channel block and things like that.

I think TV is bad at times, but it can be good; like the educational channels and Discovery channel. Too much TV is not good, but it an enjoyable way to relax. Some channels are stupid and shouldn't be on the air. Some are for men who like blood and gore. Some are for women, like beauty channels.

In conclusion, kids and TV can be good or bad depending on what they watch. It's fine if you watch a little, but too much is not good. If TV wasn't invented, I would be disappointed because when I'm bored, I like to watch. TV is not important in life, but it can give us something to do to help us relax.

Richard LeVan
Grade 6

We Should Help

One day I was on vacation with my family, when my three-year-old sister, Grace, got lost. It was a very foggy day that day.

My dad had been watching her, but he turned around to look at me, and Grace ran to our tent. But there were a lot of tents and it was confusing for her. She got lost on the way, so she just wandered around in between the tents and umbrellas. She must have been really scared. She wandered, trying to find our tent.

About an hour later, the police found her walking around looking for our tent.

We are all very thankful that she was safe, but later my mom wondered why people had seen a scared three-year-old running around the beach without a parent, and not told the lifeguards.

I think we should help others. If someone had helped Grace, she might not have been lost even five minutes.

So help others!

Emma Doerfler
Grade 4

Hobbies

I have a lot of hobbies. I enjoy watching and playing football. Soccer is my favorite sport. I would consider it one of my hobbies. I enjoy going to my school's football games. I like to play all sports with my friends.

Reading is also a hobby of mine. Reading takes my head off things. When I read a good book I could picture what's going on. It seems to feel like I'm in the book. Books that I enjoy reading are the *Harry Potter* series and *The Series of Unfortunate Events*. Reading is great. It's just something I enjoy doing. I like to read when I'm stressed. Reading calms me down.

Going to the beach is great. I have a boat. I usually take my boat to Fire Island. The ocean is a little cold sometimes, but it feels good when it's really hot outside. In the winter my friends Julia, Gabby, and I go to the beach. I enjoy the beach.

Hanging out with my friends is fun. My friends and I go to a lot of places together. We love to have sleepovers and hang out when we can. When we go to Gabby's house we usually go quadding or dirtbiking in her backyard.

Christina Dutcher
Grade 6

The Important Hamster

The thing that is most important to me is my hamster. All I've wanted my whole life is a hamster. Now he is the most important thing in my life.

When I got my hamster, the Petsmart guy told me a lot of what I needed. But the coolest thing is that I got him on my birthday. So he's really important. I always care for him and hold him, and I always give him food and water when he needs it. But most importantly I love him. He's like part of the family.

Cody Martin
Grade 5

Dance a Dream

Many people have dreams. They keep their dreams inside themselves like a turtle keeps its head in its shell. I also have a dream, but I don't keep it inside of me. I let it flow out with music like a dream should. You probably are asking, what helps me make my dream come out and how do I do it. Well, what helps me is ballet. How I do it, well, I dance!

Ballet is basically dancing a story or a dream. It is a flowing, graceful motion. If you take ballet classes, you must wear little leather slippers on your feet. Girls must wear leotards and boys must wear a t-shirt tucked into tight shorts. Also, girls must wear tights and boys must wear socks. In the winter when it's cold, you can wear tight sweaters and leg warmers. As your dancing gets more and more advanced, you learn how to dance on pointe. That means you get harder leather shoes and in them you can stand on the tips of your toes. Also, as your level of dancing gets higher, you will be picked to participate and dance in ballets such as Cinderella, The Nutcracker, and Sleeping Beauty.

You don't have special requirements to dance. You can dance your heart out and tell your dream in ballet, nobody will stop you. In ballet, there is no wrong way to do something. Everyone is graceful and beautiful in his/her own way.

Ellen Sukharevsky
Grade 5

Basketball

Basketball is my favorite sport of all. Basketball is the best sport that I've played. I play guard and forward. I've played basketball for seven years. Once I had a basketball game and I scored 30 points and we won 25-50. My basketball shooting skills are great but my trick moves is what I have to improve on. I practice every day so I can get better at this sport. Basketball is okay for me because you don't get as hurt as football. When I go to college I want to play basketball there and get accepted to the NBA.

My favorite basketball teams are the New Jersey Nets and Detroit Pistons. My favorite basketball players are Michael Jordan, Vince Carter, and Jason Kidd. My favorite college team is the Uconn Huskies. Basket ball is interesting to me because it's not a boring sport.

My favorite high school basketball team is the Immaculate Mustangs. I go to Sacred Heart School and the name of the basketball team is the Sacred Heart Stallions. I love basketball so much that I practice with my brother who is in Immaculate High School. I even have video games about basketball. I even have a game named Shot Block. Basketball was my future dream to me. My friend and I are the best on the team. I tell my basketball team that there's no I in team and we should all have team spirit when we play our basketball games. Basketball is my dream come true.

Jason Mendes
Grade 6

The Awesome Shot

My whole body was shaking. I thought I was going to lose my balance. I got my pass. My suede gloves felt so wet. My hands felt like they were prickling inside. I felt as if everything was a blur. The wind rushed in my face. My eyes were blinking. I could do it.

The goalie seemed as if he were packing a Thanksgiving turkey with stuffing. I wrapped my hands around my stick tightly to get a good grip. I felt so sticky and wet. I whacked the puck. The puck went flying!

All of a sudden, the puck hit the back post in the net. I threw my stick in the air. I had scored. The cheers and shouts were filling my ears. Hockey is awesome!

Kristina Ushakova
Grade 4

The Perfect Snow Day with My Family and Friends!

The perfect snow day would be with my friends and my family, just having a great time. It would be the best snow day, throwing snowballs at each other, taking a break, and having some hot chocolate with whipped cream. We'd start laughing at each other because we have whipped cream on our faces and we'd just be having a great time. My sister would make a fool out of herself with the whipped cream on her face and so her friends would laugh at her; we would all laugh. Then when we get back outside, we all would make snow angels and throw some more snowballs. Soon when it got dark, we would all come and we'd run around like goofballs or go in the Jacuzzi and splash each other with water. Then we would relax and have more hot chocolate. Soon, when everyone left, we would talk on the phone or the computer, or they would all go home and get stuff so they could sleep over. We would talk and talk all night and laugh so much! That would be the best snow day ever!

Pauline Rusciano
Grade 6

Soccer vs Softball

Soccer and softball are my two favorite sports. They are alike and different in many ways. I will tell you why.

Soccer and softball are alike in many different ways. They both use balls and they both have teammates. Each sport involves running and lots of practice. Both sports even have certain positions for each game. They are alike in a lot of ways.

Soccer and softball are not only alike in many ways, but they're different, too. In soccer you play with your feet and in softball you play with your hands. In both sports the balls are different sizes. Softball you score runs, but in soccer you score goals. For soccer you have halves and for softball you have innings. I told you there is a lot of differences to both sports.

Soccer and softball are very interesting and they both have a lot of things in common and a lot of things different. I love soccer and softball. Do you?

Ashley Hurey
Grade 6

Hurricane Katrina

On August 29, 2005, in the city of New Orleans, the most deadly natural disaster in the history of the United States occurred. Many died because of this tragedy. Most of the land was flooded and there were many fires. People held on to their lives for as long as they could.

Hurricane Katrina contributed to engulfing 80 percent of New Orleans underwater. Thousands of humans were stranded in different places. People were stranded on bridges, highways, and even in baseball stadiums. There was water everywhere. People were stuck where they were until the rescue workers came to save them.

When Hurricane Katrina flew through New Orleans it left no food for the people. Many people died each day because they had no access to any edible items. This went on for about four or five days. Every day, children all around the world whine and complain because they do not like what they are having for dinner, when some people that were hit by the hurricane didn't even have food to eat for days.

The rescue workers tried hard to save everyone, but there were still people out there that needed help. Firemen worked day in and day out to put out fires in New Orleans. Even though most of the humans lived, they will always remember the loss they experienced on that tragic day when Hurricane Katrina hit New Orleans.

Abby Gettig
Grade 6

Nothing But Net

Basketball is not only my passion but also something I share with my dad. It makes my dad and me extremely close. I call him my coach because he constantly helps me with my game. He makes me a better player all around and teaches me the importance of basketball. Not only does he inspire me to be a good basketball player, but he helps me be a better student.

I have had a dream for as along as I can remember to play basketball and get a full scholarship to the University of Connecticut. I've always wanted to be the starting point guard for the Huskies. Over the past summer my team played in a tournament in Connecticut. One of the games was at the home court where the Huskies play. You can imagine how excited I was to be standing on the court where all the great athletes played! My favorite player was the captain of the Huskies, Diana Turasie. My friends and I were so excited. We went up and down the stands a thousand times taking millions of pictures. I felt like the luckiest person in the world.

As the day came to an end I took one last shot and kissed the floor, knowing someday I'll win a championship on that court! I know that my mom and dad will be there to support my dreams and cheer me on all the way to victory.

Halle Majorana
Grade 6

Saying Good Bye

When I was little I had a black and white cat. His name was Poochi. He was really special to me because I got to name him. I loved him more than I had loved any other cat. He would play with me, he would come when I called him, and he would sleep with me at night. Years later my mom and I started to notice he was getting sick. For a while we just let him be, thinking he would get better…but he didn't. Once and a while his nose would start to bleed and he would cough a lot.

One day my mom and I went to the vet. The vet said he would get better. As a few months went by I could tell he was getting weaker and weaker. He didn't want to play anymore, he just wanted to sleep all day. One day when I got home from school I called him, but he didn't come. My mom said not to worry and that she would let him in later.

I felt lonely that night. The next morning when I got up, he was in the kitchen wrapped in a towel. My mom found him outside. She said that she thought he was dead, but as she was carrying him inside he moved. As I was standing there I started to cry. All I know is at least I got to say GOODBYE.

Erika Johnson
Grade 6

The Fuse

For Christmas I got a rocket. Five weeks passed by and my dad and I constructed the rocket. We put the parachute into the tube, the engine into the tube, the wires on, and now in exactly 3-2-1 I pressed the button and boom I heard (in my head). It wouldn't go. I didn't know what to say. I tried but it wouldn't work. Soon I got grounded because I needed my mom's candlewicks and my dad's matches to make a fuse. I built it again and shot it back up. Out came the parachute and I was ready to launch it again.

Logan Gardner
Grade 4

An Elementary School Memory Boo Hoo

I went to Red House Run. My favorite memory was my graduation. It was tear-jerking and happy. It's sad because I had to leave everybody I felt comfortable with especially my two best friends in the whole world. Their names are Kim and Ifeoma. But, holding the certificate made me feel proud. Then they showed a slide show and they showed me and my friends together. I'll always remember those memories that we shared with each other. Then it was party time! I only stayed for a couple of minutes. When I said goodbye to Kim and Ifeoma it took so long.

Me, Kim and Ifeoma still call each other. Then I had a party and it was fun. I swam, ate cake, and had all kinds of food and drinks. That night I put my papers and binder and all that good stuff in a box to remember the memories. I took pictures of everyone like my teacher Ms. Quinn. This is why graduation was sad and cheerful, mostly sad.

Tracy Cochran
Grade 6

The Importance of Education

Education is very important in your life. It can help determine whether you are going to be an architect or a garbage man. It all starts in preschool and goes on from there. Think about it. A good education can lead you to a good college, a good job, and lots of money. Do you want a good education?

College is very important. It leads you toward what you are going to do for a living, depending on what you major in. The best colleges are ivy league schools. To get into college, you apply for the ones you want to go to and then take a test to get into it. That is how you get to college.

A good job is very important. It helps you survive. A good one helps you make lots of money. If you don't have a good job, you may be homeless begging for money. That is why a good job is very important.

For most things, you have to get them for money. If you had a good education and a good job, you would have lots of money to get things. You can have a mansion and a Hummer if you had lots of money. That is what you can have with lots of money.

Now you know where education could get you in life. Hopefully, all the things I said will urge you to get a good education. Remember, nothing's impossible!

Andrew Branagan
Grade 6

A Start of Something New

Beep, beep! I stepped nervously onto the bus. My first All-County practice was going to be starting in about a half-hour! I was so excited. Garden City Middle School seemed far away from Shelter Rock Elementary, but we got there quite quickly.

When we arrived at the school, Mr. Capidacasa, the chaperone, told us to follow the signs to our practice rooms. I listened to his directions and found my room. It was a large, unfamiliar auditorium.

When I entered the auditorium, I saw people sitting in cliques. I, on the other hand, didn't know anyone so I sat all by myself. But, I had a feeling things would get much better.

Soon I found myself sitting next to a very nice girl. She introduced herself as Toniann. We conversed until it was time to start singing.

After the "captain" of All-County introduced herself and the conductor, we got started right away. We sang beautifully!

After our dinner break, we sang for about two more hours. Finally, it was time to find our district and get back on the bus. I couldn't wait to go home!

As I was sitting on the cold seat of the bus, I realized for the next few days I would be experiencing events that only come once in a lifetime, and I knew that I had gotten off to a good start.

Delaney Parker
Grade 6

One Life's Struggle

When General Lee surrendered to General Grant, that's when it all ended. Life in Virginia changed for everyone. After the Civil War, life was hard for some people. Some had lost loved ones, like the Robert family. In my mind I could see the mother and her daughter sitting by the father and son's graves. You could feel the cold wet tear drops, hear their loud cries, and still smell the black powder. Deep down inside you knew it's got to hurt to lose a loved one. So just imagine what these two innocent people went through.

The mother felt a lot of pain. Her husband and son just died in the war. She felt lost and doesn't know what to do. She suffered from sadness, remembering the good times the family had — on Christmas opening presents by the fire, or on her son's birthday by their pond.

The daughter, Katy, is only five. She didn't know why her daddy and brother were not coming back, but she felt pain. The daughter heard her momma crying. She saw her momma struggling, but she didn't know why.

It's gotta be hard for Mrs. Robert to be the momma and daddy. It must have been even harder for Katy to understand what happened to her daddy and brother. Life for the Robert family will never be the same. Millions died fighting in the Civil War. This was an account of one life's struggle.

Brandon Heath
Grade 5

Staying Fit

Does staying fit give you a healthy body and prevent stress and diseases?

Staying fit is important. Daily physical activity can help your body to be fit and helps to prevent diseases and stress. Your body is very important. If you're unhealthy, you're at risk for dying. If you're fit you have more control over your body. Staying fit helps you look and feel better.

Staying fit prevents high blood pressure, coronary heart disease, stroke, gallbladder disease, osteoarthritis, and sleep apnea. These are just some of the diseases that staying fit helps prevent. Being obese is one of the most common causes of heart-attacks. If you have a pain in your heart DON'T IGNORE the PAIN. Go straight to the doctor's because you might have heart disease. To avoid all of these diseases there is only one thing to do; GO OUT AND EXERCISE!!!

In order to stay fit you must eat a healthy diet. Going to fast food restaurants all the time is bad. If you do go to fast food restaurants, only get a salad or yogurt. It's a fact, when you cook at home, the food you cook has less fat in it and it tastes better. Also, think of something to try to stop eating so much. If you eat just to chew, try some gum so you won't have the desire to chew anymore.

I hope after reading this article you will change your mind about staying fit.

Elizabeth Palesano
Grade 4

Battery Wagner

The story of Battery Wagner is little known. This was an important battle because for the first time since the Revolutionary War black troops were used. The Union used them knowing it would be a difficult engagement.

Battery Wagner was a Confederate controlled sand fortress. The Union needed control of this Battery to bombard Charleston, South Carolina for two reasons. The first was because the British would have helped the Confederacy in exchange for cotton for British textile mills. The second reason was because if Charleston was not taken, the South would have had the capability to unload needed supplies from Europe.

The newly formed 54th Massachusetts Colored Infantry was to head the attack! Colonel Robert Shaw, the son of a Boston abolitionist, was in charge. Shaw had already seen action at Antietam in September, 1862 where he was wounded by shrapnel.

The Union forces began the attack on July 18, 1863. Battery Wagner had been bombarded by sea and land, but none of the shells managed to cause much damage to the Battery. When the 54th charged the Battery they were greeted by canister. The 54th did make it to the Battery's parapet and a man named Sergeant Carney planted the Union flag on it. Heavy hand-to-hand combat took place.

The aftermath of the battle was tremendous! The Union's losses were estimated at 1,689 men. The Confederacy lost only 174 men. The Battery was not taken until after a siege. Colonel Shaw was killed in action.

Adam Wilson
Grade 6

Friendship

A gift that cannot be wrapped in a box is friendship. You can consider yourself a lucky person when you have a friend. A friend is someone that is always there for you, when you're sick, sad, or happy, or when you just want to be in the company of someone you feel comfortable with. When I lost my grandma my friend was right there for me. She made me cards, brought me flowers and kept my mind off the sadness. Another important part of friendship is that it is not one-sided. My friend was there for me, so when her father had a heart attack I spent the week with her. We did everything together. She knew that I felt her pain and worried right alongside with her. The best thing about friendship is that you can always be yourself. You don't have to think about things to say or feel funny when there is nothing to say. Conversation is easy and laughing feels natural. A true friend will accept you no matter what you say and will be there to help you if you need it.

Whenever I need someone my best friends Megan and Melinda are always there for me. I never hesitate to ask them what they think of something or to help me out when I need them. Without close friends my life would be boring and lonely. With them I share some of the best times of my life.

Lauren Lorenzo
Grade 6

Movies

The first movie shown in the U.S. was shown on an outdoor screen on June 28, 1896. Since then, movies have grown greatly in popularity. They are popular first because there is a big screen on which to watch the show. Secondly, there are many treats available for sale at the theatre. Finally, there are a variety of different movie options. Going to the movies is one of the best forms of entertainment.

A large screen seems to make movies come alive. Having a large screen makes you feel like you are really there. Many people can watch the show at once. Watching a movie with a large crowd raises the level of excitement!

If a jumbo screen is not enough, there are snacks also. There are lots of different treats you can buy, and a larger selection than most people have at home. Parents will more likely say yes to candy at the movies than at home. Treats add to the fun of the event.

There are numerous movies to choose from. You can see any recent movie you desire. Once you have seen one, you can see another. No matter your age, there is usually a movie playing that you would like. Watching a movie is an exciting pastime! The extra large screen, various tasty treats available, and several options of movie choices should convince you that movies are a great recreational option. Thank goodness they have been enriching our lives since 1896!

Kyle Wilson
Grade 5

Amerigo Vespucci

Amerigo Vespucci was born in Florence, Italy on March 18th, 1454. He was an Italian explorer. Amerigo had three brothers Girolamo, Antonio, and Bernardo. Amerigo was also called Americus Vespucci. When Amerigo was a little kid his hobby was copying maps. He also was interested in astronomy when he was a boy. He died of Malaria in 1512.

In May 1499, Amerigo was 45. He showed the Spanish court his plan for finding an Asian route to the New World. They reached South America in 24 days. They went South and located Brazil's coast. Amerigo was the first person to find the mouth of the Amazon River. Amerigo kidnapped 500 Native Americans.

In 1501 he sailed for Portugal. He landed near the eastern tip of Brazil. He went as far south as Argentina.

South and North America were named after him in 1507. Amerigo was the first to state that North and South America were not connected to Asia. Amerigo later thought of a system to measure the Earth.

Amerigo Vespucci went on four voyages and brought back riches and many other items. I think Amerigo was very important and special. I also think he plays an important part on how the world got its name. Without Amerigo I wonder if America would be like the America it is today.

Hailey Tyminski
Grade 5

The Amazing White House

There have been 43 presidents in the U.S. There was only one president that didn't live in the White House. That person was George Washington. I'd heard that Thomas Jefferson's guests said they liked his macaroni, waffles, and his famous ice cream.

The White House has a blue room, green room, and a ballroom, and several dinning rooms and living rooms. Also if you want to get really excited check out this, at Christmas they make two 100 pound ginger bread houses that look like the White House.

President Bush has been elected 2 times over the past 4 years. In 2008 Bush has been president for 8 years. The president's dog's name is Barney.

Lauren Ashley Godissart
Grade 4

German Shepards

German Shepards are one of the most fascinating dogs in the world. They are one of the most fun pets to have because of their playing abilities. They are known for their work with the police officers as K-9 dogs. They are also used in competition and dog shows. Those are just some facts about German Shepards.

They are such fun pets because of many reasons. One because they are so active and are always willing to play with you. They are so furry and cuddly at night and are always protecting you. Finally, because if you are sad they will try to make you feel better by playing with you. German Shepards are lots of fun.

They are most known for being a K-9 dog. In police work they are used for sniffing out drugs because they have one of the strongest noses. They are also used for chasing people because of their bite and speed. Finally, they are used for going in places where the officers can't go. These dogs play an important role in police work.

These dogs are used in many competitions and dog shows. The competitions are for best police dog. Another competition is for best partner and dog. The dog shows are for best look and style. These dogs are very beautiful.

Now you know why I picked German Shepards. I did because they are smart, they are beautiful, and they are one of the best dogs in the world. That is why.

Brendan Leary
Grade 6

Football

My favorite TV show is football. It comes on only on Sundays because it was the playoffs. The Super Bowl is on a Sunday. The reason I like football is because I used to play it. I like watching it because I like to see who wins the games, and how badly the other team loses. The team I love is the Philadelphia Eagles. They did badly this year. They need better draft picks. If they do, all they need to do is win and not get hurt. Next year, I'm playing football again.

Bryan Jackson
Grade 4

We Must Save Brandy Station

Brandy Station was where one of the early Civil War battles took place. There, the Union and the Confederate Calvary fought to a draw. In the beginning, J.E.B. Stuart was reviewing his troops when the Union attacked the Confederates. The battle raged throughout the day. The reason for the Union attack was because of the train station there. By the end of the day both armies retreated. Now we must save this piece of history from destruction.

Daniel Comyn
Grade 5

Big Foot

I was traveling down the hallway when all of a sudden, I tumbled swiftly over something and slid across the hall. "Whoops!" I exclaimed. I stood up, peering down, I gazed at what had caused this unpleasant accident. It was worse than I thought, there were two of them!

Every day is the same, but today was different. I walked down the hall to get a drink but I tripped over something. I went to see what it was. It was my feet! Kids saw what happened and they laughed. I burst into tears. As I sobbed down to the bathroom kids giggled and snickered at me.

"Ha, ha, Alyssa fell over her big feet!" they yelled. Even in the bathroom girls said, "Did you hear? Some fourth-grader tripped over her feet!" The girls giggled, "She is a bigfoot!" I was so embarrassed! When I got home my mom asked me what was wrong. I told her and she made me feel better. The next day nobody laughed at me. I was happy.

Alyssa Ryan
Grade 5

What Freedom Means to Me

I think to be free means that you aren't always being told what to do. In the United States we have many freedoms that other countries don't. We can vote, speak freely, express our feelings about the government, own weapons, have a variety of television and radio programs, and we can practice whatever religion we choose to. Having freedom is a big responsibility also. Having too much freedom can cause problems. It is a very fine balance between the two. On September 11, 2001, after the terrorist attacks, we lost some of our feelings of freedom…possibly forever. We can never feel totally safe again. In some countries, they have never felt safe due to total government control. The men that founded this country protected our freedoms in the Constitution, a very important document. Our government would like all countries to have the freedoms that we enjoy. We are trying to establish that in Iraq now through setting up voting and fighting off terrorists that are trying to take over the country and run it their way. Everyone has a right to have freedom because no one owns another person or has the right to totally control their life. I hope someday everyone in the world can experience at least some of the freedoms that we take for granted.

Joshua Keiple
Grade 4

My First Christmas Eve

Clocks ticking, time passing backwards on Christmas Eve, 1994, my first Christmas Eve. In my little town of Honeyville it is usually quiet all year 'round, but when the Christmas holidays come around, everyone rocks around the Christmas tree.

This year, I don't think anyone will ever forget this Christmas Eve.

When I finally fell asleep, a teenager yelled, "TIME IS RUNNING BACKWARDS!" She woke up the entire town! Then, one little boy yelled Santa's not coming and sat down and cried. As I watched the clock, it turned 12:59, 12:58, 12:57 and so on.

When the sun came up, everyone was walking, talking and running backwards, even I was jogging backwards. All of the store signs said CLOSED, the fountain water went up instead of down and citizens' clothes were inside out and backwards. It was just like opposite, except the clock kept running backwards, tock tick, tock tick.

When the clocks finally started tick tocking again, it seemed like magic. Everyone's clothes were on appropriately, the fountain sprayed water down and the stores were open for business in the morning. This was my worst Christmas Eve ever.

I believed towards the end of the backwards day, everyone just wanted to have a normal day again like last Christmas Eve and the one before that and so on. To me, my gift from Santa was that the clocks ran regularly again, tick tock, tick tock.

Lauren Gedeon
Grade 5

My Family

I have a family not like most families. My brother is so cool! He loves me and I love him. He takes me places like the movies, pool places, to hang out somewhere. Even though we fight, when it's over we're back doing the same old thing. He's 21 and in college.

My mom, she's to me a hero. I look up to her for advice. I look up to her for help. She is the one who works in the family. She works hard and somehow she always pulls through. My dad is invincible. He does magic. He does cool adventure stuff. We go four-wheeling and river rafting. Together, my mom and dad protect me. Together, they help me. Together, they love me and I love them.

Another someone in my family is my dog. She is a good guard dog. She's playful at times and at times she's lazy.

My grandparents are cool. They are Italian. My grandfather is an excellent cook. My grandma knits some cool blankets. My Nana is the funniest out of our whole family. She's old, but fun and cool. She's my dad's mom. She's a great babysitter. My uncle Mark is an amazing artist. He draws things that I consider to be masterpieces.

Ray Howard
Grade 6

What Is Inside of Me

Inside of me is a whole lot of love, a whole lot of fun, and a lot of glee. Inside of me is my family and friends, my pets and my neighbors, and me, myself, and I. But the most important thing inside of me is an

F, for all the fun things I've done with this word.

A, for an awesome time with this word.

M, for the many, many, many, etc…exciting things I've done with this word.

I, for I can't believe I've been with this word so long.

L, for all the loving and caring this word has given me, and last, but not least,

Y, for "y" is this essay about this word so long?

I think that you have figured out what this word is. It is FAMILY. I have spelled this word because I love this word, and it loves me!

David Matvey
Grade 4

Baseball vs Softball

Do you know some differences between softball or baseball? If not, I could definitely tell you some. I hope you enjoy hearing about differences and things that are alike about two really fun sports.

Things that are the same about softball and baseball are: you use a ball. For both of the sports you can play on the same field. There are the same amount of bases. There aren't many things that are alike.

There are a lot of differences between the two sports. In softball you use a bigger ball and it is yellow. In baseball the ball is smaller and it is white. For these sports you have to use a different size bat. Because the ball is bigger in softball you have to use a larger glove. The pitching is different in both sports. In softball you swing your arm back and then snap your wrist. In baseball you bring your arm back in an "L" position then throw.

I really enjoy playing both sports. Even though the sports seem very different they're actually a lot alike. I hope you learned about the two sports!

Chelsy Lalama
Grade 6

Belonging

I think I don't belong in a new school sometimes. First of all I don't know anybody in my school. Secondly meeting the wrong kind of people can affect the other friends you have. The wrong people can be mean to your real friends and you will have to pick between the two friends you have. Also, getting on the bad side of bullies can get you into a lot of trouble. Third of all, sometimes you won't have anybody to sit next to in class. Getting assigned seats can get you put in the wrong position. Something might go wrong and you will get separated from your friends and not like the person you are assigned next to. In conclusion, belonging is important in this world.

Brittany Johnson
Grade 6

Tap vs Ballet

Many people who don't know very much about dance often wonder what the differences between tap and ballet are. Well, there are MANY differences between them. For one thing, they use very different shoes.

In tap, your shoes have a slight heel, and they're tight fitting. In ballet, you use tight fitting shoes also, but they have soft soles. Ballet moves are all named from French words, while tap moves are created by whoever started the move. Tap dancing is usually done to jazzy, upbeat music. Ballet is done to classical music or any music made by a piano. Ballets are very calm shows, where there is no speaking done. Popular ballets are Swan Lake, the Nutcracker, Sleeping Beauty, and Romeo and Juliet. Tap dances are mostly done in musicals. There are not very many shows completely focused on tap.

Even though tap and ballet have many differences, they also have may similarities. Both were originated in the 1600s. This was a time when a lot of other dance forms were created. They are also types of dance that are performed around the world.

In their own ways, they are different, and yet the same. Between the shoes and origins, you can tell that they are very complicated things to do.

Alyx Mance
Grade 6

Family Far Away

Have you ever missed someone so much, you would do anything to see them? My cousins, Adrian, and Isabel live in Madrid, Spain. I enjoy seeing them when they come to the United States. Even though we live in different cultures, it's amazing to see how many things we have in common.

My Aunt Shari, a school teacher, teaches English. My cousin Adrian plays soccer for his school, he is very talented. Every summer, they come to visit. We teach each other a lot of things. We teach them how to play baseball, basketball, and football. They teach me how to speak Spanish and Adrian teaches me how to count to one hundred in Spanish. They also bring candy. My favorite is the Pop Rocks, which tastes like strawberry.

My cousins and I are different in many ways. I speak and write in English and they speak and write in Spanish. They only play soccer, while I play many sports, basketball and football.

There are many ways in which my cousins and I are alike. We both speak English well and we like the same foods, pasta and chicken. I love it when Adrian and Isabel come to visit and I can't wait until the summer.

Having family far away can be a great experience. Whether you have family far away or close, spend time with them.

Emily Wahl
Grade 6

Saturday Morning Orchestra

It's Saturday, 9:30 a.m. Over fifty kids are attempting to wake up. The room is filled with sounds of chairs being unstacked, music stands being erected and the clattering of instruments being unpacked.

Initially, my ears only tune into the sounds of the strings; pluck, pluck, screech, screech, piiinnnggg!! The flutes and clarinets add to the mix, an array of high and low whistles and chirps. The room is beginning to come alive.

I try to wake up. I stretch and tap my fingers across the strings. The lead violinists' stands up and asks for an "A" from the oboe. With my bow rosined up and ready to go I screech and squeal to find that perfect note. I found my "A," it's music to my ears. Notes of every kind are flying around the room.

The conductor is ready to begin. Enthusiastically but stern, he raises his arms high into the air. Every note comes to a screeching halt. Dead silence…Swoop, his hands drop. I feel the cold steel strings of the cello vibrate, as my fingers fly swiftly over them. The rosin dust from by bow flies off as it races across each string. The conductor's arms flail every which way, telling whom to play when.

A mix of maple sap rosin and the snacks of people eating and listening begin to permeate around me. As I play E# (sharp), it feels just right. I know this will be a good rehearsal.

Louis Di Bonaventura
Grade 6

Seizing the Day

After school most of my friends go home and either turn on the TV or go on the internet. They are wasting time doing that instead of studying or doing their homework. Most kids who do that and put their homework aside, say they will do it after their show is finished. Then they watch another show and it never gets done. Many kids do this, but so do many adults. They may have to do a big business report on a different company and put it aside until the last minute. Then it may have to be at least four pages long, so they will have to work on it all day instead of doing something they want to do.

Instead of wasting the time you should seize the day. Seizing the day means getting past wasting the day on video games and sitting around. You also should exercise to seize the day. Like when you exercise you burn calories, but you also burn time. Activities are good for seizing the day too. When you do an activity, either an active one or one like chess, you are still using time wisely.

Seizing the day is not hard when you are really bored. You can just go outside or have your parents take you to the park. If you live in the city you can also read a book or volunteer for a shelter. Now remember don't waste time, seize the day.

Michalla Martin
Grade 6

The Big Fat Jump

I stood in the snow like a bird without wings. I was so nervous, my legs were trembling. My feet felt like they were on fire. The wind was whipping my face. I knew I had to do it. All the other kids did.

I was ready to do it, even though my stomach felt like it had 67 wrestlers in it. I gave myself a push. I shot down the slope, over the jump, and landed.

I couldn't believe it! I made it over the jump. It was almost like a miracle. I felt like I was on ground too much. Suddenly I said, "Let's go. There are more jumps!" I think I should go pro.

Siobhan McSweeney
Grade 4

My Family Cruise

"Whoa, this ship is huge!" I yelled to my parents. When we rode up nine stories in the glass elevator, and looked down, I hung onto my dad because I got scared.

Later that day, people brought our luggage to our room. They gave us bath towels shaped as different animals different days.

At dinnertime, we met a family from England. They have three kids named Matthew, Jon, and Katherine. Katherine played dolls with my sister. Matt and Jon played hide and seek with my brother and me.

On the cruise we went to Mexico, Jamaica, and the Grand Cayman Islands.

On Grand Cayman, we got to swim with stingrays. It felt weird, because the skin of the stingrays felt like soft jello. We went to a turtle farm and picked up huge turtles.

At Mexico, we saw the old Mayan Ruins.

At Jamaica, we climbed Duns Waterfalls, a huge waterfall. Would you like to go on a cruise?

Ryan Christopher
Grade 4

My Family Is Important to Me

Is your family important to you? My family is the most important thing to me in my life. Whenever something is wrong they take care of me. They give me a good education in school. They help me with my homework if I need help. They come to my soccer games and my basketball games. Some kids don't have family and I am lucky because I do. They will always give you a hug and a kiss before you go to bed. Sometimes they are mad at you but they still love you. They always celebrate your birthday. If I don't understand something they help me with it. It is much more fun if your family comes with you to do things. My grandparents are important to me because when I go over to their house they treat me with something. Every August my cousins from Virginia come to my house. We go to Ocean City and go crabbing with each other. That is very FUN! Every summer we go in our nice pool. Every Thanksgiving I go over to my aunt's house for the best family dinner ever.

Michael Kraus
Grade 5

Juan Ponce de Leon

Juan Ponce de Leon is a famous explorer who founded Florida. He also sailed for Christopher Columbus. They were a good team.

Juan Ponce de Leon is famous for everything he did when he was an explorer. As a kid he always wanted to be a Spanish explorer. He also was a Spanish soldier.

Ponce de Leon had interesting facts, like he named Florida after the Spanish weeds of Easter Pacua de Florida because it was the Easter season when he landed there. He also had goals. He wanted to find gold and the so-called legendary fountain of youth. He also set foot in Florida in 1513. That's also where he explored the coast of Florida.

Juan Ponce de Leon was born in 1460. He died in 1521 in Pascua de Florida by Native Americans. He ran into many Native Americans. He also fought many Native Americans. One of the Native Americans shot him once in the stomach. hen he got shot in the back, then in the heart with a poisoned arrow. One more in the back.

He also went to Puerto Rico, Florida and Cuba. Then he went in to the Gulf of Mexico. This all happened in 1513. He met many more explorers.

As you can see, Ponce de Leon is a really awesome explorer. I want to have adventures in space though.

Michael Knobel
Grade 5

The Outstanding People in My Family

My family is very important to me. Every one of us care for each other. My family is very loving. No matter what we stick together. My family is caring to anyone who steps in our house.

Out of my family my mom Kim, my aunt Kaia, and myself (Shayla) are really close. My mom has two kids including myself. She has two girls. My sister's name is Shaabria. We're ok, but we are not really close. My aunt has three kids. She has two boys and one girl. The boys' names are Nasir and Javell. The girl's name is Tajana. We are not really close, she's closer to my sister. I'm really close to my aunt's boys. They think of me as an aunt. My aunt Kaia is a LPN. My entire family supports her every move. Whenever we're sick she knows what to do. It's nice having her around.

My family is very fun and funny. Every time one of us receives a reward or something else important, our family is always behind us. If we don't succeed at something, my family is still proud of us. They say, "No matter what I'm always proud of you."

A family is a special thing to have. Without a family you're nothing because you can't do everything by yourself. You need help at some point. If you have a family, never take advantage of it. A family is important and you should always be thankful to have it.

Shayla Robinson
Grade 6

My Brother

For 9 years of my life I was an only child, until my brother came.

On August 6, 2003 I couldn't wait to see my new sibling. My stomach was filled with butterflies. As my grandma drove me to the hospital, I couldn't wait to see what my new brother would look like.

When I got to the hospital I held my brother for the first time. He was light, pleasant, and as red as a tomato. When he looked at me with his eyes half open, I knew we were going to get along.

When we took him home from the hospital I watched him lay on the floor for hours. He was cute and gentle. When he was 3 months old, he opened his eyes and smiled at me, and I played with him a lot. After he grew older he could walk and he was starting to talk. I played with him for the rest of the day when I got home from school.

Now that he is almost three years old, he is always getting in trouble. Now I don't think he is so pleasant anymore, because he's always ruining everything I own.

Even though my brother is still a pain, I love him whether he gets on my nerves or not. I just wish that I could call my brother that cute, gentle, pleasant baby I first met.

Christen Sedlak
Grade 6

On the Farm

Do you have pets? I have six chickens, one rabbit, one degu, two cows, and two dogs.

I always like to say "Hi" to my pets in the morning and say "Good Night" to them in the evening. I always go out to tell them secrets. Whenever I get angry, I go out to my chicken pen or rabbit pen and tell them; and then I feel better. I was very sad when my favorite chicken and rabbit died. They like it when I give them a treat. I like to play with my degu; it is from the kangaroo family. They look like a rat and a kangaroo but are smaller. I have dogs named J.R. and Sniffles. J.R. gives me a hug every day when I see him.

I think everybody should have a pet. They can teach you responsibility, and you can have a lot of fun with them at the same time. It is fun to take care of them in the morning, at night, and in between.

Dana Herrick
Grade 5

All About Me

My favorite thing about my life is spending time with my family and friends. What I like to do is just hang out and talk about stuff. My favorite thing about my friends is that they make me happy when I am sad. My friends are Kristin, Alexis, Lindsay, Bianca, Brianna, and Alanna. My favorite food is ice cream. My favorite sport is basketball. Sports are a great way for me to make new friends. My friends make me happiest because we can talk forever and when we get together we have a blast.

Jessica Trester
Grade 6

Valentine's Day

Have you ever wondered why Valentine's Day is important? Why is it a holiday? Is it a day of love, flowers or chocolate? Well I can tell you!

So people wonder…Why is Valentine's Day important to so many people? My opinion is that people need a holiday to love. Not just to spend time with family, but with the love of your life! You could go to the movies or go to get ice cream and even get a kiss from your crush!

You may be asking…What does Cupid have to do with anything? Well, Cupid is an angel who can make people fall in love!! With his arrows, he shoots at 2 people and they "magically" fall in love! He's a mascot for Valentine's Day!

And what is up with cards called Valentines? Well, they are like getting flowers or chocolates, only they are cards that say sweet things like "I love you" or "Be mine!" It is most common for secret admirers to send them, or even your family members!

And how are hearts involved with Valentine's Day? Hearts are a symbol of love and since Valentine's Day is a "love" holiday, they go really great together!

So, I hope I made Valentine's Day pretty clear for you! If you want to know more, look in the encyclopedias or on the Internet! I hope you do know somewhat about Valentine's Day now! And don't forget that Valentine's Day is a "love" holiday, so crush on!!!

Alexandra Steen
Grade 5

Imagination

Having an imagination can lead to many problems, but it can also lead you to another world. So try to imagine somewhere where you wouldn't miss anything, or even try to imagine somewhere where you're allowed to imagine.

Imagination is hard to get past in school because you run into problems with not paying attention to anything. The problems people run into with imagining at school are missing what the teacher is talking about because of imagination. Also imagination can lead to a problem in front of anyone like your parents and your friends. The way it involves your parents and friends are that you don't pay attention to what your parents or friends have to say when they are talking to you, which causes those people to get mad at you. Imagination can help you while you are reading. Well imagination can help you, because it helps you understand what you are reading. So imagination can be bad in school but it can also help you.

How does imagining take you into another world? It takes you into another world because you barely know what's going on around you. It also takes you into another world because you have different characters, a different setting and different places in your imagination every time you imagine. When people imagine they normally have a place where they would like to visit, a person that they really like or someone they think is nice. So have fun and imagine!

Elise Kaveney
Grade 6

Citizenship in My Life

Citizenship is a very important part of my life. I have many examples of what I have done to be a good citizen. One of them is through Boy Scouts. I have done many activities with my Boy Scout Troop. One of them is gravel bagging. We put gravel in bags and the local power companies use them to keep the power poles in place. Also, every year we go up to Graves Mountain Lodge to help out with their Apple Festival. The troop helps with serving food and helping people with their trays. We also take care of the trash around the Lodge. Since Graves Mountain is an apple orchard we help customers take the apples back to their cars. Another activity I participated in was selling Poinsettias door to door on a Saturday, so I could raise money to help my Boy Scout Troop and the nursery where we got the plants.

I have written to a couple of local newspapers about my school and lack of any activities, especially for 6th graders. One paper published my letter to the editor. My family took part in Operation Christmas Child which is a charity. We bought items for needy children such as gloves and toys so that they could have a good Christmas.

These are some examples of my citizenship. I believe that citizenship is a major part of life. The younger a person starts to develop their citizenship, the better off they will be later in life.

Shane Haislip
Grade 6

Sailing Camp

I was at sailing camp and we were starting to rig the boats, so I got my shoes on and ran out to help. There was no wind and I didn't see the point of sailing all the way across Sodus Bay just to eat lunch.

We got rigged up and stared sailing over to my instructor's place to have lunch. I was in a boat with my friends Shelby and Sam. We were assigned to the lazer called Ice Mann.

We got into the middle of the bay and the wind started to pickup so we tugged in the sail and I was standing. The boat jerked with speed and I fell off the back. The boat wasn't going that fast, but it seemed fast to us because we were hardly moving before, so it was big change. I got back in. The boys in the JY15 next to us were laughing their heads off. They were starting to pull ahead of us so we started paddling with our hands. Chris, my instructor, came over to us with the motor boat and took our bow line. He pulled us right up to his dock.

After we tied up our boat we got our lunch and it was really hot so I asked if Sam, Shelby and I could go into Chris's house. Only I could because he's my cousin.

We sailed back and derigged. Then I went to Chris's house. I had a good day after all.

Angela Tassone
Grade 6

Martin Luther King Jr.

Martin Luther King Jr. was born in Atlanta, Georgia on January 15, 1929. Martin Luther King Jr. was named after his father Martin Luther King. In 1948 he graduated from Morehouse College in Atlanta, Georgia. In 1951 he received his Bachelor's Degree in Divinity from the Crozier Theological Seminary.

Martin got married to Coretta Scott in 1953. He was a graduate of Antioch College and a student in the New England Conservatory of Music in Boston. He was a pastor of the Dextor Avenue Baptist Church in Montgomery, Alabama. He received his Doctorate in Theology from Boston University. Between 1955-1956 he received national attention for his role in organizing a successful black boycott of Montgomery, Alabama. He founded the Southern Christian Leadership Conference in order to educate blacks in the methods of nonviolence and to take effective action to end segregation. Martin Luther King Jr. delivered his famous "I Have a Dream" speech before more than 200,000 blacks and whites in a march in Washington D.C. Martin organized demonstrations on behalf of sanitation workers in Birmingham, Alabama. Martin received the Nobel Peace Prize in 1964. He was the youngest person honored in this way by the Norwegian Parliament. He organized a campaign for voter registration in Selma, Alabama. Martin Luther King Jr. organized "Poor People's Campaign" in Washington, D.C.

April 4, 1968 was a sad day. Martin Luther King Jr. was assassinated. He was shot on his front steps. That is the story of his life.

Michael Smith
Grade 6

T.J.

One day, my dad woke me and said, "We are going to look at puppies." This was so exciting for me! So, that morning we drove to Connecticut. It took a long time but it was worth it. I couldn't wait!

I really wanted a Wheaten Terrier because they were so adorable. One feisty one jumped right into my hand. I put him on the floor and he started nibbling on my pants and shoes. I put him back, he was getting too feisty. The next puppy was very calm. She licked me like there was no tomorrow. It tickled a lot. I knew she was the one.

My dad agreed with me. I knew exactly what to name her: T.J., for Tara and John. John is my brother. If I was ever going to get a dog I was always planning on naming her T.J. This was one of the happiest days of my life. I just couldn't believe it! I got a dog! Unfortunately we had to wait until Monday to take T.J. home.

That Monday when we got off the bus my brother and I sprinted to my house. I gave T.J. a huge hug. My brother thought she was the cutest puppy. My mom didn't really want a dog but when she saw her, she fell in love and so did our whole family. T.J. is now not only a dog but a part of our family.

Tara Prufeta
Grade 6

The Cat

Once when I was about 2 years of age, a stray cat wandered across our yard. My dad and I found it, and my family and I welcomed it to our home. She had no name, for I couldn't talk. My parents simply called her *Cat*. She was very cute, black and white fur, small as well, for she was a kitten. I have vague memories of her jumping on the table and sitting near the salt and pepper. Sadly, *Cat* and I did not get along well. I put her in cardboard boxes, she scratched me. My parents thought we would have to get rid of her. We also had to consider that we were getting ready to move. We searched all around for someone we could give *Cat* to. After a couple of days we found a cat breeder! We tried to convince her to take *Cat*, but it wasn't easy! In the end the cat breeder took *Cat*, and I'm sure she is very happy. I have no clue if someone else bought her from the breeder or if she died but I know she is still a good kitty where ever she is!

Lani Wyman
Grade 5

When Duty Calls

My name is Tim Arnold. I am going to tell you about World War II. Most of you think of Pearl Harbor, of Nazi Germany, but there is much more than that!

America didn't come into WWII until *after* Pearl Harbor; and if you thought the Japanese and Germans were the only enemy, there were French, Italians, and some Russians! Japan needed more help and fast, so they found the Russian General Borough. They thought they could find a Russian to make peace with Germany and use the Russian to get the Germans to help Japan later known as the Axis. Germany was ready to fight the Americans and had been slaughtering many Jewish people. North Africa in 1943, the first infantry division (Big Red One) had their first real battle. The Big Red One's motto was "No job too big. No mission too great. Duty first."

The greatest Nazi achievements were the magnetic mine, the Messerschmidt #1, and the Turpitz. The magnetic mine was planted in the Pacific Ocean. The Messerschmidt #1was used to complete a small trip around a town and perform a quick, and stealthy attack. It was so small only one pilot could fit in it!

Finally, the Turpitz. This was the greatest battleship ever, it was very powerful. It was used to attack the coast of Britain. After brutal attacks pummeled Britain's defenses, Britain's power crumbled. The British army knew what they had to do. They attacked the only dock that was big enough for Turpitz to land on. It was St. Nazaire, France. Most everyone said it was a suicide mission. Although it was in France, it was German occupied and heavily guarded. The British soldiers successfully planted charges on Turpitz and destroyed it. That is why I think World War II is so fascinating.

Tim Arnold
Grade 5

Alligators vs Crocodiles

Do you agree that animals can be alike and different like alligators and crocodiles? Well, I think so. I'm going to compare and contrast alligators and crocodiles in my next two paragraphs.

In this paragraph I'm going to compare alligators and crocodiles. Alligators and crocodiles both have long snouts, four short legs, sharp teeth, and a long tail. They can go in water and land and they eat the same prey. Alligators and crocodiles both lay eggs and build nests.

This paragraph is going to contrast alligators and crocodiles. Alligators are greenish while crocodiles are light brown. The snout of the crocodile is shaped like a V. The alligator's is shaped like a U. Crocodiles live in saltwater unlike the alligator who lives in freshwater. In China and America is where the alligators live; crocodiles live in Africa, Asia, and Australia. The alligator's teeth can be seen hanging down over the lower jaw unlike the crocodiles whose upper and lower teeth can be seen hanging down over both jaws. The nest of the crocodile is made of leaves, branches, twigs or sand banks, while the alligator's is made of water plants and mud. Crocodiles will attack humans, but alligators usually won't. Crocodiles are more aggressive than alligators, weigh more, and swim faster.

Alligators and crocodiles are amazing animals. They're alike and different in many ways. If we want them on Earth we're going to have to help preserve them. Otherwise they will become extinct.

Jocelin Teachout
Grade 6

Being Physically Fit

Do you like to be physically fit? I sure do! You get healthier and even stronger! Eat healthy foods and lift weights, those make you healthier and stronger. If you want to be fast then jog a lot, and if you don't want to be lazy then jump rope! It's fun and you're not lazy when you do it. Doing all of these things will make your body healthy and that's why you should be physically fit! You could try sports like basketball, baseball, soccer, and hockey. Soccer is my favorite.

If you don't know what kind of food is healthy, then try these: apples, carrots, corn, lettuce, broccoli, and peas too. Theses are all good foods. Come on, get active, don't be lazy! You can do many things if you are strong and healthy, then your brain is healthy and you will be more intelligent. When you're intelligent you can answer a lot of questions. I do all of these things, that's why I'm strong and have a healthy body. It can be tiring, but you can do it. In the beginning, some things can be tough but if you practice you will do great. So please be physically fit. You can do many things when you are physically fit.

Dylan Thompson
Grade 4

My Family Relationship

There are many people in my family I have a relationship with. First is my father, I play games with him like football, golf, and basketball. We talk about sports and we also watch sports on TV. Next is my mother, she listens when I play my instrument. We talk about how I do in school. I also like to shop with her. Also, my brother, Jordan, I like to play on the X-Box, PS2, and Gamecube with him. I like to play in the outdoors with him. We also like playing with our pets together.

Next is my grandfather, who I call Pop Pop, I play board games with him. I love to watch wrestling with him. Last is my grandmother, who I call Mom Mom, I play card games with her. I also learn some sign language from her. In conclusion, this is the relationship I have with my family, which I think is pretty great.

Jesse Bradley
Grade 6

Holiday Traditions with My Family

My family's Thanksgiving went very well. We always spend Thanksgiving at my dad's uncle's house in Pennsylvania. This year we had green beans with ham, turkey, cranberries, and mashed potatoes. For dessert we had pumpkin pie, red velvet cake, and 2 other different kinds of cake. My family and I also enjoy spending Christmas, Easter, the New Year and vacation time together.

At Christmas, I always like the salad, the biscuits and many more things we have. Every Christmas we go over to my granny's house or they come over to my house. My grandparents visit us every year on Christmas day. Sometimes our cousins from out of town come over to my granny's house and stay for the week. I like this because I don't get to see them very often. This is what I chose to write about.

Harlee Ellifritz
Grade 6

Dinner with Benjamin Franklin

Benjamin Franklin was born in Boston on January 17, 1706. He was known as a brilliant man that created many great inventions in his time. Among these inventions are the printing press, bifocals, an iron furnace stove, an odometer, and a long arm. Ben was the tenth son of a soap maker named Josiah Franklin. At the age of twelve years old Ben was apprenticed to James, his brother, in which he helped James compile pamphlets and set type which he would later sell in the streets.

If Benjamin Franklin was at my house for dinner I think we would have a great time. First of all, I would ask him what kind of technology they had back in his time. Then I would tell Ben about how his inventions have impacted our lives today. He would probably be surprised by how much technology has developed from his time. Last of all, I would ask him if he had any suggestions of inventions that could improve our everyday life.

Joey Titus
Grade 6

The Silver Bracelet

One of the most precious things that I have ever received is the bracelet that my Grandmother Nora gave to me two years ago. The bracelet is important to me because I don't get to see my grandma every day like some people. Some kids are so fortunate because they get to see their grandmother every day. I only get so see my grandmother for five days when she comes to America to visit.

The first day Grandma Nora gave me the silver bracelet she said, "*Shaniece, I am giving you this bracelet because I love you. I want you to promise that you will always keep it and never lose it.*"

I said, "*I promise, Grandma.*" I knew that the bracelet was a prized possession of her's too. She told me that she got the beautiful bracelet in Trinidad. I knew when she gave it to me that I would keep it forever. I knew that I would keep my silver bracelet long after my grandmother's visits stop.

The bracelet is silver with two silver ends that meet to go around my wrist. On the band is a star in the corner. I wear the bracelet every day.

My silver bracelet is precious to me because it reminds me of my Grandmother Nora and all the love that is passed down in our family from generation to generation.

Shaniece DeSouza
Grade 5

My Home

My home is important to me because it is where I live. It is perfect for my family and me. It is small, warm, cozy, and cool. My home has a lot of rooms, so we have guests over. My home is great. My family is my home too. They are so comforting and warm. They all love God and love each other. They are so great and so fun.

My home is great to have parties at in the summer. I have a really big backyard and a big pool. We have a lot of things to play with like volley ball, soccer, baseball, and tether ball. We play those things for hours. We always have a good time at parties.

In my house it is warm and cozy. We have a wood fireplace that warms up the whole house in two minutes. We have a small/medium size house on the inside so the heat travels fast. At night we get together and watch movies, so it is really warm.

My house is full of love and joy because of my family. Everyone is cheerful and happy. It is also filled with God's love. It is so comfortable to be there knowing you're safe and accepted. Everyone is willing to help. I love my home.

My home is great and perfect for my family. We have great times there. There is always love and acceptance. Everyone in my family is thankful for my home. My home is awesome.

Jessica Griffin
Grade 6

Back at Villa Cresta Elementary

Back at Villa Cresta my favorite field trip was going to Camp Ramblewood. We got on the bus and rode for at least 2 hours! Finally we got there and tried a new game. It was fun so. We got in our cabins and discovered who our cabin mates were (Alan-Michael, Jermy, Nickolas, Jim, Brett, Gram, Paul). We went to lunch then played capture the flag. We went back to our cabins and played around with each other. Then we went to sleep. We went to breakfast, went hiking and then played a web game. Then we played kickball and capture the flag. Then we were going home to end our journey!!

Cameron Hughes
Grade 6

Three Special People to Me

In my life there are three memorable people: my mom, my Aunt Connie, and my Uncle Timmie.

My mom is a very significant person in my life because she is loving, kind, and compassionate. But she can be strict at times too. I love her very much and no other mom could be like her.

Now my Aunt Connie is just like my mom. She laughs boisterously and likes jokes. She is always worried about me. She is an incomparable aunt.

Finally is my Uncle Timmie. He is very cool. He lets me ride his four-wheeler. He also does enjoyable activities with me. You would not find another uncle like him.

So that's the three special people to me. I hope you have three special people in your life too. I love them very much, and I hope you love yours too.

Jordan Gray
Grade 5

The Puppies

One day in the winter of 2005 my grandparents bought a puppy. It's a York Sheteria. They bought the kind that only weighs up to 2 or 3 pounds.

It was a boy. They named it Charlie R. S. Lane. R. stands for Robert, my grandfather's name, S. stands for Susan, my grandmother's name. Lane is their last name.

He got pneumonia, but he did not die. It is very easy for them to die, because they're so small.

Ok, back to the story. He was a good dog. He got a lot of attention. But he needed a friend. So guess what? Yeah, he got a sister. They named her Angel. Charlie and Angel. Charlie's Angel.

They're both the same color. Brown-yellowish/orangish with a little black. Charlie is 1 year and almost 1 month. His birthday is on Christmas. Angel is about 11 months. Her birthday is someday in February.

I have to say Angel is a little feisty and rough. She likes to go after my cousin's dog, which is probably 3 times its size. I love them, and wish I had dogs like them. They're the greatest!

Kristen Lane
Grade 6

I Wish I Was a Little Kid Again!

One thing I miss most about being a little kid is that my mom and dad don't hold me anymore. They don't hold me anymore because I'm getting bigger and they're getting older. Also, I miss not sleeping in a crib because sometimes I roll, and I don't want to roll off the bed and get hurt. Last, what I miss is learning how to ride a bike, do the ABC's, and learning numbers. I miss that because they were all things that I did when I was a little kid. The good thing is now I'm learning new and more important things like numbers and words in Spanish. I miss being a little kid, but I also like learning new things.

Maria Totoro
Grade 6

Girls Can Do Anything That Boys Can Do

A lot of boys think that girls shouldn't and don't play sports, but I can prove them wrong. I play many sports and I personally love them. I play football every day at school before school starts with boys and I'm the only girl that plays; I feel proud. Sometimes when I play football in the morning boys say, "I can throw so much further than you. I'm so much stronger than you." Every time they say that I think of the stereotypes about boys being stronger than girls and that really bugs me. Also when they say that I think that they say that on purpose just because I'm a girl.

Besides football I play another rough sport, I play hockey. I play on an all girls team and I'm kind of glad because if I played on a boys team they might say that I don't belong on the team because I'm a girl. I'm also glad that I play sports with boys because pretty much all my friends that are boys respect me for that.

Karina Alfisher
Grade 5

Animals vs Humans

Humans and animals are alike and different in many different ways. Like both can run fast and slow. They are different by the animals walk on four feet and we walk on two feet.

Animals can do many things humans can do. Since I am human, I think humans are better, but animals are good hunters too! Animals can run very slow like some of humans. But some animals can run very fast, like our track stars. I also think that animals and humans are very important to our environments.

Humans are different from animals by, they have fur and we have hair. We are also different by they live in the wild and we live in homes. Another way humans and animals are different is how we dress but animals do not get dressed. Also, some of the other animals have babies in an egg, but humans don't.

In conclusion, it seems like humans do more than animals. I like humans more than animals. Also, you can tell that humans and animals can do many things the same.

Rachel Link
Grade 6

Fantastic Ferret Facts

Did you know that ferrets have been around since the 1940's? Well they became popular due to the efforts of Mr. George Marshall, owner of the Marshall Research Farms located in Wolcott, New York. He began raising ferrets in the backyard of his family farm in 1939. Various articles claim that ferrets have been kept as pets and hunters since as early as 1000-400 BC.

Ferrets are fearless, very curious, and have very short attention spans. Unlike cats and dogs, ferrets seem to rely more on tactical sense (touch) rather than sent or vision, as they explore new objects. Their love for exploration and squeezing into tight places sometimes leads to dangerous situations. When they are awake they are busy checking out things around them. These periods "of checking things out" however, do not last long since ferrets sleep at least 18 hours of the day.

Different ferrets have different names. Unspayed females are called "Jills." Unuttered males are called "Hobs." Neutered males are called "Gibs." Baby ferrets are called "Kits." The traditional coat color is called "Fitch" (sable). I hope now you are more knowledgeable about ferrets!

Audrey Hulsizer
Grade 5

My Summer Vacation

Every year since I was born we go on vacation to the Finger Lakes in New York. We go to a lake called Keuka Lake. We rent cabins that are right on the lake. My dad has a bass boat and we go fishing and tubing. We always go on vacation in August. Every year we go with our family and friends.

Last year was the best year because I caught two of my biggest fish yet. They were both almost four pounds and they both were small mouth bass. After we took pictures of them, I threw them both back in the lake.

My Uncle John's friend brought his speed boat. He had a wakeboard and a kneeboard. Most of the older people used the wakeboard but my favorite was the kneeboard. Then on Wednesday, another friend came up to the lake and he had two jet skis. They were fun to ride on. They can go up to 60 miles per hour.

My Uncle Bob owns a restaurant so he brings all the food and my Aunt Sara cooks lunch and dinner for everybody. But, you had to bring your own breakfast food and make that by yourself.

It is really fun to go to Keuka Lake for a week on vacation. You get to go fishing and tubing and play all day. Everyone should go to a lake even for a day. You can rent a boat and camp out at a camp site if you don't want to rent a cabin. It is a fun vacation and you get to be with your family and friends.

Daniel Ofier
Grade 5

Biking

Many people like biking, but not so many like to B.M.X. B.M.X. is when you do tricks on your bike. I get to do it at the bike park or at home with my friend, Cody, every summer. There is only one problem, we do not know how to do many tricks. Two years ago is when I learned how to do my first cool trick.

Two years ago I had a fear of doing tricks that I have never done. My friend, Cody, invited me to go to the bike park with him. His mom took Cody and I to the bike park. A pro-biker was there and he was doing a 360 bar spin. He taught me how to do it. After, he said try it on the big ramp. I was terrified when he said that. So I kept doing what I wanted for a half hour.

After a while I decided to try the 360 bar spin. My friend was watching me, I peddled as fast as I could and hit the ramp. I spun my bars and did a 360. In the air I was terrified. I almost fell but I held on. I had landed a little crooked but still landed. After Cody's mom picked us up from the park they took me home.

In conclusion, biking is my favorite thing that I can do. I also learned that biking is fun even if you can or can't do tricks. Now I can do different tricks on my ramp at home. When Cody comes over we practice doing tricks together. Now, I have no fear of biking.

Nick Trumbull
Grade 5

I Am a Person with a Little Brother with Autism

I have a little brother with autism. It affects my whole family and is painful inside, but we go on.

My little brother Tyler is seven and very cute. He should be in second grade, but he's not because when he was two he was diagnosed with autism, and there is no cure. This disease runs in my family.

Autistic kids aren't very affectionate, but my brother is! We love Tyler and we can tell he loves us. However, he has problems he can't control, including hurting himself. He can't speak and gets frustrated. He makes verbal noises, and he bangs his forehead, making it thicker. He hurts us with bruises sometimes. It can really hurt! But through all of this, we love him.

It's hard for our family to do things together. I have to watch Tyler, and I admit, I'm not always good about it. Everyone sacrifices. I shouldn't complain because I'm fortunate and healthy. Tyler's schedule rules everything. We only go to events that Tyler can attend, and that limits a lot! I think Tyler sacrifices the most.

Thinking about Tyler's future breaks my heart. Once he's 21, the school will no longer teach him, so we don't have much time. Autism lasts forever. My parents say they will provide for him. I can't imagine what will happen when they're gone.

I'm a person with an autistic angel for a little brother. I love him and he loves me, and I will always be there for him.

Cheyenne Begley
Grade 6

Arctic Perishings*

What happens when you turn on your television or use modern day devices? Most modern day devices, including the television, are destroying our environment and animals' habitats, leading to global warming.

The average temperatures have increased by up to 10 degrees Fahrenheit in the past 40-50 years. This is extremely bad news for polar bears. The polar ice cap is disappearing. Therefore, a polar bear might have to swim 60 miles to get to another sheet of ice, causing many polar bears to drown.

Not only are polar bears and other Arctic animals in danger, but people in New Guinea and Vanuatu are abandoning their homes. Scientists predict that by 2015, melted glaciers will cover these islands with water. By 2070 the Arctic could be ice-free during summers. Thus, many species of plants and animals in the Arctic will be killed.

What are people doing to try to keep global warming from happening? World leaders met in Montreal to discuss the issue. In 1997, they agreed to cut down on 5% of the greenhouse. Recently, leaders agreed to lower this percentage even more. Even though the United States spends 3 billion dollars trying to develop energy-saving technology, they did not sign this agreement because they use much of this modern day technology. Despite the U.S.'s noncompliance, scientists are optimistic that efforts to reduce global warming will make a difference.

What can you do to help save the world and keep global warming from happening?

Jack Voigt
Grade 6
*Response to "Polar Peril"

Hope for My Cousin

Some people say that the biggest and most expensive gift is the best gift of all. I think that people who think that are absolutely wrong. The best gift that you can give is one that comes from the heart, not something you pay for or wrapped very nicely. That is why I am giving my cousin Nicky the gift of hope, because he had to get surgery on his head. When he was little he almost died from something that had happened to his head and now it has happened again. Now I am giving all of the hope in the world that I can give. I am hoping that this never happens again and he makes it through this. I know for a fact that he would give me the same gift because he is considerate and the kindest of my cousins. He never would make fun of anybody so he doesn't deserve this to happen to him. I am sure that he will make it through this because he is such a good person. He has all my hope in the world right now and all I can think about is him. In conclusion, the biggest present isn't always the best one, like my cousin Nick's condition he wouldn't want any other gift except the gift of hope.

Robert Berardi
Grade 6

Recycling

Mr. Art Feltes works as a recycling coordinator for Montgomery County. He came to our school and gave a presentation to our class. An interesting fact is how much you weigh is equal to how much you waste per month. Another fact is a dinosaur could have drunk from the water we drink now because it is recycled. Recycled means making something new out of something old.

People recycle newspapers, soda cans, and paper. Americans throw away enough soda bottles every year to go around the earth four times! There are five percent of Americans in the world, but they make 30% of the trash! We waste a lot!

It takes two months to turn something recycled into a new product. A lot of clothes are made of plastic! In most carpets these days there are soda cans! There is a machine called a compressor. It is a recycling machine in this case. It puts newspapers, soda cans and paper into a cube.

Recycling one aluminum can can save enough energy to run a television for three hours! It makes me want to recycle more. Does this make you want to recycle more? Here's how you can! You can save cans, bottles, newspapers, and some plastics. They can be turned into beaches, clothes and play ground equipment.

Mr. Feltes has taught me more about recycling than I ever thought I would know!

James Dierkes
Grade 5

The Worst Meal Ever!

There have been many disgusting dinners that I've had to eat but unfortunately, this has been the worst of all. It all started out when I was at my glorious house…Let me take you back. "Yay!" two years ago, I ran to the kitchen table, almost knocking down three chairs in my way. The chairs wobbled, rocking back and forth, and then stood still as a statue. "ALISON!" my acrimonious mom was shriveled up in lividness. "Sorry, mom," I cried.

It was a peaceful and beautifully calm Sunday night and I was extremely excited. The only noise that irritated the house were the crazy, crying crabs bubbling up as the hot, steamy and boiling water strangled them on the black stove. Then, the crying crabs died. My mom, dad, brother, and I gathered around the kitchen table. Everyone loved the dinner. I was (of course) stuffing my face!

Then, suddenly, my stomach growled like an angry mob of people. It cried, STOP!! DON'T TAKE ANY MORE BITES! It kept on growling and growling. I knew that the moment would be such a black-letter moment to me, my life, and my family. I ran to the bathroom because of the horrible feeling gripping my stomach. Then, it happened. I threw up. From then on I have never tried a crab and I never will again!

Alison Calamoneri
Grade 4

Cumulonimbus

Hi I'm a cumulonimbus cloud on my way to Texas to create a big storm. People are about to go in cause they see me making a big thunder storm. I have a very busy schedule. I have to bring rain to sunny California and thunder to mild Virginia. Now I'm on my way to dazzling France to make rain so kids can't play. See how evil I am? It's finally midnight and I'm going to my moon house. Today I had a 7:14 workout (a clouds gotta stay fit over London and dark over Africa) Next I'm on my way to tropical wild Madagascar to make rain for the villages' crops, then to New Mexico for a big tornado.

Well gotta go to see my friend cumulus, see ya later.

Bryana Steele
Grade 4

Me

Hi, I'm Jessica Lylyk. I live in Hudson Falls. I was born in Cambridge. My birthday is April 9th, 1995. I am 10 years old.

I am an active kid. I like a lot of sports. Some sports are soccer, baseball, basketball, and bowling. My most favorite sports are cheerleading and gymnastics.

I like a lot of things. My favorite colors are green, orange, blue, and hot pink. My favorite animals are frogs, pigs, and monkeys.

I have long brown hair. I have brown eyes. I love school. My favorite subjects are science, art, music, and math. My most favorite subject is gym.

I play the clarinet. I learned 10 notes so far. My favorite music is Aunt Rodie's Apatite. It is long. I like it because it is difficult. My favorite music on the radio is pop and rock.

I think it is fun to know a lot about yourself. If you know about yourself you can do what you like.

Jessica Lylyk
Grade 5

Winter vs Summer

Hi my name is Justin Ascencio. I'm comparing and contrasting winter and summer. They are both awesome seasons, that is why I picked those two seasons. There are a lot of interesting things about the two seasons.

There are many ways that these seasons are alike. A reason these two are alike is that both seasons have extreme weather conditions. Another reason is that they both hold the Olympics. The third reason is that the season spans over a month. The final reason is that they both have solstices.

There are also many ways that they are different. The first reason is that winter is cold and summer is warm. The second reason is because summer has longer days than winter. The third reason is because in Imperial we have to go to school in the winter but not the summer. The last reason is that in the winter trees are covered in snow, but they have no leaves, in summer the trees have a lot of leaves on them, but no snow.

Justin Ascencio
Grade 6

Hershey Park Vacation 2005

Some families go to theme parks for vacations. Others may go to resorts. My family went to Hershey Park for a vacation last year. We go there almost every year. We went there in July after the Fourth of July. We left at about eleven a.m. and we didn't hit traffic. After about three hours, we were there checking into the hotel.

We went to the indoor pool so we had something to do while the maids got our room ready. After they were done we went to unpack everything. After we did, we went to the park and rode a few rides. It was getting late so we went back to our room and went to bed.

The next day, we got dressed and went to have breakfast. After that we entered the park. We went on some rides. Then, we saw my aunt, uncle, and cousins unexpectedly. We all rode Hershey Park's newest attraction, the Storm Runner. We all went to go on some water rides. Then we went over to the food area and got some pizza for lunch. After we went on more rides, it was after dusk, and my knees started to hurt and my sister was tired, so we went back to our room.

The next day my aunt told us that there was a blackout in the park right after we left the park the night before. One of the generators had broken down.

It was our last day. We all got on our favorite rides once again. We bought souvenirs and gifts for the rest of the family and said our goodbyes.

We checked out of our hotel and left. We were on the road again. We were home in no time and that was the end of the Hershey Park vacation.

Andrew Fenn
Grade 6

Save the Environment

I think we need to save the environment so that none of the animals die out. The bald eagle is almost gone and people are polluting the water. Toxic waste and garbage is being put in the water also. I think it is important to save the trees. I think we need to keep the air safe and give animals a home, like birds and owls. We do not want the polar bear to become extinct.

Plants and flowers should not be harmed in any way. People should care about the environment. Animals, plants, and trees should not be harmed either. Air should not get polluted and trees should not be cut down for paper and other things like that. The environment is a special place for living things, it should be treated as a nice home.

Air pollution is bad for the air and people. The trees help the environment by giving animals a home, and making some shade in the summer. Animals help the environment by keeping the environment clean.

Please help us to keep the environment clean so that we have a healthy place to live and breathe.

James DuHamel
Grade 4

The Declaration of Independence

Among the many events of our nation's history, the most important one was the Declaration of Independence. This document informs the birth and freedom of America. Though patriots believed in liberty, loyalists insisted on being under the king's rules.

Later on, Patrick Henry, a patriot from Virginia, made a speech. Patrick said in that speech, "Give me liberty, or give me death." Thomas Paine had heard of this speech and joined in the struggle for freedom. Thomas Pain wrote a pamphlet called *Common Sense*. This stated that the colonies were treated unfairly and that we needed independence. As said in *Common Sense* the colonists had nothing to gain, but much to loose. 100,000 copies of *Common Sense* were sold. *Common Sense* was written in January of 1776.

John Adams was a patriot also. On June 7, 1776 a Virginia delegate asked Congress of independence. Thomas Jefferson wrote the Declaration of Independence with four others. Rights such as the Declaration of Independence are freedoms protected by a government's law. Thomas said colonists have a right to live, have freedom, and happiness. Kathrine Goddard printed the Declaration of Independence. John Hancock was the president of Congress. The Declaration was written on Independence Day.

So, in conclusion, the history of the Declaration of Independence is very important. It celebrates our nation's freedom. If it was not for the Declaration of Independence, we would still be ruled by Britain.

Neisha Meacham
Grade 5

Grandma

When I think of my grandma, I become full of sadness. She has P.S.P., Progressive Supranucleur Palsy, a disease that destroys your brain cells. You will lose your ability to talk, walk and eat. This disease can happen to anyone in his or her middle ages but nobody is sure when or why it happens.

Last year my grandmother went to the hospital. She had pneumonia because she aspirated her food. That means her food went down the wrong way. My whole family was devastated. The hospital tried feeding her but she kept choking. They inserted a feeding tube right above her belly button. She stayed in the hospital for a month.

Next it was off to a nursing home. Bedridden, she was left to watch TV 'till my grandpa would come to visit. Every day he would sit there and watch her. She sleeps all day and is awake all night. She has become nocturnal. She speaks very little. Most of the time she mumbles. She stayed in the nursing home a few months.

She came home on our first day of school. We had a bed and wheelchair ready for her. She has two nurses aides. Some days she will sit in the living room for a while; other times she won't. Most of the time my grandma stays in her room. I wish she would get well.

Alyssa M. Boller
Grade 6

Do You Know Why People Like to Do Gymnastics?

People choose to do gymnastics to get in better shape and just to have fun. Some people like to be competitive, so they try out for a team. Remember, just have fun!

How does it feel to be on a team?

To be on a team you feel honored, because you are picked out of a lot of people to go up to the next level! It's good to be on a team, because when you mess up your team still cheers for you and if you do something well you feel proud. Also when you go to gymnastics practice your team is nice to you and you can get rid of your energy.

Do you know any famous gymnasts or teams?

This year the U.S.A. team won second place in the Olympics. Carly Patterson was our female all around champion this year. Our male champion was Paul Hamm who then changed to second.

How does it feel to compete?

When I am competing, I get very nervous, but excited too. I always concentrate on my hard events, while I relax on beam and floor! I tell myself I can do it and never give up trying to make myself believe I can do it!

Part of gymnastics is to be a nice teammate, to have a role model to look up to, and to know how it feels to compete! Remember, you can do whatever sport you want to as long as you are having fun!

Kia Ponader
Grade 6

Camp Towanda

In the summer, I go to sleep away camp in Honesdale, Pennsylvania. I love sleep away camp because I am away from my annoying sister, and I have a lot of fun. Last summer, I went to sleep away camp called Camp Towanda. My counselors were from everywhere around the world. They were from places such as Israel, England, Spain, Canada, and the United States. In camp, I had seven male counselors and one female counselor.

My bunk was filled with other ten-year-old boys. We were all part of the Middies age group. Some of my friends were Cory, Jeff, and Brett. They were also on the travel soccer team with me. Our team traveled to camps all over Wayne County. We had three games and won them all. After winning the finals we got a trophy!

My two favorite activities were porch breakfast and free play. My favorite breakfast was "porch breakfast." This was when we got cereal and delicious Krispy Krème doughnuts. We would eat our breakfast on our bunk porch. I really loved those doughnuts. During free play, which occurred right after dinner, you could do any activity on boys' campus. On a Tuesday or Saturday during this time, you would get two packs of any choice of candy. These are some of the fun activities that I do at Camp Towanda.

Ben Sabin
Grade 5

Cumulonimbus Cloud

I'm the cumulonimbus cloud. I'm the biggest and the badest cloud. I will bring rain and very bad thunderstorms. I form in heaps in the sky. I am the cumulonimbus cloud and I will hurt you.

Shallah Allen
Grade 4

Skating

Do you know how cold ice can be? I do! Ice skating isn't just having fun. It's also a sport. Many skaters enjoy it, like Michelle Kwan. Some people just think skating is going forward, but it isn't. It can be jumping, spinning, and going backward. I know people that don't even know how to skate, like Jessie Mcartney or Britney Spears. When they get on the ice they might fall, but not me. Skating to me is being a champ. I love skating. I like how you can zoom past and it will feel good. When you start skating you will think that skating is important to you. I love how you get to pick a routine to skate to. I really believe skating is important to my life. I just love it. It can give you some exercise. If you don't know a sport to join, join skating PLEASE!

Melissa Porr
Grade 5

My Grandma!

Nancy J. Polumbo has been a very special person in my life. Born February 1, 1925, she lived through "The Great Depression" and World War II. She has one sister. She was married for seventeen years (before her husband died). She is the mother of five children, grandmother of eight.

During World War II, she volunteered as a nurse's aid at the age of sixteen. She took temperatures and changed beds. Her uniform was a white apron with a white hat. She served from 1943-1944. Her sister, Philomena Manna, volunteered as a riveter on airplanes that were built to carry soldiers. This was the way young women supported the war effort in those days.

I asked my Grandma about her time as a volunteer and she told me some very interesting stories. She worked in a hospital to relieve the nurses of some minor duties. She moved patients from room to room. "I wrapped bandages, washed patients who couldn't do it themselves. One time I was so busy a lady asked for a glass of water (her mouth was always dry) but I was so busy that I forgot! Still to this day I can hear her voice. I am real sorry." "My favorite part of working at the hospital was the baby ward. I loved it," she said. She wished she could have done more because the babies looked so helpless and she thought about them all the time.

When one of her children or a grandchild is sick she comes over, brings movies, and makes snacks (always our favorite). The thing she does the best is loves us. She's my Grandma! I like to think I take after my Grandma, because I like to volunteer and take care of little children.

Danielle Polumbo-Miller
Grade 6

Anne Frank

This essay is about Anne Frank. She was born on June 12, 1929 in Frankfort, Germany. She died in March of 1945. She was the second child to Otto and Edith Frank. She had a sister named Margot. For her 13th birthday she got a diary. She never wanted anything to happen to her diary. She always knew what to do. She was bright, intelligent, lively, playful, and happy. She wanted her diary to be her best friend. She called her diary Kitty. In the hideout there was another family. They had a boy named Peter. Anne loved Peter. Anne disliked her mom a lot.

Her message was that she wanted poor people to be treated like rich people. For example, if you step on someone's foot you should say 'sorry' just like you would to a rich person.

After she was found she was put in a concentration camp for 7 1/2 months and then she died of typhus. Her diary was published in more than 55 languages.

Anne's father published her diary. So, a lot of people wrote letters to her father and he responded to more than 30,000 of them.

Allison Antonowicz
Grade 6

Buddhism

Buddhism is a religion based on the teachings of Buddha. It is widely practiced around eastern and central Asia. Buddhism isn't based on belief in a supreme creator. Instead, Buddhists respect Buddha and his teachings. Buddhists believe you should not be too attached to the material world. Freedom from greed and hatred will open your mind to wisdom and your heart to kindness and compassion.

Siddhartha Guatama was born around 566 B.C. As a teen, Guatama led an extravagant life because his father was a king, but then he grew bored of the royal life. He traveled out into the world in search of meaning and understanding. Guatama soon renounced his princely title and became a monk. He gave away all of his possessions in hopes of finding the meaning of life. One day, while meditating under a tree, Guatama finally understood freedom from suffering and the achieving of salvation. After this experience, Guatama became known as Buddha, which means the "Enlightened One." Buddha spent the rest of his life teaching what he had come to understand. He died around 480 B.C.

The goal of every Buddhist is to reach nirvana. Nirvana is the end of all suffering and the cycle of birth and rebirth. Many people have reached nirvana but Buddha was the first. To reach nirvana you must understand the 4 Noble Truths: suffering exists, suffering has a cause, there's an end to suffering, and there's a path that leads to the end of suffering. This path is called the Noble Eightfold Path and it is to have right understanding, right thought, right speech, right action, right livelihood, right effort, right mindfulness, and right concentration.

Thor Vutcharangkul
Grade 5

Being a Good Writer

Being a good writer is challenging; it depends on if you are writing an essay or a story. If you are writing a story, you want it to have an exciting beginning. If you are writing an essay then you want to start with the main idea. For me, it's easy because I like to write exciting beginnings and start with the main idea.

If you are writing a story with a problem, you want to have a problem, three ways to solve the problem and the solution which is the third way. An essay you want to have three examples and a conclusion. For a story you want to have a satisfying ending. I still have challenges writing stories and essays because no one is perfect. That is how to become a good writer.

Madison Conroy
Grade 4

Swimming in the Water

I'm real good at swimming. If I am famous I would have an indoor swimming pool that is 12 feet deep with a board 8 feet high. I would swim twice a week and be the best swimmer in history.

I would be competing in the Olympics and live in a big house. I would try to be a model and a mentor to kids who like swimming. I'd like to do tricks like superman float, backstroke, elementary backstroke, free style, back float, and somersault.

I would like to represent the country in many events for dignity, glory, and honor to my country and fellow kids. My life would be spent swimming. When I grow up I will be the best in my family at swimming and the best when I face my friends. I'll love swimming all my life forever and ever.

Aaron Meimban
Grade 4

Doing the Impossible

My legs were shaking. My heart was pounding as I walked toward the board. My brother was there watching. The diving seemed so scary. My hands were sweating. I looked brave on the outside but on the inside, I was horrified of going through with it. I stepped on the board, and now I had to go through with it.

I started bouncing a little. My hair was blowing. My legs now felt stiff as boards. The hurt in my stomach felt like it was about to explode. I started bouncing. My body was so high. I jumped three times. I jumped for one last time. I flew off the diving board and into the water.

I hit the bottom of the pool. My heart beat at a slow pace now. The bottom of the pool felt like heaven. I began to swim up. I did it. My body felt all relaxed now. I swam to the edge. I felt like I did the impossible. I want to do it again.

Ashley LaBombard
Grade 4

I'm Not Four!

I train at Mt. Snow to race and ski freestyle. I was placed in level five. That is the expert level, but that wasn't too hard for me. I stayed in level five for a few months. It didn't seem too hard, but one day I was not prepared. The coach made me go back to level four!

In four I stood out. I was too fast. I did things that were too hard. There was nothing to be competitive about. This was TOO EASY! I was not happy in this level. Racing was not challenging. I won most of the time. I felt like my skiing was not improving at all.

As time went by I kept on wanting to go back to level five. Finally my coach agreed. She felt that this level would better prepare me to race. Racing was now more challenging, and my times became faster.

After moving back to level five I was always prepared. I had learned that there were consequences if I didn't do what was expected. Now I appreciate being in level five. I always try my best. I know that I really am not four. I am five!

Katarina Krug
Grade 6

Fencing

To me fencing is very, very important. I know you think fencing is building fences. Well it is not. Fencing is fighting with swords. Don't worry the blades are flat on the top. We also wear protective armor. We wear chest protectors, an underarm protector, a jacket, and if you fence electrically you wear a lame. Yes you still get hurt even with the protective armor. I am only 10-years-old and I have won 5 tournaments! One of them was youth 12 which has people with two years more worth of experience. I started when I was six. When I was seven I was so good I was put in the advanced group. I was put up against youth 14 fencers! When I was eight I started winning. Before I go on I will explain ratings. The ratings are E-D-C-B and A. Most people in the advanced groups have E's. The ratings are not like school grades. An E is very good. I am not rated but I have beaten 30 E's, 20 D's, 10 C's, and 1 A! I am frustrated about that. That is why I absolutely love to fence.

Gianfranco Trovato
Grade 5

Orlando Florida

This is a story about my trip to Orlando Florida. First, we found our hotel. The hotel had bamboo in it. The hotel room we stayed in had two beds, a big television and two paintings on the wall. We went on a boat across a little lake from out hotel to the park. When we got to the park, we saw a water park for little kids. We went on a Jaws ride. I got a toy that walks up windows from a Men in Black ride. I won a prize in a water gun shootout. We went to the big water park. In fact we went on one ride four or five times. There was a lot of rides. I ran around so much that I almost got lost. Soon it was time to go, and we went home.

Brandon Glass
Grade 4

Leonardo da Vinci

I picked Leonardo da Vinci because I am interested in art, and he is one of my favorite artists.

Leonardo da Vinci was born in 1452. Leonardo wasn't very interested in art until he was older. He lived with his mother at first, but then she didn't want a child. Then he moved in with his dad. Then he was too busy to take care of him. When he was five, he moved with his grandfather. They lived in a village called Vinci.

Da Vinci looked for something he was good at, and he found it. It was art. He started to love art more than he ever did. He had an art teacher named Andrea del Verrocchio. Leonardo moved into Andrea's workshop. Leonardo liked living there.

When he got older, he started to paint pictures. His first drawing was drawn August 5, 1472. It was done in pen and ink. He painted a few more pictures. Then he painted the Mona Lisa in 1516, and that painting was the most famous one of all. Some people think that the Mona Lisa has a creepy look. Her eyes stare just one way. The background is all smoky and damp. It looks creepy to me. Then just a few years later, in 1519, he died.

Now you know a little about Leonardo da Vinci. Maybe you would like to be a painter, too. Maybe you could become a great painter, too.

Tamika Matthews
Grade 5

My Siblings

I don't know what I would do without my siblings, and I don't ever want to find out! My siblings will always be a part of my life. They are friendly, but annoying. They're also very intelligent. In other words, my siblings will never be out of my life!

My three siblings are friendly. My older brother is known by teachers, peers, and etc. Wherever he goes he's highly respected! My older sister has many friends in many places. My younger sister always gets phone calls every day. It's evident that my siblings are very friendly.

My siblings are sometimes annoying. My brother continuously hogs the television. My older sister always talks about boys! My younger sister does everything I do! Now you know how annoying my siblings are.

My brother and sisters are very intelligent. My sister is in all honors classes. She is also a straight "A" student! My brother is on the honor roll every marking period. My younger sister always gets A's and B's on her tests. You can see how intelligent my siblings are!

My brother and sisters will always be a part of my life! So now you know that I am blessed with multitalented brother and sisters who are annoying, intelligent, and friendly! Finally, you know about my siblings.

Chinwendu Opara
Grade 6

All About Art

In China, art was from a beautiful dragon, which is Asia's main animal. Asia was born from a dragon so the people seem to love the dragons for their color and they love the dragons for their arts of dancing and creativity. I know all of this because my great ancestors were born from a dragon.

North America's arts are different kinds of art. Music arts are very nice. The Massachusetts' national anthem is "All Hail Massachusetts." Their arts are like a melting pot. Comic books are amazing. It shows lots of imagination and interesting things.

In India they make clay pots to hold water and flowers. Also lots of other things. I love pots as much as I love comics. I wanted to make a real pot like the people from India. Their music is very interesting. I hope one day I could make a pot like them. Russia is a very nice place with arts and great music. There are dolls that can go in another. It can go long enough to become the size of a piece of rice. The story is a man was thinking what to get for a little boy's birthday and the man made a doll that can turn out the size of a piece of rice. Now it's popular in Russia. Told you it was all about the arts.

Monique Vo
Grade 4

D.A.R.E.

DARE was a great program! I have learned some skills in the DARE program, here they are: stay away from drugs, if someone offers you a cigarette there are at least nine different ways to say NO and we learned them. That is what DARE is all about so obviously that's what DARE has taught us.

Here are some details about what we learned. If I never learned about staying away from drugs and how they can harm you, I might not of. If I didn't know marijuana was illegal I might have taken some when I was older. I might have been unsure on how to say no when I should be confident. Those are some things DARE has taught me.

DARE taught me to stay away from cigarettes and/or drugs. I have learned to not use things that harm my body. Alcohol makes you high which is bad for you. About 3,000 nonsmokers die a year from breathing other people's smoke. Those are some things I learned in DARE.

My pledge statement was:

I promise that I will never use tobacco, too much alcohol, cigarettes, marijuana, and other drugs. I will never go in a car with a drunk person.

DARE was a great program. I think teaching DARE should be one of Massachusetts' laws. The DARE program taught kids to stay away from drugs, alcohol, and cigarettes. If Massachusetts passed this law then more people would be alive instead of being killed by smoking or drunk driving.

Lauren Sheehan
Grade 6

Stop Pollution

Pollution could and should be stopped. Pollution harms the environment, animals, and humans. Pollution kills fish, plants, and whales. Pollution causes global warming. Global warming warms up the temperature more than usual.

To stop pollution is to stop global warming. People should stop throwing trash, gas, or oil in our oceans. Instead of using gas or oil in your car, we should use battery or electric powered cars to stop the gas fumes from going into the air.

Global warming might cause the end of the world with a new Ice Age or the end of the human race. No President should miss looking at pollution as an issue. People shouldn't feel comfortable about this.

I think it is everyone's responsibility, not only the President to worry about pollution. We could all help fight pollution, and we can start now.

Ryan Cortez
Grade 5

Sports

A lot of things are important to me, but one of the things I like is sports. In this story I'm going to tell you which sports I like and why I like them.

I'm pretty good at most of the sports, but the one I think I'm best at is baseball. The next sport that I like is football. I like football because the game could change with one play. The last two sports that I like are hockey and basketball. I like hockey because it's a fast paced game and I like basketball because I get to play the most.

That is one thing that I think is important to me. What is important to you?

Matt Rowe
Grade 5

The Gift of Time

The gift of time, I would give this gift to my uncle Phil. I would choose the gift of time so my uncle could rewind time so he and I could see each other many more times. I say this because my uncle passed away when I was very young. In my whole entire life I only saw him 4 times, and I enjoyed every moment I was with him. I liked spending time with him because he would take me to his favorite place (a creek hidden in the woods that was on his farm) and tell me stories when he was fighting in World War 2 and when he used to drive trucks all the way across the United States in 2 days. He was extremely entertaining. One of the fondest memories I have of him is when he bought a baby horse and said I could name him, so I named him Spots. I named him this because he had a black coat with white spots all over him. After I named him my uncle said he was mine. I wanted to bring him home but my parents said, "No." To this day my aunt takes care of Spots. That is why I would like to give the gift of time to my uncle Phil, so he could rewind the time and we could have many more fun times together.

Nicholas Walker
Grade 6

Overpaid Baseball Players

Some baseball players are overpaid. Players that sit on the bench and are paid over $20 million is way too much for them to be paid. Half of that money that is paid to the players can be given to hospitals that can use it for cures. Baseball players use it for things that they do not need. Many baseball players do not earn their money; they use steroids or go on the DL. Certain baseball players like Jorge Posada donates his money to the Jorge Posada foundation that he made to raise money for the awareness of carniosynostosis. Carniosynostosis is a congenital or birth defect, characterized by the premature closure of one or more sutures, which causes an abnormally shaped skull. The skull is normally composed of bones which are separated by sutures. As an infant's brain grows, open sutures allow them to expand and develop a relatively normal head shape. When one or more sutures close early, it can cause the skull to expand in the direction of the open sutures. This often results in an abnormal head shape and in severe cases, places excessive and damaging amounts of pressure on a growing brain.

The New York Yankees have a lot of overpaid players. Jhonny Damon was paid $30 million for a 1 year contract. That is too much money for an outfielder for 1 year. Alex Rodriguez broke the record for the most money for his contract. I think that players should donate their money to charity.

Jessie Koerner
Grade 5

Gum

One warm summer afternoon in Arizona, my sister and I were playing Monopoly while our dad was taking a shower. While we were playing my sister asked, "Where did you get that gum?" she said with a smirk.

"It's in my purse…but you can't have any."

Then she got up, so I asked, "Where are you going?"

"Oh mmmmm…just to the bathroom."

But she didn't go to the bathroom…she went in my room. So I went in my room and there she was, looking in my purse. I thought to myself, *she totally manipulated me.* I felt so hurt. She was taking everything out of my purse and then she found the gum. She took three pieces and then started coming back. When she came back I asked, "Where did you go?"

"I told you…to the bathroom!"

"Oh really? Where did you get the gum?"

"Ok! I took some out of your purse!"

When she said that I felt so sabotaged. I didn't think I could trust her anymore! "Never do that again," I said.

"I'm sorry!" she said.

And she never did it again. And now when she looks at my stuff, I watch her like a hawk!

Molly Hurlbert
Grade 5

My Beautiful Mom

"Good morning mom," I said as I ran towards her to give her a hug. Her eyes shined at me as she smiled to show that she missed me too. I quickly opened my backpack and showed her my awards. She looked at my awards, then looked at me and said, "I love you."

My mom looks beautiful in her own way. She has dark brown chin length hair, she is very tall, with dark brown eyes and very high cheek bones. There are certain phrases my mom says, like, "Get up and try again." If someone says something about the way I look, she says, "You're always beautiful to me." And if I stand by her, she says, "you're almost as tall as me."

I feel my mom is the best mom in the world. I feel my mom is a very nice person because, she gave me my life and the roof over my head. I feel my mom is the best mom in the world because she is my beautiful mom and also my hero. She is everything that I need. She plays a very important role as a mother and a father. And that's why I love her so much. She's mine and always will be.

Deijah Wilson
Grade 4

Can Science Go too Far in Its Advancements?

Can science go too far in its advancements? Some people say yes, others say no. I say yes. Why? I have three different reasons.

One reason is that to make scientific discoveries, you need money. It costs a lot to launch rockets, and hire people to help, and to do experiments. People pay to help scientists. The government helps too. If this goes on, the government will lose money. Then the people will lose money. Soon the country will be in the middle of another Great Depression.

Another reason is that the environment might suffer. People might cut down more trees to make space for labs for experiments. Or they will do it to make products for scientists. Also, fumes from experiments might cause acid rain. Scientific discoveries might be important, but the environment is important, too.

Also, products that have been discovered because of these experiments might be dangerous to people. For example, sodium chlorate was once used as ragweed killer in New Zealand.[1] More and more people bought it because scientists said it was a very good ragweed killer. Sodium chlorate, however, when mixed with organic fibers, became a dangerous explosive. The chemical mixed with the farmer's trousers, causing them to explode. Washing did not do any good.

I think scientific experiments should have limits. Otherwise, we might have disasters like an air shortage because of loss of trees. After all, regulations are better than an epidemic of exploding pants!

Jessica Yamada
Grade 4

[1]Pain, Stephanie. "Farmer Buckley's Exploding Trousers." Muse Nov./Dec. 2005: 16-20.

The Future of Public School

Will schools be safe? Will there be enough teachers to educate students? These are the questions we have to ask ourselves about the future of public schools because there might not even be school in the future. One reason is because of the increasing violence in schools. More and more fights are going on in schools and more shootings and stabbings are occurring too. Another reason is because of the loss of teachers. More teachers are quitting their jobs because of the low salary they get for their hard work and because of abusive children. Lastly, there is not enough money to buy teaching equipment such as books and computers to educate students.

To solve these problems we should work together to better schools. We can improve the security in schools and even find a way to increase the amount of money used to fund schools. By doing these things we can improve the public schools of today and even prevent them from suffering an unpleasant future.

Rotimi Babalola
Grade 6

The Day I Went to the Zoo

One day I went to the zoo! I was so excited when I walked in it looked like a jungle! The first thing I saw was monkeys! They were going wild in the cage. They were spider monkeys! I wanted to pet them but the sign said no petting aloud! As I went on I saw pretty birds they all had different colors on them like blue, red, and yellow. They are so pretty! After awhile it got hot so I went to a store. My mom bought me a blue fan and a shirt with a giraffe on it, I love giraffes! Then I went to the food court to get lunch. I got a hot-dog, it had ketchup on it, it was so good! As I went on I watched an alligator show. It was so cool, the person also told us what they eat and how fast they go! So I learned that alligators eat meat. As I went on something caught my eye, it was a giraffe! I got to pet it and feed it carrots. I named him Jerry the giraffe. As it got dark I had to go home! When I got home I really missed Jerry but I will see him next year.

Caroline Metz
Grade 4

The Perfect Sit Spin

Do you know how to ice skate? If you do, can you do a sit spin? If you want to learn how, I will tell you.

First, you should start by slowly spinning on your blade. Next, you will need to find your balance and pull your arms in. You will need to practice this a lot until you feel good with the spinning.

For this next step, you will need to skate in a line like you are sitting in a chair. Next, you will need to lift up your right leg and lock it at the knee. Then, you will need to spin on your left leg. Finally, you will need to put all of the steps together and you will have yourself a sit spin.

Caraline Barkley
Grade 5

Apollo 13

On April 11th, 1970, James Lowell (commander), Jack Swigert (commander module pilot), and Fred Haise (lunar module pilot) boarded the spacecraft Apollo 13 at the Kennedy Space Center in Florida. They checked and secured the spaceship before they launched. They launched at 2:13 exactly. Was 13 a sign of bad things to come? It was to be the third mission to the moon and hopefully, was going to be a successful one. From Earth to the moon it took 142 hours, 54 minutes, and 41 seconds.

Everything was going fine for the first two days. The configuration of Apollo 13 spacecraft was nearly identical to Apollo 12. The structure of the command module was reinforced to accommodate higher parachute loads to increased weight. It was intended as the third lunar landing mission, Apollo 13 had a full schedule of activities (experiments, sampling, etc.) planned. The mission had to be aborted after nearly 56 hours of the flight because the oxygen tank exploded. The result was the loss of the capability to generate electricity or to provide oxygen or water. This led to the famous quote by James Lowell, "Houston, we have a problem."

After the accident, virtually all activities were related to returning quickly and safely to Earth. In spite of the Apollo 13 accident, some of the scientific investigations planned for the mission were carried out. The mission made a single pass around the moon and no orbital experiments were performed. Apollo 13 safely landed April 17, within site of recovery ship Iwo Jima.

Patrick Kearney
Grade 5

When I Grow Up

I am ten years old. I have many interests and talents such as playing the piano, being involved in Boy Scouts, and building with Legos and K'nex. I am not afraid to get dirty. I have a great imagination. I am good at math and I play and work hard.

My ideal career would be an engineer. It would be my first choice. I would build things and help people with the inventions I create. My second choice would be a game designer for computer generated games. To reach this goal I would have to get a four year Bachelor of Science degree. I hope to go to Virginia Polytechnic Institute. My dad will pay for it. My majors would be electrical and mechanical.

I would be very happy with this career because I will earn a lot of money and will get to build things that I create. The starting salary is about $45,000 a year and can grow to $135,000 a year. One of the accomplishments I wish to achieve is an automatic homework machine. You put your homework in it and it does it for you. The result is a perfect grade every time!

Daryl Intravatola
Grade 4

Susan B. Anthony

Susan B. Anthony was born on February 15, 1820. She was raised by a Quaker family, when she was young. When she grew older, she taught for fifteen years. She never got married. After teaching for fifteen years, she became an agent for the American Anti-Slavery Society in 1856. There, she arranged meetings, made speeches, put up posters, and distributed leaflets (pamphlets). Also, she encountered hostile mobs, armed threats, and things being thrown at her.

In 1863, she organized a Women's National Loyal League to support the petitions for the thirteenth amendment outlawing slavery. She also attacked lynching and racial prejudice in the Rochester newspaper in the 1890's. Also in 1846 she took the position of the head of the Girls Department at Canajoharie Academy. She was only twenty-six and it was her first paid position other than her teaching.

In 1859 she spoke before the states' teachers convention in Troy New York and at the Massachusetts teachers convention, arguing for coeducation and claiming there were no differences between the minds of men and women. She also called for equal educational opportunities for all regardless of race.

When she died on March 13, 1906, an amendment had been made in her honor. Women were now able to have the right to vote.

I chose Susan B. Anthony because she helped women to vote. If it wasn't for her we would be bored. It's also because she technically gave up her life to do this for women.

Rebecca Biancardi
Grade 5

Howler Monkeys vs Giant Pandas

Here are some things that I learned about Howler Monkeys and Giant Pandas. I learned how they are the same and how they are different.

They are the same by they both have tails, but they're not the same size. They also have partly the same color fur. Pandas and Howler Monkeys both eat leaves and berries too.

Some reasons that they are different are that they have different colors. Howler Monkeys are black and the Panda Bears are black and white. Another reason is that they live in different places in the world. Panda Bears live in China and Howler Monkeys live in the Amazon Rainforest. The weights of the Panda Bear and the Howler Monkey are different also. The Panda Bear's weight at one year old is 75 lbs. and the weight of a Howler Monkey at age one is 10 lbs. They also eat *some* different things too. Howler Monkeys eat leaves, flowers and fruit while Panda Bears love to eat bamboo and its leaves.

If you forget what I just told you then I well tell you it again. I stated the differences between a Panda Bear and a Howler Monkey. Some of them were what they eat, and what they look like. And some of the same things are they both have tails and they both have fur. That is pretty much all I told you.

Mary Trax
Grade 6

The Gift of Self-Esteem

The gift that I would give to somebody is self-esteem. I would give this gift to the kids on my sports team because I think that anyone can do anything if they tried hard enough. Another reason I would give this gift is because I have seen kids say they stink, but when they try and believe in themselves they begin to play better and have courage in themselves. One important concept of self-esteem is to give it your all; no matter what. One always feels their best when they have self confidence. For it is not only emotionally positive, it is physically positive as well. There have been kids on my team that have thought they can't hit the ball, catch the football, shoot a basketball, score a goal in hockey, or kick the ball in soccer. Once they practice and hold their head up high with courage in themselves, they play well. I can relate this characteristic to a story called *The Little Engine that Could*. There is a relationship between them because in *The Little Engine that Could* the engine never gave up, and tried his hardest to get up the hill. He just said over and over, "I think I can, I think I can…"

So, that means, never give up, and try your hardest. In conclusion, if "The Little Engine" could climb up a very steep hill, a kid trying his best in a sport that he likes can achieve his goal also!

Chris Sherlock
Grade 6

Physically Fit

Being physically fit is a mammoth problem in the world, but mostly in the United States. The problem is obesity. This is a problem because if people keep gaining weight the population will begin to drop and it is basically a lose/lose situation.

The children in fifth grade have not been getting all the exercise they need. Boys have been packing on the pounds and not working them off as they should be. Girls have been eating less and exercising more. Both of these situations are terrible, they can both end with eating disorders. Most kids think that the only exercise they need is done in gym, swimming, and recess. When they get home they are like a donkey that all they want to do is play games.

When your parents were children, their society was not much better with the physically fit factor. Now their eating habits are causing their bones to become breakable and unreliable. Hopefully this will begin to change and the adults can become as healthy as a watered plant.

If you would like to be fit I advise you to be on the right diet. Your diet could cause you to be unfit, you never know. If you want an excellent diet, go see your doctor about it and he could tell you what you need. You would be surprised how much you could change within a couple of months. Get outside and play, make some noise, and enjoy the fresh air.

Michael Giovinco
Grade 5

The Coca-Cola Story

Dr. John Pemberton, a pharmacist from Atlanta Georgia, was trying to find a soda to cure headaches and that's where he found the formula for Coca-Cola. Pemberton liked the taste and brought it to Jacob's Pharmacy, the biggest pharmacy in Atlanta. John asked the store manager, Willis Venable, to add water with his soda and sell it at the store. Venable agreed to sell it for 5 cents.

Pemberton's partner and bookkeeper, Frank Robinson, suggested the name, "Coca-Cola." Robinson said that the two C's would look good in advertising. The way he drew the letters are the way they are written today.

That same year someone accidentally put in carbonated water instead of regular water into the syrup. Customers tried the new drink and liked it better. The drink would be put in a glass bottle. Coca-Cola has been made that way ever since.

Pemberton's health was failing and he couldn't keep up with his business. He had no choice, Pemberton sold his company to a man named Asa Candler in 1891 for $2,300. Candler was interested in the drink because he suffered from headaches and heard it would ease them. He tried and it worked.

Candler wanted to sell more of the drink so he put the Coca-Cola name on coasters, calendars, clocks, posters, and other items. Then people started calling Coca-Cola by a nickname, Coke. In 1945, the Coke company registered the name "Coke" as a trademark.

Today, Coke is making new flavors and has new owners, but every day Coke will have the same great taste.

Cody Martin
Grade 5

Special Cookies

One time my dad bought some cookies. I did not know who they were for, and I didn't ask anyone if I could have some. I had my friend over and we decided to sneak some of the cookies. We hid behind the door and we tasted one. We thought they were okay. Then we took another bite and, oh, how we loved them! Not for long, though. I told my dad, "These cookies are good." We were scared for a little bit that we were in trouble. We finally asked, "What did we do?" My dog had that look on her face like when someone just took something dear to you. I could see she was sad.

So, back to the cookies. My dad said, "Those cookies right there?" "Yes," we said. My dad started to giggle. We asked, "What?" "You ate dog cookies," he said laughing. We were so mad. We started to rinse and wash our mouth out. That will teach us to ask first. We called the doctor and asked him if the cookies were poisonous. He said, "Make sure you drink a lot of water." We drank like crazy!

Skylar Hottois
Grade 6

Sports and My Family

Sports are great! They foster such things as teamwork, honesty, punctuality, and they develop hard work. Playing sports has made me who I am. I really like soccer, baseball, football and many other sports. My coaches make me a better person no matter how hard they may push me. The feeling of making a good pass and getting a hit makes me feel great. When I play sports it makes all my troubles or worries in the world go away.

My family is really supportive when it comes to sports. My mom is the manager of my travel soccer team, and my dad is the coach. My family makes me feel safe and really happy. My parents always do what is best for my sister and me. And when I need them my family is always there for me through the good times and the bad.

My parents accept me for who I am. They never compare my sister and me to each other. Whenever I make a bad play my parents encourage me to keep on trying. They also tell me that I can be whatever I want if I try hard enough.

If baseball, soccer and football aren't your sports, there are so many other sports you can try. These are the reasons sports and my family are important to me.

Liam Isola
Grade 4

My Fantastic Family

My family is awesome! They are very important to me. I am very thankful God gave me my family. My family helps me, they spend time with me, and they help me learn.

My family always helps me. My dad helps me with my math homework; he is really good. My mom helps me with my science and history homework. My brothers help me carry my things.

My family spends time with me. My brothers play games with me a lot. My dad watches TV with me. My mom plays cards with me. She also takes me places with her. Sometimes we all play games together.

My family teaches me things. My mom teaches me how to cook and clean. My dad teaches me how to fix things around the house. My brothers help me help people.

I am grateful that my family does what they do for me. They are very loving and caring. I am grateful for my family.

Sidney Fallon
Grade 6

My First Goal of the Season

I excitedly waited in the locker room. The zamboni was almost done. We went onto the ice, then the horn went off. We started the face-off. I skated up to the ice. My heart was pounding. I shot the puck and I missed.

The puck came around the boards. My teammate passed it to me. I caught it on my stick, and I took the shot, and I scored. The crowd cheered!

I did it! I scored my first goal of the season. I was so happy. My team cheered. Hockey is great.

Tommy Burchard
Grade 4

My Best Friend Anthony

My best friend, Anthony, is the best friend you could ever have. He makes me laugh to cheer me up. Anthony is great at sports; Anthony and I both play basketball and baseball. He and I are both good at basketball. I have known Anthony since I was three years old. His favorite color is green. He is mean sometimes, and sometimes nice. Anthony is obsessed with video games and baseball. His hobby is collecting basketball and baseball cards. His favorite things are playing video games and being lazy.

Keanu L. Tomey
Grade 5

Cows

Did you know that the main part of the cow's body is the heart? All of the blood runs to it. Did you know that there are 5 gallons of blood in every cow's body?

Cows weigh over 500 pounds. That is a lot if you ask me. They have four stomachs. Not all cows are the same color. Some cows are brown, white, and black, and some are even blue. The blue cow is called a blue Belgium cow.

Every day at least 7 cows get milked each day. Cows give milk for us to drink. They eat hay, grass, and grains. When cows are heifers, you have to nurse them and care for them for 10 days. You can pet cows, but not bulls! Sometimes you can pet them, but I wouldn't; only if they are nice, but good luck to you.

My kitten came from a farm you know. Cows can run up to 15 miles per hour. People use cows to ride on. They have a magnet put down their throat to collect tools. People have cows for pets. They have to pull logs out of the woods. Many cows have mad cow disease.

Vets have to come and test them to see if they have the disease. My uncle has a rendering house. He has to do a lot.

Daniel West
Grade 5

My Favorite Sport

My favorite sport is baseball. I have been playing for three seasons. There are usually 16 games in one season. I wish there were more. They seem to go really fast to me because I enjoy playing so much.

My favorite position is catcher, because it gets a lot of action. Although it does get very hot under the gear! My second favorite position is third base. I like it because you get to tag the runners. When I started I played third base a lot. I have grounded many balls from that base. I want to play all the positions in the future.

I have had the same coach for two years. I think he is really nice because he as helped me so much for the last two seasons. He has helped me learn to pitch better. I hope he is my coach for this upcoming season.

I would like to play for my high school or college team, but if I can't I will play in a community league. I hope to play my whole life.

Matthew Crusan
Grade 4

Dinosaurs

Dinosaurs are one of the most interesting animals to walk the face of the Earth. We have learned and are still learning many things about dinosaurs through their fossils and bones.

The Age of the Dinosaurs began about 200 million years ago. There were many kinds of dinosaurs, all their own shapes and sizes. Some were meat-eaters and others were plant-eaters. Not all the animals that lived during the time of the dinosaurs were dinosaurs. Some were reptiles that swam in the water or flew in the sky.

Early meat-eating dinosaurs were small. They walked on two hind legs and had short front legs. Later on, as time progressed meat-eating dinosaurs became larger. The name of the dinosaur was Allosaurus. Allosaurus was over 35 feet long. It had strong legs and teeth to hunt even the largest of plant-eaters. Then came an even larger meat-eater called Tyrannosaurus Rex. This dinosaur was 50 feet long. It had strong hind legs with claws, strong jaws, and very sharp teeth that were over six inches long.

Some dinosaurs had armor or horns for protection. Others had bones, spikes, or hard plates. Triceratops had three horns and a bony shield on its head.

The duck-billed dinosaur was an herbivore. Fossil remains from its stomach show they ate leaves, seeds, twigs, and fruit. Some duck-billed dinosaurs had high crests on their heads. They walked on their hind legs.

Today scientists are still following the trail left by dinosaurs. By studying their fossils, scientists hope to learn more of the mysteries of the past. It is a fascinating mystery to solve.

Tassawar Farooq
Grade 6

Last Stop Education Station

Do you really care about getting a good education? I surely do. That education will mean everything to you when you get older. If you don't care you can't get into college. You won't get a job to feed your family. I know that sounds very intense but that's life. You need to try your hardest. You could get a scholarship to a high school or a college. That will save you a lot of money. That would make me feel so proud of myself. Just to think that I will have a great education. I know that I have a good education. For example, I have great teachers who help me every step of the way. I always work to my fullest and try to succeed. I love the feeling of acing a test. When you study all night until 11:00 and your parents were telling you to go to bed every 5 seconds. When people I knew fooled around and didn't do their work, their grades dropped. I don't always succeed in all that I do. But my education is the one thing that keeps me going. Work to your fullest potential, your future relies on it.

Alexandra Nowak
Grade 5

Imagine

John Winston Lennon was a singer, guitarist, poet, and the most influential songwriter of the 20th century. Lennon was born in Liverpool, England on October 9, 1940. His mother could not care for him when he was young, so he was raised by his aunt. Lennon developed an illness and had to wear a circular pair of wire rimmed glasses, which would become his signature item later.

John had a unique influence on rock and roll during the 1960's. His songs "Strawberry Fields Forever" and "I am the Walrus" are excellent examples of his unique style. His partnership began with Paul McCartney after his mother died in 1958. Paul introduced him to George Harrison. Pete Best joined the band as a drummer, but was replaced by Ringo Starr in 1962. The Beatles were officially born. With their growth in popularity among teens and their lack of popularity among religious leaders, the band soared on the charts. When John met Yoko Ono, the beginning of the end for the Beatles occurred.

In 1969, Lennon decided he would quit from the Beatles because of the band's hostility to Yoko. Soon after that McCartney publicly announced that he also quit. Lennon went into a solo career. In 1971, he wrote his most powerful song, "Imagine." Later, in 1980, an obsessed fan took his life. The possibility of the Beatles ever reuniting tragically ended. During his life, John Lennon influenced millions of people through his music.

David Diaz
Grade 6

Who Wants a Taste?

Gourmet Club is an enjoyable club. In gourmet club you do many entertaining things such as cooking and learning how to cook. It is pleasurable because you get to be around your friends and eat!

Gourmet club is where you get to cook. The teacher teaches you what to do and then you become the chef! You and your partner each have a stove where you cook. Next to the stove there is a microwave and a sink. You make lots of exciting food. You and your partner first get the sheet with the directions on it and then you take whatever supplies and food and you do what the teacher tells you to do with it. Then you make the food and enjoy! The teachers, Ms. Oertel and Ms. Powell, are very nice. She gives you the directions how to make the food and gives examples.

In gourmet club you do many things like cooking food and learning how to make food. It is enjoyable going every Tuesday after school. There is one thing that you have to do after cooking and making the food. That thing is always washing the dishes! You have to scrub everything off the plates and wash them in water.

Every time you go to gourmet club you make food, obviously. You make foods such as dumplings, cinnamon buns and calzones. Each of the food has steps to make them. All of the foods you make are delicious!

Swaroop Suri
Grade 6

Dad

You might think my dad is as harsh as yours, but he's not. He's amazing! My dad is loving, is supporting, and buys me a lot of things. Having a dad that is loving and supporting is cool! I love it when my dad buys me things that I want. I think it is amazing to have a father that is loving, is supporting, and buys you stuff.

My dad is loving. When I come home from school, he always asks me how school went. I love it when my dad hugs me when I come home from school. Sometimes he annoys me when he checks up on me every nine minutes. My father is loving, but sometimes annoying.

My dad is supporting. It's good to know that my dad encourages me when I have a test. He always helps me with my homework when I need it. He never screams at me. I think having a dad that is supporting is cool!

Having your dad buy you stuff is cool! He bought me a computer when I was three. He bought me a camera when I was five years old. He bought me a piano when I was seven years old. Now I'm obsessed with pianos!

Having a dad that loves, supports and buys you things is cool! I bet you would be jealous to have a dad like mine after reading all this.

Roma Gandhi
Grade 6

We Are the Champions

We came to the final championship game wanting to win. The order was the same as usual and we were sure it was perfect. We played great, made some awesome hits and plays. We moved into the fourth inning with a 6-0 score in our favor. That inning, Stephan had tired out after his amazing start, and let up 5 runs making it a close game as we neared the end. We held them to that score.

We went into the bottom of the last inning with a 1 run ball game. After a strikeout and a ground ball to me at short, the fans cheered us on telling us how close we were and how great we have played. Matthew pitched the ball…a lazy pop up to Trevor!!! WE WON! We were ecstatic! We even poured Gatorade on our coach! After we finished celebrating we sprinted into the pavilion and waited for our trophies. We clapped like crazy for everyone on the team as the coaches called our teammates up. It won't be easy for me to forget running that victory lap and having a great time with my team full of friends.

After, I ran around the field, gave high fives, talked to Adam who throughout the season had turned out to be one of my best friends. I thought all that work between the playoffs and 2 championship games was worth it. We got a trophy and a memory. We were the champs!

I love this game.

Quinlan McCarthy
Grade 6

Got Icicles?

It's a beautiful snowy day, and you're off from school. As you stare through a foggy kitchen window at the gently falling snow, you notice something. Glistening in the sunlight at the top of your window is a shining point. It is an icicle.

Icicles form when water is slowly dripped off a surface. Icicles usually form off of angled surfaces because the water drips faster and more often. The slower the water freezes and drips, the longer the icicle will be. Places where water drips more often form shorter icicles. An icicle is really just a "stack" of ice. As layers upon layers of water drip on top of each other and freeze, the width of the icicle decreases, until it ends in a point.

You may think that icicles only occur after snow. This is not true. All icicles need is temperatures under 32 degrees Fahrenheit. Therefore, icicles can form at many times.

In the summer, you may see water dripping from somewhere on your home. If you do see this, during winter months you will see an increased number of icicles there. Icicles are fun to play with and come in a variety of sizes. So, next time its cold where you live, look and see if you've "Got Icicles?"

Lauren Mayer
Grade 6

My New Year Resolution

Though I am not old and perfect, the best period to start a great brand new year is in January. I made some changes in some promises I made to myself earlier this year. I made some promises to practice on my favorite hobbies such as artwork and fashion designing during the year. However, I changed my mind and decided to spend some more time with my brother and sister by starting to do some chores around the home to earn some allowance.

I will earn my allowance by doing three different types of chores daily, such as cleaning, washing dishes and teaching my sister and brother. This will help me gain some experience and be more responsible when I grow up. The chores will also allow me to spend some time with my family. I will spend some of my earned allowance on purchasing art supplies and save the rest in the bank.

I will practice my artwork and fashion designing projects at every spare time I get after I complete my homework and chores. I will seek help from experienced adults to help me meet my goals. I will also work very hard on my projects to make them perfect. I believe that practicing often will make me better in the future.

My New Years resolution is good and I promise to work very hard in school to keep my good grades, because my parents have promised me a trip to North Carolina this summer.

Nathalyn Nunoo
Grade 4

Sweet Sara

The hardest thing I've ever done was to see my cousin, who was like a sister, suffer. She had a pediatric brain tumor from when she was five until seven.

She passed away recently. I miss her very much. It was hard to say goodbye. The person I loved so dearly that whenever she kissed me I would get this weird but wonderful feeling, is now gone. I know I won't be able to feel that feeling again. Sara and I had a wonderful connection that no one else can replace.

I felt mad at myself, like it was my fault she died. Maybe I should have prayed every second. Or, maybe if I gave her my stone that always helped me, it would have helped her, too.

I'm still scared that I will not be able to survive without her in my life. I have a huge gap in my heart, but I know she's not suffering anymore. At the ceremony, I cried a lot, but I also got to read aloud two poems about Sara that I wrote from my heart. I knew it made Sara happy.

Sara always loved butterflies. We all believe that Sara is now a butterfly, free from pain. I see butterflies all the time now. Sometimes they even follow me. Sara didn't want anything more than her nails painted. She couldn't do much. She couldn't walk or talk. She had to communicate through her eyes. She will always be my sweet Sara. God bless her.

Laura Schoenmeier
Grade 5

The Great Wall of China

I am going to tell the history of the Great Wall of China.

The Great Wall of China is 6,700 kilometers long. The Wall starts in western China and stretches to the east side of China. The Wall is in the northern part of China. Since the Great Wall is so long it is one of the Eight Wonders of the World.

The Great Wall of China was officially ordered to be built by the first Emperor of China. During the Ming Dynasty, the workers around Beijing used bricks and granite to improve the dirt and wood wall. Some of this structure still stands today. Overall, the Emperors of the Ming Dynasty had the Wall improved eighteen times to protect them from the strong northern tribes.

The Great Wall averages 10 meters high and 5 meters wide. The Wall included watch and signal (beacon) towers for soldiers. The Wall also included passes (gates) that allowed traders through. Guards were stationed at all of these areas to watch for invaders. Since the Great Wall was far from the cities, the soldiers lived in the Wall's barracks.

There was over a thousand watch towers in the Great Wall, each manned by about sixty men. The Wall protected the northern part of China from the nomad tribes (Huns). No tribes ever breached the Great Wall of China, but in 1644 a traitor let the army of Manchu through the gate and into the Forbidden City (in Peking or now Beijing).

Would you want to go to the Great Wall of China and walk on a 2000 year old wall?

Matthew Siegel
Grade 5

What Freedom Means to Me

Freedom means a lot to me. To be free means to do more that you want, and to be able to do more. Have freedom to have other friends. Have freedom to live a life that's good. Have freedom to be with anyone and to do more of what you want to do. If there was not Dr. King to help make African Americans free to do like others, I could not be friends with Ainiah (and she's one of my best friends) that would not be fair. Freedom to do more.

Well, freedom means a lot to me and a lot to other people. Freedom was a big deal in the U.S. I would hate to grow up to know all the rules and follow them. I think what they did before was unfair and bad. Well I'm happy it is over. To be free to do more is freedom, but to have true freedom the world would have to have peace. That would be a great world. The thing is the world is not a great place, well not yet. I wish people could see me and I could make a big difference, like Dr. Martin King or Rosa Parks, but I'm one kid, what could I do now? A lot of other people wish that. Freedom means a lot to me. Well, you just heard/read what I said about freedom. Freedom means a lot. So that is what I think about freedom of the U.S.A.

Amanda Stafford
Grade 6

What Freedom Means to Me

On July 4th, our country celebrates Independence Day. We gained independence from our families from long ago. This is the day that we appreciate the freedoms that all Americans enjoy. Many people seem to forget the true meaning of the holiday and the sacrifices that our fellow Americans endured. July 4th became little more than a day off from work or an excuse for family and friends to get together for cookouts and fireworks. Since September 11th, the meaning of Independence Day is different to me. We are not free in the same way we were before September 11th. Those events changed America and woke people out of a sort of "sleep." It reminds people what our freedom is really worth. The bad events of that day made me realize how lucky we are to be able to do all the things in life that we want to do. I hope every person in the world will remember the faces that came across our television screens of the people we lost on that day. Those people's lives were taken because of a bad terrorist attempt to make us feel guilty for being free. I feel sorry for all of the families who lost their loved ones. They are all heroes to me because we are still free to do as we want and terrorists can never change that. I know that as a free American, I can become anything I want to become when I grow up. If I want to be a doctor, I can. If I want to be a stay-at-home mom, I can. It is having the ability to make my own choices in my life that makes me proud to be free.

Alexie Isom
Grade 4

The War in Iraq

The war in Iraq has been going on for more than 2 years now. People in America risk their lives every day for the Iraqi people to have freedom. Some people in Iraq call the war "The War on Terror." As for me I agree with them!

Some soldiers are lucky enough to go home for the holidays. Also, they only get small portions for all meals. In Iraq it is very hot and the soldiers have to fight in the blazing sun!

Once you join the army, you can't quit until your term is over. And every day you have to take long walks with all your equipment on, and you have to fight, rain or shine.

My opinion about the war in Iraq is very complicated. I'm glad the people in our country are willing to risk their lives to help the Iraqi people but I wish that we didn't have to war to help them be free.

In conclusion, the war in Iraq is scary to Iraqi people, the soldiers, and their families. The Iraqi people also just had elections (in 2005) so our soldiers might even come home soon. I hope every soldier that is in Iraq right now can/will come home safely.

Sarah Strahan
Grade 5

A Good Friend

I think a friend should be encouraging. So if you feel bad, they will say it's okay. If you fall down, they will help you up. They will let you play with someone else.

When you are down, they find a way to cheer you up. They can have a positive attitude. They will help you with your work.

A friend is nice, kind, and loves to play with you.

Mary Elise Jacobs
Grade 4

My Cat Oliver

Have you ever had a pet for so long that you can't remember what life was like without it? Life has been like that for me since I got my cat, Oliver. He is a mix between a tabby and a Persian white. Oliver arrived with his little head peeking out of the top of my mom's work bag. My sister, Seanna, and I couldn't have been happier with the surprise, and here our story begins.

When we moved from Philly to Montgomeryville, Oliver had to come with us. There was no question about it. The switch was hard for him, but he got used to it. As long as Seanna and I had Oliver, the move was more bearable for all of us.

Oh, and did I mention his first present? Yes, his first gift to us was a mouse. Not just any mouse, but a big, fat mouse. We managed to snap a picture and get it on tape before Mom saw it and Oliver had to leave it outside. Poor Ollie.

Oliver is going on eight years old, and I am going on twelve. I couldn't love him more, and for years to come I will love him as much as I do now.

Devyn Gregorio
Grade 6

Me

My name is Kaitlyn Schmitt. I've been to the Great Escape, Florida, Montreal, and Boston. I've moved three times. I used to live in my grandparents' apartment. It was sort of their basement.

I had six pets and still have some of them. Their names are Petie the rabbit, Marvin and Stevi the fish, Kado and Buddy the dogs, Corduroy the cat, and Hog the guinea pig. I'm taking care of him for my cousin.

I used to live in South Burlington right near the airport. The most annoying thing about that place was the jets, because they went off too late.

My favorite singers are Chris Brown and David Bowie. The band I cherish is Queen. The thing I worship most is my family, my dad, Eric, my mom, Bonnie, and my little sister, Olivia. My favorite baseball team is the Boston Red Sox. My favorite movie is *Old Yeller* because it reminds me of my dog Buddy. And well, that's me, Kaitlyn Schmitt.

Kaitlyn Schmitt
Grade 5

Amazing Grandma

Since I moved to America, I really miss my grandmother in Africa. In Africa we did lots of things together. My grandmother is amazing because she does things for me I never imagined. Three things that make her special are she is active, fun, and helpful.

My grandmother is active. She likes to go walking with me. Also, she likes to go swimming in the pool. I think she looks funny when she is in the water because she always splashed the water.

She is fun because she tells me jokes and likes to play games with me. She likes to have fun cooking for our family. She likes to tell jokes. I like her jokes because they are funny.

My grandmother is helpful because she helps me clean the house so I can go play. She also helps me with my homework so we can have time to go walking. I like it when she helps me with my house cleaning. She teaches me how to cook.

My grandmother is lovely. I miss her and wish she lived closer to me. She is a wonderful woman. I know I am lucky to have her for my grandmother.

Tele Wilson-Bahoun
Grade 5

Music in the World

My music is my life. Without music the world would be a different place. Without music the world would be a boring place.

You use music in so many ways, more than you know. You use music at Mass, there is music on TV! Some people, like me, play musical instruments for fun! Some people use music for a job! So always remember how important music is.

Alan Ludwikowski
Grade 4

Extra Point

Billy (our quarterback) had just run a sweep reverse play. Our wide receiver (Mac) was sprinting as fast as he could go. Then all of a sudden, he broke free from the defense. Nobody could catch him! He ran almost the whole field, Touchdown!! Oh no, this was bad. We were tied, and the game depended on me to kick the extra point! I was really nervous! The ball was snapped. All I could do now was try my best. I ran up to the ball and kicked it as hard as I could. As soon as I kicked it I knew I had made the point, but I prayed anyway. I watched the ball fly, right through the goal posts! The crowd cheered! Unbelievable, I did it!

I got ready for defense. We held them, but not too many yards away from the end zone. There was 13 seconds left. They ran a sweep play. My team came and stopped him. The whistle blew. Then all of a sudden he broke away — he hadn't been tackled! Touchdown! Everyone was confused. It turned out the score didn't count because the whistle had already blown. We won!!! My team beat the other team 7 to 6. We were really happy they made that call. That was the best game I've ever played! For once I got to be the big hero who saves the game, like I always wanted to be.

Daniel Carey
Grade 5

Family

"All happy families resemble each other; every unhappy family is unhappy in their own way." This famous quote describes my family. They give me a lot of things that other people may not get. For example, love and happiness. I also earn special treats like money. Read on and you shall find more examples of the love and happiness I get.

One important thing my family gives me is happiness. Such as, my aunt spends time with my sisters and me going shopping. During vacations at the beach, my dad and I like to swim in monster waves. On another vacation to Puerto Rico, I loved playing with my cousins. The simple things we do make me happy.

Another thing my family gives me is love. At Christmas there are always lots of hugs, smiles and kisses. It's really loving when it's time to go to bed. I always get hugs and kisses and "I love you" from mom. These are just a few ways I get love.

Some children don't get what I get from my family, so I'm lucky. My dad rewards us for earning good grades by taking us out to dinner. My grandmother gives us five dollars for allowance. Last but not least on a special occasion like a birthday, my mom gives me lots attention. As you can see, my family cares for each other. My love and happiness come mostly from my family, making us a happy family that resemble each other.

Gabriella Snead
Grade 6

Baseball Benefits

Do you play baseball? I play for the Scott Township Little League baseball. Through my participation on the team, I have found many benefits of baseball. Playing keeps you in physical shape, helps make new friends and strengthens relationships that already exist.

Playing baseball keeps you in good physical condition. You keep in physical shape by running laps around the field. We also condition by jumping rope, running the bases, hitting the baseball, and running the hill.

Playing baseball helps strengthen relationships because you have to communicate on and off the field with teammates. You can also meet new people and new friends who could eventually be your best friend. I have played on a baseball team for five years and some of my best friends are my teammates.

Baseball may be hard, but if you put your heart and soul into the game you will a better person on and off the field. You will develop teamwork, keep yourself healthy and may even get some lasting friendships.

Jason Restich
Grade 6

The Importance of a Good Education

Education is the key to success. Without an education, it might be impossible to find a good job or to make a lot of money. A good education will provide a better life and opportunities for many. The lack of education is a source for failure and unhappiness for many. Education is power. That power will help increase a sense of confidence in many.

Having a good education is better than being illiterate and ignorant. It can bring happiness and success in many ways. It can provide a good paying job that can help buy the important and less important things in life. The money earned from being educated can buy beautiful homes, nice clothes, food and medicine for the sick. It can also buy toys for the kids and even better, video games, which are important and appreciated by most kids.

Education is very important. It helps many people become scientists, doctors, lawyers, teachers and many other qualified people. The qualified people are important in many ways. Some find cures for diseases, some teach us and some give us the right medicines when we are sick. Education is knowledge and this knowledge makes a better and healthier life.

It is very important to have a good education. Everyone should get one. It will make life much more comfortable and less confusing to many. Without it, the poor will remain poor and hungry. It is better to be smart than to be stupid. Education gives some people the strength and confidence to achieve many things in life. Without it, some people might be afraid to try new things and that can cause a lot of failures. Remember, education is knowledge and knowledge is power. So don't forget to educate yourself to become successful and powerful.

Xylon Charles
Grade 4

Raptors

65,000,000 years ago in the world of dinosaurs there was one dinosaur that was the smartest and most dangerous of them all. The raptor. The raptor came in all shapes and sizes. When you first look at a raptor, you might say it looks like a six foot turkey. But don't be fooled. The raptor was equipped with everything it needed to hunt and kill. They were equipped with a large beak like snout, a long tail for balance when running, and of course a large hook like claw on each third toe for slashing their prey open. Raptors could run at their highest pace over 60 miles per hour. Raptors were pack hunters that would corner their prey. The largest of these predators was the Utah raptor which grew to 10 ft tall and 15 ft long. A later form of a raptor was the copy. Copys are 1 ft and a half long, 11 inch high dinosaurs. They hunted in packs like raptors and cornered their prey like them. Copys didn't have a torso claw on their toe. Luckily for us these monsters are extinct today. HOPEFULLY...

Carmelo Guglielmino
Grade 6

My Memory of 5th Grade

My memory of 5th grade is a year of being taught that we needed to grow up and be independent. We were responsible for writing down our homework at the beginning of each class. I remember having teachers that I thought were mean, but now realize they were just trying to help us out. I became friends with new friends during the year like Brian, Josh, and Paul. All 5th grade students went on two memorable field trips together. The first was a 3 days 2 nights camping trip to Camp Ramblewood. We learned how it feels to be inside a bubble and some students participated in a talent show. We were able to see snakes, an eagle, and other wild animals in a controlled environment.

The second memorable field trip was to Philadelphia, PA. We were able to visit Independence Hall, Liberty Bell, and the Constitution. We had a graduation ceremony to recognize all 5th graders and our achievements. The PTA gave us a 5th grade luncheon and party.

During my fifth grade school year I also had a memory that was memorable but not enjoyable. One Sunday afternoon in January, I went to visit a friend to hang out for a few hours before my dad was to pick me up. My friend's dog attacked me (a Rottweiler). I ended up being rushed to John Hopkins Hospital and taken into emergency surgery to have my wounds cleaned and closed. When I awoke I had 15 staples in my head, 2 staples and 8 stitches in my right upper arm, 2 stitches each in 4 different areas of my lower left arm, and many puncture wounds over my chest, back, and arms. These are the memories that I had in 5th grade, some were exciting and some were not.

Johnathon Becker
Grade 6

My Mom

When I see black, curly hair waving in the air I know it is my mom. My mom is more than just my mom, she is my best friend. I tell her all of my secrets. I can trust her. When I need her help, there she is. All I do is scream, "MOM!" When I hear her footsteps I know she is on her way.

When I had a problem with my best friend at school I asked my mom for advice. She said I should talk to my friend and try to solve the problem. Her advice really helped. I always come to her because she understands me.

If I am not feeling well, or if I'm up to something, my mom knows right away. One time when I was trying to eat a cookie before dinner my mom, from all the way in her room, said, "Don't go anywhere near those cookies!" It's like she has cameras watching. I guess it is true when she says, "I know what you are up to." When I don't feel good, my mom can tell right away from the look on my face.

If there is one person in the world who will always be there for me, it is my mom. I know I can always count on her. When I have school plays or recitals, she is there in the crowd supporting me. My mom knows how special it is for me to have her there.

Diana Arevalo
Grade 6

Giant Pandas

Eight thousand to twelve thousand feet on top of the Chinese mountains roam the giant panda. The mountains are in the Szechuan Province in western China. There are only one thousand of these endangered animals left in the world. They are endangered because food is running low. Farming and logging are partly to blame since they take away the bamboo. A giant panda needs up to forty pounds of food each day. Another problem is hunting which people still do even though it is against the law. I feel that there should be more because one thousand is not enough for a species.

I really think pandas would be extremely missed if they were to go. I also think it would be really bad because they are important. They are important to me and a lot of other people since they are a part of nature and Earth's environment. Pandas are very much loved. I hope they do not become extinct.

Saving pandas is a very big job. To preserve them people are making special areas on mountain tops. One of these special areas is a sanctuary called Wanglang Preserve. They are safe from hunters and poachers. No one is allowed in without permission. The Chinese people are also trying to make bamboo that is stronger. That is really nice to know because pandas should not go. People should do more to help their population grow. I don't think pandas will ever not be my favorite animal.

Catie Yanchak
Grade 4

My First Soccer Game

About two years ago, I decided to play soccer. On the team was Jonathan LaDieu, Kyle Sprague, Sierra and Zach Snow, Sean Pulsifer, Luke Peduzzi, Aaron Connor, and Jack Fenton. I was very nervous at first, but my mother and my coaches, Roby Baer and Leo Sprague, helped me. They taught me how to overcome being nervous and how to be a good soccer player. My coaches made the season fun for me.

I was very excited as we did our laps and stretches. I would be playing as right halfback in the second quarter. As I sat on the bench, our team scored our first two goals by Sean. When it was my turn to play, I would help Kyle move the ball up the field. When the half was over, the score was 3-0, because Kyle had scored with my help. In the third quarter, Sean scored his third goal and Luke scored after him. In the fourth quarter, I was a left forward. The score was 5-0. Kyle was going for a goal when the ball was kicked away from him. Sierra recovered it and passed it to me. I dribbled a little way, and then I centered it for Kyle. With one minute left, he kicked the ball to the top right corner of the goal and scored our sixth and last goal.

At the end of the game, I was proud and sweaty. It was our first game and I could just imagine how much fun the other nine would be. Soccer can be a lot of fun when you work hard at it. It is also fun when you play with a nice team, like the one I was on. As you can see, I enjoy playing soccer.

Zander Connor
Grade 5

Gift of Friendship

The gift of friendship is something that can't be wrapped. It can make people feel cared about and happy. Friends can help kids boost their self-esteem. Some friends even help kids make new friends. Sometimes friends have fights but they can have good times too. The gift of friendship can help you if you are lonely or sad because they allow you to have someone to be with.

The gift of friendship is very special and is very important to have. It can help you so you don't make bad choices. Friends can make better decisions together. It can also help a child who may be feeling left out. Friendships can also help you when you don't feel well. Friends help make you feel better. Friends can also help you when you are stuck on a question or you need help with schoolwork or homework. Friends can also look out for you and protect you so that you are safe. They can also stick up for you against bullies. They can help break up fights or help you with something that you cannot do by yourself. Sometimes friends even get into arguments, but in the end they usually end up laughing at the whole thing.

In conclusion, friendships are a special gift that can't be wrapped. You can't buy them or sell them. You can't get them in a store. You can make them, and keep your friendships lasting forever.

Anthony Vitale
Grade 6

The Pete Rose Ball

Something that means a lot to me is my autographed Pete Rose baseball. I got it at the Trump Marina in Brigantine, New Jersey.

We had to wait in line for at least a half and hour! It was worth the wait though. It wasn't just Pete Rose either! It was all of the 1980 Philly's team. I got to meet Pete Rose, Mike Schmidt, plus Steve Carlton! I also got Steve Carlton's autograph, too!

When I met Pete Rose, I was so excited. My dad was even more excited than me. When he signed the ball, he signed his first and last name and the number of hits he had as a baseball player. He had 4,000 hits or so! That's amazing. I also got to take a picture with him!

I think that the ball could sell for a couple hundred dollars. I'd never sell it though. It was so cool that I got to meet him. It's like a once in a life time chance! He was one of the all time greats. It's too bad that he had to bet on baseball, and now he will most likely not be going to the Hall of Fame. It's so cool that I met a legend like that!

After I got the ball, though, I lost it! You're probably thinking what happened. Well, Pete Rose was nice enough to sign another baseball! I'm very lucky. What I said before, I'm never selling that ball! Ever!

Seth Lipshutz
Grade 6

My Favorite Memory of Elementary

My favorite memory of elementary is Pre-K because you got to get off at 12:00 and you got to take naps during school which I would like to do during middle school. Also, in Pre-K we had a graduation party when we passed Pre-K and my teacher Mrs. Henry was really nice and Mrs. White the assistant helper. I met a lot of my friends in that class like Kelsie, Brett, Jack, and a whole lot more. We would play a lot of games and have recess, play jump-rope, hopscotch, and can hang on the monkey bars. Another one of my favorite memories are in Kindergarten was we got to do an egg hunt, finger paint, hand paint, and we had easy homework.

My favorite memory in all of the school year Pre-K through 5th grade was all of the nice teachers we had, just like the teachers in middle school. In middle school Mrs. Posten is the nicest teacher I have, also what sucks is that they have no air conditioning, only in like 4 rooms. Middle school is way harder than elementary school because you keep going up grades which get harder every step that you make. It was a tough time for me to go to a different grade and school.

Well that is all I've got to say and that is my favorite memory at the elementary and little bits and parts of middle school.

Alyson Cole
Grade 6

Sharks

Sharks are a type of fish. They eat animals and humans. They are colored white or gray. There are different kinds of sharks; for example, the Sand Tiger Shark, Silvertip Shark, Giant Pacific Manta Ray Shark, Large Tooth Sawfish, Great White Shark, Scalloped Hammer Head Shark, Gray Reef Shark, and Whale Shark. Sharks have no bones in their body. Their sizes are usually 5.0 to 5.8 feet. Sharks have a sleek, streamlined design which helps them swim without using up a lot of energy. They need to conserve their energy because they never really sleep and most of them never stop swimming. A mother shark carriers her babies inside her body while they develop, sometimes for more than year. Even so, some sharks are born inside an egg which they have to crack open. They spend early portions of their lives in nursery grounds. Some of the advantages sharks have over people are that they keep growing new teeth, they don't have breakable bones, and they are not prone to get cancer. Sharks can move very fast.

Taysiir Aubdoollah
Grade 5

Boston University Hockey

Boston University was established in 1839. By 1916, the university's student body had really grown, and it was becoming obvious that it had a large group of students with the athletic potential. Though the school didn't even have an athletic field at the time, it would come to be known more and more for its athletics.

The Boston University Men's Hockey Team was started in 1920. Like the other official sports teams forming at this time at the University, it was started mostly by the dedication of the student athletes themselves. Their mascot is the terrier dog named Rhett and the school's colors are red and white. Since then, generations of talented and enthusiastic athletes, faculty and fans have transformed B.U. into the major national college competitor. They also have an organized support group called "Terrier Pride," which helps raise money for the sports programs.

Today B.U.'s hockey coach, Jack Parker, has a lot to be proud of. In his 33 years as head coach, he has led the team to many victories. One of the highlights for a player is to play in the "Bean Pot Hockey Championship." The Bean Pot is made up of the four "Division 1" college hockey teams in Boston. These teams are Boston University, Boston College, Harvard University and Northeastern University. This year they'll be competing for the 54th Bean Pot Championship. B.U. has made the finals in 23 of the last 24 years and has won the title 27 times.

At a recent game there were 15,565 fans. There's a group of dedicated fans named the "Dog Pound." Their mission at each game is to "hound" the opposing team by making the B.U. spirit known, loud and clear. These member get discounts at the games and concessions and more! GO TEAM!

Michael Cronin
Grade 5

Benjamin Franklin

Benjamin Franklin lived from 1706 to 1790. He was brave and talented. He was brave because he signed the Declaration of Independence, which made him a traitor of the king. He was talented as a scientist, inventor, statesman, printer, musician and economist.

He was a great inventor because he was always looking for practical and useful ways to make life easier or to complete tasks better. He had poor vision but he got tired of putting on different glasses so he combined both lenses to make bifocals. He made the lightning rod to protect buildings and ships from lightning damage. Everybody used to have to keep warm by burning wood. He knew that it was not safe to do that, so he knew he had to do something about it, so he invented a furnace made out of iron so people could heat their homes less dangerously and with less wood. That furnace was and still is known as the Franklin Stove. He also established the first fire company and fire insurance company.

He became postmaster and had to measure routes. He invented an odometer and attached it to his carriage. When he was older and retired from business and public service he spent his time reading. Even then he invented a tool called a "long arm" to reach the high books. It was a long wooden pole with a grasping claw on the end.

In conclusion, Benjamin Franklin was a brave patriot and talented inventor of colonial times.

Alex Rowden
Grade 4

A Book

An adventure anywhere in the world. How could you get there? A book is how. No one can stop you from reading but yourself. A book is a way to travel anywhere whatsoever. A book is far better than a cartoon or a video game. The best thing is; you can compose your own books. It can be about anything at all; a dog, cat, the moon, a space adventure, or even a made-up universe. There are no limits as to what you can write. There are no such things as stupid books, for they all are a significant way that the author can express himself/herself freely. I, myself try to write books, and it makes me feel great. Reading is one of the most phenomenal experiences for me. You can travel to anyplace and stay in that same chair. I love to read books about a big family living in a friendly neighborhood. I also enjoy books on old England. I love books where people who are thought of as a nuisance becomes king or queen. I love books by Dickens, Twain, and Lewis. I love books so much but I do not know what I would do without them. Reading and writing books develops creative minds. It makes me wonder about things. Books are wonderful!

Jimmy Humphrey
Grade 5

Playing Basketball

Basketball is a fun and enjoyable way to get exercise. In basketball you have fun by faking, passing, and dribbling. Basketball is fun because you get to play against other teams. You get to play with your friends if they play basketball. It is fun to take long shots from the three-point line. You learn things during the game that you have never learned before. It is exciting to win trophies if your team places first. Basketball is an enjoyable way to exercise your muscles.

Isaac Watson
Grade 6

Sports

Do you play any sports, such as football, soccer, softball, or maybe even gymnastics? Well, I do and I love it! Sports are fun for everyone and they can also help kids with their weight!

It's always nice to be able to feel the air rushing through your hair, or the feeling that you get when you win a game or score a point. But most important, it's about the fun you're having!! Sports are a great exercise and they can make people feel better about themselves. Perhaps when someone is going too hard on themselves, maybe they can play sports and relieve more stress. Sports can also make kids feel much better about their weight, so try getting outside and make a neighborhood sports team, it could be fun!

Sports aren't about winning or losing, it's about having fun. If you lose a game, don't take it out on any one person, you're a team. So get out there and play!!

Rachel Steelman
Grade 5

Equestrian at the Circus

Wow! I would love working at the circus. Working with horses would make it even better. This is how my day would usually go under the big top.

First, I would saddle up and groom my wonderful horse. I bet it's really a lot of work! Next, I would get on my horse and practice my stunts. My stunts would be extremely hard. I would have to stand on the horse, then jump in the air, do a flip, and land on my horse again. Practicing is what makes me better at my job. After practicing, I would put on my costume. My costume would be a lavender suit, white tights, a blue skirt, and everything would have feathers and sequins on it.

Time for the show! The show would last about two hours, but my part would only last ten minutes. Once the show is done I would unsaddle my beloved horse and give him a tasty treat and pat. I would also give out autographs to my extraordinary fans in the audience. I would change into comfortable sweats and then go home to a warm fire and a cup of steaming hot tea.

This is how my hectic day would usually be. I bet I would love my exciting job at the circus! What would you like to do under this marvelous tent?

Jenna Di Rito
Grade 4

My Life

My life isn't a walk through the park. I am very busy during the week. I do lots of extra-curricular activities after school.

On Mondays, I wake up early and then go to school. After school, I go to library club and then go to basketball practice. I like basketball.

On Tuesdays, I do my usual routine. After school I play the saxophone in band, then have piano lessons, then dance class. I finally get home at 7:00 pm, eat dinner, and do my homework.

On Wednesdays, I go to school, then go to science club, then basketball practice.

On Thursdays after school, I have choir practice. After choir, I go home to do my homework, practice my piano and eat a quick dinner. I have a late jazz class and don't get home until 9:00 pm.

On Fridays after school I have some free time and then go to dance class. On Fridays, I can do whatever I want!

On Saturdays, I wake up later and go to my basketball games. When the game is over, my family and I go to church.

On Sundays, I usually do a ski race. Last year I came in first place. I like skiing, except for the fact that I have to wake up earlier than usual on weekends.

I do many things during the week and sometimes I just want to stay home or play with friends. My mom keeps telling me I will thank her for all this some day, but to me, that day can't come fast enough.

Nicole Episalla
Grade 6

Snow Day

On Monday, February 13, we had a snow day. It was really nice to have a three day weekend. I got to sleep until ten o'clock. When I got up, I made sure it was a snow day. My dad was teasing me and told me it was a two hour delay. So I rushed upstairs and got dressed. When I cam downstairs he said, "Got ya!" I was so made at him. Since I was dressed, I went outside. My brother was building a moat.

I told him to come get the sleds with me. We went behind the shed to get them. When we found them, we decided to go sled down the pool stairs. After a while it kind of hurt falling off and since they were steep, they hurt. So we decided to make a path on the deck so we could run and slide down the stairs. I did it a lot. After a while, Brett went inside but I kept going.

When I came inside, I got into warm clothes and took a hot shower. I played on the computer for a while, then we went to the movies. We saw *Curious George*. It was really funny. Then I played in the snow and had dinner. I watched TV and went to bed. I had a good snow day! I can't wait until we have another fun, awesome snow day. I wonder what I will do the next snow day. I hope we don't get too much more snow!

Bryce Geiger
Grade 6

My Sleep Over Party

When I was going to turn nine, I had a sleep over party. It was awesome. My birthday is on August 23. My party was on August 22 until August 23. The people who were at my party were here on my birthday. I invited seven girls. We had a lot of fun.

First, we went outside and played tag. My little brother, Eric, played with us, too. Whenever Eric got tagged, we all had to go slow. After, we did a different game of tag. Two people would be horses. Everyone else would run away from the horses. After we were done playing that, we had cake. It was delicious. We had a chocolate cake. Oh yeah, we had music on outside, too. Eric did the Twist and everybody thought it was funny. After we were done eating, we went inside my house.

We first had to wash up. After that, I opened my presents. They were really nice. Then we went to my playroom. That's where we were going to sleep. We were going to sleep on the floor. We did my karaoke machine, played Barbies, and played with my Care Bears. After that, we did Twister. Some of the girls got hungry so they went downstairs for a snack. We went to sleep at 3:00 am. I slept in a cozy Tweety Bird sleeping bag. When we woke up, we had bagels. They were good. Then we played outside in my playhouse. That was a fun sleep over party!

Kim Connolly
Grade 4

Moving On

Some people say they can't live without their best friend. In my case, it's the complete opposite. Every day for two years, I have been put to the same misery, not seeing my best friend. In 4th grade, I heard the appalling truth. My best friend and I were blissful and full of laughter until…she told me. She said she was going to depart to New Jersey over the summer. At that moment it felt like the world came to a sudden halt. The rest of the day, I was speechless.

See, it's hard to move on. Every day I expect to see her massive smile and her attentive attitude. I feel that excruciating pain in my stomach, thinking she will be walking through the school doors saying she just came in late. She visits us seldom, maybe two or three times a year. Her Manhasset friends are starting to fade away from the picture. The last day we saw each other, we promised to never let go, that we would always stay in touch. We still have a section reserved for her in our town and in our hearts.

Although now all she sees is a slight silhouette of us, we still love her. She was, still is, and always will be my best friend. One day she may forget entirely, but I know I won't. Her moving is an emotional scar that will never go away. After all, we all need to move on.

Katherine Nevitt
Grade 6

Watership Down

Watership Down is my favorite book. In this book two rabbits are sitting in the grass. They decide to leave their home, so they get as many rabbits as they can, and get ready to leave the warren they have been living in. Hazel and his friends travel to a hill to look for a place to live. They dig burrows to live in and call the area Watership Down.

They need to find does so they can have babies and continue their race. They find another warren called Efrafa. They ask to take some of the Efrafan does back with them, but they are not allowed. They eventually escape and go back home. They return later and take some of the does. The Efrafan rabbits chase them, but the Watership Down rabbits get away by jumping on a boat and sailing down a river.

They return to Watership Down, and soon the Efrafan rabbits attack, but some of the rabbits escape. They go down to the farm and get a dog to set on the Efrafan rabbits. Hazel and his rabbits stayed at Watership Down forever and ever.

This book is important to me because it is my favorite book I've ever read. I think everyone in the world should read it. On the front of the book cover readers are told, "Everyone who can read English should read it." I think if I can only have one book to read forever, it would be *Watership Down*.

Nicholas Bowser
Grade 6

My Camp

My camp is Hidden Valley Camp in Maine. I have been going for the past two summers and love it. Some things I like about my camp are the fun activities, great food, nice counselors and campers. These are the reasons I love my camp.

My camp has a lot of the fun activities. My favorite activities were rock band and bad dancing. In bad dancing we would think of crazy dance moves, put a show together, and perform in front of the whole camp. In rock band we pick a song, practice a lot and then perform. There are also other great activities such as wind surfing.

Another reason I love my camp is because of the great food. A typical breakfast is bacon, eggs, cereal, plus other choices. For lunch there is a salad bar, sandwich meats, and leftovers from last night's meal. For dinner we have all sorts of food such as Mexican, Chinese, Indian, American, and a lot more. The cooks are great.

The last reason I love my camp is because of the nice counselors and campers. The counselors were best at making me feel more at home. The campers made me have more fun. My favorite counselors name was Gavin. He was from Scotland. My best friends from camp were Andrew, Jared, and Alex; they were awesome.

These are some of the reasons I love my camp. My camp is the best month each year, I always look forward to it. When I'm older I want to be a counselor there. I LOVE MY CAMP.

Gabe Pepe
Grade 5

My Animals

My animals are the best! I have one dog and four cats. My dog's name is Chelsea. My cat's names are Siike, Coco, Savanna, and Cleo. Savanna and Cleo are the most playful cats I have ever seen. They always eat. They always claw up the couch. Siike and Coco sleep a lot. Chelsea likes to follow my mom around all day. My favorite animals are cats and dogs.

I love animals! They are so cute and cuddly. When my animals get tired they love to cuddle with you. My grandma's cat Shugie was the best. She always cuddled up with you and always came when you called her. One day she was bumping into walls and my grandma took her to the vet and she was blind. Then a month or a year later she passed away. I hope my animals don't pass away for a very very very long time.

My animals mean so much to me. I would be so mad if an animal I know very well passes away. Chelsea, my dog, knows 3 tricks, sit, lay down, and roll over. Chelsea got hit by a truck when she was young. The truck did not even stop. My mom had to run all the way up the driveway (we have a long driveway). Chelsea was the only dog I ever had. It is going to be hard to let her go. She is fourteen or fifteen I am not sure. She is always there when I am sad. My cats stay for a while and then leave me.

Chelsea is my only dog I had since I was born.

Shannon Dorsi
Grade 6

My Life

My life was hard growing up. When I was just eight months old I had my head cut open for skull surgery. I was in the emergency room for a long time. My mom had a hard time.

The doctor reshaped my skull so my forehead won't be all the way out and the back of my head won't be dented in. I also had surgery on my fingers. When I was a baby I had my hands in a fist. So the doctor had to pull my fingers out. And still to this day my fingers are crooked.

When I was one years old my father left my mother, my brothers, and I. I didn't even know my dad. I can't remember anything about him. Then my mom met someone else named Greg. He is a very nice man and helped me a lot. I started to call Greg my dad. When I was three or four, I used to run in my mom's room while she was at work and lay in the bed and watch TV with Greg.

When I was six my mom was pregnant with the twins Marcus and Maxxine but unfortunately they died and I never got to see them. When I was eight I had a little sister named Gioanah. She is just like my mom. When I turned ten I broke my leg. I got hit by a Bronco truck. The wheel was on my foot. On my leg the cast hurted badly.

Reginald Sinclair
Grade 6

The Family Trip

My family and I were lucky enough to travel to Seaworld in San Diego, California. When we drove on the highway we were stuck in traffic like mashed potatoes jammed between us. When we finally arrived at Seaworld we had a great time together looking at the animals.

My family was exhausted and hungry, so my mom bought us cinnamon sticks to eat. When my mom lifted her hand up to take a bite, a seagull smelled the sweet taste of the cinnamon stick and dove right through the sky like an airplane with blownup engines and snatched the cinnamon stick out of her hand. She yelled at the seagull. So I started to laugh. I laughed so hard that my lungs burst out with air. It was funny.

We had so much fun looking at animals doing tricks. We went to look at the dolphins and we saw only two dolphins doing tricks with workers. When my family took a seat, we watched the dolphins swimming around the tank until the show started. Finally in a few minutes it started and it was fun.

The dolphins splashed at us like someone trying to go swimming in a pool.

After the show was over, my brother was very tired, so we went home. When my family left Seaworld I saw a candy shop, so I went there. I bought a lollipop to eat, it was the size of a soccer ball.

After that wonderful day we all went home.

Diane Keo
Grade 6

The Best Gift

Not all gifts can be bought. Most gifts, like the gift I will give are just being nice to someone. The best gift I can give is being nice to my brother. He was always nice to me, but I wasn't nice back. That is why the best possible gift I can give him is just to be nice to him.

Tyler, my brother, was always so generous to me. When I wanted to watch something else on television and he was watching something else he would change the channel. If he ever asked to watch something while I was watching television I would tell him to go away. For Christmas he spent a month making something for me because he gave me his money to get a video game for me. I never let him play. When he gave it to me I just threw it in my closet. When I think about it, I didn't get Tyler anything for Christmas. I can't believe I was always so mean to such a nice person.

Now I know what the perfect gift is: to be nice to the person who was always as nice as he could be to me. My brother was always nice to me even after I was so mean to him. That is completely unfair to Tyler. So I am going to make it up to him by being as nice as he was to me.

Kevin Meaney
Grade 6

The Gift of a Cure

There are many gifts to give and many people to give gifts to. There is one gift that I would love to give to a very special person. The gift I would like to give is the gift of a cure. I would give this gift to my grandma who had passed away from cancer. I would give her this gift because I miss her a lot. I would also give her this gift because she was so miserable when she was diagnosed with cancer. It hurt me to see her sick with something life threatening, but the thing that was so hard was not knowing if she was going to live or not. The next reason I would give her this gift is because all the holidays seem so dim and dull without her. I would give her this gift so she could see my brother and I grow up. When she was alive that's all she ever talked about. Another reason why I would give her this gift is for the sound of her voice. I miss her telling stories of when I was a baby. My grandma inspired me to be the best that I could be by being the best she could be even though she was sick. If I could give my grandma a cure I would.

Nicole Avellino
Grade 6

Camping

Get your sleeping bag, food, firewood, and tent together and let's go camping. I love to go camping, do you? When I go camping, I like to go on trails that lead to the woods. I just like to sit down and watch the sunset at night. Once I went camping and it was so much fun. We were there for two nights. When we got there we unloaded all of our stuff and made it into a beautiful home. When we were there we knew not to litter anywhere, it could hurt the animals and the environment. When we got there we shot a bow and arrow at targets. There was a lake nearby and it was pretty deep. In the lake there was crawfish and maybe water snakes. There was a tree and we tied rope on the tree and swung into the water. On the second day my cousin broke his leg and went to the hospital. Also on the second day we sadly all went home. Well we all had a great time and we were all happy.

Brenna Butts
Grade 5

Moving

When I was eight years old, I moved from Camphill to Etters and I changed schools. I didn't want to leave my friends. I really like our new house, but I miss my old house because that's the house I was in until I was eight.

We had to move because there wasn't a lot of room. At my new house, I have a bigger room. Then I started school at Fishing Creek Elementary. I was scared, but I made new friends and my computer teacher was the same one from my old school. I was in third grade in Mrs. Bourque's class, but there were so many kids that I was moved to Mrs. Shandra's room. Now I'm 10 and in Mr. Richcrick's 4th grade class.

I miss my friends and my old school, but I love Fishing Creek Elementary.

Tess Henderson
Grade 4

My Mom

My mom has done so many things for me and I really love her. She is so loving, caring and motherly. I can't ask for her to be any different. She is my best friend.

My mom understand me very well and I have a special bond with her for that very reason. She cares about me so much and she only wants what's best for me. She helps me with my homework and my personal problems. She is so helpful!

She is the closest thing to a guardian angel to me. My mom sometimes gets strict when I don't do what I am told to do but that rarely occurs. Like I said, she only wants what's best for me. I wouldn't want her any other way. I love the way she does everything for me and she is very considerate of others.

When my sister, my mom, and I came to America, my mom had to work two jobs; one a secretary and two at Burger King for minimum wage. She worked twice as hard to support my sister and me because she is a single parent and therefore she takes the place of my dad.

Due to my mom's enthusiasm to support us, she now has a far better job and is able to provide us with more. This also provides us with a better standard of living. I strongly believe that my mom is capable of taking care of us, as a single parent, until I can take care of myself. I love my mom!

Aliyah Gafoor
Grade 6

My Style, My Way

All through my life I have loved to write. Stories, essays, anything that can allow me to express myself without stating a word. After writing my first book in first grade, I have been addicted to writing, mostly performing my passion during leisure time. While other kids my age detest having to write a single paragraph, I spring at the opportunity and append as much as I possibly can. Inside of me, I can feel the words welling up until I have to pick up a pencil and let them encourage me to write what I feel, which helps me from getting my feelings bottled up inside. Not to mention, writing also is a way to show imagination, an astounding feeling. You can make up characters and setting and even plots. Then, when you're done, you have an established source of revere that can inspire you to write more and more until your writing is a symbol of who you are and your capabilities as an individual. Anyone can write what they want, too. The only thing you have to do is decide what your topic is and let the words pour out of you and onto a piece of paper. No doubt that in the end you'll be proud of yourself and see a side of you that no one has seen before. In other words, writing can show you who you really are on the inside and will show others what a talented, magnificent person you can be.

Kristen Kennefick
Grade 6

Tae Kwon Do

I do many activities in my pastime. I enjoy all of them. The activity I enjoy the most is Tae Kwon Do.

Tae Kwon Do is a very fun sport. I started Tae Kwon Do six years ago, when I was seven years old. I stopped taking Tae Kwon Do about five months ago because the school closed.

Tae Kwon Do taught me many things. But most importantly it helped me to defend myself. Tae Kwon Do has many belts and levels. I stopped Tae Kwon Do when I was a black belt.

It takes many years to get the black belt. You have to do many tests to get your black belt. I had to run three miles, do one hundred pushups, one hundred sit-ups, one hundred jumping jacks and one hundred squats and write two essays.

Tae Kwon Do helped me in many ways. Tae Kwon Do helped me concentrate in everything, and believe in myself.

Josue Huertero
Grade 6

Reading

Why read? Because it's fun! Reading is fun. It's educational and cool. It's better than TV. Reading is nice.

Reading is educational. Books are full of information. You can study from books. You may find out facts you never knew. Books are educational.

Reading is cool. It may be action or adventure. It may be fantasy or fiction. It may be futuristic, historical, or modern. Books are cool.

Reading is better than TV. It doesn't rot your brain. You can put it down at any time and start where you left off any time later. You never have to miss anything. Books are better than TV.

Reading is nice. It's educational, cool, and better than TV. In other words, reading is fun.

Drew Gensey
Grade 6

Sacagawea

Sacagawea was born around 1787 in a Shoshone village in what is now eastern Idaho. When she was eleven years old she was kidnapped and was brought to the Missouri River. Later, she was married to a French fur trapper, Toussaint Charbonneau.

Sacagawea and her husband joined the Lewis and Clark expedition in 1804. She took on many responsibilities and quickly earned the respect of Lewis and Clark. Once she rescued important papers from the Missouri River when Lewis and Clark's canoe capsized. She also looked after her newborn son, Jean Baptiste, on her journey. Sacagawea's brother, a Shoshone chief, did not want to help the explorers continue their trip until Sacagawea convinced him to.

Sacagawea and her husband returned to Fort Mandan in 1806 after Sacagawea became a translator for the expedition. That is some information on Sacagawea's life and expeditions.

Briane Bilbao
Grade 5

Life or Death

Hello, my name is Kailyn Canini. I have had a *huge* life crisis. It was when my sister, Kristin, almost died.

Kristin was in 4th grade and we were visiting my grandparents in Salem, New York. We were walking around outside and there was a bee's nest on the ground. My sister stepped on it by accident and she got stung 5 or 6 times by them. She started to swell up right away and couldn't breathe. I thought she was going to die. She was rushed to the hospital and got right in to see a doctor. She had hives for a few days but now she has to carry an Epi-pen around. She is deathly allergic to bees, but we didn't know that until that day.

That's how I had a very big family crisis. As you can see, I believe she has a guardian angel looking down on her!

Kailyn Canini
Grade 5

The Miracle

I jumped out of bed to wash the sleep from my face and realized it was one freezing cold morning! I usually use the fresh clean water like an alarm clock to wake me up. This morning was different because I heard a whining noise coming from my bedroom window. I was so cold that I looked like an already frozen ice cube. I could hear wailing sounds as I jumped back into bed. I didn't stay long because I decided to get up and put on my soft robe to keep me even warmer and I got the shock of my life!

The bedroom window blew open: Boom! I was so scared. It is hard to even imagine what was going through my mind. I somehow got close enough to look out the window and I saw a little frozen flake of snow swirling through the air. Then a strong wind blew through my room. I felt wind sweeping right through as I was thrown to the floor. I was shocked. The curtains were blowing around and my school notebooks were opening in the wind. I was so scared! Who could ever imagine that a storm could blow up so fast and let itself into my room?

Luckily I didn't get hurt but I sure was frightened! Everyone in my house said, "It was a miracle that something worse didn't happen."

Waverly Williams
Grade 5

My Family Is Important to Me

The things that are important to me are more than some toy or a book; it is my family. My family is there when I need them for a math problem or a spelling word. But they're always there when I'm hurt or sick. They get me the things I need and sometimes the things I don't need.

They teach me right from wrong and feed me when I'm hungry and give me water when I'm thirsty. My family tells me the right friends to make and the right things to do. They punish me when I'm bad and reward me when I'm good. Now you see why I want to be with my family.

Seth Fuss
Grade 4

Monet

My essay is on the impressionist artist Monet. Claude Monet was born on November 14, 1840 in Paris. When he was five-years-old, his family moved to the port city of Le Harve. At age seventeen, he was well known in his town as a skilled portrait artist. During the next year, Monet met Eug'ene Boudin, who encouraged him to paint nature, not just people.

In 1859, Monet went to Paris and entered the Swiss Academy of Art. In 1860, Monet met fellow artists Pissaro and Courbet, who inspired him greatly. Three years later, Monet discovered Manet's painting and painted *en plein air* in the Fontainebleau forest. In 1864, Monet stayed in Hofleur with Boudin, Bazille, and Jongkind and met his first art lover, Gaudibert. Three years later, Monet exhibited *Impressionist Sunrise* at the first impressionist exhibition.

In 1881, Monet rented a house in Giverny where he lived for forty-three years. Seven years later, Monet bought it and began digging the water-lily pond. In the next two years, Monet painted a series of haystacks, poplars, and the Rouen Cathedral. In 1990, he painted several views of the Japanese Bridge.

In 1907, Monet first had problems with his eyes. Things started getting blurry and colors changed. From 1916 to 1926, Monet worked on twelve large canvases, *The Water Lilies*. Monet offered to donate them to France. These paintings were installed in an architectural space designed specifically for them in a museum in Paris.

Michaela Welch
Grade 5

Whale Sharks: Aquatic Wonders

A Whale Shark is the largest species of shark in the world known to man. It's scientific name Rhincodon typus. A fully grown Whale Shark can be about 50 feet (16 meters) long and weigh more than 15 tons. It usually travels alone and is seldom seen by humans, but is also harmless to them. It has spotted skin and about 6 fins.

Whale Sharks mainly feast on plankton, but will occasionally eat anchovies and sardines. They swim with their mouth open to eat and use gill rakers to sort out food from water. The gill rakers are bristly body parts that trap the food and let the water out through the 5 gill slits. The Whale Shark gives birth to living young. Females can hold hundreds of young each about 2 feet (60 centimeters) long. They live near the Equator in open seas near the surface.

The Whale Shark is an astonishing creature and we can't let it become endangered. Humans need to protect the Whale Shark and let it live on in nature. It needs to be safe from humans waste so, don't litter and keep our oceans clean.

Ana Opishinski
Grade 6

The Money Jar

My sister and I took a small jar to save money for a pet. We are thinking of getting an iguana and it only took us two weeks to save the money. My sister and I take turns every week taking the trash out to the curb for our vovô. He gives us two dollars every time one of us does it. We also emptied out our wallets and bankbooks to add money to the jar. We almost had enough, but I had to buy food for my frogs, and my dad had no money for coffee in the morning. We let him borrow some. Monday he gave us the money he owed us and then more dollars for it.

We finally had enough. We have twenty two dollars and still didn't get the iguana so we still have the jar. We're thinking of getting any lizard if we can't get an iguana. Maybe a house gecko, or a green lizard. That's not the real name, but I don't know what the real name is. By the time I get a pet I'll have more than thirty dollars in the jar because I still help my vovô and it'll be a while until I get anything.

Zachary Arruda
Grade 6

Cassie

It was a cold damp day when I went to pick up my seven week old Cockapoo. When we got her she was whining but when we returned home, she stopped. Before I set up her six foot playpen and her black iron crate, I played with her for a while. After playing, I set up her playpen along with her food and water. While she was in her pen I hurried upstairs to set up her crate. I put the crate on the right side of my bureau. Then I went downstairs to get her, but she was already sleeping like a giant, fluffy dust ball, in the corner of the pen so I let her stay there. It was the most beautiful sight I've ever witnessed.

Joseph Long
Grade 6

Ben Roethlisberger vs Willie Parker

I compared two football players from the Pittsburgh Steelers. Their names are Ben Roethlisberger and Willie Parker.

These two football players are very different from each other. Willie Parker is running back for the Steelers. He started playing on the field in his second year playing for the Steelers. Parker is number 39. His college was North Carolina.

Ben Roethlisberger is quarterback for the Steelers. He played out on the field his first year playing for the Steelers. Roethlisberger's number is 7. He went to college in Miami, Ohio.

Roethlisberger and Parker were both in the NFL for two years. They both play for the Pittsburgh Steelers. These two players are very well recognized out on the field.

Ben Roethlisberger and Willie Parker are mostly different. They aren't a lot alike, but they are in some ways. That's how Ben Roethlisberger and Willie Parker are alike and different.

Mary Holmes
Grade 6

Drug Free

Being drug free is very important to me. I wouldn't know what to do in life if I were on drugs. Drug free is a very good thing because it is harmful to your health; it can kill others, and waste precious years.

Drugs can harm your health. So many people do drugs and they don't even know what it is doing to them. They think they are in their own world and they are floating, but they could be in the middle of the street and get run over by a massive truck. Those illegal drugs numb them.

Drug dealers sell drugs to people that are addicted to them. Those dealers know the drugs can kill them. The people that want the drugs would do anything to get it. The drug can be costly just for a piece of it. They are willing to even rob banks to get the money needed to get to their drugs.

Illegal drugs also can waste your precious years. People doing those drugs are just sitting there doing their drugs. They could be a rich lawyer instead of wasting all that time. That money could buy nicer things such as jewelry, rings, and cars which are way better than drugs.

Drugs are just not worth the time or money. They just burn all of it away when you could have saved up for something better than drugs. You waste time, money, family, and yourself by doing illegal drugs. They just waste everything.

Alex Ng
Grade 6

Loose Screw

I was in first grade and it was an ordinary day until I bumped into a kid older and bigger than I was. When I bumped into the kid, I fell on the pavement. I cracked my skull. Till this day I do not know who it was. I did not know my skull now had a four inch crack.

I left school as soon as my parents came. My mom took me to the doctors office and he said I look ok. I stayed home from school because it still hurt. On the third day, my dad kissed me on the head to thank me for helping him put the cd's back in the cases with him that day. He looked shocked and worried, and said my head felt like a wet sponge.

He called a doctor he knew and then took me to Moses Taylor Hospital where they put me in a big tube to get pictures of the inside of my head. I then went in an ambulance to Children's Hospital where they operated on me and took out a piece of my skull that a doorknob could fit in. I now have a plate in my head that is held in with titanium screws. I left there for home on Halloween day, five days after the operation.

The whole entire school sent me letters and I still have every one of those letters! After a while the screws started to shift but the bone healed. I now have 2 loose screws.

Tyler Sepcoski
Grade 5

The Titanic

Today I will talk to you about the Titanic. The Titanic was built at the Harland and Wolff shipyards, next to its sister ship. She (the Titanic) was to be better. Finally in 1912 she was launched.

Now I am going to talk about her voyage (her only one). There were three classes: first class, second class, and third class. She was the most luxurious ship ever, holding 2,200 people. She had enough food to feed a small town for months.

Now I want to talk about the horrible ending. For a while she had iceberg warnings but the crew ignored them. Then late at night they saw a huge figure in front of them. They closed the watertight doors and tried to turn but they hit. After that they knew they had two hours at most. It was time to launch the lifeboats, but they only had 20. They could hold 70 people at the most but they were only loading them with barely half of their capacity. "Women and children first," they called out. Only 700 people out of 2,200 lived. Her survivors were picked up by the Carpathia.

The Titanic has been made into movies, and lots of museums (I have been to many of them). But without it sinking, many lifeboat laws would not have changed. So when you hear the name Titanic just think about what I had to say.

Peter Lang
Grade 6

This Is Important to Me

Wonder to yourself. What kind of wasteland would the world be without art and color? For me, art and color play a major role in my life. People consider a lot of things to be art: sculpting, writing, poetry, script writing, culinary art, technological design, architectural design, automotive design and animation. Also, various kinds of fighting arts, such as Thai chi and Tai Kwan Do are considered art.

Just think if DaVinci or VanGogh hadn't discovered their wonderful art in painting. The same goes for Mozart, Beethoven, and Bach, with their lovely talents in the art of music. All of our favorite movies, plays, dramas, sitcoms, movies, and books wouldn't be possible without the art of writing and script writing.

There are a lot of artists in my family, like my aunt Philis who is a sculptor, my uncle Andy, who paints and owns a tattoo shop, and my uncle Joe, who owns a body shop. They all have pretty cool jobs…at least that's what I think.

I'm very much interested in art myself. I practice animation. And, I picked art and color to be the most important thing to me because without art and color, my life would be changed forever.

I'm Albert Trego, and I love art!

Albert Trego
Grade 6

The Gifts of Love and Appreciation

In life not all gifts can be handed to someone. The very best gifts in life are the ones that can't be handed over. I give so many gifts in life. My grandmother is one of those people who has accepted my gift. I give her the gift of love. The gift of love is a gift that means so much to her. She is the type of person that just wants love. Whenever I give her a hug it is like the whole world to her. My grandmother is not the only one who accepts my gifts. My sister does too. I give my sister the gift of appreciation. My sister is just one of the many people who show me appreciation. That is why I must show appreciation to her. Whenever we may start an argument, I will not argue back. That is the least I can do. Those two gifts mean so much. Those two people are just two of the many people who deserve special gifts. When I say gifts, I mean something that cannot be handed over or wrapped in a box. For example, love and appreciation are two gifts. These two gifts do not have a shape and do not have a size, but what they do have is a meaning. They have a very strong meaning.

Jessica Quinn
Grade 6

Magical Vacation Spot

Exciting, thrilling, and beautiful, the Outer Banks in North Carolina is my favorite vacation place to be. These are some of the joyful things that I do on this trip. First, I have the time of my life with my family. Second, I competitively fish with the National Seashore Rangers. I caught four fish.

There is also delicious food to eat. I devour the scrumptious, mouthwatering food from Bubba's Restaurant. Fourth, I lounge and play at the luxurious beach. Fifth, the ocean waves are as rough as the Grand Canyon. I boogie board until I drop! Sixth, the fireworks on the beach at night are colorful, brilliant and ear-shattering. Seventh, we speed to victory on the go cart course. The Outer Banks in North Carolina is like a magical playground.

Nick Pietri
Grade 4

Grandpop

My grandfather is my best friend. He has done a lot of things. He helped me take my first steps. My grandfather is a great person.

My grandfather, James Hedgeman, had some affects on me. Pop-pop (my grandfather) was always with me when I was young. That was a way of him saying, "You're never alone." Pop-pop had taught me to try to be kind, always.

Now that my Pop-pop is deceased he still has affects on me. I still know that I'm never alone. My grandfather is always with me. He taught me that I've gotten further being nice than I would have if I were mean.

My grandfather is a great person in my opinion. He is always in my heart and always in the sky. I loved him as my grandfather and my best friend.

Alexis Jackson
Grade 5

Spring Vacation

For spring vacation I am going to Yellowstone National Park. I'm going to rent a car and buy a tent. I'm going to go see all the animals. Also, I'm going to see Old Faithful. Also, I am going to see many beautiful sights. Finally, I'm going to see buffalos.

Here are a couple other things I'm going to see and do. I'm going to see waterfalls there. Also, swim in the lakes. Lastly, I'm going to hike through the forest there. Those are some of the other things I am doing for spring vacation.

Another thing I am going to do is hike in the deserts. Also, I am going to rock climb. Also, I'm going to see many canyons. Finally, I am going to camp in the desert. That is what I am going to do for spring vacation this year.

Jeff O'Brien
Grade 4

The Heroes of Flight 93

On September 11, 2001 men and women entered a plane. There were three men on the plane who were on a mission, a terrorist mission. Their goals was to crash into the White House. They entered the plane that was flying from Newark, New Jersey to San Francisco. The terrorists had a bomb, and mace. On the flight, they put their red bandanas on and started the attack. One guy called his wife and she said to overtake the plane. They gathered all their stuff from seat cushions, to soda cans, even hot tea. They used the food tray and smashed it into the guy with a bomb. After breaking down the cockpit door, the plane started going down. It crashed in an open field in Pennsylvania. That is the story of Flight 93.

Nick Dartt
Grade 6

The Gift of a Hug

If I could get my dad a gift that can't be bought, I would give him a big hug.

I would give him a big hug because he was the one who encouraged me to play soccer, encouraged me to try out for travel soccer and play goalie. I made the team and I give all the credit to my dad. If it wasn't for him I don't know what I would be. Another reason I would give my dad a hug is that he helped me get through things like fighting with my friends and yelling and fighting with my brother. Even though my dad and I don't get along at times I love him and still do and he loves me and still does. That is another reason why I would give my dad a big huge hug. I would also give him a hug because he is my dad and I love him. Another reason is that when we had to put our yellow lab Copper to sleep my dad told me of all the weird things she did like getting stuck on top of her cage and all of the silly things I did to her, such as playing pony on her back. That shows how much he cared about me in hard times. That's why I love my dad so much.

That is why I would give my dad a hug from me to him. I hope there are many more reasons why to come.

Melissa Maini
Grade 6

Mom, I Caught One!

My family and I went to Florida to visit my Uncle Paul. He took us to his new house. In his backyard is a bird sanctuary on an island. It is surrounded by a flowing river. We went to his old house to pick up some fishing poles and a tackle box. When Uncle Paul and I got back to his house, my brother and I each got one of the fishing poles, went to the backyard and started to fish. We were fishing for about an hour and didn't catch one fish.

So, we asked Uncle Paul if we could use his kayak to go out further. We got in the kayak and went out, I cast my fishing line out into the river. I got a bite. I had a lure on my pole so it would attract a fish. The kayak turned to the left because of the fish. The fish got away.

We went back and fished until about 5:00 p.m. Then I made a fishing pole out of a stick, fishing line, a hook, and a hot dog and some turkey as bait. I cast it in the water, I got a bite. It got away again. My brother watched me getting all these bites and he made a fishing pole too. We tried for hours, and then dinner was ready. I was reeling in my fish stick and I got a bite. I pulled as hard as I could. The fish jumped out of the water. I yelled "Mom, I caught one!"

David Schneider
Grade 6

Tribute to George Cacavas

My grandpa, George Cacavas, was a great and modest man who died when I was too young to remember. Never would he brag about his baseball card collection or his great inventions. He put the people he cared about before him, always persevering until he succeeded in any task.

My parents have told me all about my grandpa. He would never rest until everyone in my family was happy. He didn't give up on anything, even if there wasn't any hope. My grandpa was a loving person. If there was a problem he would be out to fix it almost instantly.

Grandpa George was very creative also. As an inventor, he made the Curly-Q fry machine, but a friend of his stole the invention! Instead of retaliating, he stopped talking to him. Grandpa was gracious. He would share anything with any good intentioned person.

My grandpa would always take advantage of opportunities, understanding that he wouldn't always be around. Never once did he give up the opportunity to see us when we visited. My grandpa was courteous.

I have a picture of him, and although I feel so terrible looking at it, I also get an assurance, like a bright light gleaming in my soul. The picture reminds me of all the great things he has accomplished. Hopefully I'll be like him. Though nobody can see him anymore, I'm positive that every moment of my life, he is standing right next to me.

Cole Schietinger
Grade 6

Studies

Have you ever tried studying without the right ways? If not check this out. Studies. Behave and concentrate. Also, work hard. These are the ways to study.

Behave. Behave at the classroom to concentrate on the teacher. Do not be mean to your teacher for something. Control your anger. Do not laugh or talk during class. You can do it during lunch time. These are the ways to behave at the classroom to study.

Concentrate. Focus on your studies. Be sure to ask questions if you have a doubt about something. Or you can tell the problem to your parents. These are the ways to concentrate, focus on your studies.

Work. Work real hard to get to the career you want. You need As and/or Bs to pass the test. Work in a quiet place from distraction. It is important because you need to concentrate on it. Be sure of the answer you wrote. It is also important because you need right answers to study for a test/quiz. These are the ways to work.

One of the important things are studies. The ways you can study are behave, concentrate, and work. These ways can help you study more to get to your career in your future.

Alen Saju
Grade 6

Following Your Dreams

Following your dreams is like being something you really want to be. For example, if you want to be a vet you would have to go through elementary school, middle school, high school, and college (university.) Following your dreams is imagining yourself being something and trying to do everything to become that. There are times when we choose a particular career but many external things cause us not to continue along the path to that career. Instead of following our dreams we falter and fail. It can be a life changing experience to succeed in college and end up in the career of which you dreamt.

Some things that cause people not to follow their dreams are listening to the wrong type of music and watching the wrong type of TV shows. We might be influenced by our friends or negative opinions from the wrong people. They might also unfortunately get ill or suffer from a medical condition which deters them from continuing to pursue their initial dreams.

My dream is to be a doctor. My dad said if I want to become a doctor I would have to go through prep school, middle school, high school and succeed in college (university) and graduate school. I have a medical book that teaches me how to be a doctor. It talks about diseases and cures. It's an authoritative text and is a resource to both patients and healthcare providers.

This is one of the many books that I know I would have to read in order to reach my goal. It takes hard work to follow your dreams but nothing compares to the fulfillment of having God answer our prayers.

Iniko Dixon
Grade 4

The First Snow Day of the Year

Yesterday, on February 13th I had my first snow day of the year. It has not been snowing much at all here in Long Island, New York. We got 20 inches about. The city (NY city) broke a record with about 27 inches. That's the most they've ever gotten. Well that we know of. There might be one bigger thousands of years ago before people kept records. I can't believe how much snow New York got. I thought we weren't going to get much snow because other than 3 inches one day that quickly melted, that was the first time we got snow all year. Everyone was excited.

Because of all that snow that we got on February twelfth adults had no work and kids had no school. So we missed a Monday. Also on Friday we have no school because we start winter vacation that day. So I only have a three day school week. My parents have work. My sister comes home from college for winter break on Friday also. My friends and I went snowboarding and sledding all day on Sunday and Monday. If there is still snow on the ground my friends and I are going to go sledding that day.

I heard that Long Island is going to warm weather throughout the week. That should melt the snow. If it does melt my friends and I are going to play outside all day.

Stephen Cunningham
Grade 6

Legos

Imagine starting with one inch long bricks and ending up with the Chrysler Building. These bricks are called Legos. With Legos you can build anything. I've see Lego creations three times the size of man and I am five feet tall. In Disney World Florida there is a huge Lego sea monster half submerged under water. Also in Florida there is a Lego shop with Legos galore. They were organized by color. You could take a special Lego cup and fill it up with Legos. Then you pay for it and take it home. In Times Square New York there was an exhibit of the Empire State Building made entirely of Legos.

I have seen transparent blue, green, red and crystal-clear Legos. The weirdest solid color Legos I have seen are brown, pink and yellow-green. In fact, when I was building a ship called the Arc 170 Fighter from Star Wars Episode III I used a yellow-green Lego piece. There are even Lego trees and bushes. I have seen Lego bushes that are red!

A model of the White House has been built out of Legos that stretched 7 feet 4 inches wide. A replica of the Statue of Liberty weighed 418 pounds and took 12,000 Legos to build. The Chrysler building was built out of Legos and just the spire was 1 meter, (but the whole building was 15 feet high). Larger Lego projects are built outdoors because they are too tall to stand in a normal room.

Derek Lillestolen
Grade 4

A Gift That Cannot Be Wrapped

If I had the power to give a gift that could not be wrapped, I'd give the gift of wisdom. I'd give wisdom to everybody on Earth who needs it. If people were wise, they would make responsible decisions. Children wouldn't be teased, picked on, or even bullied. Children would not be influenced by others who take drugs, hurt people, or steal, because they know it isn't what they should be doing. With wisdom comes great responsibilities. You would normally make better life decisions. People who are wise can judge what's right and wrong. Wise people act without boasting and do what they think is the right thing to do. Wisdom is a great thing if you use it in the right way. However, not everybody can do that. Wisdom is too powerful for everybody to have. People who are born wise are special. Having the gift to be born wise is a blessing. Being wise means that you can decipher the difference between good and bad. The world is filled with people who are very wise. With wisdom we can recognize these people and follow their examples. Being wise also means you need to be patient. Through experience you can learn from your mistakes. Without making mistakes you cannot know other roads which you could travel. Wisdom is one of the greatest gifts you can receive, because many good things come with it. But it makes you feel better if you earn it yourself, by experience!

Christian Romanelli
Grade 6

The Greatest Pet

Chinchilla's make the greatest pets! I know this because I have a ten month old, female Chinchilla named Zoey.

She is very soft and very unique looking. I think she is cute because she has ears like a mouse, eyes like a Koala Bear, a rabbit's body and a bushy squirrel-like tail. She is also only a little bigger than a softball.

Zoey needs a lot of attention and care. I have to clean her cage once a week, give her fresh water and food everyday and spend a lot of time with her. She has a special diet that consists of Timmothy Hay and Chinchilla pellets. I also give her raisins, dry oatmeal and she has to have pumice to chew on so that her teeth stay healthy.

Every other day I have to give her a bath. She has a bath house with bath dust in it. She gets in the bath house and rolls around to dry clean herself. Sometimes I forget to take it out of her cage and she flings it all over her cage and room. It's not fun cleaning that mess up.

She is the best pet ever because she barks at me to get my attention. She loves when I hold her and play with her. When I play video games she sits on my back. Best of all though, is when I am sad she listens to me then does something silly to make me laugh.

Jake Deemer
Grade 6

Having Good Friends

Having good friends is wonderful because most friends are grateful, friendly, and caring people.

I have four best friends. We look after each other. Sometimes we fight and then we get back together. Our favorite TV show is "That's So Raven." My friends and I are 10 years old. We are excited about growing up so we can travel, hang out at the mall, and go to new places.

I have lots of fun with my friends when we put together a dance or play for the school shows. Last Christmas we did a Christmas play. We did a dance which was performed wonderfully. We were so happy that day. Our parents took us out to celebrate at the diner. We danced to all types of music: hip-hop, reggae, and soca. Last year we did reggae dance and we did so well we got an award. Last summer we did a hip-hop dance. It was so much fun to dance together. In a couple of weeks we are going to do a reggae dance for Black History Month. We are so excited about it.

Having good friends makes it feel like they are a part of my family.

Colleen Ashwood
Grade 5

The Lion King

If I was in the circus, I would want to be a lion tamer. I would learn all about lions. I would teach them to do tricks and all kinds of cool stuff.

I would wear bright colors so that the lion could see me. I would also have a whip so that the lion will do what I tell it to do.

It would be a fun job to have because I would get to know the lions and learn more about these big cats. I think the toughest part would be training them to do the right things. If we practiced enough, I think they would be able to learn. Maybe I could give them a treat for a good job!

This is why I think I'd like to be a lion tamer.

Christopher Jacobson
Grade 4

Vanessa Is a Pest

My sister Vanessa is nice and all but sometimes she can be a pest.

Vanessa always hogs the bathroom just to do her nails. I can't stand it. When she comes out the smell gives me a headache. I have to open the window just to get rid of the stench.

Another thing is she always wastes the hot water. When I go in the shower the water is freezing. So I have to take a shower with cold water. So our mom and dad have to take a shower with freezing water. So I had to take a shower fast. I can't stand that too.

So when I'm watching television she comes and changes the channel. I can't believe she does that. So I have to fight for the remote. I have to hide the remote for special things. But sometimes I let her get it or she tells.

Lucas Tejada
Grade 4

My Friends and Family

There are lots of people you meet in your life. You may meet a person who can do two things at once or meet a funny person. My friends and family are the most precious people in my life. My friends and family can be one of my favorite things to write about.

My friends and family are very nice to me. I like the way they treat me. I know that I am safe around them. I know if I was in trouble they would help me. I wouldn't want it any other way.

My friends and family are always helping me. They are always doing everything for my benefit. My friends are like family and my family are my friends. They may be hard to get along with sometimes but they're just trying to help.

Even though they are both alike, they have their differences. Well, for starters, my friends are very "do everything at the last minute;" on the other hand most of my family is not. Another is that my friends like to rush through things but my family searches for an answer one by one. Also, my friends like wrestling and my family disagrees. Even though they are different, they are still my friends and family.

A great family is cool and fun friends are cool, put them together and what do you get? The ride of your life.

Jesse Montanez
Grade 5

Dulles Sportsplex

Walking across the parking lot after a long struggle of an early awakening the frigid wind bites me as a lion would his prey. My body shivers with goose bumps the size of plums as each leg moves a step forward. Upon entering the Dulles Sportsplex, I notice it is as large as a football field and busier than the Town Center Mall. Parents, siblings, and players are everywhere. Some siblings watch every game while others are free to waste their quarters on mindless games. Parents grab coffee and donuts and settle in at the cafeteria, while over-involved moms and dads escort their child with great eagerness to their fields. I am standing, waiting, patiently for other teammates to arrive when a roll of thunder rushes at me like an ocean wave crashing against the shore. Boom! A ball deflects against the transparent plexiglass. Bodies hit the white wall. One girl lays silent as she recovers from her injuries. The opposing player steals the ball and scores! No penalty kick is awarded. The lighted scoreboard increments by a goal. The games are fast-paced and the game never pauses for out-of-bounds. Scores jump to the double-digits. There is nothing more exhilarating than hitting the net! Going to the Sportsplex, in the dead of winter, to have the thrill of triumphant games, the shout of approval from parents and siblings, and the camaraderie of my teammates is the best way to fight the winter blues.

Tabitha McHale
Grade 6

Heroes Forever

Every day many people throughout the world risk their lives to save another's. Some of these people are firemen. They are always ready to go into a burning building to save a life.

Some of us do not realize how important firemen are until something tragic happens. This is unfortunate, because firemen are like food and water to us. If we did not have any firemen who would put out a burning building? Who would save a precious life?

Firemen risk everything once they step into a burning building. Some may have a family, and they'd lose their family if they died. They would lose their life and lose everything in their life, families, friends, home, and everything they have.

Sometimes in the news we hear about a fireman who died bravely. All we do is think, 'How sad!' and then forget about it sooner or later. Well, what about the family members of the fireman? As soon as they hear about the death, they would feel as if their world was breaking apart. They would grieve for the lost family member for a long time. On 9-11 hundreds of firemen died. This tragic event helped Americans realize how important firemen are and what brave heroes they could be.

So I think that from time to time we should think about the courageous firemen. Next time you hear about a fireman who lost his life, take a moment to think about how he was a hero in someone's life.

Ellis Young-Eun Kim
Grade 6

Veterans Remembrance

My father, Mark Birmingham, served in the navy about 20 years ago. His job was a boatswain's mate and was responsible for preservation of all topside surfaces, some gunnery and the care and operation of the ship's three small boats. My father was also an enlisted surface warfare specialist, an officer of the deck, and division leading petty officer.

Enlisted rank runs from E1-E9 and my dad was an E-5 when he left the Navy after four and a half years. The ship he served on was a destroyer, the U.S.S. Mahan DDG-42. He traveled to Europe, the Caribbean, Asia, and other exotic places. One experience he had that he remembers was once in 1983 in the Mediterranean Sea, he and his crewmates had to stay at sea for more than 90 days due to conditions in Beirut Lebanon. They relied on other ships to supply them with food and fuel. My father said, "Life was really different from what it is here at home, there were different languages and different customs." He mentioned becoming seasick on occasion. His father, George Birmingham, also served in the military.

My father, now a mechanic, finds pleasure reading books on navy boats and other boats after work. War books are also a common checkout in the library for him.

Jacob Birmingham
Grade 6

The Dirtbike

In the summer I went to a dirtbike dealership. The dealer is a big place. It is about the size of Davol School. It had all types of motorcycles, dirtbikes, cruisers, sportbikes, jet bikes, and more.

When we were on our way we got lost in Fall River because it's back roads. We went to a country-like scene, then a city like where did that come from?

The style of my dirtbike is offroad. It is a 125 cc. It is also a Kawasaki. A 2004 left over. It goes 55-60 MPH!!! It has about 150 miles. My friend has a racing 85 faster than my dirtbike. I was supposed to get 65 but it was too small.

I am really thankful for my dad getting me it. My mom didn't want to get me one, but I was lucky. The dealer gave me a deal. But now I'm going to race. That is my memoir.

Aaron Gagnon
Grade 6

George Washington's Early Life

George Washington was born in Westmoreland County, VA, on Feb. 22, 1732. He was the eldest son of Augustine Washington. George Washington was not always in the army fighting wars. At first, he spent his early childhood years on the family's land on Pope's Creek along the Potomac River. George had basic education; math and such. His father died in 1743 when George was only 11. Soon after the death, George went to live with his half brother, Lawrence. Lawrence lived in Mount Vernon, on "Lawrence's plantation" on the Potomac. George's half brother soon married into the Fairfox family. The family helped launch young George's career. George had always wanted to go to sea, but his mother had effectively discouraged that thought. So, he turned to survey Lord Fairfox's land in Shenandoah Valley. Later he helped lay out the Virginia town of Belhaven, now Alexandria. In 1749, he was appointed surveyor for Culpepper County. George had to go to Barbados in an effort to cure his brother from tuberculosis. However, Lawrence died in 1752. Soon after, George inherited the Mount Vernon estate. By 1753 the rivalry for control of the Ohio Valley soon grew into the French and Indian War [1754-1763] which created new opportunities for the young, ambitious Washington who became part of the war.

Angela Kazar
Grade 6

Sports

My favorite things are sports. I love surfing. Surfing is definitely my favorite sport. The runner up is baseball. The only thing bad about baseball is that it's a long, slow game. I also love karate. Karate is fun because the season never stops, like surfing. Cross-country is my fourth favorite sport because it helps me stay in shape. There are so many more things that I like. I like skateboarding at skate parks and going to surfing contests. As you can see, I like a lot of things.

Matt Fineran
Grade 6

Earth Day

Earth Day is a day in April when people try to clean their yard. Dudley Middle School should start participating in Earth Day. We would need a group of kids to help. We would raise money, put more trash cans up, and plant trees.

Volunteers are needed for Earth Day so we can get a group of kids by asking friends, classmates, or teammates. We could tell them it will be fun because they could hang out with friends and you would be doing something good. We could also get people, like friends and family from other towns to help.

We could raise money by having a bake sale. All of those volunteers could help bake cookies and cakes to earn money. Everyone can sell marigolds at a concession stand. We would sell things to get supplies like plants, trash cans, rakes, and trees.

This group could help plant trees in areas where they had been cut down. We can also put trash cans up around town. Picking up trash is another thing the group could do. Like in the parks where there is trash we can pick it up.

That's how the Dudley Middle School should have their Earth Day. We are going to get a group of kids, raise money, and clean the environment. We will have a great time doing it! Please help clean on Earth Day.

Samantha Savoie
Grade 5

The Games That People Play

There are different games that people play. There are good games and there are bad games. Good games can lead to a lot of fun. Bad games can cause injuries or death or influence people to do bad things. Most people like to play good games, while some people play bad games because they like taking risks.

There are some good games people play: board games like checkers, chess, and Scrabble. People also play good video games like Need for Speed, Spyro, MarioKart, and Midnight Club. There are also good computer games like Hotwheels Speedtrack. There are handheld games that you can play on a Nintendo DS, PSP, Gameboy Advance, and Gameboy Micro. My favorite games are video games…

People also play dangerous games. There is a game called the choking game. This dangerous game can lead to brain damage or death. Two bad games to avoid are the Simpson's Hit and Run and Grand Theft Auto. There are other violent and bloody games that people should not play.

My advice to everyone is to play good games that will help you to learn good things. Some good things you can learn are to properly focus, good hand skills and good hand and eye coordination. So never play bad games. Always play good games. Will you?

Adrian Warren
Grade 6

A Boy's Faith

Hebrews II:6 states the following: "But without faith it is impossible to please him; for he that cometh to God must believe that he is, and that he is a rewarder of them that diligently seek him." This verse trains me to "step out on faith and place my life in God's hands."

My belief in God and faith has helped me to endure and overcome the obstacles of my life and my school year. Some of the major obstacles that I have faced include changes in my school life, grades, and in my parents' and teachers' expectation of me.

February is African American History Month and I have been inspired by great African Americans who have made economic, political, and social contributions to society. Some of my favorites include Langston Hughes, my favorite writer, and Benjamin Banneker, a noted astronomer, gifted mathematician, farmer and creator who also helped with the designing of the city of Washington D.C. Benjamin Banneker was a multitalented leader who seemed to be successful at everything that he dreamed of or touched. I definitely want to follow in his footsteps as well as my dad's footsteps.

In closing, I know that God will train me to be a strong Christian and multitalented leader just as He has trained Mr. Banneker and my dad who are two God-trained leaders.

Many are called but few are chosen to become God's disciples and I pray that I will continue to be a part of God's chosen ones.

Donald Gibson
Grade 6

Gift of Kindness

Kindness can often be defined as a gift that can't be either wrapped or touched. No present or purchased merchandise is truly kindness, kindness is something that is priceless. Priceless meaning kindness that comes from the heart, and that is certainly not purchased and wrapped to be handed to someone.

Kindness is a great gift because even if you don't like someone or if they are disabled, by you being kind to them or even just saying hi, it could make their day. Another good gift of kindness is that if you get a gift and you don't really like it, you shouldn't say, "Wow, this is dumb," or, "I hate this." You should thank them for them for the thought of the present and be content with what you have been given. If you said that to someone who got you a gift, they would feel sad and even heartbroken. A person would also feel saddened if you ate a food that they had cooked or prepared and you said, "Eww, this is disgusting." If you don't like something, there are a few options that are respectful. You could just avoid eating it and say that you are full, eat it and say it is very good, or just suck it up and eat it.

In conclusion, kindness from the heart is the great aspect of kindness that can be given to anyone. Anyone, no matter what color, where you live, or anything of that sort, can show and give kindness.

Sean Vinberg
Grade 6

My Puppy

My puppy is important to me because he knows my emotions. He licks me when I'm crying, plays with me and even sleeps with me. Even though I had a dog and lots of birds, this is the first time I have the true experience of a pet.

For years I annoyed my dad to get a puppy. As we were driving to the breeder's house he told me about the responsibilities of having a pet. We arrived and right before my eyes were two little adorable Yorkshire Terriers. I stuck my hand in their playpen as they were wrestling each other to get to me, but I had to wait two weeks to get one.

Two weeks passed. I was so excited, but what to name him? I thought Brownie, but my dad said it was too girlie. I thought Cinnamon, but I realized that when he was grown it wouldn't fit him. My mom suggested Chocolate. It didn't feel right either.

I couldn't wait to grasp that puppy in my hands. I picked him up and he licked my face. Then my dad asked me, "So what did you decide to call the little rascal, honey?"

"Cody Olivier," I said, happily holding him in my arms.

Now my dog is nine months and jumping off the walls. When I come home from school, he's by the door waiting for me. He jumps on me as a greeting. I know he loves me.

Martine Olivier
Grade 6

Look Out for the Environment

Have you ever looked around to see what's happening to the environment?

Plants and animals are dying every day because people all over the country are throwing their trash on the side of the roads. Sailors and other people at sea are throwing their waste into the water. Where does it all go? It all goes down into the water and is affecting animals and plants. You may not think that you are harming anything, but you could be. Harmless ducks can get tangled in the plastic soda can holders and die. Fish and other sea creatures mistake floating trash for food and choke on it. This has to be stopped! Harmless animals are dying because we are not disposing of our trash in a good way.

Some easy ways to prevent these horrible situations are to:

Recycle as much materials as we can. Not only will this save the animals, it will save their homes. By recycling paper we will save trees that animals live in.

Cut up or break up things that are going in the trash that animals could hurt themselves on or get stuck in. Things like plastic soda can holders, metal cans and can lids, cardboard boxes, and plastic bags are dangerous for animals.

Help pick up trash in an area of your neighborhood. You don't have to do it alone; get a group of people and have a cleanup party. Have fun and help the environment!

Jennifer Johnson
Grade 6

My Family Vacation

Last year I went to Ogunquit, Maine with my family. I really loved it because I got to spend day and night, while we were there, with my family. I also got to stay in a very nice hotel called Anchorage by the Sea. When we were there we walked around window shopping and looking for places to eat dinner. When we got tired we went back to the hotel, rested a little while, and then went for a nice dinner at The Lobster Pound. They had great food! Once we got back, we got ready to go to the pool. My sister and I went swimming, and then we went into the hot sauna. Finally we went back to the room and went to bed. The next day we got up and went to breakfast. Then a little bit later we went walking on the Marginal Way. Once we were a little bit into the trail we saw a couple getting married on a cliff beside the ocean. After our walk we went back to the room. Then we went window shopping again and got Maine sweatshirts. That night we went to the pool again. It was very cold to walk from the pool back to the room. When we got back we went to bed. Once our two fun days together were over we drove back home.

Leah Benson
Grade 4

The Creator and Preserver

Who created the earth? Who protects and preserves the world? Who destroys the universe? These questions have been lingering in our minds for quite a while. Hindus believe that creating and protecting is done by Vishnu and Brahma. Brahma creates the world that Vishnu protects from destruction. This cycle of creating and preserving all starts with a god named Brahma.

Brahma's role is very important in the Hindu religion. His role is to create this enormous world when it is destroyed. Brahma, the creator who is also known as the god of wisdom has four heads and hands that face the four corners of the earth. These unusual features show his powers. Even though Brahma has done many good deeds like creating the world, giving life to people and symbolizing peace, he is rarely worshiped. When Brahma was first creating the world, there was a horrendous flood. Vishnu was the only man who protected it from being destroyed.

Vishnu is a kind god as he has visited the earth nine times in nine different forms to protect it from destruction. Vishnu is often born as a human to protect the world and he was born in nine different forms as a human. Vishnu is worshiped with a lot of devotion as he saved the earth nine times. Vishnu is worshiped by singing the Vishnu Sahasram.

Most religions believe that their god is the greatest of all but god itself is one. Brahma and Vishnu are one god that plays different roles.

Sharan Gottumukkala
Grade 6

My Inspiration

The reason why I am writing about Dwayne Wade is because whenever I feel like stopping I think about him. He is my inspiration to keep going. He is more than a NBA basketball player to me.

His name is Dwayne Tyrone Wade, Jr. He was born on January 17, 1982, in Chicago, Illinois. Dwayne started to get involved in sports, particularly football and basketball. He never thought about playing professional. His dad coached a basketball team of teenagers. His dad often took him to the practices. Dwayne began to love to play basketball.

For high school, Dwayne went to H.L. Richardson High School in Oak Lawn, Illinois. The school was known as a football powerhouse. The Bulldogs were in the process of building one of the areas top basketball programs. Initially, Dwayne made a bigger impression on the football coaches a Richardson High School than he did on the basketball coaches.

Determined to earn a regular spot on the varsity basketball team, Dwayne worked out all summer. His junior year he averaged 20.7 points and 7.6 rebounds. His senior year, Dwayne was becoming a hot commodity among the mid west schools. Marquette, DePaul and Illinois State were all interested in him, but he did not get a scholarship. He went to Marquette for college and played basketball. He was the Miami Heats first pick in the NBA draft. That is the reason why he is my inspiration.

Tommy Weidle
Grade 6

My Really Best Friends

My really best friends are funny, awesome, cool, and great friends. They always stick by my side and play with me. You will read about some of my really best friends.

One of them is Frenchie, (a.k.a. Nate French). He is really funny, awesome, and a great friend. Frenchie is funny because he acts silly a lot of times. He is also cool, with a K.

Another one of my friends is Jake (a.k.a. Jacob Whiting). He is really funny, cool, awesome, and a great friend. He is all of these things because he can always make me laugh. He is also my partner in everything like games we do in gym, and other partner games as well.

Third of all is Fishy (a.k.a. David Fish). He is one of the best friends that I have. He was the first friend I made when I came here. He is funny, awesome, cool, and everything else. He is everything because when I was lonely he was there for me.

Another best friend is Sarah Derway. She is funny, awesome, and a great friend. She is all of these characteristics because she can make me laugh.

In conclusion, all of my friends are very nice, cool, funny, awesome, and great amigos. All of my friends have stayed by my side, and played with me. These are some of my friends that you just read about. So if you like to laugh a lot, you would like all of my friends a lot!

Josue Estrada
Grade 5

Sidney Crosby vs Alexander Ovechkin

Hockey players are all different, but they each have some likenesses. In this essay you will hear about Alex Ovechkin and Sideny Crosby.

Some of the things they have that are alike will be found in this paragraph. These two are both major rookies in the NHL. Both rookies traded hockey stick that they each signed. Many people say that these two are very mature for being rookies. Another likeness is that they both wear visors on their helmets.

In this paragraph, you will hear some differences between the two. They play for different teams. Crosby is two years younger than Ovechkin. That makes Crosby seem like a better player than Ovechkin. Ovechkin has scored four more points than Crosby. Crosby plays for the Pittsburgh Penguins. Ovechkin plays for the Washington Capitals. Crosby is from Canada, while Ovechkin is from Russia.

I hope these facts help you see which hockey player is better. There are many more differences and likenesses between these two. I only listed a few.

Rebecca Will
Grade 6

Sharks*

"Sharks are shy, docile creatures." Sharks roam all over the world's oceans. Almost everyone who has swam in the ocean has seen a shark. All sharks are flesh-eaters, but no humans are in a shark's natural diet. Sharks will not eat humans if they are fed very well. "There are over one millions sharks in the world." Sharks are so much like their ancestors that some people call sharks living fossils. Sharks are one of the most dangerous animals in the world. The most dangerous shark is the Great White Shark.

The diet of a shark consists of many different types of food. Most sharks eat small fish or invertebrates. "Three large species filter food, known as plankton, from the sea." Some sharks hunt large animals, such as sea lions and also other sharks.

"The world's ocean is the shark's domain." A few species such as the blue shark are found throughout the warmer parts of this vast area, but many are restricted to certain coasts or types of watery habitat, such as muddy bays or the edges of coral reefs. "The majority live in the well lit surface zone, but others are found in deep water."

"A person is more likely to get struck by lightning than to be attacked by a shark." "Although experts disagree, it has been suggested that since 1940 there have been an average of only 28 attacks each year." These figures include attacks made by sharks in self defense.

Krista Merryman
Grade 5
*Information in quotes from "Pocket Sharks"
written by Joyce Pope.

Where Did It Go?

I live in a house surrounded by woods. The woods are about a mile wide and long. I play in the woods a lot and I mean a lot. My neighbor's tree house is in those woods. Nothing bad ever happens in the woods or to the woods. But now people are going to cut down the trees! They already started to! Now the woods are only a half a mile long! But the worst thing is that they are cutting down trees for a pool and houses! What they don't think about is when they build houses they're destroying someone else's. Deer and rabbits are always in front of my house because it's also their home. So people are cutting down trees for homes when they could keep some trees for the animals.

Connor Ferguson
Grade 5

The Gift from My Heart

I give the invisible gift of love and affection to my dog Dutchess. I do this in a various amount of ways for a bunch of different reasons. I can show her this by rubbing her stomach, or by scratching her head. I can also show my affection towards her by giving her a chew toy or a delicious treat. Another way I show my love is by playing with her. We play ball or if there is snow we have a snowball fight in which she kicks the snow with her feet. We can also snuggle on the couch and watch television. I love her so much and she shows her affection back. For example, she would lick my feet, which might seem disgusting but she will not do this to anyone else. She would also rub her face against my leg just like a cat might. Another reason is because she is so loyal and can really cheer me up when I'm down. She can tell when I am feeling sad and she'll come to me and just lay on my lap giving me her puppy eyes like she wants to say what's wrong. In conclusion, there are many ways I show love to Dutchess and different reasons for me to do so.

David Stewart
Grade 6

The Fear I Had

Everyone has or had a fear. It may be going on a roller coaster, flying in an airplane, and so on. My fear was skiing. This past winter I took ski lessons at Whiteface Mountain. Now, that I took the lessons at Whiteface, I'm having a blast skiing. When I first started my lessons I was scared of the ski lifts. I was even scared to do the mixing bowl (the beginner hill). To get over my fear I just kept practicing and practicing. Now, because I put so much time and effort into my skiing, I can do any of the hills/trails between the mixing bowl to the top of mid station. I still have not got rid of my fear of snowboarders hitting me and when the trails are really icy.

In conclusion, I'm very glad I got rid of my fear of skiing. But I could not have done it without the help of my 3 ski instructors. If I was able to overcome my fear of skiing, anyone can overcome any one of their fears.

Allison Archer
Grade 5

School Long Ago

About fifty years ago, school was hard. The boys would have to wear dress pants (no jeans) and a nice shirt. The girls would have to wear a skirt or dress.

Back then you would not need much school supplies. Just a notebook and a pencil.

Long ago, you had to walk to school, imagine the winter. "Brrrr."

Fifty years ago you most likely had a timeout, or a whack on the knuckles.

If you were in kindergarten you would share a room with first graders, and if you were in second grade you would share a room with third graders, and so on. Pretty crowded huh?

Matt Dolegowski
Grade 5

My Favorite Holiday

Christmas is my favorite holiday of the year for many reasons. The biggest reason, and should be everyone else's, is that Jesus Christ was born on this day. Almost every year my family either goes down to Georgia to visit grandparents, or they come up to visit us in Pennsylvania. Another reason is, since I live up north, we get a lot of snow at this time of year, and I enjoy building snowmen and making igloos. I always hope that there will be a bunch of presents under the Christmas tree by Christmas Day. I look forward to Christmas because we get a long Christmas break from school, also. Christmas is my favorite holiday, and I hope it is yours, too.

Benjamin Paget
Grade 6

In the Poconos

I go up to the Poconos every weekend, we own a house there. For Christmas break, we stay up there extra long for the long weekend. We all go there: my brother, my mom, and my brother's good friend.

Sometimes there is a snowboarding contest; my brother and his friend enter. Last year, my brother did really well, he got 2nd place! My brother's friend didn't do as well. This year, kids that live there that were friends with each other would hold up their snowboards so when they did a jump, the board would hit them. On my brother's first run, he got one of the highest airs I ever saw in a half pipe, and he landed it! The other kids all got a lot better.

This year my mom let me go out of the house for New Years. I got a snowmobile ride and went sledding on the mountain. I also spied on my brother. We have renters next to us, and it's funny to watch them get drunk. One year, when we first got the house, it was all guys, and they all got drunk and got an air mattress. They rode down the half pipe run, right next to us, and they went off a huge jump!

I love going up to the Poconos. I'm really good at skiing, but I want to learn how to snowboard, and I am learning. I can't wait to get better.

Mallory Siligato
Grade 6

My Favorite Sport

"It takes no talent to hustle." That's what my coaches always told me. Playing on a basketball team is beneficial because it keeps you physically fit, it takes a lot of practice, and teaches teamwork.

It keeps you fit because you spend hours running and practicing drills, and the games are very fast-paced. Since there is usually between thirty and forty minutes of playing time, you need to keep up and not become exhausted. This is important because you have to outplay the other team to win the game.

Basketball takes a lot of practice, usually at least twelve hours per week. You do a lot of running laps and suicides. It is very important to practice shooting and ball-handling. Ball-handling is something very difficult because you have to dribble well and protect the ball. Passes also need to be quick and sharp if you want to be a good player.

Most importantly, basketball teaches teamwork. It takes five players working together to move the ball around the court. If another player is open for the shot, you should pass the ball to them. To be a team player, you need to be unselfish and do what's best for the team.

Physical fitness, practice, and teamwork are the benefits of playing on a basketball team. Join a team and stay healthy today.

Emily Irwin
Grade 6

Accomplishments Are Important to Everybody

One day do you want to be famous, or get a job, or even be filthy rich? In order to live your dreams you must first accomplish your daily goals. Things like getting into college because you got good grades. I'll give you an example. Did you know that the famous quarterback of the Minnesota Vikings Dante Culpepper was an orphan? His parents didn't take him to school so that he can study.

While he was at the orphanage it was his job to study. He was a straight A student and went to college. So the reason he is in the NFL was because he accomplished his goals in order to get to college and get drafted. Another way to accomplish your goals is by never giving up. As Thomas Alva Edison used to quote, "Some people give up but don't know but they are actually very close."

That fact is very true, because one day at basketball practice my teammate had to pass the ball in to me. Eventually he was too late because the beset defender came up court to press. Then I was frustrated and I turned around. I had just realized he had just faked him out but he couldn't pass it to me because I had given up. This time I will never ever give up. This time I will accomplish goals and fulfill my dreams.

Zahir Ramos
Grade 5

My Mom the Role Model

I admire my mom because she is loving and caring. The impact my mom has on me is she provides me good clothes to wear. She also provides me a house to live in. The most important thing about my mom is that she loves me.

If my mother did not exist I would not be here today. My life would not be right. If she wasn't here I would not be the respectable boy I am.

Anthony Holland
Grade 6

Mrs. Kondella

This essay is about Mrs. Kondella. Mrs. Kondella is a very smart teacher. She is kind, caring and never gives up her hopes.

In the beginning of the school year I was having some problems in math and science. I owe her so many math corrections and so much science too. See, I never raised my hand in class and that is why I had trouble on most of my work. The only reason why I did not raise my hand is because I thought that kids would make fun of me and say, "How can you not know that, that is so easy!" So at the end of the month I got a bad report card. When I got home, my mother spoke to me about it. She said she was very disappointed and punished me until I got my grades up.

When I went back to school I did not understand how they did some things in math, so I raised my hand and I told Mrs. Kondella that I did not understand it. Surprisingly, no one laughed at me or said anything. Mrs. Kondella explained it to me. Then after she was done I understood. My grades are now better.

DeVanté McNair
Grade 6

Kayla and Her King

I am a big brother. My baby sister, Kayla, is almost four years old. I have loved her since before she was born.

I like being a big brother because I get to teach K.K. a lot of cool things. I've taught her how to play baseball, tell jokes and wrestle. Mom doesn't like that we wrestle but we still do it anyway.

Sometimes K.K. is really whiny and won't share the TV, which annoys me. Most of the time she makes me laugh because she does crazy things. She sings really loud and wraps her dolls in dishtowels. Tonight, she pulled her shirt over her head and said that she was a ghost.

It's a big responsibility being a big brother. Whatever I do, Kayla does too. I didn't realize that she'd look up to me like a king. I try showing her good things but it's too much fun showing her the bad things!

K.K. likes to hang out with my friends and me and my friends think K.K. is cool. She likes to ride her motorcycle and do wheelies with us.

I really love my sister and I know she loves me too. No matter how old we get, that will never change.

Michael Fusco
Grade 5

Lots and Lots of Cape May

My family and I love going to Cape May. On the first day of our trip we get up really early and leave (it's a really long trip). On the way my grandma and I play bridge and license plates. When we are finally there, we get into our suite and start to unpack. When we are done we get dressed, go to church, and go out to eat at Manga! Manga! Then we go home to play games and go to bed.

When we wake up the next morning we go out to Uncle Bill's. I usually get toast. Then when we are done, we go to get our bathing suits on and go to the beach. We build sandcastles, go boogie-boarding, and lay out in the sun. When we go back to the hotel, we have my grandma's delicious mac 'n cheese. After we eat we go down to the hotel's pool for the rest of the afternoon. After that we come back up to either have my grandma's cooking or go out to eat. Then we decide if we are going to the arcade or mini golf. When we decide, we go and have fun. After we do that we go to get ice-cream and go shopping. Basically our trip is very exciting. I love Cape May!

Molly Greb
Grade 4

Tyrannosaurus Rex's Movie Career

Tyrannosaurus Rex was a huge discovery. It was also the beginning of a great movie monster. T-Rex had some downfalls in his career but in the end he was back at the top.

T-Rex was discovered by a British man and his crew of paleontologists. I am not comfortable using the exact location of where T-Rex was found. When his, or her, bones were dug up they were sent to the boss of the British man. After many hours of thinking they thought of the name Tyrannosaurus Rex, or the "Giant Lizard King" but most formally known as T-Rex.

A famous movie T-Rex starred in was *The Ghost of Slumber Mountain*. It was a great movie to see back then, and the directors made millions! It wowed many people in the United States. Another famous movie T-Rex was in was *The New World*. First it was a book that most people read, then it was turned into a hit movie.

Compared to *King Kong* those movies were wimpy. Although King Kong was the main character, Tyrannosaurus Rex did the big battle scene where King Kong shows off his strength. Then computer animation came to the movie world. Steven Spielberg found the talent of T-Rex and put him in *Jurassic Park*. That was the turning point of T-Rex's career.

As you can see, T-Rex was close to losing his job. He came back to the top. He was a great science discovery. He was also the "Monster of the movie theater" and struck fear into many people's hearts.

Jacob John Whiting
Grade 5

The Two Minute Adventure

Have you been on an adventure where you knew where you were but you were lost? I have, and it was an adventure that lasted for about two minutes! Two minutes to the world felt like two hours to me.

It started on an island called Lemnos, Greece. My family and I were staying with the Leondis' for a week. My sister Britten and I wanted to go kayaking with Devon (my best friend) and her older sister Christie. I had to go with Christie who is two years older than me to balance the weight.

We started paddling out as I started humming "Row, Row, Row Your Boat." Soon the humming turned into singing, and then the singing turned into yelling! Christie didn't want to hear any more so she chucked my oar off the kayak! Although I was wearing a lifejacket, I didn't want to go swimming after my oar. I knew I had to, so I jumped off the kayak.

When I got my oar I turned around to see Christie paddling away! I screamed to tell her to stop but she didn't listen! I started swimming around trying to find out where I was.

One minute had passed when I saw Britten and Devon coming towards me! They asked me where Christie was and I told them what had happened. I jumped on their kayak as we started paddling to shore. That was my two minute adventure, and it was the shortest adventure I've ever had!

Courtney Reilly
Grade 6

Gift of Friendship

A gift that I would want to give that cannot be wrapped is being a good friend. To be a good friend you have to keep several things in mind. Some of these things are loyalty, compromise and keeping promises. Loyalty is important because you do not turn your back on your friends. An example of loyalty is that if your friend is made fun of you would still be friends with your friend and support him. Compromise is necessary because your ideas will not always be accepted. An example of this is when one of your friends wants to play tennis, your other friend wants to play soccer and you want to play hockey. You could find a way to do all of those things at different times, or come to some agreement. To promise is important because you have to keep your promises with your friends. For example, if your friends asked you to go play baseball and you say yes. Then, later your other friends asked you to play golf and you go with your other friends to play golf. You would turn down your other friend. Lastly, it is important to be considerate to the other person. You would not want to do or to say anything to make your friend sad. In closing, I would give this gift to anyone that I would call my friend.

William Myles
Grade 6

The Importance of Staying Drug Free!!

A subject I feel very strong about is staying drug free. When you stay drug free you are benefiting your heath and your social life, so it is best to stay drug free.

When you are drug free it benefits your health and social life. Your health is affected when you are taking drugs. Your internal organs are damaged. This may cause serious cancer, heavy coughing, and a weak immune system. Your social life is also affected when you are taking drugs. Nobody will want to be near you. Your looks are also affected. Your teeth, over time, will start to turn yellow, and your breath will stink.

Based on this evidence I provide for you here, you can see that being drug free is the best way to be. So, the choice is yours, you can take drugs, or stay drug free. I hope this will prove to you that staying drug free is the best policy! Remember the people you love and care about! My motto is, when you never start, you never have to quit.

Rachel Halek
Grade 6

My Family and Dog

The most important thing to me is my family and dog. My dog's name is Princess. She's always been there for me when I'm sad and miserable. She'll come running to my aid.

My family is much more important than my dog because they provide me with food, water, and shelter. Also they assist me when I'm in need of help. Also, when I was young they would care and play with me. My mother's name is Angie, my father's name is Ben, and my brother's name is Ben also. That concludes the most important thing to me.

Alan Berry
Grade 5

The Invisible Gifts

There are many gifts that I would love to give to people. Many of these gifts are very expensive and not affordable. However, some of these gifts don't even cost a penny and everybody can give them. Two of these "invisible gifts" that I would give are joy and trust. I would give joy to my brother Robert and trust to my friends and family. I would give joy to my brother Robert. Giving joy would be easy. To give joy you could make someone laugh or smile or anything else you could think of doing. I could make my brother laugh in many ways. One way is to tell him a joke. I could also sing a funny song or dance a funny dance. These are also ways I could make him smile. Also I could tell him a funny story. I could also give trust to my friends and family in many ways. One way is to never lie to them. Also always tell the truth. Also when I promise them something I will always come through with my promise. I will also never tell any of their personal secrets. These are some ways to give these gifts. In conclusion, these two gifts are special and come from the heart. These gifts can't be put in a box, wrapped up, or have a bow on them. These gifts are given in all different ways, all people give and receive them in different ways.

Lauren Wozniak
Grade 6

Friends

My friends are the most important people to me. On a snowy winter day, I was bored. I finally decided what to do. I would invite my friend Lauren over. When she arrived, we went outside to sled ride. We became bored doing that. Finally I had an idea; we could go into my woods and see how hard the ice was.

We walked into my woods. The two of us walked for about ten minutes when I saw what I thought was a shallow puddle of water covered with hard ice. I jumped on the ice and started to slide. It was fun! Immediately Lauren said, "Emily that ice is going to break if you don't get off it." I ignored her comment and continued to slide. Soon after she warned me, I fell right through the ice into the cold icy water. My whole body was underwater and I could not see a thing. Suddenly I felt something grab me. It was a hand! Lauren had grabbed me out of the water! I had nearly drowned in zero degree water and now I was standing outside in thirty degree weather. Limping from coldness Lauren and I walked home. (Lauren was helping me walk.) If Lauren wasn't there I would have drowned. That is why my friends are the most important people to me.

Emily Tallmadge
Grade 6

Animals vs Humans

I'm going to tell a nonfiction story about humans vs animals. The title of my story is "Animals vs Humans." I will be telling you about the differences and comparisons between humans and animals.

Animals are surprisingly more similar to us humans than anyone thought. Just like us animals have mates and children. They also have some of the same body parts such as legs and arms. Animals are also very different from us. For example instead of having hair like we do they have fur and sometimes even nothing at all. They also have paws instead of hands and feet. Unlike us humans living in regular every day houses in a regular neighborhood, animals live in dens and forests and other places.

As you can tell animals and humans have their comparisons and their differences. Still there is much more to talk about. For example the behind the scenes story for animals vs humans, like how one human may set a world record, but if you try and compare it to an animal then you would fin a big difference. One of the examples I would use is a sprinting competition. A cheetah could beat a man's record by forty-seven miles or more. Also a triple jump competition. A kangaroo could beat a man's by thirty-two point eight-two miles or more.

I hope you enjoyed my nonfiction story. This story was enjoyable to write. I hope you learned something from it.

Sam Otis
Grade 6

Snakes

Snakes are reptiles. They are cold-blooded, so they need the sun to heat up and shade to cool down. There are three different body shapes for snakes. A flattened body for sea snakes, a loaf of bread shape for tree snakes, and a circular body for ground-dwelling snakes.

Snakes also shed their skin. They do this when their old skin is too small for them. To do this, the snake rubs its nose on a hard surface and wriggles out of its old skin. Snakes have different kinds of scales. There are three kinds of scales. Keeled-scaled for wetland snakes that help them move; smooth scales for burrowing snakes that need smooth scales to slide through sand; and granular scales for sea snakes that help the snake catch slippery prey like fish.

Snakes have a resting jaw and an extended jaw. The resting jaw is normal size but when it uses its extended jaw, its mouth gets stretched at least twice the size of its head! Some snakes are venomous, so they use venom to kill their prey. Some of these snakes have warning colors that show predators it's poisonous. But some snakes have false colors so they look like a venomous snake! Other snakes may hide and be camouflaged, look dead, or make itself bigger.

Charlie Lin
Grade 5

Whales vs Fish

Do you know anything about whales and fish? I know a lot about them. They have many things similar and even more things different. I hope you enjoy learning about these two amazing creatures.

Some things that are similar about whales and fish are that they both swim in the ocean. Another reason why they are alike is because they both migrate through the ocean according to the season. There are many different types of these creatures. At one time both of them were being killed rapidly.

Whales and fish are different because whales breathe through their blow hole and fish breathe through gills. Whales have blubber, but fish don't. Fish have things called scales. Whales are mammals and fish aren't.

These are just a couple facts about whales and fish. There are a lot more. I love learning about sea creatures. That is why I did my report on them. I hope you enjoyed learning about whales and fish.

Joseph Mort
Grade 6

Cirris Is Me

Hi, my name is C Cloud, I'm puffy. I form on sunny days, I have a good eye so watch yourself. When I look down on Earth and feel it's hot I may throw water down on you. Make you feel cool like a tall glass of ice tea. I see criminals. Criminals you may think you are fast, but you never can out run me. I'll scare you so bad your socks will come off. Time for me to go Cumulonimbus is coming.

Marcus Stith
Grade 4

Music

Music is a way for your feelings to fly. Music never dies. I have one question to ask you, just one; where will we be without music?

Some people say they would be in their graves. Many say they will make their own music. Lots say they will be in their room, rocking back and forth saying "where did it go?" Lots are lost without music.

There are different types of music. One type of music is punk. It is my favorite type of music. There are different bands such as "Angels and Airwaves." They are new, but awesome.

Music is one way to make friends. If you and a friend like the same music, you are going to be better friends than before. So many people hang out with their friends just to listen to music. That's what my friends and I do.

Last week my friend said "I will give you ten dollars if you go three days without music." I couldn't do it. I really can't. I hate when I get grounded, then I can't listen to music. So this is what I do, I sing. That is what I do without music.

So what are you to do when you're in your room with nothing to do? I know what I would do if I was bored out of my mind. I would listen to music.

Alexis Antelmi
Grade 5

Evolution and Intelligent Design in the Classroom

The theory of evolution and the theory of intelligent design should be taught in the classroom. The theory of evolution should be taught as part of a science class and the theory of intelligent design should be taught as part of a comparative religion course. Evolution is supported by science based facts. Intelligent design is based on belief. People should have the opportunity to learn about all of the theories that are out there, and then make their own choice about what they want to believe. No one theory should ever be pushed on an individual.

Charles Darwin created the theory of evolution while in the Galapagos Islands. His findings showed that an animal species that began the same, when placed in two different environments, would adapt their physical bodies to better suit their new surroundings. The theory of intelligent design says that God created all life and existence on Earth. The theory also reasons that God puts new species on the planet.

The main reason both evolution and intelligent design should be taught in the classroom is because people need the knowledge to make their own choice. By educating society on both theories, people will be given the opportunity to grow as individuals, and learn to understand and be tolerant of other people and their beliefs, whether science or faith based.

Dylan Almeida
Grade 6

The Hurricane

When the powerful hurricane hit New Orleans, it became all over the news! Everybody was shocked when they heard about it. When I heard about the hurricane I felt very bad for the people that have lost a family in New Orleans that were involved in the storm.

Lots of the houses are gone or knocked down from the powerful, and strong winds during the storm. Hurricane Katrina could be one of the worst disasters to ever hit the United States!

The whole entire area where the hurricane had hit became extremely flooded. I hope that lots of people will donate some money to help the people that went through this storm. At the Talbot Middle School students have also donated some money. Our principal said that we donated over one thousand dollars to the fund. Many students have helped out donating money to the Hurricane Katrina fund.

Ashley Machado
Grade 6

The Younger Days

One thing I miss about being a little kid is not going to school and having sleepovers and playing with my friends. I also miss going to Panama to visit my family and seeing my home videos of myself. I miss having family reunions. Now that I'm at school, it's very hard to go to Panama. I miss going to carnivals and going fishing. I also miss getting a lot of attention when I was first born and in preschool. When I was in preschool, we would play "Go Fish," paint anything we wanted, and we even took naps which was my favorite part in class. Last, I miss being carried by my parents soft and toasty hands.

Alex Morales
Grade 6

My Mom as a Medic in the Army

My mother served in the United States Army for six years. She went to basic training at Fort Jackson, South Carolina. This army base was named after Andrew Jackson. She did her medical training in Fort Sam Houston, Texas. After all her training she was considered a medical specialist and her rank was SP5, which is the same as a sergeant in the army. She was stationed at the Letterman Army Medical Center in San Francisco, California. She took care of a lot of veterans from the Vietnam War.

When the soldiers had field duty my mom stayed in the field in order to give them emergency care if necessary. She also flew in an army medical emergency helicopter, which was known as medovacs, for those soldiers who needed emergency care. My mom stated that she loved serving her country in the United States Army and would do it again if she had the opportunity. She also recommends it for all others, just to get the experience and feeling of serving for their country. I am so proud of my mom and all those who are willing to serve their country.

Daniel Roberts
Grade 6

What a Good Education Means to Me

A good education is very important to me! Education is a very long process. I started school in kindergarten and will continue my education through college. I am fortunate to go to a Catholic school where I learn religion every day. This has helped me to appreciate what I have. I have learned that a good education is extremely valuable. A good education can help you find a new or better job.

I have learned that studying hard will get you good grades. This will help me to choose a good high school. After high school, I will attend college. I plan to study education. My college education will allow me to do many things.

I hope to become a teacher. I enjoy being with children, and I like to help others learn. I would love to teach children in elementary school. Being a teacher is my dream. Beginning with a good education can make my dream come true!

Katie Bierbrauer
Grade 6

Exercise Is Fun!

Yesterday, I rode my bike for a half an hour. I like to exercise because it keeps my heart strong and healthy and prevents overweight. It also builds up my muscles and brings me closer to my friends. Sometimes if I have a big test the next day riding my bike gets rid of most of my stress. Another reason I like to ride my bike is because I like to have healthy blood and the more I exercise the more healthy blood for my body. Another thing is it's one of my favorite hobbies and if you try it, it could become one of yours too! I also like to take dance class too because it makes me move a lot more and faster and I get healthier. That's why you should exercise every day.

Kylie Campbell
Grade 4

I'm a Fashion Designer

When I grow up I might be famous at fashion designing. My day might be: I wake up and tons of people are standing in front of my pink bed. Then I would go to the kitchen to eat pancakes with syrup for breakfast. The photographers and reporters would follow me until I answer their questions and let them take pictures of me. After they leave I would get dressed and go to work.

As I walk in my job, reporters and photographers would follow me again. At work I would have to design a couple of outfits for models. While I make the outfits, the Paparazzi would come and watch me design. When I'm done, I might go to the Rag Shop to get more pretty materials. Then I'll go home and sketch some ideas for clothes and accessories.

While out to dinner, the Paparazzi would take pictures again. My waiter will serve me London broil with mashed potatoes and vegetables. After I eat dinner, I will watch TV. Finally, I would get to sleep. What a day!

Angela Calasso
Grade 4

What We Can Do

Have you ever noticed how our world is changing? Our world seems so polluted and dirty, but the strange part is, it is cleaner than it was 35 years ago. Yet, we can change it more and make it a better place for everyone. In the future, children and adults should be able to have a beautiful planet like we do, hopefully better. Earth day is coming up and we can make a difference by cleaning outside. We can get started by letting people know about Earth day, we can organized a group to help.

My classmates and I like the idea of cleaning our school and making a difference. We would start by letting people know what's going on in our environment. We can make posters and on the morning announcements students can inform the school about the ideas. I feel strongly about this that I am willing to make a speech to the school.

On earth day we can start cleaning outside. We can do this for 60 minutes. Some can put out trash cans so less trash will be thrown on the ground. We can recycle paper, glass, and plastic.

My classmates and I would love this activity because we can make our school a better place. Working together with friends will get everyone motivated. This would be so enjoyable! Thank you for reading my ideas. I hope you take them into consideration. I know all of us will benefit from making our world a better place!

Alie Bates
Grade 5

Friendship

Being a new student at P.S.2, it is difficult to choose who my friends are. My basis on choosing a friend is when he or she brings out the best in me. That is when he or she is true.

In choosing a friend I base it on common interest, like card collections, favorite P.S.2 games, or even sports. Anybody can be a friend, like someone you see frequently at a grocery store or in church, or even when taking the subway. For a long time friends can help build up our dreams. He or she can be very supportive and help build my self-esteem. A friend can make you smile and will try not to make you frown. If I have a good friend the friendship can last more than ten years and is still growing. A true friend will always be there for me until the day I am old and gray. A friend can be my companion even when I get old, through good times and bad times. In school I know a friend can give me a hard time. A friend can stand by me and walk beside me. A friend is there to listen, he is there to talk to me and play with me.

Sometimes a friend can be in pain or in tears and not happy all the time. We can have sad moments too. But no matter what I know a friend is there to give me comfort, they are who is next to my family. So isn't it easy to have a friend?

Kurt Dee
Grade 5

Michael

Michael is my cousin. That is, he was, until April 10, 2005.

Michael was 13 years old, like my older sister. He had a brother, a father, and a mother. He also had cancer.

Michael struggled with lymphoma, a cancer of the lymph system, from May 2004. Although he had a serious case, Michael still lived life to its fullest. You almost never saw him not wearing his favorite sweatshirt, which said in big letters across the front, "Cancer Sucks!" He took his friends on a march for cancer victims, their families, and their supporters, to raise money for cancer research. Then he strutted up to the mayor of San Francisco (with his "Cancer Sucks" sweatshirt on) and announced, "These streets have way too many potholes."

Michael was brave and funny. When he died at the age of 13, it may have been the saddest day of my life.

At his funeral, I cried. I cried remembering him. I remembered how he once ate five pieces of mushroom pizza, then begged his mother to take him on a carousel. I remembered how when we had gone to California for a week, a butterfly landed on his pink shirt, and he stood stock still so that it wouldn't be disturbed. I remembered how he drew whole notebooks full of aliens. I miss him.

Michael is still with me. Every time I wear my own "Cancer Sucks" shirt, I wear it to honor Michael, and I think of him and smile.

Zoe Huber-Weiss
Grade 5

Bats

Bats can be very helpful to our community, by being nature's best environmentalists. As you might know, bats are not vampires and they do not suck your blood. Actually, they are furry flying mammals. They eat flies and mosquitoes that get in your food or ruin a backyard barbecue.

The bats should be protected because bats hardly ever hurt people. There are only 20 species of bats and some of them may be on the endangered-species list. As homes are being built, we are taking the forests where they live, and making them live closer to us. The droppings that bats make is called guano. It is used as a fertilizer that is very rich in nutrients and used to help crops grow.

Other communities have protected the bats by making it wrong and illegal to kill bats, such as in Florida. In Mexico, bats transfer pollen from cactus to cactus and spread the seeds around and the bats are called "Johnny cactus-seeds of the desert."

Like I was saying, in Florida it's illegal to kill bats because in Florida people think bats are helpful. I think bats are helpful because they don't hurt people. Bats should be protected because they help us so we should help them. Bats should have a home like us. They picked our state so now we need them to feel like home in our state. Do you know what? We are just like them.

Alexis Kraska
Grade 4

A Frosty Night with Grandpa

The rain was pouring down like a melting popsicle, the wind roared like lions stuck in cages. It was a cold December night. My grandpa and I stood above the stove watching the top explode off from the jiffy pop. The aroma of salty, buttery popcorn filled the air. I climbed on the counter top and reached for two large bowls. It was my grandpa's idea to make the popcorn, it was too cold and rainy to go outside. My papa would basically be my baby sitter, while my mother and sister were at her girl scout trip.

While my papa was with me, he said I could help him paint the walls in the bedroom that he'd promised he'd do. It was a sky mural on one of my walls, shooting stars and a crescent moon. He piled down popcorn in our bowls and we briskly walked over to the sofa, the commercials were nearly over when we got back. He plopped on the sofa and I copied him.

Our movie came back on — "How We Saved Christmas." I saw the brightly covered tree in the movie and looked at our own well decorated tree. I reached for the warm wool blanket and put it around us. We curled up and enjoyed the rest of the movie. The movie is one of my favorite movies to this day. I can't find it anywhere, I flipped through tons of channels around Christmastime, but I never found anything.

Allegra Maldonado
Grade 5

My Pets

Have you ever had a pet? Cats are great because you can play together. When you get home, they are waiting. When you are feeling sad, they are there for you. You can get a cat at your local shelter and give it a good home.

My pets' names are Cuddles, a black and white female medium hair cat, and Snuggles, a solid black male short hair cat. I love them because they are loving and caring! My mom said, "Those cats would have died within the next week because they were being starved." Luckily, we took them home and we gave them food.

Cuddles and Snuggles were skinny, had bald spots in their fur, and Cuddles refused to eat, at first. By constant attention and small handfuls of food, my new pets improved their appearance and appetite.

My grandmother liked Boots for one of the names, since one had black furred paws. However, Cuddles and Snuggles are perfect names because what I enjoy most about my cats is cuddling and snuggling with them, especially after a sad or tough day.

Taking care of a cat is easy. All you need is a litter box, food and water and your cat will be happy. Go to an animal shelter and save a cat's life. No matter what name you give it, it will return love to you.

Juliana Dishner
Grade 6

Hockey Life

Hockey is my life. All I do is play hockey. When I finish my homework I go outside to work on my shots with my brother. I love the way I glide across the blue lines and rip the small black puck right past the net liner like a falcon ripping past its nest. Although I work hard at hockey I also have to thank my mother for letting me practice and chauffeuring me around from practice to practice.

I have been playing hockey since I was three. My sister picked up figure skating, but my dad did not want me to figure skate, so he started me with hockey. I've kept with it ever since.

Hockey is not the only sport I play. I also play football and I go to Colorado to ski and snowboard. I have been going to Colorado since I was three. I go four times a year to ski, and I've gotten really good at it. Now I can go down anything, although last year I started snowboarding.

My favorite hockey team is the Devils. I skated with the whole team and even met Marten Brodeur's children when I was snowboarding. Martin Brodeur is the world's best goalie and one of my idols. He works hard and is a great player. I will keep working on my hockey skills so that one day maybe I will be in Martin Brodeur's league.

Andrew Boisselle
Grade 6

My Friends Are the Best

I have a lot of friends! They are all very nice and friendly. They all have different talents and qualities which make them different and unique. They all respect me and care about me. All of them are fun to hang out with and fun to chat with. I have shared a lot of wonderful moments with them that I will remember forever.

My friends are mostly girls. I do have some guy friends though. My closest friends are Marissa, Katie, Eddie, Sammie, Bionca, Nicky, Rebeca, and Greg. I mostly hang out with them. We have a lot of fun together. All nine of us.

All nine of us are very close to each other. Katie and Marissa are my closest friends though. I've known Katie since I was about eight months old. She was about six months old. Katie and I like doing crafts together and making each other laugh. We have A LOT of fun together.

I've known Marissa since 3rd grade, we were about eight years old. We like to go shopping together and just do things together. We have a *very* strong friendship that will probably last a lifetime.

All my friends are awesome! They are so wonderful it's hard to explain them. I hope our friendship goes on! They cheer me up when I am sad. And help me when I need it! They are probably the most important people in my life, and I love them all!!

Elysa Schuhmacher
Grade 6

Navy Men

I have many relatives that served in the Navy. They were my Pop, Poppie, and PopPop Steve (great-grandparent.) They are not in the military any more because they got kind of old. I like being a grandchild of a military member of our country. If I would choose to be a representative of our country, I would pick the Navy because I love the water and to swim. I have the outfit of my Poppie's uniform; I love the hat of the outfit. So, I want to thank all of the people I do know or don't know for serving and representing our country for us, the people of freedom, respect, who trust in God throughout the world.

Jennifer Donnelly
Grade 6

Comparing Dolphins and Sharks

Have you ever compared two animals? Well, in this writing assignment, that's exactly what I'll be doing. The animals I'll be talking about are the shark and the dolphin; how they're alike and how they're different.

Dolphins and sharks are very alike. For example, they both need water to survive. They also have fins and tails to help them navigate through the water. Both of them are carnivores and both of them have different species. Some shark species are the Tiger and Great White and some dolphin species are the White Beaked and the Striped.

Dolphins and sharks are also very different. For example, dolphins are mammals and sharks are fish. Dolphins have blowholes and sharks have gills. Dolphins use echolocation while some sharks lay egg cases. Don't be fooled by their similarities, dolphins and sharks are still two totally different species!

I just compared dolphins and sharks and pointed out their similarities and differences. Dolphins and sharks are pretty alike and different. I guess to find out if they're more different or the same some more research would be needed. Based on what I told you, what do you think?

Brandon McCracken
Grade 6

Snapping Turtles vs Pet Turtles

My essay is about turtles. One of them is a snapping turtle and the other is a pet turtle.

Both turtles have a lot in common. They both have shells, claws, eyes, and mouths. They swim and lay eggs if they are females. Turtles need access to water and land and use their jaws to catch their prey.

What the turtles don't have in common is that the pet turtle doesn't snap or live in the wild. They live in a cage and can be held, bought in a store, and are friendly. A wild turtle is mean, can't be bought in a store, lives in the wild, and can't be held.

I think both turtles have some in common but not everything. I picked turtles because they are one of my favorite animals. I also think that turtles are cool.

Chelsie Kline
Grade 6

Working Hard

When a teacher or a parent tells me that I have to work hard at something I am not always thrilled, but when you do work hard it can be very rewarding. That is why working hard is very important to me. For example, joke telling is a talent of mine. Even though it may come easy for me I still have to work hard at it. Lots of people see me as being funny. Knowing the right time to make someone laugh is very important. You wouldn't want to crack a joke when someone does not want to talk to you. So if you want to make somebody laugh, you have to work hard at knowing when to make somebody laugh. That's why a lot of people think I am funny. My timing in telling a joke is a key to my success. Working hard at something may not be easy, it's worth it in the end. Working hard in school is one of the most important things I do. If I don't make sure to work hard in class and at home I may not do well. That is why I work hard to always get some reading time in at home. Every time we have to read at school I make sure I read as much as possible. So next time a teacher or parent tells me to work hard I will do it without complaining.

Maverick Vicars
Grade 5

Rent

Rent. Most people when they hear this word think of renting a movie, but this essay is about the Broadway musical *Rent*.

The creator of *Rent* was Jonathan Larson. He was born on February 4, 1960. This composer from New York always loved to write music. He made the musicals *Rent* and *Tick, Tick…BOOM!* Sadly this amazing composer died unexpectedly from an undiagnosed aortic dissection and died the night before the preview of *Rent*, on January 25, 1996.

Behind the songs and dances is a hardworking group of stars. Anthony Rapp plays Mark, a poor filmmaker. Adam Pascal plays Roger, a guitarist and is Mark's roommate. Daphne Rubin-Vega plays Mimi, a woman addicted to drugs. Taye Diggs plays Benny, who once was Mark's roommate. Jesse Martin plays Collins, a gay man who knows Roger. Wilson Herdia plays Angel, a gay man that is Collin's partner. Fredi Walker plays Joanne, a lesbian lawyer. Idena Menzel plays Maureen, a lesbian that is Joanne's girlfriend.

This musical is about friends learning to live like there's no day but today. It's a story of love and friendship. The friends need to pay their rent before they get evicted, that's how this movie got its name.

Rent is about friends and their life together for a year. This musical has wonderful actors and a magnificent creator. If you liked reading my essay and would like to see the musical, you can rent the movie on February 21, 2006.

Carianne Lee
Grade 5

How I Met My Best Friend

I was very happy! School was here! It was a new school year. We were in 4th grade. This new girl came from Colorado and her name was Sara and my name is Gabrielle. I wasn't crazy about her at first. One thing that was weird about Sara is that she is never cold! Well duh, she is from Colorado! But later in September I asked to be her friend. She said yes! Yaaa!!! When I started being friends with Sara some got jealous. Then I stopped being Sara's friend! But the next day we made up. We talk all the time on the phone. Then in January I started skating. We had a problem. See, we wanted to be in the same class. Sara's mom begged. Guess what, she is in with me!! But now, Sara is going back to Colorado so good-by Sara. But…we will be on the phone, so hello phone good-bye Sara!

Sara Moles and Gabrielle Yameen
Grade 4

The Similarities and Differences of Piano and Baton

Do you have two items that you would like to compare and contrast? Well, I do, they are piano and baton. I am going to share how these two items sound totally different, but can be alike.

First, I am going to tell you how piano and baton are alike. They are alike because they are both hobbies, and you have to use hands and fingers for them. Next, you can take lessons to learn them. Finally, you can have recitals for both (or at least I do)! I hope you now know how I think baton and piano are alike.

Now you are going to learn the differences of baton and piano. The first difference is, the baton you twirl and the piano you play. Also, baton is more like a sport, and piano is like an art. Finally, the piano is a musical instrument, and the baton is not.

Now you know the similarities and differences of baton and piano. I hope you can find two items to compare and contrast. It is a lot of fun to see how two items can be so much alike and still be different.

Kayla McGoran
Grade 6

Halloween

Yes, my family celebrates Halloween. Some of the traditions we do are, we dress up in funny, scary, weird, costumes and scare each other. We also go trick-or-treating to get lots of candy. We decorate by putting up witches and skeletons. We always give candy and put out fake stunts. We also have a party usually the day before Halloween or after Halloween.

We always have a fun dinner because we put fake spiders and stuff in it and we make like ants on a stick and spiders in cupcakes and other jokes. We usually stay up late and watch very scary movies like *Scary Movie*, and more scary movies. We go outside when it gets dark and play flash light tag usually with the neighborhood.

Lindy Burruss
Grade 6

The Big Block

There I was, trembling, running harder than ever before. I put one foot in front of the other, while sweat poured down my face like a waterfall. The ball was pounding against the ground like a humungous block being thrown at a tin wall. Will I ever catch up?

My arms were being dragged behind me in flailing streamers. Oh no! I had stumbled. But I picked myself up and started to raise my arms like an eagle's wing. The ground was disappearing from underneath me. My hands whacked the ball. My hands stung. The ball was in *my* hands.

I felt the great rush of gladness go down my body. Me, I was sweating but I didn't care. My opponent looked at me like "wow." I think I might go on with this game called basketball.

Lucy Bradshaw
Grade 4

Sugar

Sugar is my guinea pig. She is 3 years old. She loves to run laps around her house! Sugar and her brother Snickers live in our playroom. Sugar is my favorite. Sugar is black with a white poof. Her cage is green and tan. She loves to chew on a hole in her house. She loves to eat lettuce and carrots. Her favorite is dry food. She drinks water. I play with her every day except Sunday. She is soft and fuzzy. I love her like Sugar is a real person. Sugar loves me like I am one of her kind. She is the best guinea pig in the whole wide world.

Skyler Phillips
Grade 4

My Family's Life

What is your family like? Are they respectful, caring, truthful, helpful, or honest? My family is always like that. They take good care of me when I am sick, upset, or lonely. My family appreciates me and I appreciate them too because they are always there for me when I need them. The family that I live with is always quiet, not noisy, and they mind their own business. My family never says bad things about people because my family cares about people. They have a good heart for people and a good mind because they want everyone to live a good life. Whenever someone needs help, they always help them. My family is always there for people.

They want everyone to be pleased with what they have because a lot of people don't cherish what they have in life. If I need something that is really important, they get it for me whenever I need it. Sometimes when someone says bad things to someone else and the person that says it laughs, it is not funny. My family cheers that person up so they don't feel like they're the only person that feels like that. That is why I always keep my family in my heart and my family always comes first in my mind. That is why I love my family so much!

Amy Ramjatan
Grade 4

Honda Is the Best!

Have you ever ridden on an ATV and were not able to get it started and it conk out on you, or is always getting stuck? Well if that's happening to you, you might want to get a Honda. Honda is the best ATV maker because they make very good motors which always start right up. They make cars and trucks too. They got two awards for both car and truck which is very hard! That also proves that they make good motors.

Honda's products work better than Yamaha because I have a Yamaha Raptor and my dad has a Honda Rancher. My Yamaha was just running the other day and it didn't start the next day. After lots of tending to, it worked. But my dad's had been sitting there for five months. After we charged its battery it worked great.

Lots of famous people ride Hondas ATV's and dirt bikes. Honda's prices are good. There are a lot of good sales and a salesperson can make you an even better deal. Honda has great power like when we just had a foot of snow and I got stuck but one of the reasons is the size of the motor but my dad got through it no problem because he has four wheel drive, which most makers don't have. So from my evidence Honda is the best ATV maker.

Reed Shuttle
Grade 6

How to Win a Swim Race

There are many things you have to think about during a swim race. How do you win a swim race? I will tell you.

First comes your dive. There are three things you have to think about: Mr. Starter, so you don't miss your starting cue; your diving forms, because if you have a good dive, that will really help you win; and last, think about capturing that gold! Those are important things to think about.

Second, you must display a long, tight streamline. During your streamline do your butterfly or freestyle kick unless you're in your breaststroke race. If so, you have to do a pullout. If your streamline isn't how it's supposed to be, you will get behind.

Finally, you've started your race! Now you have to pay attention to your stroke. You really want to stretch yourself out. Surprisingly, it's what helps you win. Also, you should save most of your energy for your second lap. If only swimming one lap sprint the whole way. Always remember, your stroke form is VERY important!

The next skill you need to know for swimming is flip turns. You only need to use flip turns if you're swimming freestyle or backstroke. Make sure your flip is tight, and then get a good push off the wall for a stream line.

Now you know how to swim a race! Hopefully, my advice will help you win too!

Molly McWilliams
Grade 6

A Weekend to Remember

An event in my life that made me cry my eyes out uncontrollably was when my mom got married. My mom got married on October 8, 2005. The wedding took place at a hotel called Congress Hall in Cape May, New Jersey. When my mom started walking down the spiral steps in her wedding dress, I started to cry because she looked so beautiful. When she walked up to me and said, "You look so pretty," I said, "Don't look at me," because I would start to automatically cry. I would cry mostly because I couldn't believe this was really happening.

Way before the wedding, my mom had mentioned that she wanted me to write a little speech or something to read during the ceremony. I did. When I read the speech, I was practically bawling my eyes out. At the end of the ceremony, we had the reception in a room right next to the room where the ceremony took place. The room was hot pink! When everyone walked in, they were very surprised that is was PINK! At the reception, everyone, I mean everyone, came up to me and said my reading was so pretty. I kind of felt bad because I made almost everyone cry; but then I realized that it wasn't a bad thing. During the reception, we had THREE HOURS of pictures! I was really starting to get bored. I had a great time, though. This is an incredible event I won't forget.

Michaela Day
Grade 6

What Can I Do?

Obesity is a problem that continues to grow, not as much in my town. Some people feel obesity is difficult to solve. To help stop the growing problem of obesity, people need to be educated, even the very young, about healthy eating habits and daily exercise.

People can do this in many ways but probably the best way is to eat healthier. You could simply eat healthy foods like fruits and vegetables and less snacks like candy. I would probably choose to eat smaller portions and healthier snacks like peanut butter crackers. Since I love fruits, I would choose to substitute junk food with fruits. I know there are other ways to lose weight like crash diets, but those are dangerous, not intelligent, and can cause physical health issues.

Exercise is another way to keep you from becoming overweight or help you lose weight. An excellent exercise is walking or running and for entertainment one can listen to music. One of my favorite ways to exercise is to do jumping jacks or sit-ups during TV commercials. If you add up the commercial time, you will be exercising for twenty minutes per hour. Exercise not only helps overcome obesity but can keep your heart healthy and decrease cholesterol. Exercising can be exciting if you are creative.

Obesity is a major health concern among the young and old. If people choose healthy eating habits and exercise more, then there should be a decrease in the number of obese people.

Jacqueline Flood
Grade 6

A Crazy Little Friend

"Charlie no!" These are the words that are typically being screamed in my house every day now. Charlie is my pet dog; he is a chocolate colored Dachshund that is only six months old. Charlie is my crazy little friend, that's what I call him. Whenever I get home from school he runs up to me, jumps, and then attacks me! "I'm pleased to see you too," I usually say.

But there are times when I wonder why he goes so crazy. It's crazy, I know! It all started on Christmas day; we fed Charlie some human food. First there was turkey, then there was salad, then there was so much more! It wasn't funny.

It's not always easy to stay away from something tempting such as a bag of potato chips. Tempting was the word I was looking for, to this day we always feed Charlie our leftovers. Yesterday we let Charlie into the garage where he found a garbage bag with a lollipop inside. He sniffed it out, and he wanted it. Now it was going to get ugly!

Ten minutes later I opened the garage door, and you will not believe what I saw! All over the garage floor was a ripped garbage bag with old tissues in it and other things. "Charlie no!" I screamed. Mom's in for a surprise! There you are my crazy little friend sucking on the tastiest lollipop of your dreams.

Claudia Wasilewski
Grade 6

My Grandfather

In this essay I will be talking about when my grandfather passed away and how I still have faith he is still living. It may make me cry, but it is worth it.

When I was only seven and my sister was just turning six, my grandfather passed away from a heart attack in his sleep. My grandfather was the only one who could get me to smile. My grandfather could play the guitar, and man could he play. My grandfather's name is Earl H. White. My grandfather was there for my sister's birthday, he made a carrot cake for my sister. My grandfather also gave my sister a great big teddy bear. My sister named the teddy bear after the size of the bear, the name was Big Bear. My grandfather was an influence to me because he was a great guitar player and a song writer, but an even better person.

I was sad when my grandfather passed away, but I got through it. The people who helped me get through it the most were my grandparents Dotty and Dan. I always give my Papa a hug every time I see him because he is my only grandfather left. My Nana helped me get through by telling me everything would be all right. My dad also helped me get through by spending time with me and my sister. My mom also helped me get through it by also spending a lot of time with me.

Erica White
Grade 6

Indoor Soccer

Have you ever played indoor soccer? It's a very good sport to play because it builds teamwork, is inexpensive, and doesn't require hours of practice. It is soccer action at its best! Indoor soccer is fifty minutes of nonstop action. Twenty five minutes are played each half. There are ten games played each session. I'm in my third season of indoor soccer. I play goal keeper and defense. I rarely ever play offense. By playing these positions, it makes me realize indoor soccer is an exciting sport.

When playing indoor soccer all of the positions are important. Without a man playing his position the team loses. If one player can't cooperate the team may struggle.

Indoor soccer isn't an extremely expensive sport to play. It costs around ninety dollars per session. Most players like to purchase indoor shoes. They cost anywhere from twenty dollars and up, although you can wear your tennis shoes if you can't purchase a pair before your first game.

Most teams don't practice, but if you want to practice you can rent the field for one hour at a time. It costs five to fifteen dollars per hour. My team doesn't practice, but some teams invite us to scrimmage them. If you want to practice without having to pay you can go to a gym.

I like indoor soccer because it builds teamwork, doesn't require a lot of practice, and doesn't cost much. Go ahead, give it a shot and score big by playing indoor soccer.

Vincent Centore
Grade 6

Memory

I would love to give the gift of memory to my grandmother. My grandmother has short-term memory loss, and sometimes forgets what she is talking about. If I could give the gift of memory to my grandmother she would not forget. To remember is a true gift; otherwise you won't know where you are or why you're there, and you could get injured. Knowing who you are is extremely valuable. For example, how you act, dress, talk, walk, eat and live. You need to know what you're doing and why. Knowing yourself is grave to everyday life. If you lose your memory you can't know what your purpose is, whether it is to be sympathetic to a person that is being teased or to assist a person finding their way. Remembering is so essential to everyday life that I can't imagine living without it. I look up to my grandmother for conquering everyday life and occasionally forgetting. This doesn't stop my grandmother from doing normal chores. She still shops with my grandfather, comes to my school events and sometimes goes to my games. My grandmother is still active and is an astonishing woman. I admire my grandmother highly and hope she will still succeed and improve.

Bradly Florio
Grade 6

Don't Get Mad Get Glad

People can tell when I am angry because I do not talk. When I am happy I'm loud, some people do like when I am loud. They also say it's annoying. When I am mad my friends ask me what's wrong. My friend Janae who is like my sister can tell when I am mad. My sisters Jessica and Jamesia can tell too. I think sometimes my friends miss my loudness when I am not in school. I think people think I am ghetto, but I'm not. My friends don't like when I cry because it's a painful feeling to them. I think I bring all the fun to my friends when I meet them. When they're mad I cheer them up. All of my friends say I am fun to hang around with. That is my story about my life with friends and sisters knowing I'm glad or mad.

Rolonda Drakeford
Grade 6

The Big Dolphins

Dolphins are air-breathing mammals, but they spend their entire lives in water. There are many different species of dolphins. They live in oceans, seas, lakes and rivers. Dolphins live in groups called schools, herds or pools. The most popular dolphin is the Bottlenose, which is famous for its friendliness toward people. It is also the dolphin most commonly kept in marine aquariums.

Dolphins and their close cousins, whales and porpoises, are together known as cetaceans. Female Bottlenose dolphins usually have only one calf every two to four years. A baby dolphin calf may weigh as much as 45 lbs. and be more than 3 ft. long. The calf feeds on its mother's milk at least four times an hour. The mother tries to protect her calf from predators. Females may live up to fifty years, and males only thirty years. We should be careful not to pollute the ocean so we don't harm the dolphins.

Jason Mitchell
Grade 5

My Family

Your family can't beat mine. My family is the best. They are helpful and they are nice. They supply me with a lot. If you looked up the best family in the dictionary, you would find the Kohut family in the definition.

My family is helpful. If I need help with my homework, they are always there to help me find the answers. They all help me out when I am down. If I am sick they help me to get better. Helpful is my family.

My family is nice. They make me do my homework then they check it. They clean my room. They feed my pets. My family is the nicest family ever.

They supply me with a lot. They get me everything I need. They give me food and water. They give me a place to live. Everyone in my family gives me what I need.

My family is the best you can ever get. My family is helpful, nice, and they supply me with a lot. My family is the best!

Cody Kohut
Grade 6

Dance Is Great!

I don't know what I would do without dance! Dance has been so fun lately. I get to learn new steps, and I get to go to lessons just about every day. Everyone at dance is like my family.

Every class I get to learn fun new steps. Whenever I go to class, I get to go across the dance floor with new steps. A few neat moves are illusions, inverts, and axles. There are different types of moves in each class. A move in tap is a draw back, and a move in ballet is a tondu. They are very different. Sometimes I get special parts in dances because I work very hard on my moves.

I have dance class everyday except for Saturday and sometimes Friday. I stay to work hard on my technique. I'm even on a competitive team to increase my level even more. Sometimes our team practices eight hours straight. The types of dances that I do are jazz, tap, acro, ballet, and lyrical. They're all extremely fun.

Everyone at dance is nice and acts like family. After dance, we always go to restaurants together. We do this mainly after competitions. Whenever I have a problem, I can talk to the people at the studio. They always have great answers. Together, we always play games and talk. There is always so much to say.

Dance has been extraordinary! Sometimes the dance studio feels like a second home!

Lillie Capone
Grade 6

Ski Area History

Here is the history of New England ski areas. You will be told what the ski area was like when it first opened and what it is like today.

The first ski area to open in New England was Stowe, Vermont. Stowe opened in 1934 with two trails. Today Stowe has the tallest skiable mountain in New England, Mt. Mansfield.

In 1936 Bromley opened in Southern Vermont with a J-bar and one trail. What makes Bromley unique is that it faces south, meaning that it needs a larger snowmaking capacity than most ski areas because they have more sunny weather, which causes the snow to melt faster.

Mad River Glen came in 1949 with a single chair lift and is still a very popular area. Now the ski area remains as it was back in the old days, with only 15% snowmaking.

The 1950s was a major time for skiing and a lot of ski areas opened during this time. In 1960 through 1970, skiing spread to Southern New England and a lot of ski areas opened there. However, there were still ski areas opening in Northern New England. I hope you liked my brief history of New England ski areas.

Coleman Whiteley
Grade 5

My Family

Have you ever wondered what life is like without family? My family supports and helps me. They also love me. Thank you family.

My family helps me. My brother helps me with homework. If I don't understand a problem he'll help. My mom helps me study. She will give me tests. My mom gets me prepared. For my skateboard she made sure I had tools.

My family loves me a lot. My mom says it all the time. She will just say it out of the blue. My grandmom says it every time I go over to her house. She also gives me big hugs. On birthdays I get cards that say it.

My family supports me. I get allowance. I can buy anything. My mom makes sure I have clothes. My mom buys me clothes when she goes shopping. My mom cheers me up when I'm sad. If I'm sad about a bad grade my mom cheers me up.

My family is very supportive and they love me very much. They also help me. I love my family.

Avery Arce
Grade 6

Football

My favorite sport is football. My favorite NFL team is the Philadelphia Eagles. I like football because of the aggressiveness in it. The plays make it competitive. The NFL, I think, tries to have the best skills so that they can win the Super Bowl.

I think that playing football is the best. At school we have to play two-hand touch. I like tackle better. I think that football is a cool sport. The cool thing about it is that you can have fun while exercising, and if you exercise, you will become more fit to play football better. That's why football is my favorite sport.

Kyle Hamilton
Grade 4

Michelle Kwan vs Kristi Yamaguchi

Kristi Yamaguchi is very different than Michelle Kwan. Although they can be similar in many ways. Both are still famous figure skaters that are well known.

Kristi and Michelle are similar because they are both famous figure skaters. They were both from California and born in July. Each of their families are Chinese. Also they have many fan sites. They are both Winter Olympic medalists, too.

Both are very different because of these reasons. Kristi Yamaguchi is older by 10 years. Also she is married to Bret Hedican who is an NHL player. She has two children with him. Michelle has a good luck necklace from her grandma and a pet squirrel. Michelle is also the youngest of three children.

You see, these two girls are very similar. Yet still very, very different. In conclusion, both have their differences but are similar and role models to me.

Kristina Rosus
Grade 6

Freedom in America

A lot of people risked their lives to give us freedom. There have been many wars throughout history that led us up to the freedoms that we have today. One of the wars was the Revolutionary War. Another war that was important to our freedom was the Civil War.

The Revolutionary War was about freedom from England. Another reason that the war was fought was because of taxation laws. This process is called "taxation without representation." The colonists got furious and wanted to break away from England because the British thought that they could tax the colonists for the cost of the French and Indian War. The colonists won the war, and we got freedom from England.

The Civil War was about slavery and states' rights. The North was trying to make a law that would abolish slavery. The North was trying to make the South obey that law. The South did not want to abolish slavery so the plantation owners could afford to run their large farms. They started a war that took almost four years. There were a lot of battles. The North won the Civil War, and slavery was abolished.

Freedom in America is very important and everyone should remember all of those people who died to free us. We should look at all of the people in other countries that don't have freedom, like Cuba. These wars, and a lot more, helped us gain our freedom. I like freedom in America, and you should too.

Michael Fowler
Grade 5

Baseball

Do you know what I desire? Well, you are about to find out. I desire baseball. I think baseball is a fun but a challenging sport. Sometimes when it's raining and there's nothing to do inside, I'll go out and play baseball in the rain.

Baseball is a good sport for anyone. There are nine different positions for nine different kinds of abilities, like a catcher for example. Most catchers aren't always fast, but they can sometimes hit, and of course, they can catch.

The game of baseball is 50% mental and 50% physical. In the game of hitting, it's more mental than physical, actually. In batting you have to know what's going on. You can use physical speed in the field to make plays. Sometimes if you're on the pitcher's mound and you mess up, you can get frustrated, but you have to keep your cool. Also, you can be the best player on your team, but if you have a bad attitude you can get kicked off the team.

Just like any other sport, baseball is very hard, so you need lots of practice. My favorite active baseball player is Derek Jeter. These are reasons why I like baseball, and I hope my guidelines for baseball are helpful.

Liam Werner
Grade 4

The Last Shot

I dribbled the ball down the court. My calves were burning like a blazing inferno of fire. I knew I could do it but all of the other players stood there staring at me like hungry vultures waiting for their prey. I sprang by like a pogo stick. I thought I could make it. My legs were like jelly as I ran down the court. My strides were strong and long like a heron's. The anticipation was terrible.

I could feel my fingers trembling as I raised my arms. Swish! I made it. I realized what I had done. My hair was drenched with sweat. I could taste sweat as it trickled down to my mouth. I had done it.

I heard the crowd cheering as I realized what had happened. My teammates came out to the court. I felt stunned at first, but I heard somebody say, "Noah, you did it."

Basketball is a great sport.

Noah Lipman
Grade 4

Good Health

Good health can be achieved by developing good health habits. You should always eat healthy foods so you do not become obese. Exercising daily can help build strong muscles. Taking care of your body helps, like keeping clean and washing your body. A lot of body sweat can cause a rash. Every day you should floss and brush your teeth to keep them healthy. Celery, carrots, fruit, yogurt, cheese and milk are healthy foods to eat. Eating chips, fast food, candy, salt, ice-cream and sweet foods are not healthy foods. Do not eat before bed because it can cause excess body fat. Getting a lot of rest is good for your health. Developing good health habits is important.

Megan Hoover
Grade 6

Cheetah vs Lion

Do you know anything about cheetahs and lions? Well you should read this and find out about them. I also hope you enjoy reading about these amazing creatures.

Cheetahs and lions are kind of similar. This is how they are: they both run fast. A couple other ones are they both are carnivores. They both grow the same height, they both weigh the same, and they both live to be about 13 years old.

They are pretty different. The reasons they are different is only the lion lives in Africa. The cheetah lives somewhere else. The lions group is called a pride. The lion also roars a lot louder than the cheetah. It can be heard from almost 5 miles away. Cheetahs don't roar very loud because they don't roar that much. They only roar if they get hurt but it's because they're crying or just mad. If you ever get one of these animals mad you will get hurt or die because they both are carnivores and they have razor sharp teeth. If you get too close to a cheetah it will charge at you, but if you get about 100 ft away they will not charge at you. The same things with lions.

Troy Joseph
Grade 6

My Favorite Holiday

My favorite holiday is exciting. You see far away relatives and you are close to family. Usually you and your sibling are nice to each other. Some people just like the presents and don't give. But do they know what Christmas is all about? Well if you're one of those people listen.

One thing I love is to be with my relatives. They comfort me in hard times and tell me their opinions on what to do. I love to give presents to relatives. I love to see smiles on other peoples faces. It brings joy to my heart.

On Christmas day my brothers and I are very nice to each other. My eldest brother wakes me up or I will wake him up. We don't wake up the rest of the house. We open up our stockings and go back to bed. Then we show my mom and dad what we got.

I love presents. That is okay. But just to ask for presents is greedy. It won't hurt to buy something for somebody else. It is also okay to pray to Jesus. Of course this is my opinion and you don't have to agree with it. What I am saying is the presents isn't what Christmas is all about.

This is why I love this holiday. It brings joy to my heart. It brings my family together. And those greedy people know something about Christmas and maybe will take my advice.

Rebecca Kent
Grade 6

Clara Barton

Have you ever wondered what it would be like to be the, "angel of the battle?"

Clara Barton was sometimes called the "angel of the battlefield." Clara Barton was the founder of the American Red Cross. She began the American Red Cross on May 21, 1881. Clara's first battle was in 1862. It was the Battle of Antietam in Maryland.

Clara Barton was born on Dec. 25, 1821. Clara was the youngest out of seven children. Although she was shy and small, she possessed courage and perseverance. She had to take care of her invalid brother when she was 11 years old.

Clara worked as a government clerk in Washington, D.C. She won her fame as a battlefield nursing volunteer.[1] Clara Barton frequently risked her life throughout the conflict of the Civil War.[2] She aided the sick and wounded, at many hospitals and on the battlefield during the war.

Clara carried all her things she needed on a wagon. Two very big oxen pulled the wagon. Things she carried were medical supplies for the sick and wounded people. Also, she carried some quilts in case the people got cold. She then took the sick and wounded back to the hospital.

Sadly, the "angel of the battlefield" died on April 12, 1912 at the age of 81 years old. Even though Barton died, the American Red Cross still goes on today and helps with disasters like hurricanes, floods, earthquakes, forest fires, and other things.

[1] & [2] Civil War, John Stanchak, Dorling Kindersley, 2000.

Samantha Muller
Grade 5

Kenya

Imagine living in the eastern region of Africa. It would be different, but you would get used to their lifestyle. Their religion is part of their amazing culture that happens every day.

Kenyans have lifestyles that are impacted by their location. In Kenya, culture is a big part of the people's lives. The main religion in Kenya today is Catholicism. Herders from the bordering countries, such as Ethiopia, Sudan, and Uganda came to Kenya to find new farmland. They didn't know at that time, but they had also brought a new religion. Before the herders came, Kenyan tribes believed in witchcraft, ghosts, and a god. They believed that if someone did something wrong, a ghost would come from the dead and try to kill you. As the 20's began, railroads were built, and churches were, too. Now that a railroad was built other religions came into Kenya, such as Islamic and Arabian. The geography of Kenya impacts the religion because it is then able to spread out and be practiced.

All in all, Kenya has its own identity. They have a very interesting lifestyle living in Kenya. I know that I would have never guessed that their main religion was brought to them by herders.

Shelby Butwell
Grade 6

I'm Free!

It does not matter. Stories do not have to be real when I write them. I can have fun making characters, working on my stories, and the topics I write about are unlimited.

Creating characters out of nothing can be fun. If I try, I can make each become a real person. Any person can do anything if I want them to. Pictures appear on any piece of paper and everything happens right in front of me. I can create any person if I want to.

I like to keep improving my stories as often as I can. Subjects come clearer and more regularly when I do. Awkward words drop out and they start to flow. When I draw more, I can make every person with more personality. Every shape has more realness and looks better.

In stories I have endless topics to choose from. A story can be about a hippopotamus ice-skating or a little girl getting glasses, anything I want. I can write about anything that is serious or fairy tale-like. My drawings can be of whatever I want, even if the story is grim. The lady can be stout and the crowd can have green dotted suits instead of pinstriped ones.

Writing gives me freedom to draw or make anything, I improve my stories and my characters are made out of anything. I can write something anywhere; all I need is a pen and paper. I am free to do anything.

Caila Stapleton
Grade 6

School Uniforms...Bad or Good?

Uniforms...I think kids should not have to wear uniforms. We should be able to wear what we want to wear to an extent. We have to follow a lot of rules, but we shouldn't have to follow this rule.

A lot of kids like to pick out what they wear in the morning. I know I do. I think it would make a lot of kids depressed. Every kid is different; not one of us is the same so why should we have to wear the same clothes as each other every day? Would you like to dress the same every day? The way you dress shows your personality. We all have different tastes in clothes; they are not the same. That is my opinion on school uniforms. So please don't make us wear school uniforms.

Josh Parker
Grade 6

My Granddad

I have never met this man, but from what I hear he was a very wise, kind, and knowledgeable man. He died when I was very young. I hear great stories about him that inspire me. He's my granddad. He believed you could learn something from everyone, and how everyone has value. This has inspired me the most.

Have you ever looked at someone and thought they were useless or not smart? My granddad never did. My granddad was open to other people's points of views, and I think everyone should be like that. It would make the world a more peaceful place.

My granddad was from the "old days," "old days" meaning not everyone went to school. He quit school in 2nd grade and taught himself to read and write. Most of the things he knew, he learned from listening to other people. Ever heard the saying "to see other people's handwriting might make yours better?" I have. Try listening to everyone; it will make you a better and more knowledgeable person.

This story has inspired me, will it inspire you?

Kristen Lilly
Grade 6

The Puppies Are Here!

My dog had puppies last Saturday and there are ten. My dog's name is Suzy Q. We have only decided one puppy's name so far, Diamond because of the diamond on his back. Suzy is so nice. She lets me pet her puppies. They are so cute, and they look like baby mice. They haven't opened their eyes yet! I'm not keeping them though because Mom says she's selling them. The puppies whine a lot, but I can still sleep through that! It's Suzy's breath I can't stand. When the puppies open their eyes, I have to clean up their "messes." Only one pup whines for no reason. It goes "mmm, mmm, mmm and waa waa waa!" I try to calm it, but it keeps whining and carrying on. The puppies should be able to leave their mommy in about seven to eight more weeks. When they go I am going to miss them.

Stephanie Smith
Grade 4

How to Survive a Bad Day

Have you ever had a bad day when you think everything in life has gone wrong? Well, I have had a few of those! One of which, I will never forget, is getting a detention on my birthday and then getting punished at home. That was the worst. Well, I have a system of dealing with those rotten days and it works!

First, I pray and ask God for forgiveness and to make my punishment shorter. Secondly, I think about doing my favorite activities. For example, I imagine that I am outside playing soccer with my friends or on the computer playing video games. You must have a good imagination to try my system.

Once, my best friend had a bad day and I suggested that he try my method. He said, "I imagined I was in Trinidad with my cousin having fun." He told me the punishment went by fast. Although he missed his favorite show, he was happy because he remembered all the good times he had with his cousin. I felt proud that I was able to help my friend when he was down and out for the count.

In conclusion, I would like to share my system to help others through their problems. The only thing I can say about this method is that it's simple, but it works. I want others to realize that an active imagination can really go a long way.

Cody I. Israel
Grade 6

Native Americans!

Native Americans from around the world have been quite interesting people. I myself have been interested in these people because I have a little Native American in me!

Today scientists don't know how Native Americans came to the Americas, but of course they have theories. One theory is that they came over a land bridge between Asia and North America. This land bridge was called Beringia.

Beringia was a cool wetland where many animals lived. The humans hunted the biggest of the animals. Over the years, they followed these animals across Beringia and into North America. This is how we got the Paleo Indians (Paleo means *past*).

There were a lot of different Paleo tribes, like the Adena, the Hopewell, and the Mississippians. These tribes were also called mound builders. Mound builders built mounds that usually looked like animals or symbols.

There was also a tribe called the Aztecs. They ruled in Central Mexico for about 200 years. The beginning of their reign probably started around 1300. The Aztecs also had a capital called Tenochtitlán (Teno-sheet-lon). This is why Native Americans from around the world are quite interesting people, to me!

Kyla Hayes
Grade 5

My Unforgettable Birthday

All birthdays are fun and exciting, but some birthdays are just too good to forget! My tenth birthday was the birthday I would never forget. Many unforgettable things happened on this birthday!

First of all, I received a birthday present that I have dreamed for long time. It was a great DELL computer! This computer helped me type essays and prepare presentations. More interestingly, together with a web camera, it allows me to talk with and see my grandparents who live on the other side of the globe. On the night of my birthday, my cousins connected with me over the web and sang "Happy Birthday" to me! It was full of fun, and made this birthday a very special one.

I have always been fascinated in computer technology and how it impacts people's daily life. Although most of my relatives live overseas, now we can interact each other easily using a web camera. This gadget from my birthday gift really strengthened our family ties beyond imagination.

Being ten years old means a lot to me. Now my age goes up from one to double digits, which means more responsibilities and more challenges, such as learning how to give not just to be given, managing my time better, more focusing, and caring more for my family. I'm confident that I can accomplish all these goals!

With all these unique happenings on my tenth birthday, I'm sure that I will remember it for all of my life!

Alexander Lin
Grade 4

Do You Hear What I Hear?

Do you feel what I feel? Do you see what I see? Winter is my favorite season. I feel the cold, wet feeling of the winter snow. I see the thoughts inside my head. I hear the peaceful sound of Christmas carols when I close my eyes. Is this how you judge what your favorite season is?

The feeling of winter is different than any other season. Feel the cold snowball bouncing off your face. Notice the tingle in the tips of your fingers and toes. Feel the sting of warmth on your bare hands. Why is the feeling of winter so important?

You see a lot of things in winter. But can you explain what you see? When I see things in winter, I don't see them like I see snow on the ground. I see them in my heart and in my head. Is that how you see things in your favorite season?

Hear the sound of children playing. Hear the whistle of the wind behind your ear. Hear the peaceful sound of nothing. Do you hear these things in any other season?

When I think of winter as my favorite season I think of what I feel, see, and what I smell. The things I find are what makes winter my favorite season. Do you hear what I hear?

Laura Dockery
Grade 5

Tae-Kwon-Do

Tae-Kwon-Do is a physical and mental activity that focuses on self-defense and self-control. It involves progressing from no belt to white belt to yellow belt to orange belt to green belt all the way to 9th degree black belt. I am currently a 1st degree black belt.

There are 4 main curriculums for a 1st degree black belt: self defense, Il Soo Shi (one-step sparring), kicking combinations, and form (Poom Se Koryo and the Pagwe forms). The mental education that I am working on is the Black Belt Principles, which focuses on the treatment of others and yourself.

Here is an excerpt from the Black Belt Principles:
Virtue comes from humility
Wisdom comes from calm thinking
Disaster comes from greed
Wrongdoing comes from no patience
This explains how good things come from good, and bad things come from evil.

In self defense, we learn how to block an attack and flip the attacker. We also have to learn how to get flipped ourselves! We have learned how to easily avoid stabs from knives, escape headlocks, and pin people to the ground, too.

During earlier belts, we had to learn to count in Korean. We have also learned simple expressions. Since Tae-Kwon-Do originated in Korea, students must learn much Korean.

Finally, children have to learn the mental education and training. This consists of phrases that you learn in English and Korean that are things you can do to make the world a better place. For both your mind and body, it is a great thing to work at Tae-Kwon-Do!

Jake Stepansky
Grade 5

If Kids Ruled the World

If kids ruled the world no one would be who they are today because kids, would not go to school. I know because I am one. Right now for example, as I sit in class, I would prefer to go to water parks or amusement parks, like Six Flags in New Jersey. Wouldn't that be fun?

If kids ruled the world, school would be closed during the winter months. We would visit the toy stores instead and jump on trampolines, ride bikes, play games, and run around the store. Of course, this would drive the salespeople crazy, but they could not do anything because kids rule!

If kids ruled the world they would change their eating habits. Kids would not eat their daily requirements of fruits and vegetables. Junk food would be at the top of the list. Just imagine candy for breakfast, burgers and fries for lunch and pasta with butter for dinner. There would be unlimited sodas to wash their food down.

Now in my heart of hearts I am really glad that adults are still in charge. But for this moment it's enjoyable to think about the long lasting fun we would have, if kids ruled the world.

Minahil Khan
Grade 4

My Special Things

I have a lot of interesting things. My grandparents are very special to me, and my room is important to me. I'm thankful for my parents. I have many interests.

My grandparents are very special to me because they're very nice; they buy lots of things for me, even when I don't ask. They are very wealthy, but that's not why they're special. It's because they care about me. They also let us spend the night over at their house; they are the best you could ever have.

My room is important to me because I love my room. It is a pretty place. It has all the stuff I need in it. My room has private stuff in it. No one is allowed to go in my room; it is like a diary waiting for me to open it. My room is special; it does not need anyone else but me. I have my own room. I'm glad because my room is my castle. That's why my room is important to me.

I'm thankful for my parents because without my parents I would not be here right now. That's why I love them. They also feed me. They get me lots of things; if I did not have them, I don't know what I'd do. My parents have rules, but I'm still loving them always.

I have assorted interests that are important to me. I'm thankful to have them and all of my other special things.

Asia Whitsett
Grade 6

You Can Make a Difference

One child can make a difference for others in so many ways. My school, St. Ambrose, goes to Rest Haven. All those people get so happy. When we sing to them, some women start to cry. We make cards for whatever holiday it is. Once I gave cards to a woman, and she said to me, "Take some of my cards; you won't have enough for all the other people."

I had to tell her that we had plenty of cards; those were for her. She was so happy.

A kid in my class's mother had surgery. We got pieces of paper and we all made a huge paper quilt. She loved it.

My uncle had an operation on his rotator cuff. I prayed for him in school. The next day I made a card for him, and I had everyone in my class sign it. Then on Saturday I went to see how he was doing, and I gave him the card. He absolutely loved it. He must have looked at it for a good ten minutes.

A girl in my class's father was in Iraq, and a man from around our area was in Kuwait. We sent them both a package of Christmas cards.

It feels very good in your heart when you do something nice for someone. You can do anything as simple as a card, and it makes people feel good. You feel good too, just because you're one simple act made a difference.

Alexa Sangregorio
Grade 5

A Scary Vacation

One day my cousin Katie was in Erie, Pennsylvania. Her hotel was called "The El Patio." Katie and her friend Heather were playing on the grass, and all of a sudden these scary guys ran out of their car that was behind a bush. Katie and Heather were so scared that they screamed loudly, ran back to their hotel room, slammed the door and locked it. No one was home because the parents were out shopping, so Katie and Heather just relaxed and ate snacks. When the parents came back Katie and Heather told them all about it! So next time they were more careful when they were alone!

Julianna Kon
Grade 4

Berlin, Germany

Today people read and learn about Berlin. This story I hope will do the same. Berlin may be known as the place with the wall or the people that hated the Jews. There once was a wall that divided East and West Berlin. One side had freedom and the other side was Communist.

The war between the Jews and the Germans came to be known as World War II. It was a brutal battle, all the Germans, wanted to do was to kills the Jews; just for being Jewish. They finally put the war to rest and said it was not necessary. Soon afterwards they decided to tear down the wall.

Germany has several interesting facts compared to the United States. They use the metric system for everything. They also have a different form of money called the Euro. Germany is six hours ahead of us and their flag colors are black, and red, and yellow.

Shannon Bushway
Grade 5

Miss Marks

My favorite teacher is Miss Marks. She is my favorite teacher because she teaches one of my favorite subjects, science. Miss Marks is also my favorite teacher because she is very kind and always helps me on a question when I am confused. Another reason why she is my favorite teacher is because the curriculum she teaches is different from any other teacher. One of the reasons why I like her curriculum is because we mostly learn what she teaches the class with hands-on activities instead of reading out of the textbook, which I find very dull.

I also like Miss Marks because instead of working by ourselves, she divides our class into groups and we work together. I find this more fun and helpful because we all help each other understand what we are doing, and I find it more fun to work together. Another reason why I idolize her is because she will explain one question twelve different ways until you understand it. My parents also think she is a wonderful teacher and very thoughtful. Miss Marks is an excellent teacher, and of all the teachers I have had she clearly stands above the rest.

Rachael Reich
Grade 6

Self Portrait

Many people are interested in different kinds of art. I, myself, am no different. I enjoy visual arts like drawing, painting, and photography. I enjoy performing arts like acting and dancing. I enjoy culinary arts. I even like writing literature and poetry. Though, I mostly specialize in visual art.

I spend a lot of my time at a table or desk drawing. I have learned my own cartoon styles, my own way of coloring, and even my own characters. Though, what I usually draw is Japanese style of art, called Manga. Manga is really a graphic novel in Japan, but they use a certain style, so many people call that style Manga.

I usually draw Manga, but the actual style of art that got me started on drawing is Anthro, which is short for Anthropomorphic. Anthro is when the characters are more like animals with human features. I have created many characters who are drawn in this style, and people who have seen my work know me for it.

Ever since I learned how to pick up a crayon, I've been drawing. Art has been a great influence on my friends, my family, but mostly me. I'm glad I'm able to express myself in my art, in many forms and ways. I hope that someday in the future, when my art has really improved, that I am able to express my talents, and give people something nice to look at. I draw, therefore, I am.

Christin Bongiorni
Grade 6

A Family Christmas

Do you celebrate Christmas with your family? I do! The three ways my family celebrates Christmas are decorating, going to Mass on Christmas Eve, and eating together on Christmas Day.

The first thing my family does is decorate. We always decorate the Christmas tree, the dining room, playroom and outside. My brother and I always love putting up the Christmas tree but it's a big part for my parents because they always have to take all the decorating stuff out and put them back away after Christmas. My parents love my brother and I to make pictures and crafts.

One of my favorite parts of Christmas is the Christmas Mass! When I go with my family we always look at all the decorating all over the church. One of my favorite parts of Mass is the story of Jesus Christ. I always listen to what the priests say. Families should always go to Mass on Christmas or Christmas Eve.

After Mass my family goes to dinner. My family eats a lot of different kinds of foods. Does your family eat different kinds like turkey, ham, green beans, or peas? I love having dinner with my family!

The best part about having Christmas with your family is the decorating, going to Mass, and eating together on Christmas Day. So remember get your family together for Christmas.

Caitlin McNamara
Grade 6

The Christmas Tree

A few days before Christmas I was with my friend at my house. She was sleeping over at my house. My mom and I had already put the Christmas decorations up. We also had a Christmas tree up in the corner of the living room. I had ten cats at the time and some of them liked to climb in the tree. One in particular, his name was Chippy. The tree was like his hideout. It was hard to see Chippy when he was in the tree.

That night I woke up in the middle of the night because I heard a noise. Then I woke my best friend up because I saw something weird. When she saw what I was talking about she couldn't believe her eyes. We were looking at the Christmas tree. It looked like it had a face. A frightening, but familiar face. It looked like Oogey Boogey's face when he is smiling. Oogey Boogey is the Boogey man in the movie, *The Nightmare Before Christmas*. The tree also looked like it was moving. It was really Chippy in the tree all along. We ended up staying up all night. After that we practically laughed our brains out. We both had a lot of fun. I will always remember this time.

Virginia King
Grade 6

One Parent

My mom and dad were together when I was a baby. My dad and mom separated a couple of times and tried to work things out. My sisters Brooke, Ashley, and Amber were born during these times. One time my dad left and it was permanent. Dad left and moved to Florida. My mom and I were so sad. I had lost a father, and she had lost a husband.

When Dad left we had to move in with Grandpa, Grandma, and Aunt Dawn. My mom, my sisters, and I all had to sleep in one room. Eventually we moved into our own apartment. There was only two bedrooms. I had to share a room with my sister Brooke. My mom shared a room with my sisters Ashley and Amber. There was only one bathroom. Five girls and one bathroom…big problem. There was not a lot of room in this apartment.

My uncle and aunt moved out of their apartment and we moved in. The apartment we live in now is bigger, but I still have to share a room with Brooke. Ashley and Amber share a room and Mom has her own room. We now have our own bathroom and Mom has her own too. My mom works at McNeil and Company in the billing office to get us food, rent money, clothes, beds, and warmth. My mom works from 8:00 am to 5:00 pm at night for us. Mom also works overtime a lot.

We love that our dad comes to visit for Christmas and birthdays. We visit him too. We talk on the phone and we tell jokes. I feel sad when I think about my dad. I love him so much. My family and I really, really miss him so much.

Barbara Benjamin
Grade 4

"Yea" for My Survival

If I was stranded out in the wilderness I would use my money to start a fire with. I would do this because money is useless out in the wilderness, you can use it to start a fire with. I wouldn't do this if the bill was more than $50.

I would make a fire by ripping the bill into tiny little pieces, and then putting them into a tiny pile. Next I would take a rock of some sort and strike another hard wall of rock to make sparks. I would then try to get the sparks to catch the bill on fire. Last I would cup my hands over the little fire so the wind wouldn't blow it out, and then I would blow the fire very gently.

Actually, I really wouldn't care if the bill was more than $50 because my life is more valuable than money. This is what I would do if my life was at stake in the middle of nowhere.

Heather E. Whaley
Grade 6

My First Buzzer Beater

My first buzzer beater was awesome. But leading up to this was not so awesome. Before I hit that shot I was so scared. My teammates were giving me a hard time about not shooting at the buzzer. I was terrified to shoot at the buzzer.

The person that helped me was Broady Douglass. He was the one who helped me overcome my fear at the buzzer. He encouraged me when I was down. He was one person who believed I could do it. He thought I could make a buzzer beater. Then one day it was going to happen. Then one day my team and I were beating this team 41-35 in the 4th quarter. I was on the bench getting a drink of Powerade when my coach said, "Justin, get in there and shoot." They had come back to lead by one. There were two seconds left. Broady threw the ball to me, I dribbled to half court and let it fly. It didn't go in, but I overcame my fear at the buzzer.

Justin Bombard
Grade 5

Family

My family is one of the most important things to me. They make me laugh and pick me up when I am down. My family is truly the best.

Laugh, laugh, laugh! That is what my family makes me do all of the time. They are always there for me. They make a joke or act funny. If I do not feel healthy they nurse me back to health. If I'm having a problem at school, my family tells me ways to handle the problem. We always stick together.

My family has tons of effects on me. If they smile, I smile back at them. When my family makes me laugh my day goes a bundle more smoothly. If they are upset I share it with them and cheer them up. I am there for them just like they are there for me.

Family is one of the most important things in the world. I would not be able to live without them. My family is absolutely the best.

Dominique DeFilippis
Grade 5

Two Great People

Luisa and Sierra are my two great best friends, and all of what I'm writing is just about them.

First, I'll tell you about Luisa. She is so cool, and she doesn't really care what other people think. She just does what her heart tells her. She is originally from Columbia, but she also has lived in Margate, Ventnor, and Atlantic City. Now she is moving to E.H.T. I'm going to miss her so so much, but we'll still keep in touch and still play with each other a lot. What makes her such a great best friend is that she is the kind of person I can just kid around with and laugh with. We have had so many great times together, and having such a great best friend like Luisa makes me really appreciate and be thankful to have her by my side.

Now, I will tell you about Sierra. She is from Margate and goes back and forth to Massachusetts. She's a really great person because she's really different and like no on else I've ever met. I can't really explain except by saying she's down to earth and also a fun person to be around. That is why she is a great best friend. These are my two awesome best friends.

We have had so many great times together, and I can't thank them enough for always being there for me. Thanks a lot, Luisa and Sierra.

Samantha Cherry
Grade 6

The Unimaginable Incident

All I remember is a giant crash. My head went flying forward, then whipped back to the seat. My body was trembling as I heard two voices screaming. For a while I couldn't quite place the voices, until I realized it was me and my mom. My eyes were wide with terror. The truck hit the left side of our car where my brother was innocently sitting before. I was afraid to look…but I pulled myself together and forced myself to turn my head. He was beat up badly, but luckily he seemed all right. I didn't believe it possible because the car hit him directly. It seemed as if an angel had come down and placed a blanket of safety over him.

I held my brother tight and cradled him in my arms to make sure he knew he was safe. My mom was on her knees on the side of the car. She was afraid to check the back seat…she didn't know what she would discover. She jumped to her feet clutching us both tightly, making me feel secure. I tried to stay strong…for everybody's sake. Luckily, we all came out in one piece.

That day was one of the most traumatizing experiences of my life and made me stop and think how fragile and valuable life really is. I realized how lucky I am to be alive and how thankful I should be for all the wonderful things I am blessed with.

Rebecca Delman
Grade 6

A Special Gift

One gift that I want to give that I cannot wrap is a home to a homeless family. One reason I want to give a house to this homeless family is because when I go to the city with my parents every other weekend we see this family sleeping outside and they look sick and cold. My second reason is that I feel so sad sleeping in my nice warm house while I see hundreds of families sleeping on the streets. Also I will collect old clothes from my neighbors and give the homeless people new clothes, shoes, and other things. Week after week after week I went into the city and kept on seeing just this one family in particular. The one day I asked my parents if I could ask them a question. Then my mom said, "What is it honey?" and I said, "Can I ask the homeless family that lives near the newsstand for their names?" My mom said, "Ok but what for?" and then I said, "You'll see." Then when I got home I entered the homeless people's names into *America's Home Makeover*. I should get a response in one week they said. One week passed by and I got a call from *America's Home Makeover* and they said I won. Then I went to New York and told the family. They were so happy. Now they are living in a home in Vermont.

Timmy Stackpole
Grade 6

Grandmother

She filled everyone's hearts with unconditional love and laughter. She brought out the best in us, pushed us to pursue our dreams, and was the shoulder we could cry on. She was my grandmother.

We all looked up to her for different reasons because she was so strong and supportive. After all the things she'd been through she still managed to put a smile on our faces when all other hope was lost. When nobody else believed in me, she gave me the support and strength I needed to carry on. She had so many incredible experiences throughout her life. I would love to follow in her footsteps.

Like they always say, "Bad things happen to good people." Later in her life she was diagnosed with skin cancer and leukemia. For three years the battle for her life raged. Unfortunately she was not strong enough to overcome the battle and sadly took her last few breaths on January 27, 2006. We were all in shock even though we knew she was going to pass away. We were preparing ourselves for this terrible loss. I knew that when it actually happened it wouldn't be easy, but the hardest part was waiting and waiting…

My grandmother taught me to live life to the fullest and never live a day without meaning. I suppose that if I had never met my extraordinary grandmother I would be incomplete, not only in my mind, but also in my heart.

Nicolette Base
Grade 6

Swimming

Swimming — a way that I am active, a huge amount of fun! Swimming is moving my body and gliding in the water like a toothbrush that glides back and forth while the toothpaste tickles my teeth. The bristles move back and forth like the way I move my arms doing the front and back crawl.

When I enter a pool by diving from a diving board into the sky blue water, it is like my own miniature world of shimmering sapphire. It's so quiet that I can't hear anything. It's relaxing like a spa treatment. I get a manicure and pedicure with the jets from the pool thrusting on my back. To me it's a superlative sensation.

The chlorine water burns my eyes like the scorching fire on the brown, rugged logs that are in my fireplace. Then I explore the water with delight like an adventure around the world to London, Paris, and maybe even Tokyo. I love the moist, deep, azure water. It's so refreshing and feels so tranquil when I first place my foot into the top surface of the water.

Swimming makes me relaxed. It makes me feel great about myself. It takes all the pressure away which builds my confidence. It is fun, yet a way that I get in shape.

Michaela Young
Grade 6

Friends Are Special to Me

What are friends? Friends are someone I can always count on. They can always tell if I'm happy or sad. My friends always have my back. No matter what the case, friends always find a way out of it. If you need help friends just don't walk away, they run over and help you get through anything and everything. If you're scared, or want to do something, they will encourage you to do it. Never will they make you do something that you don't want to do. They would never hurt you or want you to get hurt. They would always want you to get better. If you need help, even if it's in the middle of the night, they'll rush over, give you a big hug and help you with whatever you need. Friends care and love you. There isn't anything they won't do to make you happy. I can always count on my friends!

Lauren Brungo
Grade 4

Winnie the Pooh

I have a stuffed animal and it is Winnie the Pooh. It was given to me when I was three, and I still have it. My godfather gave it to me on my birthday; I love it so much, I keep it on my bed just sitting there like royalty or something.

When I go home I put my books away, say, "Hi," and walk out. Every now and then I would call my godfather and say, "I still have your stuffed animal." He often responds with, "You better!"

I love my Winnie the Pooh. He is the best because he is short and stubby like me. I also love him because he is special, everything from my godfather is special. I love him.

Jocelyn McNamara
Grade 6

Acting: The Way It Affects Me

I am obsessed with the joy of being someone else. It's not that I don't like being myself; it's just enjoyable to get a sense of being someone else. Nothing else in the world matters.

As a performer, when I play a mean character the devil travels with me. Playing a pleasant role is easy and simple, while playing a mean role has so many more opportunities for the actor.

The applause makes me feel like I'm flying. Wouldn't you love to hear the roar of the crowd all standing up and clapping until their hands are sore?

I was Alice in the play *Alice in Wonderland.* In a dance number, I was supposed to spin and fall down. I fell down hard and I really hurt myself. I heard laughter. The laughter was growing like people in the audience were laughing hyenas. I looked around. I saw my wig on the ground. I put a look of shock on my face. I got even more compliments than usual! The audience loved it!

I also like when I first go to practice for a live performance. I audition for the part I want. It's so competitive, almost like sports without the athletic part.

The theater has a part for everyone: director, actor, stage crew, or audience. For me, it's acting. I will never stop. The theater has marked me for life!

Victoria Scaramucci
Grade 6

My Kindergarten Frogs

When I was in kindergarten we had class pets and they were frogs. They started out in eggs and then we watched them hatch. It was so cool, the little slimy tadpoles. They started to grow legs one day, we were so amazed.

We had to clean the tank almost every day, because they were so messy. When I came in the classroom every morning I would check on the frogs. As soon as they started to get arms we were just so excited.

They were African Claw frogs. They lived in the water. After about a week went by the frogs were full grown. Their color is a grayish, brownish, greenish.

They are so awesome. At the end of the year anybody in our class could take as many frogs as they wanted. I took home two frogs. I had a female and a male. The female is bigger than the male, I think it is weird.

My two frogs started to mate. When I washed their tank all the eggs would go down the drain, it was so sad. The two frogs got so big we had to get another tank. We had to separate the two frogs so they wouldn't mate anymore.

One day they got sooo big we had to put them in my kiddy pool. I love my frogs, but I don't have them anymore. Something must have eaten them. I named the male Rocket and the female Star. I loved my frogs.

Justina Babcock
Grade 4

Disaster Hits New Orleans

On August twenty-ninth in the year of 2005 a natural disaster hit New Orleans — HURRICANE KATRINA. Hurricane Katrina has killed thousands. It has also injured many. Hurricane Katrina ended September third, but flooding still goes on.

The people down in New Orleans are in desperate need of a home because the homes they lived in are now destroyed. Some people down in New Orleans have to sit by their family that may be dead, and the body must be covered up. The children have gotten very sick from Hurricane Katrina because they had to live on the streets. Not only that, some kids have even been separated from their family. Those poor children.

Some homes have been wiped out by Katrina's powerful winds. People that have no place to live have been taken to alternate places to live. They have been taken to places like baseball stadiums, football stadiums, and hospitals. Some people had decided to ride out Katrina's storm. People lived and people died. The houses they had before are now nothing but a pile of rubble.

As you can see, Hurricane Katrina was one of the most deadly hurricanes to ever hit the United States. It was a category four hurricane. Hurricane Katrina was a very devastating hurricane. They are planning on rebuilding New Orleans. Hurricane Katrina is a natural tragedy of the United States.

Keirsey Hackenberg
Grade 6

Epiphone SG

Do you play the guitar? I do. I play an Epiphone SG. Playing the guitar is beneficial because of the great songs, the awesome sounds, and the pure fun of playing.

One of the best parts of playing guitar is the great songs! There are all kinds of songs from great artists like Led Zeppelin, Giant, Queen, The Who, Rush, and all kinds of others. My favorite song is New World Man by Rush, and my favorite song to play is Spirit of Radio also by Rush.

The first concert I ever went to was December 18th to see the Trans Siberian Orchestra or TSO. They were awesome! We were there for three hours, but it was worth it.

Another great part is the awesome sounds. There are so many sounds! There's regular sounds, to distortion, to different pedals. There's wah wah pedals, to different distortion pedals, and all kinds. The sounds are one of the best parts of the guitar. The best part is the look. My SG is red with chrome plated hummbuckers, silver plated knobs, a cream toggle switch, down to every piece in particular, it looks great.

The best part of playing the guitar is the pure fun. You get so much fun out of all the bends, slides, power chords, and solos. I think power chords are the best.

I think the best part of playing the guitar is, the songs, the awesome sounds, and the pure fun. Learn to play the guitar.

Mike Maloy
Grade 6

Catastrophes — Horrible Things that Strike Our World

Catastrophes are horrible. They kill lots of people but I have been wondering, "What causes catastrophes to happen?" There are also many other questions I have about catastrophes. My friends told me about their experiences with catastrophes. All they mostly say is that it was awful! They were in a car accident. It was only a man-made catastrophe but it still caused a lot of damage. In the next few paragraphs, I will tell you more about catastrophes.

Catastrophes are bad but I think there is also a good end to catastrophes. I think there is a good end because people still survive catastrophes. A natural catastrophe includes volcano eruptions. After volcano eruptions, new flowers grow. That is considered good. Did you know that from 2004 to 2005, 13 hurricanes hit the USA and 10 typhoons hit Japan? Oh yeah, I almost forgot to include the tsunami that happened in India. Can you believe all those catastrophes? But then again, lots of people still survived all those catastrophes and lived to tell the tale.

There are two kinds of catastrophes. One kind is a natural catastrophe and the other kind is a man-made catastrophe. Natural catastrophes are caused by nature. Some natural catastrophes include typhoons, hurricanes, tornadoes, hurricanes, etc. Man-made catastrophes are catastrophes that humans make. Man-made catastrophes include car accidents, plane crashes, fires, structure failures, etc. This is all about catastrophes.

Yaxin Liu
Grade 5

Transportation: A Brief Timeline of Inventions in America

Through the years, inventions of modes of transportation have grown to provide travel on land, the sea and in the air.

In 1829, George Stephenson invented the first steam engine named Rocket which reached a speed of 38 mph. This speed was unknown until then. In 1903, the Wright brothers' first plane flew 120 feet in twelve seconds at Kitty Hawk, North Carolina. Later, in 1908, Henry Ford's Model T car was released into the market. By 1927, about 15 million Model T cars were sold. Thirty-one years later, in 1939, the Heinkel He 178 jet airplane was invented by Hans Von Ohain and it flew 470 mph. In 1944, aircraft carriers were a great way to store aircraft overseas. 1950 was the year the cable-car became a historical part of San Francisco. Its main duty was to take people up the many hills in that city. In 1957 the Cadillac, otherwise known today as a "Caddy," was a car that was meant to show the owner's personality. They were gas-guzzlers but were created in a time when gas was cheap.

In the years following the introduction of the inventions mentioned, many different types of vehicles have been created and all have a very important influence on our history. Updated models of each type of transportation are designed every year.

Derek King
Grade 4

The Speedy Cheetah vs the Olympic Gold Medalist Michael Johnson

The animal and human I am comparing and contrasting are the cheetah and the one and only Michael Johnson. The cheetah and Johnson have many reasons how they are alike. There are a lot of reasons how they are different. First I'll name all the reasons how Johnson and the cheetah are different.

The first reason is that a cheetah is an animal and Michael Johnson is human. Michael Johnson runs on two legs. The cheetah runs on four legs. Cheetahs have fur. Humans only have skin. Cheetahs can run up to 65 miles per hour. Michael Johnson was only able to run up to 23 miles per hour. I'm pretty sure Johnson lives in a house. Cheetahs live in a cave or outside.

The first reason how they are the same is that they are both mammals. Another reason is that they both are fast runners. Michael Johnson and the cheetah each hold world records. Johnson holds the record for the fastest 200 meter sprint in Olympic history. The cheetah holds the record for being the fastest land mammal.

Those are all the reasons how the cheetah and Michael Johnson are alike and different. I gave you many reasons for why they are alike and why they are different. If they were in a race I would have to say that the cheetah would win.

Levi Seifert
Grade 6

My First Days at Parkville Middle School and Center of Technology

My first days at Parkville Middle School were very easy, for one because I had a map to lead me around the school. At the same time it was difficult because I was not used to seeing that many people. When I got to Mod9 the class split up; I had applied engineering in Room 113 with Mr. Kopp where we learned about the basic rules and regulations. The next day I went to violin practice in Room 100, the Dungeon, with Ms. Hoyt. I had gotten wrong directions, instead of going downstairs I went up. Then I got scared because there was 1 door then 2 sets of stairs, but there were Post-it notes on the floor to guide me. Then I saw a sign that said 'Room 100' then I went down and got there — late.

Miebaka Kalama
Grade 6

Blizzard of 2005

"The Blizzard of 2005" was coming and everybody was at the market buying things that they needed such as peanut butter, bread, etc. There were people at the hardware store buying shovels and salt. The gas station was packed with cars and trucks filling up their vehicles with gas and oil.

It was snowing hard and it was cold with gusty winds. When there was about a half inch of snow on the ground I got ready. I put all of my snow gear on and then I went to fill up my salt spreader with salt, and gassed up my snow blowers. I started plowing streets, sidewalks, driveways, and parking lots. I was really busy because I have my own company Justin's Landscaping and Construction. I plowed and shoveled for a long time but it was worth it.

It snowed so much that school was canceled for a week. That week I had a lot of fun but we had to make it up at the end of the year.

Justin Braga
Grade 6

Collies vs Shelties

The Sheltie vs the Collie. They are both great dogs. They also have differences and similarities. The breeds are different. They both like people. There are other differences and similarities too.

Both of the dogs are very social. They are also great family pets. Both dogs are loving too. They can look alike too. They also don't like to be chained up or to be in kennels.

Collies are smaller sized dogs. Shelties are medium sized dogs. Collies and Shelties look alike but they are two different breeds. Their fur color varies too. They can be brown, black, or white. They can have long or short legs. They can also have long or short coats.

Collies and Shelties are different and the same. They love people and love to please. They are family dogs. They are different and the same.

Michelle Bartha
Grade 6

Which One Would You Pick?

Flute, clarinet, saxophone, violin, drums, which one would you play? I think it's important for children to play an instrument.

My first reason is if you practice at it you could be a famous player one day. You can play on a stage, travel, or give autographs like Wynton Marsalis.

My second reason is right after a performance with your instrument your parents will be very proud of you. It makes you feel so good when you play.

Finally, if you play an instrument you will score higher on tests. For example N.J. asks for math tests. The quarter notes and 8th will help you with fractions. Also, keeping the beat is mathematical. So go to a concert, listen to the instruments, and pick one out.

Valenza Stearns
Grade 4

Eagles!

Eagles are our state animal. There are 59 different eagles in the world. Eagles are feathery animals. Antarctica is the only place that does not have eagles on the continent. Only two out of 59 types of eagles live in our continent.

The eagle is a strong bird. Baby eagles are called eaglets. An eagle can grow up to 6-7.5 feet. The Golden Eagle is more timid and harder to approach than the Bald Eagle. An eagle's talons grip so well that it is in no danger of falling off its perch even when it sleeps. Golden Eagles soar higher and more often than Bald Eagles do. At 10 weeks of age young eagles bravely flap their wings while balancing on the nest's edge. The Bald Eagle is probably North America's most admired bird. The Golden Eagle is a native of Europe, Asia and North America. It lives mainly in the mountainous regions of the west. The Bald Eagle has approximately 7000 feathers to keep clean and tidy. That takes a lot of preening!

This young Bald Eagle's bill will remain black until it is about 3 years old at which time it will turn into a beautiful golden corn color. The skeleton of an eagle is very light, weighting just over 270 grams (half a pound.) The Bald Eagle's intensity makes it look more fierce than it really is. Believe it or not an eagle's eye is larger than yours! An experienced fishing party, an eagle nest could well outlast the original owner's. It may then be taken over by a different pair of eagles. Finding food for himself and his mate keeps this father to be very, very busy.

Kyle Stem
Grade 4

Hidden History

The past, present, and future are all mysteries to us. But the past is always more confusing than the present or future. When I get older I plan on being a historian. A historian is someone who tries to learn about the past.

All my life my favorite subject has been social studies. I love to discover things that nobody else knows about. Then after my discovery I would show everyone and I would feel so proud, and that feeling I loved. I don't just want that feeling in my memories, I want it to be with me all the time. I want to share my discoveries with everyone.

Historians aren't your average person driving to a same old day at work, they go day to day where every day is different. Say Monday they could be on the computer doing research, but the next day they could be going on an adventure through the Sahara Desert. Nobody knows what's going to happen next.

I want to become a historian, not only to learn about the past, but I want to unlock hidden secrets of the future. I also want to show everyone my discoveries so they get the same feeling I do.

Devin Foster
Grade 5

Travis Barker

Travis Landon Barker, born November 14, 1975 in Fontana, California is an amazing drummer, in my opinion. He has played with so many bands, such as Boxcar Racer, Plus 44, The Aquabats, The Transplants, and my favorite band of all time, Blink-182. About 3 years ago, I went to one of his shows in Buffalo, and I saw one of his drum solos. He was about 20 feet away from me. It blew my mind at how fast-paced his drumming was.

Travis also has a show on MTV, called Meet the Barkers. It's a show about his life pretty much, there isn't a script or anything, they just film what Travis does and everything. The other people on the show are his wife, Shanna, and his 2 kids, Landon and Atiana.

Another very interesting thing about Travis is his tattoos. He has over 250 tattoos inked onto his body, and just about every one has a story/meaning behind it.

Travis started playing drums when he was 4 years old. His drum teacher taught more jazz music. Travis joined the drum corps for quite a while, then he decided to pass up jazz drumming and move on to rock drumming. Most of his experience came from playing with earlier bands, like The Suicide Machines, The Aquabats, and Feeble.

Also, Travis has accomplished so many things. He made his own shoe with DC Shoes called the Alias Remix, and has played live on TV many times, such as on the Conan O'Brian show. Travis also has his very own clothing company, called Famous Stars and Straps.

Overall, I think Travis Barker is truly amazing and will definitely go down in history along with other great rock drummers such as Tre Cool, Carmine Appice, Keith Moon, and Tommy Lee.

Cody Smith
Grade 6

The Clear Blue Water

I peered nervously into the clear blue water. My stomach churned wildly at the thought of what I was about to do. I stepped onto the white stairs one trembling leg after the other. I stopped and thought, what's going to happen? I kept going. My feet were like two heavy stones with gum on the bottom. My warm suit started to become like a leech clinging to my body. I was very determined. I was half way there. Just a few more frightening seconds and it would happen. No turning back now.

The water seemed as cold as the North Pole. I said one thing, in one slow breath. "I can do this." I reached like a giraffe reaching for leaves in trees. I kicked off as hard as I could. I had no idea what was going to happen next. My heart felt like a balloon about to pop. Finally I noticed, I was swimming!

I couldn't believe it! I had swum! I bobbed out of the water, as my hair matted down. I had a grin from ear to ear spread across my face. I felt like I was going to burst with excitement. I had finally learned how to swim.

Brennan Lynch
Grade 5

My Traditions

My family does not celebrate Halloween. But the traditions we do are Thanksgiving and Christmas. What my family does for Thanksgiving is every year we go to my aunt's and uncle's house in New Jersey. When we get there we go and settle down, then the next day it is Thanksgiving and my aunt and uncle invite people over and we have a Thanksgiving party or we have a Thanksgiving dinner. This Thanksgiving I'm hoping I will go to my cousin's house in North Carolina. This is one of the traditions my family does.

Another tradition my family does is Christmas and what we do is my family stays at my house and this time people come from out of state to my family and we exchange presents and later on we go to a Christmas party. That is what my traditions are.

Ogechi Nwaigwe
Grade 6

Harriet Tubman (1819-1913)

Harriet Tubman was born in 1819, in Dorchester County, Maryland. Before Tubman was married her name was Araminta Ross. Ross was born in times of slavery. Her harsh childhood was spent as a slave. She would get whipped for little or big mistakes. At the age of six, her master, Edward Brodas, let her work for a couple. Her first job was to weave. She was careless at that job and was beaten up harshly. Her second job was to check on muskrat traps. Ross fell sick during this job and was sent back to Brodas.

In 1844, at the age of 25, she was married to John Tubman. Tubman knew that since her and John were slaves, one day they may be split apart. Tubman started to think about escaping to the north. She told John to escape with her. John said no, and told her if she tried to escape he would tell their master. John was serious, but that didn't stop Tubman.

In 1849, she left her husband and escaped to Philadelphia. Many whites helped Tubman get to Philadelphia. Over there, slavery was illegal. Tubman got a job in Philadelphia. She saved her salary to help slaves escape. She also started to work at the Underground Railroad.

The Underground Railroad was a secret way for slaves to escape to the north. Tubman helped many slaves. She made more than 18 trips and helped over 300 slaves. She helped her parents escape. She went to free her husband, but John had married someone else and refused to go up north. Tubman was a hero.

On March 10, 1913, Tubman passed away. Tubman is still a hero today. She left us with many memories. We hope that today we still have people like Harriet Tubman who care for others.

Samia Sheikh
Grade 5

My Trip to Universal Studios

When I went to Florida, I had an awesome time! We went to visit my grandma and grandpa. While we were there, we went to Universal Studios (it's an amusement park). We woke up at 5 a.m. because Orlando was a long way from where we were. When we got there, our first ride was called SpiderMan, it was a really long line. Our next ride was a dinosaur ride, it's one of my favorite rides. You go in a raft on a river (it's sort of like a tour) but then you heard, "Danger." We made a sharp turn, and there was a humongous dinosaur. It looked like it was about to eat us. I thought it was a T-Rex! Soon, we started getting closer and closer, but then we were right by its mouth. Then we slid right between its legs. After that, my sister and my dad went on The Hulk! I would have went on, but I was not tall enough. After my sister and my dad went on it twice, my sister and I went on a ride called Doctor Doom that was one of the fastest rides ever! Then my next ride was brand new, when you first go in there it's really dark, and it goes so fast it feels like you are going upside down. That ride was so fast that they made sure you didn't bring anything on it. I had an awesome time at Universal Studios!

Meagan Costello
Grade 4

My Grandma

On December 8, 2005, at 2:04 a.m. my phone rang. My mom picked up. The phone call was very short. I got scared because nobody ever calls that late. I started to cry in my room because at 10:00 p.m. that night St. Charles called and said your grandma stopped breathing and started again. I knew that this was the call.

The phone call that made my grandma disappear. All I heard was crying sounds and my brother crying and yelling "my grandma" over and over. I knew this was it. But, I was too heartbroken to find out if it was true. So, I went back to sleep.

In the morning I woke up. My mom and dad didn't go to work. I went in and laid on my mom and dad's bed. My daddy said, "Grandma is with the angels now." It hit me, then I broke.

My grandma is an extraordinary woman. She touched everyone's life. If you talked to my grandma more than a few seconds, you automatically loved her. At my grandma's funeral all her grandchildren had to write a speech. That moment I froze and no words came out. I ran out crying. I didn't want to go back in. But, I knew my grandma would tell me to and to wipe my tears away. So that's what I did. My grandma will never be forgotten! Her lessons will be brought down by generations by generations. Her lessons will guide me through life forever.

Christina Martinez
Grade 6

My Favorite Buffalo Sabre

Who is the best Buffalo Sabre ever? Daniel Briere is my favorite Buffalo Sabre. He is the captain of the Buffalo Sabres. He is also a great leader of the team. He not only plays great hockey, but he's a caring person. He visits sick kids at hospitals to make them feel better. This report will discuss his childhood, career, stats, team, and his injury.

During his childhood Briere played a lot of hockey. He was born in Gatineau, Quebec on October 6, 1977. Even when he was a young boy, he dreamed of being a professional hockey player.

During his career he first played for the Phoenix Coyotes. Then, in the 2004 NHL draft he was selected by the Buffalo Sabres. Some of his teammates are J.P. Dumont, Tim Connoly, Chris Drury, and Adam Mair. They like Briere as their captain.

In this season so far, he has 14 assists, and 23 points. He's ranked 7th in the NHL. He was a first round draft in 1996 by the Phoenix Coyotes hockey team. His coach is Lindy Ruff, a former Buffalo Sabre. Briere has signed a four year contract to play at the center position.

On December 17, 2005, Briere got a sport's hernia. When he got hurt the fans were very disappointed and sad. I was looking forward to watching him play more hockey. He's the best!

Daniel Briere is my favorite hockey player. He's a super player and a great captain. I was lucky to meet him with my dad 3 weeks ago. He signed my hockey jersey, "To Alex thanks for your support." I was very happy to meet him. This is why he's an awesome leader and captain for the Sabres. He really cares about kids and people. I hope he never gets traded!

Alexander Kovacs
Grade 4

Watching Movies

Everyone loves to watch movies. There are so many ways to watch movies. Like watching it on television, DVD, on tapes, on different kinds of portable game systems, and going to the theater. Many people like to go to the theater so they can see the latest movies. Some people just wait until it comes on DVD or tape because everyone is different.

My mom told me that years ago they used projectors on the wall and someone would have to turn the film. A lot has changed since then. Now it is automatic. Everyone likes to watch it on the modern things.

My family makes movie watching a big thing on the holidays. Most of my family likes to see action, comedy, and scary movies. That reminds me that there are different kinds of movies. I think most people like every kind of movie I named. I love to watch comedy and action movies.

See, there are many ways to see movies. There are different kinds of movies. There are different ways to watch movies. Whoever doesn't watch movies they don't know what they're missing.

Rashard Rae
Grade 6

Softball…It's a Girl Sport

My favorite sport is softball. I've played softball for two years. That's not a lot, but I like this sport, and I play a good game.

When I started playing, I wasn't good, but I got better the more I practiced. I prefer shortstop and pitching because I can always get the ball. When I'm up to bat, I always get nervous, but I keep my eye on the ball and try my best. When I throw the ball, I throw it as hard as I can.

My last team was the Orioles. Our colors were light blue and white. We usually did a good job at the games. Our team always tried our best; we didn't care if we lost, we just played the game and had fun. We even had a snack after every game! I'm pretty sure we won half of all the games we played.

I got really mad one day because the coach said that I could pitch, but I never did in ANY game I ever played for the Orioles. When I played shortstop, I would always get so nervous because the ball always came over to my position. One time when I was playing shortstop, the ball went under my legs. It was really embarrassing, but I got over my embarrassment; everybody makes mistakes, even embarrassing ones.

I've played softball for two great years, and I look forward to many more fun times on the diamond.

Kristen Tann
Grade 5

My Brother

For my essay I chose to write about my brother. I chose to write about him because, he means the world to me.

My brother's name is Cody. He is seventeen. Cody is good at so many things that it is sometimes too hard to count. Cody is very athletic. He plays a lot of sports like, baseball, basketball, football, and volleyball.

In baseball his best positions are pitcher and first baseman. Sometimes when he's playing first base he might do the splits in order to get the runner out. I love it when he does that! He is a really good pitcher too.

My brother is also talented. When he was in the sixth grade he and a couple of his friends were in the talent show singing a song called, "All the Small Things" by Blink 182.

Cody likes to play video games. He's really into the game called, Madden. I think he really likes it!

My brother has a job working at Ruby Tuesday's. At Ruby Tuesday's Cody works the To-Go area.

Cody is nice to mostly everyone around him. He really loves his family and his girlfriend, Missy. He also really cares about his cat, Dutchess.

I know my brother is a really great person and I really do love him.

McKenna Sheridan
Grade 6

My Vacation in Aruba

My family and I all went to Aruba by plane. During our flight the movie *Jersey Girl* was on. You were given headphones so the sound of the movie was not disturbing the people who did not want to watch it. My brother slept through some of the movie. They gave you a little tray with food on it.

When we got there we rode a bus to our condo. The condo was Aruba Beach Club. There we got in our room and picked where we wanted to sleep.

I loved going to the pool and going to the beach. The water at the beach was a teal color and the sand was white. At the beach I went swimming and a high wave came and I fell on sharp shells!!! It really hurt, so because of that I liked swimming in the pool more.

While we were there I met someone named Nikita; she was really nice and funny. She introduced me to other people too. We had a lot of fun together.

I joined an activity where you stay in a room for a while and play games and activities. There I met many friends that I hope to see again. They had fun parties and movies.

In Aruba I got my hair braided, with beads at the bottom. When they were doing my hair it was very knotted and tangled from going in the pool, so it was hard.

I had a really good time in Aruba and a hard time saying goodbye, but I was happy to be home.

Grace Eskew
Grade 4

My Fear

I have many fears. One is riding on the Boomerang at the Great Escape. I had no clue how to overcome my fear. Every time I went to the Great Escape I got so scared seeing the roller coaster and hearing the sounds of the roller coaster. When it went up around the loop and back around the loop it scared me. I could hear people scream. It made me even more frightened.

My biggest fear is riding the Boomerang, it's the biggest roller coaster at the Great Escape. My brother is always telling me to go on it, it's not scary, I still didn't believe him. I was thinking of going on it, but I was so terrified. My head hurt so bad I felt light headed. My whole body was shaking, I could not stay in a still motion.

So, I finally decided to go on the Boomerang. I sat in the middle. My brother wanted to sit in the front. I got so scared and said, "No, you are sitting in the middle with me." He said, "Fine, if you are so scared, I will sit next to you." I was happy that my brother was sitting next to me. At least this way I didn't feel as scared.

After I went on the Boomerang, I felt proud and a lot better. I was so happy I overcame my fear. I learned roller coasters are not that scary. There are some things I can trust my brother on, too. He talked me into going on the Boomerang. He told me it wasn't scary. I called him a liar, but he was right, it's not scary. That's my biggest fear.

Alexandra Leon
Grade 5

Computer Games

The pros of computer games are that they help people with eye-hand coordination, which can really help in the future if you work with your hands. Also they are fun and relaxing. Another benefit is the variety of types on the market so you will never get bored. Lastly; having ratings informs parents so they will know what you should or shouldn't play.

The cons of computer games are that it eats up time because it is very addictive. Kids have no time for reading, writing or homework. One major problem with computer games is that if you play too much you could damage your vision. Sometimes parents don't care about the ratings and if it is rated M for mature and the kid is younger than 18, he/she can get very violent.

My two favorite computer games are Diablo 2 and Warcraft 3. Although it is a violent game it is very competitive and fun. For me the game can be talked about in school so school can be fun to go to which can decrease stress and increase happiness.

Brandon Chu
Grade 6

Cinnamon

I'm going to tell you how I got my dog Cinnamon.

One day I said to my mom, "Can we get a dog?" She said, "Sure." Next, I went to search for a dog online. In a few minutes, we found a playful dog called a viszla. A viszla is like a weimaraner, but a little shorter.

A few days later, we drove to Wichita, Kansas to get a viszla. When we got there, the viszlas were huge. On our way home, Cinnamon, our new dog, slept on my lap instead of the box we bought her because it was too small! It took us eleven hours to get home, but finally Cinnamon was home.

Jacob Rominger
Grade 4

A Little Addition, a Lot of Change

Before my baby brother was born, my life was normal. It was the same old thing, day after day. My life revolved around homework and piano during the week, and video games and basketball on the weekends. Life became boring and uneventful. I wanted a change.

Then one night, my wish was granted. A new noise came into my life, one I was anxiously waiting for, but not prepared for. My baby brother was born. The fun began, or so I thought. There was a lot of responsibility, but I didn't care. I have been able to play, read books, and communicate in a new language. I have learned to smile in a different way, and my heart has grown a little bigger to accommodate the additional chaos. By playing with my little brother, it has reminded me of my earlier childhood and it makes me smile.

So overall, the good outweighs the bad, sometimes. Besides the smelly diapers, crying, late nights, responsibility, and extra chores, it has been a lot of fun. Sometimes he even smiles at me! "Ugh, he's crying again!"

Michael Cislo
Grade 6

The Gift of Peace

If I had to give a gift to anyone in the family it would be to my mom. I would give her the gift of peace. This gift is a very important gift. She would definitely love it. The house would be quiet and she could relax.

My siblings and I fight a lot, too much. It is so much that it gets aggravating. If there was no fighting the house would be quiet and my mom would not be aggravated. Life would be much easier. My mom would have time to garden, work on P.T.A. things and read while everyone else would be quiet and not disturb her. She could sit down and watch TV or do anything else that she desires to do. I think she would just be relieved with the gift of peace. Everyone else would be relieved too, but she would be the most. My mom would not have to give punishments that my siblings and I don't like and we wouldn't mind being together as one happy family. This gift would be the best gift for my mom.

The gift of peace would be a great gift for anyone, but my mom deserves it. If there was no fighting my mom could have a good time and enjoy herself. If I did give a gift to anyone in my family that you cannot touch it would be the gift of peace and it would be to my mom.

Andréa Bourgal
Grade 6

Football: The Game of Many Talents

In my opinion, football is the most superb sport on Earth. It takes raw talent and excellent teamwork to even stand a slim chance of winning. Luck is something seen vaguely in football, unlike any other game or sport.

In the wonderful sport of football, if one player makes a mistake, that play will mean zilch. In football, there are many positions. In offense, there's the quarterback, the halfback, the fullback, a few wide receivers, tight ends (those two both depend on which play it is), and the offensive line. In defense, there's the linebacker, safeties, and the D line.

One of my favorite plays is the lateral (mostly at the end of the game, if the team is losing). Also the PA option featured in Madden '06. I like that because it throws off the defensive backs. My favorite play is the 24 blast because I'm the running back!

On and off the field, sportsmanship is wicked important. For instance, Terrell Owens, a former wide receiver for the Philadelphia Eagles, said some bad things about his teammates and, more importantly, his coach. In other words, he was suspended from the team and later was deactivated from the team.

That's all about my favorite sport of football. All teams (especially pros) use teamwork to help win games. Maybe even someday I bet teamwork guides a lucky team to the Super Bowl!!

Nate French
Grade 5

If I Met Colin Mochrie

I am a huge fan of Colin Mochrie from "*Whose Line is it Anyway?*" If I could have an interview with him, it would be awesome. I would first ask him why he doesn't just buy hair growth pills since he's bald. Then, I would ask him where he went to college. He must've gotten funny somewhere. My last question would be how he got a show on "*Whose Line.*"

He is really funny. He is a bad singer, so in songs he just blurts out any random word that pops in his head. He is really good at translating the gibberish foreign languages into funny sentences.

Talking to him would change my life…a little. It would definitely answer most of my questions about "*Whose Line*" and Colin himself. It would also probably give me a few more laughs in life…maybe. I would like to perform with him one day.

Ben Thieberger
Grade 6

Madison

I love my dog Madison. She is an English Setter, and I call her Maddy for short. We got her from one of my mom's friends. We weren't expecting her to be so big, but we still love her. Whenever we play, she acts like a puppy. Whenever you walk out of the door, she crouches down and jumps up.

One day my dad put a pile of leaves behind our house and Maddy jumped into them. Then we played in the leaves all day and we had a great time. I really like it when I get to talk to her and tell her about my day. I also like it when we investigate the things we hear. At the end of the day, we both snuggle up on a rug and watch TV. She also keeps me warm on cold days. Those are the reasons I love my dog.

Troy Shelton
Grade 5

Respect for My Parents

The one thing I want to give my parents more than anything in the world, which I cannot wrap, is respect. I choose respect because sometimes I do not give respect to my parents. I ignore my parents at times, as well as answer back. Sometimes I do not do things right away as I am told to do I wait until I am asked many times. I can give them respect by being a good listener. I can also do things I am told to do right away instead of being told several times. My parents would like it if I do things without being told, like put my clothes away and cleaning up after I have a snack.

When I leave a drink downstairs and it's not empty my parents yell at me because I did not bring it upstairs and put it into the refrigerator. I can be more thoughtful and nice to my sister and stop being a pest to her. When we go out my parents always tell me to hold the door open for other people and say please and thank you and to be thoughtful to others and not just think of myself. I would be respecting my parents if I did do all these things and that would make them very happy.

Paul Rescigno
Grade 6

Hawaii and Alaska

Alaska and Hawaii are two different states. In ways they are alike and in ways they are not. In the rest of this writing, I will compare and contrast them both.

Both Alaska and Hawaii are states in the United States of America. Being the forty-ninth and fiftieth states of this country they both became a state in 1959. Another thing they have in common is they both are separated from what is called the mainland. The mainland is the other connecting forty-eight states of the U.S.

Alaska's climate is entirely different from Hawaii's. Alaska gets snow and low temperatures while Hawaii is normally in the seventies all year round. Hawaii also is a group of islands and Alaska is connected to Canada. The leading exports of Hawaii are pineapple and sugarcane. Alaska's leading export is seafood.

In conclusion, Alaska and Hawaii are two different places that have some things in common. Whether you like skiing down freshly snow covered mountains or laying on the beach all day, both places can be paradise.

Amanda Gannon
Grade 6

Scary Storm Surrounding Scranton

A few weeks ago, my father and I decided to take a trip upstate. Although the season had not treated us with snow in the city, there was plenty of it on our way to visit my grandparents. We took our usual way through the Poconos since mom got sick from the winding mountainous roads. We had a great start and the trip was scenic as always until I shouted, "Oh no!" Dad asked what was the matter and then he could see as we entered into what I thought was the twilight zone. The weather was clear and sunny one minute and blizzard-like the next. We couldn't see a thing except the huge snowflakes falling. It lasted for what seemed like forever so we decided to talk. I could tell Dad was trying to make me feel comfortable, but I knew he had trouble seeing the road. I suggested that we pull over and stay in a motel for a while, but Dad knew something I didn't. Just as he said that, I couldn't believe my eyes. The snow stopped, just like that! Dad said it's always like that upstate; sunny in one state and snowing blankets in the next.

We have made many trips upstate and mom never likes to travel in the winter because she knows how weird the weather is. She always tells us the story of when we were little. It was Easter and we drove right into a snowstorm in Binghamton. She said that day it took us seven hours to get home and swore she saw angels guiding us to safety. So, we never travel upstate in the winter. We eventually made it to our destination safe and sound and though the trip was scary, I knew the angels were still with us.

Frankie Catarisano
Grade 6

My Hero

My hero is my grandpa because he fought in the army. He was a medic there. Whenever he came home we would spend time together. We would eat pumpkin pie and he would take me fishing. When he died I was so sad I could not go fishing anymore. He died of smoking. I begged him to stop but he said, "I will try." But he never did.

I miss him really bad. His name was Ralph. When he retired from the army he worked at a school. When I was 4 he took me to Amsterdam on a train. My grandfather drove his car. We went back in the car and it took us at least an hour and a half.

I think 2 years before he died he showed me all his army stuff. It is cool. He showed me his badges and his uniform. He had tons and tons of badges. His uniform had 20 badges on it. It was a dark green. I always wanted to be in the army ever since he showed me all of his stuff.

When he died, he left all of his stuff to me. I miss him but I still have my grandma. He inspired me because he was a good man and he fought for our country with honor.

Matt Colangelo
Grade 6

Muslims in America

I am a Muslim girl who lives in America. It is a challenge being Muslim in America.

First of all you have to wear your scarf at a certain age. Some people look at you because you have your scarf on. When you attend a public school, you have off days for Christmas and Thanksgiving, but not for Eid-ul-adha and Eid-ul-fitr. Eid-ul-fitr is a holiday Muslims celebrate to the finishing of the holy month of Ramadan. Ramadan is a month when Muslims fast each day for 29 or 30 days from dawn to dusk. When it comes to eating it's very hard. Suppose you wanted to eat out tonight and you want to eat whatever they have in the restaurant, but you can't just eat any food that is harmful to your body. You have to avoid fatty foods and as a Muslim you have to follow restrictions on pork products.

Muslims have to pray five times a day. Since there are very few Masjids, it would have been easier for people to get together as a community to worship, and to help each other if there were more Masjids. Also people might work where it is not convenient for them to pray while working and because of that they miss the opportunity to pray on time.

Families also sacrifice a very important aspect of a Muslim life. Families don't get together at the dinner table. They do not spend time to walk, jog, bike, and even play together. I think we have to improve a lot of things that I mentioned above to make it even more exciting to live in the United States of America.

Siham Beshir
Grade 6

We Need to Preserve Natural History

I think it is important to save national parks and natural wonders. Examples of natural wonders to save are the Natural Bridge, Grand Canyon, and Niagara Falls. We also need to save all national parks around the world.

National parks should be saved so that wildlife doesn't become extinct. Wildlife helps keep arthropods and other annoying living creatures and plant populations down. Wildlife also gives food to people around the planet.

We also need to save natural wonders so we can see incredible views and learn so much about them. Some people can even make money off of some natural wonders.

I hope I have proven a point to you. National parks and natural wonders need to be saved like the Grand Canyon, Natural Bridge, and Shenandoah National Park. They need to be saved so humankind and wildlife can survive.

Shawn Blanchard
Grade 5

Kobe Bryant vs Allen Iverson

Kobe Bryant and Allen Iverson are considered two of the NBA's best players. Both are guards that score a lot of points. Compared stat-wise Kobe is the better player. He is first in 10 categories.

Kobe and Allen are both point guards. When they shoot, they both make over 40%. That helps them both have over 30 points per game. They both are over 6 feet tall, and they are in great shape. Both play over 40 minutes per game.

A couple of things that are different are that Kobe leads the league in 10 stat categories. Iverson only leads in 1. Although this is fact, Iverson is second to 7 of Kobe's firsts. Also, Kobe's career high, 81, is higher than Iverson's 61.

I guess with this Kobe is better, but it is very arguable. Both equally help their teams.

Garrett Browning
Grade 6

My First Chorus Concert

Many people have hidden fears. Mine happened to be stage fright. When I was younger I had stage fright then, too. At my school winter concert I had it but it wasn't that bad.

On the night of my chorus concert we went into Mr. Colliers room. Everyone was nervous, but my stomach was in knots. I was real warm and scared. I felt like I was burning up. I didn't think I had stage fright until I stepped out to center stage! When Mrs. Carter said, "Lets, go, it's our turn," my back got chills.

When I came out onto the stage I was scared. Then I saw my mom, sister, and dad. I felt a little better and I was happier. Still I was shaky though. After this experience I felt relieved.

After this experience I learned some things about myself. I've learned that I don't have to be nervous. I have also learned I'm not a bad singer. Stage fright is not my only hidden fear!

Olivia Worden
Grade 5

How Did Martin Change the World?

What would our lives be like if Martin Luther King Jr. never lived? Maybe there would still be segregation. This would cause blacks and whites to go to different schools. In black schools, children weren't treated with respect. Kids probably only got one piece of paper, one pencil and that was it. The conditions of these schools were horrible. On the other hand, the white people were treated with a lot of respect. They had buses, books, pencils and their buildings were very nicely maintained.

Martin Luther King Jr.'s goal was to achieve peace. In the March on Washington he said his famous speech, "I have a dream that one day this nation will rise up and live out the true meaning of its creed. We hold theses truths to be self-evident that all men are created equal."

MLK believed in nonviolence. One achievement was to stop the buses from being segregated with a boycott. He did this to help Rosa Parks. These were MLK's goals before his death.

After Martin Luther King died how did that change the world? When there was a problem with someone or there was fighting they all realized that Martin Luther King helped them and their society. James Earl Ray assassinated him in 1968 on April 4th in Memphis, Tennessee. He was only 39 years old.

A.J. Carnevale
Grade 6

My First Baseball Game in the Dome

One of the most memorable experiences of my life has to be my first ever baseball game in the dome. It was amazing and a lot different than regular baseball outside.

When I got there, it was almost game time. My coach had me playing first base. The games are different because they are on a time schedule and when that is up, the game is over. The whole game I was doing pretty well at first base, but not at hitting. It took me a while to get used to it because the ball is green and the pitcher's mound is farther back than in little league. Since the pitcher's mound is farther back, the ball comes slower to the plate.

The score was really close during most of the game but then the other team scored more runs but they weren't winning by too many. Then one of our teammates hit a homerun and brought the score closer and we only needed a couple more runs to tie. Then I came to the plate. I struck out the two times before and I really wanted to have a hit. So when I came up, my coach told me to take (not swing) until I got a strike and on the second pitch I got a strike. Then the next pitch was down the middle and I hit it to centerfield. I got a single! We lost that game 6-8 but I will never forget that game.

Jonathan Aston
Grade 6

Lights Out!

It started as a normal night watching television and doing homework when the lights went out and the whole neighborhood went quiet. Ronny, Rodney, Rochelle and I all sat on my Grandfather Teofilo's bed and started to make jokes to pass the time. When we stopped telling jokes it was silent.

My family sent out for Kentucky Fried Chicken. We felt our way to the kitchen and sat at the table to eat. If you were there you would have heard the box of chicken as I opened it. We didn't want to guess what we were eating so we found a candle and lit it. When we weren't eating and it was silent you could even hear us breathe. Then we went back upstairs to sleep.

When I was sleeping a bright light woke me up. The light felt like the sun on a hot day. I sat up and heard all kinds of noises: the television, radio, and things humming. I knew the electricity was back on in our neighborhood; and probably everybody woke up to shut things off again.

I did get most of my homework finished. I did have dinner even though it was mostly in the dark. My brothers and my sister and I got to tell some good jokes and stories. Every time I think of that night in the dark I feel good because I had *"quiet time"* with some of my favorite people: my family.

Romney R. Galvao
Grade 5

Galloping into Horses

There is more to know about horses than people realize. There are different sizes, colors, breeds, personalities. Personalities are important in a horse's life. For example a horse I ride, PJ, has a kind personality which makes him easier to ride though he can be quite stubborn. Shetland ponies have a friendly personality and also can be stubborn. There are also warm and cold-blooded horses. A cold-blooded horse means it has a cool and peaceful temper. Warm-blooded horses are very spirited, and they're good for sports.

Horses are measured in hands. Each hand is 4 inches. PJ is 17 hands which is 68 inches. Shetland ponies are 40 inches or 10 hands. The largest horse is a Shire and is 18 and above hands! The smallest horse is a Falabella and is 6 hands!

Many people think that a pony is a stage of a horse's life. But a pony is a small horse and stops growing below 14 hands. There are a number of breeds of ponies.

When a horse is born it's called a foal. A boy foal is called a colt and grows into a stallion. Girl foals are called fillies and grow into mares.

There is a difference between breed and color. PJ for example has a chestnut color but he is a Thoroughbred.

Horses are also used for sports such as Polo, Rodeos, racing, and show jumping. So saddle up and gallop into horses!

Emma Kaplan
Grade 4

Recycle, It Should Be the Law

We should all recycle. As a matter of fact, it should be the law!! So many people carelessly throw plastic containers and glass bottles in the trash. That may seem like the easiest thing to do. Truthfully, it really is. But guess what? It is not the *right* thing to do. Here is the behind the scenes scenario.

Suppose you tossed just one plastic container in the trash. You're thinking, "It's just one bottle, it won't hurt anybody." So Friday comes, and the trash man collects your trash. They go and dump it in the ground or water and declare themselves finished.

When you throw away paper goods, they rot and leave few remains. However, if you throw away plastic, it will stay there forever. So, if every person in the United States threw away on plastic container, the pollution will be dangerous.

What I am trying to say is *please* recycle. It really should be the law!

Latasha Easter
Grade 6

Exercise for Hours

Last night I jogged for a million miles! Okay not really a million miles but I jogged on my treadmill for a very long time. Exercising is so important we probably couldn't live without it. Exercising is great for your heart too. It keeps your heart beating at the correct rate and keeps it strong. Exercising also gives your body energy to live. It allows more oxygen to come through your body.

It gets rid of stress, too, when you're at home or school. Exercising doesn't always have to be a punishment, either. It can be fun to do, too.

You can do anything you want to do. You can exercise with a friend, in a group, or independently, and that's why you should start exercising and get heart-healthy today!

Rachel Magin
Grade 4

Help the Needy

I have had to live in Mexico. I have seen all the people sitting and living on the street without a job and without a home and it made me feel very sad. I don't think that it is fair that some people don't have a job because their parents didn't have enough money to send them to school. That means that eventually the family doesn't even have enough money to live in a house. They end up having to live on the street. The children are born into a life of having to sell things all day like food and candy, not only that but they have to beg for money to get as much as they can from cars at stoplights, so they can actually buy and eat food.

I think people like us in Southborough, Massachusetts take some things for granted. We want so much, and we think we have so little, but really, if you went to a place like Mexico, you would see that we have a lot more than most people do. Those, I think, are some very good reasons why I think people should start helping the needy.

Nicole Wrin
Grade 6

Too Much Homework

Did you ever hear your friends, sister, brother, and children say they have too much homework? I have heard them say that. Do you wish they had less homework? I wish we all had less homework.

I think we should have less homework, because it can interfere with activities you have to do. You shouldn't skip activities because of homework. What if your grandfather is in the hospital, for example? You can't do your homework while visiting him.

Homework is hard sometimes. If we did homework in class, we would have better grades. If we did homework in class, we could ask the teacher questions when we get stuck on questions. At home, you may ask your parents, but they don't always know.

Sometimes at home, your computers don't work. When you're at school they have 50-100 computers. They also have someone to fix it.

That's why I think we should do homework in school. The conditions are more favorable at school for success and better grades.

Jesse DeMasi
Grade 6

Jessica

Smart, pretty, hazel-green eyed, light sprinkled freckles, and long golden hair describes my little sister Jessica. But there is much more to this spunky little girl. Far more precious than gold, she is my treasure.

Perhaps Jessica's best qualities are that she is passionate, caring and loving. Helping others is what she does best. Whether you're sick, glum or just in a bad mood, you can never stay unhappy for long. Jessica will walk up to you, ask what's wrong, and cheer you up. She's funny, talented, and always has an ace up her sleeve!

Jessica loves ice skating, gymnastics and playing basketball. She's devoted to all of these sports, but she does it in her own *quirky* way. You might see a sparkling purple dot on the middle of the rink laughing and maybe even lying on the ground! In everything she does, she acts free spirited. You never know what to expect!

Active, playful, fun loving, her room is full of life. She knows and loves any type of game and will jump at the chance to have a play date. In summer, she is *always* in the back yard. She soars on the swings and adores the inflatable pool. I never get bored. She is full of ideas and makes me laugh nonstop!

Jessica's an amazing, unusual, loving seven-year-old. I treasure her personality and all the memories we've shared, but the best part of all is that she's my little sister and that's one thing that will never change!

Alexandra Gribbin
Grade 6

Cheetahs vs Jaguars

Ok, I'm here to tell you facts about cheetahs and jaguars. Now I know that it's going through your mind, how will dumb stupid facts interest me? Well I'm about to tell you…so read the next 2 paragraphs and you will see, see how it will interest you!

Ok let's talk about some cheetahs vs jaguars, now I know that this is going to sound boring but you've got to face the facts. Well, what to know, I'm just about to tell you some facts about cheetahs and jaguars. The first thing is that, well, this is kind of simple, they have the same colored spots. They also belong to the feline family, I think this is right, they both live in South America. The order that they fall in under is carnivore.

Now to tell you about the differences between these two animals. The first thing different between them is that jaguars mostly live in the wet Savanna, now cheetahs live in Africa. Jabiru is the kind of species cheetahs are, and Onca is the kind of species jaguars are! Now jaguars can be three colors, they can be orange, black or brown. But cheetahs can only be one color, orange! Cheetahs can only be one color, while jaguars can be three colors, that sucks!

And that's the facts I dug up. I hope you like it because I do, a lot right?

Lance Johnson
Grade 6

My Grandma

My grandma is in Maine right now. She'll be coming home soon. I can't wait to give her a hug. At Halloween we go to my grandma's house. I trick or treat in her neighborhood, get as much candy as I want from my grandma. A lot of people come to her door. My grandma is a nice, helpful, giving person.

My grandma is a nice woman. She's very generous. She mailed me money to buy some things that I wanted. She sews my clothes for me. I like it when she is nice to me.

My grandma is helpful when she invites us over for dinner. My grandma is helpful when she brings me places. I like when my grandma brings me places because I get to spend time with her.

My grandma is a giving person. She likes to help other people by giving them stuff. One time my grandma was giving is when she gave her next-door neighbor some flowers and once my grandma gave me some flowers and I thought that was being giving.

In conclusion my grandma is nice, helpful, and giving, because she is always helping my family. I think my grandma is caring because she is always helping me. I think that it is caring of my grandma to help us. My grandma makes me feel special and I feel so lucky to have her.

Michaela Beauregard
Grade 5

My Dad, My Hero

Have you had a person in your life that you look up to? I look up to my dad not just because he is taller than me, but he does a bunch of things I like to do. He takes me and my brothers on bike rides all the time in the summer. My grandparents have a pool that he takes me to a few times a week. I love to swim and my dad helps me get there.

I think I want to be a hunter like my dad. He has gotten many deer, over thirty turkeys, and even a bear on his hunting trips. I am proud of my dad and when hunting season comes around I love to go with him. I got a chance to go with him last year on the first day of deer season and it was super fun. We got up early so we could be in the woods before it got light. We sat quietly under a pine tree for about an hour. He told me to sit really still while we were there. Two does came down the trail toward us and my dad was able to get one with one shot.

I want to do things with my dad because he likes to be outside and so do I. He does a whole lot with me and my brothers and I thank him for that every day.

Clayton Miller
Grade 4

The Best Surprise Ever

On a Wednesday in fourth grade, I was supposed to go to my after school activity. Instead, my mom told me that my dad had an important meeting in Philadelphia. After we got home from school, I saw this huge limo in front of my house. We were in Philadelphia when we turned into the airport entrance. My mom pulled out her video camera and said, "We're going to Disney World!" I was speechless. My mom's parents and sister live in a city outside of Ft. Lauderdale. As we were walking in MGM to see Mickey's Giant Hat, I saw my grandparents, two aunts, my uncle, and my cousin walking towards us. I asked my mom if it was really them, and she said yes. I was so happy. That day was my brother's birthday so we were going to have this big party with my family. We went right to the restaurant when they were setting up the table. I saw them put five kid's menus on the table. As I was about to put two back, I saw my other cousins that I never see walk in. I was so excited. That was a vacation I will never forget!

Sari Krachman
Grade 6

The Dribble of It All

I love the way my hands glide the ball to the hoop, the basketball court so squeaky clean, the way my shoes make that noise. Basketball is my favorite sport. I love the way I dribble up and down the court. It is so easy, but yet still challenging. When the coach takes me off, I get a drink and I am ready to be put back in. I can let all my energy out, but yet I am fulfilled with it at the end of the game. Win or lose, I still have hope. Maybe someday I will be under all those lights having thousands of people watching me.

Logan McClelland
Grade 6

My Own Room

Ever since I was nine years old I wanted my own room. One day I thought of a crazy plan so I could have a room of my own.

I looked around my house and realized that hardly anybody used the living room. So I took all my things: my clothes, all my toys, and everything I owned and I went to the living room. I organized all my stuff all over the place and I slept on the couch and used a chair to hang my clothes. My mom discovered me sometime in the middle of the night and asked me, "What are you doing…aren't you supposed to be in your room sleeping?"

I said, "Yeah, but I want my own room and now the living room is mine!" My mom gave me the evil look and told me at 3 in the morning to pick up all my stuff and take it back to the room my sister and I shared.

After I moved back to my room I was finally able to fall asleep. My mom and I talked in the morning. Mom said, "Look, if you want a room that bad I'll let you have one since your birthday is coming up."

Today I have what I consider the best room in the house: I live in the guest room. My family helped to decorate it and I have been so happy since the problem was solved.

Thalia Valverde
Grade 5

9/11

The most tragic day of American history was September 11, 2001. That was the day when the terrorists made attacks on U.S. soil. That was the day when thousands of Americans lost their lives and when thousands of children became orphans. The terrorists attacked the Twin Towers, Somerset county, and the U.S. Department of Defense at the Pentagon. The terrorists used commercial airplanes to act as missiles. Unfortunately, their mission was successful.

The person who put this plan together was said to be Osama bin Laden. He used young, unemployed, unmarried men from Egypt, Saudi Arabia, and Lebanon to carry out his mission. They were extremely organized in their plot using commercial airplanes leaving from Boston, MA, Washington D.C., and Newark, NJ. Many of the terrorists were questioned before boarding their planes, but were let on anyway.

Two planes were targeted for the Twin Towers, which fell both 45 and 90 minutes after the hit. One plane landed in a field in Somerset County, which was not its intended target, and one plane hit the Pentagon.

One good thing that came from this horrible act is that commercial flying is safer now than ever.

To this day our country remembers this event with memorials for the heroes who risked their lives, such as police and firefighters.

Rosalee Severino
Grade 5

One More Day

So many things in life can be bought and wrapped with a pretty bow on top. Yet, the most expensive things and other inanimate objects are not always the most valuable. Some of the most important things are feelings, emotions, or even time. The best gift I could give to someone is just that. This gift would be for my grandfather. It would be for him to have just one more day with my grandmother. You see, in August almost three years ago, my grandma passed away. He misses her so much and it is hard for him to do some things without her. If I could give this to him, you can't describe the way he would feel. Seeing that, it would not only be a gift for him but for me too. I know this is impossible but at least we have the memories of her. These are more precious than anything in the world. If there was anyway possible I would give this gift. She was important to everyone in my family. I don't think there is one day where anyone in my family doesn't think of her. This is something in life that is valued more than gold or other expensive items. It is a lot more important!

Lauren Reisig
Grade 6

Surprise at the Door

I was taken by surprise when my grandparents came to America from Albania. I didn't even know! Well, when my grandparents came to America, it was my sister's birthday so we were at the party; then my grandparents came. The first thing I did was hug them. I felt like I was going to melt when I saw them. The whole time they were here, we did different things like fishing, going bowling, going to the movies, and the mall. But after a couple of months they had to go.

After they left, I learned how important my family is to me. The whole time they were here, we had tons of fun with them. Hopefully, they come again. To top it off, that was the most surprising moment of my life.

Timmy Jonuzi
Grade 6

My Trip to Maryland

On August 18, 2005 I went to Maryland for a competition. I was nine years old when I started cheerleading. It was my first year and first competition.

I was so excited when I got there. It was a huge gym, and there were a lot of people. My Red Land team was competing against six other squads. While we were practicing, we did really badly and when I stepped on the mat I got scared and nervous, but I believed in myself. Once we were done performing, everyone was cheering and screaming. I ran to my parents. They were so proud of me.

Soon it was time for awards. Our Midjets earned second place. Our Ponies also earned second place. The Peewees (my squad) earned first. We were all really happy and so was my coach. My coach was probably happier than all of us. Afterwards, we all threw a party and had a blast.

Saeda Bretz
Grade 4

There Is No One Like Me

There is no one like me because nobody else has my personality and my fingerprints and my handwriting. I have my own ways of thinking. No two people think alike. If things are not right, it bothers me. They have to be put neatly. I'm a very clean person and like things to be perfect.

I like to buy all my clothes from Limited Too stores. They have a nice selection of clothes. They also help you match your clothes. In this store, they also sell things to match for your room. Since everything in my room is pink, I find lots of cute things to buy for my room. They sell things that I buy to hang up in my room. I fix my own bed, because I like to place my stuffed animals in a certain way.

I also help my mother clean the house because she works very hard in her job and in the house. I feel bad for her, so I try to help as much as I can. She teaches me to always be a good person and be caring to others. I'm a very special girl with lots of good qualities.

Stephanie Ruiz
Grade 5

Why My Family Is Important to Me

My family is the most important thing to me. They're always there for me when I need them. They are always there for me at my soccer games, my baseball games, and my basketball games. I am always there for my brother's games too. They help me with what I need help with. A lot of the time my brother and I get in fights and arguments, but that doesn't mean we completely hate each other. If any of us have a problem we always find a way to fix it. We do lots of stuff together like going on summer vacations. On our vacation we usually go to Williamsburg and we go to an amusement park and a water park. We always have fun. Every Sunday we go to church together as a family. We usually never miss a week of church. Going to church with my family is important to me because we ask God to watch over our family. My grandparents are important to me too because I think that I am lucky to have all four of my grandparents still alive. I realized that some people don't have all their grandparents. I think that other people's family should be as important to them as mine are to me.

Bryan Caruso
Grade 5

My Trip to Europe

After a 9 hour and 30 minute flight, and after a long taxi ride, we finally got to our hotel in Greece. The room was so small, but not as small as our room in Rome, which is another story. That night I went to bed and I woke up sleepwalking. While sleeping I was saying something so my dad thought it was a dream. I was scared to death because I was in a foreign country and I was lucky that I did not walk out of the hotel. Then he woke up and came to the hall and brought me back to the room. I hope I never sleep walk again.

Doug Levine
Grade 6

All About Me

My favorite thing to do is play baseball. I have been playing since I could hold a bat and hit a ball. I have been on the Bethel travel team for 2 years in a row. That means they take best players that played the best in their league. I am going to be a pro baseball player when I grow up. I go to a hitting league each winter so I can stay in shape. When I grow up I want to play for the New York Yankees. I have been playing my hardest every game.

My other favorite thing to do is watch TV and play video games. I watch a lot of TV. One of my favorite shows to watch is called *CSI* (Crime Scene Investigation). I watch it every night. I also like to play video games. One of my favorite is called *Need for Speed Most Wanted*.

I have a lot of friends. My friends are very nice to me. We joke around all the time. They also make me laugh and I make them laugh.

My favorite color is blue. Most of the things right are in blue. The sky is blue and the uniforms are blue. That's why I like blue.

My favorite hobby is to build model cars. My dad made one but I have made about seven. I just made my favorite car, the Tony Stewart 20 car. I had so much fun making it.

I like to play football with my brother. He plays football with me all the time. He taught me to throw and catch a football. I can throw about 15 yards. He taught me all about the game.

Dennis Gehring
Grade 6

Islam

Islam means peace. Our prophets, messengers, and books have revealed Islam to us. Islam is the religion Muslims believe in. A person who makes Shahadah, belief in Allah (God,) and has faith, is a Muslim. Shahadah is when a person says 'I bear witness that there is no god but Allah and Prophet Muhammad is His messenger.' There are five pillars of Islam: Shahadah, praying to God, paying charity, fasting, and making pilgrimage.

Muslims have to do good deeds to go to Jannah. Jannah means paradise. At the end of the world there will be a judgment day when everybody will rise up and get judged. There are two places to go, Jannah or Hellfire. Hellfire is a bad and horrible place. The enemy to Muslims is Shaytan. Shaytan is bad and wants us to disobey Allah.

Salah is the second pillar of Islam. Muslims pray five times a day. When we pray to Allah we get close to Him. Also when we pray we talk to Him. Even if you can't see or hear Allah, He can see and hear you. Wudu is ablution. Wudu is the key to Salah. Wudu keeps us clean so we can be clean in front of Allah. That is about Islam.

Nuha Muktar
Grade 6

Stop Whining and Run

Running is a great sport. It keeps you in shape and keeps your heart healthy. Running is also a soothing sport. You don't have to think about anything when you run. It clears your mind. If you have a lot on your mind it gives you time to organize your thoughts.

Running can be an individual sport or a team sport. Running in races is a lot of fun. As an individual you can win prizes, trophies, and money if you are good. It is also fun to run in races when you are on a team. The better you run, the better the team does. Taking time off your previous race is always the main goal. By taking time off your previous race, you become a better runner. You should also be sure to have fun when you run. If you are not having fun, then running is not for you.

Running is a great sport to get involved in. All you need is a pair of good running shoes and time. Anyone can do it. You don't have to be coordinated or athletic. So put on your sneakers, stop whining and just RUN!

Megan Staub
Grade 5

All About Me

Hi. My name is Danny and I'm going to tell you about me. I like to go fishing. I like to watch scary movies at my friend's house. Sometimes I like to play games with AJ at the park. We like to play army. My favorite subjects in school are gym, math, science and art. I also like to draw in my notebook. I like to write in my journal.

I like to play games on the computer. I like to play chess. My favorite places are school, park, and my friend's house. My favorite teacher is Mrs. Zaino. She's the best. She rules over everyone. My favorite songs are "In Da Club" and "Window Shopper" by 50 Cent.

Danny Capotosto
Grade 4

Jeff Gordon

Jeff Gordon is the best. When I grow up I want to be just like him. He is the best racer in NASCAR. He is the fastest of all. My dream is to be just like Jeff Gordon.

Jeff Gordon is my idol. He started out racing a go-kart. After he went to a stock car. Then he would of gone to NASCAR. He joined the Hendricks Motor Sports Team. They are the best team in the world.

Jeff Gordon is my favorite star. I wish I can be just like him when I grow up. I watch every race on Sunday and sometimes Saturdays too. He is the BEST of all forty-three cars.

Jeff Gordon's paint jobs are cool. The paint job on his flame car is at least 100,000 dollars or more. His flame car is the best one of all. His # is twenty-four. I want the flame suit he has. He has a Pepsi suit too. I would love to be just like Jeff Gordon. It would be the best thing that ever happened to me. My dream is to be just like Jeff Gordon.

Todd Colomb
Grade 5

The Fryburg Fair

Every fall, I go up to New Hampshire for the annual Fryburg Fair. This is one of the best times that I have every year because I get to see my cousins for the first time every year.

I go to about three fairs every year and this fair is probably the best. We go in rain or shine, and if someone is sick, we bring them anyway, so they can watch. The tickets are on the pricey side, but I think it is worth it. One of the cool things is there is a horse racing stadium, and you can watch the horses race; it is so cool.

You can also go on plenty of rides, like the Scrambled Egg, the Ferris Wheel, Bumper Cars, and much more. You can also ride a pony for three dollars. There are also these little stores that you can buy stuff from, like candy, stuffed animals, antique stuff, and lots of clothing.

There are also food carts where you can get fries, corn dogs, chicken nuggets, and other stuff. Since you can go to the fair on a Friday, a Saturday, or a Sunday, some people bring their campers and stay there for all three days; if you want you can. There is also entertainment, like singing and magic shows. There are also animals that you can see; it is my sister's favorite part.

It would be awesome if you could see it yourself!

Katie Kokis
Grade 6

Having a Good Education/Schools

Having a good education plays a big role in your life. Your education of learning starts in preschool. There you learn how to play and share. You will also learn songs and build courtesy for your friends and teachers.

As you graduate preschool you will be promoted to a higher class, kindergarten. There you will learn the alphabet that you will use in writing everything.

From here you will go to an elementary school. There you will go through the grades 1-5. You will be taught math, English, science, and so on. After that you will go to the middle school and then the high school. After you graduate high school you will get a diploma which will allow you to go on to college.

In college you will be tested to your limits, so it would have been good if you studied and paid attention in class during your school years. While you are in college you will be taught the subjects that will relate to the job that you will want to have when you grow up.

It is good to have a good education because as you grow older you will get a job based on how smart you are and how much you know about a certain subject. It would be good if you never drop out of school or if you never skip a grade. This is why it is important to have a good education.

Ian Constantin
Grade 6

School

Hey! Did you see the new kid that is Mongolian and likes to go to school? My school is fantastic. I see great places and things in school. I meet new friends. I learn a lot in school. These things are why I go to school.

I see great places and things in school. I went to museums and different places in school on trips, and it was great. In school I went to places that I haven't been with my family. These show that schools take us to many places.

I've met new kids in school. I spend a lot of time with my friends. My friends and I have fun together and eat lunch together. On holidays we give each other gifts and make each other happy. Therefore, I have many friends in school.

I learn many new things in school. I learned some new facts about history. One of the best ones was how to be healthy. If we go to school, we will learn lots and have a better life. In conclusion without the school the world wouldn't be a good place to live.

School is one of the important things in my life. Great things happen in school. Only the best place to learn education is school. I think school is the place to learn.

Bumba Batyeruult
Grade 6

Recycling

Did you know that glass melts at 1,200 degrees Fahrenheit? Glass can be recycled forever. It never wears out. Glass is made from sand.

Shirts, rugs, and pencils can be made out of recycled plastic. Plastic comes from fossil fuels. Fossil fuels are biodegraded animals and plants. It takes millions of years to create oil. Oil cannot be reused or recycled it is a finite resource.

Plastic can only be recycled once. Today the United States can make plastic out of vegetables and fruit. Plastic can be made into many things such as toys, bottles and more. If you incinerate plastic, it produces a harmful chemical that causes cancer.

Tin melts at 1,500 Fahrenheit. Tin can be recycled. Tin is mined from the ground. For every hundred pounds of rock, there is only one pound of tin. Every tin can recycled saves enough electricity to power a TV for three hours.

Every gallon of oil dumped in storm drains ends up in the ocean. It effects exactly half a million gallons of water. There is only a certain amount of water on Earth. In fact, there has been the same amount of water on the earth for millions of years. Only one percent of water in the world is drinkable. Imagine if there was a huge oil spill and it affected one percent of drinkable water. We would be in trouble.

In conclusion, we have to recycle more and protect Mother Nature and her children.

Jared Cooper
Grade 5

Who Are Today's Patriots?!

Who are today's patriots? There are only so many. A patriot is someone who serves America, who values freedom, who's loyal to America, who loves America, and someone who obeys American laws.

I will name groups or people who are today's patriots. The first group I will be talking about is the president. He is loyal to America, he obeys, and cares for the people of the United States. He is the ruler of our country. Another person or group is our government. The government is a group of people who pass and reject laws that people think that are right. Also, the military is a group of patriots. The soldiers defend our country in war. Also, the Navy Seals are a group who is loyal to our country. They fight by using boats and huge ships. They also risk their lives to serve our country. The second to last person or groups that I will be talking about is the mayors of each state. They all serve, and love America. A mayor is a person who gets elected for mayor, like a president. They pass some laws for their state. Those are almost all of the people or groups from the past and present.

Now, I will be talking about one more person...Me! I'm loyal, I love America, and I serve America. Even though I'm ten years old, I still help my country every day! Even if you're just nice to somebody, you can be a patriot too.

Kelly Curran
Grade 5

The Benefits of Life in Soccer

Some people may think that soccer is just kicking a ball around and running, but it's not. Soccer provides many important benefits.

First, there's teamwork. Teamwork means to work together. Without teamwork in life you probably won't be able to work with a partner in your job when you grow up. For instance, I want to grow up to be a professional soccer player. If I accomplish teamwork now, when I am young, it won't be a problem when I'm grown.

Next, is fitness. Fitness means the quality or state of being healthy. This is especially important. Most likely if you're fit, you have less chances of getting sick. Also, if you exercise when you're young, your body will probably get adapted to all the physical activity. So, when you're older, you'll probably want to exercise everyday.

Last, the most important benefit of all is friendship! Just imagine yourself without friendship! I can. I can imagine myself on the field with the soccerball, all the soccer goals, and me. As I always say, it doesn't matter how many friends you have, because you only need one to support you in everything you do. Friendship also goes along with teamwork. When everybody works together, which is teamwork, people tend to make bonds of friendship by seeing what they can accomplish as a team.

Do you see now? Soccer isn't just kicking a ball around and running. It's about teamwork, fitness, and friendship!

Autumn Francis
Grade 5

People Use Too Much Water

"Shut off the water!" That is a common phrase that tells people they aren't saving enough water in their household. My two reasons to prove that not enough people conserve water in their household are that people leave the water running constantly and people use too much ground water. I hope my essay will convince you to save water.

My first reason proving that people use too much water is that people leave the water running constantly inside and outside their house which later can cause droughts. Here in Ridgewood NJ we've experienced numerous droughts. This does not just take place in Ridgewood; it's nationwide. Near the top of the list of reasons behind the water supply crisis is developing countries' governments' inability to regulate, manage and invest in water. Scientists are predicting a big decrease in water supplies as deserts expand and evaporation rates increase.

My second reason proving that people use too much water is we use too much ground water. For example, Delhi is predicted to run out of ground water by 2015 at current usage rates. By 2025 the amount of water needed for food production across the world will rise by 50%, due to population growth and higher standards of living.

I think my two reasons, people leave the water running constantly and people use too much ground water. That proves people waste too much water.

Daniel Jacobini
Grade 5

Uncle Floyd

I know that I am supposed to write about something important to me. Lots of things are important in my life, including family. But the one person that comes to mind when I'm asked this question, "What is important to me?" is my great-uncle Floyd.

I am sad to say that he passed away in May of 2005, but I will never forget him. I will miss seeing him at all of the high school football games. You see, he went to every high school sports event in the county. He was a big supporter of the county and almost everyone in Madison, Virginia knew him.

He always came to Sunday lunch at my grandparents' house. We would all watch a sports event or the playoffs in the basement after lunch. He was funny, and he loved everyone in the family. He showed that he loved us because he came to all the family parties like birthdays, Christmas, and Thanksgiving. I think that what I'll miss the most is the way his truck beeped when he backed out of the driveway. He had a device that beeped when he went into reverse on his Ford Ranger, and we always knew when he was leaving.

I wrote this paper to honor the best great-uncle I could ask for, my Uncle Floyd, who was always there for me.

Drew Kelliher
Grade 5

A Special Talent

You may not know it, but I'm a great tap dancer. I started tap dancing in third grade. At first it was really difficult. I had no idea what I was doing. I kept pushing myself further and further. Now I'm a fifth-grader in advanced tap in and out of school.

My hero is Savion Glover. I've looked up to him since I saw one of his performances. He is amazing! I really try my hardest now to achieve one goal and that is, being at least half as good as Savion.

Tap dancing is harder than you would think. You can't just throw on a pair of tap shoes and expect yourself to be able to do a routine. You really have to love the sport to dedicate enough time to it. You always have to be willing to pressure yourself. Also, one important thing that you shouldn't do that will drive your teacher through the wall is saying these two words, "I can't."

I always feel tired and annoyed when I go to tap lessons, but I come out feeling excited and happy for no reason at all. I've realized that even if I'm younger than everyone else, I can still push myself harder than I ever thought. I love my talent, and I bet if you tried tap dancing you might love it too!

Ariana Wescott
Grade 5

My Hero Dad

My dad is my hero because he has fought for me to live with him. It feels like he carries me on his shoulders, especially right now because I am struggling with school. He also puts a roof over my head, and gets me all my needs, takes care of me also. That is why I love my dad. If I could I would fulfill his dreams, never make him scream, give him a crown and never make him frown.

Michael Stiemly
Grade 6

Basketball vs Soccer

In my paper "Basketball vs Soccer," I will compare and contrast soccer and basketball. There will be four things that are the same about each other and for reasons they're not alike.

In this paragraph I will compare soccer and basketball. The first one is that they both use balls. The next one is you can score points in each game. The third one is in these sports you need offensive and defensive people. The last one is that both girls and boys can play either sport.

This paragraph will contrast both sports. In the sports they use different size balls. The second one is in basketball you dribble with your hands and in soccer you dribble with your feet. The third one is you wear shin pads in soccer and you wear kneepads in basketball. The last reason is in soccer you wear cleats and in basketball you wear basketball shoes.

I hope you liked my paper on basketball and soccer. I also hope you understood my compare and contrast reasons.

Morgan Seybold
Grade 6

Mastodons and Mammoths

What is a mastodon? Mastodons were an elephant-like mammal that lived during the Ice Age. This species is the American Mastodon. Mastodons are related to mammoths and modern elephants. They are all members of a group of mammals known as the Proboscideans.

What was the difference between a Mastodon and a mammoth? Mammoths had teeth with hard ridges for grinding dry vegetation and grazed in open grasslands. Some reached 16 feet in height and had enormous curved tusks. Mastodons had blunt coned teeth and probably were browsers on softer plants, such as herbs and leaves. They were found mostly in forested and brushy areas.

When did Mastodons live? The American Mastodon roamed much of North America during the Pliocene and Pleistocene Epochs, from at least 3.75 million to 10,000 years ago.

Why did they become extinct? The last Mastodon lived about 10,000 years ago. The reason they died out is not completely understood. The changing climate at the close of the Ice Age is thought to have played an important part. Over-hunting by humans or disease may also have contributed to their extinction.

Thomas M. Mirra
Grade 4

The Hurricane

In 2005 a disastrous hurricane storm hit Mississippi, Louisiana and New Orleans. Many people were found dead and hurt. One of the dams broke and those places flooded. Many people are now living on the streets.

My friend and her aunt had a bake sale and the money they raised they sent to the Red Cross for the victims of Hurricane Katrina. They raised three-thousand-five-hundred dollars.

This hurricane made me feel sad because many people were hurt and killed. Many victims felt angry and sad because they lost their homes.

Sheila Soares
Grade 6

Gorillas vs Monkeys

Gorillas and monkeys are two very interesting animals. They are both cute. I am going to tell you how monkeys and gorillas are different and alike.

Gorillas and monkeys have different personalities. Monkeys are normally small and most gorillas are big. Monkeys normally live in trees. Gorillas make nests on the ground. There are many other ways they're different.

They are also alike in some ways. They both eat the same things. They are basically in the same family. They're both vegetarians. They probably have a lot of other things alike.

Monkeys and gorillas are both really cute. They are my favorite animals. They are both unique in different ways. We will always love them both no matter what.

Madeleine Thurston
Grade 6

My Little Sister

My little sister is so cute. Her name is Jackie, and she is only six months old. She laughs all the time, and is a very happy baby. I think her favorite color will be pink, because she is never sad in pink clothes.

She was born on August 10, 2005, in Mountainside Hospital. She weighed 6 pounds, 11 ounces, and looked like a little angel.

Jackie always tries to chew on things, and those things that she chews on are usually my things. Now it will be even worse because she can roll over and be more accessible to things, so now I have to keep everything off the floor.

Her first word was Mama, which she says whenever she wants her mom (I have seen her say it in her sleep). There is only one thing I would change about her. That she wouldn't turn night into day. She wakes up in the middle of the night, waking everyone else up. However, all babies do that, so I cannot be mad at her.

My family calls her Birdie because she sounds like a bird when she is calling for us. My father gave her the nickname when she was very young, so she was a Birdie when she was born. Jackie was named after my aunt on my father's side. Jackie looks just like I did when I was a baby.

I think she is the cutest thing in the world.

Julian Lee
Grade 5

My Individuality

Being an individual means being different from others. It means you are unique and you stand out. I am an individual because of my skills in cooking, baking, and the way I dress.

I like cooking because when I am finished, it is satisfying to taste what I have made. My mother cooks and makes up recipes often, so I have been experimenting since I was little. I like to make soups and salads. Soups are challenging, but salads are easy to make. Now that I make soup, I want to try different stews. They are almost the same, but thicker.

I am also an individual because of my skills in baking. This is certainly because of my mom, who has been baking forever, and I guess so have I. I like making cookies, cakes, pies, and other desserts. My friends tell me I am an excellent baker, but I want to keep getting better.

Another way I am an individual is the way I dress. I never buy full outfits, just random shirts and pants so I can mix and match, which is much more fun. I love the way I dress and do not want it to change. Who knows? Maybe I could do this for a living some day.

My cooking, baking, and the way I dress are all the ways I am an individual. These things will probably take me into the future, and not change much. They describe me, who I am, an individual!

Madeline Pifer
Grade 5

Queen of the Honey

I'm going to tell you about the queen bee's food, life cycle, and her job.

Any bee larva can become a queen by being fed royal jelly. Worker bees secrete this jelly from glands in their head. Other larva get fed bee bread and bee milk which is less nutritious. Queen bees are the biggest bees in the hive measuring three quarters of an inch long.

The life cycle of a queen bee starts with an egg which lasts three days. The second stage is the larvae stage which takes six days. The pupa stage is the third stage and goes on for six days. The queen is then an adult and can live up to four years. She might produce 1,500,000 eggs in that time. Queens do little other than lay eggs. They don't even feed themselves as they get workers to do that.

There can only be one queen in the hive. If she sees another queen, they will fight for control of the hive. When the fight is over, the winner goes on a marriage flight. She mates with about ten drones. She is now head of the hive and will start to lay her eggs.

I hope you enjoyed reading about the queen bee's food, life cycle, and job.

Phillip Roshon
Grade 4

Dear Diary

Dear Diary,

Today, I met Ms. Lantz, a ballet teacher. She was surprisingly understanding, and while we had simple steps, the way she put together combinations made them interesting, and challenging.

Instead of criticizing me like other ballet teachers, she offered a smile and a nice way to say "Hold your stomach in" or "Shoulders down." She offered me tricks to make my neck seem longer, and make me work very hard on steps, so I could master them without trouble. The steps were pretty challenging, but somehow she made them enjoyable for me.

I never really enjoyed ballet very much. I had always thought it was just stretching your leg to the back, or kicking it in the front. I thought it was just some hard exercises invented for a grueling hour and a half workout. I thought all this, before I had a class with Ms. Lantz.

"Girls and boys, anyone can kick their leg in the air. When you look at it that way, ballet is easy. We could ask a policeman off the street to come join class and ask him to do kicks to the front. Being a dancer isn't all about technical things. It's about the way your fingers stretch front, your expression, the quality of the exercise. Being a dancer is about grace." As she spoke, I had an epiphany.

Dancing isn't about kicking your leg to the front. It is about expressing your feelings through movement. It's about grace.

Thanks, Ms. Lantz.

Love,

Julia Pingeton

Julia Pingeton
Grade 6

My One Special Gift

If I could give one special gift to someone that couldn't be wrapped I would give the gift of comfort. I would give this gift to my ninety-nine-year-old great-grandmother. I would give this gift to her for numerous reasons. One reason why I would give this gift to her is because she is turning one-hundred in November and has several aching bones. With sadness in her eyes I know that she is feeling pain that no one deserves to feel. Another reason why I would give this gift to her is because she lives all by herself in a retirement home, and her son (my grandfather) lives very far away from her. It kills me inside when I see her all alone with the feeling that she is on her own. With this gift she will finally know that I still love her even though our good times have been slowly fading away with her old age. If I could give this gift to her I would give it to her in a hospital, where our memories first started and where they will end. I would mostly give her this gift because I love her dearly and have countless memories with her and I know that she isn't going to be around forever. With the gift of comfort I know that she will leave this world without pain. This gift could change her life.

Suzanne Fuccillo
Grade 6

Alexander the Great

Why is Alexander the Great called great and not good? Alexander was strong, good looking, and hard working since he was a little boy. He was also very clever and good in every sport. But Alexander had to work for his name.

Alexander the Great had a wonderful father and mother (Philip and Olimpias) who wanted the best for him. According to legend Alexander was the son of Hercules. His real mother gave him excellent tutors like Aristotle. He also knew how to show respect. When he was king he went to see a poor philosopher. When Alexander asked the philosopher what he could do for him, the philosopher replied "stop standing in-between me and the Sun" and Alexander didn't get mad. Alexander was a soldier and commanded in the army at the age of 16. When his father died he took over the army and became king at 20 years old! He led his army of 5,000 to conquer Babylon, Macedonia, Gaugamela, Cyprus, Tyre, Athens, and Persia. He also conquered Perseopolis, Susa, and Bucephalus. In all, Alexander took over all of the eastern Mediterranean and founded 70 cities, 16 of which were named Alexandria after him.

He died at 32 but throughout his lifetime he bettered rich ideas, cultures, and customs. Alexander was trusting and noble and although he was like a superman in his time, he taught the world today what hard work can do. He definitely earned his name as Alexander the Great!

Courtney Flynn
Grade 6

A Hero for All

My hero is Mia Hamm. She played a forward on the women's U.S. national soccer team. Mia is now retired. Many people refer to her as their hero. She had an extremely successful career as a soccer player.

On March 17, 1972 Mia Hamm was born in Alabama. Mia's first appearance on the team was in 1987 and she was 15 years old. Mia Hamm's my inspiration because she was an excellent player. Not only did she play well, but she's open hearted. In 1997 Mia Hamm's brother Garrett died from bone marrow disease. Garrett was one of her heroes. This caused her a lot of pain. After that she decided to take action. Mia decided to start what's called the Mia Hamm Foundation to raise money and awareness for bone marrow transplant patients and their families. She tries to provide more opportunities for girls in sports. She's an excellent role model for girls of all ages. As an all-around best women's soccer player, Mia's scored more than 150 goals! Mia developed concepts of teamwork. Mia's my hero.

A very inspirational quote once spoken by Mia is, "I am a member of a team. I rely on the team. The team, not the player, is the champion." This quote acknowledges determination and teamwork. Mia never gave up, which made her a hero and an outstanding player. She didn't brag, and she did her very best. Even though Mia Hamm's retired, she's still remembered and by far "my hero."

Megan O'Connell
Grade 6

Good or Bad?

On the day before Halloween, The Willows Equestrian Center had a Hunter Jumper show. I'm leasing a horse named "Paddy" because my horse "Blue" had a foot injury and she can't jump anymore. My instructor Nancy said I'm ready to try 2'3" jumps in a course. Paddy is very moody sometimes, and it's hard to work her through her problems. Sadly, the day of the show she was having a moody day. We went over the first jump, it was AWESOME! Then we were heading for the outside line. She was getting her really bad sulky canter. "Well, Okay," I thought. I was ready to go over the first jump in the line she was about to go over, but she didn't! I went flying over the hay bales and hit the pole on the jump.

We tried to go over two more times, but she didn't go over. Nancy took me back in the schooling ring to try to go over a cross rail in there. She refused in there, too. Her owner, Kiley, got on and took her in the show ring to see if she would go over. Paddy went over the jump with a crack on the butt and fussiness over the jump. Nancy had another jumping show next weekend. I showed and I got through the whole course. Yay!!

Madison Strony
Grade 5

My Christmas Tree

Just one Christmas tree can light up an entire home, and that is exactly what mind does. My Christmas tree is eight feet tall. Hundreds of red and green ornaments dangle from its thin, dark, green branches. The beautiful tree lets out a fragrant aroma which gives my home a nice pine smell. Lights are strung around the tree and are shining brightly, filling the whole room with the joy of Christmas. Small plastic icicles hang from the many branches of the tree. Below the tree, gifts piled on top of each other wait to be opened on Christmas Day. A star on the top completes the wondrous, natural creation that reminds us that it is the holiday season, and it is time to celebrate!

Nicholas Hartmann
Grade 6

Cheetah vs Michael Johnson

I picked the cheetah and Michael Johnson because they had the most facts. They are alike because they can both run. My second thing why are they alike because they can both run quick. And when I say quick I mean quick. The cheetah can run 113 kph (70 mph). And Michael Johnson got an Olympic world record. He ran 200 m in 19.32 seconds. That is 37 kph (23 mph). And of course they both have feet. That is all I can talk about right now.

They are different because…the cheetah has four legs and feet. The cheetah can run way faster than any human being in the world. And Michael Johnson is the fastest person in the whole United States. And also Michael Johnson does not have a muzzle. That is the difference between the cheetah and Michael Johnson.

Ashley Gerhart
Grade 6

Bowling

My all time favorite sport is bowling! This sport can be frustrating, but it is fun. I bowl at Broadway Lanes. There, before you bowl you have a chance to practice. You have to bowl three games. You also have to pick your team name.

My favorite thing about bowling is that when you bowl a good game you get rewarded. For a reward you get a patch that says what you bowled on it. For example, say that my highest game was 125 then they would have 125 on it. I also like hanging out with my friends or family there. Whenever you have plans on the day you bowl you can pre-bowl. Pre-bowling means you bowl before the day you're supposed to bowl.

The worst thing about bowling is when you bowl straight but you still have one or two pins left. That's called being robbed. Being robbed means that you should have gotten a strike, but you didn't.

It's fun when you go with your family. I've bowled for two years, and I think this sport is awesome, and fun. I think everybody should try this sport. My highest game ever was a 125.

Taylor Winney
Grade 5

Family

I'm a nine year old boy. Many things are important to me like my school, my friends and my toys; but most of all my family is important to me.

I have a small family. My family members are: my mother, my father my grandma and grandpa, my Aunt Ruby, and my Uncle Cesar. I'm the only child in my family.

My mother is important to me because she takes care of me. She teaches me to be a good boy with values and morals. We spend quality time together. She was the one to teach me to swim and to ride a bike. She checks my homework and takes me to church on Sunday. My father lives in Florida. We talk over the phone quite often. Even though we don't spend time together, he is important to me.

Another member of my family is my grandma, Maria. She is special to me. My grandma picks me up from school in the afternoon. She takes care of me until my mom returns from work in the evening. My grandma and I have many things in common. We like books and gardening. I always help my grandma with her flowers and plants in the summer. All the members of my family are important to me.

I appreciate the teachings and love I receive from my family. Every day I give thanks to God for my family.

Julio Rivas
Grade 4

Life Skills

Life Skills is one of the many favorite cycles at Grover Middle School. In Life Skills the comical teacher, Ms. Jinx, has a variety of subjects to choose from. Some of the enjoyed topics are sewing, bullying, and projects that are not too difficult. Also included is cooking, a favored component in the class.

In the segment of cooking, a few of the favorites are Chex mix, cheese quesadillas, English muffin pizza and my favorite; Orange Julius. Too bad you only make snack sized portions because many wouldn't mind more than a sample. Each recipe takes the entire class time to make so you are limited to the amount of snacks.

The smoothie named The Orange Julius has been greatly talked about all over the school. You may be wondering, "Is it really a healthy snack?" Well, here's your answer; yes. The entire pitcher only contains about one third of a cup of sugar for four servings. Now that's not too much for the average teenage body. In fact, it's quite a healthy snack. All you need to make this is one third of a cup of sugar, ten ice cubes, a cup of milk, a cup of water, a teaspoon of vanilla extract, and a container of frozen concentrated orange juice. Then you just blend it until its as creamy as a whipped cream.

And that is why most students at Grover Middle School enjoy the class and look forward to going to Life Skills.

Gregory Fox
Grade 6

My Parents

I have two parents named Ricky and Lisa Erb and they are special to me. I wish everybody could have parents like mine. They are good to me and to everyone they meet.

My dad is on the fire department. My dad also takes me up to the firehouse to play. He works at V.H.I.S. Builders. He builds houses, and does plumbing and electric work. I don't know what I would do without my dad.

My mother is also very special. She works at Autumn Care of Madison. She works as a social director. She lets people come to live there and has worked there for sixteen years. I don't know what I would do without her.

I would like my dad to be remembered for letting people have a place to live and for saving people's houses. My mom should be remembered for letting people have a place to live and for taking care of old people. My mom or dad could never be replaced because of their caring and kindness.

Abby Erb
Grade 5

My Family

I learned a lot about my family. Now I'm going to tell you about them. My brother is seven and sometimes he is funny. He likes to pull pranks. He loves hot cocoa and his hobbies are football and basketball.

My mom is thirty-seven and she makes great pizza. She likes shopping and riding bicycles. Her hobbies are watching the WNBA, riding bicycles and snowboarding. When my mom was little, she had three dogs and eight cats.

My dad was a CCR Basketball Champion and he works at the United Nations. His hobby is watching the NHL games, playing hockey, and playing basketball. The coolest thing about my dad is that he can make pancakes.

Next, the moment we have been waiting for. Now I'm going to tell you about me. I'm ten and I will turn eleven on February fifth. I love my dad's pancakes and my mom's pizza. My hobbies are riding roller coasters and playing sports. On every Monday, I walk my neighbor's dog, Max.

Kirill Ivanov
Grade 4

Lacrosse

Have you ever heard of the sport lacrosse before? First, you need speed for the game. The field is one-hundred-ten yards. There are a minimum of ten players allowed on the field. The players all have pads on. It is a difficult sport because everyone attacks the ball.

Next, you need a mouthpiece. There are two kinds of Lax sticks. The goal is shaped like a triangle. It has a large net. Whoever gets the most points wins.

Finally, you need to be strong. You will have to practice. The ball is white, small, and made of rubber. The team who has seven or more points when the other team doesn't have more than seven gives the ball to the lower point team. This is a hard, hurtful, and fun sport.

Donald Moeller
Grade 4

My Role Models

Hi, my name is Hannah Girard and there are two people in my life that I look up to; people who I admire for who they are and for their absolute wonderful and lively personality. They're Mrs. MacDuff and Miss McLaughlin.

Mrs. MacDuff is my first role model. She is a fourth grade, nice, fun, and energetic teacher. I want to become a teacher and she was the one who inspired me. She's the one I look up to and when I get older, I want to have her energy and her way of being fun while students are learning.

My second role model is Miss McLaughlin. She's an organized, fun, and happy 5th grade teacher. She's my teacher. She and Mrs. MacDuff are my favorite teachers. I want to have her organization. I'm not very organized. She's very.

Those are my two role models that I look up to in my life.

Hannah Girard
Grade 5

The Gift of Sound

The gift that I want to give is the gift of sound. In the fall of 1999 my dad became deaf in his left ear. He woke up one morning and realized that he had no sound in his left ear. First we thought that it was an ear infection, but after seeing many doctors they determined that it was a virus that destroyed the nerves in that ear. Life has been very difficult for my dad. For instance, when he is on the phone he can only talk in his right ear. Also, when someone is talking to him in his left ear, he can't hear him or her, so they have to scream to him. When my dad became deaf he was very much upset. My mom was heartbroken too. I know that if he got this gift that I want to give him, he would be very much delighted. So that's why I want to give my dad this gift so badly. Also, if my dad did get this gift, he wouldn't have to face all of the difficulties that he has faced. I know that it would take a miracle for my dad to get back his hearing, but I still and will always have hope.

Megan Sheehan
Grade 6

Jordan and I

Jordan is my best friend in the whole wide world. I have known Jordan since kindergarten. We became best friends ever since the first day. We always used to play with our stuffed animals. Jordan's stuffed animal is a tiger named Flapjack. My stuffed animal is a dinosaur named Barney.

Jordan and I usually played on the playground. We usually played chase the girls. It was fun!

We were together again in first grade. We weren't together in second or third grade. That made me feel sad.

Now we are together in fourth grade. I think everybody should be friends with Jordan because he is friendly, loyal, trustworthy, caring, kind, playful, nice, cheerful, respecting, peaceful, loving, encouraging, great and a very good friend.

What kind of friend do you have?

Philip John Horan
Grade 4

My Cousin Michael

My cousin, Michael, has more faith and courage than anyone I know. He was diagnosed with uncontrolled epilepsy when he was four years old.

Through the years the doctors tried many drugs to stop him from having seizures, but nothing worked.

He has never been able to be a normal kid and play sports and other activities that normal kids do. It also meant many kids treated him badly because he was different, and they didn't understand why, especially when he had a seizure because it scared them.

He is now fourteen years old, and the doctors told him they might be able to cure him of his epilepsy if they could find where in his brain the seizures were coming from and remove that part of his brain, but they also told him there was only a fifty percent chance it would work and he may die, or be paralyzed from the operation. Michael told the doctors he wanted to have the operation because he knew God would be with him and take care of him no matter what.

When I visited Michael, after his second operation I saw that his head had been cut open from ear to ear. I realized how much faith and courage he really does have, and I knew then what Michael has always known, that God really is always with him no matter what.

Taylor Patterson
Grade 6

About My Uncle

A few weeks ago I went to see a movie called *End of the Spear*, a true story about five missionaries, their families, and an Indian tribe called the Waodani in Ecuador. The Waodani Indians were a violent tribe brought up on ancient traditions of revenge and hate. They had fought and killed each other nearly to extinction. The five missionaries felt they had to show them the gospel before it was too late. When they made contact the Indians killed them. Still the families forgave them and tried again to reach them. They were miraculously successful.

That is just a very small summary of a great story with many more details. But that is beside the point. This wonderful story of forgiveness inspired my Uncle Alan to do missionary work in the Amazon. He flew planes for the same Christian organization as one of the main characters in the story.

One day my uncle was flying his plane in Venezuela with another missionary. The plane crashed due to severe engine failure. Neither my uncle nor his friend survived. I was just a little tiny baby but I still know what it meant to my family.

When I saw that movie my uncle's story became very real to me. I will always be proud of him because he answered God's call to serve.

James Weisel
Grade 6

Going to Massachusetts

Skiing is one of my favorite sports, and the best part is the ski lift. After you get all the way to the top you have to go down the hill. If you are very good at skiing you can go on the coconut trail. You have to be careful though, I sprained my ankle and had to sit out the rest of the day.

There's another fun part. There is a ramp to get to one of the ski sections and then you have to pick a trail. One trail has a steep hill. I went down the hill and fell trying to stop myself. I tried to go down the hill again, but this time I fell all the way down the hill and bumped my head on a tree. My cousin came, fell next to me, and my friend fell on the other side of me, then all of us got up. We finally made it to the end, then my brother said he wanted to have a race. My cousin was in first, my brother was in second, my brother's friend was in third, my friend was in fourth, and I was in last. When we got close to the end, my cousin fell. Then my brother and my brother's friend got into a crash. My friend Cameron was coming fast and I was right behind her. We saw everybody on the ground. Cameron and I opened our mouths wide and laughed. That was my fun skiing trip in Massachusetts.

Karma Somerville-Powell
Grade 4

My Dad

My dad taught me the three "C's," confidence, concentration, and courage. My dad coached baseball, basketball, soccer, and snowboarding. My dad is the best coach I have ever had.

My dad is usually an assistant coach for basketball and he still helps me when he can. My dad would take to the court to work on my dribbling, shooting, and lay ups. I work on point guard even though I'm not a point guard my dad helps me achieve that goal. And after every game he mentions the three "C's."

My favorite sport is baseball, my dad would play catch with me when he could. I love it when he's able to do that. Dad takes me to batting cages a lot during the off season and during the season to work on my swing. He also brings me to the field to work on my two favorite positions pitcher and short stop.

My favorite position in soccer is goalie. When my dad was a kid he played goalie so he taught me all the inside tricks of saving the ball. Now I am one of the best goalies on my team and I love it!

My dad started snowboarding and I saw him so I wanted to try it. The first day I tried snowboarding I wanted to quit. It was the worst, but my dad told me to keep with it and so I did. We go to a ski resort called Sunday River a lot so I get tons of practice.

My dad helps me so much with every sport and that's why I am such a successful athlete. And, don't forget the three "C's," they will help you to greatness in life and in sports and try your best.

Eric Lundgren
Grade 6

Brittany Barron

About two years ago my good friend was in the hospital and I was really worried about her. I asked my mom if we could visit her, but she said that Brittany is too sick. I kept on asking her questions like, "How would she learn?" My mom said that there was a camera in the classroom. Then I asked her, "What disease does she have?" and she said it was a bone marrow disease. A year went by and I kept on asking her if we could visit her and she said, "No Mallory we can't." I came back home and my mom was talking on the phone and crying at the same time. I asked her, "What was wrong?" and she said that someone died. Then I asked her who it was and she said that it was Brittany Barron. Then my mom and I started crying. After that my brother came and then he asked why we were crying and we told him that Brittany Barron died.

That Hanukkah I got an iPod. I was looking at the top one hundred songs and the best one was called Heaven. When I heard the song it made me cry. I cried until supper. We ate and my mom and I talked about Brittany and we said how nice she was to everyone. Up until this day she is still my friend forever and like my soul sister.

Mallory Schiff
Grade 5

Peer Pressure

In life there are two kinds of pressure: good peer pressure that motivates you, and bad peer pressure that makes you get in serious trouble. We all want the good peer pressure in our lives.

"Friends are the chocolate chip cookies in life…" are words written by Marcia Byalick, the author of *Quit It.* This statement is true because chocolate chips are sweet and gooey like friends. They have sweet spots where they are kind and friendly and are "gooey," and they understand your problems and comfort you.

When you are at a HUGE competition, your friends make you focus on the game and try your hardest. My friends on my softball team motivate me by cheering me on and saying, "Knock it out of the park!" They trigger my mind and help push me to my full potential.

Bad peer pressure is like a scar or a burn. It leaves a deep mark in your skin. I have witnessed bad peer pressure. At school a boy in my class said to his friend, "I have the test answers. You want them?" He took them and later was caught. I felt so bad for him. He knew it was wrong, but it's hard to turn away from things like that.

What would you rather have? A friend who gets you in trouble, or a friend who motivates you? I want a trustworthy friend who helps me all the way and steers me on the right path.

Alex Wysota
Grade 6

The Moon and Stars

There are many facts about the moon and here are some of them. The moon is 238,857 miles from the Earth. The first astronauts landed on the moon on Apollo 11 in 1969. A moon is any natural object that orbits, or circles a planet. The moon is the Earth's closest neighbor in space. The same side of the moon always faces the Earth. The moon does not have any water on it. If you go to the moon and if you weight 70 pounds on Earth, you will weight about 35 pounds. The moon may look like it has holes in it but those are called craters. The moon is covered with thousands of craters.

There are also many facts about stars. Stars are extremely bright and made of gas that gives out an enormous amount of light and heat. Stars may look small but they are very big. Alioth, a blue giant star, is the brightest star in the Big Dipper constellation. A binary star is two stars that are held together by gravity. A star cluster is a group of stars near each other in space that have similar characteristics. A neutron star is very small but extremely dense. Stars vary widely in mass, size, temperature and total energy. The brightest stars are called supernovas. They are about 10 million times more powerful than the sun. There are millions of stars in the sky even if you cannot see them at night. Those are some facts about the moon and stars.

Tiana Maylor
Grade 5

How I Met Taryn and Lauryn

One summer day I went to the wedding of my dad's friend with my family. After the wedding we went to the reception which was held outside behind the church. I went to a swing set where these two girls followed me. I started talking to the two girls whose names were Taryn and Lauryn. Then I told them that my name was Amy. It turned out that my parents and their parents were good friends.

We talked about what our favorite colors were, about where we all went to school and discussed the favorite kind of animal each one of us liked. The girls and I played in the sandbox and went on the swings. Then we went to get a snack and a drink. There was a DJ so Taryn, Lauryn and I went out on the dance floor and had a lot of fun. Then the kids of the groom and bride were giving slush drinks with little umbrellas in them so we went to get some. Taryn and I were collecting the little umbrellas which were different colors. Then we ate a little more and Lauryn was really hungry.

Later in the night Taryn, Lauryn and I were really crazy and did splits, somersaults and cartwheels. Then we got some more drinks. Then it was time to leave but before we left we made a pact to see each other again so we gave each other our email addresses.

Amy Boris
Grade 5

Crocodiles and Alligators

Do you know the similarities and differences of crocodiles and alligators? Well, I sure do. An example of how they are different is that they are from different families. Read on and you will find some more information on them.

I am going to tell you three ways that crocodiles and alligators are different from each other. For one, crocodiles are from the crocdylidae family while alligators are from the alligatoridae family. The next two things I am going to tell you can also help you tell them apart. Crocodiles have a very long, narrow, v-shaped snout, while the alligator's snout is wider and u-shaped. Also, alligators' jaws hinge on the bottom and crocodiles' hinge on the top.

I am going to tell you 2 ways the crocodiles and alligators are alike, one you probably already know is that they both live in water, they live in two different kinds of water, but they still both live in water. The other way they are alike is that they both feed on a variety of fish, water bird, mammals and other reptiles.

I have told you some information I know on crocodiles and alligators, how they are the same and how they are different. I hope you enjoyed reading this paper.

Erin Rodgers
Grade 6

I Am a Person Who Loves to Sing

I wait with anticipation, thinking, "This is it, all I've trained for is finally here; NYSSMA." The door swung open, my heart raced.

I thought to myself "Run!" but it was too late. I glanced at the judge. She was sitting on a white chair with a pen in her hand, with stacked papers that were so tall you'd have thought that it would be obscuring her vision. She was fairly pretty, with chocolate brown eyes and golden blonde hair that framed her face perfectly. A smile was painted on her extravagantly gorgeous face.

"Uh, um I — "

She cut me off. "You're Megan D'Agostino, right?" she inquired.

"Uh, um yeah," I stuttered. "Why can't I just speak normally?!" I thought.

"What song will you be singing?" she asked. "And oh by the way my, name is Ms. Harris."

"I-I'm going to be singing the-the, uh, 'The Ash Grove.'" I stuttered sheepishly.

"Okay, we'll start with some sight reading, I'll give you a few lines to sing, and you'll look at them for as long as you like and then sing it," Ms. Harris instructed.

Luckily the sight reading was extremely easy. Now it was time for the hardest part; singing "The Ash Grove." When I was done she smiled, showing her pearly white teeth, and said, "Very nice."

At that, I walked out the door to be swarmed with hugs.

I thought proudly to myself, "I did it! I actually did it!" I swear my smile was a mile wide.

Megan D'Agostino
Grade 6

Thomas Edison's Creations

Thomas Alva Edison went to school for three months and questioned everything his teachers taught. His mother had been a teacher and decided to teach him at home. At age ten he loved books, and enjoyed the encyclopedia where he learned chemistry and experimenting.

Moving to Michigan, the cellar of their house became a laboratory. Thomas was twelve years old when he started as a newspaper, magazine, and candy vendor.

Thomas' books and chemistry set fell and started a fire on a train. The conductor boxed his ears and threw him off the train.

At a different train depot, he became a hero when he rescued a boy on the tracks. An oncoming engine approached, and Thomas thought quickly and scooped the boy into his arms. Thomas' reward from the boy's father was an offer to teach telegraphy. He worked there for a while then moved to New York.

He found a job at Gold and Stock Telegraph Company. Thomas still studied chemistry, electricity, and continued experiments on telegraph machines.

Thomas sold his inventions for a large sum of money then built a factory in New Jersey for building telegraph machines. In 1876 he set up a laboratory and his chief business was making inventions.

Thomas received a medal from the Untied States Congress which set the value of his inventions at $15,599,000,000. The phonograph, motion picture cameras, and light bulbs are a few of the one thousand inventions created. He changed our lives significantly.

Dan Bish
Grade 4

My Favorite Biography

My favorite biography is about Lou Gehrig and it is called *Lou Gehrig, the Luckiest Man* by David A. Adler. It is my favorite because Lou Gehrig was not only a great baseball player, but he also was a great man. Lou Gehrig was always thankful for all of his blessings. He never complained about the bad things that happened to him, especially the terrible illness he had. Lou Gehrig never gave up and always had courage.

After I read this book, I thought of Lou Gehrig as my role model. For me, it is very easy to complain, but when I think of Lou Gehrig, I try not to complain. This man died from a terrible illness when he was only 38. Even while he had this illness, he still considered himself "the luckiest man in the world."

Lou Gehrig always had a way of being happy. That is something that we should always try to do, so that we too can achieve the most important things in life.

Marianne Lipovsky
Grade 5

Our Friendship Will Last Forever

My best friend's name is Chloe. We have been friends for as long as I can remember. We may have fights, but when we get over them, our friendship is stronger than before. We met in preschool at Troki Hebrew Academy. We only played with each other, no one else. You could call us inseparable.

The thing that I like in a best friend like her is she's someone who I can trust and talk to when I need someone to talk to. We tell each other our secrets. There are some secrets that we have told one another when we were seven, and we both have not told anyone to this day.

Some of the things that we like to do together are play games, go shopping, make up dances, and listen to music. Also in the summer, we go to my house and play "Truth or Dare" in my pool. When I go to her house, we also play with her little sister, Lanie. We did the talent show together. We danced to the song "Fighter." Our parents are as good friends as we are, maybe even better. It is really fun when we all go the mall together.

I think that even when we're older, we will still be really good friends, maybe even better friends than we are today.

Jenny Kaufman
Grade 6

On the Slope Is My Favorite Place

My favorite place is on the ski slope. It is my favorite because I love coming down the mountain really fast and having all that wind in my face. It is fun meeting kids and racing them down the mountain. Whether I win or lose, it is still a lot of fun. My brother and I race a lot, too. Most of the time, I win. If I fall, I don't care because I will get right back up and start going down the mountain again. It is awesome if I see some of my friends from school on the mountain because then I can race them. If I lose, I don't care because that just means they are faster than me. My dad is always at the bottom of the mountain taking pictures of my mom, brother and me.

Anthony Wright
Grade 6

The World Series

On the day of the World Series it was the Boston Red Sox vs the New York Yankees. It was at the Yankee Stadium. It was so huge!!! My dad and I went to his best friend's house, he has a big screen TV. My team is the Boston Red Sox. We all had Boston's jerseys on. Our jerseys were sparkling white with some ruby and silver on them. There were so many people coming to my dad's friend's house.

About 30 minutes into the game, which Curt was pitching, he cut his foot. So the cut seemed very bad. I guess he was living up to his baseball team because his sock was all dark pink from blood. When my dad and I were celebrating while we were driving home, we listened to the radio. Finally we found the station that was talking about the game. When my dad and I got home we ate a bin of fried chicken.

Colby McIlroy
Grade 6

The Drawing Queen

Someday, if I became famous, I think I'd be famous as an artist. My day would be very busy. The first thing that I would do is draw a simple picture and then go to a museum. I would enjoy walking around the beautiful pictures that I painted.

After, I will draw pictures for a book. I would speak with the author and find out what kind of illustrations she would like me to make. After lunch, I would go back to my house and watch an artist show on TV starring me.

Then, after dinner I would look up some artists' tips on the computer. The next morning, I will start my routine all over again. That would be my life as a famous artist.

Gabriella Micciche
Grade 4

Cell Phones Are Great!

The most important thing to me is my cell phone. My cell phone lets me call and talk to my cousin, Kayla, and my friends too. It also lets you call somebody in case of emergency.

Now say you get caught in traffic on your way home from work. You could call your husband or wife and tell them you got stuck in traffic. If you did not have a cell phone, what would you do?

On your way home from school, your friend asks you, "Do you want to come over for a while?" You have a phone to call your mom or dad and ask them if you could go to your friend's house.

So you're at a movie with your friend. The movie is over and no one is there to pick you up. You would have a phone to call and get a hold of somebody. So you call and the person on the other line says, "Thank goodness you had your phone. I forgot all about picking you guys up."

That's why you should have a cell phone.

Sydney Kaercher
Grade 4

Alligators vs Crocodiles

What do you think is the most dominate, the crocodile or the alligator? Both can live to be about 50 years old. Also you can only see the crocodile's fourth tooth when it's mouth is closed.

Now that you have 2 facts about alligators and crocodiles, here are 2 similarities. One of their similarities is that they can live in water and on land. Another way they are alike is both are in the same family.

In addition to the similarities listed, here are some differences. Crocodiles have larger snouts than alligators. Another way they are different is that alligators are slightly larger than crocodiles. Finally you can see an alligator's lower jaw when its mouth is closed.

With the above information do you have an answer? Mine is the alligator. I am choosing the alligator because it weighs more and it seems more vicious than the crocodile.

Derek Licktieg
Grade 6

Veteran's Day

My dad was a Marine once! My dad got 2 medals for shooting. He got a marksmanship award twice. The first award was being series high shooter. My dad was the best shooter out of 831 other people that went up for the award. When he was putting the guns together he would say 5.56 mil, light weight, air cooled, gas operated, magazine feed, shoulder firing weapon, capable of firing semiautomatic or automatic by use of a selector lever sir. He served our country for four years straight from 1987-1991. My dad was very good at shooting, and I get my shooting skills from him. He gave me both of his medals but I am not allowed to take them anywhere because he does not want them to be lost. He was very happy when I brought his jacket back and he keeps saying thank you. He even cares more about the marines because it turned an undisciplined kid into a well respected young man.

Zachery Myrick
Grade 6

My First Puppy

My mom was holding a video camera when I walked into our back room. I glanced up at her and then looked before me. What I saw was so shocking that I didn't know what to say. "When did you think of this?" My brother's and sisters' expressions changed when I screeched, "We got a puppy!"

I looked around the room filled with dog supplies. There were grooming tools, food cans and bags, toys, treats and a little bed. The puppy was so small, only one and a half pounds. I didn't want to disturb her because she was sleeping so comfortably with a stuffed animal almost bigger than her. Immediately she looked up from her sleep. I picked her up.

Behind me was my dad. "I can't believe you changed your mind!" My dad never liked dogs and was allergic to them! I did some research to prove that people with allergies weren't allergic to terriers. His reply was always, "We're not getting a dog." I almost completely gave up. That's why this was so shocking.

"What are we going to name her?" I was thinking of the name Sparky for my future dog, but now that sounded too much like a boy.

Mom replied, "I was thinking about the name Sparkles."

"Come here Sparkles." I squeaked her perfect sized hot pink bone. She came running as fast as a rocket.

That night I went to bed with Sparkles. Knowing that I had a puppy made me feel like the luckiest person in the world.

In the morning I thought I was dreaming but Sparkles was at my feet. Still in shock, I picked her up, cuddled her in my arms, and kissed her little, delicate, almost bald head. Now I believe that my greatest dreams can come true.

Kayla Winchester
Grade 6

My Life as a Cloud

Hi my name is Culunimbous. My cousins names are Cumulus, Cirrus and Stratus. We think people on Earth call us clouds. Do you want to know why I'm so black? Birds store lots of coal in their wings and throw it on me. People on airplanes open their windows and throw fire on me.

Do you want to know why we have dangerous thunder storms? I get mad, I turn red and start crying and yelling and throwing fire. Do you want to know why we have snow? Angels bring huge, big, amounts of ice and dump it on me until I let it go. I wonder why people of Earth, call us clouds.

Anthea Shaw
Grade 4

Believe It, or Not

Do you believe in the Loch Ness Monster? These stories may encourage your belief as they encouraged mine. A man was walking down a Scottish road when he was picked up by the Loch Ness Monster! It happened the same day a priest was walking down the same road, but arrived later. He saw a terrified man hanging from the jaws of the Loch Ness monster. He commanded it to put the man down in the name of the Lord, and so it did, and receded into the water.

Another time, much later, science groups from all over the world came to look for, and catch on camera, the Loch Ness Monster. One group had a set of underwater electronic equipment, and a problem. Some of the equipment was disabled, so they sent a diver to repair it. The diver slowly walked down the quickly descending underwater landscape, and he had almost reached the buoy when he saw Nessie face to face. He was terrified, and slowly began walking backwards, when Nessie quickly turned around and swam into the murk. The diver said he would never approach the Loch again. Do you believe? I do.

Jacob Young
Grade 6

The Baby

"What are you having?" "A baby!" You're only 27 years old, gosh you're young. My sisters Filipa, Marina, and Bianca didn't know, but my dad sure knew. Days and days went by and I kept seeing my mom not feeling well. My father took her to the hospital and she was ill. Then my mom and dad came home and said to my sisters that she was going to have a baby boy named Kevin.

I was so surprised and my sisters were too. Then a few days later my mom went to the hospital to have my brother. Then the doctor found that she had lost the baby. So she stayed in the hospital for a few days so she could calm down because of what happened to the baby. When she was still in the hospital we baked a cake for her. When she came home that night we showed her the biggest cake. She said, "Let's eat the cake together." Then we all ate the cake. All of us were so happy that our mom was home from the hospital and healthy.

Joana DaSilva
Grade 6

Mr. Slick

Wow, the past five years that I have watched football I have not seen a better quarterback than Michael Vick. He plays for my favorite team, the Atlanta Falcons. Yet, I haven't been to a game. I watch him every chance that I possibly have. This young fearless quarterback out of Virginia Tech can turn absolutely nothing into a ten or twenty yard gain.

Vick graduated from Virginia Tech in 2001 and has already captured the minds of young kids across the globe. He is a great quarterback and his younger brother Marcus has the potential to be just as good, if not a better ballplayer than Michael is. Mike wore the number 7 in college and still yields it today in the NFL.

His younger brother Marcus also plays for Virginia Tech, yet he wears the number 5. Or at least Marcus would if he didn't get kicked off the Virginia Tech team. Some people criticize Mike for not being a real quarterback. They think he runs the ball too often, but I think that's what makes him unique to all the other QB's that can't run to get out of trouble at all.

On game day you couldn't depend on a better QB at the line of scrimmage than Michael Vick. When you put the ball in his hands, you could almost guarantee a victory. For all of those rival teams out there, good luck stopping Mike and the rest of the Atlanta Falcons' offense.

Ethan Kelsey
Grade 5

Best Friends Forever (BFF)

I have a lot of friends and best friends. They are Alexis, Michael, and Sarah. I am so thankful for their friendship.

Alexis is my best friend. She is my best friend because her and I have a lot in common. We both love the color orange. We both like the same movies, and we both love bracelets, rings, and necklaces! When I'm down or in trouble, she's there for me all the way! The same for her, too. If she is feeling down or is in trouble I'm always there. Alexis is my best friend forever (BFF)!

Another very good friend I have is Sarah! Sarah is a good friend because she is nice, pretty, and unique! Sometimes she does her own thing and that's why she is so unique. She is kind of like Alexis. They have the same characteristics.

Michael is my very good friend too! We played soccer together. I was dark blue and he was aqua green! He can be very annoying sometimes. We call each other all the time and talk for about 2 hours! Once we had a conversation for 6 hours about nothing.

In conclusion, my best friends are the best of them all. Sarah and Alexis are my best friends forever and will always be through good times and bad times! I am so thankful that I have them for friends!

Hailey Burch
Grade 5

Hunter

I love dogs in fact I received a Beagle two years ago. My mom and my dad gave my brother, sister, and I the best gift ever. It was my new dog. They gave it to us early because they didn't want the puppy to be confused with all the people that would be visiting on Christmas Eve. He was so cute and I was so happy that I began to cry. He was a Beagle so we named him Hunter because Beagles hunt.

After about one week he started following me everywhere. I'd play with him and do everything with him. I started feeling that if I had a problem I could talk to my dog Hunter. He is a very good listener. Sometimes I even feel that he is human and that he can really understand me, he shows so much love towards me. I always show it back by hugging him, taking him for a walk and feeding him. My dog loves to sleep so when I am tired I'd sleep right next to him. It is so weird; he became my best friend within two weeks. The good thing is they give you exercise and can help you when anything ever happens. My grandma, who lived with me, was sick from lung cancer and my dog knew right away that something was wrong and seemed really sad with us. He began to follow her around. Shortly after she died Hunter was sad too! He was whimpering.

Dogs are very special, they can get you through anything. They are sensitive and fun. A dog can be your best companion.

Samantha Ardino
Grade 6

My Dog Lexi

One day my Mom and Dad went to buy a puppy. They found a place to buy a puppy by looking in the newspaper. When they got to the house which sold the puppies, my Mom picked out a puppy. All of a sudden one of the other puppies jumped on her and knocked her down. My Mom bought her instead (the alpha puppy). While my Dad was driving home, my Mom picked off some fleas that were on the puppy. She threw them out the window and did that all the way home. When my Mom and Dad got home, they introduced the puppy to her new home. They decided to name her Lexi.

When I was born, Lexi became my best friend ever! As a matter of fact, I gave Lexi her first taste of people food. I was in a highchair and I threw a Cheerio on the floor and Lexi ate it! She seemed to have liked it my Mom claims. I think she did because now she loves Cheerios! As Lexi grew up, she got paralyzed by falling down while chasing after a tennis ball in our backyard. We rushed her to a pet hospital and she was unable to walk. Now she is all right and able to walk, but not up stairs very well. I love Lexi and I'm glad that she's part of our family. Lexi still lives today at the age of 11 years old (that's 77 in dog years)!

Brett Cotten
Grade 4

The Water Cycle

A water cycle is a path that water takes as it evaporates from oceans, lakes and other sources, condenses, and falls to Earth as precipitation, and evaporates or flows back to the sea. Water is always moving on through and above Earth as it changes from one form to another in the water cycle. The steps of the water cycle include evaporation, condensation, precipitation, and runoff. These steps can be affected by temperature, pressure, wind, and the elevation of the land.

Water vapor makes up a very small fraction of the gases in the air. The particles of water vapor, like particles of other gases, are constantly moving. The sun has a major effect on the water cycle. The energy of sunlight causes most melting, evaporation, and sublimation. Energy is needed to raise water vapor to the clouds and move it by winds. This energy originally comes from the sun. When water vapor condenses into liquid water, it releases energy. This is heat. It warms the air or water in the immediate area.

Justin Rodriguez
Grade 5

Hershey Chocolate

As one of the most popular candy industries in the world, Hershey Chocolate stands high with what many say is a delicious taste. It has a lot of history and today, Hershey Chocolate is celebrated in many different ways.

Milton S. Hershey was the man who started it all by creating Hershey Chocolate. Since he was the only surviving child in his family, he had strict discipline of the Mennonite faith and was only able to finish fourth grade. When Hershey was at a high point of success in his business, he envisioned a complete new community around his factory. He added a ballroom, swimming pool, Hotel Hershey, Hershey Lodge, and the Hershey Park Arena. He also added a park, which attracted many visitors.

To be near the top, Hershey Chocolate has a whole lot of history! When Milton Hershey had a four year apprenticeship with a Lancaster candy maker, Lancaster Carmel Company came to be. Soon, Hershey became fascinated with German chocolate making and decided to focus more on his chocolate making career. Hershey sold the Lancaster Carmel Company for $1,000,000. He used the money to make his chocolate with the latest mass production techniques. When Hershey's milk chocolate first went on the market, it was the only chocolate of its kind.

Hershey Park is a theme park near the Hershey Chocolate factory that has over 60 rides and attractions! Hershey Park offers an outside tour of the Hershey factory by monorail and lets you watch chocolate being made in Chocolate World. Hotel Hershey and the Hershey Lodge are the two hotels near Hershey Park.

Hershey Chocolate sure has come a long way from when it first started! It has extended into a huge industry. With a whole lot of history, this chocolate still satisfies many people today.

Stephanie Neville
Grade 5

Canada

One summer we had a vacation to Canada. It took us five hours to get there, and when we got there it was night. Then we checked into a hotel and then we slept there for the night. Then in the morning we went to stores there and I bought souvenirs and my brother bought things for him, too.

After we stopped going in stores, we went to the arcade and my sister and my older brother found a game that they really liked and used it the whole entire time we were in there. We were in it a while, and then we got tickets for a tour on a ship. After that, we went for lunch on a boat. It had a really good menu, but they were expensive. Then, we went back to our hotel room and just stayed there for a little while until we had to leave for our tour on the ship. There was a line to get on the ship, but it wasn't that long. When we got on, they were serving supper on the middle deck. I ate only a little bit, because I was still a little full from when I ate on the boat for lunch. Then, I went on the top deck to take my first ever pictures on my camera.

It was a very long time, but soon the ship director headed back and we were almost out of film. Then when we got back, we went home.

Michael Twardowski
Grade 5

Why Litter Bugs Me

You know what bugs me? People who litter. Litter makes my town look ugly. When my friends and family come from out of town to visit, I am embarrassed. One time my dog cut his paw on glass because of someone who thought it would be cool to smash a bottle that was dropped. I worry about the environment and wildlife that we need to protect.

What can we do about all of this litter? We as knowledgeable humans need to be more responsible. If someone smokes a cigarette they shouldn't throw it on the ground. Keep a bag in your car to hold litter. Hold onto garbage until you pass a trash can.

How does litter affect us? Litter harms nature. Cigarette butts can cause fires if they are thrown on the ground still lit. Beautiful lands and national parks are also spoiled by litter and broken glass. Litter also spreads disease. Litter goes down storm drains and ends up in our oceans. Plastic bags, toys, and six-pack rings choke or make sea animals sick.

Why do people litter? Some people litter because there is no garbage can nearby. Some kids my age litter to rebel against the rules to be cool. But most of the time people litter because they're lazy. Others litter because they don't think the object they dropped is litter, such as food scraps and cigarettes.

Please help me by telling your friends that littering is bad and by picking up litter when you see it.

Ali Baranowski
Grade 6

Derek Jeter

Derek Jeter plays shortstop for the New York Yankees. In 2004 he had 482 at bats and 87 runs, with 10 homeruns and 52 RBI's. His batting average was .324. Derek Jeter was born in Pequannock, New Jersey in 1974. Derek Jeter is a 5 time All-Star and he is also the New York Yankees' team captain. His team won the World Series with him 4 times. His batting average ranks 5th in Yankees' history. That's why Derek Jeter is a good player.

Daniel Hank
Grade 4

Life or Death

My family had a scary life experience. It all started six years ago. It was a life or death situation. My mom had a brain tumor in the left part of her brain.

It all started when my mom had a tumor from when she was about ten-years-old. She had a set of MRI scans because she had a massive brain tumor on the left side of her brain. There was an eighty percent chance she'd die and a twenty percent chance she'd live. She was only thirty-years-old, now she is thirty-six-years-old.

The surgery to remove the tumor would take forty-two hours. After the surgery, she had one-hundred and seven staples in her head. She also had an eye patch over her left eye. She can't ride an amusement park ride ever again. She can't walk for a long time. She can't do the stuff she used to, but she can do what she's best at; being a mom.

My mom survived the deadly surgery. She can't do everything she used to and sometimes she gets frustrated, but it doesn't matter, at least she's still alive and that's what matters most. She always does what's best for our family.

Katelynn Elms
Grade 5

Volcanos

Volcanoes can be loud and interesting to watch, if they are still around. When they erupt or blow the top shoot rocks through the air, or a lot of people call it lava. The melted rocks are like water in a way, the lava will flow like water in a river. Eruptions, like Mount St. Helens, start out deep in the earth. Our planet has three layers: the crust, the mantle, and the core. As the eruption continued mudslides started up. The ashes and dirt mixes up and causes mud to form.

In 1980, the ground shook in Washington state, then Mount St. Helens rumbled. The side of the volcano exploded. The whole top of the mountain was gone. Rocks, ash, and gases ran down the volcano. We call that lava. Deep down in the ground 3 to 25 miles below the crust, is a soft, hot layer. The mantle contains hot, melted rock called magma.

In certain places, it pushes through the ground and makes a volcano. In Hawaii people can watch the volcanoes erupt. The Hawaii volcanoes have almost no sound when they blow. The lava can get 2,100 degrees Fahrenheit that is hot enough to melt some metals.

Nichole Miller
Grade 4

Spinach

On one treacherous night my dad made disgusting dark green spinach. I sat down at the Tiger Wood table in my cozy house as he yelled, "dinner is ready." Then it was there (I remember like it was yesterday) the spinach in their camouflage army uniforms. Just sitting there waiting to be eaten.

I took a big scoop of creamy mashed potatoes and a thick, juicy slice of ham. "No," I screamed as my dad was going to dump a colossal spoon of acrimonious spinach onto my plate. Then, he plopped it down on my plate and took another spoonful and dumped it on my navy blue plate. It seemed like they were yelling at me, "eat me, eat me."

After that, I had to eat all of it. My grandpa even watched me eat the disloyal food. Then I hid all of the little soldiers under my snow white napkin. I quickly threw the whole meal away and had no second thoughts. My spinach sat in the trash can in disbelief. I will never eat spinach again in my life, even if it was the only food in the world. That was the most wretched meal of my life, for sure!

Kathryn Zimmerman
Grade 4

I Have a Dream…

Someday I will be famous because I will find a cure for cancer. I will find a cure for cancer because my cousin had cancer and I know what it's like to have a family member that's sick. I also like to help people. I always wanted to be a doctor.

I will find a cure for cancer because I had a relative that had cancer. When my cousin got sick, she started to lose her hair. She missed *a lot* of school. I'm *so* glad that she's better now and that she doesn't have to take chemotherapy anymore. This is why I am determined to become a doctor and find a cure for cancer so this will never happen again.

I have always wanted to be a doctor. I will go to medical school. I will do research on the computer and I will read books to get into medical school.

I will also try to prevent cancer. I will try to prevent it by finding out what causes it. Since I have always wanted to be a doctor it will be easy to live this dream.

Samantha Brown
Grade 5

My Way to Florida

One day my cousin Kiki invited me to go to Florida with her. My mom said I could go. I started to pack.

It took us about 15 hours. We had to go through North Carolina, South Carolina, and Georgia just to get to Florida. When we got there, I went to sleep.

The next day I woke up and I headed straight to the pool. I went to the hot tub, it felt really relaxing.

When I got home my mom was so happy to see me, and my whole family started to hug me. I guess they missed me a lot. I was so happy to be home.

Angela Delgado
Grade 4

USA Glory

Did you ever look at a flag for a moment and feel something special? The American flag is the greatest way to feel the enjoyment of life. When I look at this flag I see the glorious freedom it has, the struggle it went through, and a marvelous future.

The reason I see freedom in this country's flag is because all men and women from any race can vote. For my eleven years, and soon to be twelve, all I have seen is love. People can practice religion, have freedom of speech, and travel freely without anyone stopping them. I have noticed almost everything in America is open to the public.

Don't ever think that America got this way without struggle. There's been a plethora of wars for America to get where it is today. Every single one of the soldiers that fought for this spectacular piece of territory is honored as a hero. We still honor heroes today, and we will forever.

I just can't wait for the future of America. With the high quality technology we have today, we may even live on the moon. Hopefully, war will end, and peace will spread across the world. At some time, we could gain more states and possibly have a female president. Living in this wonderful country makes me feel that a terrific life was meant to exist in America.

Now, don't you think America is fantastic? America is the most splendid country ever.

Ryan Ribeiro
Grade 6

The Shed

When I was 5 years old the shed was where my friends and I hung out. We picked the shed because it was where we could hide out and have fun. It was great because it was like a little house. We would only let girls in and make the boys hit the road. We didn't let boys in because when I was small it was boys vs girls. We had so much fun that my dad redid it. It now has lights, painted walls, carpeting, windows, and electricity.

As I grew older I grew out of it and turned it over to my little cousin and her friends. She made a tremendous amount of rules for the shed too. The rules that my cousin made are silly. I don't remember them well since she never really told me. She also made a little fort out front and filled a box with water balloons, with the help of me, so boys would back off.

I grew up with that shed and it was hard to give it away because I'm too old to go in, it's a new rule. Although I liked it there is no reason for me to keep it since I'm not 5. Giving it away was a big day in my life because it was a real childhood memory. If you ask my friends one day they will tell you about it and how much we enjoyed it.

Nicole Souza
Grade 6

Best Grandma in the World

Someone special to me is my Grandma, who I call Mema. She has done many things in the past for me. She has also helped me through rough times. My grandma has been through multiple things, one thing she has been through is breast cancer. I go to her house sometimes and clean it to help her out. When she is feeling okay, she takes me to the movies, the mall, and also takes me to breakfast almost every week. She has done so much for me in the past. We have so many memories and I hope for plenty more to come with her in the future!

Michael Callas
Grade 6

Mario Lemieux vs Wayne Gretzky

I am writing to settle the argument of who is better. Is it Mario Lemieux or Wayne Gretzky?

At the end of the 2003-2004 season, Mario had played 889 games, scored 683 goals and 1018 assists! This means he averaged 0.8 goals per game and 1.1 assists per game. At the end of his career, Gretzky played 1,487 games, scored 894 goals, and had 1,963 assists. He averaged 0.6 goals per game and 1.3 assists per game.

Last, what gives the best comparison between Gretzky and Lemieux? It is points and average points per game. Gretzky had 2,857 points in his career. Mario had 1,701 points up to the 2003-2004 season…Mario averages 1.913 points per game in the NHL. Gretzky averaged 1.921 points per game in his career in the NHL.

According to stats, Gretzky was better than Lemieux. It is a close fight, Lemieux only losing by 0.01 of a point per game. I guess that settles it and ends the argument.

Chris Hughes
Grade 6

My Dream

My name is Elora Leah Reilly. I am in the fourth grade, and I love singing, dancing, and acting. As soon as I came to Hillside in third grade, I set my goal to be in Traveling Troupe (a singing and acting traveling group) and to have a lead part in the school play. Unfortunately, the school drama teacher told me only 4th and 5th graders were allowed to join. I was very disappointed, but I took drama classes and chorus for the entire year.

In June 2005, the Traveling Troupe tryouts finally rolled around, and I was going to sing, "The Sun Will Come Out Tomorrow." I thought I had done perfectly and that I would get in until I saw the list of people who had made it, but I wasn't one of them!

The whole summer I practiced like mad but this year in Play Production when I tried out for Jasmine in the play *Aladdin,* the drama teacher barely paid attention to me. Instead of the part of Jasmine, I got a group part. I became a *royal* instead. I guess dreams don't always come true, at least not the way you want them to.

Elora Reilly
Grade 4

My Family

I have many good and bad memories with my family. All in all though, I love them very much! Every summer I go to Rockaway Beach. We have tons of family there. I usually go boogie boarding with my cousins or dive under the waves. We all get ices from the ice cream man.

Rockaway is not just where our summer house is and the place where we go to the beach and hang out. It fills in the pieces that are incomplete in our hearts. If the sun is shining and there is a nice, cool breeze, my mom and I walk and collect sea glass. Then at the end of the summer we get a cork board and paint it white. We put all the pieces on it and it looks like a giant jigsaw puzzle!

If there are no mosquitoes and it is still light out, we will order pizza on the beach. We all get to sit together and catch up on how the summer has been so far. We sit there on a towel and watch the gorgeous sunset.

We all love to be together and be just who we want to be whenever and wherever we want. There is no one else I enjoy being with more than my mom, my dad and my brothers! We fight sometimes, but that doesn't mean we don't love each other. Together we laugh, together we cry, together we are a family. Rockaway Beach is our special place!

Cassie DeMatteis
Grade 6

A Memory

I remember the great blizzard, it was big. When I was playing fastball outside with my friends I could hardly see them. When I threw the ball I would miss them every time. I was playing fastball with my four friends Josh, Anthony, Marcus, and CJ.

"Can you throw the ball to me instead of the snow?" Josh yelled at me like it was my fault. Josh was the type of kid that would do just about anything. He was small and skinny. Basically he looked like Eminem the rap artist. He was fun to hang with.

"Yeah, no problem." I said back to him. You think we would be dumb for playing fastball in the freezing cold. It was fun though because every time I would run the ball my foot would get stuck in the snow. It felt like snow was holding onto my leg, and then my friends would jump on me.

"You guys want to play capture the flag?" said Anthony. Anthony was a big stocky kid, very strong too, who I play football a lot with.

"OK why not," said Josh. When we hid the flag it felt like it disappeared because it snowed so much. We had to dig in the snow to find the flag. It was getting cold. So I decided to go inside and drink some hot cocoa. Then I went to bed with five blankets. That was the memory of my great blizzard.

Dillon Holmes
Grade 6

The Kick

The field looked like it was a never ending chain of grass. My legs seemed to run faster and harder like I never had before. It seemed the moment was nearer and nearer.

As I approached the goal, I felt like a mouse running for cheese in the kitchen. I swung my leg like a pro would. BAM! I kicked the ball straight in the goal.

I opened my eyes. There was a trophy in my hand. We won! My team congratulated me. This was a moment I surely would never forget.

Tera Evenson
Grade 4

The Worst Sight Ever

The most horrible sight I've ever seen is when I was watching TV, and I put the news on and I saw what Hurricane Katrina did to the people that lived in Louisiana. When I saw it, I saw a little kid who lost his home and his mom, dad, and everyone else in his family. The kid was screaming for his mom and dad. Then I thought to myself, what would I do if that happened to me, and I was the same age. I thought to myself, I don't know what I would do. Then I kept watching, and I saw dead bodies floating and houses under water. If that happened to where I live, I would probably go on top of my house, but I really don't know unless it happened to me. I thought that was scary because there are people in this world that now will never see their parents again. I would probably cry and look for family members. I hope this will never happen to me, and I will pray for the people of the Hurricane Katrina.

Anthony Mazza
Grade 6

Having Goals

I think it is important to have goals in life. My goal is to join the Navy or to become a doctor, or maybe become a doctor in the Navy. It is important to give back to America. I also want to help people or find cures for diseases. At the same time, I want to help save the rain forest. It is being cut down, burned, and bulldozed at this very moment. This is very hurtful to the environment.

But right now, I'm only ten years old. Still there are steps that I can take to reach my goals. To help the environment, I pick up trash along the road and recycle. I try to conserve energy by turning off lights and taking quick showers. Even though it's not curing cancer, I wash my hands so I don't spread germs to other people.

Since I'm not a genius, I work hard at my studies at school. It is important to develop correct study habits and to get good grades now. These things will help me later on in high school and college. Most of what I do are small steps towards meeting my goals; and they are helping the world a little bit, too. They are not rocket science, but I do have goals. Besides, I *am* only ten years old!

Brianne Lee Corey
Grade 5

Painting to Spaghetti*

When I look at this painting I think of my favorite food, spaghetti. I find it easier to compare a painting to my favorite food than to just say what I think.

The artist compares to the chef. The artist makes a beautiful painting while the chef makes a different type of masterpiece. I notice the colors, the texture, the warmth in my plate and on the canvas.

The canvas compares to the plate. Both are empty until the chef or artist begins his magic. Whether mixing ingredients or paints on the canvas or plate, every piece of art has a starting point.

The paints compare to the sauce, both with much texture and color. The sauce can be lumpy or smooth, red or red with different colored spices. The paint can be 3 dimensional or flat and can be any color of the artist's desire.

Certain colors give certain feelings. Reds and oranges give more of a mad or warm feeling and blues, grays or blacks give more of a sad or cold feeling. Greens, yellows and pinks give a HAPPY feeling.

I think that this painting feels very happy and peaceful. It has a smooth texture and a great chef. When you look at this painting you wish you were on the bridge. Look at your favorite painting and when someone asks you what you think of it, try comparing it to YOUR favorite food. It really helps to describe how you feel and it's fun too.

Shannon Abel
Grade 6
*Inspired by Monet's "Water Lily"

An Inspiring Hero!

On September 21, 2005, Nellie Flynn and I had a terrible day. We were running cross-country and a pit bull came behind us and bit us. We were so scared, and we were crying so much. Four innocent Margate kids were bitten, including Nellie and I. We all had to go to the hospital from four o'clock in the after noon until ten o'clock at night. Nellie had to get over 40 stitches. Since I only got four, I could walk.

When we were in the hospital, I wheeled myself down to Nellie's hospital bed. I was there for Nellie, and she was there for me. Now, four months later, we are closer than ever. I feel like a sister to her.

Nellie is the bravest person I know! I want to thank her for inspiring me to always be the best I can be and to always live life to its fullest. It may sound weird, but two eleven year olds, stuck in a hospital made us closer than ever!

Nellie and I will always feel like family. I feel like she is the twin I never had. Nellie is the best person I've ever met. She is so sweet. You, Nellie! I love you! I hope we are best friends forever! Whenever I hear the word pit bull, I think of Nellie. I think of her being the best.

Chloe Chipkin
Grade 6

Niagara Falls

When I was eight I went to Niagara Falls. It was beautiful. The water was a deep blue and so many other colors. I was there for three days. The first day it was a long drive; we went from Albany to Montreal, Canada. I am not sure how long it took because I was playing my Gameboy and my brother was sleeping the whole way there. When we got there my brother woke up, I stopped playing my Gameboy, and we checked into a hotel. Later my brother and I tried to go swimming but it was way too cold. So the next day we checked out of the hotel and hopped in the car and went towards Niagara Falls (Montreal was just a rest stop). This drive was the longest drive of the trip, from Montreal to Niagara Falls.

We were finally there. We went to another hotel and checked in. Then we could rest. Then we swam until about 4:30 and then we went to the falls. We watched the beautiful falls all night and then we went back to the hotel. The next day we looked at the falls one more time that day. We went and saw a movie on all the people that went down the falls and then we left.

I really liked this trip and I hope this inspires you to go, too.

Jake Fogel
Grade 5

Computers Are Important

Did you ever wonder what the world would be like without computers? I can describe this type of world in two worlds: confusing and difficult. Many jobs would be affected and so would the amount of information we are able to receive.

Librarians, for example, would have a hard time organizing books. This is because there are so many titles that have to be sorted to be easily found. Scientists could not conduct many of the helpful experiments that they can with computers. For example, without computers, there would not be space exploration. At the post office, sorting letters would be very difficult without the help of computers. Think of all the time they probably save. Some jobs have been greatly improved by computers. Some of these include jobs in the medical field, in farming, and even in restaurants.

We would not have all the amazing information that we can get with the push of a button. We can be in America and have the entire history of China in moments. We can find out what happened thousands of years ago or only yesterday just by logging on. You can talk to children in other countries without even leaving your home!

We are very fortunate to live in a time of computers. Computers make our lives easier, and they bring the world to us. That is why I feel computers are very important!

Blaze Oxier
Grade 5

All About Me

I'm a baby lover, and impatient. I love my family and I can't stand untidy things. If I see something untidy, I ask for permission to clean it up.

I'm a baby lover because I'm a babysitter. I love babies because they are so cute. They can smell really bad sometimes. (After they have gone poop.) Being a babysitter is frustrating and complicated. It's frustrating with infants because they might cry. You try everything and they don't stop crying. It's frustrating when changing a child because they squirm. (Even infants can squirm.)

I'm impatient. When someone says, "guess what?" I go, "what what what?" Also I'm impatient because I love to ask questions. Asking questions is my favorite thing to do because I ask the same question 100 times. I know how annoying it gets because people do the same thing to me as well.

I love my family and they love me. I'm the youngest. I have a mom, dad, older half brother and a sister. I have a dog. He is a Doberman. He is humongous and he's only 7 months old!

I can't stand untidy things. I love to clean. One weird thing about me is that I love to clean other people's houses but hate to clean mine. (How weird?)

In conclusion I'm a baby lover, impatient, love my family and am obsessed with cleaning. I get so excited when I do these things. All of these things are very hard!

Sara Kukobat
Grade 5

My Stoop

At age three, every so often I would go to my grandparents' house in Hewlett Harbor. When I got there I would stand on my stoop and get ready to perform. My grandparents knew what they were in for because every time I would do the same thing and they would sit down and watch. Sometimes I would perform a three-ring circus on my stoop, and run down to the basement for colorful clown hats. Other times I would dance a silly dance and sing pretty tunes. There were times when I fell off my stoop and twisted an arm out of its socket only to come back the next week or so with a smile on my face, ready to perform on my special stoop. When my sister was born one March I sang on my stoop gentle songs about how much I loved her. When years passed, and she was old enough we both stood on what had become our stoop.

Years passed, and I was getting older. My sister was now a big sister to my baby brother, and my grandparents were getting more and more tired of their house as we forgot about our special stoop. Two years ago they decided to move out of their house, and into an apartment. They had forgotten about our stoop and it was nowhere to be found in their new apartment. The memory still lives on in my heart even though my special stoop no longer exists.

Rebecca Herz
Grade 5

On Stage

Acting brings you places that might not exist. You trade in your body for someone else's. You feel like you are another person. You *are* another person. It's important to have something to wash away worries. For me, it's acting.

When I'm on stage, I don't feel like my normal self. I don't think about upcoming tests, projects due, or my homework. When I act, I have to get into character so I can know how to act like that character.

I've been acting for five years. Before I started acting, somehow I knew I loved it. That seems hard to believe, but it's true. You see, you had to be in second grade to join the drama class at Saturday Series. When I first heard about this, I was too young but I couldn't wait to join. I made a great choice. It changed my life.

I've starred in many plays, but my favorite was *Willy Wonka and the Chocolate Factory*. I starred as Willy Wonka! It felt great to be up there on stage with everybody looking at me. Everyone was amazed by my performance. Then afterwards everyone congratulated me. It felt too great for words. Complete strangers came up to me and complimented me!

I've never found anything else that gives me the same great feeling I get from acting. When I act, I become another person and let myself be free. I can be whatever I want to be. It's great to express myself through acting.

Olivia Demeri
Grade 6

An Incredible Place

Do you want an incredible vacation spot? Then Tennessee is the place for you. Tennessee has so much to offer for any sized group.

One spectacular thing is that it has an awesome theme park, the kids will love it and you will too. The park's name is Dolly Wood. You can take a train ride around the mountains on an old steam train. One of the main things is the Tennessee Tornado, it is one of the craziest roller coasters in the South. I think the kids will enjoy it.

Another marvelous thing about Tennessee is that it is the country capital of the world. One of the biggest parts is the Grand Ol' Opera. So if you like country music Tennessee is a great place for you to vacation.

Lastly I believe it is the most peaceful place in the world. I think it is the most peaceful because it has 500,000 acres of wilderness and over 150 tree species. Also without leaving your car, you may drive the 11 mile, one way, paved Loop Road. You could pass deer, bear, and wild turkey are frequently seen.

I think Tennessee is a great place to vacation. Oh and one more thing, look out for Black Bears!

Colton Fergus
Grade 4

My Best Friend

My best friend is very nice. She is one of the kindest people I know. She always helps me and is never mean. She is very smart and is very funny. She can always make me laugh. We are a lot alike. She is like a sister to me. We see each other almost every day. There could not be a better friend than her. We also like to talk on the phone a lot. I met her in first grade, she was new to our school. On the second day of school I asked her if she wanted to play and ever since then we have been best friends. We have been lucky enough to have been in the same class every year since first grade. We have a lot of play dates. When I'm sad she cheers me up. We have sleepovers. She has a great family, they are all so nice. I like to go to her house and she likes to go to my house. She is very fun to play with. We both like to play with our American Girl dolls. She has three and I have seven. In school at lunch she sits with me a lot. We use to go to Mattituck Dance Center and do dance recitals together. She wears glasses, has long curly brown hair, white skin, and greenish bluish color eyes. She's a great friend and I feel very lucky to be her best friend!

Katie Krukowski
Grade 4

My First Time on a Roller Coaster

One afternoon my family and I went to Great Escape theme park. On my way down in the car, I was thinking about what I was going to do. We went down after the first night. We were looking at some stores on the way down to the park. We went in only one store.

When we finally got to the park my dad would not stop asking me if I would go on the Screaming Demon with him. I finally said yes so he would stop bugging me.

When we were in line we were both excited, but I was a little scared. I was scared I would fall out of my seat when we went on the loop. When were on the ride, I wanted to get off, but it was too late. I couldn't see anything on the ride, all I saw was my feet. My head was shaking back and forth and I got a headache.

When we got off I said to my dad, "I do not want to go on that ride again." When we got off I felt much better. We went to a restaurant right behind the roller coaster. We could hear people screaming. From that day I hear people screaming.

Daniel McDonald
Grade 5

The Beach

My favorite possible place on earth has to be the beach. Listening to the beautiful music of the ocean pounding on the lifeguard stand is soothing to me. I watch the ocean waves tackle each other, one being bigger than the last. I feel like a tiny island in the middle of a sea of sand. When swimming I am not able to resist a mouthful of salt water. Yet, the sweet and bitter smell of salt air brings peace to me.

Ryan Fitzgerald
Grade 6

Our Country After Peril

This essay is about the heroes of nine-eleven and the soldiers who fought for our freedom. The heroes of nine-eleven died trying to save lives. Whereas the soldiers who fought for our freedom died fighting for our rights and constitution that we've grown to love.

Nine-eleven was a great tragedy that killed many of our country's citizens. Most of us Americans were sitting at home with our friends and family unable to do anything about what just happened. American people were scared and angry. We were scared because we don't always know what's going on around us; we were angry because we didn't want to believe that such a tragedy of that elevation could happen on the soil of our homeland.

The soldiers who fought for our freedom fought so that we could live our lives in peace. Many of those soldiers who fought for our freedom died. They died trying to make our country a better place, a place without fear. If we were to ask the soldiers who fought for our freedom, if they regret serving for the military, they might say no. They may even say that they enjoyed seeing all the nice, new places and meeting interesting people. If they had to do it all again they may say yes.

Nine-eleven has made American citizens much more cautious of events in other parts of the world. Tragedies like this not only happen on foreign soil, but here as well.

Angel Lints
Grade 6

Heart Stopper

Try screaming with no sound coming out. It's pretty hard, but I can do it. It all started when my family and I were going down the shore for vacation. My cousin, Megan, and I were so excited about the new ride on the boardwalk, the Atmosphere. It goes up one hundred and eighty feet and drops seventy miles per-hour. A couple of days later we went to the boardwalk. Walking up the ramp screams of laughter were ringing in our ears. As we got closer the screams became louder, they were all from one ride, the Atmosphere. The line was as long as the boardwalk itself. While waiting in line mice were running up and down my spine and butterflies were fluttering in my stomach in anticipation from the ride. Finally it was our turn. We started up and someone from a speaker started to talk, to give a space effect. As I looked down I immediately shut my eyes, since we were up about one hundred and fifty feet already. The person who was talking started to break up. Then it was just silent, hearing the latch let go was so frightening. We dropped, I tried to scream, but nothing came out of my mouth. My voice stayed at the top of the ride. In a blink of an eye the ride was over. My hands were shaking so bard that it seemed they were going to shake right off my arm. Breathing was difficult because my heart was pounding so rapidly. That was a HEART STOPPER!!!

Jessica Woltemate
Grade 6

Mada

Do you have an animal that you just couldn't live without? Well, I do. It's my pet dog Mada. She is a Peekapoo. If you don't know what that is, it's half Pekingese and half Poodle.

She is always there for me. When I'm sad, she makes me feel better. When I'm mad, she makes me feel happy. My dog, Mada, will do whatever I want to do. If I want to play, she'll play.

Mada is special to me because she is mine. She hangs out with me all the time. Mada is so smart too. She knows so many things. For example, she knows how to sit up, go get her toys, knows what bed time is, and sometimes I will hide and she'll find me.

She is like a little sister to me because I am an only child. So she is like part of my family. She loves everyone in my family, too.

She is important to me because she is like my best friend. She's always there for me. When I get home, she's waiting for me. It makes me feel happy when I see her waiting at the door. My dog is very, very friendly. She will run up to you and be really nice. She is also a very likable dog.

Mada is very special and anyone would love her. She is an awesome pet and an awesome friend. I would never give her up.

Cheyenne Svihla
Grade 6

Lost in London

SCREECH! BAM! I woke up in a startle. The dim light of five o'clock in the morning shines. It was time to go to London. At first I was terrified. It's the year the Twin Towers fell down. Tobi and Mom held my hand. They made me feel so much better. After the plane lifted off I had so much fun. I ate nachos, and watched TV; I was living the life.

The breeze filled my golden hair. As the wind blew I could smell food, hear birds, and see Big Ben, Queen's Castle, and Saint Paul's Cathedral. My mom was right the tour did make me feel better.

"It was grand it was great," quoted the guide. I was at the Queen's Castle. I went inside; it was like a dream home. Jewels and armor filled the room, and this is just one of hundreds of rooms.

Big Ben is the greatest clock in the world to everyone except me. That's where I got lost. You see, my mom and sister went to see Big Ben so my dad and I were together walking around. All of a sudden I turned around and he's not there! Bump! I look up. It's my mom, I'm saved! I will probably miss London but my home is way better! The plane ride home was ok. I couldn't get enough of those nachos; I ordered them again and watched TV. The plane started to move I was on my way home!

Elise Simon
Grade 5

My Favorite Author

My favorite author is Roald Dahl. I loved his books very much. Well, let me tell you why I loved his books. When I was 5, I loved reading books, but when I was 8 I started to think books were kind of boring. So I started not reading books. I thought I can't ever read books, never. When I was going to the library, I found a book by Roald Dahl. I thought it was interesting so I started reading. Then I really started liking it. When I went to the library the only books I got were Roald Dahl books, I almost read every book that he wrote. I really wanted to meet him. I noticed that he passed away in 1990, I was very disappointed. I was kind of sad but I was glad he wrote the books. If he had not written the books, I would have still thought books were boring. I would have thanked Roald Dahl for writing these books if he was alive. But still I thank him very much for writing these books. This is the story of why I love his books very much.

Chihiro Shimomoto
Grade 4

My Cat Callie

When I wake up on a Saturday morning I usually see Callie curled up at my feet. Callie is the stout, little, fat cat I know and love. She makes an art form out of purring a lot and having a meow similar to a broken gate. Although she has a peaceful nature around friends and family, she has quite a temper with the other cats. She may not look so great on first impression; but the more you know her, the more you find her inner beauty. Her fur is like the dark colors of the rainbow and her tongue is as tough as sandpaper. Usually, when I get home I see her on the sofa searching for attention. She may look large, but at supper time she runs like a jet engine! I think Callie is one of the best cats in the world, and I'm lucky she's mine!

Colleen Donnelly
Grade 6

There Is No One Like Me

Why is there no one like me? I don't know. But like the snowflake, none of them have the same pattern. None of us are the same because we have different lives and sufferings. We also have different feelings at different times.

I am different because I am an only child. I was raised by my mother. I was also raised by my grandma. Also, my father lives in Atlanta, and I get to visit him.

My favorite sports are swimming and anything that is on ice. I also like riding my bike. A lot of my friends like to play basketball and volleyball.

I am the only girl that is an altar server. I like being an altar server because I get to serve God. I am the only one in the class that has naturally red hair. My favorite music is rock. I am also the tallest girl in my class. There is a lot about me I want to change. But my friends say, "People would have curly hair. So, accept the person you are."

Monique Williams
Grade 5

Dogs

Did you know when a dog has lived 11 years it has lived around 100 dog years? Did you know a two-month old German Shepherd can follow a scent? I am going to tell you how dogs are the best playmates, how dogs can feel emotion, and how pretty they are. Dogs are incredible creatures for pets.

If my dog Sierra could, she would play all day. She loves playing tug-of-war with the bottom of two pant legs. She grabs them with all her might and pulls. If you start shaking them she will jump forward and shake her head in protest.

Just like a dog can sense fear it can also sense happiness. I have been sad and my dog jumped up and started licking me. When I am happy, she grabs a toy and drops it at my feet. Sometimes I get angry and she grabs a sock and helps me run my energy off. I feel like she is a mind reader!

My dog is the most beautiful dog around. When we brush her she stays pretty all day. When we give Sierra a bath (which she hates) she looks stunning. My dog also looks good after energizing walks.

Dogs are the best pets anyone could have. Dogs are complex animals. They love to play, they can sense emotion, and they are unique in their creation. Just like young dogs can catch a scent, I can smell out a good pet.

David Hedinger
Grade 6

The Best Day Ever

Everybody wants something big in their life. I wanted a dog! For all my life, I wished I had a dog. It was so important to me because at my age my mom had a dog, and I thought I could have one, too. Well, right now, you are probably wondering did I get a dog. I did! One day, my friend, Emily, told me that she was getting a dog. I didn't believe her at all! So one week later, I slept over at her house, and she said, "the dog breeder was coming down from Cherry Hill tomorrow." At my house, my family was really planning to get me a dog. So that morning, we went outside, and my brother came down, and Emily's sister was there, too.

As we all waited two hours for the breeder to come down, he finally came down in his big red truck. The truck was filled with eighteen puppies in crates. I went bananas! Later my parents came down and said to me, "Hannah, pick out your favorite puppy!" I screamed! Emily's family had already picked out a dog and their friends had, too. So I went with my dad in the back of the truck, and I pointed to the cutest puppy in the world! We all named her "Gypsy." My mom and I went to the store to buy a bed, crate, food, toys, bones, and treats. It's more than I imagined. Having a puppy is the greatest thing ever!

Hannah Marino
Grade 6

What Education Means to Me

We go to school to get an education. We need an education to get through life. Our education as a child starts in grammar school and continues through high school and sometimes college. The better the education, the better prepared we are for a good job. I go to school not only to learn about math and other subjects, but also to learn about my faith and my religion.

However, not every child can get an education. Some children cannot go to school because their parents cannot afford it or their parents need them to help with a family business to earn money. There are children that hate school and try to skip going. However, I like going to school because I learn new things every day. Some subjects come easier than others do but that is what makes going to school a challenge.

Going to school every day for me is fun. I get to learn new things, and I make new friends. That makes me feel good about myself. I am not quite sure what I want to be when I grow up but each day I feel is a work in progress. Someday, I will have the job of my dreams and be thankful that I had the opportunity to go to school and have the education that I received. This is thanks to all the dedicated teachers and my parents.

Rebecca Meyer
Grade 6

The Gift of Friendship

The gift of friendship is a special type of gift. It's a gift you can't buy or wrap up. It's special because friendship is with someone who you like being with and hanging out with a lot.

I have received and given the gift of friendship. My friend Lauren Liegmann and I have so many good times together because we are best friends. Everyone has the gift of friendship. Lauren and I have so much fun together.

There are many other types of gifts in the world. There's the gift of love, the gift of life, the gift of happy, the gift of hope, and a lot others. My favorite one is the gift of friendship because friends are special in every way and Lauren and I have something special.

The gift of friendship is helpful to me for reasons. One reason is when I am down and lonely and feel left out, Lauren would always somehow cheer me up. It's really nice to have her. You should always become friends with people who don't have friends because it's lonely for them and no fun at all.

Lauren is always there for me and I am always there for her. It's nice to have someone always there for you besides your relatives.

In conclusion I chose the gift of friendship for these reasons. I'm glad I have my friend Lauren.

Megan McKenna
Grade 6

Niagara Falls

Almost everyone has heard of Niagara Falls. To many, it may seem like a big giant waterfall that pours tons of water every day and never changes. Well, they are wrong! There are a lot more things that are going on.

Yes, water falls over the falls. It also generates electricity. There is a power plant called Sir Adam Beck Power Plant that is actually a tourist attraction. If you put out your hand to touch the waterfall from Journey Behind the Falls, it would break every bone in your hand! The water is that powerful. People have seen double and triple rainbows from the mist the falls produce. Upstream, the water from the falls creates Class 5 rapids and whirlpools. Jet boats can take brave tourists through the rapids out to the whirlpools.

There are many other things that are really interesting about Niagara Falls. For example, the river flows north! There are actually two waterfalls. One is called the Canadian Horseshoe Falls and the other is called the American Falls. They are right next to each other. The height of the Horseshoe Falls is 180 feet high, and the pool at the bottom is as deep as the Horseshoe Falls is high. The Horseshoe Falls actually recede one foot every ten years because of erosion! There are books that show how the falls have changed over time.

See, there are many things that make Niagara Falls interesting. This is a fascinating and beautiful place to visit.

Daniel Ziegler
Grade 6

The Strange Day

One day at the end of school something strange seemed to be going on: the wind was blowing strong and trees were swinging everywhere. The howling noise was enough to scare you even if you didn't look out the classroom window to see the wires hanging from the poles. A pole fell and wires were dangling everywhere. I knew electricity could give you a shock so I got scared.

Then all of a sudden an announcement came from the office. The principal started calling all the bus kids. She told the bus kids to go through the front door — not the bus doors.

It took a long time to get on my bus because we had to walk all the way down a hill to get to the bus. My legs felt like noodles. I finally did get to the bus.

On the way home a big tree fell and everyone on the bus had to wait until the tree was removed. The bus was really noisy! Our bus began to get cold and we were getting worried.

Finally, the tree was removed. The bus started on its way again. I began to talk to my friends. I talked so much I forgot to get off at my stop. When I realized what I had done I ran up to the driver and told him he had to go all the way back to get me home!

I was glad to get home!

Kayla Jefferson
Grade 5

How to Be a Nice Person

In order to be a nice person, you must be kind to everybody and accept people for who they are. People are very different. You could have a friend who wears nothing but black all the time and listens to rock music. Then you could have one who wears no black and listens to country music. It doesn't matter what people look like on the outside; it's the inside that counts in the long run. For example, there may be a person who is good looking and popular, but mean. You're not missing out on anything.

Not to pick on girls, but in most situations, there could be a mean girl; and she may be so cruel that you hide every time you see her. Just remind yourself to smile and don't let her bother you. Almost always when people are kind to one another, when they get older, they have a good job and a loving family. The cruel ones are usually stuck working at Burger King or something like that.

Make sure you don't let anything get you down. Learn how to accept yourself and everybody else, too. If you're a good person, people will remember it; and it will make you feel good about yourself. Stand tall and don't let anybody get in your way. Because the truth is, they don't have anything better to do. Follow my advice; it will help you not only in the present time but in the future, too.

Shelby Seavey
Grade 6

September 11: A Creator of War

It was a warm sunny day in the Northeast. Around 8:30 there was an out of control plane flying over New York City. Suddenly, the World Trade Center and two U.S. Airline planes burst into flames killing an unspeakable amount of people. At the same time two more planes were being hijacked as well; one hit the Pentagon, the other crashed not reaching its destination. These events on September 11, will go down in history.

September 11 lead to a disastrous war on terrorism that continues today. Almost every day I hear about a fatal car bomb, or a hostage case that involves innocent people. It seems that this "war" gets worse, not better. Our country continues to waste money on this disaster in Iraq. Billions of dollars down the drain to see soldiers and other Iraqis killed. Wouldn't this money be more beneficial helping Katrina and other natural disaster victims? After you think about that you ask yourself, "How did we get ourselves into this?" That is an unknown answer.

If all the people on Earth would learn to settle their differences without war there would be more joy and peace. All people in some way want peace in our world and that is what we need to work toward, not killing terrorists just making peace with them.

John Donnelly
Grade 6

Football

I love anything to do with football. I like playing football and playing football video games. Every day I do something involving football. I really like to play tackle football. If I get hurt I get angry and let's just say that is the game-breaker.

The positions I'm good at are safety, cornerback, and wide receiver. I am really bad at quarterback, even though I do like playing that position. One time instead of throwing the football to my friend, I threw it into my friend's car. Luckily I didn't get into trouble.

There are many places that I like to play football. My two favorite places to play football are in my backyard and in my friend's backyard. These places are the best because they are the biggest. Some other places that I like to play are at the bus stop and in the street.

Two weeks ago I was at my friend's house and we wanted to play football. It was pitch black out because it was late. We played from 8:30 until 9:00. We were having so much fun that none of us wanted to go inside.

I really enjoy watching professional football on TV. I saw both the NFC and the AFC championship games, and the Super Bowl. It was the Pittsburgh Steelers versus the Seattle Seahawks. I wanted the Steelers to win. I had an idea in my head that the Seahawks would win. The steelers won though, and it was a good game.

I am pretty sure that I won't get on an NFL team or even a college team (but that would be fun). I will try my hardest, and do my best as a kid. Hey, a kid can dream can't he? I can't resist football. Football is my passion.

Damon Holm
Grade 5

A Walk on the River

One day my friend and I went to the river and found a rock trail that ran right down the middle of the river. We took little steps on the slippery rocks. She fell in and I helped her get out, that's what a good friend should do.

Then we saw a big tree. We could not go under it because the water was too deep on the other side. I was about to suggest that we turn around but just then she suggested that we go over it. I thought that was a good plan. As my friend is taller than me, she helped me climb over and we walked to the other side. We walked on land until we could not walk on land anymore. Then we went back to the river rock trail. We fell in a few times, but we helped each other out along the way. When we had walked halfway down the river rock trail we stopped and climbed to the top of a steep hill. It was the best place to have a snack without it getting wet. Then when we were done we packed up and went back down to the river. We found a lot of rusty old car parts, rusty treasures like twisted things and metal wheels.

A walk on the river was a great adventure with many treasures, but always remember that the best treasure you can find is a good friend.

Sarah Gihr
Grade 4

Horseback Riding

Horseback riding is the best thing to do because it involves all of my favorite things to do. I walk out to the barn and go get the horse or pony and tie them up and brush them.

First, I use the currycomb and brush them off. 2nd, I use the soft brush and brush them off. 3rd, I use the hard brush and get the rest of the dirt that the soft brush and the curry comb left. 4th, I use the hoof pick, and I get the rocks that they stepped on so they won't get lame by stepping on rocks all day. 5th, I put the saddle pad on, then the saddle, then the martingale on, then the girth, then the bridle. Then, I put my chaps on, then my helmet.

Next, I walk them out and mount my horse, and I warm the horse up. First, I warm the horse up at a trot, then the canter. I then warm it up in the other direction. Then, if I'm jumping, which I do, I jump in every direction on a small jump. Next, I put the jump up to the height that I jump and do a course and practice.

Then when I'm done, I cool out the horse and untack. I brush them off and pick their feet out and put them back out in the paddock. It might sound crazy, but it's my favorite sport, horseback riding.

Jon Sterling
Grade 6

Animals

Do you like animals? Because I love them so much. I have three cats, one dog, and two guinea pigs. I take care of them every day. The guinea pigs are the hardest to take care of, but I still love them very much. Even though I have animals I want more cats and dogs because they are really cool and fun animals. You really can't do much with smaller animals. The hardest thing about all animals is getting them shots and making sure they're in good hands. I always get nervous when one of my animals are sick.

I've been wondering what the world would be like without any animals. First, we wouldn't have any eggs and no meat. Without cows we wouldn't have milk. People would be dying here and there if we had no animals and kids would be bored without animals.

There is one thing sad about animals. It is when they die from illnesses, old age, people hitting them on the road, people killing them on purpose, starvation, dehydration, and from hunters. Another one is other animals killing each other.

When I see an animal die I could cry right there. To me, it's really sad.

People who kill animals on purpose should go to jail or get a fine because that's really rude.

Well, I really love animals and you probably do too. So just think about animals getting killed and other things, that's so sad. I really take care of my animals because I love them all!

Ashley Chappell
Grade 5

What Makes Me an Individual?

Being an individual means that you are different from everybody else. It also means that you stand out. I am an individual because I love to cook, I have a birthmark on my face, and I love to travel.

What I like about cooking is that I get to spend time with my mom. I have many things I like to cook, but the one thing I like to cook with my mom is lasagna. I also like to cook sausage casserole. My favorite utensils are the measuring cups. I have all different sets of them.

I have a birthmark on my face. I like it because it makes me different from everybody else. Sometimes I don't like it because it looks kind of funny. One time my grandma tried to use makeup to cover my birthmark. I said, "No, because it looks even worse." I wiped it off and said, "I like it how it is, that's me!"

My family's love for traveling makes me special too. My favorite part about traveling is when the plane lands. I also like to see the sights. I like traveling too, because I get to spend time with my family. My favorite trip was when we went to Hawaii. We traveled at night, although it was still fun.

I know that in the future my dreams can come true. Maybe I could become a flight attendant or get a career in cooking. I know that I have been given a blessing by God.

Beth Anne Bridgeman
Grade 5

I Love Singing!

I am a singer, and a singer I shall be. I can sing. I love to sing, it's fun to do, and I love what I can sing. I am a singer.

I love to sing. I write songs to sing them. One of my dreams is to make an album. My family always asks me to sing on special occasions. I had to sing "I Believe I Can Fly" at my family reunion. I rocked. I get almost every solo at church. Because I can sing during big things, I get the solo. In conclusion I love singing.

It's fun to do. I sing when I'm bored. I sing walking home; I'm bored at that time. I sing while I clean. While washing dishes, I sing. I sing everywhere I go. I sing at home, school, while taking tests/quizzes, when I do my homework, and in church. In conclusion singing is fun for me.

What I can sing: Gospel, I sing gospel the most. Hip hop, I'm not allowed to sing hip hop, but I do anyway. Soul, I sing soul because I like the music. In conclusion I sing just about everything.

I sing when I'm happy, when I'm sad, and when I want to because I can sing. I love singing. I can sing and I sing just about everything. In conclusion I can sing. Singing is what I can do. It's my hobby.

Cornelius Robinson
Grade 6

My Papa

I think my Papa is the best grandfather in the world. My papa is a great teacher. He is also a good cook. He is very generous to me. I love him so much. We always have fun whenever we go to his house. My grandfather is very generous.

My Papa is a good teacher. He taught my brothers and me how to fish. He also taught my brothers and me how to play poker. When we go to his house we sometimes play it. We have a lot of fun.

I think my Papa is a good cook. He is good at making waffles and pancakes. His pancakes are the best pancakes I ever had. His pancakes are one of my favorite foods. I also like his eggs. They taste so good because they're light and fluffy and have a lot of syrup.

My Papa is very generous when he takes us out for Ice cream. He watches my brothers and me during the summer when we are out of camp and our mom and dad at their jobs. He is also generous when he bought my brothers and me fishing poles.

In conclusion, my essay shows that my Papa is special and important to me. He is important and special to me because he is generous and a good cook and a great teacher. He is a great grandfather to me. I want to be just like him when I grow up.

Stephanie Knight
Grade 5

Australian Shepherds

One of man's best friends for hundreds and hundreds of years. Dogs have always been there for us. Now here is the history of the Australian Shepherd.

The Australian Shepherd, or the Aussie, as some people like to call them, make great family pets. They are also great with children. If you are in danger, your Aussie will turn from a lovable pet to a ferocious guard dog! They are very intelligent and responsive. They are very energetic. Some lines of the Australian Shepherd are made more aggressive.

The fur has a double coat and is medium length. Usually it is straight, but sometimes it is wavy. The color that the fur comes in are: a blue merle, black, red merle, and all red with white markings, or without white markings. The Aussie needs minimal grooming for their coat. The coat has to be made sure that there are no burrs.

The Aussie has a bobtail and each dog sometimes has two different colored eyes or some will have half brown and half blue. This will not affect their vision at all. They are working dogs and like to herd sheep and cattle. Sometimes they also perform in search and rescue. They are a tireless worker for their owners or owner. They are strong and agile and will love their owner.

The Aussies were bred in America even though they have the name Australian Shepherd. They got this name by being with the Australian herdsmen, called the Basques.

Kasey Wolfe
Grade 5

My Inspiration

My inspiration is mostly my mom and dad. But, the person I'm most inspired by is Mia Hamm. She is the best soccer player in America, by my opinion, and I want to be just like her.

On weekends, I pass the ball around with my dad and my brother. My dad has helped me succeed in every way. I've never given up and I'm not planning to. Watching videos of learning how to become a better soccer player is great, but when I try to do the impossible, it gets interesting. I play games on weekends, during the week, and any other day in the week! I play in soccer tournaments. Sometimes we don't succeed, but we "don't quit." I've learned a lot about Mia Hamm and her soccer life, but I've also learned a bit about her social life. Mia Hamm is a regular person, just like you and me.

Once you take that first step on the field, the butterflies in your stomach multiply. You feel the soft, mowed, green grass touch your cleats and you say to yourself, "I can do this." It's great achieving your goals with a positive attitude on the field and off. Every soccer game, my dad says if I'm not playing my hardest, he's going to start singing. That's why every game I look forward to playing my hardest! I'm the next Mia Hamm!!! I will do my very best to be the best!

Natalie Streifert
Grade 6

What Am I Thankful For?

I am thankful for so many things. I am thankful for my family. I am thankful for my friends. I am thankful for teachers. I am most thankful for life. Life is precious. You should live it out while it lasts. You never know when it's your time to go.

I am ten years old and in the fifth grade. I work hard every day in school so that I can go to college. When I go to college I am going to study nursing so that I can get my degree and become a nurse. I think that it's important to have your goal set on what you would like to do in life. If you do, people can never say that you are nobody.

My mom and my dad have always taught me right from wrong. They always tell me that they love me. They tell me to never put myself down. I think that since life is short, I should take the opportunity and live it out. Life has so many adventures to it. Every night when I watch the news and hear how many people are dying in the world today, I just cry.

My family is the greatest people on the Earth. That's why I am thankful for them. My friends are so much fun to be around. That's why I am thankful for them. My teachers help me to become somebody in life. That's why I am thankful for them. Without family, friends, and teachers, life that I am most thankful for wouldn't be special.

Dayna Haffenden
Grade 5

First Day of School

Every kid dreads the day when the fun summer times come to an end, the day when the law that lets kids be free reaches its expiration date, the day when the boundary between fun and education comes crashing down, the day when the forces of the United States educational system come into action: the first day of school…

My walk down that hallway was the loneliest walk of my life, the first time I had ever been down to the sixth grade wing. My legs felt like jelly. The feeling was soon replaced by fear. What would my teacher be like?

I had heard good things about Mr. Sirof, but I had also heard he gave a lot of homework. As I strode to his door I tried to think about all the good things. He was teaching social studies, my favorite subject, and I heard he was a great writer. But this didn't stop me from sweating.

Pushing the door open drained me of all my energy. When I turned my head I froze. The teacher was not the devil who had so reluctantly jumped into my dreams the past few nights. Sitting at his desk was a kind young man with a funky tie. This was also a lucky break. As the school day progressed, I learned that he was also very forgiving and had a way with kids. All of my doubts were gone because I knew this was going to be a great school year.

Bradley Harmeyer
Grade 6

All About Me

I am a very good dancer. I take dance lessons at Lori's Center Stage Dance Studio. I can't wait to dance with all my friends. We are the best of friends and we talk about everything. We love to dance with each other. We do a recital with each other every year. We have the best teacher, Ona-May, and we have Abby, our teacher assistant. It's so much fun to dance with my friends every week. Dancing is so much fun.

I love to shop. I shop every weekend and buy new clothes, jewelry, bags, hats, sunglasses, and shoes. I have so much stuff in my closets and in my jewelry box. I'm very into fashion and I always wear new clothes every where I go. The mall is the best place to shop. They always have everything I need. I guess I just love to shop.

My favorite animals are puppies and horses. I used to have a puppy when I was younger. His name was Popcorn. I used to love to play with him and get his dog food out. I also love horses because they are so beautiful. I have a horse poster of a brown colored horse; I like looking at him every day.

I love the outdoors, too!! I like to plant flowers in the summertime. I love to see beautiful butterflies flying in the sky with the birds. I love nature.

Alexis Koukos
Grade 6

My Dream: World Peace

What is my dream, you may ask? My dream is world peace; no wars or unfairness, so the world will be like God created it.

My point is to make a group to stop wars, and the result: peace.

If the Lord made peace, we can too!

If this happens, problems will be solved with love, and everyone will be happy. Heaven will be exactly like Earth, and God will be very happy, and everyone will see Heaven.

Christopher Tabacjar
Grade 4

The Trip

I was going on a trip with my family. At first I didn't know where we were going. We ended up taking a trip to New Hampshire. We drove for a couple of hours until we reached New Hampshire. We got to a trailer park and decided that was where we were going to stay.

My family and I went to the beach. We met some friends there. We found a hideout and played cops and robbers. The bathroom was in a different house. We only had one TV. We didn't have any phones. We didn't have any radios either.

I didn't know how to ride a bike so the people at the campsite tried to teach me. It was too hard so I gave up. I decided to go to the beach with my dad instead. A short time later a storm began to happen while we were at the beach. We decided to leave just as it began raining. We ran home.

Patrick 'PJ' Walsh
Grade 4

Green Beans

There have been terrible nights before, but this one awful event was the worst of all! I was forced to eat GREEN BEANS! They were laughing on my beautiful blue plate. The terrible food wasn't laughing at a joke, they were laughing at my disgusted face.

It all began when I looked down onto my wonderful plate of surprises. I knew I was excited to eat my buttered noodles and steak, but the green grass blades in the right corner just looked hideous. My sister wailed, "I DON'T WANT IT!"

"Brynne, you have to eat your green beans. You need to have your vegetables," my mom always recites this when we don't want to eat our vegetables, which she gives us almost every night.

My mom answered calmly, "Look at Kirsten, your sister. She's going to eat it all."

"I am? Oh yeah, I am!" I replied in a not convincing way.

I took a tiny bite, it crunched, it cried, it tasted like a hair ball! I smiled, turned away and gulped it all down.

I ate it and asked, "How many more bites?"

"Two more bites," my mom sighed. CRUNCH! CRUNCH! They were gone. Memories of that terrible meal still haunt me.

Kirsten Virginia Cave
Grade 4

The Sphinx vs the American Curl

The two animals I'm writing about are the Sphinx and the American Curl. These two animals are two different types of cats. That's the reason I picked them.

As I've said, they are really different, but they do have a couple similarities. For example, they are both cats. Two, they both come in all different colors. Three, they both have one strange characteristic. As for the Sphinx, it is born with no fur. As for the American Curl, it is odd because of its ears, which are curled back. And fourth, they each have a long history about them.

Now I will discuss with you the differences between the two of them. The most obvious difference is that the Sphinx is bald and the American Curl is covered in fur. Two, the American Curl's ears are much, much smaller than those of the Sphinx's. Three, the Sphinx is born bald, the American Curl's ears take time to curl. Four, the Sphinx is a lot harder to take care of than the American Curl. The reason is because during the winter you must keep the Sphinx warm. Fifth, also you may want to groom your American Curl, you can't do that with a Sphinx. Sixth, Sphinx's body shape and the American Curl's are very different. The Sphinx's is very fine and muscular where the American Curl's is medium. Seventh, the American Curl loves affection, where the Sphinx would rather keep to itself.

In conclusion even though these two animals are in the same family they are still two drastically different cats.

Jayme Kerr
Grade 6

Who I Look Up to the Most in Life

I look up to both my mom and dad but the person in my life that I look up to is my mom. I look up to her because even though she had to leave her family back in Medllin, Colombia, she came here to be with my dad. I also look up to her because no matter how bad my brother and I behave she still loves us. I admire the way she is because if we are sad or sick she comforts us and stays with us until we're better. I look up to my mother because she tries really hard for my brother and I to not miss church and for me to be in chorus.

I chose my mom because she is fun, responsible, and caring. When I grow up I want to be at least half the person she is. I look up to my mom because I like basketball and my mom also likes basketball. I look up to her also because she cooks delicious. When I grow up I would love to cook like she cooks. My mom also likes volleyball and likes to play volleyball like me.

I admire the way my mom kept on trying to learn English and she learned by reading books. That's another thing I admire about her, she doesn't stop trying until she gets it. I admire my mom because if I need help with homework she'll be there. My mom always helps me study for test and practices basketball, volleyball, tennis, and swimming.

Lorraine Delgado
Grade 6

A Terrific Teacher

A role model is a person you look up to. A role model never does anything bad. A role model has many terrific traits like I am going to write about.

Role models are great people who you look up to. A person you admire is honest, so they won't lie to you. You can rely on your role model. A role model is also kind and has a big heart. For example, if there was only one piece of chocolate left on a plate, and there was you and someone else, if you had a big heart and were kind, you would let the other person have the piece of chocolate.

My role model is Mrs. Ostrander. Mrs. Ostrander is a fifth grade teacher at Hudson Falls Intermediate School. She is the best teacher in the whole entire universe!

Mrs. Ostrander is a very unique individual. She has many talents. One of her talents is making everyone laugh. Another thing about Mrs. Ostrander is she always has a smile on her face that never comes off. She is an amazing person to look up to! Also, she is caring for everyone nonstop. She puts all of her effort into everything she does.

In conclusion, Mrs. Ostrander is an amazing person. She has all of the terrific traits of a role model. In addition, Mrs. Ostrander is my role model. Mrs. Ostrander is a person you should always remember.

Courtney Arlington
Grade 5

My Family

When I was 5, these are the things I liked to do. Every day I do these things. I love playing with my dog, when I'm finished, I like to play with my family. I love watching TV. I've done all of these things in the past, and I still like to do them.

My dog's a playing machine. My dog eases the pain when I'm angry. When I have bad days at school, my dog gives me a "positive vibe" and I feel much better. My dog is an intruder alerter. One time when there was a car accident my dog kept on barking until we saw the accident. My dog's very fun to play with. He's very caring. He will cuddle up right next to you. That's why I like playing with my dog.

My family's the best. My family makes me very happy. When I'm sad, my family always makes me happy. I like to play with my family. Every Monday my family and I go out to play or go out to eat. My family will always be in my heart. I love my family so much that I will never forget them. That's why I love my family.

The next thing I love to do is watch TV. It's very entertaining. TVs come in a variety of colors. Finally, TVs come with cable. That's why I love watching TV.

I like doing a lot of things. That's me, you can't change me.

Terryl Williams
Grade 6

When I Learned to Water-Ski

My dad is a great water-skier. He can do it one-handed. I can do it too, but for less time. I always enjoy watching him ski. One day I decided that I wanted to try it for myself. I started out on "grown up" skis, and so it was much harder for me to learn. I got to a standing position, and then fell back into the dark, icy water. This went on for a few minutes, until finally I could stand up. But just as I thought I had figured out how to ski, I toppled back into the deep, breathtaking lake. I didn't sink because I was luckily wearing a life jacket; of course it's against the law not to. Shivering, I pushed through the water, towards the boat, where I took a rest, then jumped back into the water to try again. It was impossible to get me to give up. I started out in a crouching position, then twisted and turned, and pushed, until I finally got up. Then I looked down, and saw the icy wakes, which were as rough as the ocean. Eventually, I got better and better.

Years later (now) I have tried to do it on one ski. The falls are painful, and I don't stay up long, but I'm still trying. Now I know that practice makes perfect.

Annie Rubin
Grade 5

Unjustified Justice*

Two thousand, two hundred and twenty-five juveniles are sentenced to life without parole. Locking adolescents under the age of 18 in prison is a cruel and inhumane punishment. Areas of the brain are not fully developed in teens so their ability to control their impulses and to see long term consequences are not yet working. Let's take the case of Stacey T.

Stacey was a fourteen year old boy who had good grades and no criminal record. Then, an adult cousin asked him to help rob Stacey's girlfriend's brother, Alex. Stacey's cousin was supposed to pretend to kill Stacey and steal Alex's car. After the pretense, Stacey went home. During that time, Alex was shot to death. Stacey was charged with second-degree murder. He now has life without parole in Pennsylvania.

Imagine if you were in Stacey's shoes. How would you feel…a fourteen year old who would have no hope in life, no career, and no dreams to be fulfilled? You probably would not look forward to living.

Stacey is just one heartbreaking story of the three hundred thirty two juveniles locked away for life in Pennsylvania. And, the other 41 states have children in prison. In fact, in Nevada, children as young as eight can be locked away for life. These kids barely even know how to multiply.

Think about these horrible statistics. In 1995, one hundred fifty-two children were convicted to life in prison. Sadly, the number of convicted teen "lifers" is only growing. Let's help them!

Alison Roberto
Grade 6
*Response to "Locked Up for Life"

Taking Care of Dogs

What has four legs, a tail and a great sense of smell? The answer is a dog. A lot of people say that dogs are cute and soft, and my opinion of dogs is the same. People also say that they chew on carpet and furniture. My own dog chewed on our wooden chair when she was a puppy. Owners need to teach their dogs not to chew on furniture or carpet. This can take time for the dog to learn. Some people feel that dogs mess their house up. This can happen until a dog learns how to behave for their owner. Their great sense of smell can help them find almost anything. Since they have such great smell, that is why some breeds make great hunting dogs. My own dog likes when you throw her toys for her to go get. This activity is actually good for people and the dog. They are both getting exercise which helps keep everyone healthy. Another way to make sure your dog stays healthy is to visit a vet regularly. Dogs also need to eat twice a day and have plenty of water to drink.

Dogs are soft and cute. They need to get lots of exercise and be fed twice daily. Owners need to make sure their dogs see a vet at least once a year for a check up. If you already know that, then you are probably ready to take care of your own dog.

Jessica Dennis
Grade 6

Dreams Can Change the World!

Following your dream is very important. Just having a dream is good and I don't mean a dream while asleep. I mean a goal in life. All the great people followed their dreams and stuck with them, no matter how difficult or bad things got. That is what truly defines a person.

Some people who followed their dreams changed the world. One of them is Dr. Martin Luther King Jr. His dream was equal rights for all, no matter what skin color. His first dream was to preach at a church. He went to college. After Rosa Parks was arrested he got involved in the civil rights movement. His house was bombed. He stuck with his dreams still. Even though he was arrested thirteen times, he stuck with his dreams. They held signs and called him names. During sit-ins when people were dragged out or killed, he stuck with his dream. He protested in a peaceful manner. He wouldn't stop even though protesters were killed. He persevered. He kept trying to change the country. After he was assassinated the blacks kept protesting and persevered. They accomplished his dream. His dream changed the country for the better.

Martin Luther King Jr. followed his dream and made a difference in the country. That is why you should follow your dream. If you follow your dream you can do anything. So, always dream big.

Max Ramsey
Grade 6

Razina, My Friend

Everybody wants to make a new friend, somebody to laugh with, share things and have fun with.

I have a new best friend. Her name is Razina. The first day I came to Shelter Rock she wanted to know everything about me: where I came from, when I was born and more questions about my personal life. At my old school making a new friend was very hard. One minute you're friends and the next minute you're fighting. Girls would call each other names. It would make you cry and think about how you look. Razina is very different. We never call each other names or fight.

Razina is funny. She makes me laugh every single day. One time I was laughing so hard my eyes started to water and my stomach started to hurt. As they say, laughing is exercise. I feel like I have known her for years when I have only known her for five months. She makes me feel very good about myself. When I am upset or sad, she brings me right back up and she talks to me about my situation or whatever problem. She doesn't put me down at all.

We really support each other. Like the saying goes: "Let me see your friends and I will tell you who you are." I never had a loving friend like Razina. Once you get to know her, you will love her and she will love you back.

Etiopia Martin
Grade 6

Dinner with Larry Bird

Larry Bird is a very interesting person. During his NBA seasons he had 2,850 points, 240 steals, and 1,247 rebounds. Larry Bird was a 12 time NBA All-star and the MVP of the 1982 All-star game. Larry Bird was also the college player of the year in 1979. Larry Joe Bird was born December 7, 1956 in West Baden, Indiana. His parents were Georgia and Claude Bird. He went to Springs Valley High School and Indiana College in 1979. He was 6 feet 9 inches and weighed 220 pounds. Larry Bird was introduced to basketball by two of his four brothers, Mark and Mike, and he also had a sister. Larry Bird had a wife named Janet but got divorced after having one kid. Then he got remarried to Dinah and adopted two kids, Connor and Mariah.

I would like to have this man over for dinner because we could discuss many things because I also play basketball. We would discuss things like how to shoot the right way or what drills I could do to get better at basketball. I would like to have dinner with Larry because I could learn how to commit to things better because it must have taken a lot of commitment to have the points, steals, and rebounds that he had during his basketball career. If I had Larry over for dinner I think we would have steak because it is his favorite meal.

Christian Cotugno
Grade 6

Dolphins and Orca Whales

The topic that I am writing about is dolphins and Orca Whales. One thing that you will learn about is the difference and similarities between them.

Dolphins are different from Orca Whales. They are a grey color. Most dolphins live to be 40 years old. Their teeth are conical shaped. Also they have a distinct beak. Females only have one calf at a time. Orca Whales are also known as Killer Whales. Males grow to be 23 feet long. Females grow to be 21 feet long. Killer Whales live in pods. In the pods Orcas form hierarchies, led by females. 5-30 Orcas live in pods.

Also they're very alike. They both have flukes and fins. Dolphins and Orcas are not fish, they are mammals. Both of them use echolocation, hunt for their own food, live in pods, and are very social.

Now, do you see a difference in them? They also are very similar. If you would like to learn about them you can. You could also research anything else.

Kira Rinehart
Grade 6

The Winter

The year 2005 was big like a blizzard. There was a lot of snow and no school for a week. Mathew (my brother) and I shoveled up all the snow including the sidewalk, the driveway, and my yard.

After that we dug this humongous hole and it was cool. After we were finished we went inside the hole and hung out for a while.

But after that it got a little chilly, so we went inside the house and drank hot chocolate until we were nice and cozy. That year I will never forget because it was important to me.

Brian Aguiar
Grade 6

Hear No Evil, Speak No Evil, See No Evil

Since my mom is deaf, I'm going to explain what it is like to live with a deaf person.

My mom has been deaf since birth. My grandmother says she noticed that my mom wasn't responding to anything my grandmother said. My mom got her first pair of hearing aids when she was four years old. Mom was highly embarrassed to show her ears because of the hearing aids. My grandmother cut Mom's hair above her ears to show her that there was nothing to be embarrassed about.

My mom had my brother Seth, before me so Seth had to make phone calls for Mom when he was my age. There are only cons for this disability. For example, I can't talk to her with her back turned, and I can't talk to her on the phone. Also I have to make appointments for her, such as doctor or dental appointments.

I love my mom so it doesn't bother me that she is deaf. Even though Mom is deaf, everyone treats her like I do: with respect!

Emily Jones
Grade 6

Pet Responsibilities

Many people have pets. Cats and dogs are among the most common. I have three cats, three dogs, one bird, two hamsters, and two fish. A lot of my old pets have died, like my old hamster, Snowy, my old cat, Pepper, a few old fish, and two hermit crabs named, Crabby and Pinchy, because they were sick or too much responsibility. Some people can't and shouldn't have pets, and this is why.

Some people shouldn't have pets because they forget their responsibilities. If you forget to feed your pets, they become ravenous, cranky, and viscous. Also, they could starve. Another responsibility that children can forget with pets is to clean the cats' litter box, or the rodent's cages. This could cause both a bad smell throughout the house, and discomfort to the animals from the wood shavings. These are only a few responsibilities children can forget.

Sometimes, even though children are responsible enough to have pets, they can't. This could be because they or their parents have allergies to some animals such as cats and dogs. Another reason children can't have pets is because the building they live in doesn't allow them if they are over a certain size or weight. These are a few reasons children can't have pets.

Although I can handle my pets, it doesn't mean that everybody can. The same goes for having them in the first place and the reasons stated above are just a few. In conclusion, pets are not for everyone.

Haley Marie Cox
Grade 6

Stitch

When I was 9 years old I asked my dad for a bike. One day after school I went to my grandparents' house. A few hours later my mom and dad came and picked my brother and me up. As we got in the car I noticed that my dad had a backpack on his lap. I saw that it was moving. I asked my dad what was moving in the backpack and he unzipped it and my ferret jumped out.

My ferret has puffy brown and white fur. It is a boy and his name is Stitch. I got the name from the movie *Lilo and Stitch*. Stitch thinks he is a dog. He jumps up and down. He runs around and steals my family's socks and stuffed animals. He loves when I get a small ball about the size of someone's palm and I rub his belly with it. When I first got Stitch, I bought him a shirt that said 'killer' on the back of it.

Stitch loves to crawl in my sock drawer and sleep. Stitch eats ferret food, cat food, and once in a while he will sneak out of his cage and get into the cereal. Stitch makes a big mess out of his cage and gets pieces of newspapers all over the place. I've had Stitch for years and he is a great pet. I think he is the best pet I've ever had. I love Stitch.

Kristen Moerler
Grade 6

QRIO

The QRIO is a new interactive robot used for entertainment made by Sony. The QRIO can dance, walk, see, avoid obstacles, and even talk. The QRIO is two-feet-tall and somewhat resembles a human. It can bend its "knees" and "elbows."

The QRIO can be programmed to remember some faces and he could have a different greeting to each one. If you talk to it and play with it, it will be happy to see you, but if you are mean to it or if you abuse it, it might be sad when it sees you. The QRIO can recognize facial expressions.

The QRIO is amazing when it comes to movement. It can walk on tile, carpet, wood, and many other surfaces and it still keeps its balance. If someone did knock it over it would be able to get itself up in a matter of seconds. It can even balance on a moving platform.

I think it would be fun to spend time with the QRIO because it is responsive to you. It has a personality of its own. You can play with it and you can talk to it. It feels like you're talking to a human. It would be fun to watch it move in thick carpet and avoid obstacles.

Erica Lange
Grade 5

Pugs — Lap Dog and Playmate

The pug is described as "a lot of dog in a small package." Pugs have oriental origins with similarities to the Pekinese. The breed comes from China and then appeared in Japan and Europe. Pugs were treasured house pets of kings and queens. A pug saved the life of William the Prince of Orange, letting him know the Spaniards were coming. The silver pug named Pompey became the official dog of the House of Orange in Holland. Napolean's wife Josephine owned a pug named Fortune. The artist Hogarth had a pug named Trump and put him in several of his paintings.

Pugs have a square, stocky, compact body. They are typically 10 to 12 inches tall, 10 to 12 inches long and weigh 14 to 18 pounds. They live to be about 12 to 15 years old. Their coats come in fawn, black, and silver with a short, flat, black nose.

Pugs are not delicate eaters; they slurp and chow down. Pugs can become overweight, so they need to be kept on a good diet and get regular exercise. Clean, cool drinking water is important to a pug. Pugs have short noses so they shouldn't be over exercised and are sensitive to heat, humidity, and cold. Pugs enjoy energetic games like tug of war, fetch and chase.

Pugs need a bath at least once every two weeks. Although they have short hair, pugs have 2 coats of hair and need to be brushed regularly. Pugs have big "buglike" eyes that are easily injured. Dirt and moisture collect in their wrinkles and need to be regularly cleaned out.

Despite their different look, pugs get along with everybody and make cute, lovable pets.

Joseph Beauchamp
Grade 4

Individuality

Individuality. The word itself sounds unique. Being different is not a crime no one should be afraid to be themself.

Being an individual is extremely vital. If everyone was the same, life would be boring and nothing exciting would ever happen. Individuality helps people express themselves. Do not be afraid to be different. Be yourself. Be who you really are.

Individuality is affecting us every day. It gives us a positive attitude toward everything. It makes life more interesting. With individuality, you have a variety of different people to choose your friends from. We would be lost without it. You should not act, talk, or dress a certain way just because everyone else is acting, talking, or dressing that way. It does not matter what other people think about you. Do not care about that. Only care about what you think about yourself.

Always remember to be yourself. Sameness is like a garden of weeds. It is your job to be an individual. It is your job to become a flower.

Rachel Filippone
Grade 5

The Birthday

I remember when I turned 11 years old on March 17th, 2005. My mom made a party for me at my house. It wasn't a wild party with a lot of people, it was a party with just a few people.

The people that came were my mom, two brothers, grandmother, my mom's boyfriend, grandmother's friend and of course, me. I will always remember it because my mom spent a lot of money on all the food, gifts, and the decorations.

The food that she bought was KFC and Burger King. She also bought cake and more. The gifts that I got were clothes and money. It was great party, that is why I will always remember my 11th birthday.

Marcia Gouveia
Grade 6

Dancing Is My Thing

What do you love to do? I love dancing. I love dancing because I can dance to different types of music. Why else do I love dance? It keeps me physically fit. I also love dance because it is very, very active and creative.

Dance is really fun and it's a way to hang with and meet new friends. I feel by dancing, I can express myself and make up dances with friends that dance too. Dance is awesome!

I really get excited when I get on stage and start dancing. I sometimes get nervous. Then, once I start dancing, I feel a lot better. I feel really good when I hear the crowd shouting, whistling, and clapping. Those are the reasons why I love dancing.

Katie Bendick
Grade 5

Malti-Poos

The Malti-poo is a very smart dog, and gets along with other dogs well. They stay away from strangers, and get along great with kids. They live well inside homes, and are fairly energetic. They enjoy walks in vast open spaces.

Malti-poos are a cross-breed between a Maltese and a Poodle. Their colors are black, white, or brown. They have hair instead of fur, so they shed very little. Even if you're allergic to dogs, you can still have a Malti-poo in your home because they have no dander.

These dogs are very active. On a scale of 1-10 they range from 5-7. They like to go on walks, or play in a fenced area, like your backyard. Like most dogs, they are most active when they are puppies. They live from 12-15 years, or 84-105 in dog years.

What they look like is what Maltese and a Poodle look like put together. They have the legs, eyes, tongue, and body of a poodle. They have the snout, paws, ears, and tail of a Maltese. Like all dogs, their origin is from the wolf, despite how cute they are.

Their size depends on the size of the parents, but the usual size varies from 5-9 pounds. Their height is from 8-10 inches tall. Their breed is a toy dog, and one of the smaller dogs of all of them.

I hope you learned more about Malti-poos, thanks for reading!

Jackie Silva
Grade 5

Blazing Basketball Benefits

Are you playing on a basketball team? Well, if you're not, this will change your mind. Basketball is a great sport and it also has many benefits. It keeps you in great physical shape, teaches you teamwork, and you learn a great sport.

One advantage of playing basketball is that it keeps you in great physical shape. It keeps you in great physical shape because there is a lot of running involved. There is also stretching involved, and this prevents you from pulling a muscle.

Another benefit is that it teaches you teamwork. You learn to play like a team, win like a team, and lose like a team. Without teamwork, there would be no team success. Teamwork also teaches you great life skills that you will use for the rest of your life.

A privilege of playing basketball is that you get to learn a great sport. You learn to shoot, pass and make good plays. You also learn to have fun and always do your best!

Keeping you in great physical shape, teaching you teamwork, and learning a great sport are all great benefits of playing basketball. So join a basketball team today and you will agree with me one hundred percent!

Benjamin Aiello
Grade 6

Finding Love in Russia

As I walked through the old run-down orphanage in Lobnya, Russia, a tingle of excitement stirred within me. Continuing into a dimly lit room, I sat down on a worn-out, plum-colored couch. All around, rickety cabinets stood as still as statues topped with old toys, out of any child's reach. Screech, screech! An old rocking chair creaked continuously as my dad gently swayed back and forth. In the distance, faint Russian voices grew quieter and quieter until there was no sound at all. Worker's shoes pattered down the hallway.

While I stared out an old, dusty window, contemplating how my life was about to change, suddenly the door creaked open. The sound made me jump. When I looked to see who it was, a wide smile fell across my face as an adorable little girl quietly walked in with a social worker…my new little sister!

She was dressed in many layers and covered with mosquito bites that made her face look like a speckled egg. She wore the saddest expression I'd ever seen. Neither she nor I had any idea about the special relationship that was about to begin.

Lauren Longenecker
Grade 4

Invention of the Computer

Could you imagine our world without computers? Many people today could not live without them. Computers make life much easier, and almost every business has one. Today we have e-mail and Internet. When computers were first used, they did not have either of these programs. It took many decades, inventors, and perseverance to make the computer we have today.

The first computers were very different from today's computers. Used for military purposes, they were large, slow, and mechanical. Later they were steam-powered. When the transistor was invented in 1947, computers could store more memory and run programs. With each new invention, a different computer was made. Each computer was better than the last.

The Z1 was the first computer. It was made by Konrad Zuse, who would later make the Hollerith Machine. The Hollerith Machine kept lists of Jews and other German enemies. In 1943, the Allies made Colossus, which decoded German ciphers. Then the Mark I and ENIAC, or Electronic Numerical Integrator and Calculator, were made. The Mark I was made by Howard H. Aiken. ENIAC, 1,000X faster than the Mark I, was made by John Eckert and John Mauchly. In the 1970s, personal computers began to appear. In 1985, when Bill Gates founded Microsoft, computers became faster, with better capabilities.

Computers have greatly improved over the years. Inventors are the reason this happened. Computers are one of the greatest inventions ever, and they continue to improve and grow in popularity.

Andrew Vaccaro
Grade 5

The Magnificent Towers

Once there were two magnificent towers in New York City that attracted millions of people from all over the world. They were the tallest skyscrapers in America.

To see the towers best, take an afternoon ferry ride to the city. It's marvelous the way the beautiful sun shines upon its hundreds of crystal clear windows. At the base of the tremendous towers, one might look up to see what looks like a never-ending path leading to the glorious gates of heaven. In the lobby there are people of all nationalities. An elevator ride is necessary to reach the top. In the stuffy elevator, you feel a rush of excitement race up your spine as you speed to the top of the tower. Once you reach the observation deck of the majestic towers, you look upon the awesome city of New York, and your breath is taken away. You view the surrounding landscape and it makes you feel like a giant. When you glance upward and catch the sight of the great American flag waving proudly in the breeze you may feel a surge of American pride and shout out "God Bless America!" And those words, carried on the wings of the wind, would sound in the hearts of the people on the busy streets of New York below.

On September 11, 2001 two hijacked jet planes crashed into the towers, destroying them and killing thousands of innocent lives. Slowly, America has pulled itself together and is now stronger than ever.

Simeon Boyle
Grade 6

Football

If you think the best sport in the world is football, then you need to read this. Football is the greatest sport ever. This game has a lot of rules, but it's fun to play. I watch it on TV all the time. Football is the greatest ever.

The game is really fun to play. I play it every day with my friends in their backyard. Me and my friends make up our own teams. My brother taught me everything I know. It's fun to play.

I watch it all the time on TV. My favorite team is the Jags. The team that I think is going to win the Super Bowl is the Seahawks. My favorite player is Reggy Bush. It's a great sport to watch.

The sport has some rules you need to know. The object is to get the ball to the other end of the field. If you get taken down or fall on your knees you are down. There's two ways to get an extra point and one is if you kick the field goal from the 3 or if you get two by running or passing from the 3. The rules make it fun to play.

Watching it on TV, learning the rules, and playing it outside is the way you can get to know this game. This sport should be number one everywhere.

Joseph Winters
Grade 6

Atlantic Salmon

Fishing for Atlantic salmon used to be a way of life down east. Many friends were made on the river banks.

Atlantic salmon have become endangered in the Dennys River. Salmon are hunted by seals, birds of prey, otters, and fishermen in Greenland and Labrador. Salmon are stocked in the Dennys River. 100,000 fish are stocked every year. After two years at sea, the fish migrate back to their native river. About two or three fish return per year. The fish they get back are caught in a weir. I don't think that all of the fish go into the weir because they see it and go out to sea.

Fishing dropped in the 1970s. My father, grandfather, great grandfather, and great great grandfather, know many things about the famous fish.

The salmon come up river to spawn. They lay their eggs in good size cobbles. Where the water is swift and good in oxygen, the female deposits the eggs after she swiftly moves her tail to move the cobbles. Then after the eggs are fertilized, they are covered up.

I think the weir should be taken out for five years. Then the salmon can go upstream, and spawn while they stock some more. Eventually the salmon won't need as much stocking anymore.

There are many salmon stocked in the river every year; and in the river, the salmon are a treasure. Without salmon, Dennysville and Edmunds might not be the same again.

Ben Robinson
Grade 6

Good Teachers Make a Good Education

Many things make up a good education, but to me, good teachers are what make my education a good one.

From my experiences, I have learned that even boring topics can be interesting with a good teacher. For example, I went to a nature camp and wondered what could possibly be exciting about learning about trees? What I thought would be boring turned out to be very interesting because of the instructors who took us on hikes and didn't just give us a lecture. Also, at school I didn't think learning about China would be very interesting, but my teacher made it interesting through class discussions and telling us things about the lifestyle in China.

Good teachers also make difficult subjects easier. Some teachers have a way of explaining difficult things to help me understand them. Some teachers will let me stay after school for extra help if I have trouble with something. These teachers who help me understand things make my education a good one.

So whether I am learning at school, at home, at camps, or in sports, I think that good teachers are what make a good education.

Seth Carey
Grade 6

Christmas — How It's too Commercial

In my mind, Christmas should be a jolly, happy time for sharing and caring. But I think that some people think mostly of gifts. And that's what I think makes Christmas so commercial.

Buying gifts for other people is great, but some people find it an obligation. Why do it if you feel like that? Gift-giving is just a way to show friendship or affection.

Christmas is a great time to get people the things that they really need. An example is getting someone something like clothes or an alarm clock if they need it. Giving them things that they need shows that you really took time to think about what they really need, instead of just buying them easy things, like toys (which I feel is partly what I feel makes Christmas so commercial.) Doing that shows them that you really thought about them when you were shopping.

One other thing that makes Christmas less commercial is making donations. This Christmas, try to donate books or toys. Just because you won't be able to use them, another kid will. Another thing that you can donate is your time. Give away some of your time to charities.

The next time you think of Christmas, try to also think of the great holiness that you feel during the holidays. Try to also think about donating something this year. Doing these things will make Christmas less commercial.

Abigail Jeffers
Grade 6

Vikings

There is a magic place, a land of beautiful and majestic fjords. A place where the elusive troll is still believed to live in the deepest corners of the forest. It's a place where the fierce and mighty and brave Vikings once lived. The place is Norway!

Norway is known for its Vikings explorers and two of the most famous Vikings were father and son. They were Erik the Red and Leif Eriksson. Erik the Red got his name because his hair and beard were red and he had an awful temper. Erik the Red's father was an outlaw and forced to leave Norway because of some killings and the family then settled in Iceland. On his travels Erik the Red discovered Greenland and the family moved there. Erik the Red's son Leif Eriksson was believed to have been the first European to discover North America. They might have been outlaws, but they sure were good explorers and discoverers of new places.

Vikings were best known for their weapons and ships. Their weapons were used for sea and land warfare. Their weapons consisted of the spear, sword and sometimes the battle-axe. For defensive weapons they used the shield, a chain-linked short called the mail short and the helmet. An interesting fact about the helmet was that it did not have any horns sticking out of it like most people believe it did. Vikings were truly the best explorers and warriors in Europe from A.D. 800-1100.

Austin Rafoss
Grade 4

Put a Smile On

We all feel down sometimes. We come back from a hard day and feel mad, tired and even a little sad. What if that never happened? If I could give a gift, any gift, even if it could not be wrapped up, I would give the gift of a smile to all the people that are feeling sad in the world. Just think if everyone was happy, all the terrible things that would be stopped. If everyone would live their life with a smile on their face, it would make everything around us seem brighter. If everybody was happier they might see the world from a different point of view. Take time to stop and notice the things that we don't realize or appreciate every day, the things we take for granted. To stop and see everyone you turn to with a smile on their face, it would make you feel glad on the inside and the outside. An amazing gift to the world would be the gift of a smile. A smile cannot be wrapped up; it has to come from the heart. It's an amazing feeling inside when you see someone walking by with a smile on their face for no reason at all, they are just happy to be alive. If everyone realized that being alive is enough of a gift, people might look at the world with a different perspective, and do it with a smile.

Victoria Dillon
Grade 6

Ice Skating

My favorite hobby is skating. I like interpreting and flowing to the music. I started skating when I was seven, and you should see me now! I skate like an eagle flies! It's so much fun.

When I started skating, I was really scared. I didn't know what friends I was going to make, or how much progress I was going to make. Now, I have two really good friends that I made from going to skating: Rachel and Tori.

I've been skating for four years, and I can't wait 'til I got on to five. I have a medal collection, and over half of them are skating medals! That shows how many years I've been skating.

Every year our skating club, (Montclair Inside Edge) goes on a trip to go compete in Lake Placid. We got first place again! Can you believe it?

Sometimes it's hard to be a figure skater, and it gets frustrating. A lot of the time it's fun though. My coach is really nice, and I like her. Sometimes she *could* get a bit pushy. When I'm trying to do something on the ice, and I fall, she gets a *bit* angry.

Over everything that happens in skating, like coaches, competitions, friends, losing, winning, and even getting frustrated, it is a lot of fun! It may be hard in the beginning, but it's worth it in the end. When I grow up, I want to be a skating coach or judge.

Krista Frias
Grade 5

Astrology

A star is full of two main gases. They are hydrogen and helium. These gases are held together by gravity. At the core they are very densely packed. The belief that the movement of the sun, moon, and planets affect people's personalities and events in their lives. There are thousands of stars arranged in a compact ball. The largest stars are 1,000 times the diameter of the sun, and the smaller ones are just one fraction of its size; not much bigger than Jupiter. Stars produce energy by nuclear fusion. Within the core, hydrogen nuclei (protons) collide and fuse to form first deuterium (heavy hydrogen). The mass of the sun -1Solar mass-18s used as a standard for measuring other stars.

Francesca Caruso
Grade 5

The Mini Super Bowl

It was a hot day when a huge rivalry for school football began. It was being played by the St. Sebastian Knights and the St. Bonaventure Bobcats. This game is called the Autumn Bowl. It would be played on North Hills field.

The Knights kicked off first. St. Bonaventure scored on their opening drive. Then it was the Knights' turn. The Knights scored on their first drive too.

St. Bonaventure scored 14 unanswered points. Then it was half-time.

The coaches of the Knights gave a heck of a talk and the Knights came home with a win and a trophy.

Luke Spicer
Grade 4

I'm a Person Who Loves to Make New Friends

I'm a person who loves to make new friends. It makes my heart glow every time I meet someone new. I just want to be good friends with that person. I treat everyone the same. I love to make new friends because it's like adding another person into my family. It also makes me really happy when I make a new friend because then my relationship with everybody grows and keeps on growing. I love to hang out with my friends and whenever someone's in trouble I'm always there for them whenever they need me. I would never leave someone out. I want to be friends with everyone. I don't care if that person has different colored skin or if that person has a disability. I would still be friends with them.

When I moved to a new school I didn't know anyone there. I was scared to death. I thought that they would make fun of me or do something horrible to me until these two girls came to me and made me feel so comfortable. We became best friends and their names were Ming and Kiki. As the years went by I became friends with other people.

Having friends is like having another brother and sister. We will never hurt each other's feelings and we would always watch each other's backs. Friends are a big part of life. They are like a pot of gold.

Rachel Lii
Grade 6

Otto

What's important to me is my dog. His name is Otto. Otto is a black and brown Standard Dachshund. He weighs about 19 pounds and has brown eyes. He's small, but a big barker. One time he had heart worms. He has a medicine that he doesn't like, so we wrap it in cheese and he doesn't notice.

My first big reason that is important about my dog is that he plays with me. He plays with me because he's always active and loves to play with his tennis balls. He runs around the table like a crazy monkey.

My second big reason that is important about my dog is that he loves me. He loves me because I play with him a lot. I also feed and take care of him outside.

These are my big reasons why my dog is important to me.

Christian Edder
Grade 4

Imagination

Adults and kids use their imagination, but mostly kids. The majority of kids that use theirs are at the age of 5 to 7 years old. But when they grow up, they get real friends and imaginary friends.

It's great to have an imagination and an imaginary friend because you play with them a lot. You can pretend with your imaginary friend, you can go on an imaginary spaceship to the moon. You can use your imagination anywhere, at school, outside, at the doctor and home. A lot of kids in kindergarten and preschool like to play with their imaginary friends anywhere.

Grown-ups still have their imaginary friends. I even have one and his name is Superboy and his powers are super laser and super strength that makes him fly. In the future I hope kids will still have their imaginary friends.

Sotiris Papa
Grade 5

The Mall

I remember about five years ago my parents and I went to New Hampshire to see what it was like. We drove by a mall and we were getting restless driving around all the time so we went in.

We were in the mall and my parents were looking at some things. Then I saw a big, colorful carousel. It wasn't too far from my parents so I went to go check it out. But I was really tiny and a huge gathering of people came by me and when they left I looked towards where my parents were and they disappeared. I knew they were looking for me which meant they were moving around so it was more difficult to catch up with them.

I was lost and I was scared. I started to pace up and down the mall until I recognized a shirt that looked like my dad's. It could have been a stranger but I didn't care it was my only sign of hope. Lucky for me it was my dad. When I found my parents I had never been happier to see them.

Eric Carvalho
Grade 6

My Christmas Vacation

Finally, twice a year only, we had a great experience of fresh, mouthwatering French fries with gravy. Dark gravy straight from the fresh-smelling ski chalet's stove. Canada: your skiing and snowboarding dream. At the chalet, we definitely bought French fries with gravy plus lift tickets. Our whole family got an anytime pass for skiing anytime in 2005-2006 there at the park. We also bought lesson passes for my sister and me for the holiday.

I snowboarded this year. Our snowboard coach was incomparable. His name was Ian. We also had a crazy team name! Ours was the Shreddogs. I liked our group members, too. They were funny and friendly. I think this group IS the best. I was divided in the OK group, which was the group I was in.

There were other groups, the novice and the advanced group. We often saw the advanced group. We threw snowballs at them because "Benedict Arnold" from our group went up to the advanced group. He said that Shreddogs STINK! Therefore, we threw snowballs at him and his group!

After we had fun skiing and snowboarding, we, an exhausted family, went back to where we stayed — our friends' house. They had three sons; I had some friends to play with, too! We played games all evening. We also got Christmas presents there! I got an *Artemis Fowl* book, but I didn't care!

Canada is a great place to be. Being there is just like home! I look forward to going there again!

Edward Ma
Grade 6

Nicole, My Role Model

My name is Victoria Reilly. My role model is Nicole Middleton. Nicole is my big, 19 year old, cousin. Her wardrobe includes clothes from American Eagle, and Hollister. Nicole is 5'5" and a sophomore at St. John Fisher College. She helps me with my homework all the time. Nicole plays softball and the drums. She is my role model because Nicole is nice, pretty, and fun to be around. Nicole and I send emails to each other all the time. She has 5 best friends Benway, Maria, Miaw, Katie, Steven, and Theresa. Nicole is also on the honor role.

The cool thing is her and I share clothes, shoes, accessories, etc. Nicole is the best person in the universe. Nicole listens to rap. We both like the same song, "Gold Digger" and we both like the same fragrance. Nicole also has a Sprint camera phone. Her ring tone is "Gold Digger." Nicole is the best baby sitter. She plays with me and studies with me. When I grow up I want to be just like her. Nicole is the best person ever.

Victoria Reilly
Grade 5

A Good Friend

A good friend should be honest with you. They should not lie. If they do not have your trust because they lied, they are not a true friend.

Second, a friend should care about you. If you fall down, they should help you up. Say someone hurt your feelings, they should say, "what's the matter?"

Third, you should encourage your friend to do things. If your friend wants to start something new, you should say, "I think that you would be good at that." Those are the traits of a good friend.

Dan Jacobs
Grade 4

Hockey Freak

My favorite things to watch on TV is Hockey Night in Canada. It shows Canadian hockey teams playing against each other. There was a lockout last year so I'm really glad hockey is back. I watch it more often now because I really miss it. Since I know almost all the players, I like acting like the spokesperson. I get really mad and upset when the team I'm rooting for misses a good shot. I also get really mad when the team I'm rooting against gets a goal. I love it when it's overtime, and the team I like gets a goal and wins the game. I jump up and down.

I like hockey so much because I used to live in Canada, and we're all hockey freaks there. If there aren't any interesting games on, I'll watch cartoons or I'll watch football.

Eleni Siganos
Grade 6

Good Buddies or Not So Good?

Sometimes people get in a relationship with friends. You may think you have an honest, trustworthy friend one day, but then the next day, you hear a bunch of your friends talking about you behind your back. You don't want that to happen to you.

You may think you have one great friend, but things could change. If you're close to my age then you might be getting ready for Junior High or Middle School. Some people might call that drug time. One of your best friends might come up to you and ask you if you want any drugs. You never want to be in a group of friends that are going to ask you for drugs. You also never want friends that are going to be pretending to be your friend, but then they go and talk behind your back. Being in a little fight with your best friend is okay. It's not normal if you don't even fight once, for a little bit. The best choice is to know who your best friend is, and know that they're not going to put pressure on you.

Knowing more about your friends is good. You know you have great friends, so go enjoy life with your friends and family, and make sure you're with the people you know love and care for you!

Julie Reese
Grade 6

About Cats

Cats are very graceful. They almost always land on their feet. Also cats can use their mouths to smell prey. They also use their tails for balance and signaling to other cats. The pads on the bottoms of their feet are very sensitive. Cats make good house pets.

There are two types of cats. Cats can be domestic, meaning tame, or wild, which means free. A few wild cats are tigers, lions, and cougars. Wild cats have been around since the ice age. The best-known one from that long ago is the saber-tooth tiger. The saber-tooth had two long, sharp fangs that stuck down from their upper jaw. A more modern wild cat would be the panther or the tiger. They live in jungles.

The first domestic cat my family ever owned was a tiger cat named Puddy. She was called a tiger cat because of her small mane. My parents had gotten her before I was born. When I was born she was very fun to play with. But she died at 14 years of age.

Now we have two kittens. One is mine and one is my sister's. Mine is a she-cat whose name is Epee, which is a type of sword from fencing. Epee is gray with white streaks on her back. My sister's cat is a black and gray tom. His name is Snickers.

Thank you for listening to my essay. I hope now you will love cats too.

Nick Gude
Grade 5

Sugar

When I was about 4 years old, my family adopted a French Bulldog puppy named Sugar. Some people will call my family, "A dog family" which means we just LOVE dogs. I've grown up with dogs all my life so I can't really understand when people are afraid of my dogs.

Sugar was a sweetie. She was only a few months old when we adopted her. Sugar hated other dogs. Sugar loved chasing squirrels! One time when my mom was walking her, she came a hop, skip, and a jump from eating one whole.

When Sugar turned 5, she started walking strange. It seemed like she was in a lot of pain. We took her to the vet. The vet didn't really do too much for her. She'd be fine for two days, and then she would just walk funny again. Finally, they told my mom to put her to sleep.

When I got home from my friend's house, my house was dead silent. I asked my mom what had happened and she told me the news. I cried for what seemed like a million years, which was actually only that night and 2 days. I had never seen my dad cry but I can't say that anymore. I think about Sugar every day and how she didn't have to suffer very long. It's like we did a good deed for her.

Samantha Lotwin
Grade 5

Save a Life…an Animal's Life!

Have you ever visited an animal shelter? If you have, I'm sure you wanted to take every animal out of its cage and take it home with you!

There are too many animals waiting to be adopted in shelters across the United States. Animal shelters save the lives of animals by removing them from high-kill shelters and placing them in foster homes where they are cared for until a forever home can be found. Adopting animals from shelters, instead of buying them in a store or from a breeder, would save the lives of animals.

The reason there are so many animals in shelters is because people buy animals and they aren't ready to take care of them and love them. Animals require a lot more than food and water. People buy puppies because they are cute, but they don't understand that they need attention, like a baby. When the puppy starts to "get into trouble" people get annoyed and decide to just get rid of the puppy by leaving it on the side of the road or at a park.

Shelters have animals of all ages. If you have never been to a shelter you should pay one a visit and I'm sure you will come home with an animal.

It's sad to see animals such as dogs and cats sitting in cages waiting for the right family to come along to adopt them. Adopt an animal today or become a foster family. You will be saving a life.

Matthew Mottola
Grade 5

Dance

Dancing is one of the best sports around. You get lots of exercise. Dancing can also be competitive. Dance is tons of fun! My favorite type of dance is lyrical.

Exercise is important and dancing is a great way to get it. When you dance in ballet or lyrical, you use your arm and leg muscles. After I dance, sometimes my legs get sore, but I think it is worth it. You have to be flexible to be a dancer so we have to do a lot of stretching. Dancing is a fun way to get exercise.

Did you know that dancing could get competitive? To be in a dance competition, you have to work really hard. I really like going to competition. I think it is worth it if my group wins something. Sure it's hard work, but I think it can also be fun to be in a dance competition.

Dance is also tons of fun. You get to use up lots of energy. In my opinion, it is fun to dress up for a competition or recital. Lots of my friends dance with me, and they all like dancing, too.

If someone asks me, "Is dancing really a sport?" I always answer yes. In dance, you do the same general thing that you do in a regular sport, like baseball or basketball. In dance you work hard, get exercise, compete against other teams, and have fun! Dancing is a sport that is really worth working hard for.

Audrey Romano
Grade 6

My First Vacation

The last two summer vacations we got to go to 1000 Islands. The first time I ever went there I was excited because my mom said we were going to go on a boat to go on a tour of the islands.

When we got there we had to get tickets for the tour. The tour was very long. They showed us all the islands. They told us the whole history of 1000 Islands, like that there were a lot more islands than 1000. Soon during the tour we got to get a tour of one of the castles named Bolt Castle. The tour of Bolt Castle was very interesting. We got to look wherever we wanted. There were parts that you couldn't look at because they were redoing some of the parts. Some of the parts were like that because they said that the person who was making it made it for his wife but while he was making it she died so he stopped making it.

I took a lot of pictures on the tours. I used about three rolls of film. After the tour we went looking around. The next day we shopped for a long time. I bought some things there. Later my mom said that we had tickets for the dinner cruise on the boat. After about an hour we got back and had to get ready to go back home. Then we got to look around some more. Then we went home. It was very fun.

Blasé Twardowski
Grade 5

Audra vs Lindsey

Do you have similarities and differences? Well, I know I do! Mine has to deal with my best friend, Audra, and I've known Audra since I was three years old. Even though we grew up together, we are very different. In this writing assignment you will find out the similarities and differences between Audra and I.

First, let's start with similarities. This year, we both made Highest Honor Roll, which is all straight "A's." Also, Audra and I like to shop at Abercrombie. We could shop until we drop. Audra likes to play outside a lot, same with me. Also, Audra and I like to sit by the computer for about two hours and talk to our friends. It's pretty fun, and it helps us with our typing. That could help improve my typing skills. When we talk on the computer, we always find something new the computer can do.

Audra and I can be really different. Audra likes basketball and I like softball. Audra has brown hair and I have blonde. Also, Audra has no sisters and I have four. Audra isn't an aunt, and I am. Audra loves to read, I don't. I wear glasses, and Audra wears contacts.

Did you think Audra and I are a lot, or a little bit alike? Personally, we are very different. While I was writing, I could think of a ton of differences. Not a lot of similarities, but that won't ever stop us from being best friends!

Lindsey Wood
Grade 6

Join the Fight — Stop Poverty

My dream is for poverty to come to an end. A child dies every three seconds as a result of extreme poverty. That is honestly, just really scary, to me. Think about it. 1, 2, 3, a child dead, in this world, at this time. 1, 2, 3, another dead. If we could save this world of ours from poverty, we could save the lives of so many children. Over 33,000 people die…DAILY…from poverty. Think about the fact that if that is only each DAY, I fear to think about the number which represents each year's mortality count. Almost all of the kids who die from this dreadful, life-taking condition are usually 100% poor. I can say that these people did not get what they deserved. Those who have had their lives claimed by this threatening condition shouldn't have really, well…had to suffer at all. Living with this fact is our consequence. For some people, not contributing at all. Ending on that note, I'll now say, thank you so much for taking the time to read this essay and I hope that it has inspired you to get active in the fight against poverty. Poverty has made me just jump to my feet and put on my own MAKE POVERTY HISTORY bracelet. I hope this essay has made you become more active in the fight against poverty.

JOIN THE FIGHT — STOP POVERTY

Kristen Lilley
Grade 5

Books

One of the most important things to me are books. If there were no books no history would be known, or stories about knights and dragons. They're one of the oldest ways of entertainment. Books are very important because they are entertaining, they record history, and are helpful tools of knowledge.

I love books. There is a book on every subject you could think of. Books are ancient knowledge passed down from one generation to the next. There are fiction, science, science-fiction, mystery, history, and more. Books are an everlasting way of entertainment.

History is very important. If we save books, we save history, without history we would not know about the past. Books are also important because without them it would be hard to learn about reading and writing along with science, math, and English. I also like to read books because to me they are like an adventure in the palm of your hands.

Books are helpful tools; they contain information and directions, they contain plans for buildings and temples. Books are helpful because they can entertain me and they have the old ways of people long ago. Keeping records in books are a responsibility for us to save history. I like books because they are entertaining, they record history, and are helpful tools of knowledge.

Colton Miller
Grade 6

My Education

The most important thing to me is my education. My education is important to me because it teaches me how to respect people and to have, in the future, a professional job. It is important to study very hard to reach your goal in your future. Also, it is important to have an education because if you don't, you will end up in the streets and beg for money and will starve. If you're someone educated you would have good manners and be very smart.

I will keep on studying, for I could be an archeologist. I want to be an archeologist because I want to learn about the old centuries, how they lived, and solve mysteries. I will study hard because I want to be a professional in the future and ask God to help me.

Jessica Arias
Grade 4

Have You Ever Had to Say Goodbye to a Friend

When I moved to New York I had to say goodbye to my best friend ever. His name is Konner. We used to do everything together. If one of us got punished we both got punished. If one of us got rewarded we both got rewarded. We were practically exactly the same.

When I heard I was moving I was very upset and I even started crying. I couldn't believe that I would just have to say goodbye after being friends for so long. After hearing that I had to move we started playing together practically all the time until I had to move. When moving day came he gave me an ancient golden coin that he had found. We were both crying. It is really hard to have to say goodbye to a very, very good friend after being friends for so long. Now we only see each other about five or six times a year. I miss playing with him a lot.

Alan Probst
Grade 6

Sports

If we did not have any sports, life would not be right. Basketball, football, and baseball are fun to watch and play. Basketball and football are fun to play. Baseball is cool. Basketball, football, and baseball are cool sports.

Basketball is fun. Playing it is very fun. Basketball is nice to watch. Basketball is my favorite sport. It is the best sport in my eyes.

Football is a fun sport too. Football is my second favorite sport. I like it when teams barely win. I like watching the Super Bowl too because of the amazing plays, because they are good.

Baseball is a cool sport. Sometimes I like to play it. It is my third favorite sport. Playing baseball is very fun sometimes. Baseball is raw.

Basketball, football, and baseball are good sports. Basketball is a good sport to play. Football is a cool sport. Baseball is one of the best sports. These are three fun sports.

Jesse Wertz
Grade 6

Freedom Is Not Free

You have to remember that the freedom of the U.S. did not come free. A very large number of Americans lost their lives defending our country, and our way of life.

Freedom is a very strong word. To me it means that the civilians of the U.S. can make decisions for ourselves. We can choose our lifestyles, our cultures, our religion, to have a family, pick your job, you can wear any clothes you choose, and most importantly you can be loved. The U.S. is one of the few countries to be free. Being free is the greatest feeling in the world.

Every U.S. soldier is risking their life every day, to keep our country safe, and defend our freedom. Soldiers who have come home from the battle grounds alive are called veterans. Every person treats them with respect for their bravery, courage and defending our country. The soldiers who never return are remembered for their bravery, they have given up their lives to keep the U.S. the way it is today. Veterans and lost soldiers are the strongest people in the United States of America.

Every United States soldier who devotes their time and their *life* to protect each and every one of us are the biggest heroes in the United States of America. I thank all the U.S. soldiers for all they've done for me, and all the people of the U.S. You are truly amazing people.

Trevor Keller
Grade 6

My Pet, Spike

I chose for this essay my pet, Spike. He's part golden retriever and German shepherd. My dog, Spike, is a dark golden color. He is my most favorite pet, and I will tell you why.

Spike's special to me because he is the first dog I ever had. When I was younger, we lived in the city; and it was not so easy to have a dog. When I was six years old, my aunt's dog had puppies so my mom kept one. Also, Spike is special to me because his birthday is on February 14, Valentine's Day. Spike is very smart, and he does many things. I even taught him how to play hide-and-seek. He really loves that game because I give him treats when he finds what I hide for him. He usually finds what I hide. Spike is also very special to me because he is a great watch dog. I am never afraid when Spike is around. He often sleeps in my room near my bed.

I am glad we moved to Maine because Spike has more room to run and play. When we lived in the city, he mainly stayed in the house except when my brothers walked him on his leash. Now we let him run around our big yard. This February 14, Spike will turn five years old, thirty-five in dog years. I intend on spending all my free time playing with my special pet, Spike.

Marissa Hinojosa
Grade 5

Mahatma Gandhi

Gandhi is known as the "Father of India." After a lifetime of working for human rights, he led the people of India to independence in 1947. But his greatest gift was an idea — nonviolence. He believed in solving problems peacefully, without fighting. Gandhi was respected throughout the nation. Choosing such a path was not easy for millions of his followers, but with Gandhi as its guide, the free nation of India was born.

Nonviolence was not a new idea, of course. Most great religions of the world preach against violence. However, people have wanted to use these teachings only in their personal lives. Gandhi brought nonviolence into public life and used it to change governments and their laws. For Gandhi, nonviolence was not a sign of weakness — it was a way to make people become stronger. It could also be a powerful force for change. Nonviolence could change laws, gain freedom and equal rights, and even change entire nations.

Gandhi's Hindu religion was the most important force in his life. He wasn't interested in having money or owning things because possessions go in the way of his spiritual life. It was clear to everyone that Gandhi was a truly holy man. In fact, the Indian writer, R. Tagore, gave Gandhi the name Mahatma, which means "great soul." Through his teachings and tireless efforts, Gandhi helped millions of people gain self-rule.

Gandhi introduced many ideas to help bring about change without violence. Gandhi's ideas about nonviolence changed the lives of many people. Gandhi was a small man, but his influence was enormous.

Tanysha Anand
Grade 5

The Importance of TV

I believe that the TV was an important invention for American society. One reason I have to support that belief is that the news helps people to get to know if there are victims of some civil unrest or natural disaster that they should aid in their state of distress. Also, the weather forecast can act as a forewarning if a hurricane or other catastrophe is headed in the viewer's way, and tells them to get to a safe facility. Even though news is important, it emits a rather pessimistic attitude that only shows the bad events and people's failures.

Sports on TV can be important also, by countering the pessimistic attitude and giving people something to be happy and celebrate about. It also brings people together when a family hosts a party in which they watch football or another sport. An example would be that in my school we all are celebrating together because the Steelers have won the Super Bowl. In fact all of Pittsburgh was celebrating together despite differences they might have. Those are some reasons why I think TV was an important invention for American society.

Jeremiah Scanlan
Grade 4

Ballet's Amazing History

Ballet is one of the oldest forms of entertainment, beginning in Ancient Greece, changing during King Louis XIV's reign in France, and then evolving today as a beautiful art. Ballet began in Greece as choral drama. People danced in patterns that represented their gods. A philosopher named Cicero thought people had to be insane or drunk to dance. Over time, ballet spread to other countries in Europe and ballet changed.

During the Renaissance era Italian dancers wore their regular clothes and regular shoes while dancing in ballets. At first they used ballrooms, but later theaters were built where performances were held. Dancing masters choreographed dances where strings were attached to the dancers' backs to make it seem that they were flying.

In the early 1700s, ballet spread to France where it changed even more. The ways of moving and the rules of ballet that we use were created then. A man named Giovanni de Bologna developed the moves for hands and wrists. It was in France in the 1700s that modern ballet performances started. After the French Revolution in 1789, professional ballet companies started in France too. Later, in 1835, the first Pointe shoes were made. Pointe shoes were made to make the women look like they were floating on air.

Now ballet is a wonderful art form with ballet companies all over the world. For dancers, it is important to know the history of ballet. With each step, move, and turn you are connected with ballet's exquisite past.

Annelise Straw
Grade 5

Books

If anyone is looking for a good way to pass the time reading a book is the way to do it. Books are important to me. Books are also fun and mysterious. They can even be calming. Books are a great way to spend your time.

Books are fun. Books can take your imagination anywhere. A good book will suck you right into the plot. You never know what can and will happen. If you like surprises books are perfect for you. A good story makes reading a good experience. All in all, books are fun.

Books can also be mysterious. Mysteries can exercise your brain without even noticing. If you want to be a detective this is a good way to start. If you try to figure out who did what it's like picking out a suspect. The suspense of a thriller is amazing. In conclusion, books are mysterious.

Books can even be calming. No matter how mad you are a funny book *will* make you laugh. Books are a good way to cheer you up. When you get into a good book you forget everything and everyone around you. Sometimes books make you tired. If you're sleepy but you can't get to sleep it'll help a lot. Now you know, books can be calming.

In other words an important thing to me is books. Books are fun, mysterious, and calming. Books are great!

Amethyst Carey
Grade 6

There's No One Like Me

There's no one like me! Because I'm special. I am a boy who prays every night, because I try to follow Jesus. I always forgive others because I'm a loving boy also. I always try not to hurt anyone's feelings. When my cousins come to visit me, I usually let them play with my games. This means I'm a very good sharer. I'm a person who absolutely loves science. I think that science is a challenging subject. It's very interesting to me. Something else that drives me absolutely crazy in a good way is dinosaurs.

Another reason why there's no one else like me is because I'm one of a kind. I love to play outside and inside, it doesn't matter. I love to observe fish because they make me feel like I am part of their world. I love to imagine that I'm under the sea with all the creatures. I have a big imagination and sometimes I spend my time daydreaming.

Another reason why I am like no one else is because God made me. He decided that I was special enough to be put on Earth. God knew that I would make a difference in this world. This makes me a very happy person.

Edwin Rodriguez
Grade 5

My Family

My name is Michelle and I belong to a family of five. This family consists of my parents, my two brothers and me. Every sibling in my family plays a sport and attends piano lessons. This keeps everyone, even my grandfather who lives next door, very busy.

Sometimes I love my brothers and other times I just need to be alone. Living in my house is like living with mixed personalities. My brother Kevin is usually very nice and makes me laugh. My other brother Stephen can be the exact opposite. Even though he is often bossy, he can be very funny. They can be very watchful too, making sure I do the right thing when our parents are not around.

Being raised with two brothers has not given me a boyish personality. Instead, living with two brothers has given me a different perspective on ideas and thoughts. Yet somehow it has also made me closer to my mom, maybe because we are the only girls in the family.

I have always been very close to my brothers Stephen and Kevin. During the summer we enjoy watching movies together and playing basketball. I was never good at basketball, but that never mattered to my brothers. Stephen would usually be the one to organize and start games. Sometimes he would be a little bossy while organizing the games to prevent Kevin and I from being lazy. At times we might even argue, which I guess is normal for brothers and sisters, but it never takes us a long time to apologize and to be friends again. My family is great!

Michelle Fernando
Grade 6

The Blizzard

Last year there was a huge blizzard. It was fun. It gave us an extra week of no school. We got to go outside the entire week. Part of the time outside was shoveling. The snow was a few feet deep. The snow blower couldn't do it, so that meant we had to shovel it. By the end I was exhausted. My little brother, Bradyn, didn't like it because it was so high he couldn't walk. He stood in the snow paralyzed.

I went sledding on a steep street layered in ice. I never went so fast. I made an igloo that eventually turned into ice.

The worst thing about the blizzard was that we had to make it up at the end of the school year. We had a short summer vacation. I will never forget the blizzard of 2005 because it was the most fun winter I have ever had.

Cody Ksen
Grade 6

A Job That Can Be Fixed

"Whew" I softly whimpered to myself. That nasty garbage stunk like a skunk blasting its horrible spray. My grip squeezed my squishy nose as if there were two strong magnets sticking together from each side. I felt like a burnt hamburger sitting in the blazing heat rays of the scorching sun. Imagine every week, you have to take out the smelly garbage. I hated this because my sizzling driveway was burning my cool feet. One day I ambled down the midnight black driveway. As I was almost to the white sparkly curb, I let go of the sky blue handle. The garbage rolled down the shimmering driveway.

This looked very amusing. It seemed like an amusement park ride. Next week I pushed off the smooth driveway and sped down like a fierce cheetah to the rocky curb. This was quick and exciting! Now I could always make this terrible job enjoyable. In addition, my dad thought it would be more simple and faster. I will never forget this intelligent idea.

Jordan Steiner
Grade 4

Michael vs Cheetah

The location is a grass plain in Africa. The competitors are Michael Johnson of the USA Olympic track team and the cheetah.

The cheetah has an advantage over Michael. The cheetah is in its own environment. He has the ability to hunt for food for energy. He can also find water when he is thirsty. Michael has to plan ahead to make sure he has food and water. If he forgets to bring his food and water, he may not be able to survive.

The cheetah has four legs and Michael has just two legs. This makes the cheetah better at running short distances. Michael would also have to run in the grasslands instead of on a track. The grass would cause him to run slower.

For these reasons, I feel that the cheetah would win the sprinting contest.

Zachary Abel
Grade 6

The Big Hit

I am nervously going toward the batter's box. I am afraid of getting hit by the ball. My hands start to shake. I am frightened. I am thinking, "Bryan, you can do this!" It is all right. My mouth can taste fear. I'm thinking, "I am going to get beaned by the ball." My ears can hear the pitcher talking to me. He says, "You are going down." My heart pounds faster and faster as I get closer. I know there is no going back.

I'm in the batter's box ready for the ball. I can hardly breathe. My hands grip the bat as hard as a snakebite. The pitcher starts his wind-up. The pitcher throws the ball. I swing the bat. I slam the ball all the way to right field. I hesitate, then I run. I run as fast as I can to first base. I think I am going to make it, but I am really close.

I did it! I can hear the crowd screaming my name. I am so proud! The first baseman throws the ball home to get somebody else out, so I run to second base. The catcher overthrows, so I run to third base. I quickly slide into third base. I am so happy, I jump up and down. I can hear the crowd screaming wildly. The pitcher throws a wild pitch. I steal home and score! Baseball for life.

Bryan Vachereau
Grade 4

Celebrating Earth Day

Earth Day is a nationally observed day. People get together and clean up their community. Many schools here in the United States celebrate this day, but not my school. I want my school to do something to give back to our community, and I think this would be a great opportunity.

On Earth Day I want to go outside with students and faculty members to clean up around Dudley Middle School. I think we should also plant different flowers and trees. The woods around the school would be cleaned up. Bird houses can be built and put up outside.

I think my school should participate in this Earth Day celebration because this will make my school look better. This would also be a way for us to give back to our community. This celebration would also be fun to do. If my school does take part in this celebration, it will be educational for all the students that were involved.

To get our supplies and tools to do all these things we need to raise money. We can walk around the school in the morning and collect donations. Some people may be able to ask friends or family for donations. The administration can ask other surrounding districts to volunteer and help us raise money.

On April 22nd I want my school to work as one to change how we celebrate Earthy Day in Dudley. I hope my school can do this and help our community.

Danielle Moore
Grade 5

A Special Gift

A gift that I would want to give to my family and friends that cannot be wrapped or used is compassion. Compassion would be the gift because sometimes that's the greatest gift of all.

The character trait of compassion really means caring for someone when they're down or sad. You don't have to buy someone a fancy necklace or video games, you just have to let them know you really care. Sometimes it just takes compassion to brighten up someone's gloomy day.

You can't go to the store and buy a box of compassion; it must be part of your character, personality, and the way you act. Also, when you receive compassion you don't have to pay for it, it is the way people act. Since I go by the motto, "Treat people the way you would want to be treated," I always show compassion to people. I am grateful to all the compassionate people. Compassion is one of the most special gifts of all.

I show the gift of compassion like many other caring people. For example, when my grandparents are ill, I visit them with my mom and prepare lunch for them, and care for them. If you want to be compassionate, just care for and help people who need it.

It's never too late to learn how to be compassionate. Being compassionate is very rewarding, and truly is one of the greatest gifts of all.

Neal Vespe
Grade 6

Friends Are Not Leaders or Followers

A great author once said "Don't walk in front of me, I may not follow — don't walk behind me, I may not lead — just walk beside me and be my friend." Friendship is important to me because without friends I would not be happy. They stay beside me when I am in trouble and I stand beside them. We stick together and that's what makes us good friends. They don't take control of things and they don't follow me. We just hang out together. It's hard having friends who are bossy but you have to tell them how you feel. They will understand you if they are your real friend.

Friends should like you for who you are not for how you act or who you hang out with. Friends should always think of friends first. If someone has a chance to be the most popular person but only if they humiliate their friend, they should not do it. Friends come with virtues. You have to be patient with your friends, you have to be generous, you have to be considerate, and you have to have humility. Humility is a virtue that if you won something or you are good at something, you do not boast or brag about it because you consider your friends and you consider your relationship with them and their feelings.

Emma Shields
Grade 6

While I Was Sleeping

My worst memory began at overnight camp in Worcester, Massachusetts.

One night I was trying to get some sleep when I felt something tickle me. I didn't sleep long because I woke myself up screaming and yelling. The sting and pain was horrible. The Camp Nurse was called and she put medication on a huge spider bite.

The next day we had a game against the other cabin. I was trying to make a *steal shot in basketball* when I tripped and fell on the spider bump. The huge swollen bump exploded like a balloon! I had to go back to the nurse. The nurse put on the same medications and told me to see her every day.

The next day I looked at my wrist and it seemed to be healing a little. I went to my hockey game. The game was exciting and we got an advantage by taking out the other team's best player. Then it happened, I learned they had an advantage too: *Me*. If one of them bumped into my wrist I'd go down. So my coach took me out.

I never knew the type of spider that bit me but I know it made a lasting memory in my mind. I still can feel the pain and the hurt that it caused me. *I get really upset when I think about how that spider ruined my last days at camp and it all happened while I was sleeping!*

Michael Holliday
Grade 5

Mets Fantasy Camp

In Port St. Lucie FL, there is a great place to go. It's called Mets Fantasy Camp. While you are there you can do many things, such as play games against other fans and the pros. You get coached by former Mets who help you out a lot. There is a trainer's room with professional trainers who help you and treat you like the pros.

They give you lockers with your name on them. They also give you baseball uniforms. One grey uniform with your name on it and one pin striped uniform with your name on it. You provide your own glove and spikes.

You stay at the PGA Villas. It contains a Jacuzzi. Also a full kitchen, master bedroom with a bathroom. While you are there you can leave the hotel to practice, visit relatives, or go to amusement parks.

You can stay in Florida if you want. My dad stayed four extra days. The camp was five days. During the extra days he hung out with the pros and got many autographs. So it would be a great idea to stay.

The last night there they give out awards. My dad won the Cleon Jones award. It was for the highest batting average. Some other awards are the MVP award (most valuable player), Tom McKenna award (for injuries), and the Defensive award (best fielder). It was the best time my dad ever had. If you like the NY Mets and baseball then you would enjoy it too.

Danielle Antonucci
Grade 6

The Fiji Mermaid Hoax

In August of 1842, a man by the name of Dr. J. Griffin said he acquired a 'mermaid' in South America, even though it had been caught in the Fiji Islands. The Fiji mermaid appeared to be half mammal, half fish. The original exhibit was made popular by P.T. Barnum, but has been also been popularized by other strange-seeking people such as Robert Ripley from Ripley's Believe It Or Not. The 'mermaid' looked like it had "Died in great agony." The fish tail was a blue-green color, while the front part resembled a 'monkey corpse that was sewn onto a fish tail'. Millions over the world were astonished to find that the Fiji Mermaid was exactly that. Since then, many hoax or false 'Fiji Mermaid' have been sold worldwide. They are widely popular in America. Believers of the mermaid trick create occupations and careers of 'Mermaid Catchers'. They move deep into the South American waters looking for a tiny little monkey mermaid. Many reports of "seeing a small baby-like figure swimming in the water" are told to the police every year. They also explain when they tried to catch the mermaid, the figure darted away in the warm island waters. Amazingly so, the mermaids are still sold today. It's amazing how you can trick a million people in only a short time!

Michelle Taliento
Grade 5

Friends

What are friends? Friends are people that you can trust, people who are there for you when you need them most. Friends are not people who make you do something that you don't want to do, or people who talk about you behind your back. A big mistake people make with friends, is that they don't realize the signs that people are using them. Another mistake that people make, is that they don't branch out, or they think that if they make a new friend, they have to abandon the old friend just to make a new one.

What you don't want to do, is overdo your friendships, or spend too much time together, because you might get sick of each other. You also really don't want to prejudge someone by his of her hair, clothes, or by their first impression. That's what messes up some friendships that could be really strong or close. Remember, first impressions aren't always correct.

A good friendship should always come first. If you and your best friend both have a crush on the same guy, then your friendship should be stronger than that and you'll figure something out. Besides, you can always get a boy, but you cannot get back the same friend. Boys will come and go, but good friendships will last forever.

Friends are important, and they will last forever. So, make sure you're there for them, and they will always be there for you!

Erin Siegman
Grade 6

Dolphins

Dolphins live all over the world, from colder northern and southern waters to warm tropical waters. The Bottlenose Dolphins prefer warmer waters. Bottlenose can swim at 3 to 7 miles per hour. They can go over 20 miles per hour when they work hard. The shape of a dolphin helps it swim fast.

There are 32 species of dolphins. Bottlenoses are the most studied. They can dive down to 150 feet, but are shallow divers. They can grow to lengths of 7.5 to 8.5 feet and weigh as much as 300 lbs.

Dolphins are warm blooded. Their internal body temperature is about 98 degrees. They need to conserve their body heat in colder water. Their body is surrounded by a thick layer of fat, called blubber, just under the skin.

They eat a variety of fish and squid, depending on where they live. The dolphins' cone-shaped teeth interlock to catch fish. Their teeth are not used to chew because they swallow their food whole.

Dolphins communicate just like dogs, cats, and other mammals by using sound, vision, touch, and taste. Dolphins don't have the ability to smell. They can make a unique signature whistle that may help individual dolphins recognize each other.

Echolocation is a way of using sound to find objects. The dolphin generates a sound from its forehead, which is sent into the water. The sound bounces off objects creating an echo that returns to the dolphin. They feel the sound pulses against their jaws. Different objects or fish give off different kinds of echoes. They judge how far away the object is by how long it takes for the echo to return.

Amber Maurin
Grade 5

The Perfect Gift

The perfect gift for an average person just like you and me would not be small, expensive, rare, or even very pretty. The perfect gift would be nothing you could buy, sell, box or shelf. The perfect gift would be something every person could give no matter how rich, famous or strong you are. The perfect gift would be something from the heart, which means so much more. The perfect gift would be the gift of time. A conversation or just spending time together would be the perfect gift. Anyone can use this gift, although it may seem not like much, but one day when you are lonely you will understand. It fills your heart with goodness and joy to kingdom come. "Treat others as you want to be treated" is the best rule to go with this gift. That is because one of the best parts is that whenever you give this gift you always get it back from the person you are giving it to so you can have a gift too. The best gifts work like this. Although even when you aren't lonely and see someone who might be, just think of yourself lonely and you know that you would want to be with someone. The gift of time is the perfect gift that every person should give every day.

Danny Mignone
Grade 6

Wolves

Wolves are incredible animals. Unfortunately, people misunderstand them. Wolves eat livestock and game animals. In folklore, wolves are portrayed as evil and scary. People never bother to learn the good qualities of wolves.

Wolves live in packs which usually have about eight members. Members have a good rapport with one another. There are two ranks of wolves: dominant and subordinate. Wolves demonstrate their rank every time they meet. A dominant wolf stands straight, and a subordinate wolf crouches, puts its tail between its legs, and puts its ears back.

Wolves hunt in a pack at any time of the day. When a hunt begins, wolves howl to greet each other. They hunt in the opposite direction of the wind so that their prey does not smell them. Wolves usually eat large animals. They sometimes hunt old, sick, and injured animals helping the herd of these animals because they can be a burden.

Wolves have one to eleven pups in a litter. The pups drink their mother's milk, and when they are three weeks old, meat is brought to them by other adults in the pack. At two months old, they leave the den. Then they hunt with the adults.

People's fear of wolves has had terrible results. Many people have hunted wolves. Thousands of wolves were killed in organized hunting. The wolf is now an endangered species in the United States. Fortunately, however, the government has made regulations about hunting wolves.

Claudia Gallagher
Grade 6

My Friend

Parakeets are fluffy, chatty, active little birds. It's so amazing that they can fly. Their colorful wings cut the air and whoosh! Before you know it, they're already in the air, soaring and flipping in the sky.

Both of my buddies were bought in Petland. They have very different personalities. Bala is mean and bossy, while Fe Fe is nice and eager to be trained. I personally like Fe Fe better than Bala. He always greets me with a chirp when I am near his cage. I am glad he does because his delightful call always perks me up. He loves to learn and is scared of new objects just like the way I am. It is also funny when I eat food, he does too!

When I train him it is like I am in my own personal space. I can do anything and my bird helps me fulfill it. When he glimmers in the light, his feathers seem to shimmer with delight trying to perk me up and comfort me. The sky blue color of his feathers reminds me of the love I have for him.

Without my pets, my life would be filled with darkness. When Fe Fe and Bala keep me occupied, my life is filled with sunshine. When I am sad, holding them will relieve me. Their fluffy feathers always tickle my hand making me happy. They also entertain me with the tricks I taught them. I appreciate them and they appreciate me the same.

Jean Cheng
Grade 6

The Basilisk

The Basilisk, nicknamed the "Jesus Christ Lizard," is a type of lizard that lives in trees and rocks located near water in moist tropical rain forests in South America. The basilisk can run across the surface of water for short distances using its hind legs and holding its body almost upright, the tail acts as a counterweight. It is also a good swimmer and climber. This cold-blooded animal is territorial. Basilisk have teeth that are fused to the inner sides of their jaws. These reptiles have a long, whip-like tail, four sprawling legs, and a body covered with overlapping scales. The body is laterally compressed, tall and thin. The outer edges of the toes have long fringe-like scales that help it walk on water. A large flat, 10 bed crest, adorns the crest of the basilisk's head. Male basilisks also have a tall crest running along the back. Basilisks range for 2 to 2.5 feet. Females are smaller than males. Basilisks are carnivores, eating insects and arachnids, worms, and other small animals. Like other lizards, the basilisk stores fat in its tail. A female will dig a shallow trench.

Jamie Davis
Grade 4

Friends Are Important

Friends are very important to have. When you are going through a hard time, for example, when a loved one dies, they will help you. They also can help you with everyday things like homework, chores, and accountability. Friends can also encourage you. Whether it is to do one more push-up in gym or to study more for a big test, they are your cheerleaders. It is your decision to take their advice or let it go, but true friends will give you good advice to make you a better person. As you can see, it is very important to have friends.

Ashley Grooms
Grade 6

A Trip to Canada

One weekend, my family and I went to Canada. Our hotel room was small, but comfortable. It had two beds, a TV, a bathroom, and a deck. The hotel had a hot tub, a swimming pool, and a lobby. Behind it was a restaurant. It had great food! We saw Niagara Falls, and the U.S. Falls. We rode on a boat called "Maid of the Mist." We got soaked!

After we rode, we went to a gift shop. We purchased post cards, cups, and little toys that if you pull a string back, a cap pops out. We also visited Ripley's "Believe it or Not" Museum. That stuff sure is weird! I mean, I saw an eight-legged animal!

Niagara Falls is a great place! Those were the best two days of my life! I love Canada!

Matthew Krivanek
Grade 4

Christmas

Wow!!! What a great Christmas. It couldn't be better. My mom and grandma went crazy doing a lot of things for Christmas at my house, also my dad because he had to make a lot of cakes and cookies at our bakery. Mom and Grandma got up at 7:00 in the morning getting ready for Christmas Eve. We had over fifty people coming over to our house.

The best part of Christmas at my house was being with all my friends and family listening to Christmas music and singing along with the songs. Some of the songs we listened to were "Jingle Bells," "Santa Claus Is Coming to Town" and a lot of others.

We ate stuffed shells, pasta, mussels, shrimp and other delicious food. Before we ate we said a prayer thanking God for the food we had and wishing everybody in the world to have the best holiday ever.

After we were done eating, Santa Claus miraculously came down the staircase and gave us candy canes. We then unwrapped presents. All I saw was paper flying everywhere and getting torn up. I got an indoor basketball hoop, Xbox games, PlayStation games and clothes. I really didn't care about the presents, all I cared about was being with my family and friends.

We had hot cocoa and while we had hot cocoa we were admiring the Christmas tree and saying how nice it looked. This was probably one of the best Christmases for my family, friends and especially me!!!

Francesco Borgognone
Grade 6

Today's Trash Tomorrow's Treasures

Recycling paper is important because it helps the environment. There are many uses for recycled paper, and schools and other organizations can earn money.

Through recycling one can improve the environment. Recycling one ton of paper can save seventeen trees, six thousand nine hundred fifty three gallons of water, and four hundred sixty three gallons of oil. Littering or throwing away paper can be harmful to the environment and takes up a lot of landfill space.

Did you ever think about what is made from recycled paper? Recycled paper can be transformed into magazines, cardboard boxes, and paper cups. Just think a birthday card you give a friend could two weeks ago have been a cardboard box.

Abitibi recycling company pays schools, churches, and other organizations for recycling old newspapers, magazines, junk mail, and cardboard boxes. You don't even have to remove the ink. They will pay you by the ton. My school has earned a lot of money from Abitibi recycling company.

Recycling paper is great! Helping the environment, making new products from old ones, and fundraising for non-profitable organizations are wonderful reasons to recycle paper.

Sarah Kimutis
Grade 6

Christmas Eve

An important tradition to me is Christmas Eve. I spend every Christmas Eve and Christmas Day with my maternal grandparents. We have many rituals and traditions that we have continued over many years. All year-round I look forward to this night. Now I'd like to share some traditions.

At 7:30 every Christmas Eve, I meet my cousins, aunts, uncles, and grandparents at church. My mom, dad, and sister are there, too. When church is over, everyone goes back to my grandparents' house. The grandchildren play Santa Bingo together. We win prizes like candy and elf or Santa hats. Then, at about 8:30, my grandfather (Pappap) reads "'Twas the Night Before Christmas" to everyone.

Although presents aren't everything, everyone enjoys getting some! Another tradition we have is opening one gift on Christmas Eve. After the story, my grandmother (Mammaw) brings out eleven presents (one for each grandchild). Then we open them and show them to our aunts and uncles. Mammaw brings in plum pudding while we all sing "Happy Birthday, Dear Jesus." The last tradition we have is opening poppers. We each open a popper with a little surprise inside. The night of Christmas Eve is almost over, but our memories still thrive.

Soon everyone must go home. My family stays the night, though. Our anticipation for Christmas Day is rising, while our excitement from the night is dying. We all eventually fall asleep in our beds with visions of sugar plums dancing in our heads.

Megan Zembower
Grade 6

The Priceless Gifts in Life

Priceless gifts are the best gifts of all. Most priceless gifts come from the heart, which is more important than a gift that you could buy. Examples of priceless gifts are the gift of love and the gift of trust. I'd give both of my parents the gift of love. Even though they are divorced I still love both of them greatly. Love is important because if you lose everything you have, you still have the love inside you that everyone needs. Another great gift in life that I would give all of my family and friends is the gift of trust. Trust is good in life because if you have this, then anybody could tell you anything from a secret to what happened to him or her. Trust is also important because if you trust someone you can tell them what goes on that you normally don't tell your parents or your friends. For example, if something happened at school that upsets you then maybe if you tell your friends or family, then they can solve the problem for you. I hope one can see that the most important gifts in life are priceless. To me the gift of love and the gift of trust mean the most to me because they have the biggest impact on my life.

Justin Maurici
Grade 6

All About Me!

Hi, my name is Danielle and I am going to tell about my life. I was born on March 8, 1996 in Boston, Massachusetts. I'm nine years old. I have one older brother. His name is Alex and he is 15. I have two great parents who love me very much.

My teacher is Mrs. Zaino. She is very nice. My ethnic background is Spanish. I go to the Madeline English School; it is pretty big. I have a lot of friends at this school.

My favorite thing to do is gymnastics. I have been doing it for two years. I like playing with my cousin Jacky all the time. She is like a sister to me.

I go to El Salvador about every year with my aunt. I go there to see part of my family, like my grandparents, my aunts, my uncles, and cousins. I've been going there since I was three years old.

One of my hobbies is dancing. My favorite subject is Social Studies — well kind of.

My favorite song is "Burn It Up" by R. Kelly. I spend most of my time with my friends and family. I like making my own songs and try to make my own demo. Someday I would like to be a music artist. I like to write my own stories. I like to draw comics and much more. I like to chill in my crib and hang out. Well I hope you enjoyed hearing about me Danielle Haley!

Danielle Haley
Grade 4

Wow! My First Day at PMSCT

Wow! You would not believe my first day at PMSCT. When I first entered the room I saw my two friends, Katie and Sarah. When Mrs. Walton came into the classroom we had to be quiet so she could speak. Then we had to get assigned seats. After that we got our lockers. My locker number is 898. I'm on the purple hallway, second floor. Then it was time for lunch. We had to sit with our section, which is 612. There are 4 lunch lines and a snack line. After lunch we went on a tour with our team leader, Ms. Posten. We toured the entire school. Also we learned where to get on the bus.

After the tour we were dismissed to go to mod 9. My class was art with Mrs. Knight. We learned how to draw lines and different shapes. Also we learned everybody's name by doing a worksheet. We were drawing for two hours. I still had fun. When class was over we had to get back to our locker. The combination was tricky, but I got my lock open after several tries. I had to wait in the cafeteria for the bus. My bus number is 556. When the bus came we exited from the back door. I sat with my friend Katie on the way home. I had a much longer walk home. I had a fun first day at PMSCT.

Ebony Costello
Grade 6

Winter

Winter has months like no other. It's so magical with its white cold powder that covers the ground like a giant sheet. Winter can't relate to another season because it's months of love and magic. You think of gifts on holidays. But there's much, much more. It's about giving to others and caring for all, all through winter. You should give without expecting anything in return. Now that's the winter season.

Winter is December through March. Nothing is like winter. No season is similar. No snow shows in other seasons but winter. Winter holds Christmas, Hanukah, Kwanza, Valentine's Day, and other holidays.

You and I couldn't live without winter. There would be no snow to make snowmen or ice for icicles or no Christmas or Hanukah (and other winter holidays). Even more, you should know winter is one of the most magical and joyful seasons of them all.

Ava Graham
Grade 5

Earth Day "Blues"

Is the earth clean? Of course not! Garbage and other litter has polluted the earth from the United States to Japan. This is a worldwide problem and it needs to change. It would be a dream come true if the earths' future would be clean. The saying, "Do to others what you would want done to you," applies to the earth also. If we keep on polluting the earth, we won't have anywhere to live! I think if we have fines for people who get caught littering, they will stop. If we make a law that everyone has to recycle, the earth might get cleaner. If we change our ways, people and the earth will be happier and cleaner.

Justine Fairman
Grade 6

D-Day

D-day was a very important day for our military. Winning D-day gave our troops in Europe courage to keep fighting.

D-day was a very important day for the United States. It took place in Normandy, France, on June 6, 1944. The beaches in Normandy that D-day took place on are Omaha Beach and Utah Beach, which were invaded by the United State troops. Gold Beach and Sword Beach were invaded by the British troops. Juno Beach was invaded by the Canadian troops, even the Canadian Bicycle Division.

Within five days of June 6, 1944, sixteen divisions had invaded Normandy. There were boats, ships, planes, and tanks everywhere. Planes were bombing bridges, railroad tracks, and roads to prevent reinforcements from coming into the interior. Boats called the "Ducks" were transporting soldiers from England to the beaches of Normandy, while tanks and ships were firing at enemy bunkers.

On June 9, 1944, three days after the invasion started, the horrible battle ended.

Shane Seeley
Grade 6

A Night on the Strip

It was an excruciating summer evening and my family and I started our trip squished like tomatoes in our tightly packed van. While the rest of my family was asleep, I was looking out the car window, day dreaming about dancing at the Flamingo hotel. All of the sudden I saw a bunch of lights as bright as the sun out in the distance. As we drove closer I saw a sign that said "Las Vegas." At that moment I immediately woke everybody up while pointing to the sign. My family got wide eyed with excitement as we approached such extravagant buildings and lights.

As soon as we got to our hotel at the "Four Seasons" we immediately got ready for night on the strip! As we were walking along we strolled inside some of the hotels admiring the lobbies and casinos. We especially like Kahuna Ville. The place was packed. Everyone was jumping with excitement because the bartenders were putting on quite a show. They would juggle the bottles and were jumping onto the bar. After that we went back on the strip and toured until our feet were as sore as elephants in high heels. As we were walking back to our hotel we all agreed it was a great vacation.

Nora Watson
Grade 6

Homework

School is important to me because I love to learn in school because I want to be a straight A student. My friends are nice to me and they are generous. My friends can be nice and sometimes they could be mean. Homework is important because I want to get a good grade. I love to do homework for every subject. I love reading because it is the best homework to do. I started to like homework when I was in 2nd grade. I liked 2nd grade math homework. I start my homework everyday to get a good grade. Sometimes I don't want my grade to drop if I don't do my homework.

Gym is very important in my life. Gym is kind of fun. My favorite subject to do in gym is playing basketball. I enjoy basketball, it can be hard sometimes. I love to do push-ups, sit-ups, and games in gym. Push-ups and sit-ups are a good exercise. I have a nice gym teacher that is generous. Gym is important to me so I could get a good grade.

Class work is important because I want to finish before the teacher says it's home work. Sometimes I don't want to do class work for home work. Class work is important to me because I like to do it. Class work is the best thing to do in school except for doing nothing. Class work can be fun if I listen to the teacher. Sometimes I stop during class work because sometimes I kinda get frustrated. I like to finish class work in school instead of doing it for home work. Sometimes I help my classmates to do class work.

Carter Jenkins
Grade 6

The Big Surprise

Weekends with my dad are fun! When I was about 1 my mom and dad got separated. I lived with my mom most of the time, and spent many weekends with my dad. I always had pleasant times going over to my dad's house.

When my birthday rolled around, my dad would give me presents. When I became 5, my father came to pick me up at my mom's house. He muttered on the way to his house that he had a special surprise for me. On the way, I tried to guess what the surprise was, but I was only five, and I didn't know the things that I know now. I asked, "Is it a big toy?" But it wasn't. "Is it a pony?" Nope not that.

As we pulled into the driveway I couldn't think of what it could be. We walked in the living room and sure enough on the couch sat a tiny puppy. Once I saw the puppy I screamed on the top of my lungs, "A PUPPY!" I couldn't believe it, the thought of a puppy never crossed my mind.

After a while I tried thinking of what I should name it so I said a silly name, "Honey!" My dad didn't want to be calling, "Honey! Honey! come here."

"Everyone would think he was crazy!" he said.

"What should we call her?" I asked.

"What about — Penny?"

"Why Penny?" I asked.

"Because she has the color of a penny," he explained.

Sarah Leite
Grade 6

My Role Models!

I have three role models that I really want to be like! I would really like to be like my mom, my dad, and my sister. I want to be like them all combined!! Also they *ALL* have excellent personalities!

When I grow up I would really like to be the way my dad is, the way my mom is, and the way my sister is! I want to be like my dad because when I grow up I would like to be a woodsy person. I would like to become like my mom too, because I want to have the personality that my mom has; friendly, kind, and she is pretty! I would also like to be my sister, because my sister is beautiful, and I want to look exactly like her!

As you can see, I think that they are good role models for me because I want to be all of them combined! I want to be woodsy, I want to be friendly, and kind! Last but not least, I want to be pretty! (Like all of them!)

Mary Kill
Grade 5

Relationships

I have a relationship with my dad. We make models together. He takes me places he is going sometimes. We go to get movies. He went to math night at school with me, and he came to movie night with me. He even plays games with me when he doesn't want to.

Tony Persichitti
Grade 6

Popularity

Popularity is very impressive to some people. People will dress or act differently just to be popular. They usually try to hang around people who never noticed them before they changed. For other people, being popular is not that important. They tend to associate with people who like them just the way they are.

Sometimes people change the way they dress and act if they think it will make them more popular. I remember one day while I was at the mall, I saw a girl I know wearing a style of clothes that I never saw her wear before. Later that day, I saw her talking to a couple of other girls who were popular at our school and were wearing the same type of outfits. I think she dressed like them just to impress the girls and be accepted. She appeared to be happy and had a big smile on her face. But, I had to ask myself how could she be happy if she had to change who she was.

Popularity definitely has its good points. Entertainers and professional athletes get paid great salaries and usually have whatever they want. But it also has its down side. It's hard for them to go out to lunch or even for a walk without admirers stopping them for an autograph. They have no privacy.

For myself, I'm happy with who I am. I don't want to change just to be popular. I think it's more important to be judged for the person you are inside.

Brandon Bunting
Grade 6

My Handicapped Bird

Hey did you ever wonder what it is like to have a handicapped bird? Well, I am going to tell you about my handicapped parakeet named Lime. I love my bird and I also feel bad for it.

My bird's life is interesting for a lot of reasons. One reason is because it can do a lot of things the same way as other birds. One thing it can't do is fly. But, since he can't fly he uses his two legs to climb up the side of his cage.

Lime became handicapped in a peculiar way. He became handicapped by being at the bottom of his pile of eggs. There were ten eggs and two were squished under all of them. One of those two eggs was Lime. His legs were stretched out straight and couldn't move to certain positions like an average bird. He also can't perch like an average bird.

My bird has an amazing life. It is because he can do mostly anything an average bird can. Unlike an average bird he can't fly that far. He basically jumps and slides for his destiny. He can eat and drink from the same height as an average bird.

He is an amazing bird to me for a bunch of reasons. One reason is he gets around with some struggle, but not too much. It is astonishing because most people think that he can't do what an average bird can. He is an extraordinary bird.

Nick Maulbeck
Grade 6

Why I Think My Baby Cousin Is So Cool

I love my baby cousin Gabriel because he's just so cute. He is two, but when he first started talking he was able to say my name "Joe" although he pronounced it "Doe." He has always been my friend and whenever I leave his house he calls, "Bye buddy."

My cousin's name is Gabriel Stec, just so you know, and he is also very funny. Whenever I sleep over at my cousin's house Gabriel will wake me up at six in the morning to play guys with him. One funny story about Gabriel was when my aunt walked into the living room and there were potato chips everywhere, even on top of the bookcase. My aunt said, "What happened?" Gabriel said, "I EAT CHIPS." We have a picture of him in a lion suit with a huge smile on his face.

Gabriel loves to play ball. He is very good at throwing. Another game that he loves to play is one where he pretends to be a puppy. It is very funny also. He also likes to play with their two dogs.

I have 46 first cousins. It is awesome to have that many cousins. There are a lot of babies. But out of all of them my best friend would be my cousin Mike and my favorite baby of all is Gabriel. Don't get me wrong, I love them all, but Gabriel is the best.

Joseph Miele
Grade 6

Kleenex

Achoo, achoo, achoo! What do you use when you are coughing? What about sneezing, or if you have a runny nose? I have always loved Kleenex. Now that I am older, I don't use these tissues quite so much, but they are still very important to me. I use them for a runny nose, and I use them to decorate. I use Kleenex for everything! You can use all sorts of tissues, but my favorite is Kleenex!

Do you like how a cat feels? Then you might as well use Kleenex because these tissues feel very soft, just like a silky cat. When you take a Kleenex tissue out of the box, it unfolds. Other tissues are way too thick, unlike perfect Kleenex. Some tissues are very big and heavy. They don't stretch or feel soft. Kleenex is a whole different story.

Let's think of fashion, too. Kleenex comes in those very fancy cubed boxes picturing landscapes or trees. There are also some boxes that feature cartoons from Disney such as Lion King. Kleenex are not just helpful, they're beautiful!

When teachers or parents see that we are coughing, sneezing, or have a runny nose, they don't just say, "Go use a tissue," they say, "Go get some Kleenex!" These tissues are very important to me. Kleenex is not just a tissue; they're much more than that! Kleenex, buy one and you might even be lucky to get one free!

Jennifer Kanarskaya
Grade 6

Stitches

In our everyday lives we have to be courageous. In first grade, I had to have stitches when a girl, by accident, hit me with the corner of her bin into my eyebrow. I got sent to the nurse because I was bleeding badly. The nurse called my mom and she brought me to the hospital. I was six years old and I was crying and I was scared. The doctor said I needed stitches. When the doctor called me in, I laid down on a chair and the doctor started giving me stitches. I screamed, at first, but I knew I had to be brave and sit still. The doctor gave me six stitches. I have a small, white scar over my eyebrow to show I was a brave little boy.

Brad DaRoss
Grade 6

My Pet

Have you ever had or have a pet? I have a dog. Her name is Piper Lynn Grey. My dog is a girl and her birthday is on July 2, 2004. She has a brother named Spike. When she was little her mom and dad were sold and Piper and her brother were left homeless, so I adopted her.

Piper is a beagle. She is blackish-brown with a little bit of white under her chin. She has brown eyes and a black nose. Many people think she is a black lab but she isn't. Her fur is as dark as chocolate and she is as soft as a bunny.

In my spare time, I like to play with Piper. She has many favorite toys like a rope, a bone and many more. Her favorite thing to chew on is a rawhide. She will lay in the living room and chew on it all day long. She loves them! Also, her favorite treats are Bacon Bites. She also can do the following tricks: sit, stay, come, shake, back paws, speak, and lay down. Last but not least, she loves her dog food Ol'Roy.

These are some facts on my dog. Would you love her if you had her? I do!

Kayla Grey
Grade 5

Laundry

Do you like doing laundry? I sure don't. Especially my brothers laundry, because it is as wet and sweaty as if I poured water on it. In addition, all the dirty clothes smell like whoever was wearing them got into a flight with a skunk, and the skunk won. Furthermore, I never have anyone's help to turn on the washing machine. I needed help because the machine is like a giant and I am a mouse.

Except one amazing day I thought of an idea that would change the world or at least my life. I ambled upstairs and snatched my miniature basketball hoop. After I snatched my hoop I crept back downstairs and set up the idea that would change my life: laundry basketball. Now I can shoot hoops and put the laundry in the drier at the same time. The next day I had an urge to shoot a slam dunk. When I jumped for a dunk it felt like I was flying. Ever since that amazing day I actually asked to do the laundry.

Callum Humphrey
Grade 4

School Is Important

Want to see what is important in my life? School is the most important thing. The most important things are behaving and learning. Also there is having some fun. Now you see some of the things that are important to me.

If you want to learn, behave. If you don't behave, you will not hear the teacher. Also, you could get in trouble. If you get in trouble, you will go somewhere else and not hear the lesson. That is why it is important to behave.

Next, learn if you want to make something out of yourself. If you want nice things, you have to learn to get a job to get the things you want. Also, school is not a waste of time; it is a gain if you learn. Finally, learning will get you in a nice, warm house and not on the street. Those are reasons to learn.

Finally, it is ok to have fun. It is fine to have fun, but learn where to have fun. You can talk to your friends at lunchtime. You can also be with them at field. Now you see it is ok to have fun.

School has an impact on your life. Behaving, learning, and having fun are only some things school offers. That is why school is so important.

Katherine Fernandez
Grade 6

Baseball Team

Have you ever played on a baseball team? I have and know that playing on a baseball team is beneficial because baseball keeps you strong and fast, lifetime friendships are formed, and you learn teamwork.

Baseball keeps you strong and fast because you have many practices a week and you play games that can last for two hours. Playing nonstop for two hours is a long hard day. You are not alone. There are eight other players out there with you, and you have to work together as a team to win games.

When you play baseball, lifetime friendships are developed. If it were not for baseball, I would not have made friends so quickly when I came to Our Lady of Grace. When I was nine, I played Scott Township baseball. There I made many good friends. I moved to a new school three years ago, and today those teammates are still my best friends and may be for many years.

While playing baseball, you learn teamwork. When you play, you are playing with eight other players. If you share the ball and rely on your team you will learn to be a good team player. Working together helps you win games.

Now you know that playing baseball will help you learn teamwork, create long lasting friendships, and keep you strong for other sports.

Michael Klim
Grade 6

The Price of Freedom

Constructed in 1724, Mission San Antonio de Valero started out as a home for missionaries and their Native American converts. Beginning in the early 1800s, the Spanish stationed a cavalry unit at this former mission and renamed it the Alamo.

By 1835, a large amount of Americans were living in Texas. These American immigrants, along with their Mexican neighbors (or Tejanos) announced that year their will to secede from Mexico. Outraged, the Mexican government organized an army under General Santa Anna and marched from Mexico to put down this revolution.

These two opposing forces eventually met at the Alamo. This is where the great clash of wills began for the future of Texas. For the defenders of the Alamo, this struggle was a life or death struggle against all odds for a belief in freedom.

With certain death looming closer by the day, all but one of the Alamo defenders chose to stay and fight. These men chose to face certain death for a cause in spite of a hopeless situation.

The sacrifice of those at the Alamo means a lot to me personally. It shows that some things like freedom are worth giving your life in the pursuit of. This common belief in liberty did not fall with the Alamo. It continues today in places like Cuba, North Korea, and Libya. For as long as people yearn for equality, the spirit of the Alamo will continue.

Jack Andrew
Grade 6

Your Body and Health

Did you know your body and your health are very important? How you take care of it, what you eat, what you do to stay in shape, and a lot more. Your health is what keeps you energized. Some ways to keep yourself healthy is to exercise every day and eat more fruits and vegetables.

Since your body is what keeps you alive you should keep it healthy. This is very important because if you do not eat healthy you could die! Some suggestions are to exercise while you watch TV or go to the gym. It is easy to gain weight but it is hard to lose it!

Eating healthy is a very important thing. Fruits and vegetables can taste bad, but they make you strong. You should eat fruits and vegetables every day. If you eat healthy, your life will be better instead of eating junk food every day. Junk food is OK once in a while.

This is an important topic and you should follow the rules or ideas that were stated. If you follow a healthy diet your life will be better. I hope this has helped you learn something about your health and body!

Felicia Maisuria
Grade 6

Family

I am thankful for a lot of things. One and the most I'm thankful for is my family. Yes, sometimes my siblings are annoying but I would miss them if all of a sudden they disappeared.

I am also thankful for clean water. Without water we would all die and would have no life. We are lucky that we are alive. I am happy we all have food to eat because then we don't have to starve. I'm also thankful for clothes. We would all smell from wearing the same clothes every day. I thank all the veterans that fight for our freedom. I am also thankful for the soldiers that fight for our lives. I am also thankful for the police and the fire people that we have. Without them we could all be stolen or locked in a fire without help. They risk their lives for ours and think about us more than themselves.

All in all I learned that we should be thankful for what we have and use it.

Crystal Benedict
Grade 6

Taekwondo's Best

Taekwondo is a relaxing, but strenuous sport. During Taekwondo, you do exercises that help strengthen your muscles, which can be very strenuous at times. However, at the same time, Taekwondo is relaxing, because if you had a hard day, it can take your mind off of other daily activities.

An example of Taekwondo being relaxing and strenuous at the same time is when you are working hard on your straddle split stretch and you cannot go all the way down. When the instructor tells you to come slowly out of the stretch, you might feel a sense of relief and relaxation, which feels good. Also, Taekwondo is very relaxing because it will relieve stress as you perform movements at your own pace. Finally, Taekwondo is strenuous because you work out many of your muscles, even on simple drills.

As a benefit though, you become an even better martial artist. Taekwondo is an all around fun, stress-free sport.

Nika Anschuetz
Grade 6

Basketball

I play basketball for fun a lot. I've played it for about four years. I played in third grade and in 6th. Our team practices once a week at Antneil Gym. I like to play ball.

In my third grade year I played on a team called Sixers. On the Sixers we only won a few times, but in sixth grade we're winning all our games. So far our team has won six games and lost 2. So we're probably going to be in second place. Our team won six games in a row.

My position in basketball is center and forward, that position is getting rebounds and putting the ball back up. Our games are only on Saturdays at Park Max Middle School at different times. It lasts about an hour or two, and that's how it happens.

Jamar Bynum
Grade 6

My Top 3 Best Friends and My New Best Friend

Hello, my name is Sarah and I have many friends. They mean a whole lot to me because they are always there for me. Carleigh, Katelynn, Brianna, and Emily are my best friends.

My best friend is Carleigh. Carleigh and I have been friends forever. She is a very funny person. Carleigh loves to talk. I have known Carleigh since I was about four. Carleigh and I have had bad memories, like getting into big arguments. We have had wonderful memories, too. Carleigh and I play on the same basketball team. We rock!

Katelynn is my second best friend. I have known Katelynn since I was about six. Katelynn and I get along really well. We have never gotten into an argument. Katelynn and I are very open to each other. We can tell each other anything knowing that we won't laugh or tell anyone else.

My third best friend is Brianna. Bri and I have known each other for about 4 years. Bri and I share family. Her aunt Lisa is my cousin. When Lisa passed away, that's when we met and became friends. Brianna is funny!

Emily Forcier is my new best friend. She is a really nice person. Emily is funny. We get along great! I'm so happy Emily is my best friend.

All my best friends mean a whole lot to me. I will always be there for them. My best friends are really important.

Sarah K. Derway
Grade 5

Haunted House

Goblins scaring people away, Dracula sucking your blood, mummies walking around, witches making soup. Frankenstein peering at you. These are just a couple things you'll find in a haunted house.

There are many things inside a haunted house. Spider webs are one of the things you'll find inside. You'll also find mummies in a tomb. One last thing you'll find is ghouls and witches walking around. These are some of the things inside a haunted house.

There are many sounds in a haunted house. Some sounds are Dracula saying, "I'm going to suck your blood." Another sound is mummies saying, "Ahhh!" One last sound are owls screeching, "Hoot hoot!" These are just a couple of the sounds you'll hear inside a haunted house.

There are many people found in a haunted house. One person is greenish Frankenstein. Another person is bloodish Dracula. The last person is the ghoulish ghost. These are just a couple of people found in the haunted house.

Goblins scaring people away, Dracula sucking your blood, mummies walking around, witches making soup, and Frankenstein peering at you are just a couple of things you'll find in a haunted house.

Emili Antos
Grade 5

What Freedom Means to Me

What freedom means to me is getting to go to school. A long time ago, girls in different countries couldn't go to school, so they couldn't learn how to read or write. They would never be able to get good jobs or even go to college. That means the girls were never free, because they couldn't decide whether they wanted to go to school. All girls should have the right to do whatever boys have the right to do. I have the right to learn how to read and write, go to college, and get a good job when I get older. I am also free to pick my own classes when I get in to junior high. In some families, parents choose their kids' schedules. I am free to choose either Spanish or French (as an example). This is what freedom means to me. Freedom is important and I'm glad I'm free!

Nicole Blevins
Grade 4

Wolves

Wolves are my favorite animals in the world because they are dogs that live in the wild. Their fur is beautiful. I like the Gray Wolf more because I like the color. I think people should not hunt wolves. Wolves howl when they talk with each other or when they cry. I like their howl. I would like it if wolves lived near us. I also like wolves because they have beautiful and smooth faces. The eyes I like the most on their face because they glow in the dark. Wolves are harmless to people. Wolves are afraid of you. Wolves only kill when they are hunting or protecting their family. The black wolf is mostly the leader of the pack because they are brave and tough. Wolves are good at hunting. Their glow-in-the-dark eyes, are for hunting at night. They are good at hunting for elk, moose and deer. That's why wolves are my favorite animals.

Alex Evans
Grade 4

How to Lower Obesity

Even though you may not know, there are still many overweight people who need our help. Too many teens are starting to become overweight mostly because of the technology we have right now. Because of that we should try to make a change.

There are many creative ways that we can help overweight people, but these are probably the most effective ways. One of them would be to stop eating fast food. That would help a great amount because it would put all of the unhealthy restaurants out of business. Another possibility would be to convince gym owners to lower the price and raise the quality and prove that he/she could make a lot of money from doing that. The people who really want to make a difference could start programs (cross country, tennis, etc.) There are still many people that need our help and we can accomplish that if we try.

Chris Blanchard
Grade 6

A Boy and His Dog

My name is Damani Batchler and this essay is about my favorite person in the world, my dog, Marco Polo. My dog and I have been on a long road since the first day I got him as a Christmas present, and here is how that road began.

It all began on Christmas of 2004. My parents and I were in York, Pennsylvania at my grandmother's house. I had just finished giving and receiving the best presents ever and my parents explained to me that there was a part two to my Christmas experience. So we got in the car and drove. After the first five minutes I fell asleep. When I woke up we were at a pet shop. Immediately I was totally invigorated with excitement as we entered the pet store. There were numerous displays of pet products and in the very back was the dog area. As we entered, my parents asked me to pick one out and so I did and luckily for me it was the best dog I could ever pick. So we brought his necessary items and we left with my new found best friend. Over the months I grew more attached to Marco. To me he is the true meaning of happiness. Marco's birthday is October 14 and we happily celebrate it every year. Even though he sometimes gets on my parents and my last nerves, Marco Polo still brings joy to our household, and until the day he dies I will love him like a brother.

In conclusion, I believe my dog Marco Polo is the best, and if you don't believe me, then you should come and see him for yourself!

Damani Batchler
Grade 6

Meeting Someone New

"Come on," my big sister complained. "Hurry, papa is waiting outside!" "I know," I replied. I struggled with my boot, as I finally got it on. I strolled out, into the car. We were all going to see my baby brother. He was born at 5:00 that very morning!

Finally, the car stopped at the hospital. We all popped out of the car. Outside, there was a bone-chilling air. We slowly approached the hospital. We were nervous about seeing him. I was scratching my head like I usually do when I'm waiting for something big to happen. My father asked the lady by the desk, "Excuse me, what is Zhong's room number?" She replied, "Room 214." We finally got up to the second floor. I looked at every door until I saw 214. I knocked on the door. "Come on in," called my mother. My sister slowly opened the door. "Hi," we said in unison. "Can my brother come in?" I asked. "Sure." Mom pressed a button and said, "Please bring the baby in." A nurse strolled in with a baby. "That's him?" I asked. "That's him," my mother said.

He was like a ray of sunshine in the land of darkness. He had 10 tiny french fries for fingers. His head was like a well-blown-up balloon. His body was like an average pencil box. I felt so proud to have a brother like him. There were happy tears in my eyes.

Alina Zhong
Grade 5

Cheating in School

In school you can either cheat or do it yourself. No one wants to cheat, but some people feel they have to.

Everyone in school has the ability to cheat. People will most likely cheat when they didn't study. When I study I feel good because I know I won't be cheating. There are many ways to cheat, like copying off of someone's paper or writing it on the bottom of your shoe. When you copy the answers off of someone's paper you will most likely get caught or they could have the wrong answers. When you write it on the bottom of your shoe someone might see it and copy it or tell on you. When you cheat your stomach might be all in knots because you never cheated before. If your stomach is not in knots then you have cheated before. If I forgot to study I would try to study when I get the chance. Cheating should be the last thing on your mind. One time I forgot to bring my book home, so I couldn't study. The next day when I got to school I took the 2 periods I had to study for the test. Guess what? I got an A!

When I take a test I will never cheat because I might get a better grade than if I would have cheated. When you cheat you are not helping yourself, you are hurting yourself!!! So never cheat and do your best!

Amanda Murray
Grade 6

Rain Forests

Rain Forests are treasures to numerous kinds of animals and animal species. They are their home and their habitat which keeps them alive. They are just as important to plants, also. There are items in the rain forest that plants need to stay alive. Just think, if something happens to the rain forest, it effects the plants and animals that live in it. Some people might think that nothing happens to the rain forest, but it does. The rain forest is getting destroyed every day. It is getting destroyed by people who want wood and other products. These people don't realize when they cut down trees, burn land, and cut plants, they are killing people. When people get sick or get diseases, they rely on doctors to give them medicine. These doctors can get medicine from plants in the rain forest. The people who cut the trees down use heavy machinery like bulldozers to push out the cut trees. There used to be 14% of land that was covered by rain forests; now there is about 6% of land. One and one-half acres of rain forests are lost every second. When this happens, over 137 plant, insect, and animal species are destroyed. The rain forest isn't just important because of these facts. It is also important because it gives people a place to enjoy looking at its beauty and at the objects that live in it.

Kayla McCroskey
Grade 5

The Kick

I stepped up to the target. My body shook. I could barely feel my feet. I felt numb all over. I felt like I was going to drop down. The target was like a dark hole. It was round and big. It was coming right in front of me.

I sprang up in the air. I anxiously spun around. The wind was catching up. I felt like a top. I slammed the target with my foot. I did it!

I hit the ground. My knees felt as weak as rubber. I felt like springing up in the air. My Tae Kwan Do dream was being realized.

Amin Habibovic
Grade 4

The Water Cycle

The water cycle is one of the many cycles on Earth. The water cycle, unlike some cycles, has only three stages. A cycle is a process that keeps on going around and around. The sun powers the water cycle. The sun is the thing that makes the water evaporate.

Did you know that the three stages of the water cycle are related to each other? In evaporation the water in lakes and streams changes from a liquid to a gas to form water vapor. Condensation is all the water vapor forming into clouds and back to a liquid. When there is enough water in the clouds the water comes out as precipitation. The kind of precipitation depends on the temperature. There are four kinds of precipitation: rain, snow, sleet and hail. Precipitation is liquid or solid falling from the clouds. Aren't those stages cool?

There is also the run-off. The run-off is the water on land going to the ocean. The ground water is the water underground. We would not be able to live without the water cycle.

Jasper Barbash-Taylor
Grade 5

More Harry Potter

Good books for my peers and I have dwindled a great deal. I was thrilled when I read a good book called *Harry Potter and the Sorcerer's Stone* by J.K. Rowling. I was eager to get started on the other five of her books. I read each one with great enthusiasm. I couldn't put them down.

They were exciting and allowed me to think about things that I never knew to be possible. Her books reeled me in. I could not guess what was in the next chapter. I truly believe more authors should follow Ms. Rowling in capturing the imagination of kids and write books that will peak our interest to learn new things in a fun way.

I have recommended the six *Harry Potter* books that I have read to my friends and they all absolutely loved them. We all anxiously await the release of the 7th book in the summer of 2006. Until then, we all hope another book will capture our young and expressive minds.

Joshua Burke
Grade 4

What Freedom Means to Me

The definition of "freedom" in my student dictionary says that freedom means: "liberty, independence, being free." What freedom means to me is that you can do anything or be anything you want within the rules. It also means that you can take advantage of the opportunities that you are given. Because of freedom, with hard work, I can become anything I want…even President of the United States! I can go to school and study anything I want, anywhere in the United States. Education is available to anyone who wants it. The United States is the only country where you can be born poor and earn a lot of money if you are willing to work hard. This country does not limit how much money you can make. Freedom means you can have your own opinion and say it without getting in trouble. I have the right to dress in and choose any style I want. I have the right to choose my religion, like Christianity or Judaism, without being judged. We are very lucky to live in a country where we have so many freedoms that we take for granted.

Daniel King
Grade 4

Skating

I love figure skating. I have been taking lessons since I was three-years-old. Anyone who can walk can learn to skate. The first step and the hardest step is to learn how to stand up on the ice without falling. This requires balance. Once you learn to balance on the ice, the rest is just practice — lots and lots of practice. The difficult part of skating is learning the tricks like jumps, spins and bunny hops.

People have been skating for more than a thousand years. The author of an article I found on www.kidzworld.com said, "the first skates were made from animal bones and attached to the feet with leather straps." At first people used skates in the winter to get across frozen lakes and rivers. Later in the mid 19th century skating became a sport called figure skating. According to the author in www.kidzworld.com article, "the first World Figure Skating Championships for men were held in 1896 in Russia" and "the first World Figure Skating Championships for women were held in Switzerland in 1906."

While skating started in Europe, figure skating, as we now know it, came from an American named Jackson Haines. Jackson was born in New York in 1840. Unlike other figure skaters of his time, Jackson combined dance and skating. His style was free and expressive and not stiff and rigid. Americans did not like Jackson's style of skating, so he went to Europe to skate. The Europeans loved his skating and he became a success overnight. America did not accept his style of skating until the first decade of the 21st century.

Meghann Breton
Grade 5

Community Service Club

Did you know that at Community Service you help people around the world? Well in the club we go on field trips, have clothing drives and many more things. Mrs. Duhaylongsod is the instructor of this club.

The students at the club went on a field trip to the Recreation Department and played games with senior citizens. They also went to the Police Department to sort out toys. During the two field trips the students were having fun playing games and sorting out toys for certain families.

The Community Service club also did a clothing drive for the Pakistan earthquake. First the members of the club made posters and decorated boxes. The students made posters so that they could inform other students at Community Middle School. They put boxes in certain places in the school.

We have this club because it shows us what other people are going through. Also it's fun knowing that you are actually helping people around the world.

In conclusion students in the Community Service club had lots of fun going on field trips, doing the clothing drive, and decorating boxes and posters. Community Service club is a good way to help people around the world.

Hafsa Saleem
Grade 6

God

Who made the stars? Who knows the number of hairs on your head? Who knows where each lightning bolt strikes?

The answer to all of these is God. Who is God? An incomprehensible force that created the universe, time, and the Earth in seven days, giving us our week. Nothing else in science provides it. "So God created man in his own image," (Genesis 1:27a) God made you just like him.

God is three persons in one. This means he has three parts: Father, Son, and Holy Spirit. An example of this is water. Water has three forms: liquid, solid and vapor. No matter how you look at it, they are all water. And take eggs — they are three in one. Shell, white and yolk. How God is three in one is not understood and cannot be understood by man.

Heaven is more than we can even dream. There are walls of jasper, 12 gates of pearls, and Main Street is pure transparent gold. There is a crystal lake and deluxe concerts. Best of all we spend eternity with our Master Creator, God.

Are you going there forever? Do you believe that Jesus Christ is the one and only God? That because we are all sinners, Christ died for us? And through his sacrifice, we can live with God forever? Then you must pray to God and ask him to forgive you and put your trust in Him. Compared to Him, evolution stands not a chance.

Marinah Boyles
Grade 6

My Favorite Athletic Competition

My favorite athletic competition is karate. I am a yellow white belt. We do something called katas. The first kata is called Form One and the second kata is called Taygon. I am now learning Taygon, which is my favorite kata.

The first competition I saw was in Herkimer and the best part of the competition was the sparring and the weapons. There are 13 belts in karate before you get to black. After you get to black belt you have to go through first degree all the way to 10th degree. Karate is mostly punches and blocks, but there are kicks too. I like karate because it can increase your strength. They also do some fun things like the water challenge. The water challenge is when you have to balance a cup of water on your head while taking ten steps and ten kicks. They also have board breaking challenges. The easiest board is white and the hardest board is black. I am on the blue board and only need five more boards to break before going to black. I do many kicks, such as the front snap kick, the skip front snap, the round house kick, and side thrust kick.

There is a competition coming up on Super Bowl Sunday. I will try to compete in this competition this time. Last time I was only a white belt and only knew one kata. However, like I mentioned before, I now know half of Taygon. It is still my favorite kata. That's why karate is my favorite sport.

Tori Zecca
Grade 6

The Crazy Crumb

This past holiday season I had many enjoyable experiences, but I have to say one takes the cake, or should I say cookie?

On Christmas Eve my mom and I worked on some cookies. There was some extra dough, so I decided to make a Harry Potter cookie. I shaped the face and especially the scar giving it an ominous appearance. I put it in the oven to bake and waited.

This cookie's hand-carved face and impressive scar were like a sculpture made by a craftsman. The one problem with this cookie was that it was no bigger than my thumb!

When my mother took Harry out of the oven, I felt faint, the suspense was unbearable. Sadly, my dad didn't feel the same way. I slowly approached the tray sitting on my kitchen table, but…my dad strutted over to Harry and popped him in his mouth! It took me a couple of seconds to take in the moment, but I eventually said…well, screamed, "You just ate Harry Potter!" I couldn't believe what had just happened.

"That cookie you just ate, it was my Harry Potter cookie, why'd you eat it?!" Guess what he said!

"What? I thought it was a crumb!"

My world had just ended. Harry Potter was dead, gone, and no one but me even cared. As I silently mourned my cookie, I came to realize it really was a crumb. I still miss it, but one thing's for sure, that was one crazy crumb.

Kiki Barnes
Grade 6

Sailing

I like to sail optis and 420s in the summer. Sailing is a sport most people don't even think is a sport. Even when people think about sailing many believe it would be effortless. Sailing is a complex sport with hundreds of racing rules. To be a good racer you must know all parts of the boat and how each point of sail is related to wind directions. When racing you must go around every buoy without touching it. In small boat racing it is usually safe to cut it really close. If you touch a buoy or hit a boat you have to do a 360. A 360 is when you sail your boat in a complete circle.

The rules for the start are more difficult than the other rules. I consider the starts the hardest part in racing. A whistle is blown a specific number of times to tell racers to start the countdown to begin the race. In racing, the countdown takes five minutes. The key is to fall back and tack (change direction) and when the timer reaches around 20 seconds you head for the line. If you cross the line before the time is up you have to turn a 360 or go back across the line, then start the race. Sailing is a sport that takes skill and a lot of practice.

Nat Rogers
Grade 5

History of the Olympics

The Olympic Games were started because of a Greek legend that said that the great Herakles won a race at Olympia, a plain in the small state of Ellis, and then decreed that the race should be held every four years. Another legend said that Zeus himself had created the festival after defeating Cronus. The more likely story is that the Olympic festival was a local religious even until the year 884 BC. While Iphitus was king of Ellis, he had decided to turn it into a larger event, pan-Hallenic festival. To accomplish that he made a truce with other rules, and to allow athletes and spectators to travel peacefully to Olympia while the festival was going on.

The Greeks based their chronology on four-year periods called Olympiads, and the Olympic festival marked the beginning of each Olympiad. The festival was considered the start of the first Olympiad. The festival was a religious gathering to celebrate the worshipping of the gods, mostly Zeus.

During the first fifteen Olympics, only one race was offered to the athletes. The race was the length of the stadium which was about 200 yards. As time went on, the game that had become part of the festival grew and they became more important to win. Other races were added for more athletes to participate in.

To this day, winning an event at the Olympics is a major accomplishment for any athlete.

Caitlyn Curley
Grade 5

My Pets

My pets are faithful and cuddly, not to mention fluffy and furry! I have four pets. One of them is my rabbit Precious. He is so soft and fluffy I love him. He has red eyes, which is normal, and white fur with black points. He is about 1 1/2 years old and started out with brown points. I love him so much!

Speaking of love, I have three cats. One of my cats is named Fritzy, and the name is not in vain either. She is so hyper. I nicknamed her Boombox because she yowls so loud and so much. She is a calico, which means she has a lot of colors that look like they are splashed on her. She hisses a lot but I think she is just scared.

Speaking of scared cats, my other cat Sneakers is scared of everything! It gets annoying when he runs from every single sound. I love him but he runs even from me. It gets annoying. He loves my mom, and I mean LOVES with a capital L.

Speaking of a cat that LOVES with a capital L, my last cat I am going to talk about is my buddy Spaz. I have known him since before I was born. He was even attached to me before I was born. He is called my buddy for one simple reason, he sleeps with me and follows me everywhere.

All of these animals are loyal, faithful and cuddly, especially Spaz. They are my faithful pets. Cats are truly a woman's best friend!!!!

Tashya Krom
Grade 6

My First Trip to an Extra-Special Place

In 2004, when I went to Italy my aunt brought me on an extra-special trip to Rome.

One day in August at 7 am my dad dropped us off at the train station. The ride was 7 hours long. We played checkers the whole way.

In Rome, the hotel manager was a friend of ours and he let me choose my own room! We got settled and went to see the Coliseum. It was amazing! We saw the ruins of ancient Rome where the Gladiators once fought lions but now you can take pictures with them.

The next day we went to see the Trevi Fountain. Most of the tourists were Japanese and Americans. They were yelling, pointing and flipping coins into the water.

After that, we went to Vatican City. I didn't realize that I was crossing a country's border! I saw the Swiss guards with colorful uniforms and Pope John Paul II on a plasma screen TV. He was on vacation at the time. In the Sistine Chapel we saw the ceiling painted by Michelangelo. It was spectacular!

Back at the hotel the manager introduced me to a cloistered nun who almost never talks to anyone. She even gave me a jar of marmalade.

Before I wanted to, it was time to say goodbye to Rome. We went home on an airplane, it was much faster. I hope to go back to Rome with my whole family. I can't wait.

Gabriella Manduca
Grade 5

School

Do you know what one of the most important things to me is? School is important to me. Two reasons are that without it, I might not be able to get a job or solve everyday problems. My last reason is that without it, I wouldn't be able to make my family proud. School is very important to me.

Without school I might not get a job. I might have everything I need for a job, but I might not get it if I don't have an education. If I get a job, I might not keep it very long. I might not get a job if I can't read, write, do math, or spell.

Another reason is that I wouldn't be able to solve everyday problems without it. I might not be able to count things that are important. I might not be able to count how much money I owe someone. I might buy something and not be able to pay enough money. I might not be able to spell when I write something.

Finally, without it I wouldn't be able to make my parents and my family proud. My parents want me to have a good life, and without school I can't have that. My parents want me to be smart, and without school I can't be. Without school it would look like my family doesn't care about my education.

So, something important to me is school. Without school I can't get a job, solve problems, or make my family proud. In short, school is extremely important to me.

Tim Smith
Grade 6

My Gift

There are many people that I can mention that I do nice things for, things that you cannot buy such as chores, love, care, concern, honesty, etc. It does not matter how poorly I do it, or how perfectly I did it, the only thing that matters is that I care for them. The people that I do these things for appreciate the fact that I do these things for them. These special things that I do for these people make me feel a way that you would feel if you did these special things for the person or that they would do for you what I mentioned earlier.

There are a lot of things I do for my mother, like chores. Chores such as washing dishes, taking out the garbage, putting clothes in the washing machine, cleaning the table after dinner, and taking my puppy out for a walk. I give respect to my mother like it's her birthday every day. My mom isn't the only one I do these things for. I do these things for my aunts, uncles, cousins, and grandparents. One time my mother was on a walker because she got surgery on her foot and she was in a lot of pain, so I did everything for her around the house for nothing but love. Even though I still did something wrong every once in a while she still respected that I did it. In conclusion, I love my family the most.

Larry Skow
Grade 6

Muhammad Ali vs George Foreman

Do you know anything about Muhammad Ali or George Foreman? They are both alike and different in many ways.

Both of them were some of the greatest boxers of all time. In fact they've both won the Heavy Weight championship of the world! They were so good that both have actually gone to the Olympics.

Now that I've told you how they were alike, here's how they were different. Muhammad Ali had changed his name from Cassius Clay. George Foreman never changed his name. The name Muhammad Ali brings up another difference. He not only changed his name but his religion to Muslim. On the other hand George Foreman didn't change his religion either.

I picked these two boxers because they are two of my heroes. Now that you've heard my perspective on the two boxers you should research them more to really see how great they both were.

Paul Jeff Brandebura
Grade 6

Manga

I love Manga. What's Manga, you ask? It's a form of art that's different than most. There are hundreds of Manga artists.

Manga is a Nihongo (Japanese for the word "Japanese") form of art. It's similar to a cartoon, but that's called Animé. That's when you give Manga "life," as some say. Manga is more like a comic book.

Every Manga artist has their own style. There are many different kinds and styles of Manga. Manga is usually made into a graphic novel. Most graphic novels are published by Viz or Viz Media.

My personal favorite Manga artist is Akira Toriyami. He has written and drawn the *DragonBall* and *DragonBall Z* series and *Dr. Slump*. Manga is also put into magazines or comic books. *Shonen Jump* is a very popular magazine with lots of Manga stories in it.

Akira Toriyami's style is called "Muscle Manga." That's when the character in the Manga is very muscular, such as *DBZ*. I can draw some decent Manga, and I sometimes use part of Akira's style in my drawings. I learned how to draw Manga from a Manga drawing book and by reading *DBZ*.

Manga is a complicated style of art. Changing the way a character looks and talks gives them their personality. Usually making character's eyes smaller, bigger, rounder or sharper changes their personality from cute and bubbly to dark and mysterious. Manga is usually black and white. As they say in Rurouni Kenshin, "This one (yourself) says goodbye!"

Jacob A. Loson
Grade 6

Pollution: Should It Happen?

Do you pollute? Well I think you should stop. Pollution is very bad and it should not happen. There are two kinds of pollution, water pollution and air pollution. Pollution can kill people and animals. I will tell you more about these kinds of pollution in the next few paragraphs.

Water pollution is pollution that happens in bodies of water, like oceans. This can be caused by dumping oil in the ocean. The oil contaminates the water and can cause the animals to die. Did you know that an average of 321,000 animals die a year because of pollution? To me, that is totally unacceptable. Polluting is not fair to the animals, so we shouldn't do it.

Air pollution contaminates the air. If it gets into your lungs you can get sick and die. That's why it's important not to smoke. Smoking and secondhand smoking kills a lot of people. I get uncomfortable when I smell smoke. I always try to get other people to stop smoking.

When I ask my family what they think about pollution they say that it is bad and it should not continue. However, there are some people that will say the exact opposite. I don't get why. I can't think of one positive thing about pollution. How about you?

You aren't forced to pollute so you shouldn't do it. It's very inconsiderate and uncaring. So think twice before you're going to puff a cigar or dump oil in the ocean.

Victor Vasquez, Jr.
Grade 5

Why Are Families So Important?

What would you do without your family? I have no clue what I would do without my family. My family is very important to me. I think my family is very special and supporting. My parents took care of me since I was a baby.

My family is very special. They're very special because they are always there for me. My family is special because they'll love me no matter how I look or act. Also, my brother and sister can play with me whenever I am lonely and some people don't even have any people to talk with about their problems or anybody to play with.

Families are also very supporting. My family is very supporting because they always come to my concerts. My parents support me by saving up money for me so I can go to college. They also support me by telling me I can do anything if I try.

My parents take good care of me. My parents always dressed me, cooked for me, and taught me many things. Before I went to school my mom tried to teach me how to read and write. Also, my dad helps me with things that I don't understand.

In conclusion, I'll always love my family and no one can stop me from doing that. I really appreciate my parents for not giving up on me. My parents love me so much they'll even sacrifice their lives for me and I will do the same!

Emily Ung
Grade 6

My Family, My Freedom, My Life

If you ask me for things I am grateful for, I would have many things to say, but I am just going to list my top seven.

Number seven is my cat, and my two fish to cheer me up when I'm sad.

Number six is my friends, because they are like a family away from home for me.

Number five is all my needs, shelter to keep me dry, food and water to keep me healthy, and clothes to keep me warm and dry.

Number four is my education, so I can grow up to be a smart and independent person.

Number three is my family, it's not big, but its love is as big as a 100-story building.

Number two is my life, for being put on this planet, and to be loved like I am.

And finally, number one is my freedom. To live in America, to have a democracy, and to have the rights that I do. All the other ones I listed were important, but this one is by far the most important.

Olivia Rauktis
Grade 4

The Gift of Compassion

We can show our compassion to people on Valentine's Day this year. Compassion is a feeling of pity or a need to help. Many people don't feel very good about themselves and would enjoy having someone caring for them and showing compassion towards them. Showing someone compassion on Valentine's Day, or for any reason, can make them feel good, special, confident, or all three. Compassion can surely be a very special gift.

Performing an act of kindness when someone is in trouble is showing compassion. For example, if someone is having a problem understanding their schoolwork, instead of playing, you could help them with their studies and explain it to them. Or, if someone felt ill and needed to sit down on the bus but didn't have a seat, you could give up yours. These are just simple acts of kindness.

Other ways to show compassion are to give encouraging words to those who need them. If your friend doesn't get chosen for a team that they like they might feel unhappy. You could make them feel better by encouraging them to keep trying and that they will reach their goal in the future. Sometimes people have other problems that make them sad. Just being their friend and someone they can talk to can make them feel better. That is compassion.

This year on Valentine's Day, show someone compassion. This could be doing a good deed, giving encouraging words or just being a good friend!

Thomas Lucca
Grade 6

Dogs

I love dogs. Every dog. Any color. Long haired dogs. Short haired dogs. Allergic free dogs. Big dogs. Little dogs. Pure bred dogs, and mutts. Just dogs. Relationships between dogs and people are special. Dogs do not talk with their mouths like people. They talk with their body language, their ears, tails and noses. They use howling to express themselves, low growling to state anger and in some cases whimpering to say they hurt or are sad. Dogs also use their noses to sniff out things. They know their owner's smell from miles away and know when dinner is coming. Some dogs have great big jaws and teeth for mashing up large kibbles of food while small dogs have small teeth. Dogs also know their owner's car sound or if there are children in the family, they probably know the sound of the bus. Some people say dogs know time because when it's time for dinner some dogs sit by their food bowl.

Dogs are pack animals and like living in a family. There usually has to be a leader of the pack someone strong and know the leader's smell. Even if you wear perfume to cover up your scent your dog knows you. Some dogs have a great sense of sight while others have great hearing. The dogs with pointed ears have better hearing then the dogs with flopped down ears like cocker spaniels. No matter what kind of dog, they are the best!

Jillian Russo
Grade 6

Books

What I love to do in my spare time is to read books. I love to read, and reading can help my mind grow. Reading is the best thing that I can do for my mind. It teaches me things that I can do in real life. Books have taught me to handle problems and challenges properly. They can teach me how to start a fire, how to get water from a river, and I can learn lessons. Books are like parents who don't talk but still teach me. They can go anywhere with me and they can take me, anywhere I want to go no matter where I am. I can also be anyone that I want to be.

Once I am done with one book, I have to start another one. Everyone likes different kinds of books but personally, I like mystery books. I never know what is going to happen. Like I said, people like different books. You may like real life stories, fantasy, nonfiction, or fiction. There are many other kinds, too many genres to list. Books are wonderful and very exciting. Even if I think I know what's going to happen, they always trick me. Books are mysterious and wonderful in any kind of way. All books grab me and I never want to stop reading them at all. Books are amazing, so why aren't you reading one now?

Molly Giewont
Grade 6

The Worst Meal Ever!

There have been lots of bad foods I've eaten in my lifetime but not as bad as this. It was an inclement day. Rain fell to the ground like it was on a trampoline. Two years ago, my 2nd grade class began to munch on their luscious lunch. I was about to take a delicious bite but I noticed something was terribly wrong.

"Yuck!" I screamed. My mother accidentally put disgusting turkey on my sandwich! Lunch was now ruined. I really wished I weren't hungry but I was. In fact, I was as hungry as a big brown bear. The turkey was goo in my hands. Unluckily, my acrimonious lunch aid told me it was my fault and I had to eat it. "No, please don't make me," but the evil lunch aid had already gone.

I knew I had to do something. So I made my move. The garbage can was right next to my table. I scrunched the gelatinous sandwich into a ball and threw it right into the garbage! The lunch aid came back and my sandwich was gone. This tremendous memory will last a lifetime!

Taylor Donnellan
Grade 4

Pittsburgh vs Seattle

I am going to compare two cities, Pittsburgh and Seattle. I am going to tell you how these cities are the same and different.

I am going to tell you how these cities are the same. Well Pittsburgh and Seattle are cities. Both of their teams went to the Super Bowl. They both have football, basketball, and baseball teams. Both cities also have football fields.

Now I am going to tell you how they are different. Seattle has the Space Needle. Pittsburgh has the Steel Building. Seattle has no Super Bowl wins. Pittsburgh has five Super Bowl wins.

Now you know how Pittsburgh and Seattle are the same and different. I hope now that you will want to see how two things are the same and different.

Taylor Cavalovitch
Grade 6

My Day with Owls

Once on a street name Elliott Lane, I was waiting for my bus and saw an owl! After I saw it I said to myself I remember some things about owls. Some people think owls are evil. But I think owls are cool. Did you know that owls can fly over a graveyard without a sound? Is that cool or what. The baby owls that are called chicks stay with their mom and dad for three months. Then they are on their own. The most an owl should live for is 20 or more years old. We can live older! Do you want to know something cool about owls? They have the best night vision on earth! This big owl is endangered. This is my favorite kind of owl. I think it is a cool owl. Hey, the owl flew away and look my bus is here it was fun talking to you!

Hunter Endler
Grade 4

The Blackout That Changed My Plans

One night my family decided to watch a movie called *Friday After Next*. Grandma Feddie, Grandpa Edward, cousin Khadijah, sister Jakia, and I were watching the movie and having a good time. It was going to be fun to stay up late. Then my Grandpa Edward clapped his hands and all of a sudden the electricity went off.

Everybody began to tell Grandpa Edward to clap again and maybe it would come back on. The lights still weren't on so my grandparents told all of us kids to go to bed. My cousin went home. *My sister and I were scared and went to bed.*

We went upstairs and it was darker than I thought. When my sister and I finally got into bed we kept tapping each other to make sure that neither one of us really fell asleep. I didn't want my sister to go to sleep either because she was company for me, and kept me from being scared (even if she was younger).

We tried to stay awake all night but a strange thing happened, the next thing we knew it was morning. The noise of the television, cars on the streets outside, and lights woke us up in the morning. I thought we were going to stay up all night long but I guess things don't always happen like you plan them.

Jasmine Warren
Grade 5

The Professional Age Limit

Professional means to be paid to perform a job.

There is some controversy about how old you should be to become a professional athlete. I don't think there should be an age limit, because there are so many great athlete's in the world that are under the age of 18. So they could become professional because of their talent.

Say there was a 15 year old swimmer, who just broke 7 world records, only in a dual meet. But no one wanted to sponsor him. They would but don't want to. They think that other companies will think that they are weird for sponsoring a 15 year old.

The Olympics supervisor asks him to come to the Olympics. He went and won everything. But, no sponsor's asked him to be sponsored. It is all because of his age. I don't think that your age should affect it.

I think that anyone who gets to the Olympics should be considered a professional. Because the Olympics are for the biggest, strongest, fastest, toughest, and the best athletes in the world. So you should be considered a professional.

If you are 8 or 18, and you go to the Olympics, and you succeed in what you do, then you should be considered a professional. Your age doesn't matter. It is your talent that matters.

PJ Fallon
Grade 6

Best Friends

In my life the person, or should I say people, that I have a close relationship with are my two best friends, Meilin Lim and Michelle Farley. They go to Parkville Middle, but are not in any of my classes except Meilin, she is not in my class, she just has the same teacher as me. That teacher is Mrs. Styles.

In our hearts our relationship is strong; it always holds up no matter what. We have known each other since about kindergarten. Except Meilin, I knew her since before we were even born it seems like, because our brothers are now about 17 and they have known each other since about kindergarten.

Meilin and Michelle have always included me. We always played sports together, had sleepovers, and always have been there for each other no matter what happens between us; if one of us needs help we help. Our friendship is so nice or great we are just like sisters and for us being there for each other, that is what makes us sisters at heart. This is the relationship between my friends and I, together forever.

Sadie Spencer
Grade 6

Old Country Buffet

On Saturday August 27, 2005, I went to Old Country Buffet with my best friends. Their names were Amanda who was 18, Matt who was 14 and Shannon who was 11. We decided to eat lunch there. When we got there, we paid for our lunch and went right to eat. The foods they had were cheese pizza, French fries, ham, chicken noodle soup, green salad and chicken. When I tried the French fries I almost ate the entire bucket! They were so good that I waited until they got more. The chicken was the greatest! It was so delicious, especially with ketchup "yummm." The salad was nutritious and delicious I tried almost every dressing.

When I was done eating I went right into dessert which was the best part. They had cookies, brownies, cheese cake, chocolate cake and chocolate ice cream! I was so excited that I flew to the machine like I had wings. They even had toppings, really good toppings, such as crushed Oreos, nuts, sprinkles, fudge and butterscotch! I ate all the ice cream I took. That was the best, I mean the best ice cream I ever ate in my entire life!

When we were all done we left the paradise we were in and went back to boring old home. I really loved eating there and I hope I come back soon.

Vanessa Pires
Grade 6

Love

Love is the greatest thing in the world. Love is sharing, caring, giving, living, and praying. All that is love. You can love your family, your friends, your pet, your cousins, your aunts, your uncles, your teachers, and your grandparents. So whatever you do, love everyone.

Patrick Sennott
Grade 4

A Bad Day Fishing

It was last summer, and my dad and I were fishing in the Adirondack Mountains. The pond was clear so you could see all living creatures. There were trout, bass, sunfish, frogs, snakes, and even turtles. We had only caught a little fish so I decided that I was going to fish for frogs.

I used my fishing net, which had big holes in it, so the frogs would, unfortunately, get out. Finally I saw the momma frog. She was huge, about the size of a junior football. I slowly waded into the water and "swoosh," the frog was in the net. I walked over to show my dad and the frog leaped out of the net and landed on my leg. I kicked my leg because it was so slimy and it flew off. I landed in a pile of mud. My dad thought this was hilarious, but I was disgusted. I walked home unhappy because my clothes were covered in mud.

Austin Strang
Grade 6

A Late Night Snack

I woke up very late at night. It was very dark and cold downstairs. When I went into the dark kitchen and opened the refrigerator door, the one thing, the only thing, the best thing I would want to find inside waiting for me to discover would be cold pizza.

I love cold pizza, not just a little bit in love, but I mean my favorite snack of all time. There should be only one slice left and it would have my name written all over it. It would be wrapped in aluminum foil. I would be so happy to pick it up and unwrap it. I would gulp it down so fast that my stomach wouldn't know what hit it! My mouth would be so happy it would want to sing a cute little pizza song. Cold is just the right temperature for me. The cheese would be hard and the sauce would be nice and cool. I even like to eat the cold, hard crust. It will taste so great going down. The perfect drink to top it off with is Sprite. Straight from the bottle is best for a late night snack.

Oh yes! To get up late at night and find the one, last slice of cold pizza left in the refrigerator would be the best thing that could happen to me late at night.

Michele Mattaliano
Grade 4

My Perfect World

A perfect world would be a world where everything is reality; where all your dreams and wishes turn real; where you and your family have great friends who never let you down; where people don't treat people different because of their race. A perfect world is being spoiled. In a perfect world, you can meet celebrities. You could have your own mansion where in your backyard you have roller coasters, water parks, and arcades that you don't have to wait in a long line for your turn. In a perfect world, you can have your own limousine service. A perfect world is where you don't have to do chores. A perfect world is where there is world peace.

Ana Amorocho
Grade 6

Imagination

Imagination is exciting! It is being able to create a picture in your mind about something that is not real, something not seen, or something that you never went through. There is no limit to what you can create, invent, or use as a resource. Imagination affects many things such as books, TV shows, and games.

Story books seem to come alive because of the author's imagination. Some books like *Droon*, *Narnia*, and *Magic Tree House* are good examples of this. As you read these books a new world seems to appear.

Television is another thing imagination affects. TV shows like *Jimmy Neutron*, *Cyber Chase*, and other Nickelodeon shows are about being resourceful and inventive. The characters use what they have to make something new. These shows also make you want to create something.

Games like Candy Land, Guess Who, and Mall Madness are imaginative and creative games. The creators of these games are able to make these games exciting because of how they are played. The designs and colors also make these games fun to play.

Imagination is the process of creating a picture in your mind of something that is not like something someone has seen. Although it's not real, it makes it seem possible to be real or true. One of the greatest things our mind can do is to imagine things. It is a picture or an idea that can show up in books, TV shows, games, and anywhere else possible. An imagination has no limits!

Brianna Henry
Grade 4

Hanukkah with the Hubermans

My favorite holiday is Hanukkah. This is my favorite holiday for many reasons. One reason is because we get eight nights of presents. It is always fun getting gifts, and I usually get what I want. I also like Hanukkah because we get to eat one of the best foods, latkes. Every day for dinner or breakfast, we eat latkes. They are fried potato pancakes that we dip into applesauce, and they taste great.

Hanukkah isn't only about he presents and the food, but it is also about the Menorah and the candle lighting. Every night after sundown, we all gather around the Menorah and light the candles. We all sing the blessings and just remember why we are lighting the candles. This is a very special and happy time.

Hanukkah is the time of a miracle. It was when Judah and the Macabees won a war and when they lit the candles with only a drop of oil, which lasted for eight days. Hanukkah is a very special time, and this is why Hanukkah is my favorite holiday.

Jason Huberman
Grade 6

Skateboarding

Skateboarding is part of my life. I go to the skatepark in South Glen Falls every day. The name of it is "Halfpipe Thrills" and it used to be called "Halfpipe Mike's."

I buy my boards from there. I bought a Plan B Paul Rodriguez board. It's one of my favorites so far. On my board I have Krux trucks and Spitfire wheels, which I don't like very much. I can do many more tricks with this board than the other boards I have used. I would say in a few weeks my tail or nose is going to snap. I've been skating on it every day for at least 5 or 6 hours a day. On Fridays and Saturdays I skate 10 hours. I can't believe how much better I have gotten. I think this has changed my life. I have gotten way more mature. I do everything alone or with my friends there. My mom and dad don't stay there and watch me, they trust me and know I will not get into trouble. They pick me up when the park closes. Me and a lot of my friends just hang out and watch skate videos and then go to skate for a few hours until dinner and then we go get something to eat.

This is my daily routine. Skateboarding I think is for fun and I have a lot while doing it. It doesn't matter if I get sponsored. I would like to, but if I don't at least I will still have fun!!

Brett Bull
Grade 5

The Untold Author

When I woke up that morning, I thought it was going to be like any other Wednesday. Don't get me wrong, that's not a bad thing. I just never believed something so wonderful was about to happen to me.

That very morning, as I ambled into class, Ms. Fox said we were going to try something brand new. Since Ms. Fox teaches English, I assumed it had something to do with writing. As I sat at my desk, she began to explain the assignment. With excitement in her voice, she said, "Class, today we will be writing an essay about something we have learned." Promptly, ideas began popping into my head. Because I had only written a few paragraphs in my lifetime, I wasn't sure where to begin. I finally picked one. I chose "how to organize a paragraph." Even though the topic was so small, and slightly boring, I turned it into a fun and exciting paragraph. Once I started writing, I just couldn't stop. I realized how much I enjoyed writing. It was more fun than I ever imagined.

A week later, Ms. Fox came to my desk. She whispered in my ear, "Taylor, some day I will be reading your stories in books." She thought I really had a gift for writing. I was speechless! I was so excited! It was then my dream to become an author, in the future.

Taylor Skelton
Grade 4

My Family

What is important to me is my family because they care about me. When I am hurt they always help me. If I am in danger they protect me. They are loving and generous.

My older sister, Ruth, is always there for me. If I have a question concerning my homework she always answers it if she can. My younger sister, Lourdes, and my younger brothers, Juan and Isaias, always make me laugh because of the silly things they do. My parents are very understanding. They are the people I could go and talk to if I have a question. My baby sister doesn't really do anything but be cute.

I do not know what I would do without my family. They are very special to me. I am very grateful I have such a great family.

Susana Rosa
Grade 4

Exercise Is Important

I rode my bike for a thousand miles. Okay, not a thousand, but it did seem like that. When I was done my legs and back ached. I was exercising because exercise is very important. It is important because it keeps your heart strong and it keeps your heart pumping. It also prevents you from getting overweight.

Exercise is also fun to do and it gets rid of stress. When you exercise you can learn new things, and have fun at the same time. After school I always have stress and when I ride my bike it's like exercising makes your stress disappear. I have to go try to ride those thousand miles now.

Alison Horner
Grade 4

My Trip to France

"Goodbye!" I yelled to my grandfather as I boarded the airplane. I was so nervous on my first plane trip. I was going across the ocean to France. My family had been planning this reunion for weeks. On the plane there was a mini television in front of every seat! The trip was seven hours long so naturally, I got bored. I turned on the TV and watched, "Hide and Seek" and "Constantine."

Then after seven hours, I was there. Everything was so different and I didn't have any idea what was being said! The trip to the beach house where I was staying was three hours away. Once I got to the house I saw cousins that I knew and six I didn't know. It felt so strange to meet people who I didn't know existed in my family.

About a week later, my family and I decided to take a trip to Paris. Once we got there, we checked into our hotel. That day we went to the Notre Dame Church. Later on we went to see the Eiffel Tower. That night we saw some fireworks and visited down town.

It was time to leave. I was sad, but boy it felt good to be home!

Andrew du Bois
Grade 4

Horse Riding

This essay is about "What I enjoy doing most." Horseback riding is my favorite hobby. I take lessons with a horse trainer. When I ride I believe in myself.

When I was five to seven years old, my mom had friends who had an Arabian. Her name was Tara, we rode her. Last summer, she died at the age of twenty-nine or thirty, we were very upset. I started lessons with my trainer two and a half years ago. At first I rode a thirty-three year old Quarter Horse gelding, his name is Blondie. When I got better, I rode a sixteen two hand high Hanovarian mare, her name is Kate. After I rode Kate, my trainer leased a pony named Benleas Sea Maple (Maggie May.) She was my favorite pony. Then my trainer leased another pony, I tried riding her. During the lesson, Gracie-Lou (the new pony) bolted twice and I bailed.

Then when my trainer purchased a pony named Dora, I fell in love with her. Right away we became great partners, we even jump two foot three jumps. I have ridden her since last summer. For all the years I have ridden she is the best pony I have ever met.

That is why I enjoy horses. Right now my twin, my mom, and I are looking for a horse. I would never trade anything for getting a horse or to stop horse riding. Riding is a great passion that will last forever.

Courtney Wheeler
Grade 6

What Is the Greatest Gift of All?

The greatest gift of all is life. Life is the greatest gift because without life you couldn't do anything. Life allows me to love, be happy, and to have my religion. Life allows me to do all of this and so much more.

Life brings me love because without my love or anybody else's love, the world would not be a good place. It is good to love because one day that person may not be there. After that person is gone, you will probably wish you had loved them. Love is a very good gift in life.

Happiness is another gift in life. Happiness spreads to others and then they are happy. Without this gift, our lives would not be as wonderful. Happiness is definitely a great gift.

Without the gift of religion, there would be no God. If there was not a God, we could not pray for ourselves, family, or friends. Religion is important because it brings some of the greatest things in life. This is one gift we could not live without.

The gift of life brings me all of these wonderful things and so much more. It is so wonderful, I can't describe it. These things I couldn't live without for one minute. This is why I believe life is the greatest gift of all.

Claire Sullivan
Grade 6

My Family

My family is the best family I will ever have. I wouldn't give them up for anything, not even $1000.00. That's how much I love my family. My parents are cool. They give me shelter, food, clothing, and especially love and care. Their names are Laura and Andrew. My sister is so much fun to be with. She plays with you when you have no one to play with. Her name is GeenaMarie. My brother is so cute. If I am on a play date and come home late, he will miss me so much. He will come over and give me a big hug. This is my best buddy. His name is Andrew. He was named after my dad. This is my family. They are fun, nice, cool, and love me no matter what I do.

Jessica Rosalbo
Grade 5

Christmas

Christmas is an amazing holiday. There are many lights and merry colors. Green and red are seen all around, in storefronts and in front of homes, on wreaths and so many more. People put up Christmas trees and wreaths. Many families decorate them with lights, ribbons, bows and ornaments. Some people put up their decorations weeks before Christmas and some do it a few days before.

Around Christmas everyone is jolly and in a good mood, but when Christmas arrives everyone has presents on their mind. Children think of all of the gifts they will soon be getting and adults think of their holiday shopping list and what they need to get people. On Christmas everyone wakes up and runs to see all of their presents and children see if they got what they wanted. After opening gifts on Christmas day, people listen to Christmas carols. Christmas is a great time of year and everyone is in a great mood.

Danica Villanueva
Grade 6

The Gift

My little cousin, Dylan, has a disease called SDS (Swachmand Diamond Disease). Currently the disease has no cure. I hope for my cousin that one day it is cured. I will be with him when he is sick or lonely. He is a good person and I think he should be cured. I will try and raise money for research, but I think the most important thing is to keep him happy and treat him nicely. He is a fun loving kid and I don't think that he should ever be handicapped. He is just like the other kids and I will spend time with him whenever I can. Right now, all I can do is hope that he is going to get well and my gift to him is hope. I love spending time with him because all he wants to do is have fun. I'll watch television with him, play games or do whatever he wants. He is only 5 but he knows how to have fun. I think that if I hope for him, he will eventually get better. Until then all I can do is hang out with him and hope for a breakthrough in research. I hope Dylan gets better!

James Ziede
Grade 6

My Favorite Place to Be

My favorite place to be is Greece. It's my favorite place because most of my family lives there, and my dad owns a bar and apartments there so I go every summer and help out around the bar. I also love the pool we have, I swim in it like 24/7. All the stores are close to the bar so I can walk to any store. The bar is also really close to the beach, and I love to swim so I go to the beach a lot when I'm in Greece. It's also very sunny in Greece; that's another reason why I love Greece.

There are festivals in Greece, too. I love the festivals there. A lot of people sell things when festivals are going on. They sell jewelry, toys, and a lot of other things. To go to Greece from America by plane, it takes eight hours.

The only thing that I don't like about going to Greece is that it is far away. But I don't care that much because most of my family is there, and I love to visit them.

Fotini Thalassinos
Grade 6

Reading

Most people would rather watch TV than read a book. And I'm saying you should read instead. There is nothing you can get from television that you can't get from a good book. If you like horror movies, try some horror books like something written by Steven King or *Goosebumps* by R.L. Stine. If you like fantasy books like me try *The Amulet of Samarkand, The Golem's Eye,* or *Ptolemy's Gate* by Jonathan Stroud. They are my personal favorites. Books make you smarter and enlarge your vocabulary but TV will turn your brain to mush. It's okay to watch your favorite show every once in a while, but next time you want to turn on the TV try reaching to the bookshelf instead.

Daniel Bromberg
Grade 6

The Big Game

On a sweltering hot day in July I got ready to play the biggest game of my life. When I got to the field I immediately started warming up, as there was only one hour until game time. Championship games were tough until I learned to channel my nerves. I was playing third base and was extremely nervous, as if I was about to go skydiving. Gradually I became calm and just focused on the game. After a while my coach told me to change from third base to pitcher, I was drowning in sweat. It was nerve racking, but I did fine. Amazingly, I didn't give up any runs in two innings. That was so relieving, as if I passed a hard test. My teammates and I were so hyper, and we knew we were going to win. With two outs, my pitcher made the batter lift a fly ball, which resembled a ball reaching the heavens. My center fielder caught it for the last out. My team had won the championships. What a terrific game!

Paul Buckley
Grade 6

Road Trip!

When I was in first grade, my family and I went on a five-week road trip. You'll never guess where we drove to…California! It took a long time, but it was definitely worth it.

We started out in NJ, of course, and made our way to California from there. I had a great time at all the places we went, but one of my favorites was Nashville, Tennessee. It was so cool there. There was a weird Ripley's Believe It or Not museum there. It was interesting.

Another amazing place we went to was my cousins' house. They live in California. They had lots of pet chickens and turkeys there. California was awesome.

Sleeping, in general, was weird because one day you would be in one time zone and the next day you'd be in another. When my parents set the alarms in our hotels, we would always be so tired when we woke up. At my cousins' house I went to bed at three their time, six my time, and woke up at seven their time, ten my time. It was very hard to get used to.

The last stop we made was to Niagara Falls. Then we knew that our trip was coming to an end. We had fun anyway. We made stops at different places on the way back. So we still had a great time.

My family trip was a great experience because I got to learn new things about other places. I also got to be with my family a lot. Almost too much, but then again, you can never spend too much time with your family.

Amelia Parker
Grade 5

Falling into Fame

As I stood backstage, I was shaking with excitement. Sweat was dripping down my back and I felt as slimy as a snake. My friend, Rachel, squeezed my hand when our instructor called out, "Five minutes!" We and our class were going to perform a ballet called "The Real." I was Effie, the leading role, and had to dance with a boy. It was my first lead and I was scared. Before I knew it, like magic, the curtain was up and the music began. There was a small red string dangling from the bottom of my dress I paid no attention to it, but should have. Then about half way through out long routine I fell flat on my face like a piano falling from the roof of a tall building. As I got up I noticed five of my teeth lying on the stage. My partner and I ran off into the wings and like a broken record he repeated, "Are you ok? Are you ok?" Bloody swabs of cotton filled my mouth and aching pains shot through my jaw. Since then people have asked me, "Are you the girl that fell?" I hold my head up high and say, "Yes." It truly was a fall into fame!

Mary Guarnieri
Grade 6

The History of Basketball

Dr. James Naismith is known worldwide as the inventor of the game of basketball. He was born in the year 1861 in Ontario, Canada. The idea of basketball came from his school days where he played a simple game called duck-on-a-rock. The game involved trying to knock a "duck" off the top of a large rock by tossing another rock at it. After attending McGill University in Montreal, Canada, James became the Athletic Director there. James then moved on to the YMCA Training School in Springfield Massachusetts in 1891.

At the YMCA, James had to find a sport that was suitable for inside during the Massachusetts winters. James wanted to create a game of skill, instead of one that depended on strength. He also needed a game that could be played in a small space indoors.

The first game was played with a soccer ball and two peach baskets used as goals at each end of the local gymnasium. James made a set of thirteen rules. The object of the game is to score points by throwing the ball into the "basket" at your opponent's end of the court. Basketball is a nonviolent sport, played indoors, in which you bounce the ball, but cannot carry or kick it.

Basketball was played at the Berlin Olympics in 1936. James Naismith was flown to Berlin to watch the games. He died in Lawrence, Kansas, in 1939.

Today, basketball has become one of the world's most popular sports.

Gregory Campanile
Grade 5

My Experience

I was a little scared when we were in the elevator going to the top of Carew Tower. I did not want to go on top but my family's decision was to go to the very top of the building. When I walked out onto the platform, my heart was pumping hard. The platform at the top was outside, and that made me extra scared. The weather made a difference to me too. Thankfully, it was sunny and nice, but if the weather had been bad, I would have been super scared. That made a big difference.

At the top, the sight was awesome. Up there we had a really great view. The building is fifty stories tall. Once at the top, the building doesn't seem tall, but it really is tall. In fact, we could see all around Cincinnati. We could see buildings from other cities. From the other side of the Ohio River in Covington, Kentucky you can see Carew Tower. I had a really, really, really fun time up there.

I am glad that my parents and my brother decided to go up there that day. My brother and I went up again this year with my uncle. I think it was better the first time when I went up with my whole family. That is a day that I will remember for the rest of my life.

Connor Gregory
Grade 6

The Feeling of Soccer

The crisp fall air is beating on my skin. I feel a giant lump in my stomach that won't go away until I make this play. My pulse gets faster as the players quickly advance towards me. My heart is a drum that gets louder as my keen, trained feet move swiftly at the ball. I kick the ball so it is suspended in the air, hovering over the players as they stare in awe. I love soccer.

Soccer is skill, discipline, thrill, and passion. Everything just melts away, all the worries, problems and work. The feeling is like flying. It is exhilarating and I feel unbeatable!

Soccer teaches me many lessons, to be alert and be ready for anything. Soccer trains my mind to think fast and use my body to its advantage.

Soccer is nothing without friends; it would be a black hole of exhaustion! One time by accident I hurt the goalie, and she started crying! I felt like I murdered somebody. I felt sick. My friends noticed my awkward behavior and cheered me up. My team is like my second family.

Soccer is everything, my stress reliever, my hobby, my life! I love the adrenaline rush it gives me. I feel like a new person. When I play soccer I can terminate. I can win. I can fly! I welcome soccer with open arms, and when I embrace it, I am a new girl!!!

Claudia Steck
Grade 6

Whiskers

I got my cat, Whiskers, when I was six years old. I went to the SPCA to get him. I looked at all the cats there. I didn't want Whiskers. At the time, we already had two other cats that were boys and this time I wanted a girl cat, not Whiskers.

When I saw Whiskers in his cage at the SPCA, I knew I really didn't want him. There were a lot of other cats there and a lot of them were cleaner than he was. He was very skinny. My opinion about not wanting him did not change very quickly because he kept yanking on my hair through his cage.

Soon, we adopted Whiskers. He was a stray kitten and he was really nice. He didn't hiss or scratch and he got along well with everyone. I never knew a person who didn't like him. He was one of the kindest cats that I had ever known.

Whiskers quickly became my favorite cat. He was always loyal and nice. He never scratched me and he never did anything wrong. He didn't fight with the other cats and he never caused any trouble. Out of the two others cats I had at the time, I liked him the best. He was really nice to everyone, and although he's only a cat he had a personality of his own. He had always been my favorite cat and he still remains my favorite cat to this very day.

Morgan Biscontini
Grade 6

Books

I like books. I like books because I love learning interesting stories, and there are always at least two books I am wanting to read. I even once tried to type *Harry Potter and the Goblet of Fire* on my computer! I read in the morning, afternoon, and mostly at night because everywhere it's nice and quiet.

On every trip I take, I take a book and I usually always finish it. My favorite genres are fantasy and sometimes science fiction. Right now I am reading a fantasy book called *Inkheart,* and I'm looking forward to reading the sequel, *Inkspell.* I would recommend it. When I grow up I would like to write fantasy, and become a teacher so I can share fantasy with other children. Hopefully they will grow to also like fantasy.

Other topics that interest me are frogs, beavers, monkeys, and all different sorts of animals because I love learning about different adaptations. I have learned so much from reading and if I had never learned to read I would not be the person I am today. I love reading, and I will never stop. These are some of the reasons why I love books.

John Walden
Grade 4

Kenya

Stepping off the plane, our exhausting journey was over. We were in Kenya! When we drove to our hotel, I felt the bumps on the choppy road. I collapsed in bed thinking about the animals I would see.

I opened my droopy eyes, reluctant to rise at seven a.m. Soon we left for Nakuru. Baboons and impala were the first creatures we saw in the stunning habitat. In the park, there was a water buck, five feet from us.

On our first game drive I spotted twelve rhinos! "He's cute!" I said when looking at a baby rhino joyfully prancing like a puppy. We bumped our way to the lake and saw millions of flamingos. Later, sleep came easily with the memory of kifaru.

The next day we were off again, and we spotted Colobus monkeys lounging in a tree. We continued and saw the king of the jungle, coolest of all cats, the lion! A rush of excitement overcame my fear.

Most people have heard of leopards and think they are pretty cool. But if you have been to Kenya, you know that seeing a leopard is a BIG DEAL! The leopard, just one creature, really wraps up a trip. In a tree, we saw a silhouette. Legs, tail, spots, yes indeed, we were looking at a chui. What a way to end it!

A cat is a good thing to fall asleep with, and I definitely slept with cats and other Kenyan animals stuffed in my mind!

Jimmy Gilman
Grade 5

The Amazing Derek Jeter

Have you ever wondered about the Yankees' famous present day captain? Well, if you have, this report will tell you some interesting things.

My essay is on a mighty player called Derek Jeter. I hope that you've heard of him because he's a fantastic player. He plays baseball on the New York Yankees. I'm writing on him because I praise the New York Yankees.

Derek hit the most hits out of all the shortstops over a five-year period. He hit 1,005 hits from 1998 to 2002.

What does Jeter need to do to make the Hall of Fame? If he finishes his career in a fairly normal progression, he has a very good chance. He has a 75% chance of making it.

When Derek was six he dreamed he would play shortstop for the unstoppable New York Yankees. His friends always said you'll never make it to the majors and even if you do you probably won't play for the Yankees. But dreams do come true. Derek got to the majors by lifting weights and practicing throwing with his pitch back. If Derek's not playing baseball he might be in an Oreo stacking contest because he loves to eat and stack his Oreos.

Derek never went to AA. He was so talented that he went from A to AAA and then to the Majors. I was born on August 15, 1996, one day after Derek did a double play. I like to call that a birthday present from Derek. I didn't like the Yankees all my life. I like the Red Sox. But as I got older I kicked out the thought of liking the Red Sox and went to the Yankees.

Now I'll always pledge my soul to the great American team of the New York Yankees, I think.

Nick Hartman
Grade 6

I Love My Family

My family means everything to me. I love spending time with them. My family and I have fun together and see new things. Also, we take vacation together. I love spending time with my family.

I have fun with my family. We do fun things together. One time my whole family got in a picture together and made funny faces. We go to fun places together. We relax and have fun together. My family and I love to have fun.

I get to see new things with my family. We do new things at new places. We go places we've never been to before. We go to stores we've never been to before. My family and I do lots of new things together.

My family and I go on vacations together. We go to amusement parks. We go to new states. We sometimes have even been out of the country. My family and I love to go to new places.

Spending time with my family is something I enjoy. My family and I like to go on vacations, go to new places, and have fun together. My family is great.

Renee Robbins
Grade 6

The Crib

"Wake up! Wake up!" I screamed to my mom and dad as I jumped on them, "I want to open my gifts!" When we finally opened our gifts it felt like it took forever. We finally finished though.

I was about to go and play with my toys. When my mom screamed. "Wait, Sydney, you have one more gift!" I screamed, "Yeah!" Then I saw my mom carrying out a huge doll crib for my three dolls. I squeezed my parents so hard, and then went off to play.

A couple of days after Christmas, I was bored so I fooled around with my cat, Meko. Just then I got a brilliant idea. I told my sister, Kayla, so she would help me. She grabbed Meko and helped me shove him in the crib. We tucked him in extremely tight. He couldn't get out. We did that every night for a year. Then I was tired of the crib so I put it away.

One random day I decided to use the crib. So I took it out of the closet, then decided to forget it and just leave it there in my room. So I went downstairs to watch TV and I forgot about it in my room for a couple of days.

A week later I went back to school, when I came home I walked into my room to see Meko was asleep in the crib.

Till this very day Meko still sleeps in the crib.

Sydney Desrosiers
Grade 6

My Christmas Presents

For Christmas I got many presents. I will tell you about them. My first present was a Nintendo DS. It has two screens. One is a regular screen and the other is a touch screen. My favorite game to play on my DS is Super Mario 64 DS. You have to collect power stars. There are 150 power stars in total. I have 18 power stars. There are mini games you can play. The multiplayer games is a game where everyone that is playing VS each other and has to collect stars. Whoever has the most stars by the end wins. The characters are different colored Yoshi. There are three caps. One turns the player into Luigi, one turns the player into Wario, and one turns you into Mario.

I also got a book called *Poppy*. I already finished it. It was about a mouse name Poppy. It was a good book. There are more Poppy books. Some other Poppy books are *Poppy and Rye*, *Poppy's Return*, and *Ereth's Birthday*.

I also got two DS games. One was Mario Kart DS. I got a new player. His name is Dry Bones. I also got a game called The Ultimate Spiderman. I finished 17% of the game. The Ultimate Spiderman is multiplayer, that needs two or more game cards. Mario Kart needs only 1 game card. The multiplayer games are Balloon Battle and Shine Runners. Those are all the presents I got for Christmas this year.

Alex Chung
Grade 4

Memories of Manhattan

From the time I was born up until age 5, I lived in Manhattan. Here are some things that I remember about the city.

When you say Manhattan, the first thing I think of is the really nice man who owned the dry cleaners in my building. He loved children and always gave me a lollipop when I was in his store. The second thing I remember was going to a park with large sprinklers, which turned on automatically each day in the summertime. I also remember never using my car but walking everywhere.

One thing different about Manhattan compared with New Jersey is the amount of noise and activity. In Montclair, it's mostly quiet especially at night. In New York, there's always a lot of activity outside. I remember always hearing sirens and a lot of commotion down on the street.

When I lived in New York, I remember always being able to drive to my grandparents house in Connecticut. Now I have to go to Florida to visit them. I remember the smell of exhaust from all the cars and seeing steam coming out of holes in the street. Every year at Christmas, I remember seeing thousands of Christmas lights everywhere. When we wanted to get across town, we would always take a subway. And, when we were on the subway, the lights would always go out. I also remember not having my little sister in Manhattan. It was just my little brother Matthew and me.

I will never forget about living in Manhattan, but I am happy to be living in New Jersey now.

Daniel Ingersoll
Grade 5

My Pets

The first pet I ever remember having is Pepper. It was a dog, German Shepard and husky mixed. It was a male. He was black with little dots on his nose. He was about 4 feet and 32 pounds. I got him when he was a puppy and about 4 years later he was stolen.

About around the same time, I had a hamster. It's name was Garbage Can. He was white with brown spots. He was about 5 inches and weighed about 1 pound. I had him for about 3 years. The way he got his name was when he got out of his cage we found him in the garbage. I named him.

The next pet I am going to talk about is a bird. It was a canary. Its name was Nikey. I got it when my dad's hamster died. We would let it fly out of its cage and it would use my mom's hair as a nest.

My favorite pet is Jigg. He is a dog. He is a mix. He is small and chunky. He is white with black dots and brown rings around the dots. He is my favorite dog because I got him on my 7th birthday. I think everyone should have pets because pets are fun to have. They keep you from being lonely. They also keep you from being sad or depressed. They can always cheer you up.

Robert Ryan
Grade 6

It's Basketball

Have you ever had a hobby that you loved so much you could do it forever? Well, I didn't until I got my hobby. It is fun, and you have to work hard to play it. Yes, it is basketball! It is my favorite sport that is also my favorite hobby. It is totally awesome!

Basketball might not be important to you, but it is to me. It is important because of the experience you get from it. The most important rule is having fun. If you play good, that's good, but if you have fun, that's great.

When you're in a game, the coach starts out five players. The positions are: center, two guards, and two forwards. The center does the jump ball and plays in and out of the key. The guards guard the ball and go for the rebounds. Finally, the forwards take the ball out and play defense or offense. It takes a while to learn all of the positions, but you'll get used to them.

So, I told you basketball was important in my life and I told you why. The hard working sport, basketball, is all about the fun and the experience that you learn, and I love it a lot!

Britney Murray
Grade 6

Soccer

We have many sports. I love everything! But I love soccer more than everything because we can score, we can do many tricks, and we can play every free time.

My first reason that soccer is fun, I can score. One day during recess time, I played soccer with my friends. I dribbled across my friends. I got a chance to shoot! And I shot the ball with my full power. Then, score! I was so excited that I scored. Don't you think it's exciting? I think so.

My second reason why I love soccer is we can do many tricks. When I was in my soccer team in Korea, we used to learn more tricks. It was so fun! Tricks like turn, protect the ball, and pass the ball through other team; it was so fun! This makes me think soccer's fun! What about you?

Kunwoo Kim
Grade 5

The Best Day Ever

The best day ever would be no parents to tell us what to do. That would be great. We could go to Kennywood, go see scary movies that our parents wouldn't let us see, and play Play Station 2 all day.

But we need our parents to cook our favorite food, care for us, tuck us into bed, help us to be healthy, get us ready for school, take care of us when we're sick, and be there for us.

Oh yeah, I forgot to tell you something. The real best day ever would be me and my family playing, watching movies together, laughing, and having fun.

Gunnar Geyer
Grade 4

My Life with Horses

When I was seven, I went to summer camp. It was a horse camp and I rode every day. I rode a horse named Cutie. She was white with reddish-brown spots, and had a reddish-brown mane. Every day I would ride, and then go to the barn and do chores all day. One day I had anaphylactic shock. I couldn't breathe, and I was afraid of being bitten again, but that didn't stop me from riding. When I was better I had a competition at camp, and I won 1st place. The next year I couldn't go to camp. My mom got me lessons at a different place to make up for it, but we couldn't afford it. After a while, my mom found Greendale Farm. It was Heaven on Earth. I loved Wesley, my teacher. She made me feel wonderful every time I saw her. But the real owner was Susan, and eventually she closed the barn. I was devastated. When my birthday rolled around, my mother told me the most wonderful thing on Earth. Wesley was still working at Greendale. It was a miracle. I can't explain. She had scheduled a lesson and it was that day. I rode my heart out, and that day, I got to canter. I felt the wind run through my hair, and I knew I was going to be a Jockey when I grew up, and I am never ever going to let anyone tell me differently.

Jacquelyn Harning
Grade 5

Recycling

Recycling is very important. It saves trees and other resources. It's important to save the trees because a lot of animals have homes in the forest. Everyone should try to recycle. Recycling is good for everyone and everything.

Trees provide us and animals with many things. They provide us and animals with wood for homes, paper, fruits, nuts, shade and natural beauty. Trees play an important role in Earth's natural cycle. They help prevent erosion, and they capture carbon from carbon dioxide. But the problem is that we use more than 500,000 trees to produce the two-thirds of newspapers that are never recycled.

But listen to this: by saving one ton of paper, you save 17 trees, 6,953 gallons of water, 463 gallons of oil, 587 pounds of air pollution, 3.06 cubic yards of landfill space, and 4,077 kilowatt hours of energy. The good news is that in 1996, 42.3 million tons of paper were recycled in America. If all morning newspapers read around the country were recycled, 41,000 trees wouldn't be cut daily and 6 million tons of waste would never end up in landfills.

Did you know the average American throws out about 61 pounds of tin cans every month? About 70% of metal, used just once, is discarded. Can you believe that? It just makes me very sad. That is why my family tries to recycle as much as we can, and I suggest you do too.

Maria Rincón
Grade 5

Marshmallow and Yam

Most turkeys are worried and afraid around Thanksgiving, but two turkeys aren't. Marshmallow and Yam have both met the President of the United States, been pardoned by him, flown first-class, now live in Disneyland, and were grand marshals in the Disneyland's Thanksgiving Day parade.

Marshmallow and Yam were raised on Henning farm in Minnesota and were picked from a flock of 30 other turkeys because they know how to strut the best. They are both male and when they were 18 weeks old, they weighed 36 pounds each. Before being pardoned, a poll on a White House website was held for their names. After getting the results of the poll, their names changed from Snowball and Blizzard to Marshmallow and Yam. On November 22, 2005, Marshmallow and Yam almost met the dinner table but were saved by being pardoned by the President, George W. Bush (phew!) They were the only pardoned turkeys to ever go to Disneyland. Lucky them as they flew first-class on-stop on a flight from Washington D.C. to Disneyland. After their arrival, Marshmallow and Yam were grand marshals in the Disneyland Thanksgiving Day parade to celebrate its 50th anniversary. They now both live in an enclosure in Frontierland, near the entrance to Big Thunder Roller coaster. Marshmallow and Yam get the joy of seeing the roller coaster going up and down every day.

Marshmallow and Yam are two of the luckiest turkeys and will live a happy and wonderful life out in Disneyland.

Colette Biro
Grade 5

Special Gifts

People are constantly giving and receiving gifts. Many people just buy numerous things that they think would make people content. What if you didn't have to go out and buy gifts for people or make them yourself? What gifts would you give to people? First, to my mom and dad I would give them an absolutely immaculate room. My room is usually very grotesque and my parents keep nagging me about cleaning it. Next, to my grandma and grandpa I would call them more. I would want to do this because they say that when I call them they feel happier and better. They like to get to know us and like to see what our lives are like. To my Nana and Popi I would try and eat much healthier things. Right now carbs are my life. Every time I go to their house for any meal Nana will have her special Nana ham out. And she'll become angry with me when I refuse to eat her ham or anything healthy she makes for that matter. Sometimes I tend to be mean around my brother and sisters. their names are Jennifer, Bridget, John, and Shannon. For them I would try to be more optimistic and pleasant. I would also try to not say so many hateful words to them. As you can see, if I didn't have to go out and purchase or make people things I would give these special gifts to numerous people.

Delaney Oliveri
Grade 6

One Heroic Job

My daddy has a very important, heroic job. He is a fireman! I think he is a very hard worker! He works for the Troy Fire Department.

One exciting thing my dad has done during his career was help the family of Matthew Barnes. He was a fireman in 9/11. I am very thankful that my dad was not a fireman in that disaster.

I love to hear my dad's stories. He tells wonderful stories. They are about the different things he did throughout his day. All of the firemen he works with are very nice. Sometimes they give me soda and ice cream!

My friends and I play a game we invented called "The Fire Game." I think it's pretty cool. Real firemen must have a coat, boots, mask, helmet, gloves, and an air tank before going into a burning building. When we play "The Fire Game," we put on our snow pants, coats, gloves, and pretend fire helmets. Then we ride our bikes up to a hill, get our hoses (not real!) and in we go!

One of the best things about being a fireman's daughter is the Christmas party! We get a gift from Santa! Afterward, we go on an old-fashioned fire truck with Santa — it's so much fun! There's music and soda, candy and cocoa. I make new friends, too!

I love being a fireman's daughter! I love dad's job as a fireman! It is so awesome!

Emily Halpin
Grade 4

The Amazing Toys

This is what the future holds for me. Seeing myself become a famous toy maker and creating different kinds of toys. Today, I always seem to find ways to make a simple piece of paper into a whole new thing. It makes my creative instincts into fun and adventurous experiences for many children in my class. In the future, I hope my designs will be enjoyed not only by my class, but by children all around the world. Becoming famous for this is just one part of this success. Enjoying this time while doing it is the best part of all.

I'm sure to make a lot of kids happy and still keep their imagination alive. It is worth it for me to watch a kid play and enjoy a toy I made for them. I would love to see them share it with family and friends.

I would spend my day thinking of new toy designs, using most of the profits for materials to make new toys, making the toys, and delivering the stock of the toys, and then finally getting some deserved sleep. Even though I'm famous, my job does not attract the Paparazzi. That is what lies in my future.

Vincent Dimaya
Grade 4

Animals vs People

Did you ever wonder how far you can jump? Well, for these people and animals it comes natural to them. We will now lead our attention to the kangaroo vs Ashia Hansen, the kangaroo jumped to 25m in one jump that would make a triple jump of 82 ft! In the 1999 world championship Ashia jumped to 15.02m which would be 49.28 ft!

How fast can you run? Well, cheetahs, Michael Johnson and other great athletes can run very fast. Right now we will just focus on the cheetah vs Michael Johnson. The cheetah in this ran 113 kph (70 mph). In the 1996 Olympic games, Johnson set a world record and got a gold medal when he ran 200 m in 19.32 seconds. That's 37 kph (23 mph).

How far can you run? The ostrich and Gabriela Szabo can run long distances for a period of time. I will focus on the difference between the ostrich and Gabriela. The ostrich ran 48 kph (30 mph) for 30 minutes. Gabriela ran an indoor record in the 5,000 m run. She ran this distance in just over 14 minutes, 30 seconds.

I concluded that in all the events that the animals won. Also, that the animals they went up against were made for that event. For example, the cheetah won because that type of animal was made to run. So, it was really not fair to the other athletes, because humans are made for multiple things and don't focus on just that one thing. Did you make that same conclusion?

Amanda Dremsek
Grade 6

Being Drug-Free

Being drug-free feels GREAT! One reason I don't and can't do drugs is because I am only 9 years old. Did you know that some people start taking drugs in their teen years? Isn't that horrible? Their lungs can turn black. I know it sounds nasty, but it is part of human nature.

Do you know how drugs affect you if you take them? Drugs affect you in a very critical way. Drugs can even affect people's emotional feelings. No matter what some people say, drugs are still very bad for you.

After you do drugs, you can regret it and even after you are done using them. Sometimes when people take a lot of drugs, they act silly. Sometimes people can even feel dizzy when they take too many drugs. When people take drugs, sometimes they also start to have heart problems. Isn't that really sad?

The people who sell drugs are bad, too. They just want the money. They don't care about the people who buy them. They don't even care if the people die. I hope you learned something about why it is important to stay drug-free. I am so glad that I am drug-free!

Yasmeen Castro-Johnson
Grade 4

I Like to Build Things Like Houses

I like to build things like houses. I get to run forklifts and things like that. Here is a list of all the things I have gotten to run: backhoe, manlift, trackhoe, and chainsaw.

I have gotten to use a nail gun too. I have gotten to go forty-two feet in the air. I have gotten to go up on a 12x12 pitch roof. I have built walls and put in windows. I have run a flooring nailer. What is a flooring nailer, you are probably asking. It is what puts down wood floors. I have gotten to put in tile and pour concrete in the basement of our new house. I have helped set rafters. I have helped put in LVL's (laminated veneer lumber) which are like beams in a way. Oh, I almost forgot. I have run a bulldozer with my grandpa. I also had to fix our sewer top because my grandpa hit it with the bulldozer. I also had to run a lot of wire. We had to run over three thousand feet of wire. I helped put up twenty-one thousand square feet of sheet rock in my grandparents' house which is under ours and is a new house.

We have twenty-eight recessed lights. We have twenty-six fluorescent lights. We have fifty fluorescent light bulbs. We also have over six thousand linear feet of wood on our ceiling and we have sixty-six stairs inside and out. We have a big house.

Luke Hatch
Grade 5

The Heroes of 9-11

On September 11, 2001 several groups of terrorists hijacked four planes and planned to crash them into the Twin Towers, the Pentagon, and maybe the White House. Two of the planes crashed into the Twin Towers and the Twin Towers collapsed into the ground. One plane crashed into the Pentagon and one side of the Pentagon collapsed. Then another plane was maybe going to crash into the White House, but the passengers fought with the terrorists, then the plane crashed into the ground.

The firemen and policemen risked their lives to help and save the people who were stuck in the Twin Towers. There were also policemen and firemen from other cities and states helping the victims of this horrible plan. The firemen and the policemen did not care about themselves. They cared just about the people that were stuck in the Twin Towers. These firemen and policemen left their families to help the people in need at the moment. Saving and rescuing people was the number one thing in their mind.

The air was contaminated because of chemicals on the air, the smell of dead bodies and the smoke of the plane crash. Despite all this our heroes, the policemen and firemen, continued to work giving the true meaning to the United States of America. The 9-11 was a day of terror and death but these heroes made us feel strong and safe. I am grateful and thankful for these heroes who risked their lives for others.

Shaina Loran
Grade 4

Loving My Time in Italy

We were there. Not in a German Airport or on the plane. No, we were really in Italy.

I packed some of my stuff into my carry-on bag and slung it over my shoulder. I kept inhaling the pure Italian air. It was so fresh! The whole ride there I was jumping around with anticipation. I couldn't wait to see the villa! Then it came into sight. It was a beautiful yellow color. I ran to the back and saw what we later joked about as an olympic-sized pool. Not that it really was, but it was huge!

Ignoring my jet lag, I changed into my swimsuit and jumped right in. Most of my time spent at the villa was spent sleeping, eating, (wonderful food of course!) and swimming. I am a very active swimmer!

The rest of my time was traveling through Siena, Monte Benichi, Vinci, Florence, Rome, Pisa, Pompeii, Sorrento, and Venice. We spent most of our traveling time on trains. The rest was driving (like to Siena). Our time spent going through the cities was walking and dodging cars.

After the whole hot month of July (which includes my brother's and my birthday) I just couldn't go home. But all good things must end, so I said good-bye to Italy and hello to an 18-hour plane ride. Time to catch some Z's!

Kara Newman
Grade 5

My Family

If I didn't have my family I don't know what would happen, and I don't want to find out. I love my family so much. My family is always there to keep me company, and they love me so much. With them I have everything I need to live.

When I need my family, they are always there to keep me company. I always have someone around me. If I need help with something, or just want someone with me, they are there in a second. When I am alone or sad, they will do whatever they can to help me. I sometimes get bored. Since I have a brother, I always have someone to play with.

I am loved so much by my family. I can tell my family loves me. All of the time they are helping me. Also, they always take me where I want to go. My family loves me very much. Every day they are telling me that they love me.

With my family I have everything I need to live. My family provides me with food. It isn't just normal food that you need. It is very delicious food. I have a beautiful house that I live in. If I didn't have my family I wouldn't have a house. Also, I have my very awesome clothes. My mom and I go shopping all the time.

My family does so much for me. I don't know what I would do without them.

Nicole Fowler
Grade 6

Dare to Dance

Have you ever wanted to have some fun while exercising? Join ballet! Ballet is beneficial because it keeps your mind sharp, body healthy, and is a lot of fun. For fun, try a ballet class, it will make great use of your time and effort.

The combinations change every class to keep your mind in shape. Also, you can keep your body fit by strengthening your legs, arms, back, and ab muscles. Ballet can also be very fun because you learn things that you might want to try, the floor exercises and bar combinations can be hard, and if someone messes up then we all get a good laugh.

The greatest part of being a dancer is that you get a sense of self confidence, dignity and pride. That can come in handy when dealing with a challenge. It really helps to have all these qualities to help boost your self confidence.

Every year, I participate in The Nutcracker at my school, Pittsburgh Youth Ballet. Most people from P.Y.B. become famous. Someday, I hope I can do the same thing. Right now, I am a pretty good dancer, but I hope to improve over my years at P.Y.B.

Ballet can be fun and beneficial. In dancing, you can keep your mind sharp, your body tone and have lots of fun too! Because of all this, I just truly love ballet. Try a ballet class, it can be a great benefit to you.

Ashley David
Grade 6

Family, Education, Goals, and Friends

What is important to me are the following things: my family, my education, my career goals and of course, my friends.

First of all, my family is important to me because they are always there to cheer me up and let me know that everything will be fine when I am sad. They are the ones that will be there to advise me of what is right and wrong and to guide me in the right direction. My mom is the best one to encourage me to keep doing good because it will get me ahead in life. I know she means well even though I sometimes do not understand or might get upset at her.

My education is important to me because this is what will get me to where I want to be when I am an adult. Without my education I will not have a good future or achieve my career goals.

The other is my career goals. One of my goals in life is to become one of the best basketball players around, but if this is not possible my other goal is to become an actor. With the help of my family and good friends this will become a reality for me.

Last are my friends. My friends are also important to me because they always have my back and make me laugh when I am upset or sad about something.

I hope that all the people that I love will always be there when my goals become a reality.

Milton E. Vargas Jr.
Grade 4

The Good Memories and the Bad

When you're eleven, you just want to have fun. You want to be worry-free. Unfortunately two eleven year olds had a frightening experience that they just can't help worrying about.

On September 21, 2005, Nellie Flynn (me), Chloe Chipkin, and two other Margate students were attacked by a pit-bull at a cross-country meet. I had to get over forty stitches. My best friend Chloe had to get four stitches. Four or forty, it's the same pain. I couldn't walk for four weeks. When I couldn't come to school, my friends came over to my house to keep me company so I wouldn't feel so alone. When I first got out of the house to go for a walk, the first dog I saw, yes, you guessed it, a pit-bull. I am very scared of pit-bulls, and whenever I go outside and hear a big dog barking, I go back inside as fast as I can. Chloe and I are going through the same thing right now. Just think, an eleven year old afraid to ever go near a big dog. I can't trust anybody's dog except mine. I wish I were able to love dogs as much as I used to.

Before we were attacked, we both loved dogs more than anything, now they scare us more than anything. I hope the people that owned this dog know what they did to us innocent kids from Margate. I hope they remember the experience like we do.

Nellie Flynn
Grade 6

Let's Stop Littering!

What a thoughtless way to throw out your trash! Everyday I see people throwing litter on the ground and I am disgusted. This practice is called littering and should be stopped! Not only is littering a problem here, in the United States, but it is also a problem in other parts of the world.

Littering reduces the appeal of public places. According to researchers in Australia, cigarette butts are the leading product that is littered. Out of all the things that people throw on the ground, cigarette butts make up 21%! Not only does it reduce the appeal of public places, cigarettes can take up to five years to disintegrate, and releases up to 4,000 chemicals into the atmosphere!

Did you know littering also affects wildlife? Squirrels and other animals stop to eat plastic wrappers and sniff broken glass bottles. When the animals eat things they shouldn't they get sick and eventually die. For example, at many weddings guests throw rice. Birds eat it and die because the rice cooks in their stomach. Weird, I know! Birds cannot burp and throw up, so the rice can't be regurgitated.

Since littering is extremely bad, many governments have made up a fining system to punish those who participate in this disrespectful act. But do not lose hope! There is a possible solution to this matter. If just one person uses the trash can, other people might follow and the world would be a better place…so, DO NOT LITTER!

Malkese Edwards
Grade 5

Friends

If I didn't have my comforting and fun friends I would be lost. I look to my friends for security, and also for comfort. When I want to have fun I turn to my friends. This is why I like to have many friends.

I look to my friends for security. When there's trouble they bail you out. they are there when you're in need. They make you feel safe. That's why I look to my friends for security. I also look to my friends for comfort. They are always there to lend a helping hand. My friends always give me a shoulder to cry on. Having friends means having someone to talk to. That is why I look to them for comfort.

When I want to have fun I turn to my friends. I like to share lots of laughter with my friends. My friends and I like to have sleepovers. With my friends I always have someone to play games with. These examples show why I turn to my friends to have fun.

Being with my friends always gives me comfort and security. When I'm with my friends I have a lot of fun, and at the same time they provide me with security and comfort. These examples show why I enjoy having friends.

Alexes Duran
Grade 6

Amazing Facts About Lizards

There are many different types of lizards. Some different types are the fierce Gila monster, Komodo dragon, the Leopard gecko (and any other kind of gecko), plus long tailed lizards, Anoles and Iguanas.

Lizards can be as big as a chalkboard to as small as a thumbtack. Try to imagine that! Lizards are cold-blooded reptiles, which means they can't count on their own body for heat like we can. They would probably have to lie on a rock and let the sun do the work. The smaller lizards usually eat crickets, meal worms, and other insects. While the bigger lizards eat rats, mice, beavers, moles, groundhogs, and other small animals. They could even take down a deer if they were really hungry!

Lizards are very colorful. They can be beautiful reds, yellows, greens, oranges, browns, blacks, whites, grays, and many other colors. Does that seem colorful to you?

Lizards usually live in warm areas that don't have all 4 seasons such as Florida, Arizona, Texas, Georgia, South Carolina, and many other places.

Lizards are very nice reptiles, but when they bite you trust me it's no joke! Some lizards bite harder than others. The Komodo dragon's bite will definitely hurt more than the Leopard gecko's or the long tailed lizard's.

Those are some amazing facts about these wonderful reptiles!!

Liana Muia
Grade 4

Freedom Run

Have you ever dreamed of having something, but felt like you could never have it? I have. My dream was to have a horse. Every time I saw one, I begged my parents to get it.

When I went to an animal shop and saw the grooming supplies, I wished I had them: the brush to comb my horse's mane, the leash to lead my horse, the food to feed him/her. My sister had her dream pet, a cat. My brother had his, a dog. But I didn't. I had to share all the animals with someone, and dreamed of having mine one day. I got books about horses and drew them, and bought many toys that had something or was a horse. My mom said, "Horses are too expensive." My dad said, "No more animals." My brother and sister said, "We don't care if we have one or not." I said, "One day I'll get one."

The years passed and soon it was Christmas. We opened our presents, then my mom said, "Come on, let's go get your outside work done."

"Oh Mom, not now please," I said.

"No, I want you to get it done, so you'll have the rest of the day."

"Fine." So the whole family got dressed and went outside. On our way to the chickens' pen we heard a noise. "Oh my gosh, what was that?" my sister asked. She pushed the door open. We went in the empty part of the garage, my sister screamed, and I cried. There in the empty room was my dream come true, my horse.

We named it Franco, and even though I can't ride him because he's a miniature horse, I still have him. So you see dreams can come true, just give it time.

Kayla Huggins
Grade 5

Summertime

Summertime is one of my favorite times. In the summertime you can do a lot of things because the weather is always nice (most of the time). You can do a lot of things like go swimming, go to parks, or you could go to the beach.

What I like to do in the summertime is to go to Maine or Maryland. What I do in Maine is I go to the ocean and I walk the streets to go into stores. I also walk the boardwalk. One shop that I always go to is a toe ring shop where you have a toe ring fitted on your toe. One thing that you do is you get to pick your own design and what toe you want it on.

In Maryland I also like to go to the beach and walk the boardwalk. One of the things I do is go to shops and I always get caramel corn. At both places I like to go boogie boarding which is kind of like surfing but you don't go out into the ocean like surfing. I usually stay in a hotel or I stay at a campground in both Maine and Maryland.

Summertime is one of my favorite times of the year. I like it because I go to Maine and Maryland and because I do a lot of things there.

Courtney Britt
Grade 5

What I Think Is Important to Me

It is important to me that all of the kids should enjoy their life, because many kids don't have, don't do, and don't eat what other kids have, do, and eat.

My cousin Luiza keeps telling me, "Be happy with what you have because not a lot of people have what you have. You will never know what will happen with you."

Now she has it stuck in my mind and I DO think about WHAT IF that was me and it really hurts. It is sad how people don't think some times and waste their money on just clothes looking to be popular.

When I'm at my cousin's house, I take a lot of food, but then I never finish it, or sometimes I do. Then if I don't finish it, I would have to throw it away or just give it to someone who could actually finish it. Then Luiza would be in my mind again and I would feel bad again. I thank everybody who is always trying to help me, because I know a lot of kids my age don't get that.

Since I live by the city Erie, there is an amusement park called "Waldemeer Park." I always get to go there and I try to have fun because I know that my parents pay big bucks to go there.

I believe that every body should enjoy life, even when it is tough.

Alina Gidenko
Grade 6

My Family

I have many things that are important to me, but the one that is most important is my family. My family is important to me because they always have my back and they love me very much. I live in a family of six. I have one sister, two brothers, and my parents. Each member of my family has something special about them. Amy, my sister is always there for me when I need her. My brothers, Andrew and Justin, can get annoying at times, but if I need a laugh they're always there to cheer me up. The reason my parents are also special to me is that if I have a question, or problem, they can answer it for me so I can make the right choice. Also, they all love me!

Is your family special to you? Well, if they aren't they should be. Your family are those people who tuck you in at night, help you with your homework, and most of all, love you with all their hearts. There are even more things your family does for you, but I think that if you really love your family, you will figure that out for yourself.

I love my family more than the whole wide world and you should too. With my brothers, my sister, and my parents, I am thankful, I have a great life with a great family. That's how your family should be for you also.

Laura Groszkiewicz
Grade 6

Coretta Scott King and Her Contributions to the Civil Rights Movement

Coretta Scott King, a famous Civil Rights leader, led a life full of commitment and sorrow. Mrs. King was born on April 27, in Perry County, Alabama. Her parents were Bernice and Obie Scott. She had two siblings, Edythe and Obie. Although her family was not wealthy, Mrs. King excelled in school. Years later, Mrs. King went to Lincoln High and graduated best in her class. She accepted a scholarship to Antioch College. After graduating Antioch, she attended the New England Conservatory of Music.

At the conservatory, she met Martin Luther King, Jr. On June 18, 1953, they were married. The couple became actively involved in the Civil Rights' Movement after Rosa Parks' was arrested. Dr. King began to organize protests against racism. Mrs. King held fundraisers for the Southern Christian Leadership Conference.

On April 4, 1986, Dr. King was shot in Tennessee. It was a heartbreaking day for thousands. Mrs. King felt there should be a holiday in honor of King's great work. President Reagan signed a document to make the holiday official. In 1981, the King Center opened to the community. In was the first institution to honor an African American.

In August of 2005, Mrs. King suffered a stroke and a minor heart attack. She made her last public appearance sixteen days before she died at a ceremony honoring her husband. Coretta Scott King died in her sleep on January 30, 2006. We will remember Mrs. King's contributions to the Civil Right's Movement forever.

Caroline Wharton
Grade 5

The Old Grounds

On a cold brisk day my dad, my uncle and I set out on a fishing trip to the Old Grounds. I had to sit in the back of the boat with the horrible stench of bait. We started to move fast so I quickly grabbed something to hold onto. An hour later we arrived at the Old Grounds. I dropped my line in the water and heard the buzzing sound of my drag. Ten minutes later I felt the yanking pull of my fishing pole. I pulled back and hooked the fish in the lip. He kept taking lots of line from my reel. Finally a few minutes later he got too tired to pull. So I reeled him in toward the boat. My dad lifted him up on the boat and we weighed him and measured him. The fish weighed 14 lbs and was 24 inches. That was a day to remember.

Dominick Baker
Grade 6

Why the Declaration of Independence Is Important Today

I think the Declaration of Independence is still important today because the ideas that are said in the first few paragraphs are the whole reason why we make the laws that we do. The Declaration states "all men are created equal that they are endowed by their creator with certain inalienable rights, that among these are life, liberty, and the pursuit of happiness." The Declaration recognizes God. Many laws that are made today follow God's laws.

Thomas Jefferson wrote the Declaration of Independence in 1763. He was chosen to write it because he was a leader for the patriots in Virginia, was a lawyer, studied government, and wrote about problems with the British rule. There are also laws today to make sure all people are treated equal, like black people and women. Even in Iraq American soldiers are fighting so that other people will have life, liberty, and the pursuit of happiness. These are just a few of the ways that the Declaration of Independence is still important today.

Alexandra Neimetz
Grade 5

Peer Pressure — How You Can Stay Away from Those "So-Called Friends"

Sometimes being a good friend means doing the wrong thing, especially with all the peer pressure there is today. I'm in the sixth grade, I sure know about peer pressure and how your "so-called friends" can pressure you into doing something you don't feel comfortable with. This is one of the biggest problems with teens and preteens today. They may be young but should know right from wrong. Your peers might think if you don't do something that they're doing you can't be friends anymore. Just because your friends are doing something bad like smoking doesn't mean you have to make the same mistake. No real friend would ever make you feel uncomfortable or force you to do something that is wrong in any point in your friendship with them.

Peer pressure doesn't only deal with drugs but some cases of peer pressure have to do with weight. Some people pressure their peers to lose weight by telling them that they are too big and they can't be seen with them unless they lose weight. Personally, I think that is harassment and the person who said that may feel that there is something wrong with themselves so they have to put other people down.

I think that any case of peer pressure is wrong unless your peers are pressuring you to do something right like to stop smoking. Peer pressure can lead to serious damage in one's life.

Maegan Juul
Grade 6

Have You Changed?

Have you changed for other people so you will fit in? If you did, you probably have noticed the change, and you're disappointed. Some people change without knowing why.

I bet you have heard your parents tell you never to let people change you. Why do you change? You do it for others. You want friends. You think, if I change people will be my friend. I won't be alone. Be yourself. It's you your friends want to be with!

Be who you want to be, wear the clothes you want to wear, listen to the music you want to listen to, talk how you want to talk. Some people may not like your personality, but don't change it for them. Somewhere out there is a person just like you. You will never find the right friend for you if you change. If you change your personality to fit in it is even worse because kids don't want you to be a replica of them. The people you find as friends will like you for you. I didn't change and I found people who like me for who I am.

I'll say it again, you're you. Be who you want to be. You're your own person and no one can change that no matter what. This should be as important to you as it is to me.

Were you thinking of changing? Don't! Accept you for you, and be proud!

Marissa Flores
Grade 6

The Bermuda Triangle

The Bermuda Triangle is the greatest modern mystery of our well stood world. A region of the Atlantic ocean between Bermuda, Miami, Florida, and San Juan, Puerto Rico, where disappearances of ships, planes, and people have occurred. Charts and maps help guide you to the geography of the Bermuda Triangle, plus marking possible locations for missing ships, planes, and people.

Some people call the Bermuda Triangle the sea of the lost ships. Many ships have sunk and disappeared. Some names of those ships are Saba Bank, El Carbibe, Dancing Fathers, and El Gato. Those are some ships that sank and disappeared. The Saba Bank sank in 1974, and Dancing Fathers disappeared in 1964.

Planes have disappeared too. Some planes that have disappeared are PV-1 Ventura, SBD-5 Dauntless, PBY-5A Catalina, Star Tiger, and Flight 19. There are a lot more planes that have disappeared.

People have disappeared too. One incident in 1969, the government was missing two keepers to a lighthouse on the Bermuda Triangle. That was one incident. There are many more. That is the Bermuda Triangle and facts about the Bermuda Triangle.

Adam Gannon
Grade 5

Great White Shark

The Great White Shark is the main star in the movie "Jaws." The Great White Shark is called different names in different parts of the world. In Germany it's called Werssshai, in France, Grand Requrn Blanco, in Spain, Tiburon Blanco, in Australia, White Pointer and White Death, in Russia, Sedoraga Akula, and in Japan, Hohjirozame is the name for the Great White Shark.

The Great White Shark can grow to be nearly 20 feet long and weighing up to 5,000 pounds with its teeth as sharp as your mom's steak knife. The Great White Shark is mainly composed of cartilage. Cartilage is a stiff, flexible material that is found in the ridge of your nose and your earlobes. Its fins are called dorsal fins, pectoral fins, and caudal fins.

The Great White Shark's prey is humans, fish, other sharks, seals, and sea lions. The people who usually get bitten by them are the people who go back and try to catch the Great White Shark for a prize.

The spot that the Great White is usually found in is called Farallon Island. There has been over 1,000 attacks in south Farallon caused by the loss of blood. The loss of blood easily attracts sharks. The Great White Shark will attack in 45-90 degrees because it is hot and there are lots of swimmers out there.

I hope you liked my facts about the Great White Shark and you learned more about them. Remember swimmers, when you are out there swimming it is more important being safe than goofing around.

Jalen Wilford
Grade 5

A Thousand Meanings

A picture…is just a painting. A picture…is just a drawing. Anyone would walk up to the *Mona Lisa* and wonder, "Why is this so famous? It's just a painting." In other words: what is art? Is a drawing just a drawing? Is a painting just a painting? Two words can answer that: absolutely not! Keep reading and find out why.

Art isn't just a painting, just a drawing, just a sketch, or just a sculpture. Art is a wonderful way to express how you were feeling at that particular time. When people look at a piece of art, they just look at it. But there was one thing wrong with what they did. They didn't see the beauty in it because they didn't observe it! People just look at a painting and think, "Oh that person must have been really good," and go to the next piece of art. If that person really observed the detail, they definitely would have seen it completely differently!

The next time you look at a piece of art here's what to do: first, just scan the piece of art, don't bother about the details, just scan it. Then, really observe it, look at the shape, look at the color, and most importantly look for the tiniest details. Art is an expression. But what do I know, I'm just a kid.

Annalise Cain
Grade 4

I Love Basketball

The first time I ever played basketball was when I was 6 at my local YMCA. It was the most fun I ever had.

The kids were my age. I remember when I first scored. My dad was so proud. The more I played the better I got. By the time I was 8 I was really good. When I was in 4th grade I joined my first real Stan Evans Boys Basketball League. We were undefeated for the whole season and we won the championship. The next year I got better. I was the starting point guard. I was so excited. We only lost 1 game to Gansevoort. We made it to the semifinals but lost to Gansevoort. The players on my team were good and they were all my friends.

Now I'm in 6th grade and I am really good. I got lucky and Richard is on my team. He's about 5'3" and possibly is the best player in the league. We have some really good guys on the team. We have learned to play as a team and it has helped us. We are undefeated and have had a couple close games. This year we had 1 close game that we won by 2 points.

Who knows what basketball has in store for me. I still have a lot to learn. I keep improving. Someday I hope to be a professional basketball player. One day I want to be the best.

Drew Hinman
Grade 6

Olympic Stars

There are many rising stars and stories emerging from the Olympics. A skater who is going for the gold is Chad Hedrick. One determined skier is Lindsey Kildow. Toby Dawson is a skier who has a very interesting past. All of the Olympians are dedicated to their races.

Chad Hedrick is a speed skater from Texas. He won the gold in the five hundred meter and hopes to get five medals in the Olympics. The day of the five hundred meter was the day that his grandmother had died. He wrote her name on the front of his skates to honor her. She was looking down on him that day he won the gold.

Lindsey Kildow fell during a practice and was rushed to the hospital. She came back and placed sixth in the downhill skiing. She was stiff because of the fall; this didn't prevent her from completing the race. Kildow is a tough competitor and will not give up.

Toby Dawson was adopted at the age of three and has loved skiing all his life. It has been tough for him to fit in with others in his childhood. His mother has always supported him. He won the bronze in the men's moguls this year. Toby's time on the mountains has really paid off.

Overall, anyone can be an Olympian. Through good and bad times these stars have come through with determination. This is what makes the Olympics such a wonderful event to watch. We can all learn from their perseverance.

Heather Piekarz
Grade 6

My Exclusive Grades Affect My Incandescing Future

My exclusive grades are absolutely important to me and to the future that lies ahead. In this informative and provocative essay, I'll explain how my grades are important to me.

First of all I'll explain why my grades are important and how they help me gain personality. My grades will help me to establish an accolade winning career. As my future will brighten, almost anything will be as easy as memorizing the ABC's. People who are smart are only selected for strategic jobs, because these people are highly skilled. If I were one of those smart employees, I would be paid in millions. Also, they are important to make me a well known personality. If I'm a well known personality, jobs would come easily to me or else I would be in a miserable situation like chasing jobs or being a cat trying to nab rats and mice.

Secondly, if I get good grades now, I would be able to pass GEPA and SAT test easily and with great scores. This will also help not to take extra tuitions.

Thirdly, I would make my parents proud by showing my small way of dedication towards the family happiness and love. This would indeed give me a great satisfaction to everyone around me and above all being truthful and hardworking in the beginning of life.

As my father says, "There is no substitute to hard work," these golden words would continue to motivate me to get good grades.

Anindya Mehta
Grade 5

Ocean City

Every year my family and I go to the amazing Ocean City, New Jersey. Every day we go to the beach for about five to six hours. We go for so long because once my brothers and I get in the water it is impossible to get us out. It's like trying to get a whale out of the ocean. I love to play football, ride the waves, and eat the delicious, "Mac and Manco Pizza," all on the beach. After this we head back to our house and get cleaned up to get ready for the boardwalk. When we go to the boardwalk my brothers, Sean and Brian, and I every year get a new hat from All Campus. This store sells all college hats. I'm a big Notre Dame fan so I always get a Notre Dame hat. Then we sometimes either hit the arcade or go on the rides. Even though I am not a ride person these are still a lot of fun. We even sometimes walk the whole boardwalk which is about four miles! I really enjoy this since it is a great time to spend with your family and it's a blast. Finally we head back down to the house which takes three times as long as it would take us to walk all that. This is because we are all so tired. Then we just relax the rest of the night and do it all over again the next day.

Steve Collins
Grade 6

Siblings

Do you have a sibling problem? If you do, you're reading the right essay! I happen to have an older sister and let me tell you, she can be a pain! Always hogging the phone or the TV, or her personal favorite, picking on me. But I have come up with some simple ways to stop that, or at least the picking on part.

First, try the old "I'll tell on you if you touch me!" If that doesn't work try to get to your room and lock the door. You aren't allowed to? Tell your mom or dad the problem and either ask them to deal with your sibling, or get a lock for your room.

A little tip: I've learned to come home and separate from my sibling. That way she has no reason to pick on me. If all else fails, just try to ignore your sibling. If your parents are out, and your sibling still won't leave you alone, after trying the advice above, try to call a parent on a cell phone.

And remember, no matter how much you say you don't like your sibling, one thing remains the same: Siblings. Can't live with them and you can't with without them. I hope my tips and advice help!

WARNING: Parents may be annoyed if you try calling them a lot.

Author's note: Only children, you may want to rethink wanting siblings.

Ashley Hall
Grade 5

My Favorite Book Series and Why

My all time favorite book series is *The Adventures of Captain Underpants*. Why I enjoy the series so much is because it is funny and most invigorating. Plus its humor is usually clean. Sometimes it may be about diapers and underpants. The clean humor is when the author spells words incorrectly. When the author spells words incorrectly, it makes the book look much funnier and sillier. For instance, on the cover page, the word 'laughs' is spelled 'laffs.' I always get a kick out of that! Then it says 'Romance', but then in parentheses it says 'just kidding!' Isn't that funny to you?? Either or, I think it's funny.

Captain Underpants should get an award for being not just the funniest book ever, but also the best book ever. I think the author and the illustrator should win awards for dedicating so much of their time on writing not just one book but a whole series of books for children to read and enjoy. The pictures and words in the books are all very descriptive, decorated, and all go with the words. Not only is The Adventures of Captain Underpants cool, it is also original. It wasn't copied or stolen from another series of books.

These books are family oriented, fun-filled, exciting, and all around great! No, all around excellent!! No, all around divine!!! Yes, that's grand! All around divine.

I hope you take my advice and read one book.

Francesco Stranieri
Grade 4

Cameroon

Ever wonder what it's like to walk into a tropical rain forest and see rare animals jumping from tree to tree? In Cameroon, that's common. The geography in Cameroon has vast tropical savannas and rain forests. A wonderful geography isn't everything, Cameroon has a very poor economy. About 48% of Cameroonians are in poverty. They might be in poverty and poor, but that does not stop the culture from believing what they want to.

The country of Cameroon is located in the Middle East. There are not many water bodies in Cameroon, although there is Lake Chad. The Cameroonians also get to enjoy a small section of the Atlantic Ocean. Mt. Cameroon is a very popular landmark in Cameroon. It stands at an amazing 13,440 feet! In Cameroon, the land is covered with vast tropical savannas and tropical rain forests. The southern part of Cameroon has an average temperature of about 65-73 degrees Fahrenheit. In the northern part, the temperature will range from about 73-90 degrees Fahrenheit.

Being a rain forest, there is a lot of deforestation, causing lumber to be a big resource. Some other resources include crude oil and petroleum products, and cocoa beans. Living in the rain forest will affect the clothes the people wear, they will also eat more tropical fruit. Rain forests will also provide a lot more woodcutting jobs, causing it to be a natural resource. Cameroon is an amazing country.

Mark Luzzi
Grade 6

Why My Grandparents Are Special to Me

I have three grandparents that are great. Their names are Nana, Granpy, and Grandma. My grandma lives in Long Island. The other two live by me.

My grandma comes and visits me almost every month. The other two we see when we want to. My Granpy is a Chiropractor and my Nana helps him. My grandma works for an allergy doctor. When my family and I need to get an adjustment, we go see Granpy. We don't really go to my grandma's house, she just comes and sees us. My grandma travels a lot to all my cousins' houses. My other grandparents do not travel a lot, but they still support me. My grandparents are the best because they support me for a lot of things. When I get older I want to be just as good of a grandparent as them. My grandma is the only grandparent that travels a lot just to see her grandchildren. The other two grandparents try to see us when we are not busy.

The three people I wrote about are my grandparents and they are the best. I am very lucky to have such good grandparents that support me and when I need them they are there for me.

Nicole Anken
Grade 6

No More Food for You

Chomp went my mouth as I was eating breakfast one morning. I was as tired as a three-toed sloth.

It was a bright, sunny day when we heard a tap at the window. We listened. We turned. Mom, Anna and I saw a fat bluebird. It was as big as an elephant! We had never seen anything this big. He started to look at the food. We all froze and blinked. He started to eat. We continued watching him. He could have been a royal bird because he was so huge. If he was, he was getting a special treat at our feeder. We were so quiet, you could hear the bird eat…and we did! We were so excited to see him. We gave him a name; it was Mr.! Mr. kept eating at our feeder and we kept watching. He didn't see us because our feeder has a 2-way mirror. We saw Mr. but he couldn't see us. He was growing by the minute. He still kept eating. All of a sudden, two more bluebirds came along and started eating. We were shocked and amazed at how such fat bluebirds could eat so much.

Mr. looked like a blue dragon. I think he was a king. I thought to myself, Mr. is so fat but as peaceful as a butterfly. Just then, he flew away. He moved swiftly, like an eagle. I hope to see him again but I won't know until spring.

Michael Borinski
Grade 4

Don't Judge a Book by Its Cover

Hi! I'm Lidia. Ever heard the saying, "Don't judge a book by its cover?" Well I'm not proud to admit that I once did exactly that. Let me tell you a story about it…

Mom had just come back from work. She brings us books from the school where she works. Usually, my goal is to read all of them, as was my goal this time. When I thought I had finished them, I began to rummage my bookshelf for more books — which I found.

To my dismay, I discovered the very book I had no interest in reading. A small brown novel entitled *Anthony Burns: the Defeat and Triumph of a Fugitive Slave*. Oh brother, I thought. This looks like the type of book an adult would read for historical research, but I was determined to accomplish my goal.

Halfway through the book, I was totally into the novel. The expeditions to rescue Anthony were intense and interesting. As I finally closed the hardcover book, a wave of amusement swept over me. And you thought you'd never judge a book by its cover, I chuckled.

A few weeks later, I discovered another novel, *Pictures of Hollis Woods*. What a boring-looking adult book I thought, until Mom said it was for kids! This time, I was ready, because you shouldn't judge a book by its cover. And oh boy, did I enjoy reading it!

Lidia Ani
Grade 4

Global Warming — The Environmental Nightmare

Global warming is the rise in average temperature that the Earth experiences when certain gases called greenhouse gases trap heat from the sun. This is a weather phenomenon that is a big danger to all of us. It increases the chance of natural disasters and according to scientists, in time it will destroy the Earth.

Gases that cause global warming form an invisible shield in the atmosphere. This shield reflects the heat that is let out of the Earth, warming it in the process. This is the same thing the glass panels of a greenhouse would do, hence, global warming is also known as the greenhouse effect.

The Earth's temperature has already risen 1 degree Fahrenheit this year and next year scientists predict it will go up 2-6 more degrees. That is horrible because the temperature increases will cause more natural disasters and water rises. The heat could become stressful and even dangerous to people in warm climates. People that live in colder climates will also face great lifestyle changes and certain plants and animals would have their habitats destroyed.

A few ways that one can stop global warming are: limiting car usage, recycling and using electricity less. Cars emit carbon-monoxide from their mufflers. Methane is emitted when trash is sent to landfills, and power plants emit greenhouse gases when someone uses electricity. All these things contribute to global warming. We can stop global warming and save the Earth!

Jafari Roberts
Grade 5

All About Me

My name is Ana Clara. I have a bird and two cats. I have a mom, a dad and a brother. My mom is from Brazil. My dad is from America. I have many relatives in Brazil. I have less relatives in America. I like a lot of things. My favorite color is blue. My favorite food is pasta with butter. I have many friends and they are all very cool. I like to play soccer, it is one of my favorite sports. My dad used to be my coach, it was cool. I also like baseball, I think it is fun. I play wiffle ball in the summer at camp. I like to watch the Red Sox games. They are my favorite team. One of my hobbies is fishing. I like fishing with my dad. It is fun. One time I caught a turtle. It was heavy and hard to pull in. I thought it would break the rod, instead it broke the line. It was a snapping turtle!

When I was little I loved going to the beach. I always made sand castles. Sometimes I would chase the waves and run away from them after. Now I like exploring the beach and climbing any big rocks. I learned to knit when I was in fourth grade. Now I am knitting all sorts of things like scarves, pillows and even dolls. I have many beanie babies but I am not collecting them. That is my life so far.

Ana Clara Robison
Grade 6

The Red Truck

My name is Ryan, I am ten years old, and have an older brother named Brett. When he turned eighteen years old he bought a 1973 GMC red truck. This is the coolest truck ever!

Brett takes me fishing, we load up the poles and worms then hit the streams. The best is when he takes me hunting with him. I have been squirrel hunting, coyote hunting, and even deer hunting with his in line gun.

Every time we go in the red truck, I feel like a shot because I am with my big brother, and nothing was getting in our way. The one day we were bored so we hopped in the truck and went to Cabela's. We came home with a ton of fishing lures.

I think my brother is the best big brother ever. I will never forget the fun we had growing up. I will always remember how I felt when he would ask me if I wanted to go with him somewhere. Are we going in the truck, I would ask? He would answer yes, and with that I was putting on my shoes, grabbing my jacket, then racing out to the truck.

I look forward to when Brett comes home from college because he will play games with me on my play station, he will teach me some wrestling moves, eat all my cereal, but before he goes back, I know I will get a ride in the red truck.

Ryan Martinez
Grade 5

Family at Heart

Family. You love them. You can't live without them. You are surrounded by them 24/7. You love them dearly! But why do they drive you so crazy?

It's pretty noticeable. You are at a time when you are starting to grow up and starting to think, feel, and have opinions of your own. And just sometimes it doesn't match with your families. But don't worry! You are not an ideal family! You have your own outlooks and so do your parents.

Ok, you ask your mom if you can go somewhere and she refuses. You stomp away, shout and bawl, and even lock yourself in your room. Your parents want the best for you. So instead of being depressed, do something by yourself. And when you are relaxed, the next day go talk to them. Describe your moods and opinions.

Your family is the best medicine! If you're feeling down in the dumps, go talk to your parents. They are there for you. All they want to do is keep you secure and see you happy. So just chat with them and you'll feel better than ever!

Even though they annoy you, imagine all the times you've slammed doors in their faces, talk backed, and violated the rules. The truth. Even though you have friends, they sometimes won't be there, but your family (even siblings) will always be there for you. Forever. No matter what.

Nyamekye Coleman
Grade 5

My Dog, Wendyl!

One of the most important things to me is my dog, Wendyl. He is a chocolate Standard Poodle. He is four years old.

He is always there when I need him. His bark sounds ferocious, but he is very lovable and wouldn't hurt a flea even if it was biting him on the back. My dog always wants to play with me and doesn't want to stop. It is fun to play with him. When I am feeling sad, he comes and puts his cold, wet nose in my face. That makes me happy.

The best thing about my dog is that he is big and I can use him as a pillow. That is why my big, fluffy dog, Wendyl is important to me.

Mackenzie Keller
Grade 4

When I Went to Florida

One day when I was told that I was going to Florida, I was so excited. I packed my bags and got ready to go. My mom, sister and I were all ready to go on our trip. Finally, when it was time to get on the plane and leave, my mom, my sister and I were ready to visit my aunt. I heard my aunt's house was very nice. When I got there it was!

When I walked into the front door, there was an indoor pool. Her house isn't huge but it is nice for just one person. I slept in a bed with my sister and my mom slept on the couch. My aunt had to work, so during the day my mom, my sister and I did our own thing. One day we went to visit my mom's good friend that moved to Florida. Her house is HUGE! Her children had a school fair that they had to go to, so my family went also. The fair was delayed because the rides would always get stuck. Instead of waiting we went out to dinner. After that we went back to my aunt's house. For the rest of the week we just went to the beach and relaxed. I had a great time in Florida!!!

Nicole Ilaria
Grade 4

The Hard Hitter Patrick Kerney

Patrick had rather modest expectations when he went off to college. He wanted to be a defensive end. He was picked in the first round of the NFL draft. Now with the Atlanta Falcons more comfortable in a 4-3 defense, Kerney leads the league with 7 sacks. He was named NFC defensive player of the month. Kerney played football weighing in at 230 pounds and managed to hold his own with all the other players on scholarship.

His parents, John and Janet Kerney, were always on the go at the family's small farm in Philadelphia. Kerney tried to bulk up in the 4-3 but felt like it took away his quickness and cutting ability. He's back playing at 271 pounds, though it takes four meals a day and plenty of snacks to maintain his weight.

Drew Clark
Grade 4

What Makes Me an Individual?

Being an individual means standing out of the crowd. When you're an individual you are one of a kind. Some of the ways I am an individual are that I have unusual pets, I love to read, and I have a sister with special needs.

Mice are odd pets, but not for me! The first time I got a mouse was at Christmas. My mouse's name was Elliot Patrick Houser. Elliot liked to run on his wheel, and I loved to watch him do it. He was so soft and petting him was fun. I remember that I used to try to make leashes for him, but I could never get it right because during his fitting he was very fidgety! Elliot was a wonderful pet.

Reading is one of the best things that ever happened to me! I'll read anything that I can get my hands on. My mom and older sister both love to read and that is probably where I got the bug from. I read books by the hundreds of pages. I love reading!

Having a sister with special needs has the good points along with the bad. One of the good things about it is that it has made me more responsible. I have to balance my time between different things like school. Also, I can spend more time with Lesley in her speech therapy. Lesley needs people to work with her twenty minutes a day, about eight times! Although Lesley will not be able to do normal things, we will try. But, Lesley is worth it all the way.

It makes me feel good when I follow my own heart. Not many people have mice, or love to read, and have siblings with special needs. That's how I'm special; that's how I stand out!

Kristen Houser
Grade 5

My Puppy Jack

My puppy Jack has many bold characteristics. Some of them are being rough, kissing everyone all of the time, and being easy to get going.

Jack can be rough in many ways. One way is when someone is playing with him he bites and scratches. He can also be rough at many times. One time is when someone arrives at my house. Another time he gets rough is when my dad plays with him. This is how my puppy Jack can get rough.

There are many reasons why Jack kisses everyone all of the time. One reason is because Jack LOVES everyone. A second reason is because Jack thinks that everyone loves him. A third reason is because Jack thinks that everyone loves his kisses.

Jack's easy to get going in many ways. One way is when someone arrives at my house. A second way is when I get out the four wheeler. A third way is when my dad and I get ready to go hunting.

This is how Jack can be rough, kissing everyone all of the time, and easy to get going.

Christen Marshall
Grade 5

The Dirt Bike Kid

I got my first dirt bike when I was three years old. I could not ride it until I was four. I started on training wheels. Then went on to just two wheels.

I rode for a few years and then had my first race. My dad told me to go out without the oil injected motorcycle riders for practice. I fell but I was determined to finish. Then it came time for the race. I was shaking like a leaf on the starting line. I ended up last off the start then gradually worked my way up to eleventh. That was my overall for that day.

Then my career was started. Ever since then I have been getting faster, winning more and more races and getting lots of trophies. Of course, I have gotten many injuries since that day.

I got second at a race where pros were watching. It was a national race and track. I should have won, but trying to go your fastest for the pros, you mess up a lot.

I was eight years old. I won 24 races straight and forty out of forty-eight. I have always ridden KTM's as my bike. I have even won a race that I lapped everyone in. I have beaten pros before too. I have gotten to race some of the fastest mini riders in the country. I have been able to meet some of the best pro riders in the last three years of racing.

I am now getting on the 125's bikes and trying to get the speed and the endurance to go pro someday.

Ryan Francis
Grade 6

There Is No One Like Me

There is no one like me. I'm one of a kind. You can't find or get another of me anywhere in the world. You can try to make a clone, but no matter what, there will always be something that will never be the same and that would be the mind, love, spirit, heart and soul. These are the things that a clone will never have. No one could ever replace me. They can walk, talk, look, and even act like me. I am me and no one else. Anybody who wants to be like somebody special is a nobody. If you are yourself then you are somebody.

Everybody is somebody special in his or her own way no matter what. Being one of a kind is a gift from above that God only gives to certain people, and I love what God has given to me because those are things that only I can have in a certain way. Many people have talents like me, but don't exactly perform them like me or think the same way as me. No one is the same, everybody is different in their own way. The only way everybody is the same is that we all have one God that created us and the world. No one is the same at all. You might look a little like a person, but not exactly. So there is no one like me!

Emma Huyo
Grade 5

Endangered Animals

One of the most endangered animals is the panda. An endangered animal is an animal that has very little population left. The main reason why pandas are endangered is because people hunt them for their hides or skin. People also hunt them down for self-defense. They think that since pandas are so big, they are vicious and the panda will attack them. In reality, pandas are usually gentle beings unless they feel threatened.

There are 2 types of pandas. One is the Giant Panda. This panda is the one that we typically think of. A huge, fuzzy, black and white, teddy bear. The other type of panda is the Red Panda. Most people don't know of this panda. The Red Panda looks like small, reddish, fox-like creature that looks like it's related to a raccoon. Even though they have their differences, both eat the same foods. Bamboo. They also both originated in China.

These creatures were here long before we were. Just because you want to make some money, does that really give you the right to kill an innocent animal? Just because you aren't sure if an animal is going to attack you, does that give you the right to kill an animal? I think not. Every living creature is great in its own way. Why would you ever want to harm one?

Kira Farrell
Grade 6

Tae Kwon Do

An important thing to me is Tae Kwon Do. I have been doing Tae Kwon Do for over four years, and I don't want to stop. I have a 1st degree Black Belt, and I may test for my second degree in six months.

Someday I would like to go to the Olympics for Martial Arts. I have watched the Olympics on TV and I know it's what I want to do.

I love sparring class. Sparring is when you kick and punch other opponents for points. The rounds are five minutes long, or last until someone gets five points. You get points by kicking your opponent in the chest or head.

Another thing we do in Tae Kwon Do is our forms. Forms are a series or set of techniques, such as crescent kicks or backfists. We need to know our forms to test for the next belt.

I have Karate on Tuesdays, Thursdays, Fridays, and Saturdays. I like how sometimes my cousin and I carpool with each other, because we both take Tae Kwon Do at the same place.

Testing is when we have a test to see if we get to pass to the next belt or mid-term. During testing, you must do your form without messing up. (MISTAKES ARE EVEN WORSE WHEN YOU ARE A HIGHER BELT).

I am glad I do Tae Kwon Do, and I encourage you to try it also!

Douglas Squires
Grade 6

Friendship

Friendship is a gift that can't be wrapped, because it is very special. Friendship is not about how you look, it is about being nice and being trustworthy to the other person. Making friends usually happens when you and the other person are interested in the same things, like movies and sports.

By being good friends, you should still be friends, even if they are sad. When that happens, you should go talk to them. Being best friends forever is showing that you should help your friend in school and with homework. You should never say to another kid that your friend did something bad or did not do something bad like rumors. Even if you try to buy friendship, you can't, because your friends like you the way you are.

If there is a new kid at your school and he or she does not have any friends, you should talk to them and try to be their friend. Friendship is very important. It could make your day a lot better, than if you're having a bad day. You can also find a friend by going on vacation. For example, if you are waiting on a long line for a ride, then you find out the kid next to you likes the same things as you. By the end of the ride you become friends. Therefore, in many different ways, friendship is a gift that can't be wrapped.

Sean Kilcullen
Grade 6

The Friend

"I forgot about this picture." I said to myself. It was the first day of kindergarten. The teacher was as mean as the devil himself. She would yell a lot especially when I bit my nails.

I had no idea how I was going to make it through the day. Until at recess. When a lady started to play with me. This wonderful lady's name was Mrs. Hallal. She was as pretty as a flower and as tall as a cornstalk. She had shiny brown hair, and shimmering brown eyes. Her voice was as calm as a mother's voice when she was happy. I liked to be around her when I was sad, because she would make me so happy. She was my only friend. She didn't have a son or daughter, but she treated her students like they were hers.

I lost my only friend during the summer of 2004 on a hot July day. She was in Arizona on vacation. On the way to the airport when she passed away. No one knew how bad her heart problems were until then. When my dad told me I didn't want to listen. But after a while when she wasn't around I got the point that she was gone. I went to her funeral. It was really emotional seeing her lay there.

I'll never forget her sweet voice and the way she looked at me, and the fact that she was my best friend.

Sarah Monte
Grade 6

Allen Iverson "The Staying Dog"

Allen Iverson is a living legend who is one phenomenal player for the Philadelphia 76er's. Some people think that he is one of the most talented players on the NBA court, winning games for the 76er's every season.

One time when the 76er's were playing against the Bucks, they were down by ten points with just 55.2 seconds left on the clock. Iverson was fouled by another player, and earned the right to shoot three foul shots. Amazingly, he made all three foul shots, and then went on to score two three point baskets with just 5.6 seconds on the clock. The Philadelphia 76er's were still down by one point.

The crowd was cheering wildly, and Iverson then managed to steal the ball and dribble down the court, firing the ball into the basket, scoring another two points for the 76er's! Iverson helped win the game for his team by just one point before the clock ran out!

Allen Iverson is an athlete who doesn't cave under pressure. No matter how stressful the game may be, he never gives up or adopts a negative attitude. Since this victory against the Bucks, Iverson has been nicknamed "The Staying Dog." The nickname suits him because he certainly has a tremendous amount of "staying power" on and off the court, and he moves down the court with the speed and agility of a dog on the prowl…for the victory!

C.J. Puzo
Grade 6

Drugs

Living above the influence is how people thrive and learn. So when it comes to drugs, living above the influence of illegal drugs is how the world becomes a better place, one person at a time.

For many people, drugs are a hard thing to talk about. But it's something everyone needs to hear because if they don't, that one decision to do drugs will enable them to make other decisions. Drugs are chemicals that can be powerful and addictive, they also damage your heart, lungs, and other vital organs. There are ways you can tell if a person is taking drugs; they tend to lose interest in school, and have a hard time concentrating. People taking drugs often ask to be alone, get in fights and become moody, negative, cranky, and worried. Drugs also affect your appearance; you may lose or gain weight, frequently cough, get a runny noise, and puffy eyes. All of those things would affect me very much, so being drug free is important.

I think it is clear that drugs can be bad, and affect a person's life. So when a child is well informed, the need to do drugs is diminished. When a person has a problem sometimes they think drugs are the answer. Then, before they know it, they are addicted, and that's when the problem really starts. I want to live life to the fullest, with no regrets so I chose to live above the influence.

Madeline Wigon
Grade 6

Life Changes Even When You're Young

It was another school year, I was entering the fourth grade. The year was going just fine, but there were rumors that the school was going to close. I remembered when I was in second grade the same rumors had occurred. Nothing happened then so I figured nothing was going to change. Rumors — that is all they were.

Was I ever wrong. The news broke after the new year and there was no turning back. There would be no more school next year. Now, what was I going to do, where would I go, what about all of my friends? I was so upset.

The rest of the school year was tough. It was the last of everything that we would ever do together in the same school. All the parents were very upset and put up signs and had rallies to save the school. No luck, it was going to close.

The last day of school had come and we had a school mass and let balloons go in the sky. It was so sad and memorable.

The next school year I entered fifth grade. I was nervous. Who would be there and how would the teachers be? Most of my friends were there and the teachers were all very nice.

I'm at my new school again and I love it! I miss my old school, but it was for the best. Change is okay and it happens to everyone, even us young kids.

Ali Quinn
Grade 6

The Scaring of a Lifetime

Last Halloween, I was trick-or-treating, and then I saw a huge, white, haunted house. Kyle (my friend) and I went in. It was scary. We heard music, and then we went in the next room and we saw a skeleton dancing! In the hallway there was a grim reaper who followed us with a lantern. When we turned around, he was gone.

There were so many rooms! In one room was a smoke machine. There were so many skeletons hanging around everywhere. In all the windows were flashing lights. We saw a real black cat walking in our path. Fountains of fake blood appeared around every corner. There were many spider webs, home to fake spiders.

We were scared because we worried that people could jump out from behind walls. Kyle and I could each feel our hearts beating so fast that it felt as though our hearts were going to pop out of our chests! I didn't know if people were following us or not. I thought I was going to die. Kyle was about to pass out, so was I. Then a real spider dangled in front of my face. There was a step I didn't notice, and I fell, but I was okay. At the end we were greeted by a man with a fake beard and wearing a cloak. He said "take one." He had at least one hundred packs of candy lying on a table!

Ryan Facchine
Grade 5

The Fab Four

John, Paul, George, Ringo. Names that will be remembered forever. The Beatles, one of the greatest bands ever, that will be remembered forever.

Peace, love, joy. That is what the Beatles sang about. Songs like "All You Need Is Love," "Here Comes the Sun," and "Come Together" are just a few. John sang songs like "Give Peace a Chance."

Their songs helped thousands of people. If the Beatles were never a band, those people would have to find a different output for their problems: violence.

Their rise to fame was astounding, with five movies and millions of dollars. They had Beatles hairspray and Beatles tablecloths; anything they could put the Beatles faces on. An era called Beatle mania. During concerts, the Beatles were stressed. John said, "They are cheering so loud you can't hear the music."

As you can see, the Beatles were one of the greatest bands ever. Paul and Ringo are still alive. The Beatles will always be remembered for their change for the world, and the millions they helped.

Matt Mazzone
Grade 5

Pluto

Have you ever thought about traveling to the planet Pluto? There are a lot of interesting facts about Pluto. Did you know that Pluto does not look like any other planet? If you read my essay you will learn a lot about Pluto.

Pluto has one moon named Charon. Charon and Pluto could fit into the borders of the United States of America. Charon is named for the God who ferried the dead across the River Acheron into the underworld. Pluto's name in Greek means Hades. Hades was the God of the underworld.

Charon and Pluto keep the same face towards each other at all times. This means that imaginary aliens living on one side of Charon would never see Pluto, and imaginary aliens living on the opposite side of Pluto would never see Charon.

Through a telescope on Earth, Charon and Pluto look like they are the same object. However, in 1978 Jim Christy discovered that what we used to think was one object was really two. Beyond Pluto lies a huge ring of frozen rocks known as the Kuiper Belt. Astronomers think a few of these rocks might be bigger than Pluto.

Pluto is the ninth planet from the Sun. Inside Pluto is a rock, icy core. Pluto is so far away that no satellites have ever been sent there. All scientists can do is guess what Pluto looks like. The tip of Pluto is nitrogen ice.

I really enjoyed learning about the planet Pluto. Maybe someday I can visit Pluto!!

Julia Kelly
Grade 4

Penguins

Penguins have been around 50 to 60 million years. They have clues by fossils. There are so many names of the bird; for example, the Chinstrap is named for its special marking, and the Rockhoppers name is called that because of its fancy footwork. There are so many different species of penguins; there are 17. The Emperor is the second largest of all, the Fairy Penguin is the smallest, the Macaroni for its unique air style, and the Yellow-eyed is called that because of its yellow eye.

Some penguins live only under the Equator and some live in South America, Africa, Australia, and New Zealand. Most birds have thin bones, but penguins have heavy and thick bodies to keep them warm. The Rockhoppers will jump up to 70 feet. To move faster on ice the penguins have to go on their bellies. The food that penguins eat are fish and grill; they can chew on the food because they have a sharp bill with hooks that fit together.

To feed the young, they have crops, a special pouch in their trout, and in that crop there is undigested food. The penguins spread out their arms to show they like each other. The male does things to get a mate; for example, they call and they walk as a fancy man. They have many predators that eat them or their baby — sea eagles, blue-tongue lizards, sheathbills, and the leopard seal. People do many things to protect penguins.

Joann Estrella
Grade 5

The Humuhumunukunukuapua'a; Hawaii's State Fish

The Humuhumunukunukuapua'a is Hawaii's state fish. This fish's nickname is "Tiger Fish" because of its sharp spiked dorsal fin. Although there is no official meaning of Humuhumunukunukuapua'a, some people say it means, "fish with a snout like a pig." Others say it means, "fish that comes out of water and sounds like a pig." When it is brought out of water it puffs up and that makes it snort. It can also wedge itself between rocks or coral. It grows to be eight to nine inches in length. The tiger fish is also found in Polynesia, Australia, Melanesia, the Philippines, and all over the Indian Ocean.

The tiger fish has a diamond-shaped body, a dark strip across its belly, and pale blue fins. This bizarre looking fish has almost clear looking fins and a tiny eye with an orange ring around it. Its lips stick out as if it were sucking in its cheeks. At the end of its tail there is an orange ring. A thick black line separates the bright yellow on its body. Its face is white except for the blue ring around its lips. The tiger fish eats seaweed and worms. The female takes care of the fertilized eggs and the nest until the eggs hatch and swim away.

This interesting fish is fascinating, fun to watch, and a mouthful to pronounce.

Audrey Re
Grade 5

Soccer Champs!!!

Usually I give my mom a difficult time waking up in the morning, but this day was different. I was the first one awake. Everyone else was still in bed not aware of my excitement. Soon, I started to kick the soccer ball around, mom woke, wondering what all the racket was all about. I reminded her that today was the soccer tournament. I began by practicing my kicks, then blocks with my brother. Then with my uniform on, water bottle ready, we headed for the field.

The coach gave us last minute instructions before the beginning whistle. When the referee blew the whistle we took our positions on the field. My job was defense, to defend the ball from getting into the goal. The first two quarters went by quickly, with both teams scoring two goals. The third quarter began with a collision between two players but they were all right. In the next play I did exactly what I was supposed to do and the opponents did not score a goal because I blocked the shot. Therefore, no points were scored.

The fourth and last quarter was the best. I defended the ball up field and scored. After another goal from one of my teammates, we defended the ball to the best of our ability. No more goals were scored and the Stoners were names winners of the County Cup Tournament. With our medals around our necks we celebrated. The day ended with as much, if not more excitement as it began.

Bradley McKitish
Grade 6

My Family

Imagine a little boy sitting on his bed in an empty house wondering what to do with his life. That would be me if I didn't have my family. My family is important to me. My mom and dad love me and care for me. My siblings care about me. My family is everything to me.

My mom loves me. She always wants to hear my high and low points of the day. She makes sure I get better when I'm sick. She helps me keep my grades up. My mother treats me very kindly.

My dad cares for me. He always awards me for my hard work. He makes sure I learn from my mistakes. If someone was going to hurt me, he wouldn't hesitate to take the hit. My father loves me.

My siblings care about me. My brother stands up for me. My sister supports me. She always tells me what a great job I'm doing. My siblings keep me entertained. My siblings are there for me.

My family means everything to me. My mom and dad love me a lot, and my siblings are there for me. Without my family, I'd be incomplete.

Ezequiel Dávila
Grade 6

My Hero

My mom is my hero. She taught me everything I am capable of now. She instructed me all the important things such as, how to feel, speak, love, and care for other people. I wouldn't be happy if my mom wasn't with me.

To illustrate, her dad died during her final test of her last year of elementary school. Although she was in a grief, she got good grades because she studied very well all year long. This experience taught me to be prepared for any surprises and emergencies. After her dad passed away, they had limited money. My mom told me that she learned the value of the money. Therefore, I try not to spend money on unnecessary things.

When my mom was in junior high, she learned how to type. She wanted to learn a skill to find a job to support her family. My hero was always top student until she graduated from college with a bachelor degree in business. My mom could not find a job matching her degree. Thus, she took advantage of her skill and worked as a typist. Just as she was a top student; I am working hard to be a top student too.

My mom still helps me with her life experience. The best thing that I like about my mom is that she helps people when they have problems. Namely, she donated money for hurricane Katrina. I always donate money out of my allowance to poor people.

Nisma Zakria
Grade 5

Making a Commitment

I play basketball, baseball and football. I have also joined the Natural Helpers in school. Once you join a team you should go to all the practices, games and meetings. This helps you to know what plays the team is running or activities the group has coming up. It isn't fair to the other people that are always going to practice and meetings, if a person that misses them doesn't know what is going on and ruins the plans.

Sometimes you miss things that you really want to do, because you made a commitment to the team or group. I have missed parties and given up tickets to see Giants football games because I am committed to my team. It's hard to make the decision to miss something you really want to do, but I think I would feel bad if I didn't go and my team lost because of me.

Making a commitment means trying your hardest and not fooling around during practices or meetings. It makes the people that are trying hard upset when other people aren't working as hard. When everyone makes a commitment to work hard the team or group has a better chance to succeed.

Before you make the decision to join the team, you should check to see if you have the time and if you want to work hard. The only reason you should miss practice is if you have schoolwork or if you aren't getting good grades.

Michael Foss
Grade 6

Amerigo Vespucci

Amerigo Vespucci was an Italian explorer. He was born in Florence, Italy in March 1451. He died in 1512 of Malaria. As a little boy he studied the stars. He was also known as Americus Vespucci. He had three brothers.

During Amerigo's voyages he discovered many things. One thing he found was North and South America. North and South America were named after him. He also found the mouth of the Amazon River. He tried to find a quicker route to Asia by going west. It took him 24 days to get to South America. He went south and found Brazil's coast.

Amerigo Vespucci made many voyages. He sailed for Spain in 1499. When he sailed for Spain he tried to find the New World. Amerigo also sailed for Portugal in 1499. When he sailed for Portugal he landed at the eastern tip of Brazil. On one of his voyages he kidnapped 500 Native Americans. He took many voyages to the New World which is North America. His first instructions were from his uncle, Giorgeo Antonio.

Amerigo Vespucci took many voyages and found many things. If it weren't for him North and South American probably wouldn't be named America. I think that Amerigo is very important in history.

Lauren Daley
Grade 5

The Titanic

April 10, 1912. The seas were smooth and calm as the R.M.S. (Royal Mail Steamer) Titanic began its maiden voyage.

Many of the world's most famous millionaires were traveling on this ship. Many would not live to see the end of the voyage. John Jacob Astor was the richest man on board the ship. He was traveling in 1st class. You may have heard of the "Unsinkable Molly Brown." Her story is one of the most famous on the subject of the Titanic. She was also traveling 1st class. The Titanic was the most luxurious ship ever built. Its main features included a gymnasium, a Turkish bath, a first-class dining saloon, and a saltwater swimming pool. Its most amazing feature was a grand staircase that ran from A deck all the way down to G deck.

Even 2nd and 3rd class staterooms were bigger and had more facilities than many would have at home. The Titanic itself was an extremely large ship — she ran 882 1/2 feet in length and was over 45,000 tons. Besides carrying over 2,200 people and over a million supplies, the Titanic also carried mail.

On April 14, watcher Fredrick Fleet spotted an iceberg ahead. "Iceberg right ahead!" He cried, but it was too late. The iceberg scraped the side of the ship, and water rushed in. The Titanic was doomed. As the life boats escaped, the ship broke in half and the bow sank. The stern bobbled cork-like and sank after it. The "unsinkable" Titanic had sunk.

Samoree Jean-Marie
Grade 5

The Perfect Present

My birthday was in December and I got the best present ever. I received a puppy! I couldn't believe it!

My puppy is so cute. It's a girl and she's a puggle. A puggle is a mix between a pug and a beagle. She is a tan color with black on the tip of her tail. She is very adorable.

After a while I decided to name her Roxy. It was either Roxy or Sandy; I thought Roxy had more Pizzazz to it. I'm very happy with the name that I chose.

Roxy has a great personality. She is very energetic and playful, but at the end of the day when you are tired and you lay down, she lays down right next to you. Her personality is one of her great qualities.

My puppy is so popular. When my friends come over to my house all they want to do is play with Roxy. Everyone loves Roxy!

Another thing Roxy does is bite everything. She has bitten everything from fingers, to candles, to backpacks. But Roxy's favorite is my stuffed animals. In my room I have a big pile of them. Roxy pulls the stuffed animals out one by one. It's not much fun for me because I have to clean it up, but Roxy seems to enjoy it!

I love Roxy so much and I wouldn't change her for the world. Roxy is not just the best present, she's the perfect present!

Lisa Swenson
Grade 5

My Favorite Sport Is Football

My favorite sport is football. I like the sport because you can tackle people and then they start crying and whining. At one football game in Norwich, my friends and I tackled a kid and broke his leg. Then an ambulance came, then paramedics came out of the truck and laid him on the gurney. Then they took him away in the ambulance. Although we lost the game, it was still fun. The one reason we lost the game is because they were the best team in the league.

The next game was next weekend and my coach said to come off of the field. I said ok. Then the ref said there weren't enough men on the field so he told me to go back out on the field in right center. Then he said, "Corey, go on the left side of the field." So I went there and the runningback came there. Then he started running backwards. Then I went to tackle him. I was running with him in the air and I dropped him in the end zone. That was really cool.

The way I got into football is every Thanksgiving my family would watch football and I thought it was stupid. Then I started to watch it and I really liked it so I signed up. I have liked it ever since then.

Corey Hanson
Grade 6

Teen Obesity and Health Concerns

As more fast food restaurants are being created, more teens stop moving and the world freezes. Since 1970, fast food restaurants have been increasing their population and teens become inactive because eating becomes their main habit. Every day those couch potatoes eat junk that slows their metabolism and energy. Now, most high school students don't take physical education. On television, commercials appear more often which lets kids notice fast food.

Inch by inch, we can achieve. Someone could open a group. Examples are playing sports or running marathons. Kids and preteens can join a YMCA or sports club to avoid problems later. Other kids can change their diets and start eating a balanced meal. They can avoid soda and high sugar foods and instead, they can have fruits and vegetables dipped in their favorite sauce. Both choices are equally tasty, but one is healthier. Every kid should exercise at least one hour each week. Overweight people should exercise even more. They can go to fast food restaurants limitedly and have television systems that block all commercials during a show.

Usually teens get obese and overweight. This is because when kids turn into teens, they get lazier. Afterwards, they get into a habit of eating whatever and whenever. This turns them into obese and overweight children. This affects the United States the most, but countries like China are developing more fast food restaurants and eventually, the citizens are going to become corpulent. They would have to develop a system to decrease their weight.

Erin Yang
Grade 6

Walt Disney World

Orlando is a very cosmopolitan area in the state of Florida. Orlando has a lot of nightlife restaurants and cafés. But, everyone really goes to Walt Disney World. Disney World has a lot of cool parks, great food, and huge hotels.

When I go to Walt Disney World, I visit all of the parks. The parks are Magic Kingdom, EPCOT, M.G.M., and Animal Kingdom. All of these parks have great restaurants. They all have a lot of rides and firework spectaculars.

Disney World has a lot of great restaurants at each park. At the Magic Kingdom, you can dine at the Crystal Palace. At EPCOT, you can dine at The Land. At M.G.M you can dine at 50's Prime Time Café and at Animal Kingdom, you can dine at the Rainforest Café.

Every year when my family and I go to Walt Disney World we stay at The Yacht Club. There is a huge pool and water slide. There is an old ice cream parlor called Beaches and Cream.

I chose this nonfiction topic because I feel that every kid should get to go to Walt Disney World at least twice. Twice because there is so much to do and it takes more than one trip to experience all of the magic.

David Heim
Grade 6

Favorite Frog

My essay is about Poison Arrow Dart frog. Do you know why this Frog is endangered? Also how poisonous it is? And do you know how big it is?

The Poison Arrow Dart Frog is endangered. Do you know why? People used the poison for arrows and other weapons. A law was cast in 1991 so humans couldn't kill them for their poison. The Poison Arrow Dart frogs are in South America.

The Poison Darted Arrow Frog is highly poisonous, it can kill 3 dogs and 2 humans per day. If a predator comes like a snake they try to eat the frog. Once the snake tries to eat it, it releases a toxic gas which comes out of its glands. Its skin is also poisonous. It's the most poisonous frog in the world. Did you know if you drink the poison you will live. If you touch the skin you will get terribly sick and die.

The Poison Arrow Dart frog is unbelievably small, it can sit on a penny. The frog's size helps it hide from predators. The highly poisonous frog is small, but it can take on 5 of its same type. (Yes, frogs do fight over moist places).

The Poison Arrow Dart frog is a very interesting amphibian. There are many different types of Poison Arrow Dart frogs. They are poisonous, endangered, and very small but they have a lot of colors too. They are my favorite frog. They are what made me realize that frogs are awesome!

Kaly Jones
Grade 6

Things I Have Learned in My Life About People

When I was in the third grade I would go to visit Grandmother Mella in the Dominican Republic and I'd stay the whole summer with her.

One day Grandmother Mella asked me to go to the store. She said, *"Angie, tell the man to give you one-third cup of sugar, and three and one-half dozen eggs."*

I said, "Yes!" I went to the store and the man took a pail and measured out one-third cup of brown sugar from a big bag. He put that sugar in a pail then put it in a little bag. Then, he counted out the eggs and put them on a tray. He had measured out exactly what my grandmother wanted. I thought that was strange.

You might think I am telling stories but they are true. At another time it was a holiday. It was like the Fourth of July. the big party started in the evening and lasted until the next day. Everybody dressed up in a costume and made a parade. The parade looked like the kind we have in America on the Fourth of July.

So, in my life I have learned that different people celebrate things in similar ways when they are happy. I have learned that people live differently and do things different. I know now that all people are unique and wonderful.

Angie Cotto
Grade 5

More Recess for the Sixth Grade Students

The sixth grade students and I are having some issues with the time we have at recess. We think we are not getting enough recess. I have many reasons why we should have more recess. A poll also said that many other sixth graders share my opinions.

I think we should have more recess because we would be able to get all our energy out. If we got all our energy out we would be able to have an easier time paying attention because we wouldn't have enough energy to play around inside. We would also have enough time to chat with our friends if we wanted to tell them something.

Another reason is getting fresh air. The sixth graders need more fresh air since they are always working hard and doggedly. It is also very hard to keep our minds straight without some relaxing time. Personally I think it feels nice and refreshing to get outside and run around for a little. I always feel calm and tired after recess. School comes so easy to me after recess.

I really hope you're on my side with the sixth grade. I would love it if we could have some more recess. Don't forget about all the great reasons for the hardworking sixth grade to have more recess.

Chris Boroch
Grade 6

My Skiing Memory

My memorable moment in my 6th grade ski trip. We went right before I changed schools. It was the first time I went skiing with people from my school. It took four hours to get there. When we got to the hotel, we unpacked our stuff and ate dinner. Then, we had a dance party. After dancing, we went upstairs and played in the halls. Lock down was at 12:30 A.M. They locked and taped the doors. We weren't allowed to talk on the phone. We had to wake up at 7:00 A.M. and eat breakfast at 7:30 A.M.

The next day, we ate; then as fast as we could, we got our ski clothes on. It took about fifteen minutes to get to the mountains. We all had to take lessons, even if we knew how to ski. I ended up doing well. My friend smashed into another girl, and her asthma started acting up. She was pulled away and had to go back to the hotel. Our friend saw what happened and went with her.

We finished skiing and went back to the hotel. When we got there, we all went to the pool. After, we had dinner and another dance. This time, lock down was at 11:30 P.M. because everyone stayed up too late. We were all tired from skiing. They next day, we went tubing; then, we packed up. This was the best way to say good-bye to all my friends. I'm really thankful for my trip.

Jessica Garry
Grade 6

The Enchanting World of the Monarch

Monarchs are one of the most incredible and beautiful kinds of butterfly. The monarch starts as a tiny egg and dies as a beautiful orange butterfly. The changes are remarkable from beginning to end.

The caterpillar hatches from a tiny egg and eats its shell for protein. Then this small caterpillar goes and eats up to 30 big milkweed leaves. In the process, it sheds four times growing big and fat. It finds a good place to make its chrysalis and makes what's called a button onto whatever object or plant it wants to hold onto once it is in its chrysalis. The caterpillar uses its spinneret to make a chrysalis around itself.

The caterpillar turns into a green soup inside the chrysalis. The butterfly forms out of this. The chrysalis turns clear when the butterfly is about to hatch. If you look at it at this stage, you can see the wings through the clear chrysalis. The newly formed butterfly pushes itself out of its chrysalis and pumps its wings to get fluid pumping through its veins, and to dry them.

Before winter the butterfly will journey all the way to Mexico where it will stay for the winter. On the way back, the butterfly will stop and lay its eggs. After laying them, it will die. Amazingly the babies will continue the migration the parents started.

The life cycle of the monarch butterfly is full of wonderful miracles. The smallest things in life are usually the most enchanting.

Amy Garland
Grade 5

What Makes Me an Individual

Being an individual means being different. It means you are special and you are not like everyone else. Three ways I'm an individual are that I have a very big family, I am funny, and I like to cook.

I have a big family. I think I have 26 cousins on one side and 22 on the other side. Whenever we have a family reunion or just a party, we play a game of dodge ball! It's really brutal, and at least one person gets hurt by the end of the game.

I am really funny sometimes. My goal at school is to make at least one person laugh a day. Morgan doesn't count. She's too easy. Once in the library, I told her the name of a book and she started cracking up.

I like to cook, it's one of my favorite hobbies. I can and like to cook many things, especially coconut pound cake. The reason I like to make it is because it's challenging. I have to separate six egg yolks from the egg whites. I like making it, but I really don't like eating it.

All and all I think I'm a pretty good individual. Maybe these qualities will help me in the future. I hope so. I enjoy these qualities.

Matt Flynn
Grade 5

Italy

For my essay I did Italy. Italy's capital is Rome. Rome is the largest city of in Italy. Vatican City is the world center of the Roman Catholic Church. The Vatican City lies completely within Rome.

The land of Italy is a peninsula that extends into the Mediterranean Sea from southern Europe. Rome has about 2,816,000 people. The longest river is 405 miles. The mainland coastline stretches for over 1,400 miles. Italy has been one of the world's most popular tourist destinations for years.

8 million people come to see the city of Venice each year, and its own population is 80,000. The evening Promade is an important social occasion in small villages and large cities alike. The name Italy comes from the Italic tribes who lived in the south in ancient times.

The Roman Empire in Italy stretched from Scotland to Egypt, from the Atlantic Ocean. Italy has three major physical regions, the Alps, the Po Valley, and the Apennines. The Alps are in the North.

Mont. Blanc, western Europe's highest peak, lies partly in Italy. The Po Valley, at the base of the Alps, is a relatively flat, triangular plain. It extends from the vicinity of Turin to the head of the Adriatic where the plain has a maximum width of about 150 miles. That is some facts I learned about Italy.

Alana Vecchiarello
Grade 5

My Family's Important to Me

I don't know what I'd do without my family, and I don't plan to know. My family is important to me. We care for each other and are there for each other. We also do things together. In conclusion, that's why my family is important to me.

My family and I care for each other. I help my mom with her typing. When she doesn't know where a key is, I show her where it is. In return she helps me with my homework. She takes me through the steps in math. I also help her with groceries. We really care for each other.

We care for each other. I'm there for my little brother when he is sick. He cheers me up when I'm mad. If he is hurt, I'm there to help him. In conclusion, my family will always be there for me.

Finally, my family and I do things together. We go to parties, like my birthday party. We go on family trips. Also we go to picnics. We go everywhere together.

My family is important to me. I don't know what I'd do without them. We do things together. We care for each other. We are also there for each other. My family is the world to me.

Norman Hamilton
Grade 6

Being Drug-Free

As you grow up, peer pressure starts. Sometimes your peers might pressure you to do drugs. You have to make healthy decisions to be drug-free. These decisions include not giving in to peer pressure, walking away, or giving the cold shoulder. Another way to be drug-free is to avoid places where people use drugs. These are some ways to make healthy decisions.

Alcohol, tobacco and marijuana are very harmful to the body. Marijuana is addictive. Loss of concentration and short-term memory loss are some effects of smoking marijuana. This is probably why it is illegal in the United States.

Alcohol is found in beer, wine and liquor. It is illegal for anyone under the age of twenty-one. It also slows down the brain and the body. It can damage every organ in the body.

Lastly is tobacco. Tobacco is found in cigarettes. Smoking cigarettes causes breathing problems and heart disease. Although it is not illegal in the United States, I think it should be. People die every year from lung cancer or heart disease because they have smoked. In my opinion, it's just like paying for your lungs to be damaged; or like buying your own death. The reasons above tell how dangerous and harmful tobacco, alcohol and marijuana can be.

Some people might think that drugs seem exciting and cool. Others might think it makes you look tough. They are wrong. Drugs are very harmful to your body. No matter what, you should always say no to drugs.

Bianca Ignacio
Grade 6

Football

The reasons you should play football are to keep in good physical shape, make friends, and have fun. I played football since I was seven, and now I'm twelve. Playing football for five years has kept me in good health, provided me with friends, and has been very enjoyable.

Football keeps you in very good shape. You have to practice for two hours or more. And in practice you run, do pushups, sit ups, and scrimmage your own team while wearing heavy equipment. It makes you stronger, faster, healthier, and it raises your stamina. You can work harder and longer each week.

It lets you meet new friends, or sometimes even old friends. It teaches you how to share because you give away the ball to teammates. Being a member of a football team teaches you to get along with your teammates. Sometimes if you get a good play, more people will like you.

Playing football is a lot of fun. Some fun things are catching, running, and throwing. Other things are even more fun like playing in the mud or making tackles.

Keeping in good shape, making friends, and having fun are just some of the benefits of playing football.

Patrick Morgan
Grade 6

Search for a True NASCAR Hero: Mark Martin

When I was young my father bought me a Mark Martin Lego car set. Immediately Mark became my favorite driver. Since then I've been buying Mark Martin memorabilia. I watch every race that he is in. Two summers ago I went to the Pocono Raceway. It was the first time I ever saw his car close up. As the car came around the third turn and passed in front of me, I was amazed at how fast and loud it was.

The next year I again went back to watch another round of qualifying. My grandma bought me pit passes only to find out that I was too young to go in the pits. We went to the Mark Martin souvenir trailer and bought more items for my collection.

My mom picked me up from school early to go to Tom Hesser Ford to see Mark who was supposed to be there to sign autographs. When we got there we were disappointed to find out that he could not be there because he had to qualify for a race. I met his car owner Jack Roush who signed a die cast car and a picture for me. I also met Benny Parsons, Mr. and Mrs. Matiolli who own the Pocono Raceway.

I thought the 2005 season was Mark's last season. Mark said that after he won the all-star event, he would come back for another season if someone would offer him a ride. After winning the Kansas race he announced he would return in the number 6 car.

2006 may end up being my lucky year. I may finally get a chance to meet my true NASCAR hero, Mark Martin!

Bryan Russo
Grade 5

Glistening Snowflakes

My perfect snow day would start when I fall asleep in my cozy bed dreaming of snowflakes falling from the dark gray sky. As the snow adds a layer of pure white glistening snow to the city's streets and sidewalks, I am lying in bed on a Sunday night before school. I wake-up. I look out the window hoping for snow. The window is frosted over by a couple of layers of ice. I lie back into bed and think to myself, well, it's just a little flurry. At 7:00 A.M, I wake-up. It has snowed! My parents turn on the news. After the weather lady tells us about the commute to work and how much the streets are covered, then come the school closings. The newscasters storm down the lists of schools; my school is closed. I run back into my cozy warm bed, put my head on my soft cushiony pillow, and shut my eyes. I dream of what I am going to do on this wonderful day of pure, white, glistening snow. I go downstairs and eat breakfast. I get dressed and bundle up. I run out the door and slip on ice. Minor setback. I then pick up a patch of snow and mold it into a snowball. My sister runs outside, slips once, and I throw a snowball at her. She throws one right back. I am going to have a great day. It will be filled with glistening snow and fun.

Courtney Flank
Grade 6

Dinner with Jesus

I would pick to go to dinner with Jesus. Jesus was born on December 25th. His mother was Mary, His father was God, and His stepfather was Joseph. Jesus never sinned in His life. God sent an angel to Mary at the age of thirteen. Jesus had twelve disciples. Jesus was 33 when He was crucified. He resurrected three days later. What was Jesus' last name? Nobody knows what Jesus' last name was. Most think that Jesus' last name is Christ, but it is not. The truth is that Jesus never revealed His last name to us. When He died He said, "Christ has died, Christ has risen, Christ will come again." When He comes again He will reveal His last name.

I would pick to go to dinner with Jesus. I would pick Him because He would tell me and teach me a lot. He would tell me all about Heaven, God, and lots of other mysteries about the world. Jesus would teach me many life lessons. He could teach me so many things. Some of the many things He could teach me would be: how to love everyone, to be a better person, and just to love God. Jesus would be a great person to go to dinner with. When I die I look forward to my dinner with Jesus.

Lauren Spence
Grade 6

The Person I Look Up To

The person I look up to the most is my grandmother. She is by far the nicest person I have ever met. No matter what you do or say, she will still love you. I hope I can be half as nice a person as she is.

Whenever I go over to my grandmother's house, I am a king. I barely have to lift a finger when I'm over there. She cooks food for me when I'm hungry and plays with me when I'm bored. I have so much fun over there that I never want to leave!

My grandmother has never and probably never will think anything bad about anybody. She is friends with everyone she meets, and everyone who knows her loves her. If somebody does something against me I would get mad, but she is not like that at all. She forgives and forgets in a second, which is very difficult to do for many of us. She is truly something to be admired.

I have known my grandmother all my life and all that I know of her is good. She has had a hard life yet she always looks on the bright side. My life has been great, I get everything I want and I still complain. I look up to my grandmother because she is just about perfect to me. She is loving, caring and nice. I want to be just like her in so many ways. If everyone could be just like her the world would be a much better and nicer place. That is why I look up to her so much. She is a great person and a great grandmother to me.

Thomas Murphy
Grade 6

The Ideal Preschool

If I would open my own preschool, I would want to make it an interesting place for kids to come and play. I would divide the classroom into four sections.

In one section would be a painting area. I would display many different colors and paintbrushes, and of course, smocks so you don't get dirty.

Another section would be called, "Storytime." It would have a little carpet to sit on and different kinds of books. It would be comfortable because you wouldn't have to sit on the floor and you get to read the books you want.

There would be a learning section. There you learn the ABCs and I would have a poster on the wall so if you forgot the ABCs, you could look at it. In this section would also be headphones and tape recorders with different tapes. That can help you learn as you hear different things from the tape.

The last section would be the play area. It would have different games, puzzles, and blocks. There would be a closet filled with many supplies like glitter, glue, and stuff like that. That means they make a lot of projects. They would also have a computer.

This preschool would be the best place for a kid to spend a year!

Joyce Greenstein
Grade 6

Dogs

Dogs are very nice pets. There are about 250 different breeds of dog. There are 2 different kinds of dog; mutts and purebred. Mutts are a mix between 2 or more purebred dogs. Some examples of purebreds are Pomeranians, Bichon Frises and Cocker Spaniels. Some examples of mutts are Puggles, Cockapoos and Labradoodles.

Dogs come in different shapes and sizes. The smallest dog in the world is the Chihuahua. Chihuahuas can weigh from 4-6 pounds. Chihuahuas came from Mexico. The largest dog in the world is the Wolfhound. Wolfhounds can weigh up to 200 pounds! Wolfhounds came from Ireland.

The most popular breed of dog in the USA is the Golden Retriever. Golden Retrievers came from the United Kingdom. Golden Retrievers are very gentle and nice. Golden Retrievers are called Golden Retrievers because they were bred to retrieve animals and other things. Golden Retrievers can sometimes be very stubborn. All dogs originated from the wolf.

My dog's name is Spike. He is a Bichon Frise. Spike is very cute and nice to everyone. Spike loves being around people. Once when my family and I had to go somewhere for 2 days Spike wouldn't eat or drink anything until we came back. This proves how much dogs love us and care about us.

When I grow up I want to be a vet. I want to be a vet because I love all animals. My favorites are dogs and small animals. I love dogs and dogs will be my passion forever.

Mara Zafrina
Grade 5

What a Great Veteran

My mom is a veteran she was in the US Navy. My mom started when she was 19 years old, my mom was in the Navy for 4 years. When my mom started she went to Boot Camp in Orlando, Florida. When she went it was her first flight on an airplane. She was stationed in Fort Meade, Maryland at Naval Security. My mom dealt with lots of discipline. She learned how to lay out and write a magazine she also learned how to develop pictures. My mom had to learn how to make military knots just in case of emergencies. My mom had several rates (jobs). Those jobs were working in a Personal Office and maintaining entitled officers vacations. My mom took a class in Public Relations to become a journalist so she can write stories, take pictures, and attend ceremonies. My mom was working with really great people.

My mother enjoyed the Navy because she learned a lot. She learned all types of skills that have helped her in present occupations. Dealing with difficult situations, talking with all types of people and taking orders. She also met different people from different states and countries. Her most enjoyable experience in the Navy was being close to home and getting to learn many skills that has helped her in her everyday life.

Shawn Evins
Grade 6

The Greatest Gift of All

There are so many kinds of gifts. To me, the greatest gift is my family. My family shows love, happiness, and friendship.

My family shows love by coming to my basketball games, helps me when I am sick, or just helps me with my problems. They really love me!

My family shows happiness by either helping me with school work or just making me laugh. We also go to parks almost every weekend and have a lot of fun! They all mean so much to me. We are a very happy family.

My family has really good friendships. We all are really good friends although, I sometimes fight with my siblings. We all still love each other, and they all mean so much to me. They really do. We all are not just a family, we are great friends. I don't need anyone else in my life other than them to make me happy!

Family is the greatest gift of all. Family shows love, happiness, and friendship. Some people are not lucky to have parents and a family. Just think about it; no one but you. It would be very lonely. I strongly believe the greatest gift of all is family. I also thank God for giving me a wonderful family and life. I would never be happy without them. What is your favorite gift now?

Sarah Canfield
Grade 6

Brandy's New Friend

I always wondered if my dog Brandy would meet my cousin Maria's dog Sugar. Since Maria lived all the way in Delaware, Brandy could not see her. But one day before Thanksgiving she and Sugar came to visit.

At first Brandy barked at her but he soon got to trust her. They played the whole time Maria was visiting. Brandy would chase her all around the house. When my mom was giving her treats, Brandy tried to steal them. Every time we would hold her Brandy would bark or growl at her. Before Maria left we gave Sugar a rawhide bone. Brandy also tried to steal the bone off her. She did not appear to be chewing it a lot but we let her have it anyway. As soon as she left Brandy went by our front door and he laid there.

But soon, almost one month later, the day before Christmas Eve, Maria and Sugar came back for another visit. When Sugar and Brandy played Sugar chased Brandy instead. He was very curious about her. Sometimes when I would bounce the ball to her, Brandy would get it. We also fed her these little Snausage treats which she really, and I mean *really,* liked. When it was time for Maria and Sugar to go we gave her yet another rawhide bone. Brandy once again went to our front door and laid there as soon as they left. I looked at Brandy and I just knew he would miss her.

Jacob Kozak
Grade 5

How to Pick Your Friends

I think that choosing a good friend is important. When choosing a friend, you should choose someone who would not use you. He or she could take you for granted and maybe take your money; that would be horrible!

You could find someone who embarrasses you by doing something behind your back so that no one likes you. He could also try to use you to make others feel jealous or pretend to be your friend until he gets someone else and then leaves you. This friend could make you do stuff you wouldn't have done. For example, he could make you be a bully. He could get you suspended for something you didn't do. He could also teach you to be bad by doing things that are wrong. This is why you should choose your friends wisely.

A good friend helps you and plays with you. They try not to hurt you or leave you alone. A good friend makes your life a little bit better, he or she is a great person to be around. This person is someone who stands up for you when a bully tries to attack you. You should never take advantage of your friend. Don't let him do so much for you that people will think that you're a bully and that he's afraid of you. You must have respect for each other. That's what a good friend is like. They should treat you like a true friend.

Antunee Adams
Grade 4

Rain Forest Animals

Many animals live in the lush, green, quiet rain forest. I'm writing to tell you about the wonderful animals.

I think the lizards are the most magnificent creatures. The iguana is about five feet long including their long tails. They live in trees and burrow under ground. They go as fast as six mph. Iguanas are excellent swimmers. Iguanas eat plants and small nuts. The Basilisk is a relative of the iguana but, eats rodents, birds and vegetables. It is about two feet long. They have long tails and many predators like snakes and electric eels.

There are mammals in the rain forest, too. The anteater eats ants, termites and other insects. They have long skulls, thick fur and long tails. The three-toed sloth eats leaves, buds and young twigs from the trees. This animal almost never comes to the ground and usually hangs upside down. They also have no tails or ears and have peg-like teeth and long coarse hair. Their three toes on each leg help them grip the branches they hang on. Wow, I think the sloth is cool!!

There are snakes in the rain forest, too!! One kind is the Anaconda, which is one of the world's largest and heaviest snakes. It spends a lot of time in the water and eats fish, deer, and other animals.

I like to learn about endangered animals. Many rain forest animals are endangered. So now you know more about the wonderful creatures and their unique body features.

Carrie Zilhaver
Grade 4

Meowing!

One beautiful spring day I was visiting my aunt Angie. She lives on a small farm in and old two story farmhouse with a swing on the front porch. There is an old barn, which was built by my great-grandfather, a chicken coop, and plenty of pasture land to run and play on. I helped feed the horses while my aunt and little brother, Reid, fed the chickens. When they came back, I told them I had heard meowing!

Reid squeezed through a hold in the fence and ran to get a flashlight. Meanwhile, Angie and I searched the lighted area throughout the barn. When I got near the hay loft, the meowing sounded stronger! Soon Reid returned with the flashlight and I crawled up into the hay loft.

I searched and soon found them huddled in a corner. There were two gray tabbies, a calico (it was black with orange stripes) and a fuzzy yellow one. The kittens' eyes were opened halfway. Reid got Uncle Jeff and we showed the kittens to him. What a pleasant surprise! I love animals, especially the babies.

When I went back again a few days later, the mom had moved them. I looked and looked but could not find them! I'm sure the mom was trying to protect her little ones, but I surely was disappointed.

Hanna F. Artrip
Grade 5

The Gift of Nature

If I were to give a gift to anyone that could not be bought with money, it would be the gift of nature and I would give it to my friends.

I would give the gift of nature to my friends because here on Long Island we do not get a lot of nature experience in our lives. This is because our area is polluted and doesn't have a lot of forests and animals. I would give this gift by taking my friends to my house upstate. Our home upstate is in the Catskills. At our house we do a lot of events involving nature. For instance, ride on our quads, go for walks in the woods, and play in the snow, ice skating, skiing, tubing and more fun things that involve nature. Another activity that we can do that involves natures is go deer spotting or go to the lake. Nearby there is a dairy farm where we can feed horses, watch cows get milked, we have experienced baby calves born twice! What you can also do is go see a phenomenal place called Point Lookout. You can view five different states at the same time! What we also do is sit at night and look at the millions of stars; we cannot do this on Long Island because of the light pollution.

In conclusion, I believe we could do more nature things upstate than here on Long Island. We need more nature in our lives!

Dana Ahrens
Grade 6

Parents: You Can't Live Without Them

My parents are everything to me. They are an inspiration. Without them I would not be here right now so thank you Mom and Dad.

I know I can go through whatever I have to go through with them beside me. If I get hurt they come and help me. When I have a problem with my friends or at school they will try to help me find a solution. When I am sick they are right beside me. When I am down they extend a hand to offer help. They correct my homework even if they are sick. They support me in all I do and they are there for me at all times.

Lots of kids are very unfortunate not to have loving parents, but my parents love me no matter what I do. They tell me that they love me every day.

It is the little things that count. They get me to the doctor's right away when I am sick. They drive me to sports. They help me study for a test. Last but not least they do their job as being my parents.

Of course you can tell by what I have written that I am allowed to say that I am blessed because I have great parents. I cannot survive without my parents. They put the food right on that table. I may put the silverware on but who cares. We kids need our parents, no doubt about that.

Nathan Grimley
Grade 6

Melissa's Funeral*

On June 29, 2005 at four fifteen p.m. Melissa McCartney died. At eight o'clock at night my sister's best friend called and said Melissa died. My sister was crying and I just could not believe this was happening. The sad thing was, my sister Kim and Melissa had just become really great friends.

Two days later was Melissa's funeral. When we walked into the funeral home Kim's best friend Taylor burst into tears because Melissa was Taylor's best friend as well. The hardest part was Melissa was only 17 years old. When my mom and I walked up to her casket we hugged Melissa's mom, dad, brother and sister. Then my mom said, "Kelly (Melissa's sister) did a beautiful job with Melissa's make-up and she looks just like she's sleeping." The next day we went to her church and they sang and talked about her life. People got up and said a little something about what Melissa meant to them. After the service was over, everyone walked over to the cemetery across the street from the church. I am glad it was such a beautiful day and not raining. A few days later I saw Melissa's family at her grave. I thought to myself, 'How could this have happened to Melissa and her family?'

The next day me and my mom dropped Kim off at Taylor's house so Kim could comfort Taylor. Then Kim and Taylor walked over to Melissa's house and gave the family a fruit platter. A few days later Taylor's mom Sharon bought a beautiful bench for Melissa's grave. When it gets warmer out, me and my mom are going to go to Melissa's grave and sit on the bench and talk to Melissa. It will be a great comfort to me. I'll never ever forget Melissa.

Sarah Richardson
Grade 4
*About a girl in my mom's Girl Scout troop
who passed away.

What Is the Greatest Gift of All?

The greatest gift of all is family because they support you, they love you, and they teach you.

Your family supports you no matter what. They support your dreams and encourage you to go for them. Your family keeps you going when you are ready to give up. That is why family is the greatest gift.

Your family loves you your entire life. They love you and show affection. Your family loves you even when you do wrongs. That is why your family is the greatest gift.

Your family teaches you the important things about life. They teach you what is right and wrong. Family teaches you how to live your life wisely. Your family teaches you love, kindness, and caring. That is why your family is the greatest gift.

Your family is the greatest gift of all because they are the key to living a happy life. They support you, they love you, and they teach you. That is why your family will always be the greatest gift.

Madeline Lee
Grade 6

Guiding Me Through the Water

Sue Guertin is like the Olympic gold medal to me. She guides me through the water just like she guides me through my life. Sue has always taught me that school is first and swimming is second. Sue never gives up trying to make me faster. The YMCA's motto is honesty, caring, respect and responsibility, and Sue lives by this creed.

The first thing she does to be the gold is guiding me through my life. She always says that the best thing to be in life is a great person. Whenever there is a disagreement between us because of a relay or who goes first in the lane, she always reminds us that in the end the best relationship would be between us and the other person than the ribbon or the wall.

Sue has always taught me that school comes before swimming. Although I would love to have a professional swimming career, she knows that being educated would make me more successful. Swimming can lead me to a great education but I would rather have my education make me a great swimmer. Being educated can get me to Harvard but swimming cannot. Sue cares about my future that's why she believes education comes before swimming.

Sue Guertin is anymore than anyone could every ask for, a coach, a mentor. Being there for me ever since she taught me to swim, always putting in the same effort.

Toireasa Rafferty-Millett
Grade 6

My Christmas

On Christmas when I was little, I used to wonder what Santa looked like, so every year I would try to stay up and get a good look at him. I kept on falling asleep, though, so I never saw him. When I asked my mom what he looked like, she always said she didn't know! After that I was so desperate, that I asked everyone in my house, even my dog, but of course she just looked at me in her cute way.

Still I wanted to know. No one knew what Santa looked like! Then when I was six years old I, decided to drink a lot of Pepsi so I could stay up Christmas Eve. I was off to a good start. It was about one thirty, and I was still up. There was no sign of Santa. About three thirty I fell asleep. When I woke up I was in my bed and all the presents were wrapped and under the tree! I could hear voices outside, so I went to look and it was my family! They all came inside to open presents. When I was opening my presents, I found a note from Santa! I remember it saying something about that he could never be seen because he knows who's awake, and he won't come 'til everyone is asleep. If he was asleep the elves would make him create toys. That was my best Christmas ever!

Katherine Michael
Grade 6

Great-Grandma

G.G. is my Great-Grandma. We took the first letter out of each word, great grandma, and we came up with G.G. I am writing about her for many reasons. Number one, she is am awesome grandma. Number two, she said to me when I was about six years old that she was going to stay alive to watch me compete in the Olympics for gymnastics. I am determined to win the Olympics just for her.

Every year on my birthday she usually gives me money. G.G. usually gives somewhere around twenty dollars. I try to tell her not to give me so much, but she ignores me and refuses to take it back. She is a very generous woman, and I love her very much!

G.G. lives in a small apartment all alone and does not usually get company. On her 90th birthday we decided to throw a surprise birthday party at my aunt's lake. We thought that we would do something different for a change. Everyone enjoys the lake. We go water skiing, knee boarding, tubing, and canoeing. Last year she just sat in her apartment all alone. We all felt a lot better because she was there with the whole family.

I love my grandma so much and I hope she really does live until I compete in the Olympics. I will do anything I can to make it to the Olympics just for her. She is the best grandma ever!

Danny Roberts
Grade 6

Eagles Company

"Aaahhh" my friend and I both screamed "there's an earthquake, abort, abort, abort the basement." STOP...Whoa, Whoa, Whoa. Okay, you're probably wondering why my friend and I are both screaming. Well, about that...um, oh, yeah, I found a way to explain that. The Eagles made it to the Super Bowl in 2005. They were up against the New England Patriots. My family had a party that day. My parents had friends come over, and it just so happened they had a girl just my age.

"Aaahhh" my friend and I screamed...again. "Yes, the Eagles scored" all of the adults above us yelled. When I say adults, I mean parents and their friends. All the people upstairs began jumping up AND down, screaming AND yelling, making a huge commotion, which seemed to be similar to an earthquake (although I've never really been in an earthquake). Unfortunately, we had to be beneath all the excitement. The walls shook, the lights flickered, the drinks almost spilled. We were terrified.

Finally, the game was over and we found out that there really was never an earthquake, it was just the so-called "mature" adults out of control, but it did feel, look and sound like one. My friend and I managed to survive.

Moral of the story; never be in a room below people whose hometown team is in the Super Bowl!

Dana Barth
Grade 4

The Best Pet Ever!

I have a cat named Carly. She is 6 years old. Her birthday is May 9th, the same day as my grandma's. She is a long haired calico cat.

When I was younger, I had always wanted a cat. So when my mom and dad went on their honeymoon, my grandparents took me to the humane society. There were so many cats and we couldn't decide. I was holding a Siamese cat and asked my grandma if she wanted to hold her. She said yes. When she took the cat, it tried to claw her. So she dropped it, and it went under the cages. After that incident, my grandma was playing with a cat with her purse strap. She kept saying, "Look at this cat." But I didn't like her that much. But after a while I got tired of looking for a cat. I started to play with the cat my grandma was playing with. When she looked at me, she had beautiful green eyes. She was so tiny she fit in my hand. She had two other sisters and her mom in the cage.

After a couple of minutes of playing with her, I decided I wanted to buy her. We couldn't take her home that day because I will still at my grandparents' house. So the next Tuesday, we went and got her. For these reasons, Carly is the best pet I ever had!

Danielle Parsons
Grade 6

Gasho's

One of my favorite dinners took place in Gasho's with one of my best friends, Louis. He is in third grade and should be turning nine pretty soon. It is really fun watching the chefs cook and do tricks in front of you.

Gasho's is a Japanese restaurant that is supposed to look like it is old. While you are waiting for your food they might flick broccoli into your mouth. When you are done with your dinner you can have dessert. Outside of Gasho's is a pool with fish in it. There is also a big field with woods near it, so everyone went exploring in the back. It was awesome to see what was behind it. The reason I went was because it was Louis' birthday. His other friend Silke and his brother Ted were there too. Silke and Louis' mom had chicken. The rest had steak. After that we all got tasty ice cream. Then they sang "Happy Birthday" to Louis and hit him on the head eight times with a plastic hammer that when it hits something it will make a funny, squeaky sound. It was funny.

When we got back to his house we played a game. When we went inside we played a lot of card games. The only bad part was I got sick and had to go home, but the whole thing had been really fun anyway. I went to Gasho's one other time, when it was my brother's birthday. He went with me, my mom, my dad and a friend. He went there a few years ago so I don't remember much, but it was really fun. Gasho's is a cool restaurant. They also sing in Japanese. Next time I have a birthday party I will probably go there.

Brendan Goldberg
Grade 4

What a Good Education Means to Me

A good education is very important to me. There are many times when I wish I weren't in school. Then I think about if I was not in school I would miss learning new things. I am very lucky I can go to school because in other countries, they don't let girls go to school. I think those girls wish they were in school too.

Without school I wouldn't be very smart. No one would. This morning I was listening to the radio and I heard a story about a robber. He was robbing a bank and he said, "Hi! I'm (his name) and I'm going to rob this bank." Without school, people make other poor decisions like smoking, taking drugs, and drinking alcohol. Without an education people also get poorer jobs.

Going to school would make me smarter so I wouldn't have to rob a bank. School also leads to a better job. With an education, I can become a doctor, a lawyer, a vet, a teacher, or almost anything. Teachers can also inspire me to get a certain job.

My parents want me to have a better education. That is why they send me to a private school. That proves that both my parents and I want me to have a better education.

Callan Piazza
Grade 6

Spectacular Fall!

The beautiful colors of red, yellow, brown, and orange swirl and twirl in the cool breeze. I love walking outside and hearing the crisp leaves crackle under my feet. Fall is about the leaves.

Seeing the gentle leaves tumbling into piles is magnificent. I walk towards the pile. Suddenly, a small, multicolored mass jumps out screaming.

Struck with fear I fall back. Then noticing it is my sister, I tackle her and we plunge under the leaves. Right there, on our front lawn, we play our favorite game: leaf fight. These times are the happiest times of my life.

Smack! "Oh, there's a deep drive to center field, it's back, back, GONE!" Baseball is also a big part of the fall. What is more exciting to watch than the World Series! It is so exhilarating to watch one of the greats like Roger Clemens striking someone out. These moments mean a lot to me.

Finally, the most important part of fall is Thanksgiving. Having my loving family surrounding me is great. Laughing and playing in the family room is great.

Then we all sit down to watch the Thanksgiving Day Parade with its giant balloons in their most magical splendor.

Sadly, it is time to say goodbye to my family, but I will see them again next month for Christmas. Unfortunately, I will not see this splendorous season for another year.

Ryan Murray
Grade 6

A New Experience

Nicole ran up to me and said I had to see Mr. C., our school band director. I had been playing French horn for 1 1/2 years. I pondered why he wanted to see me. I hadn't missed any rehearsals and I didn't have music lessons on Tuesdays. Thinking I was in trouble, I nervously walked to his room.

When I got there he said, "This is very serious." Then he handed me a black folder decorated with white music notes. Written at the top was "All-County Band."

All-County is an ensemble for the best instrument players in the whole county! I glanced at the label to make sure it was mine. It clearly said "Maggie Pavlovich." WOW!

One half of my mind wanted to jump for joy. The other half wanted to snatch the music out of the folder and practice. In the end I just stared at it.

Being in All-County was different from normal band. The music was harder, and after 3 three-hour rehearsals we performed at the Tilles Center! Almost every famous musician ever has performed there. I was very nervous. If I made a mistake it would be recorded on microphones and over 300 CDs! Also, my family was in the audience.

I was grateful at the end of the concert. It had gone smoothly. This experience made me think about being a professional musician. But I still have many more notes to play before I have to make that decision.

Maggie Pavlovich
Grade 6

Magaly Molina

The person I look up to is Magaly Molina. The reason is because she immigrated from Cuba to give her son a better life. She's been here in America for 10 years already. She has a grandson, Dennis. She raised him from when he was a baby and helped her son out. Her job here, in America, is doing nails in her gorgeous house. This lady has suffered from bad times and has always found a way to fix it. She is a loving mother, grandmother, and a great friend. That is why I look up to her. Magaly has done so much for the people that she has loved. She has taught me how to relate to different cultures, that there is nothing in life you can't obtain, and once you set your goals you will succeed.

Her latest achievement is a dream that she's had which is about to come true. Her sister has won the lottery and is being allowed to leave Cuba along with her husband and son as permanent residents to the United States. Magaly is adding an addition to her house, making an apartment for her relatives. Her sister is going to be a beautician here, as that is her profession in Cuba. Her husband is a construction worker and is also going to work here so one day they can obtain their goals for a better life. Until then, Magaly will subsidize them any way she can. I admire Magaly for her strength and willpower.

Amanda Fragoso
Grade 6

Nature

Mother Nature is beautiful, especially the flowers that grow in the spring and the leaves that change color in autumn. Land on Earth is also part of nature. It has nature itself in it. Animals are part of nature. There are all kinds of animals. They are big, small, furry, feathery, soft and rough. Even humans are part of nature. We are important because we share the natural sense. Also about trees, there are different kinds of trees. Some grow flowers, some don't. Some are big, some are small. Oil, gold, diamonds, waterfalls, and even rocks, are natural, but they don't have life. Humans, animals, and plants have life.

Some people love nature, but they don't realize they're nature. I believe Earth is Mother Nature itself. We must keep it clean so nature can live happy in a clean Earth. The seasons are part of nature too. They are great, but the best is autumn. Since cold weather is coming, leaves are starting to dry and that causes them to change color. After that, comes winter. Trees are left without leaves. Snow falls from the sky. After that, comes spring. The flowers start to grow. Trees grow flowers first, and then they grow leaves. After that, comes the summer. There's hot weather in the summer because the sun rays are much stronger. The trees are filled with leaves.

Gabriela Mantilla
Grade 5

Freedom

Freedom is something I wish that everyone could have. Unfortunately, people in many countries all over the world are restricted, and instead, live in poverty, hunger, and tyranny. They cannot say or do anything they want, which I can't imagine my life without.

To me freedom means free will, liberty, choice, and independence. Without free will, I might not be able to go to school, or say what I want because I am a girl. In many countries girls and women are limited to staying at home to cook and clean. Liberty means to do what you want, like protest, go outside, or work where you want. Choice is very important to me, with it I can go where I want and do what I want. I can choose so many things like where I want to eat, what I want to buy, and who my friends are. Independence means that I can do things without someone else's help. In many Middle Eastern countries women and children cannot go out side or even speak, without their husbands permission.

I feel lucky that my family has the money for a house and food, because so many don't. These are all the reasons I am thankful for my freedom, and being born and living in the free United States of America.

Sara-Paige Silvestro
Grade 6

How Important Is Soccer to You?

"How important is soccer to you?" Soccer is one of the things I enjoy and is important in my life, besides family. Two things about soccer that I like are the fun and also all of the friends you get out of it. Next, a good thing is the coaches who are basically the teams' leaders.

From the sport soccer you get loads and loads of fun. First, soccer parties are an example of fun. Also, when we have practices on Saturday and we did a really good job we get rewarded with a mini game. A thing I love about them are if you make a mistake we all laugh together and make fun of it. Last, you get to see the people and friends who you love to be around.

Coaches are people who are loved and important to have in the soccer society. I love having coaches because they help the team through the rough times. Secondly, they keep the team organized. Last, the coaches motivate you to do better.

Friends are something you get from playing soccer. Soccer friends are important to me because they're like sisters of my own. Soccer friends will make you feel like you're never alone and hated. Lastly, soccer friends are worth something, because in a game if you make a mistake they'll cheer you on.

Now you know why soccer is one of the most important things in my life, and all the things that come with it.

Kaitlyn Coulton
Grade 6

Being in the Zone

Do you ever go in a zone of your own? When I play the drums I get so focused. I have no clue what is happening around me. When I am on stage with people staring at me, I am nervous at first but after a while, I don't pay attention to the cheering. I just play my heart out. Somebody might think I am crazy when I am in my zone because I stare straight ahead and just go off in my own world, playing.

Do you play an instrument or a sport? For me, I only get in this zone when I play the drums. When I play the cello it is not the same experience! My mom always has to push me to practice the cello. I don't need to be told to practice the drums, I just run downstairs and bang on my blue, sparkly drum set. When I play the drums, I don't get distracted by anything! I have fun! I play songs that I know, popular songs played on the radio. Cello music is classical. When I get in my zone, it lifts me up and into a zone of happiness and relaxation. Nothing else matters.

I can sometimes play the drums forever and not realize until I stop to take a break and look at my watch. I am in the zone!

Charlotte Burch
Grade 6

How to Care for Your Bunny

Rabbits surprisingly are not rodents they are lagomorphs. They are actually closely related to the horse due to their diet and digestive system. One of the calmest breeds is Holland Lops. As you may know they have floppy ears.

Rabbits are very smart, you can even teach them how to do tricks with a lot of training. If a rabbit is happy it will do a "binky." If you witness a binky, you will probably think to call a vet, but no, this is normal. The third most popular house pet in America is the rabbit. Also one more upside to rabbits is that you can potty train them. Just buy your bunny litter box and every day work on potty training with your bunny. Rabbits live an average of 5-10 years. Bunnies are very loving animals if you treat them well. If you don't they might make a deep growling noise to say, "back off I need my space." If your bunny believes that he owns something and he loves it very much, he will rub his chin on it. If you treat your bunny well, he might even rub his chin on you!

Rabbits love carrot tops and will eat carrots if they aren't cold. Certain lettuce isn't good for your bunny, and so are some other veggies. So feed your bunny the right foods, give your bunny plenty of attention (but not too much), exercise, and love!

Haley Sienkiewicz
Grade 5

Once Upon a Child

Do you know how it feels when you leave home on the first day? Becoming scared and afraid that on your first day of kindergarten, knowing not a soul, you will screw up…or…get in trouble…maybe not even wanting to go back ever again. But then, the feeling of coming home after a hard day's work and telling your parents how great it was, and asking if your new best friends can come over after lunch.

Everyone in his or her whole life goes through that stage. And when it's over, having felt like you're all grown up, you can make your own decisions and feel like you have nothing to lose, except the memories and the great times.

Reading the first paragraph, you will notice that you mentally change. It's like your whole elementary school involved life was based on going from "Hmmm…should I play kitchen with Jill?" to "OH! Did you hear that? Sam has a crush on Lilly!" You later get involved with things you will eventually regret like gossiping, or sorting your friends into groups (the nerds, braniacs, popular kids, etc.) And if you try to avoid doing these things, then maybe you would have a successful life. It's like telling somebody that you don't need to do all these things, because you have better choices to make.

In my experience, I made some great choices and some bad ones, where I learned my lesson. I hope my essay helped inspire you to be *you*.

Meghan Carron
Grade 5

Eric Gagne

Eric Gagne is a famous baseball player. He is a pitcher for the Los Angeles Dodgers. He played in the minor leagues until he was called up to the majors on September 7, 1999. He plays at Dodger Stadium in Los Angeles, California. He is a very good pitcher.

Gagne grew up in Quebec, Canada. He started throwing a baseball when he was 2. As a child he enjoyed both baseball and hockey. When he was 7 he was asked what he wanted to be when he grew up, and he answered he wanted to be a major league baseball pitcher. At age 17 he had to choose between hockey and baseball. He chose baseball.

Gagne was drafted by the Chicago White Sox, but decided to go to college instead. He didn't speak any English so he watched hours of MTV to learn the language. He lost his first 6 games as a pro because his parents were going through a divorce. Another reason he was losing the games is because he injured his elbow. After speaking to his team doctor, he won 9 games straight. In 2003 he set a major league record by winning all 55 games that he played. He received the Cy Young award in that same season.

He always pictures himself striking the batter out before he releases the ball. Gagne always has a positive attitude no matter what he is doing whether it's life or baseball.

Matthew Maltese
Grade 4

Publishing Words

I have a unique imagination. I write stories. I've written 3 books so far and I've called them *The Karen Series* which tell of me living with a family of 13. I someday will publish my books, but for now I just write them. I've always loved writing books and essays and I always get good grades in English language arts.

My stories express me. I'm influenced by Ann M. Martin who writes *The Babysitter Series* and the woman who wrote *Black Beauty,* a nonfiction story. I love books and to write stories. I'm also writing about a girl named Samantha who takes care of horses and tames horses. I call the book *Sam's Horses.* I'm also influenced by my parents and Mr. Lanzi. My stories are my life. I even once sent a story on the internet. It was called "Spy Acara." It is about a creature named Annie who meets this fairy and learns how to become a spy. I don't know if it was published or not, but I'm glad I sent it.

If I keep believing in myself, I'll really make a difference. I've even written a book called *Taking Care of a Unicorn* and another that's half finished called *Being Something Else,* including another called *Midnite Mare.* Though all of my stories are fiction, I am thinking about writing about myself. Maybe I could write about something new or about horses.

Melissa Falzarano
Grade 6

Kitty Cat

Guess who wants to be your playful, cuddling, and furry friend? Your favorite and loving pet cat. Cats are playful, require responsibilities, and they long for loving.

Playful cats and kittens need interesting toys for playing. So you need to get some toys. Most cats like toys on strings, or jingling balls that smell like catnip. After you get some toys you can make superior forts if you want to. You can make first-rate forts out of sofas, sofa cushions, and paper bags. Now you and your cat can play.

In addition, you have responsibilities. You have to clean the smelly and yucky litter box. Next, you have to fill its bowl with food and water daily. If your cat hurls a slobbery, stomach-smelling hair ball, you have to clean it up.

Also, cats will meow for eternal loving. They enjoy sleeping in bed, so you have to be careful you don't squish them. Plus, they come for cuddling when you're sitting down. They like scratching under their chins.

In conclusion, cats can be playful, require responsibilities, and adore loving. I think cats can be very loving. I think cats would be good pets.

Peter Wise
Grade 5

My Hero

My hero is my Uncle Bob. I chose him because he was dedicated to children, for his positive outlook on life, and for his love of his friends and family. His personality and smile would warm the hearts of those he knew or would meet.

Uncle Bob had a great love for hockey. He always played the game hard, fast, and physical. His motto was "play to win." His love for the game continued, even when he no longer could play, by coaching younger children. Bob had a unique way with children. He would teach them by example and this helped the children to reach their potential. He had respect for each player and they respected him. The lessons he taught them didn't end when practice was over. Their self-confidence and respect for others was seen on and off the ice. He showed them how important it was not only to be a player but to be a successful player and how to be part of a team on and off the ice.

Another reason for choosing Uncle Bob was his positive attitude. No matter what his day brought him he'd never complain. He always tried to find a positive to everything. He would always greet you with a smile and be concerned about you, even when he wasn't feeling well. His positive outlook and courage enabled him to enjoy his life until he died.

My Uncle Bob didn't live a long life but he lived a fulfilled one. He touched the lives of many. He showed me by the way he lived that it's important to make the most of each day in a positive way. He also gave me encouragement to accomplish what I set out to do and that I can make a difference in the world.

Joshua Luczak
Grade 6

Gift

If I could choose a person in the world to give a gift that can't be touched or wrapped it would be my grandmother. I don't call her grandma, but I do call her mom because she is just like another mom to me. I choose my grandmother because she's the most loving person you will ever meet. My grandma is sweet, nice, caring, respectful, and her heart is filled with pure love. The main gift I would want to give my grandma is a cure for her sickness. My grandma is always down because she is sick and when she is happy is just brightens my day. I think a cure would be the perfect gift to give my grandma because she deserves the best, and the best would be to give her a cure so she could be happier. And like I said, it seems as if when she's happy the whole world is happy. My grandma inspires me so much for many reasons, but one is that she always has a smile on her face. I think that if I could choose who my grandma is mostly like I would declare her as an angel because she has all the power to be the best. In conclusion, I feel my grandma deserves a cure for her sickness because she's the most loyal person you will ever meet. This is why my grandma inspires me to be all that I can be.

Josephine Christodoulou
Grade 6

Marie Antoinette

Marie was born on November 2, 1775 in Vienna, Austria. She was the youngest of 15 children and the daughter of Emperor Louis I and Marie Theresa. She had a poor education and hated to read but was very artistic and well behaved.

In 1770, Marie married Prince Louis XVI of France at the age of 15 and four years later became Queen. Marie gambled a lot, went to fancy balls, and theater shows because she was bored with her life as Queen. Marie tried to fire the government workers of France because they wanted to stop her from spending so much money.

King Louis controlled the French government. The people paid high taxes and were starving. In 1789, a hungry crowd marched to the castle of Versailles in Paris. Marie asked why they were so angry "because they have no bread." "Then let them eat cake," she replied. The people of France only got angrier.

When France went to war with Austria and Prussia, Marie passed war secrets to the enemy. She was later caught and thrown into prison. In October 1793, they cut Marie's hair, tied her hands behind her back, put her in a slow moving cart, and paraded her through Paris. She was executed on the guillotine, her head displayed to a cheering crowd, and her body buried in an unmarked grave.

There is a movie about her life coming to theaters this year. She was a powerful queen, but her power was her downfall.

Alexandria Paige Holbrook
Grade 5

The Plunge into Oblivion

I looked up at what seemed like thousands of stairs. Legs shaking, I saw another person go down. I was shaking wildly. I looked behind me. More people started to line up, anticipating the moment of pure energy. They wanted to go up. But I didn't, although I saw now that there was no turning back. Soon I would have to face my fate. The hot sun blazing overhead, I realized what had to be done. I'd have to take the plunge into oblivion. The moment was now. If I wanted to back out, well, I couldn't. My stomach felt like the arena of a horse race. The lifeguard told me it was okay, so I closed my eyes and jumped. Holding my breath I dove in, my now wet bathing suit clinging to my skin. I was racing down at the speed of light! I could taste saltwater in my mouth as I rapidly approached the pool. I can do this! Happiness spread through my cold, wet body. And then I plunged into the pool. Diving under the water, I kicked my legs like it was the fourth of July, until my head popped out of the water. I was floating! I made my way to the edge of the pool, salt water burned my tender eyes as I blinked in amazement. As my body pulled itself out of the water, a smile bigger than Kentucky crossed my face as I realized that now, I could do anything.

Alex Brinkman
Grade 5

Dinner with Raphael

Raphael was an Italian painter and architect born in 1483 in Urabino. Raphael was best known for his big figure compositions in the Vatican. The Vatican is located in Rome. The first painting that Raphael did was done in 1495. Raphael did most of his paintings in Rome and was called by Pope Julius II to come to Rome for the architect Donato Bramante. Raphael has many other names that he is known by. For example: Raffaello Sanzio, Raffael Santi, and Rafael Sanzio de Urbino. The four Teenage Mutant Ninja Turtles are named after the four biggest painters: Raphael, Michelangelo, Leonardo, and Donatello.

If I was able to have dinner with Raphael it would be so amazing. I'd be happy and shocked to eat dinner with one of the most famous painters. I would ask him to paint a picture of me. If he did that I would show our whole school. I don't think I would ever want to give it up. Raphael is a big role model for me. He has inspired me and I have learned that if you put your mind to something you can do anything. I would ask Raphael so many questions. I would ask him how it feels to be one of the most famous painters in the whole entire world. I would ask Raphael if he ever got nervous or scared, if he would ever mess up on a painting, would he keep trying or would he just give up?

Ashley Darby
Grade 6

Mother Teresa of Calcutta

Mother Teresa was born on August 26, 1910. She was born with the name Agnes Gonxha Bojaxhiu and was Albanian. Mother Teresa joined the Sisters of Loreto in 1928 and taught for 17 years at the Order's school in Calcutta. She experienced her "divine call" to devote herself to caring for the sick and poor in 1946. She founded the Order of the Missionaries of Charity, which would become a pontifical congregation in 1965. She established Nirmal Hriday, a hospice where those poor and near death could die with dignity. She received the name Sister Mary Teresa after St. Therese of Lisieux. She made her First Profession of Vows in May 1931 and was assigned to the Loreto Entally community in Calcutta and taught at St. Mary's School for girls. On May 24, 1937, Sister Teresa made her Final Profession of Vows, becoming, as she said, the "spouse of Jesus" for "all eternity." From that time on she was called Mother Teresa.

She continued teaching at St. Mary's and in 1944 became the school's principal. On September 10, 1946 Mother Teresa received her "inspiration," her "call within a call." From that day on she washed lepers and carried babies who were alone off the streets of Calcutta to take care of them. She was called the "Mother of the Poor."

Being a Catholic student you do different essays on different Saints but I never got the chance to do an essay on Mother Teresa, until now. She means so much to me and she made a huge difference in many peoples' lives. I look up to her as an unbelievable role model because her message of peace, love, and hospitality touched the hearts of many people. I know it touched mine.

Samantha Martin
Grade 5

My Best Friend

One of my best friends is Anthony. He is my best friend because he is very humorous. He is funny because sometimes he will lie, but the lie is hilarious. Another reason he is funny is that he can make up great jokes right off the top of his head. For example, this one time he and my other friend Steve made a great joke about Pokemon in about five minutes.

Anthony is also my friend because we have so much in common. The first way is that we both love to trade Pokemon cards. Next, we like all kinds of sports like football, baseball, and basketball. We also like video games and any time we get a cheat code, we will tell each other. One time we were playing James Bond and Anthony and I were on a team, and he blew up the building that I was in.

The last reason Anthony is my best friend is that he is very generous. He is generous because he invites me to his house, birthday parties, and he offers me food. Also we were on eBay and he offered to pay. For all of these reasons, Anthony is a great friend.

Troy MacPherson
Grade 4

Animals vs Humans

Do you think your life is hard? Well, animals have it really tough! In the Olympics, humans compete for medals. In the wild, animals compete for life. In this essay I will explore some similarities and differences between animals and humans as they compete in the world. You'll learn some of the ways humans and animals have made adaptations to their environments, using their strengths and abilities.

Animals and humans are very similar in these ways. Both animals and humans can do the same things. For example sprinting, jumping, and surviving. All of us have made adaptations to the conditions we live in. Cheetahs have the ability to run fast, ostriches to run for long periods of time, and kangaroos to jump very high. Humans and animals were born with special abilities that help them along the way.

Now, let's take a look at the differences between animals and humans. Even though we do the same things, animals can often do it at a greater speed, height, time, etc. Doing the research for this essay has made me realize how amazing animals are. Another reason why animals are different from humans is because they use their muscles daily. Humans have to take the time to train their muscles. Animals and humans are very different, but in a way a lot alike.

Kristen Rohm
Grade 6

Soccer

Soccer is my favorite sport. I love to play soccer. I would play soccer outside or inside. Even in a video game. I love kicking and passing the ball. I can play soccer a whole day without getting tired. I play soccer with my friends. I play in a team. I play it by myself.

I invent different games with a soccer ball. Like kicking it and not letting it bounce more than once. I can juggle. I'm good at soccer too. My dad plays with me sometimes. He taught me how to play soccer. My dad always tells me if I want to get better I have to practice.

I practice a lot so that's why I'm good at soccer. I need to get better. I want to be a professional soccer player. When I grow up I want to play for USA. If they pick me for their team I will practice and play as hard and as good as I can. If I ever become famous I will share my money with my family.

If I play for their team I would want kids to yell out my name and ask me for my autograph. I would also want them to use me as an example. I would give money to the poor. I wouldn't be greedy. That will be wrong. I would never miss a practice. If I'm on the team. When it's time for the game, I will be ready and confident so we can win. If we don't win it doesn't matter. All it matters is to have fun and play your best.

Marco Vasconez
Grade 6

My Family

Have you ever written about your family? Even though my family is different from others, they are special to me.

Everyone in my family does things for me, which makes me feel special. When I get sick, someone is always there to take care of me and make sure I have everything that I need. If I get upset, they are always there to hug me and let me know that everything will be okay. My family is very generous. If I'm at my mom's, dad's or my grandparent's house they always have presents for me. If I'm bad, I don't get anything at all! They are also very helpful. They help me with my homework if I ask them.

The best thing about my family is they are loving. They take me places like the toy store, restaurants, or even the mall to buy clothes. They always make sure that I have a good time wherever I go. My family takes me on vacations to Virginia, Disney, and a Dude Ranch. In the summer, I go to my grandma's to crab or even jet ski!

When I need to get my hair done, my aunt can do it for me since she is a hairdresser. I also can get my teeth cleaned for free since my mom works for a dentist.

Although my family is different, I love them. Do you love your family as much as I love mine?

Amanda Driscoll
Grade 4

My Role Model

Do you have a role model? I do; her name is Carrie. She is 15 years old and is in 10th grade. She has the best qualities of a role model. She gets good grades in school. She is a great friend. But, most of all, she is a great dancer. This is great because I love dancing almost as much as she does.

She gets great grades in school. She even takes extra classes before and after school. She is a member of the Fellowship of Christian Athletes, and an active member of her church.

She is also a great friend. She always listens to your ideas, even when some aren't the greatest. She doesn't care if they're good or bad. If you look 'friend' up in the dictionary you'll find her name in bold print.

She loves to dance so much. I think she takes about eight or nine dance classes and is an apprentice in one class. She can do just about any kind of dance; from Acro to Pointe she can do them all. She is a very graceful dancer. All we do is dance, all summer long.

So, do you have a role model yet? Well, if you don't, and if you need a good friend with good grades and who has a passion for dancing, she is the one for you. I mean, who can beat that? That's why she's my role model.

Taylor Nicole Cline
Grade 6

Jets!!

Did you ever hear of the New York Jets? Well, I'm going to talk about some players on the Jets. First, Chad Pennington was one of the quarterbacks on the Jets. He was number ten; he had five-hundred-thirty pass yards. He is six foot three, two-hundred-twenty-five pounds; he made two touchdowns, and his ratings is 70.9.

Brooks Bollinger is now the new quarterback because Chad broke his arm. Brooks is number five; he is a quarterback. He is six foot five, two-hundred-thirty-five pounds; he has seven-hundred-seventy-seven pass yards. He got one touchdown, and his rating is 59.4.

Finally, Curtis Martin is a running back. His number is twenty-eight; he is five foot one. He has two-hundred-thirty-five rushing yards, and five touchdowns. Those are some people from the Jets.

Justin R. Moretto
Grade 4

My Best Friend

I was at one of my cottages in Pennsylvania. We were going to do the "Olympics" with everybody there. But my dad called from our other cottage and said that he wanted us to come over there. My brothers and I didn't want to go. We didn't want to miss the best day of our lives, doing the Olympics.

My mom was on my dad's side so she threw us in the car. We were all mad at her. When we got to our other cottage my brothers and I pouted in the car, and we weren't getting out, no way, definitely not. My dad came up looking for us and he had the best thing in his hand, a little puppy on a leash. At that moment we were all out of the car in a jiffy. We were so excited. I think the puppy was scared. If I had known that my dad had a new dog I would have made my mom go 110 mph on all the roads. We were so excited to see a new dog. Now he is my best friend in the whole world.

Gardy Webber
Grade 6

The Taste

I eyed the food placed before me. My hands were trembling when I reached for it. I pulled it up and looked at it. My stomach fluttered like butterflies. Maybe I would like it, maybe I would not. What if I couldn't get the taste out of my mouth? I looked at the small plastic plate. There were 3 pieces. I gulped.

I brought the sushi up to my mouth. My arms felt like lead. I felt like I was sweating. I nervously bit down. I knew there was no turning back now.

I swallowed the rice, fish, and seaweed. I thought about the taste. Yum! Delicious! I grabbed another and decided to dip it in soy sauce. Then I had the third. You have to try sushi!

Morgan Gillespie
Grade 4

Great Friends

Great friends look out for each other; help each other in time of need, and like you for who you are. Great friends help you get through the day and it is a friendly responsibility to be very truthful and comforting in times of despair. When I think of my best friend, I feel happy because I know what a treasure he is to me and the people around him. I thank God for wonderful friends and continue to pray for good friends.

When we have homework and one of us is absent, we each make sure the other person gets the homework information as soon as possible, so the homework is not late. We make sure we follow school rules and remind each other of our obligations. Friendship means being there for each other in good and bad times. We run errands for each other and carry books for each other when the need arises. We do not complain about the sacrifices we make nor do we take what we do for each other for granted.

Others may not appreciate or take us for who we are, but being the great friends we have become, we do cherish every moment we share. We learn to appreciate and respect people. We accept them for who they are, and that is what makes us what we are; Great Friends.

Bryan Fondufe
Grade 6

A Winter Miracle

It was a few days after Christmas I had gone to my dad's house over vacation. My mom was sick and in the hospital a day or two later with a bleeding ulcer. They patched her stomach and sent her home. A few more days later and she was in the hospital again. They did the same procedure and sent her home. She was in the hospital a third time so they did a Gastro bypass.

If in any way I could say thanks to Saint Francis Hospital I would want to say thanks for giving me my best friend back. And I would want to tell them that my mom is healthy. At the hospital the nurses are extremely nice. Because of those nurses, doctors, and surgeons my mom is alive right now. The Ashford Volunteer Fire Department also helped by giving my mom a ride in an ambulance to the hospital.

My mom is healthy now. She can't eat as much as most adults and some foods or a lot of stress can give her a stomach ache.

If I could turn the clocks back I would. I would go back to before my mom was sick. I am so happy for my mom. Thanks to everyone that helped her. I recommend Saint Francis Hospital because they really help. I wish that I could say to everyone who helps people with ulcers, works at a hospital, has an ulcer, or knows someone with an ulcer: Merry Christmas.

Cassandra Svelnys
Grade 6

Jump!

Jump-roping is a sport. I like it and my friends like it. When you are jump-roping you can do a lot of things like doing tricks and when you are jump-roping you are also exercising.

First, I can do tricks like skiing, bell, and jumping jacks! I can do a lot more tricks but those are my favorites. When I do skiing I jump from side to side. You have to be careful because you could lose your balance easily. When I do a half twist I jump kind of from side to side only I twist halfway. That is my favorite trick! Finally, when you do jumping jacks you move your feet like you do when you do jumping jacks only you don't move your arms. That can get a little tricky.

Second, you have fun. My friends and I do all sorts of tricks. We also listen to music and that's how we have the fun! However, you can have competitions like pros. We also raise money for Jump Rope for Heart.

Yet, you can exercise while you have fun. A lot of young kids are obese, so if you jump-rope you can exercise at the same time. Also, you can make yourself healthier and lose weight at the same time. I jump-rope because my grandpa died of a heart attack so I want to keep my heart healthy. In conclusion, I like to jump-rope.

Allison Steffy
Grade 5

Riding My Bike

It was about 5 years ago when I was ready to take off my training wheels on my bike. I was down at the beach house when I wanted to take off my training wheels. My mother went to Plattsburgh. So, I was at the beach house with my Grandma, Grandpa, Courtney, Conner, Cody, my Uncle Jay, and Aunt Laurie. My bike was down at the beach house.

That day my Uncle Jay and Aunt Laurie dared me to ride my bike without training wheels. So, I did because I did not want to be a chicken. So, I put on my helmet, elbow pads, my kneepads, and my hand guards. My Uncle Jay and Aunt Laurie took off my training wheels and sat them off to the side and helped me to the wobbly bike. I was shaking and sweating. I was so nervous.

That day it was hot and humid, it made it worse because I was still sweating. When I was riding my bike I felt shaky still. Also, I felt calm and confident in myself. When an hour went by, I felt like I could ride my bike without anyone walking behind me. It was like learning the ABC's or tying my shoes, I loved it!

By the end of the day, my mom came to the beach house. She saw me riding around on my bike. She was so proud of me. When I got off my bike my mom asked me, "Who taught you how to ride your bike with no training wheels?" She looked at my Uncle Jay and Aunt Laurie and I said, "They did, mom!" Till this very day, I am better than ever at riding my bike!

Miranda Douglas
Grade 5

The Boat

Well one day early in the morning about 5:00 a.m. my dad and 2 of his friends went fishing on a boat. I wanted to go but my dad said no because it was all boys. Then my mother said that she would go so my dad exclaimed yes. This is my first time on the boat but it was the second time for the others. This kind of boat is a sea ray. So we went fishing in the Taunton River.

On the way back my dad's friend, Peter, noticed that there was smoke coming from the engine. So my dad went downstairs where the beds were. He went to get a bucket. My dad passed the bucket to his friend so he could put water on the engine so it could cool off. He shut the boat off in a rough current. Finally it cooled off but my dad had to go slow.

When we were on shore my dad had to put it on the trailer. He tried to fix it but he couldn't because the wire ripped. So I told my dad that it was the first and last time I would go on a boat. Maybe I was the one who brought the bad luck.

Shawna Reis
Grade 6

Charles Schultz

Charles Schultz, the man behind "Peanuts" cartoons, died on February 12, 2000, on the eve of his last cartoon strip, which included a farewell letter.

The 77-year-old Schultz had been battling colon cancer since January, 2000. As the world's most widely syndicated cartoon artist, he was honored by many awards, including International Cartoonist of the year in 1978, two Reuben Awards in 1955 and 1964, and France Commanders of Arts and Letters in 1990.

"Peanuts" became the most popular cartoon in history. The 1967 *Life* magazine featured Snoopy and Charlie Brown on the cover.

Schultz himself sketched and wrote every running of Peanuts for 50 years, and had a clause inserted into his contract preventing anyone else from releasing new "Peanuts" cartoons after his death. *A Charlie Brown Christmas* has aired every year since 1965. In all, there were 50 TV specials, and 1,400 books, selling more than 300 million copies. "Peanuts" was running in 2,600 papers and was read by around 355 million in 75 countries. The strip inspired some household phrases: "security blanket" after Linus' prop, and "happiness is a warm puppy," of course, after Snoopy.

Many of his characters were based on real people in Schultz' life. His childhood dog, Spike, was behind Snoopy. The little red-haired girl was based on a girlfriend who rejected his proposal for marriage. An art school friend of his inspired the character Charlie Brown.

This was the life of comedian Charles Schultz.

Shiven Patel
Grade 5

Enslaved

When Coretta Scott King died, I asked Mom did she think there was going to be slavery again. Mom said that slavery is still today. Mom said that in the old days it was blacks being taken by the whites, but today other things make people become slaves. If you look in the dictionary, the definition of the word "slave" is one who is submissive or subject to a person or influence. A master is one who has control over something.

If you do drugs, you are a slave to drugs. Drugs will become the master. When this happens, you will lose your dignity. Another kind of slavery happens when people commit crimes and go to jail. The master is the police that tell criminals what to do. They are slaves because their freedom is taken away. Education is important in helping to not become a slave. Education is the key to getting somewhere in life. If you do not get a good education you will be poor and it can cause you to become a slave because you cannot do the things you want like having a career, buy a house, a car, and living in a nice area.

When I grow up I would like to become a judge and the first black female president. I would like to be independent and not afraid to make the world a better place. I want to serve my master which is God. God is a master good to serve.

Cyndria Kishen
Grade 5

Family Fun

My family is the best in my life and I love them. They're always there for me. My parents are the people who comfort when I'm sad. They feed me and care for me. They do so many things. My parents are the best at comforting me but the most amazing thing they do is help with work. When I get a bad grade they yell. Then they give me a positive statement, which encourages me. When I get mad and don't talk to anyone they find a way to gently get the truth right out. It's like they are a truth magnet. That's why I love them. When I run out of clothes that fit they will buy me new ones. In the time I spend with them I am usually shopping. Sometimes we have a mother daughter day together. It's when my mom and I go shopping for anything that's not expensive and then we have lunch together. I also have a father daughter day. It's when we go to where he like to go which are mostly the golf stores. They're the most important people in my life and I don't want to lose them. They're my family and they comfort me in my time of need. They buy things when needed, and feed me. We have so much fun on our shopping spree and other fun things we do together. Thank you mom and dad you are the best.

Sarah Peoples
Grade 6

Having Good Friends

Having good friends feels like heaven. If you need help on work, friends will help. I have these five best friends: Natalie, Sarah, Hannah, Jackie and Courtney. They always make me laugh, even when I am feeling bad. They're always there for me. I also have this nice friend Melissa. My friends and I always help each other out. I also have this friend that I've been friends with forever. We always used to laugh. We still do today.

My friends always make fun of me because I like this one boy, but I know they're just playing around. It is impossible to stop us from laughing. They make fun of Garrett about me. It is so funny though. Natalie and I are best, best friends. You can't tear us apart. We always sit next to each other anywhere, well most of the time. Jackie laughs all the time. Even if you say "pudding" she will keep on laughing. Sara is just a tough girl. Courtney is really smart. Hannah is just so funny. Melissa is so nice. Natalie is a good friend. Amanda is my very best friend. We always go shopping. We do a lot of stuff together. That's the girl I told you that we still laugh. Amanda and I go to Enchanted Forest every summer. We have so much fun together. We rides bikes and go swimming. We are so crazy. Nobody can stop us. These are my friends I have just told you about.

Melissa Witek
Grade 6

Baseball

Baseball is one of the best sports ever. You get to run, field, hit, pitch, and win championships. You also get to have lots of fun. You also have to wear special equipment like spikes which are shoes that make you have better traction on the dirt, a glove that catches a ball, pants which will protect your legs when you slide, and jerseys to make you look cool.

First, I would like to take you through the hitting steps. To begin you must get into the right stance. Next you would watch the ball if you think it's a strike then swing at the right time and you will hit the ball. Hitting also has its downside, you can strike out. To strike out the ball has to be pitched over the plate, but not too high or too low. If it is pitched too high or too low it is a ball. You can also get hit by the ball though, that hurts. Next is fielding. In my opinion fielding is the best because it seems that it has the most action. When you are in the field you need a glove and a position, infield or outfield. There are several positions, first base, second base, short stop, and third base. In the outfield there is the right field, center field, and left field. The infield is supposed to get the ground balls that are hit and not let any of them passed you. Outfield is supposed to get the balls that go past the infield and the fly balls.

Hitting and fielding are the most basic parts of baseball. You can hit, field, run, throw, and have fun all at the same time. That's why baseball is the best sport.

Kevin O'Brien
Grade 6

I Have a Dream

Football is a great sport. It has been played for more than a hundred years. I have a dream that I could get drafted into the NFL and be a star in it.

Football is a great sport because you get paid a lot of money. You also are famous and get to be on TV. You can also be in video games, that kids play and they could be playing you in the game. People look up to you and treat you with a lot of respect. On away games you travel to many different places and see places you never saw before. Also it can be not as great. You have to put a lot of time into practicing. You only get a month or two to be with your family. You can be traded which means you will have to move and take your family. You also get picked by the teams and you could either be on a good team or a bad team. Lastly, if you are hurt it could last you the rest of your life.

My dream will be hard to accomplish, but I will work hard to fulfill my dream. There are a lot of hardships to my dream, but I will overcome them and hopefully be successful.

Peter Galiano
Grade 6

Space

If you don't know a lot about space then this essay will tell you a lot about space, like what it's like, what's in it, and what revolves around what.

First thing this writing will teach you about space is what it's like. Space is never ending, or endless. Some say that the universe is endless but it's really space that is endless because there are different parallel. Everything in space is surrounded by blankness because space is endless, and is encased in total darkness.

The second thing this will teach you about space is what is in it. Space consists of a lot of different things. Some things it holds are planets, galaxies, and the biggest things, universes. The smaller objects in it are meteors, meteorites, comets, asteroids, and scattered chunks of space ice which are really dirty.

The third thing this will teach you about space is what objects revolve around what. In space, different objects revolve around bigger objects. In our solar system, all the planets revolve around the sun. Other things that revolve around the sun are comets and a lot of asteroids. Even some planets have something revolving around them, they're called moons. But some planets have large rings that expand around the planet. The most known planet that has rings is Saturn. Saturn has thousands of rings made out of chunks of ice. There are also galaxies and universes that revolve around each other.

Finally, this has hopefully taught you a lot about space.

Ian Wilt
Grade 5

The Gift of Laughter

I will give the gift of laughter. I will give this because I like to make people laugh and it makes me feel great. I will give this to all of my friends that need some laughter in their lives. When I give laughter I'm clearing stress of the kids that are laughing. I'm doing something good for my friends and something good for me too. Someone might have so much on their mind that they just want to get rid of it. So that is where me making them laugh kicks in.

Teachers and parents might think it is annoying, but it is good for them because they have more stress. Once my friend got a bad grade on his math test and forgot his homework. I made him laugh that he wasn't so stressed and he almost forgot about it, but it came back. I will make them laugh by saying a joke or talking in a funny way, but either way I'm making them laugh. A gift is something someone enjoys. Laughing is something someone enjoys as much as a toy or a video game. Some people don't realize laughing is a gift like love or life. It should be realized as a gift not as an annoying noise. Therefore, my gift to my friends is laughter.

Brian Poole
Grade 6

Stay Away and Be Okay

No one plans on being a drug addict. No one wants to be an alcoholic when they grow up. These things happen because people think they can do things once, or just a little, and then they get hooked and can't stop. Some people start doing bad things because of peer pressure, or because they want to look cool. Drinking, smoking and drugs are not cool. Addiction means you can't stop doing something even if you want to. Addictions can ruin lives.

Drugs are illegal, and they can kill. Among the worst are heroin, cocaine, and marijuana. Drugs are very addictive. You can get hooked right away. Drugs have no value, so do not try them.

Drinking beer, wine, and other types of alcohol is very bad as well. It is illegal for anyone under 21 years old. If you are caught drinking while driving you could lose your license. Drinking damages your health and personality.

Smoking is also very harmful. It is illegal for anyone less than 18 years old. It is very addictive. If you smoke, you are endangering others also, because secondhand smoke can kill even nonsmokers.

A class that teaches the evils of drug is DARE. DARE shows you what happens when you take drugs. It teaches you that drugs are harmful and addictive. DARE is very fun and helpful. I am happy we have DARE, because it will prepare me if I am asked to take drugs in the future. Stay away and be okay.

Jake Bassinder
Grade 5

Lacrosse

"Ball down!" kids hear. "Pass!" one yells. "Shoot!" another kid shouts. Lacrosse history is interesting; the game is exciting for more and more American kids, while the professionals are entertaining to watch.

Amazing, did you know that lacrosse was invented around the time of the 1600s? The Native Americans invented the game of lacrosse in the 1630s. Two Native Americans named Seneca and Mohawk made up the rules of the game one evening as they met in one of their villages. At this time only men played, unlike today. They played from sunrise to sunset. They played for an amazing amount of time: for about 3 to 4 days in a row! They used to play with around 100 to 1,000 people, according to the lax history site.

The players now wear even more protection because they get more physical and they have to be more protected. A team in the pros is usually made up of about 16 to 20 people, just in case someone gets hurt. There are 10 people on each team: three midfielders, three defenders, and three attackers, and the one goalie. The attackers have to score points. Defenders stop the opposite team from scoring on them. The midfielders have the hardest job of doing both defending and attacking, and the goalie as you know stops the shots from getting in the goal. Now that you know of the history, its popularity, and the pro game, try it out, it's fun!

Michael Davila
Grade 6

Underage Drinking

Did you know that a normal high school student has or could have consumed eighty-one percent of alcohol? Also, that a normal teenager could drink at least five times a month? This is the topic I chose because I don't like people that drink alcoholic beverages that are under the age of twenty-one. Also I don't like people getting drunk or drinking beer, liquor, or a very strong beverage that can kill you if you drink too much of it. Drinking can get you in serious trouble because you can go to jail, also you can die.

I feel very strong with the topic I chose because drinking under age can damage your memory and also you usually forget many things; for example, what you were doing at the time you were drunk. Drinking can hurt you physically and it can hurt other people like your family and friends emotionally. Drinking can involve many things like drugs, stealing, and also even abuse. It even can turn you into an alcoholic. I do not understand why people keep on hurting themselves when they don't even know.

As you can tell, drinking alcohol is bad if you drink it too much and you can't trust any teenagers because you don't know when they're lying to you, but there are some people that do not drink. I can clarify to you that I will never drink or do drugs, and I will never steal, and of course I will never, ever do abuse!

Nicole Ponguta
Grade 6

Animals vs Humans

Have you ever wondered how champions that have won gold medals compare to animals that have the same talents? You would be very surprised if you knew. I was when I researched this topic. Many people will be surprised to know what I am about to tell you. I will tell you how animals-vs-humans are different and how they are alike.

There are many ways the two are different. One is that animals are faster than humans. Animals survive the wild through their natural speed. Humans need to build up their bodies to have great speed.

A way in which humans and animals are alike. Both are very fast, and both never quit until what they need to get done is done. In the animals case, if they do not use their natural skills, the skills will leave and the animal will die. Humans will lose only their talent and will not have anything special to do in the Olympics.

I have explained how animals and humans are alike and different. I was very surprised when I found out animals were faster than humans. I think it is great to get involved in learning new things. Thank you for reading. So try reading more, you will be surprised what you learn.

Melissa Ayoob
Grade 6

A Forever Friendship

My best friend is Ashley. I have known Ashley since I was two years old. I met her when I moved into my house. As soon as we met, we became friends. Aimee, my sister, is one year younger than Ashley's brother, and I'm one year younger than Ashley. My sister and Brandon, Ashley's brother, would always hang out. All of us would always play outside together. I grew up with Ashley living next door to me, feeling like my family is her family and her family is mine. Our grandma's both lived next door to each other when they were younger and were best friends, too. That's the cool thing about our friendship. It helps to have Ashley only one year ahead of me in school to tell me about things.

When I'm upset, Ashley's there for me. When I'm happy, Ashley's there to share the joy. When I'm bored, Ashley's there to entertain me. Ashley's there when I'm having a bad day, and she makes it a good one. When I need a cheerleader, Ashley's there, sitting on the sidelines screaming, "Go Sally!" When I need a friend to go crazy with and have a good time with, Ashley's sitting there on my couch, waiting for me to turn up the music and plug in "Dance Dance Revolution."

Ashley's my best friend. She's always there for me through thick and thin, always on my side to make me happy. I love her like a sister.

Sally Reilert
Grade 6

Stay in School

I think many things are important, but the most important thing I think is to stay in school. Many things could go wrong if you drop out of school. You could lose everything if you don't stay in school, and not get a good job. That is one thing you could do to make everything go wrong. If you want to get far in life you must stay in school.

If you don't stay in school you won't be able to get a good job. If you are planning to drop out of school, and get a well paying job you're wrong! Most jobs that you go to; unless it's Burger King or other places like that you need a high school and college degree. Of course unless you are still in school trying to find a job. I am planning to be a marine biologist and I am not going to be able to do that if I drop out of school and don't go to college. Most people plan on having a family, and you can't have a well balanced family if you have a minimum wage job. You should stay in school and get a good job.

Stay in school, go to college have a good life. Don't drop out of school. I believe everyone should go to college, get a good job, and have a great life. Everyone should work their hardest and be the best they can be.

Sydney Lesseski
Grade 6

Emperor Penguins

Have you ever heard of a type of bird that can't fly but can only swim? Well, the emperor penguin can! It cannot fly but swims the depths of the Arctic Ocean. This is the only bird in the world that cannot fly but can swim!

All emperor penguins, unless in captivity, live in the Arctic regions, in Antarctica, but not alone. Penguins stay together in packs of over one hundred. This is because of the harsh weather, they keep each other warm. They move still in packs during breeding seasons to their birth spots to lay an egg. Then the penguins split into females and males. All the males or fathers stay and try to protect the egg. All the females or mothers are starved and go back to water to get food. Then after they have eaten their fill, the mothers come back together to see their baby. This is the only time the penguins split up. The only other time is if you get left behind, they will go on without you.

In the penguins' only feeding spots, the frigid water, they feast on shrimp, small fish, and other little sea creatures, but they also have one predator in the ocean unfortunately also. This is the leopard seal.

Did you know that emperor penguins can go under the deep depths of the Arctic waters for 18 minutes? They can also go as deep as one hundred seventy feet under water! Penguins also go over one hundred eighty endless days without food and sometimes die for their babies. Penguins are also one of the few animals that can belly slide and waddle!

Amber Carroll
Grade 5

Facts About the Ocean

Do you like the ocean? I'll give you a few reasons why I like the ocean and then you'll see if you do.

First off, there is a lot of wildlife in the ocean. For instance, there are hundreds of thousands of animals in the sea. Another reason is that life is quiet under the sea. After all, animals can't talk like us! If they could talk, the earth would be one big jukebox. Trust me, the Earth is fine just the way it is.

Another great thing about the ocean is that if you go deep enough you'll sleep in the water because the water will eventually become pitch black.

Lastly, most fish are not deadly. Some fish are deadly but most of them aren't deadly. In fact some fish you can keep as pets! So do you like the ocean? If not, I've got a few more reasons to like it. However, don't go too deep, otherwise you'll end up getting crushed by the water weight. Besides, you use water to take a bath, to drink, and to cool off in the summer. How do you feel about the ocean?

Andrew Pawelczak
Grade 4

Muhammad Ali: Sports Hero

Boxing in the early 1960's, largely controlled by the Mob, was in a bad state until Muhammad Ali — Cassius Clay, as he was known in those days — appeared on the scene. Floating, stinging, punching, prophesying, he transformed the sport and became the world's most adored athlete.

One of his most famous fights was with Sonny Liston, the current heavyweight champion. "Sonny Liston has spat out his mouth guard! The fight is over, Clay wins!" screamed the announcer. That was the fight that made Cassius Clay feel immortal. This boxing newborn had defeated the heavyweight champion of the world and earned himself the reputation of a lifetime. Before the fight, Cassius stated that Liston was, "too ugly to be a heavyweight champion!" That was in 1964, Clay had already won a gold medal in the Olympics and had never lost a fight. At the time experts did not think much of his boxing. Clay was just another big shot, punk, black kid who didn't stand a chance. Little did they know that one amazing upset was not what Clay was looking for — he didn't want to be a one hit wonder. After changing his name to Muhammad Ali and becoming a Muslim he continued to fight. He lost the title and regained it in 1974 after knocking out George Foreman in the famous "Rumble in the Jungle" which became a permanent chapter in boxing history. The "Rumble in the Jungle" could not hold a torch however to 1975's "Thrilla in Manilla" where Ali beat boxer Joe Frazier. Was it his physical presence, his social commentary, his clever, cocky rhymes, or his humanitarian endeavors? Maybe it's all of the above for the many who have been inspired, uplifted, and touched by the greatest champion of all time, Muhammad Ali.

Nicholas Vitale
Grade 5

Alexander Graham Bell

Alexander Graham Bell was born on March 3, 1847, in Edinburgh, Scotland. He was an inventor and a scientist. He went to school and graduated from Royal High School in Scotland when he was 13. When he was 16, he was a grammar and music teacher at the Weston House Academy in Scotland. From there he went on to teach at Somersetshire College, where he became interested in acoustics.

On March 7, 1876 the US Patent Office granted a patent for a communication device for transmitting vocal or other sounds telegraphically. This invention is known today as the telephone. He demonstrated his invention to the people on June 25, 1876. He made an ear phonoautograph from a piece of hay and a dead man's ear. He talked into the ear and the hay traced the sound. Alexander had 18 patents granted to him alone, and 12 more with others.

In 1882, Alexander Graham Bell became a citizen of the United States of America. He was one of the founding members of the National Geographic Society, and he received many honors. He was married to Mabel Hubbard who was deaf and mute, just like his mother. The telephone was something that he was trying to create to communicate with his wife and his mother. Alexander Graham Bell died on August 2, 1922 in Baddeck, Canada. Now you know who invented our telephone, and why Alexander Graham Bell was named one of the "American Greats."

Thomas Dropik
Grade 4

Friends

Do you think that a friend is a special person in your life? A friend to me is an exceptional person in your life. A friend is someone who is kind, caring, and trustworthy. A true friend is someone you can rely on. You can tell if they aren't your friend if they are using you. You can share secrets, hang out, and play sports together, and they have your back when you get in turmoil.

Those are the good things. The bad thing about having a friendship is fighting. When you fight, you sometimes say things you don't really mean. Sometimes we even say that we don't want to be friends anymore, but in the end we always end up staying friends.

Making a friend can be easy. You just have to treat them like you would like to be treated. If there is a new person at school, then go up to them and introduce yourself. Nine times out of ten they will become your friend.

I think that having friends in life is important because they keep you company and they give you somebody to talk to. So from this essay you should have learned how important friends are and that they are the key to life.

Timberly Deane
Grade 5

The History of Ice Cream

There are many different facts about ice cream in the world. Some facts many know by heart, while others give puzzled looks or will make you want to say, "I would have never guessed!" Well, the facts I am going to tell you now may make you like ice cream even more than you do already.

There are many different types of ice cream around the world. Did you know that French ice cream is ice cream that is enriched with egg yolks? Did you know that parfait and mousse are ice creams that are not beaten during the freezing process? Did you know that Spumoni is ice cream that is mousse with fruits and nuts? Not only does ice cream come in different flavors, but also in different places, it is made differently.

There are many fun facts about ice cream that you probably didn't know. You probably didn't know that July is National Ice Cream month, did you? Did you know that the most ice cream is sold on Sunday each week? Did you know that people ages 2-12 and over 45 eat the most ice cream? Not even the smartest person in the world would be able to figure those out!

There are many facts about ice cream flavors. This first fact is very easy to believe: that vanilla is the most popular ice cream flavor in the world. Did you know that there are over 150 different ice cream flavors in the world?

Those are the facts I know on the long history of ice cream.

Bridget Cauley
Grade 4

My Dad, My Hero

He's unforgettable and always there for me. He's my dad, always filled with enthusiasm, pride, and humor. He lights my way through total darkness. He may not be perfect but he's my dad and I'm proud of him.

His smile is unbeatable. His smile reflects his thoughts, like when he's proud of me. A shiver of love flows through my body. His smile is the best and most meaningful in the whole world. My dad and his smile together are unbeatable.

My dad is my hero. He knows every time I need him, and he is there in a second. He knows how I feel without even asking. My dad is always there for me, supporting me. When I'm around my dad, my worries go away. He always has good advice for me whether in the middle of the night or at the crack of dawn.

My dad and I both love lacrosse. He teaches me how to throw and catch better, to cradle like a professional and get goals like no one is blocking me. I look up to him. Someday I want to be like my dad, helping other people, always being there for the family, and best of all, being one of the best parents in the whole world. A day with my dad is like a vacation from all my worries. He's my coach, he's my hero, he's my worry taker, and best of all, he's my dad.

Kelsey J. Brown
Grade 6

What Freedom Means to Me

Freedom; not many people have it, but I do. Some people try their whole lives to find freedom while some take it for granted. When I think of freedom I think of every one having the right to say what they want to say. I think of women having rights and being able to do anything.

On July Fourth Seventeen Seventy-six America signed the Declaration of Independence and became free from Britain. When I hear about my country becoming free I think of all the poor men who died and to all the people who lost a family member. I am happy that our country is free, but I still feel bad for their families. Even today people in different countries are still trying to find freedom. I wish everyone could be free so men and women would not die.

Even though America is free, we still have rules. You cannot just walk up to the bank and rob it, you would be thrown in jail. The people who are in jail are abusing their freedom; those are the people who no longer have rights to do anything.

I believe freedom is something to cherish, I think some people do not notice how important their freedom is to other people who want freedom; they are willing to die. To me freedom is something you will have for the rest of your life you will never have to give it back. I love having freedom.

Emma Haggerty
Grade 6

One for the Team

I'm on the scratchy blue mat waiting to start, thinking about what I'm about to do. My heart pounded like it has never pounded before. I felt sweat dripping down my body like I was a popsicle melting in the sun. I heard people chanting my name saying "Deanna, Deanna." I felt like my stomach was a punching bag. There was no turning back. I had to go through with it.

I saw the eyes of the crowd. They seemed like they were coming closer to me. I heard my teammate calling my name, saying, "Are you ready?" I felt like a turtle that wanted to hide in my shell. But I slowly said, "Yes." Soon I heard our name get called. It was time. I heard the music start. I was doing what I needed to do. I felt like I was in a dream. Was it true? I was doing cheerleading in front of a big crowd. I am standing there with my arms in a high V starting to go into a jump. After I did my jump I started to do my dance. We were great!

I was amazed at what I just accomplished. I just did cheerleading in front of a huge crowd. It was amazing. I felt like I could do it again. It was so fun. I could not believe it, we won first place! I am proud to be a great cheerleader. I can't wait 'till next year to do it again.

Deanna Ploesser
Grade 5

What a Good Education Means to Me

According to *Webster's Dictionary*, the definition of an education is "the process of gaining or giving knowledge and skills." Having a good education is very important. Some people can't afford to go to school and learn. I am lucky to go to an excellent school where I am able to learn.

A good education, to me, means succeeding later in life. If I have a good education, I can succeed in my future and I can afford nice things. It also means to learn new things. Learning new things is fun and exciting. Education also means becoming smarter. If I am learning new things, I am becoming more intelligent. Education can also actually help me to become a better person. When I have a good education, I feel good about myself. A good education is something no one can take away from me.

I think getting a good education is important. Education really can help me succeed in life. Also, education will really help me to be a confident adult. I think a good education is important for a happy and successful life!

Emilie Kovacs
Grade 6

The Life and Story of Harriet Tubman

In this essay, I will tell you about Harriet Tubman. She was a famous African American and respected woman who was born into slavery. She was a woman of faith and courage.

Harriet Tubman was born in 1812, in Bucktown, Maryland, to Harriet Green and Benjamin Ross. Harriet's parents were born slaves. Harriet's parents named her Araminta but people called her by her mother's name, Harriet. Harriet, her parents, and ten brothers and sisters lived and worked in Brodess, a large plantation near Bucktown. Harriet was just 8 years old when she started to work. She had to baby-sit. When Harriet did something wrong, they would punish her with beatings.

At age twenty, Harriet's life had changed, she married John Tubman. John Tubman was a free African American who lived near the plantation. When Harriet got married to John she was still a slave. Harriet told her husband she wanted to run away, but her husband did not like the idea. One night, Harriet and her two brothers snuck out. Her brother's changed their minds, Harriet went alone. Harriet had directions to the house of a woman she did not know. She found a place to live. She missed her family. She went back to free her family. She was a tough leader, she carried a gun. Harriet went on her mission back in Maryland to pick up her family and free them.

Harriet was born a slave but was determined that she was not going to die a slave. Harriet died at the age of 93.

Shalice Hunt
Grade 4

The Ball Game

When I heard the coach call out my name, I almost choked on my salt sunflower seeds. Immediately jumping down from the bench, I grabbed my favorite bat. I felt drops of sweat slither down my quivering back. As I stood by home plate, time stopped and my mind was racing as fast as the Energizer Bunny.

The other teams cheering rang in my mind. Finally, Kelsey, the pitcher on the other team, pitched a fastball to me. Slamming the ball far out of the field in Burhome Park, I bolted around the bases. The four of us slid on home plate and jubilantly jumped for joy.

After the game we devoured doughnuts and congratulated one another. Next, we rolled down an enormous hill in the park and reminisced about the game. Effort, teamwork and luck are what it takes to achieve your goal and that is what we had on that special, special day.

Kate Larkin
Grade 6

All About Me

Hi! My name is Ann Marie. I am ten years old. I will tell you about some of the things that I like to do. I like to do a lot of things, especially fun things. I hope you enjoy all about my life. It's really fun learning all about me.

I'll tell you some of the things I like to do. I like to play tag with my sisters. My favorite board games are Monopoly and Risk. I love to play them! My favorite video game is Tomb Raider. My favorite book is *Goosebumps: The Curse of the Mummy's Tomb*. My favorite food is pizza.

Now, I'll tell you what I like to do. I like to play with my sisters. I like to play with my friends too. I like to go to school and I love to go to Girl Scouts!

My favorite kind of season is winter because you get to go sledding and you can have snowball fights. I like writing because it is fun. I get to express myself and write what I want to write.

Ann Marie Taylor
Grade 4

Exercise Every Day

Did you know if you exercise every day you can make your heart strong; it can prevent being overweight, builds all the muscles in your body, and it really helps your blood flow. You can give your body energy by doing sports like soccer and basketball. Any kind of change in your life, can cause stress. Stress can put a strain on your heart. If you want to be really strong you can lift weights, run every day, and stretch. If you lift weights every day for a year you can gain 25 pounds. If you run every day for a year you can put a lot of energy into your body. If you always stretch every muscle in your body, you can be really muscular. Keep exercising and you'll look like a muscular machine.

Eric Simpson
Grade 4

Dogs

There are lots of dog breeds. Some dogs are hunters and some are just house pets. There are dogs that are wild like wolves or coyotes. Wolves can be nice but can be protective. Some wolves will take you in as part of the pack and they will treat you like their own. Coyotes are not nice and they can get real mean at times and they do not like people. Coyotes use facial expressions to tell people and other animals how they feel. There are also foxes. Foxes tend to be clever and they are hard to catch because they are very fast. They eat rabbits, fruits and garbage.

House pets eat dog food and get walked on a leash. All dogs are part of the wolf family. The one thing dogs don't like is a cat. Some dogs chase cats and some just ignore them.

Lots of dogs are very nice and some are not. Some dogs do agility, disc catching, or obedience. In agility, dogs are timed and they have to complete many obstacles that you might think a dog could never do. In disc catching, a dog has to catch a flying disc and earn points. In obedience training a dog has to listen to their owner and do things like sit and lie down for a certain amount of time.

Francesca Valeri
Grade 5

Hop, Hop, Hop

Looking for a new version of Hopscotch? This new way will keep you playing for hours. Few supplies are needed, the procedure is a snap, and the cleanup is a breeze.

The supplies needed include chalk, a pavement driveway, a sunny day, and throwing stones. Collect five friends and a hose.

Procedure is fun and easy. Draw boxes on the driveway with chalk. Draw one box and on top of that, draw two boxes side by side. The middle of the two boxes should line up with the middle of the single box. The final box should be one big box. Second, sketch the numbers in the boxes. The numbers should start with one and end with the final number in the big box. Next, pick the order of people. Usually it goes from youngest to oldest. Throw the rocks onto the Hopscotch boxes and hop. Hop to the number your rock landed on, pick it up, and then come back to the start. If anyone touches a line, it's an out. Afterward, pick the winner or the person who didn't touch lines or touched the fewest.

Cleanup is a snap. Spray the driveway with water from the hose. Meanwhile, put the rocks and chalk away. Afterward, let the pavement dry in the hot sun. At last, give the overall winner an awesome prize.

So, isn't this a fun new version of Hopscotch? With a little labor, everyone will be able to have lots of fun.

Jacqueline Zuhse
Grade 6

Sharks

Sharks are very interesting. Sharks have no bones, they have cartilage instead. When sharks break or lose a tooth a new one grows in its place. Most other fish have a gill slit for breathing. On both sides of a shark it has five or six even seven gills. Most fish have a flap over their gills but sharks do not. Sharks have very sensitive ears. They can hear much lower sounds than a human can. Some sharks can hear up to 700 feet away.

The most dangerous shark is the Great White Shark. It can grow fifty feet long. It can weigh more than two tons. They like warm water. There are more than three hundred fifty kinds of sharks.

Sharks usually eat only what they need to function. Sharks that live on the floor of the ocean blend in. Some sharks can smell blood in the water from a mile away. A hungry shark will eat anything it can find. Sharks mainly feed on other fish.

The largest shark in the world has teeth so small they are useless. There are between 3,000 and 6,000 of them. Whale sharks weigh up to 8 to 10 tons. Sharks are very interesting creatures.

Leo Cleveland
Grade 4

My Childhood vs My Mom's

Was it better living in my mom's childhood or mine? Whose was safer? Some people would answer these questions with "Today's world," but I have some points that might change your mind.

In my mom's childhood, she didn't have any violent situations. For example, my mom's parents would leave her in her stroller outside to take a nap. People wouldn't do this today because they hear of kidnappings and other things on the news. She didn't have lockdowns either. She didn't have these because nobody brought weapons to school. She didn't have situations like September 11 in her childhood. Her parents could even leave her in the car when they went into Wawa to get a drink or snack! People wouldn't do this nowadays because there are carjackings and other offenses like that.

My childhood isn't as safe as it was when my parents were growing up. One of the reasons it's not safe is because people are filling their minds with violent videogames. In my childhood, nobody goes out and makes friends, either. You have to be very careful about kidnappings and killings. It seems that almost every day said on the news someone was hurt, murdered, or kidnapped.

In the future, I hope that everything goes back to the way it used to be. The only problem is, just because someone wants something to happen, doesn't mean it will.

I hope I changed your point of view. Remember, many people can change something together.

Bobby Kelly
Grade 5

Thomas Alva Edison

I chose to write about Thomas Edison because I believe he is a very interesting person. He was born on February 11, 1847, in the city of Milan, Ohio. In 1854 Thomas Edison's family moved to the vibrant city of Port Huron, Michigan.

Thomas Edison's mother decided to home school him at age seven because he was in a one-room school house with 38 other students. His mother felt that by teaching him she would help him achieve his potential. Thomas Edison loved to read. His parents encouraged his reading by teaching him how to use the public library. He swore that he would read every book in the library. However, his parents could not keep up with him. He had too many questions about science and physics. At age 14 he developed scarlet fever and it is believed that later in life this caused him to become deaf. He was totally deaf in his left ear and 80% deaf in his right ear and because of this he could not go to school.

Edison's first job was selling newspapers, snacks and candy on the railroad. He then began publishing a newspaper called the *Weekly Herald*. At the age of 15 he became a "brass pounder" or a telegraph operator. It was during this time that Edison began working on his experiments.

On October 18, 1931, Thomas Edison died at the age of 84. He is still hailed as one of the greatest inventors there ever was.

Joshua Dennis
Grade 4

All About Me!

My name is Rosa Marie Hodges. I have two very nice brothers and one very cute and funny sister. My brothers' names are Zach and Tyler. Zach is 16 and Tyler is 10. My sister's name is Isabella, who is one. I also have my mom and dad.

I am 11 years old. I was born on May 26, 1994. I was adopted from Omsk, Russia in an orphanage. I am a friendly person and I have brown hair. I also have brown eyes and I weight 80 pounds. I have tan skin and I am 4'9" tall.

I am interested in lots of stuff, but the most that I'm interested in is horses. I love horses very much. I want to learn more about them because I want to breed horses when I'm older.

In school I do very well and get lots of good grades. In school, my favorite subjects are art, writing, and gym. My least favorite subjects are math, English, language arts, and social studies.

I have one pet that is my brother's. It is a lizard. I used to have many like dogs, a chinchilla, mice, hamsters, birds, ferrets, and more, but they're all gone now.

Some things I enjoy for fun are drawing horses and people. I also like to play sports like basketball, soccer, and swimming.

Rosa Marie Hodges
Grade 5

The Aurora Mystery

Among airplane fanatics (like me), there are many mysteries and legends. One of the current and most famous of these legends is of the Aurora. This mysterious airplane is a high speed and high altitude U.S. spy plane. It is known only as the Aurora Project to the public. Only a few people know what it really looks like and many less have seen it. The Aurora flies in dangerous, heavily guarded enemy territory to take reconnaissance pictures. Experts believe that it probably takes these photos from more than 80,000 feet and with enough precision to read a license plate on a car. Definitely not your average camera lens! It may seem outrageous, but there are private organizations devoted to trying to find the Aurora. According to "sightings," enthusiasts say it looks somewhat like the space shuttle. Sightings of 'donuts-on-a-rope' contrails indicate that if these were made by the Aurora then it would have some type of pulsejet or ramjet engines.

In addition to the Aurora, fame and glory surround many other Air Force planes like the amazing Lockheed Martin Fleet, including the SR-71 Blackbird, the fastest known air breathing machine in the history of the world, the U-2 and TR-1, otherwise known as the inline wheel planes, and the F-117 Nighthawk, the first stealth airplane. I believe the Aurora is Lockheed's newest addition to this fleet. The courage of the designers and pilots who keep pushing the limits of aviation make the history and future of flight glorious.

Rich Eberheim
Grade 5

Girl Scouts

One thing that I am interested in and involved in is Girl Scouts. There are many things about Girl Scouts that I like to do. These things are very fun, and educational, too.

One thing I enjoy about Girl Scouts is camping with my friends. We have gone to several different camps, including Camp Timberlake, Camp Roy Weller, Camp Henry Kaufman, and Camp Skymeadow. We learned how to canoe and ride horseback which was lots of fun. I also like to go on day trips to different places with my troop. We have gone bowling at Holiday Lanes, and we went to see the new Harry Potter movie on the big screen at the Carnegie Science Center.

I also enjoy selling Girl Scout cookies. I like to go around and sell to my neighbors. If we sell a certain amount of cookies, we even get T-shirts. We sell cookies to benefit the troops overseas. We send them a lot of cookies each year to help remind them of home.

Girl Scouts is very fun for me, and I would like to stay with it until I am a Senior Girl Scout. Then I can become a leader if I want to.

Alyssa Lynn
Grade 5

Religion in School

"I pledge allegiance to the flag of the United States of America and to the republic for which it stands one nation, under God, indivisible, with liberty and justice for all."

Those are the words millions of American students recite in public schools each day. But I wonder, are we really one nation under God? The Bible tells us that we should not deny our beliefs for any reason and that our testimonies are important to witness to non-believers everywhere. But the fact that we cannot do this in educational facilities nearly contradicts this thought.

I think it is really important to express your religion in school or any place else. I believe that it shows your character, traditions, and who you represent as a person. I also think that it is an important factor in your culture. For instance, in school there are always issues in which people fight or have disputes over religion, color, or background. If these topics were discussed in places such as school, we would be able to go into the real world with a positive mindset regarding these problems. This would also help reduce war and violence because everybody would respect each other.

In conclusion, I really do hope that people start to be open minded about religion. But hoping doesn't change much. So, now I've decided to pray on the matter.

Briana Savage
Grade 6

Favorite Vacation

My favorite vacation was last year, 2005. I went to St. John, St. Thomas, and Tortola. I have a young brother. My mom stayed back with him and my two other siblings. I traveled with my dad.

The trip was eight days. The first day we were in St. Thomas at a hotel. It was neat because when you walked out of your room, there was a desk with games to play. Also, it was right next to the gate that led outside. It felt like an island hotel.

The next seven nights we were in St. John. We stayed in two different places. The first place we stayed in a cabin with screens for windows and doors. The rain smelled so fresh. There was no hot water so we had to take cold showers.

The last three nights we camped out! We got a tent that had a curtain so we each had a separate room. We took a ferry to Tortola for a day. We also went canoeing to a small island. We went on a boat that took us to uninhabited islands where we could go snorkeling. The colors were as beautiful as the rainbow. I had a lot of tropical smoothies and great food.

When we were getting on the airplane, we walked onto the runway and walked right on. It was the best vacation. The only thing that would have made it better was to have the rest of my family there.

Rachel Lilienfeld
Grade 6

My Wonderful Family

My family is very important to me. If I had no family I would be so sad at an orphanage. Everything I have is from my family.

Parents are the most important part of the family for me. I see them the most; they take care of me. My mother cooks for me and checks my homework. My dad plays with me and has fun with me. My mother is a good cook. My father is good at cooking meat. Sometimes my mom also has fun with me. We play board games like Monopoly.

Other than parents grandparents are also important. Grandparents have lots of stories to tell. Sometimes they even give you money. They also have many interesting items that I have never seen before. My Grandmother takes care of me too. She is there for me if I need to stay there. She checks my homework and feeds me when I am there too. My grandmother is great.

The other parts of the family other than grandparents are aunts, uncles, and cousins. I only see my uncle four to five times a year. I see my aunt and cousin every other Friday. Christmas brings the whole family together, I love seeing them all.

I love my family. Who would cook for me if I do not have a family? Who would be there to have fun with me?

Nicholas Burnell
Grade 6

100 Stitches

When I was four, on a hot, sunny Fourth of July, I was at my grandparents' at one of their Fourth of July cookouts. But it was about ninety eight degrees and I wanted to go home and go swimming. So my mom, dad and I went home. When we got there my parents were out on the deck and I was in the house getting my bathing suit on. On my way outside I got mad and started banging on the back door glass window. That time I hit it a little too hard — my arms went through it! My parents came right in and my dad wrapped my arms up in towels. Then I said to my dad, "I think I'm bleeding." The whole floor was red. My grandparents came down in not even a minute later and said, "Did somebody gut a deer?"

Then the ambulance came. It was freezing in there, because I still had my bathing suit on. When I got to the hospital I was screaming when they put the hundred stitches in and glued one up. My mom almost passed out; they had to bring my dad in. They gave me about 3 needles that were supposed to make me forget everything but it didn't work.

Right after I got out of the hospital, my mom, dad and I went to see fireworks. The next day I went swimming with a bread bag on each arm. I got the stitches out and I went home and jumped right in the pool.

Kimberly Chesniak
Grade 5

Family

My family is important to me because they help me when I need help in my life. When I am sick they look after me. We even pray a morning prayer together. My family cares about me and loves me so much that they put me in a well-educated school. When we eat dinner we pray and give grace.

When I am back from school I don't understand my homework and my parents help me with it. My family provides me good, healthy and tasty food every day.

They take me to fun places like Chuckie Cheese and Downy Park in the summer. My parents buy me good quality clothes. They also provide me a good home.

My brother loves me so much that he is always thankful to God that he has a good sister like me. I love my family so much, I am thankful to God that I have a good family. They make sure that I am happy and they are looking forward to seeing me getting a good education and I am trying for them, to make them happy. They will protect me and take good care of me all the time.

Nidhi Patel
Grade 4

Michelle Kwan

Michelle Kwan is a 25 year old American figure skater; one of the world's best skaters in the late 1990s and early 2000s. She is a six-time United States national champion and four-time world champion. Being a figure skater takes a lot of talent, time, athletic ability, and confidence.

She was born on July 7, 1980 in Torrance, California to parents who came to the United States from Hong Kong and China. She became interested in ice skating at a young age while watching her older brother play ice hockey. Soon she began skating at the highly regarded Ice Castle International Training Center in Lake Arrowhead, California.

In 1993, at age 12, she finished in sixth place at the U.S. national championships. In 1996 she won her first national and world titles in women's figure skating. She has received more perfect scores than any other skater in the history of the U.S. national championships. At the 1998 Winter Olympics in Nagano, Japan, she finished in second place and received a silver medal. Later that year she won the 1998 world championships. She was U.S. champion in 1999, 2000, 2001, and 2002, and won world titles in 2000 and 2001. She finished third at the 2002 Winter Olympics and second at the 2002 world championships. She is the first American female skater to win four world titles since Carol Heiss won five straight from 1956 to 1960.

She was recently selected to be a member of the United States 2006 figure skating team which is to perform in Torino, Italy. On Saturday, February 11, 2006, she suffered an injury that would keep her out of the Olympics. She was replaced by Emily Hughes of New York. Emily's sister is former Olympic Gold Medalist, Sarah Hughes.

Christian Roberts
Grade 5

National Park Zoo

In Washington DC there is a zoo that is called the National Park Zoo. National Park Zoo is in the eastern part of Washington DC. If you live in Alexandra, you would have to take the metro. The National Park Zoo can get very hot outside.

When I went to the National Park Zoo, it was very hot outside. There were a lot of animals. Some of the animals were pandas. One of the female pandas had a baby cub. Some other animals there were monkeys. The monkeys were hiding in the trees. My mother and I also got to see lions and tigers. The lions were males and the tigers were females. We also got to see baby cheetahs. The cheetahs were very cute. Some of them were running very fast. When cheetahs are young they can run about 35 mph. Another animal that I saw was a hippo. The hippos had a very small cage with water, but they can come outside whenever they want. We also got to see elephants. One of them was giving its young a bath. The elephants had a very big trunk where they can have their water. It was very hot outside so whenever we found a misty spout, we would go under it.

In conclusion, the National Park Zoo is a really fun place. The zoo is in Washington DC. All of the things at the zoo were a lot of fun. I loved the reptile room.

Erin Noonan
Grade 5

An Invisible Gift

The invisible gift I would give is the gift of health to my grandmother. This would give her the freedom to do more things. This gift you cannot put in a box wrapped and put a bow on it. I would give my grandmother one of my kidneys. My grandmother's kidneys do not work anymore because they both have failed. She has to go to dialysis three times a week and it makes her very tired and weak. She is limited in what she can do and where she can go. If I was to give her one of my kidneys, she would be able to live a more fulfilling and independent life. In addition, it would relieve a lot of stress and would make her mentally stronger.

Giving up one of my kidneys to my grandmother would effect my own life, but it would be worth it to help her live a normal and healthier life. I would have to watch my health a little more, but at least my grandmother would be around with me longer. If that really did happen, she could go on vacation with me and could visit more often. Additionally, she may be around longer to watch my sisters and I grow up. She wouldn't have to depend on others to take care of her and she could do more things for herself.

So this is my invisible gift. This gift cannot be wrapped or seen, but is a real and special gift from me.

Kristi Thom
Grade 6

Leaving a Best Friend

I had a friend named Geun-Young Moon in Korea. This all began when I moved to a new apartment. I went to only one week of school and I had a vacation.

When the school reopened, I was in fourth grade. I went to a new class and the first day passed quickly. I saw a boy entering an apartment that I lived in. At the front of the elevator, I asked him if he was in my classroom. He said, "I'm not sure…what class are you in?"

"I'm in 4-2," I answered.

"Me too, what floor do you live on?" "I live on the 4th floor," I answered. We quickly became friendlier and friendlier as time passed on. By the time I was in 5th grade, my dad's company sent us to America. I was so sad that I had to leave my friend and my relatives. We visited every one of them and we all said goodbye. I gave my friend a cake as I said goodbye to him.

We communicate with each other through emails. I really want to see him very much although I want to stay in the United States. I want him to send me some photographs, but he never does. Anyway, he is my best friend and it was sad leaving him in Korea. I really miss Geun-Young Moon.

Sungjay Yoo
Grade 6

Who Do I Admire?

Do you have some people you admire? I admire my Papa Joe, my Grandma Donna, and my mom and dad. I admire them because they love, care, and help me.

When I come to visit my Papa Joe, he likes to talk about sports. He loves to help me with math. When I call him about good report cards, I get twenty dollars, and if I get bad grades I get ten. Whenever we practice plays together, we go to the YMCA. I never really see him much because he lives so far away.

My Grandma Donna always makes me smile. She tries to play basketball with me, but she's not very good. She's great at volleyball and she's always there for me when I get hurt, and I am always there for her when she needs help with cooking.

My grandparents are not the only two people who inspire me I still have my mom and dad. They help me a lot with everything like homework, and comfort me when I'm sad. When they go out, I am the one they tell to baby-sit. My parents provide me with a good home, food, but more importantly they are a good role model for me.

The next time you visit your grandparents or sit down with your parents have a nice talk about anything that happened in school or ask them what happened at work. Love, care, and help are the ways they inspire me!

Elizabeth Novelli
Grade 6

Still a Rivalry?

For years, the Cleveland Browns and the Pittsburgh Steelers had one of the greatest rivalries in all of sports. Recently, however, fans and players alike have realized that both teams must have an equal chance of winning for there to actually be a rivalry. Coming into the latest installment of this "rivalry," it seemed as if the Steelers' overwhelming superiority would once again amount to a win.

The biggest story coming into the November 13 *Sunday Night Football* game on ESPN was Ben Roethlisberger's injured knee. "Big Ben" had sat out the previous game, a win against the Packers. Instead of putting Tommy Maddox in to start after his abysmal performance in a loss against the Jaguars, when he threw three interceptions, one for the game-winning interception return for a touchdown in overtime, and one fumble, Charlie Batch led the Steelers to a victory. Steelers head coach Bill Cowher must have had faith in the veteran backup quarterback to repeat that success, making him the starter for the second week in a row.

This game was not only a big one in terms of bragging rights, but it was also important in the AFC North division standings. The Steelers, with a record of 6-2, were tied for the division lead with the Cincinnati Bengals, but they held the tie-breaker with a win over the Bengals earlier in the season.

In the end, Charlie Batch would lead the Steelers to another convincing win, defeating the Browns, 34-21.

Aidan Murphey
Grade 6

Falling Up

One winter day, I was playing outside in the snow. I was trying to build a snowman but that didn't happen. It was getting boring outside so I planned to go inside.

At my house there are four steps to get up to my back door. Since it was boring outside, I went to put away the shovel that I used to collect snow with. It started to snow again and I almost fell just walking one mile an hour because the snow covered up the ice.

When I finally reached the steps, I stopped to call my dog. So she walked up the slippery steps just fine. I started to walk up the steps and I noticed that my boot somehow got stuck. Then I fell up on my knees, and since I was falling so fast I hit my wrist on the edge of the step. I was in so much pain that I was crying. I got myself up and crawled into the house.

After two days we finally knew my wrist was broken because of the way I was forced to hold it. The x-rays were negative (meaning not broken), but my doctor didn't believe that. So she sent me to the cast place and I got a cast from my thumb to my arm pit. It was awful. After some time it got better and I got a shorter cast. So yes, you can *fall up* the steps.

Lesley Hogan
Grade 6

Across America in My Traveling Truck

My traveling truck is traveling through many states. First it went to Florida and saw Disney World. I saw Mickey Mouse on a roller coaster. I went on it too and I sat with him. Next, I went to NASA Space Center and I saw Mars on a video. Then I saw an alligator and it was covered with mud.

Also I went to Maine and I saw a lighthouse and I went in the light room. It was bright! I also went on an airplane over the town. The houses seemed very small. I saw a really big battle ship, and went fishing on Penobscot River.

My traveling truck also went to Mississippi and I saw a REALLY big field with all different types of flowers: blue, yellow, white, green, tall, and short flowers. I also saw millions of chickens in a chicken farm. At the harbor there was a really big boat being built. Then I went fishing for lobsters.

Next, I went to Hawaii in an airplane. I saw a volcano. I went to the top of it but there was no lava in it! I also went to a beach and went swimming. The water was cold. Then I went to an aquarium and saw a bunch of fish and lots of sharks too. I also swam with dolphins. I went surfing on big waves and fell a lot of times. That is what I did in Hawaii.

And that is where my traveling truck went!

Kyle Thibeault
Grade 4

The Patriots

One hot day in the summer around August my mom was listening to the radio on the way home. They were talking about the Patriots. How the Patriots are going to have practice games. So when my dad got home from work my mom told my dad about it. My dad said we should go.

My cousin, Lizz, was over at our house so she went with us. We went in our RV. We all were very happy because we love football and the Patriots. When we got there we saw all blow up stuff and other games. When we got out we were all wondering where the Patriots were.

Then we were walking past all the kiddy games and we saw a big blow up football. We walked through the football gate. So we passed that and we saw the field and bleachers. So we sat in the grass. Then we moved down closer to the rope.

Only my cousin, my sisters, and I moved towards the rope. We were taking pictures of the players. A couple hours later everybody started standing up so we did. We were standing up for a couple of minutes.

Then the players got up and started signing papers. I got a couple autographs. Tom Brady, my favorite player, walked by us but I got a good picture of him and other players. We had an incredible time.

Mikayla Cabral
Grade 6

Scott's Accident

One accident could change someone for years, but here is a guy who had one accident that changed his entire life. His name is Scott Remington. One beech tree on May 25, 1999 fell and crushed his back. Amazingly, not one drop of blood was found at the scene. There was not one cut, or bruise on him, but he was paralyzed! He is amazing, so what we do for him is have a benefit every year.

My second cousin Scott is very caring. He loves everyone around him. He loves his children, John and Jenna, very much. He does amazing things for people. He would go on a camping trip with somebody. He is very caring. He loves everybody around him.

Today he is very active and can do a lot of things. One activity he does is he hunts deer and black bears in a wheelchair! One time he went hunting and killed three deer and two black bears! He also rides snowmobiles with the wheelchair on the back. He rides jet skis, and a dune buggy, paralyzed.

He is very cool. He can do a lot of things to this day. He can do a lot of things on his own. He sometimes goes hunting by himself. He was paralyzed from the waist down.

That is what happened to Scott Remington. He will go down in history in my family. Maybe some other families too if they read his amazing, spectacular book.

Zachary Van Every
Grade 5

The Hockey Game

On a Saturday afternoon I was at my championship hockey games. It was at the old Frank M. Silvia School gymnasium. My team was really good and we were the Senators. We were playing against the Capitals for the championship trophy. They were also very good. The game began and everybody was ready to start the 1st period. My team was passing a lot. Then we scored a goal. We were still playing in the 1st period and the other team was passing well and scored. So now it was a tie 1-1. I said "Oh man they scored. We will have to try harder."

We had a break for 5 minutes. We resumed playing the second period. Nobody scored! Now it was the 3rd, and the last period. I could feel that everybody was really nervous and excited. Nobody scored until there were 2 minutes left. My team tried really hard and pushed the other team away from the ball when they were just about to score. We were passing good and kept control. Then we had a perfect shot and we scored in the last 10 seconds of the game. Everybody in the room started yelling and they were really happy that we were giving each other high fives and running around. The other team never scored and we won.

The hockey league that I play for had a banquet at White's Restaurant. My team received a big trophy that said "Champions" on it and it was really nice.

Kaitlyn Berube
Grade 6

Moving from Place to Place

May, 1996, I was born. My mother Dawn was very happy. When I was a baby, I was very colic. My mother was the first one to hold me. When I was two, I started going to my aunt's daycare. I went there until I was five. When it was my sixth birthday we moved from Florida, my birth state, to Alabama. Moving to Alabama really hurt me because I missed my friends, but we kept in touch. Two years after we moved to Alabama, my grandfather passed. My brother and I stayed at a friend's house while my mom and dad went down to Florida. We were very upset. While we were in Alabama, I attended Brewbaker school. When I turned eight, we moved to Pennsylvania. In May I turned nine. So far I'm having a great time in PA, I've been doing very well in school. My teacher is very nice. My principal is very nice. I really like this school.

Cody Cooke
Grade 4

Friends

I have a lot of friends. I have big friends and little friends. There is Alex, he is a little crazy. There is Kimmy, she sits in front of me. She is really nice. There's Justina, she is really good at sports. She and I are really good friends. I've known Drew since we were three. My best friend is Mike. He and I have a lot in common. There is Brian, he is my lawyer. Michel M. is crazy like Alex. There's Tim. He's cool. Chris is on my dad's travel team. John, James and Will are on my basketball team. Anthony is on my bus. Caroline is good at hockey, so is Jeff. I've known Abby since I was in kindergarten. Giuliana sits next to me. Katie was in my class last year.

In kindergarten my best friend was Brian. In first grade it was Jeff. In second grade it was Charlie, he moved. In third grade it was Mike.

Robert Mahony
Grade 4

My Special Dog Hurricane

My dog is a very special dog because he found his way back to my house before a hurricane hit land. That is why we named him Hurricane.

Hurricane is a miniature terrier. He is also very hyper. He always makes me laugh just by the way he looks at me with his big eyes and his ears poked straight while wagging his stubby tail. Without Hurricane, I do not know what I would do to make me laugh. Hurricane also knows a lot of tricks. He can roll over, give you his paw, stand on his back legs, and he can play dead. He can also make a noise when he yawns that makes me laugh every time.

Hurricane is a very special dog; he makes you laugh and makes you happy. That is why Hurricane is so important to me.

Douglas Howell II
Grade 6

Fantasy Football

Fantasy Football is amazing. I didn't know what Fantasy Football was, until my sister's boyfriend Elliot told me about it. Elliot said he would help me set up a team. When he told me about it I was very excited. He told me to go to the Fantasy section on the Internet. Elliot then said I had to pick a team name. The name I chose was the Hurricanes. Next, I picked my players. I thought my team was very good.

The first game was a disaster for my team. We lost by 21 points! During the week I made helpful changes in my lineup. The next Sunday my team survived a scare by winning by 3 points. The day after I won my game, all I talked about was Fantasy Football.

During the next few weeks my team got awesome. My team's record was 5-1 at this point. Coming up was my huge match up against Sport Stud, also with a 5-1 record. On the day of the game, I kept checking the score. My team came back from behind and won by 2 points in a thriller. The next week I played the best team, and killed them! This past week my team crushed a very bad team. At this point in the year my best players are QB Jake Plummer and WR Steve Smith. Someday I hope to win the league, and earn a plaque. Fantasy Football is fascinating.

Kenneth McGrain
Grade 5

My Autobiography

My name is Kayla Mangan. I was born on October 23, 1995. Ever since I was little I've always wanted to be famous. I love to sing and act. I attend plays and it might help me when I'm older. It's a lot of hard work but in the end it is really worth it.

I also play softball. I started playing baseball when I was like three. Then when I got older I went to softball. I usually play second base. I have team spirit and I cheer on my team. You get hurt a lot in softball, especially if you're small like me. I get run over by big people. I just get back up in the game.

A lot of the time I hang out with my friends. That's something that I love to do. We go on vacations together and everything. We practically see each other every day. We get into fights sometimes but we make up in about one minute. Friends are the best thing I can ask for!

Dogs are my favorite animal. I have one now. I used to have another one but he died. It was my dog Willy's twin brother. His name was Bobby. We adopted them in 2003. We were really lucky to get them because thousands of people wanted them but they had to be bought together. And we were the only ones who would take both of them. Bobby died in 2005. I still have my dog Willy.

Kayla Mangan
Grade 4

September Eleventh, 2001

On September 11, 2001, terrorist hijacked plane flights American Airlines, flight 11, and United Airlines 175. The two flights had a total of 137 people. Both terrorist flew their stolen planes into the Twin Towers. United Airlines, flight 175, crashed into the South Tower at the World Trade Center, while American Airlines, flight 11, crashed into the North Tower. President George W. Bush was informed of the news while giving a speech to the students at a Florida school. President Bush called the White House and ordered everyone to evacuate the area.

Workers spent days searching for survivors and found many buried under layers of rocks, cement, and debris. Later on that day, the Pentagon was hit by American Airlines, flight 77, carrying 64 on board. Another tragedy that happen was United Airlines, flight 93, which had 45 passengers, crashed southeast of Pittsburgh. These 4 crashes cost the government millions of dollars in damage. Most of the money went to destruction of the Twin Towers.

The collapsed building sent a huge shock-wave into the surrounding areas. The collapsed building created a colossal amount of dust, which covered many city blocks. The dust cloud was so big, it left New York City in darkness. People in the Twin Towers rushed out as fast as they could. Some made it out, others did not make it out unhurt or alive. Around the area, people tried to run from the oncoming dust which made total darkness for a while. A month later, the president found out the name of the person who hired the terrorist. His name is Osama Bin-Laden.

Alex Martino
Grade 5

My Allergy

"What's going on? Why are my eyes blowing up?" Those were the only words I could find as my eyes expanded. This is the story of me, when I found out I was allergic to shellfish.

I was so frightened. Just to look into a mirror and not be able to see my face the way it always looked was scary enough. This all started when I was going out to a lobster dinner with one of my best friends. I was looking forward to this scrumptious meal!

When we arrived at the restaurant I smelled the delightful lobster smothered in butter. I knew I had to order it. As I started to eat, I realized that something wasn't the same. Something was happening. My eye started to itch; it wouldn't go away! My left eye blew up and before I knew it so did my right.

It has been a while since I have had shellfish. You may think that this allergy is not that important, but it has changed my life. I always have to make sure when I go somewhere that no shellfish is near my food. If they touched, I would have to go through another terrifying experience. Lobster and shrimp — off the menu!

Anne Hull
Grade 6

Star of the Week

I was always the last Star of the Week, but when Mrs. Kukan picked my number I was so excited! I was not the last Star of the Week! I got to bring in pictures about me. Today I also picked the *Goodness Gorilla* from the bucket. I can't wait 'til Friday. I'm bringing a snack.

Yesterday they didn't ask me much about the pictures, only Karl did. But he didn't ask me about my favorite.

My favorite is the picture of my guinea pig, Little Johnny, because he looks like an angel in the picture. Someone asked me about my hippy picture. I had to dress up like a hippy for the camp I go to. I think it's so cool being the Star.

I already know what I'm bringing in. Here's a hint, my mom already got the mix. Today is Thursday, and I brought in my seven tamas. They are little hand-held games.

I told the class that last night I got two more. I got a mini and a best friend's tama with my friend Molly. Now I have so many!

Today is Friday and I can tell you what I'm bringing in. I'm bringing in — are you sure you want to hear it? Well, ok, I'm bringing in *cupcakes*. I think everyone liked them!

Dana Spagnola
Grade 4

Larry Bird

Larry Bird was born on December 7, 1956, in West Baden, Indiana. He is 6-foot-9 and weighs 220 pounds. He attended Springs Valley High School from 1976 to 1979. Bird led Indiana State to the 1979 National Collegiate Athletic Association (NCAA) championship against Michigan State, and to a season record of 81-13, and to a home record of 50-1. Bird holds 30 Indiana state records including most points scored, 2,850, 240 steals, and 1,427 rebounds. He won 32 awards throughout his college career.

Larry Bird entered the NBA in 1978 when he was drafted by the Boston Celtics as the sixth overall pick. He played for the Celtics from 1979 to 1992. He won 18 awards in the NBA including Rookie of the Year and Most Valuable Player from 1984 to 1986. He also was a long distance shoot-out winner, NBA finals MVP, won three NBA championships with the Boston Celtics, and was a member of a gold medal Olympic team. His nickname became "Larry Legend."

Another basketball superstar, "Magic" Johnson, said Bird was the most dedicated athlete imaginable and that basketball was not just a job for him, it was his life.

Larry Bird retired from professional basketball in 1992, and the Celtics retired his number 33. He then coached the Indiana Pacers from 1997 to 2000 and was named Coach of the Year in 1998. Today, Larry Bird is the Pacer's President of Basketball Operations.

Sean Mahar
Grade 5

The Gift of Kindness

Kindness is a gift that can't be wrapped up in colorful wrapping paper or have a sparkling bow. Kindness is a quality that we should all share. The gift of kindness is a good gift; because when you feel sad all you need is a friend to comfort and be kind to you. I'm going to give the gift of kindness to my sister, Tara. My sister is very enthusiastic and has a great character. She's a great sister to me. However, sometimes we get in fights and I don't like it when we fight. I would really like to fix this so I'm going to give my sister the gift of kindness. One way that I could give her this is by trying to work out problems by listening to her side of the story. This is a good idea because then we could work things out easier and there would be less of a problem. Another way I could give this gift to her is by trying to play with her more often so she won't be so lonely all the time. This would be helpful because I get to act more like a sister to her, and it would help for me to get to know my sister better. The gift of kindness is just one of the many special and personal gifts that you could give to someone.

Shannon McBrien
Grade 6

Christmas

I am wondering, do you like Christmas as much as I do? Why do I like Christmas? What decorations do I put up for Christmas? Where do I celebrate Christmas? These are all questions that you will get to hear the answers to, later on in my essay.

The reason that I like Christmas isn't just because I want to get the presents from other people, it's because I get to see most of my family on one special day. I also like seeing the happy faces on other people when I give them their present that I gave them too!

When I put up decorations for Christmas I usually like to keep them plain and simple. But, my family usually puts up lights in front of the house like hanging icicles. We always put up a Christmas tree and decorate it with tinsel and ornaments. Sometimes we like to spiff up the house with some decorations by having tinsel on the railing, mistletoe hanging in the doorway, or having some mini Christmas trees around the house.

When I celebrate Christmas I celebrate it with a lot of people! I usually start off by going to my dad's house and sleeping over his house for the night. In the morning I open some presents there, then later I go over to my step-aunt's house to open more presents. Next my dad drops me off at my grandmother's house and then my mom comes and picks me up and I go to her house.

So this Christmas try and make it one of the best ones!!!

Jessica Badger
Grade 6

Being Drug Free Is for Me!

Do you know why drugs are bad for you? Drugs can do a lot of bad things to you. Drugs can hurt your brain and body very badly. If you take drugs and drive a car you could get in an accident.

Do you know how to refuse drugs? It is an easy thing to do. Just say no! Stick to sports and other activities such as joining clubs, getting a job after school, or volunteering. Always hang out with drug free people.

Drugs are against the law. You will get in trouble and go to jail if you do drugs. You will lose your freedom and not see your family or friends.

You will be a criminal if you do or sell drugs. Being drug free is very good and it makes you very cool! Your mom and dad will be very proud of you, and you will be very proud of yourself! You can be a role model to all your friends. All of these reasons should make you stay away from drugs. I say again, say no to drugs!

Paul Cano
Grade 4

Baboons

The baboon is an interesting animal that is a large type of monkey.

A baboon can survive in a few different habitats. One of the habitats that they live in is rocky open lands. This helps them by letting them run around free. It also helps the baboons because they can find food to help them survive. Another place they live in is tall trees. This helps them survive because they can swing from trees and they can avoid dangerous animals. Baboons like it because it is a better place to sleep in. Cliff faces are another good habitat for baboons. Cliff faces help the baboons to survive because the baboons can see if any trouble is ahead and also helps them find food.

A baboon has a large head and long sharp teeth. The baboon's arms are as long as its legs. Male baboons are much larger than the females. The male baboons almost weigh up to 90 pounds. The female weighs up to 24 pounds. Infant baboons depend on their mothers for food and protection.

There are different types of baboons. The Hamadryas Baboon lives on the plains and rocky hills. You can find these baboons in Arabia, Egypt and Ethiopia. The Hamadryas Baboon lives in harems that have one male, several females and their babies. Another type of baboon is the Chacma Baboon. They live in southern Africa in the rocky and woodland areas.

Even though baboons are different and live in different areas of the world they still eat the same foods. Baboons eat eggs, fruit, grass, insects and roots.

Baboons are very resourceful because they can survive in many different habitats.

Molly Meka
Grade 4

I Am a Person Who Misses His Old Town

It was March 2004 when I was informed that I was moving. I began thinking of what I would tell my friends and wondered if I would fit in with the new people. I realized that moving was like going on vacation except you are never coming back.

I lived in Valley Stream for all my life. I accomplished everything in Valley Stream. I felt so devastated because I had to leave all my friends that I've known since my diaper days. I just couldn't get over the thought of me leaving my friends.

On the last day of school in Valley Stream, I was heartbroken to leave my friends behind. It was like watching a family member board a plane and fly away from you. Before I left they presented me with *William's Memory Book,* a book that will stay in my heart forever. Before we left the room they embraced me and I left feeling so miserable.

Although I made a lot of new friends in my new town, whenever I see my old school I feel so depressed. I wish I could have known my friends even longer. I can never forget about my old friends and all of the great moments we had. All the memories I had in Valley Stream will never be forgotten. Although I know I moved for my own benefit, I will forever miss my old town, Valley Stream.

William Kim
Grade 6

Animals vs Humans

Carl Lewis is an Olympic gold medal champion. Lewis was born on July 1, 1961, Birmingham, Alabama. Can you imagine being at the Olympics during a race of his? You might say, "Wow he runs like a cheetah!" Let's compare Carl Lewis to a cheetah right now!

Here's a simple comparing fact: their names both start with "C." Being like the cheetah, Carl Lewis was obviously built for speed. Both creatures can jump really far. Also, did you know that both are able to eat meat? Where do you think all those muscles came from?

Now, lets contrast the two of them and see how they're different. A cheetah can run 71 miles per hour. Carl Lewis can run 28 mph. That may seem like small amount to a cheetah, but it sure is fast for us! The life span of a cheetah is totally different from ours. A wild cheetah only lives up to about 10 years old. Carl Lewis was born in 1961, so he is 44 years old. That is definitely longer than a cheetah's life!

Now, a cheetah weighs from a range of 80 to 140 pounds. Carl Lewis's weight was 175 lbs. They may have different weights, but they are positively lean. Did you know that while the cheetah is the fastest land animal, Lewis is the fastest animal on the track. I'm sure plenty still think so to this day. Yeah, I agree, Carl Lewis does seem like a cheetah!

Marina Lauff
Grade 6

Libya

Have you ever wondered how Libya's geography affects how the people live? With a long stretch of Mediterranean coastline, Libya is a hot Mediterranean vacation spot even though three quarters of the inland is part of the Sahara Desert. Libya has an abundance of desert and tropical animal life and is spotted with a number of Berbers, Arabs, Italians and many ancient Roman and Greek ruins. Libya is highly influenced by its Mediterranean and Arabian neighbors.

Libya's coastline is beautiful but the desert is very dangerous. Many Chadian rebels hide in the rocky outcropping. Over ninety percent of Libya's inland is desert. On the southern border is the Sahara, which is a barren wasteland with twelve inches of rain every two to three years. The Libyan Desert, south of the Green Mountains, houses two large oasis settlements, Sabha and Murzug. Sabha, the more famous of the two, houses a fortification once used by a French garrison on the settlement's outskirts. The abandoned building now is used as a headquarters and outpost for the Libyan police. Tripoli, Libya's coastline capital, has highly influenced Libya's economy because of its many ports, offshore activities and long white-sand beaches.

Overall, Libya is an interesting country with a great offshore community, good oil business, limitless cultures and a powerful government. Bonded by a Mediterranean outlook and Arab ideas and customs, Libya is growing fast.

Mitchell Samal
Grade 6

Hockey

Have you ever watched or played hockey? If you have then you know how cool it is. I've been playing hockey since I was three, and let me tell you it's a great experience. Hockey is a great sport to play because it takes lots of practice, is easy to learn, and keeps you physically fit.

Hockey is a physical sport. Hockey is a contact sport. You can check and trip. The positions are center, left wing, right wing, left defenseman, right defenseman, and goalie. Playing any of these positions will keep you in a good physical condition. Hockey can be tough, but if you have the right gear then you'll be O.K.

Hockey is a fun sport to play. I live in Pittsburgh, Pennsylvania and our home team is the Pittsburgh Penguins. The National Hockey League (NHL) is made up of all the National teams in the U.S. and Canada. I played hockey for the Mt. Lebanon Hornets and won the PHLA championship.

Hockey requires practice. At practice, you will learn how to handle the puck and skate well. If you want to be a good hockey player, then you need to practice.

Hockey is a fun sport and is really easy to play and learn. All you need is a stick, a puck, and skates. So play some hockey today and keep yourself physically fit.

Derek Yanosick
Grade 6

Interesting Wars

This essay is about one of the interesting questions about history. This question is whether or not the result of any single battle can tell you which side will win. I will explain this question by showing you three different battles of The American Revolution. Based on my evidence, I will make a conclusion at the end.

In May 1775, the Patriots captured Fort Ticonderoga from the British. This was in the beginning of the war. However, the Patriots in their next important battle could not hold onto New York City. Joseph Martin wrote in his letter that the British were *too powerful* at that moment and they had to retreat. On July 6, 1777, the British got back Fort Ticonderoga.

Then, in October 1777, General Burgoyne surrendered to George Washington at Saratoga. In a painting about that battle it shows the American flag and cannons still up, and Burgoyne is giving his sword to George Washington. There are only two Redcoats present and those Redcoats are surrounded by Patriots. At this time, it looks like the Patriots are going to win. Even though this looked positive, the end was still four more years to go. Finally, the American Patriots won.

My conclusion is that you can't tell who's going to win till the last battle when the other side gives up. I have made my point by showing that the winnings of these battles went back and forth several times before the Revolutionary War ended.

Rachel Scaman
Grade 5

My Family

My mom, dad, sister, and I make up my big loving family. Hi, my name is Ashley Muschiatti and I'm ten years old. My family and I love sports. My dad coaches football. My mom is a Creative Memories Consultant and she passed it down to me. My sister Kelly, on the other hand, is a soccer girl. She loves soccer and gymnastics. Me, well let's just say I LOVE basketball. The Muschiatti family spends a lot of time together. We're like four peas in a pod. We have so many memories to share.

Let me tell you more about my family. When my sister, my parents, or I participate in something, the rest of my family is there to support each other. Each summer we go down to my grandparent's house in Ocean Pines, MD. We have so much fun! Our household gets crazy sometimes because we have four dogs, my rabbit Missy, fish, and me and my sister. We were a huge loving family until summer '05 when my parents split up. We're still a big loving family but we're not as big as we used to be. Right now I'm going to skip that thought. Sometimes Kelly and I don't know how good we have it. We have a loving mom and dad that care about us. Some people don't have that. Hopefully you think about what I just said and be thankful for what you have.

Ashley Muschiatti
Grade 4

If Only I Could

We all know we only get to experience one day once, and it will never be back again. However, not too many people pay attention to that.

Say if it's your first birthday, or the first time you go to a different state or country. People dream that they could go back in time just once. You may have memories of that special day in time, like a relative's wedding, but it's gone the next day. You may think that day was bad, but no day is bad. Maybe you wish that day never happened, but in the back of your mind you liked that day. Some people just say they want to skip a few days 'til they go on a trip. Without that time in between, there is no excitement! Then people just don't have enough time to wait, but you always have the time: you just don't know it. If you go on your first airplane ride, that day only lasts once. People sometimes hate each other for silly little fights, but then they miss their friends. But their friends don't miss them so they wish they could go back in time to fix the problem.

Every day goes by, but every day you get older until you die. If only I could go back and change some things. If I'm ever offered the chance to, I know what I'm going to say: "YES!"

Anthony Hinojosa
Grade 6

The Worst Summer Ever

One summer vacation, I fell and hurt my leg. I was playing with my cousins and I fell and hit a stick. Then my cousins got my mom and I went to the hospital. There I got five stitches and then went home.

My leg took two weeks to get better. I was worried that I wouldn't be able to go on the fishing trips that my grandfather and I were going on. I got my stitches out a few days before I was going to leave. After the cut healed, it left a big v-shaped scar on my left calf.

That was the summer that my dad sold his store and started to work at the Juvenile Detention Center. So that year we didn't get to go on a vacation. Instead we went to Claws and Paws Zoo. After that we went to Promised Land State Park.

On one of the last days of summer, I was fishing with my cousin. When we were going to a different spot I ran over a bees' nest in a log. I jumped off and then ran, but they followed me. I got stung by one hundred bees.

When I went to the hospital they said I was close to going into shock. They kept me there a long time. Then the poison from the bees made me tired so I slept. When I woke up it was dark outside. My grandparents were there. Then we went home and I slept.

John Paul Ameen
Grade 6

The Tennis Tournament

On a wet and cloudy morning, I was on my way to Westwood for a tennis tournament.

"You'll be fine," my mother assured me.

"Whatever…" I murmured.

Trembling, I walked into the Westwood lobby.

"Good Morning!" said the coach. "Are you R.J. Petrella?"

"Yes," I said.

"Well if you'll be so good as to wait over there, your first match will begin shortly."

About 10 minutes later, I was walking down to the court with my opponent. Within minutes, I realized that I shouldn't have gotten so nervous about this match: I won it with a score of 6-0, 6-0. What an easy first round!

In about an hour, I was scheduled a second match.

"You're DEAD!!" said my opponent.

"Right," I retorted. Actually, no matter what he said, I still beat him with another score of 6-0, 6-0. These two simple rounds had gotten me to the finals.

The next morning, my mother, once again, drove me to Westwood for the finals.

"Just play like it's practice," consoled my mother.

"Nothing will make me less nervous," I whispered.

I was more nervous as the match began, which made me begin losing 0-2. Eventually, I was able to revive my momentum and win the first and second sets (the match) 6-2, 6-2! I walked back to the lobby and beamed as I accepted the 14-and-under singles trophy and my place as the 14-and-under champion.

Richard Petrella
Grade 6

Singing Out Loud!

I spend most of my time singing. Mostly I sing songs of what I'm going through in my life and what I love to do. I enjoy listening to songs on the radio and I usually remember lyrics to the songs.

I am thankful for my family and friends because they are my little audience and they support me. Without singing I don't think my life would be as easy because I wouldn't be able to let out my emotions and personal feelings for someone or something I love. I think through singing it made me a stronger person. My role model for singing is Kelly Clarkson. She sings about how her life was as a kid, teen and adult. I really love her voice. I want to become a singer and try out for *American Idol* just like she did. I don't think I have a super voice but I know I have a pretty awesome one for a twelve year old.

I like writing my own lyrics and singing to them because I can make my own beat to the song and sing it as high and low as I want. I keep all my lyrics in a book. When I am finished with a song I perform it for my family. They support me and I'm glad I will sing out loud!

Alysha Nelbach
Grade 6

Our Trip to New York

My father, my sister, and I arrived in New York at the end of September of 2005. The trip on the plane was quite an excitement because we had mixed feelings. We were sad because we left our mom, sisters and other members of our family in Ecuador and at the same time we were going to meet our other family here. Also, this was the first time we flew on a plane. When we were on the plane, we cried a lot and were very upset because we were coming to a whole new world.

When we arrived and got off the plane, we had to go through the immigration part and we met many people there who were asking us many questions. In the beginning we felt lost because we could not understand one word the people were saying to us. Then someone who spoke Spanish came to help and translated everything for us. When we got out it was a relief because we finally were with our family. My grandparents, my aunts, uncles and cousins were there waiting for us.

We have been here for four months and it has been very hard for me and my family to adjust to all the changes. Now, I am working very hard so I can learn as much as I can. I am doing this essay with the help of my aunt who is taking care of me and my family.

Genesis Lopez
Grade 5

Time

Allie opened the garage door letting a fall chill rush in, with me following in her footsteps. We looked for the rake and finally found it. I went back inside our toasty home, opened the door as it creaked, and shouted for my dad to come get the rake for us. He gave it to Allie, as she tried to hold the rake for it was still heavy for her.

We walked down our driveway to the front yard. Allie had the rake, so I just looked at her. All our memories together flashed by my eyes. We sure do have something special between us, a special love bigger than the universe. Allie snapped me back to life, calling my name, telling me she raked one pile of leaves.

We made a huge pile of leaves and named it. Allie and I jumped into the leaves. Allie and I laughed and giggled at how funny we looked with all these leaves stuck in our hair, and created a new memory that we'll always remember.

Until this day we run and play in that one special time, seeing leaves of scarlet, auburn, gold and russet scattered all over the front yard, only in that special time. Allie can reach for the rake and I take the red wagon to play and create a new special time. But most importantly, it's my special time with my sister.

Samantha Castellanos
Grade 6

The Sound of Music

I love the arts. I love them all, especially music. It is great, the beats and rhythms that I hear.

My favorite type of music may not seem typical, but I really love it. I have been in love with rock and roll since before I could remember. I like the old music: AC/DC, Def Leopard, Judas Priest, Led Zeppelin, and many more. I credit my dad for introducing me to the music. My favorite band is AC/DC. I know a lot about them. I even have a guitar like Angus Young's. Angus Young is my hero. He is an amazing guitarist. He still managed to keep his family close to him by having his brother, Malcolm Young, play the rhythm guitar. They started out with Bon Scott as their singer, but he died on February 19, 1980. He was replaced with Brian Johnson. Well, not completely, nobody could fill the shoes of Bon Scott. Brian was willing to give it a try. With Phill Rudd on the drums and Cliff Williams on the bass, they rocked! Angus Young stuck to his school boy image and he was in junior high when he started the band.

AC/DC was a great band with a great sound. They wanted to be famous and they were. In the words of AC/DC, it's a long way to the top if you want to rock and roll. I think that AC/DC is the greatest band in history.

Sara Luczak
Grade 6

Interference in Baseball

In the past we have had sports figures like Lou Gherig. Gherig was also known as the "Iron Man." He had a record for the most consecutive games played despite the Lou Gherig Disease. Cal Ripkin Jr. later shattered that record and finalized the record number upon retirement. Gherig's record might still exist if the disease had not hit him. Drugs and health problems interfere with baseball.

Steroids are interfering with baseball. Barry Bonds is who I think about when somebody says, "steroids." He was once an average guy on the Pirates. Then he started steroids and is now huge. In 2001 he shattered Mark McGuire's record for the most homers in a single season. McGuire was taking steroids. He broke the record held traditionally, by Babe Ruth and Roger Maris. There is also Jason Giambi. He took steroids and was a good player. But then, he got sick for nearly a season.

Illness and death can cause interferences too. Lou Gherig was diagnosed with the "Lou Gherig Disease." The disease didn't only kill a man. It erased something from baseball that will never again come. Not only the most consecutive games played but maybe more records. He was such a tremendous player that he could have set other records.

Interference in baseball is dreadful. It can destroy some of the greatest things to happen. Either drugs or disease, it is still interference.

Tom McLaughlin
Grade 6

My Friend Tricia Robinson

I have a friend and her name is Tricia Robinson. Tricia and I go to the same school and same class. Also we've known each other for 7 years.

Tricia has bluish green eyes and wears glasses. Her full name is Tricia Marie Robinson. She has golden brown/dark brown hair. Her dog is a black Labrador, named MISS COE. Tricia's a little chubby like me but that's okay. She and I are both insane about animals.

Tricia's had her ears pierced twice, once in the lobe and once in the cartilage. She told me to definitely DO NOT do that ever. It really hurts. She sits right next to me in class. We're both in Mr. Porter's or Mr. P's classroom. She wears a fluffy jacket and it's blue. Her favorite color is obviously blue.

I've known her since pree/k. That's 7 years. We never knew about that.

She hates school. She loves to read. Her favorite subject is math. Tricia's teacher is Mr. Porter or Mr. P. Her favorite shirt is a brown shirt that says girls rule. She's kind of good in social studies. Today in school she wore a pink paradise shirt with blue jeans.

Today Trish and I just figured out that we were in the same pree/k class and third grade and fifth grade. That's so cool.

My essay was all about Tricia Robinson and I. She is the best friend ever. She can be *really funny* other times *grumpy*.

Shaylene Stewart
Grade 5

As I Grow Older...

As us kids grow older, we become stronger and braver, because we will soon have to live on our own.

But why? Why do we have to fend for ourselves? Well, because eight or nine years from now, we'll be through with college, living on our own. No one's going to buy us toys to play with, give us clothing, or give us allowance money. Most of all, no one is going to feed us.

When you're a kid, life might seem hard, but when life as a kid seems hard, being an adult must be like suicide. Adults pay bills, rent, taxes and buy food, and on top of that, there's getting a good job to support you and your family! As a kid, we take a lot for granted, as if it's just always there.

There's always food in the fridge, you always have clothes in your drawer, and toys, but as an adult, you *buy* them *by* getting a job.

So when you say, "It's not fair! It's not fair!!!" you should rethink what you are saying because nothing is fair as an adult.

Daniel R. Glass
Grade 6

Grandmother

Everyone has one special person in their life, one person who they love, who always fills their heart with joy. My person is my grandmother. Even though Gran has 19 grandchildren she finds enough love in her for every one of us.

My grandmother has a special way of showing her love to others. She has one special signal, her smile. Her smile is sure to make my day better. It isn't just the smile that shows her love, but how her face automatically changes when I walk into the room. It's my sunshine on a rainy day.

There is one time that my grandma showed me special care. My grandparents had taken my family out to dinner and told us we could have ice cream when we got home. My brother became excited and on our way home he accidentally pushed me over and my knee was cut. My grandmother did everything she could to make sure I was okay. She set up pillows so I wouldn't have to limp to my room. I was so grateful and so was my brother when she said she wouldn't tell our parents how I really fell.

This story doesn't really sound like much. The reason it's special is the way Gran made me feel. The way she treated my wound with such care, it showed me the love and joy she could bring. I love Gran with all my heart. In my hectic world, my grandma holds me together.

Julia Smaldone
Grade 6

Ice Cream, Ice Cream, Ice Cream

Looking for a good way to make an ice cream sundae? This technique makes a great ice cream sundae. The things needed are some equipment, a procedure that won't take long, and cleanup, which is really easy.

To make a sundae, a few things will be needed. They are ice cream, syrup, sprinkles, whipped cream, an ice cream scooper, a bowl or sundae dish, and a spoon.

The procedure is easy. First, open a favorite ice cream. Next, use an ice cream scooper to put as much ice cream as wanted into a bowl or sundae dish. Then, put syrup on the ice cream. Afterward, put whipped cream on top of everything. Finally, use a spoon to eat and enjoy.

Cleanup doesn't take long. To begin, put the ice cream, sprinkles, and whipped cream away. Now, turn the sink on to warm or hot water. Meanwhile, put the bowl, spoon, and ice cream scooper under warm or hot running water, put soap on them, and scrub with a sponge. Lastly, turn the water off, dry the items with a cloth and put them away.

So what better way is there to make a sundae? With such a small amount of preparation your sundae will taste even better!

Brian Havens
Grade 6

Have You Ever Lost a Friend?

Have you ever met someone who meant everything to you, someone that you know will stick by your side through anything? That's a true friend. Now imagine having that taken away. That's what happened to me when my Aunt Valerie died.

It was March 15, 2005. It was an average day. Right when I was drifting off to sleep the phone rang. Who would be calling at 11 o'clock? It was my mom's brother who lived in Florida. A couple of minutes later I started to hear Mom cry. I heard her yell out to Dad as if she were in pain. I ran in and saw her crying. I said, "What's going on?" My mom whispered in a little voice that was barely audible, "Tonight, your Aunt Val died."

Then reality hit me like a truck on the highway. I'd never see my Aunt Val again. Never again will we play our card tournaments of Rummy or War. We'd never do anything ever again. Although it took an emotional toll on me, my mom looked like someone ripped her heart out and put it in a blender.

The next day we departed to Florida. Many tears were shed during this trip and there were hundreds of memories being brought up like old toys under a bed. I lost more than an aunt that pinches your cheek every time you see her. I lost a true friend.

Michael Christofer
Grade 6

A Special Gift

The most special gift you can give can be neither wrapped nor bought; yet it is more precious than gold. It is friendship. When the time was ripe, I was offered this gift, and eagerly accepted it. I had just hopped into the family Honda, unnerved, staring in awe at the menacing moving truck with all of the family's belongings inside, except for a few toys I kept tightly clutched in my hand. We moved to a new neighborhood and I was the "new kid" at school. I felt way outside all of the unwritten social divisions of my new complex environment. To put it plainly, I was alone. However, soon I was taken in by someone and smiled gleefully. Eventually the time came for me to share this gift. I was carrying my tray to my class's lunch table. There was a boy sitting alone at the center of the yogurt-stained table and I figured I'd go talk to him. It turned out that we both enjoyed the same games and movies, so I introduced him to my friends. I smiled as I watched them chat and laugh together. Material possessions, money and the likes matter not; what really makes a difference in yours and others' lives is friendship and kindness. A little bit of kindness goes a long way towards sharing the ultimate gift, happiness. After all, spreading joy and being considerate to one another makes the world a better place.

Matthew Goldenberg
Grade 6

What I Did Last Summer

One of the most exciting things that I did last summer was go to the Rock and Mineral Show at Saint Joseph's Oblates. There were dealers there from all over the country with many different rocks, fossils, and minerals.

The fossils were the most interesting because they were very old. There were dinosaur eggs, sharks' teeth, and plant fossils pressed into the stones. The one dealer had many different minerals and rocks. Among them were samples of uranium rocks which glowed in the dark. He also had many colorful gemstones that were in their raw form. There was a young man who brought up samples of geodes from Mexico. A geode looks just like a round rock until it is split open. Each geode has a different substance and colorful inside. A way to pick a good geode is to get one that's really light.

Everyone's admission ticket was put in a raffle to be drawn for a prize during the show. It must have been my lucky day because the second number picked was mine. The prize that I received was a sample of raw copper. As I was leaving the show there was a sand pit where you could dig for rocks and fossils. One of the items that I found was a saber-toothed tiger's tooth which was over millions of years old. I had a great time at the Rock and Mineral Show and I hope that I can go there again this summer.

Amy Mozeleski
Grade 6

The Thrill of the Race

There is nothing as exciting as swimming a good race and feeling like you have done your best. Swimming is a sport that takes a lot of discipline and work to be able to swim fast. The beginning and the middle of the race is the hardest part, but when you finish you feel like you have accomplished something.

The start is one of the most important parts of the race. Before you race, you must be focused and in the starting position. When the official blows his whistle, the race begins. Having a fast start gives you an advantage because it is like getting a head start.

During the race you have to swim your hardest, which gets your adrenaline pumping. As you are racing toward the wall, your mind is set on doing a perfect turn. Then, when racing your competition to the finish, you have to think, "Make the other person quit first."

At the end of your race, you feel exhausted. When you get out of the pool, you want to collapse, but it is always exciting to see what your time was and how you placed. After swimming a good race, you want to jump up and down and scream you are so excited.

In conclusion, there is nothing more thrilling than knowing you swam your best in a race. Swimming is a difficult sport, but if you put time and effort into it the results are so worth it.

Kendall Hough
Grade 6

My Vacation

My vacation was very exciting. I was so excited I got packed a few days early. A couple days later it was time to go. So we went to the airport and got on the plane. It took a while to get there. But when we got there we had a hard time finding the hotel, but when we found it we unpacked and went to bed. The next day we went over to our uncle's house and he took us over to the ocean on his speedboat. It was really fun. He took us to this island where we swam in the ocean. It was a fun day.

The next day we went to the Magic Kingdom in Disney World. We went on all different kinds of rides. We went into gift shops and restaurants. The next day we went to Sea World. We had a lot of fun at Sea World. We went on this one ride. It was so cool; the ride was called Journey to Atlantis. It was a roller coaster and a water ride. It was really fun.

We also got to pet the dolphins and stingrays and we got to see the Shamu show. That was really neat. We sat in the splash zone but we didn't get wet one bit. After a couple days it was time to go home. We packed our things and went to the airport. We got on the plane and went home. I was glad to be home.

Katie George
Grade 5

A Snow Day to Remember

Ughh! Another Monday morning after a great weekend. So I get up, tired of course, and wake up my parents. I was surprised that they were already awake. Then I looked at the TV and they were posting school closings. I ran out of the room and looked out my window, the backyard was totally snow covered. I ran back into my parents' room, the TV was still naming schools. Finally!!! Margate Schools were listed. "Yes," I screamed "It's closed!" I went back into my room for more sleep but I was too excited. Still in my pajamas, I went downstairs to find my mom making breakfast. As I was eating my chocolate chips pancakes, I called my friends to come over and play. When they came, we made snow angels, had a snowball fight, and ice-skated. After skating in my backyard, we went over to my friends, Courtney and Nicole's home for hot chocolate. When we were warm, we went back outside and made a snow fort. It was huge and all five of us could fit in it. Eventually we all had to go home, but the day wasn't over for me. Every year my family and I make a snowman together. Afterwards we went inside for more hot chocolate and a movie. It was the perfect snow day. The only thing that could make it better would be for the next day to be another snow day.

Amanda McCabe
Grade 6

A Special Picture

It was a dark night, rain pounding, lightning flashing, I sat on my bed looking through my photograph album. Then I came across a picture I hardly recognized. I was standing on the beach with my family. The small figure perched on my shoulder jogged my memory, and I remembered that day.

The small figure on my shoulder was a lizard I named Sydney. After finding her at our beach house, she spent every moment with me. The picture was taken after my eight-year-old birthday, but we were not celebrating my birthday, it was actually my aunt's wedding.

I was a flower girl, along with my two younger cousins. So much commotion that day; cameras flashing, dresses swooshing, we all hopped into the limo to the church. Although my two younger cousins were so scared that they forgot to throw flowers, the wedding was wonderful.

Sun setting, the wedding reception took place on the beach. My favorite part of the reception was the chocolate cake, I love cake! Then, my family gathered on the beach for the perfect picture. I placed Sydney on my shoulder and then click, a wonderful memory was stored that we would never forget.

It was hard to believe that I did not remember that great day at first. Smiling, I slowly closed the photograph album and got ready for bed. I turned off the lamp, walked over to my night stand, and wished my lizard friend Sidney, "good night."

Sarah Straka
Grade 5

Falstaff

I used to have two dogs. Now I have only one. Ariel and Falstaff were great dogs. Then one day Falstaff died.

Weeks before he passed away, he was very sick so we put him on medicine. We started taking him on walks and thought he was doing much better. We were wrong.

One day his back legs stopped working. Frosty (Falstaff's nickname) couldn't walk or even stand. I went to sit with him outside that Sunday morning, but he barked at me because he was in so much pain.

I was crying and didn't want to go to Hebrew School, but I went. We pulled up to the synagogue in the car and my brother and I said good-bye.

We came home and Frosty was gone. He went to the vet and they put him to sleep.

My brother and my mom were in tears that day, but my dad and I were okay. I had already cried that morning but in my heart I felt awful.

I know it was the right thing to do because Falstaff didn't suffer. Every night I think about him and know he is okay now. I still miss him a lot. I can't even believe he is gone for good.

Alison Peltz
Grade 5

The Miracle

My hockey team had a horrible year. We lost almost every game and tournament. Then, during one game that we needed to win, (or we would not go to the finals) we were losing 5-1. However, with about three minutes left of the game, we scored. The only problem was the score was 2-5. We were losing.

Then the coach must have said something to the players, I do not know because I was on the ice, but my team scored three goals in about twenty-five seconds. It was amazing! With about a minute left, the game was tied.

We went into an overtime shootout. I was tense, nervous, and just wished I was not there. The other team scored and then my coach wanted me to shoot. I was afraid. The team needed me to score or we would lose. I started skating from the middle of the ice and started at the goalie. I got real close and pretended to shoot. The goalie slipped, I shot, and scored. My team had another chance.

The other team missed their next shot and my team had won the game. We came back from a game that was almost a loss, it was truly a miracle.

It will be a game I will never forget. One of my favorite trophies is the one I got that day, as the most valuable player.

Cody Murphy
Grade 6

Chihuahua

There are many types of Chihuahuas. Some types of Chihuahuas are short hair, long hair, tea cup and just an average Chihuahua. They also come in many colors such as tan, white, black or you can get a mixed color. The average size of a Chihuahua is six to eight inches. Its average weight is two to six pounds. The Chihuahua life span is fourteen years to eighteen years old.

The Chihuahua was originally bred to be a companion. This dog usually bonds with one person. The Chihuahua originally came from Mexico. The Chihuahua is very playful and loves to be around people. The Chihuahua is a big dog in a little body. They are very lively and are very playful. They are friendly to others. Chihuahuas are wary of boisterous children and dogs that are much larger than they are.

The Chihuahua does not need a lot of room to run, so a Chihuahua would be a great pet for someone who lives in an apartment. The Chihuahua is good around other pets. They are friendly to strangers and unfamiliar dogs. A perfect owner for a Chihuahua would be someone who is gentle, affectionate and someone who will play with it and take care of this tiny dog. I think that Chihuahuas are adorable, and hope to have one someday.

Hannah Schmitt
Grade 6

I Can Do Anything When I Believe in Myself...

Basketballs were flying down the court at the speed of light. My team and I were in the 4th quarter of our championship game and time was running out. There were 7 seconds left on the clock and we were down by 3 points. The score was 35 to 38. It would be a miracle if we brought home the championship trophy.

No matter how many points we were down by, I didn't give up. I kept believing in myself and I told myself that I can do anything that I put my mind to.

I gazed back at the clock with confidence and the ball was in my possession. So there was only one thing left to do and it was to get as close to the basket as I possibly could then shoot. That's exactly what I did. But while I was shooting the ball, I was fouled by a player from the other team. On top of that I made the shot. Then the buzzer rung, but the game wasn't over yet because I still had two foul shots to shoot from being fouled. So that meant we still had a chance to win. I was so overwhelmed that I almost fell to the ground with astonishment.

So, if you ever get into a tough situation like I did, just remember to always believe in yourself and to set your goals high.

Mariah Puchyr
Grade 6

Jason Giambi

Did you know that Jason Giambi hit 38 home runs and had a .300 batting average? In addition to that he gets paid well and gets to be a Yankee. This is why I chose to be Jason Giambi for a day.

If I were Jason Giambi I would get paid $250,000 a game. If I got paid like that I'd be able to buy a convertible, Hummer, or even a Jaguar. With some more of my money I'd donate to hurricane relief foundations just like Jason. Having his money would be one of the best things in the world.

If I was able to be Jason Giambi for a day, I would be able to travel all around the world like Montreal, San Diego, and Arizona. In addition to that if I were Jason I would get batting titles almost all the time. Almost every game I would be able to meet new and old players all the time. Playing baseball all day is one of the best things to do in my free time. In baseball you can just hit and run but you also can be with your friends all day.

Getting to be a Yankee is one of the best things ever. If I were Jason I would be able to hang out in the clubhouse. I would be able to sign autographs. I would be able to play against the Red Sox. I would be able to play all day too.

There are many other people in the world that are like Jason. That's why I would love to be a Yankee and get paid like Jason Giambi. These are the reasons I would like to be Jason for a day.

John Delfino
Grade 5

Cancer

Many people have cancer. I am one of the cancer veterans. I had leukemia. I am grateful to be alive right now. If it weren't for my caring doctors, I might not be here to tell the tale.

I was diagnosed with cancer when I was only six years old. When I entered the hospital, the doctors stuck an IV in my arm. I stayed at the hospital night and day for a week. However, that was only the beginning of my long and raging battle against cancer.

About a year later, two people from the Make a Wish foundation came to my house. The Make a Wish foundation is an organization that grants wishes for kids who have a life-threatening disease. I wished for a trip to Disney World. I got more than that. I got to live for a week in Give Kids the World, a town built only for kids with life-threatening diseases. I got to eat in a gingerbread house, have ice cream for breakfast, play video games at the arcade, and swim and play in the water park and pool. Best of all, it's close to Disney World, Sea World, and Universal Studios.

Think about what having cancer would be like. Every second, every time you go to school, every time you sleep, every time you do anything, a battle would be raging in your body. It was tough, but here I am.

Philip Lowe
Grade 6

Bad Day

A time with my Mom I will never forget was when I was laying on a bed in an ambulance with my Mom right there next to me. I split my lip in half and chipped my tooth. It was horrible! My grandmother (Cheryl) was watching me and my two brothers, Tony and Caleb. Caleb was pushing me on a skateboard and the front wheel hit a crack in the sidewalk. That is when I smashed my face on the ground. BAM!!! At first I didn't know what happened.

When I felt the pain I burst into tears. As soon as I started to cry my friend's mom came over to help me. By the time my Mom got there, the ambulance was already there. The paramedics put me on a bed with wheels. My mom got in the ambulance with me and the paramedics.

When we got to the hospital the doctor had to stick an enormous needle into my gum to inject Novocain. It felt like a giant pinch. After that they put ten stitches in my lip. My mom was so upset. She wanted to hit the doctor for making me scream. My mom had to be taken out of the room because she was so upset. After that, my mom and dad spent $50.00 to $60.00 on toys for me. My mom says I looked like Bart Simpson because my top lip was hanging way past my bottom lip.

Brandon Sulli
Grade 6

Save the Animals

We can save the animals by doing some changes, one of the things is we do not have to cut down the homes of animals. How would you feel if someone cut down your home? When you cut down an animal's home, the animal could die. If you cut down woods, make sure no animals live there. If there is, put the animal in a zoo or shelter. Or just move and cut down trees somewhere else. Sometimes it is okay to cut down an animal's home, but not too much. If you choose to cut one down, leave a little bit of the trees behind so you do not destroy a real good home. Do not kill, hurt, or poison the sweet animals. The animals and I want you to make a change.

Kaylee Lowe
Grade 4

A Day at the Circus

If I had to pick a circus act, I would like to be an acrobat girl and flip in the air. I would have to be very flexible. I would also need to know how to do gymnastics. It would take alot of practice to do my job. I would have to do it everyday to get better.

My hot pink costume would be one of the best things about doing this job. It would look like a bodysuit with a little shirt and a skirt. The shirt has beautiful sequins on it, so it would sparkle.

A day at the circus is a lot of hours and hard work. I have to put in a lot of time and really concentrate. If an acrobat didn't concentrate the circus will be messed up. Practice is every day even on weekends, but it will be worth it because we would hear the applause of the audience at every show.

Tiffany Foley
Grade 4

My Shadow

Don't think it's impossible to get scared by your shadow, it happened to me. I was at my friend's house just having fun like usual. My friend's mom said we should go outside since we were all wound up and it was pretty warm. It was dark outside but we decided to go out anyway and shoot some hoops. When we got outside we started playing a little and taking turns shooting. Then the ball rolled down the hill and my friend went to get it. When I turned around I saw a shadow and screamed! I thought it was a stranger or kidnapper. Then I realized it was my shadow. To make matters worse, when my friend was getting the ball, her shoe got stuck in mud so she ended up with a muddy shoe. I'll remind you though, I'm terribly afraid of someone attacking me in the dark. As you can see, it's not impossible to get scared by your own shadow.

Kayla Fessler
Grade 6

Duke Is the School for You!

Do you want to be on the top college basketball team? If you do then Duke is the school for you. You can meet stars like senior J.J. Reddick. Their team is ranked number 2 in the league. Duke has a spectacular team.

My second reason is they have first class coaching. Coach Krewzewski is a phenomenal coach. Since 1990 he won 3 NCAA championships with Duke. He is a great coach.

My third reason is they are one of the greatest universities. In academics they are rated number 5 according to the national news. If you don't want to play sports you can get a good job afterwards.

Duke is a tremendous college to go to.

Joey Natale
Grade 4

When My Cat Died!!!

My cat died two weeks ago. She had a tumor in her stomach about the size of my dad's fist. She died on January 21, 2006 at 12:00 p.m. Or, in other words, at lunch time. I was crying for the rest of the day. So here it goes…

One day I woke up at 7:00 a.m. on a Saturday. I went downstairs to go feed my cat. I called her upstairs and she wouldn't come upstairs, so I went downstairs and picked her up with the towel (so she wouldn't scratch me.) When I brought her up to her bowls, then took the towel off of her, I realized that her bottom was soaking. So I called my mom and dad downstairs and asked my dad to go get the meat container. I got Twe a piece of meat and she ate it. Then my mom wrapped her in the towel and said to Daddy, "You need to take her to the pet hospital." Two and a half hours later my dad called with the news that Twe was dead! I cried for the rest of the day and the next day I prayed for her at church. The rest of the day was very dull for everybody because we all loved Twe very much. I really miss her a lot.

Now wasn't that story sad? I thought so.

Ariana Y. Saccoccio
Grade 4

My Dog, Brody

One of the things that are important to me is my dog, Brody. He is important to me for a lot of reasons.

First, he makes me laugh when he runs around the house in circles. Next, he always wants to play, so I'm never bored. Another reason is because he is always beside me, no matter where I go.

Finally, he is important to me because I take care of him and love him. He is a great pet because he is easy to take care of. He can keep himself company with his toys or fighting with our cat, Remi.

I love Brody and those are some of the reasons why he is important to me.

Kayla Majors
Grade 4

The Pup

Wait till you see my new pup! His name is Zorro. Guess why? He actually has a Z on the back of his neck. His original owners were gonna put him to sleep because no one would want him, but we couldn't let that happen to him. Zorro is a boxer. They are fast, brave, and highly protective of their family.

He gets along well with my other two dogs, Chyna and Dozer. Chyna and Dozer are both bulldogs, Chyna is English/American and Dozer is English which is a pure-breed. Chyna is the bulldog and Dozer is the male bulldog. When we had to bring Zorro to our house he was so thrilled that he wouldn't stop jumping around for 5 minutes. We had to make sure that Dozer and Chyna would like him and they did, but Zorro didn't like our cat, Kookie.

Zorro really likes my mom because he likes following her around. She likes to call him Dubee which is his nickname. When Zorro can't find my mom he starts to cry and he lays down in front of my back door, but mostly she's cooking something outside like steak tips, hamburgers and steak, but Zorro doesn't know about that. Zorro likes to nibble my mom's feet and my feet, but if you want him to stop just say, "Zorro want to do numb a numbs."

Zorro is an excellent puppy for our family. He gives us a lot of love. That's why my family loves Zorro.

Jordan D'Amaral
Grade 6

Disney World

I am going to write about when I went to Disney World. We had to wake up at six in the morning, so we wouldn't catch much traffic on the way. It was a boring ride. We stopped at a motel when it was about eleven p.m. We woke up again at six a.m. It was a two day trip to Florida, for us anyway. When we got to Florida we went to a hotel (much better than the motel, and bigger). When I got to my room I went straight to the pool.

My cousins came too, Ariadne and her brother Oseias. We were about four, or five rooms apart. My other cousin, Lucas, was in the other side of the hotel. Ariadne is nine. Oseias is six. That's why we play with each other. On the other hand, Lucas is thirteen and I am ten. It doesn't seem right for us to play with each other. Plus he's a trouble maker. Well anyway, the pool was great. They even had a hot tub. The next day we were ready to go to Disney World. I think it was about one hour to get there.

It was a lot of fun. There was this Huck Roller Coaster that I wanted to go on but was too short. So I went on the spinning tea cup. I also went on the Spiderman ride. I went on a whole lot of rides, but I can't tell you about it.

Laynara Barboza
Grade 4

My Great Love for Pets

My pets are very important to me. I love them so much! I love to cuddle and play. My dogs and I have fun all summer and winter. I am glad I have my pets in my life.

Pets are cool! They come in all shapes and sizes. Each one different just like you. They even have their own personalities, they play, and eat, and sleep. They love you just the way you are! Pets love your company like you enjoy theirs. That's how pets are cool!

Pets in general are special friends. They are so much fun. They play and run and like to be silly. Just like me! They sleep on the end of your bed and keep your toes warm. But best of all they comfort you when you are sad.

The sad part about having a pet is when they pass away. You loved them so much and now they are gone in one bad day. I should know, I have lost 10 pets. I was very sad. It's hard to lose a special friend especially if you loved them. You will be sad for a long time. But you should try to be happy, because you know that your pet is happy in Heaven. Also, you will eventually be with your pet again if you accept Jesus Christ as your savior.

Pets are great. They play and they care. But most of all they listen. You can tell them everything. I am glad God created pets!

Leanora Gibb
Grade 6

The Panda Bear

The most famous endangered animal is probably the panda bear. Some pandas live in six small areas all located in China. In China they call the pandas the xiongmas which means in their country "giant cat bears."

Some people believed that the panda's powers could ward off natural disasters and evil spirits. There are writings about pandas that have been traced back to be 3,000 years old. The panda bears were also kept as pets by the Chinese emperors. The pandas first were introduced to the western world by 1869 by a French missionary. They sent a pelt to a museum in Paris.

There are fifteen kinds of bamboo panda bears eat. They eat for 12 to 16 hours a day. Pandas eat 22 to 40 pounds of bamboo each day. When the pandas eat a shoot of fresh bamboo they eat about 84 pounds a day. They only live in damp and cold coniferous forest. For the bamboo to survive the elevation needs to range from 3,000 to 11,000 feet high. Panda bears compete with the farmers in the rivers, valleys, and the mountains. There are approximately 700 to 1,000 giant panda bears still alive in the wild. They will remain in danger because bamboo is hard to find. Bamboo goes through a renewal cycle and can cause pandas to starve and cause death! Male pandas weigh 10% to 20% more than female pandas.

Alexsis Kuriatnyk
Grade 4

Teachers

We need teachers. My teachers are important to me. They challenge us so we can learn better and they give an understanding of what we learn. Teachers help us learn important things. They are required to challenge us for the better. They sometimes give us hard work because they believe we can do it. Our math teacher challenges us a lot, but it gets better. So when we don't understand the work he helps us until we do. Teachers may offer us extra credit work or extra help.

They give us an understanding of what to do. Before we move on to something else our teachers first explain it. A few days ago we learned about ratios and rates, but first the teacher explained what it was. When something is hard we go over it. Sometimes in class people don't understand the work, so we review it. Teachers work hard to give us an education. They don't prepare hard lessons to be mean, just to help us.

Important things are fed to the students from teachers. In kindergarten we were introduced to addition. Now we use it practically everyday. So without teachers education would not be possible. We learned about rates and ratios. So if we enter a line of work that requires us to know this we will not need it to be taught to us. I've learned a lot from teachers and the work they give us. Teachers challenge us on purpose, help us understand and teach us important things. In short teachers are needed.

Brielle Allison
Grade 6

The Big Move

It was a hot, muggy day in the middle of August. Everyone was coming over to help us pack the moving van. My family and I packed for days like little squirrels packing nuts in their house for winter, and we couldn't wait. Soon enough, everyone came and we were ready to go. Already sweating, my dad and uncle picked up the couch and headed for the door. They were grunting angrily trying to get it through the door. Finally they got it through. Everyone cheered as they put it in the moving van. We all knew that was a sign that it wasn't going to be a very easy day. But we kept putting things in the truck, and soon we were ready to go to the new house. We got in the car and sadly stared as we left the house.

After half an hour of driving, we finally got there. Everyone loved the new house. Especially the kids because there was a swing-set in the backyard. So the kids ran off and played as the parents unloaded the truck.

Soon it was 9:00 p.m. and everyone was getting ready to leave. We said our goodbyes and thank yous as they walked out the door. We were very happy and tired at the same time. I said goodnight to my parents and went to bed in my new room.

Anastasia Weckerly
Grade 6

My Hero

My dad is my hero. His name is Yaser Zakria. He is an engineer. Now, he owns a tile store in Queens. He taught me many things such as, being kind and caring for people.

My dad was born in Egypt. He did not come from a rich family. My hero had seven brothers and sisters. My dad was a hard worker. He studied very hard to get fifth and six grades together in one school year. He continued to study very hard until he finished college and became an engineer. Currently, I am trying to study very hard to be top student like him.

Afterwards, my dad tried to look for a good job. When he could not find one, he decided to travel to Iraq. He worked there for five years as an engineer. He spent all the money he made on his family. His experience taught me to be kind and helpful with my family.

After my dad finished his contract in Iraq, he decided to come to America. When he came here, he could not find an engineering job. He took advantage of being handy. He learned how to install tiles. I believe that everybody has to have a skill as a helpful way to find a job.

To summarize, my hero is a nice, kind and hard worker. I learn from him to be helpful and supportive to my family. I also try to be a good student to have a good career like him.

Ahmed Zakria
Grade 4

The Challenge

One day at the crack of dawn in Colorado my family and friends decided to do early tracks. Early tracks is skiing on a really powdery day early in the morning. I was so excited. There was only one lift open, the Gondola. We got our skis and got on the lift. We could see the whole mountain and the beautiful, white, glistening snow.

Then we all headed down the mountain to a trail called Rolex. It is a double black diamond trail. I flew down the mountain like a hawk soaring through the sky.

When we finally passed the steep part of the mountain and were getting to the bottom, I felt like I was being taken out of a cookie jar and being dipped into a glass of milk. It was so foggy. It is hard to imagine, I know, but it is true.

When I got off of the run I was dizzy and in shock that I didn't crash into anything. Everyone else who went down the hill lost their balance. I think that I was the only one in my family who didn't fall, and everyone else had much more experience than I have.

Early tracks was one of the most challenging things that I have ever done. In two weeks, for winter vacation, we are going to Utah. I'm sure there will be more challenges, but doing early tracks in Colorado will always be on my mind!

Victoria H. Wang
Grade 6

How I Got My Dog

The Coassolo family was lonely with no animal companion at their side. The date was December 29, 2002 and we were home on Christmas vacation from school. We were trying to decide what fun thing to do for that day. We thought about going to the movies but then we decided to go to the S.P.C.A. We went in hopes of finding a puppy that would be just right for our family.

The helpers at the S.P.C.A. showed us some big dogs and some little dogs. My brother Christian liked the big dogs, but the rest of us wanted a puppy. So none of those dogs were right for us. Then we walked by this one kennel that had the cutest little puppies in it. We asked if we could take the puppies out of the kennel so that we could hold them and play with them. One puppy was curious. She looked at everything and sniffed at everything. The other one was very scared. He stood in one place and shook all over. He looked so cute. We had to have him. We named him Lucky and brought him home.

We quietly came in our home and down the hall to where my dad was asleep. We opened the door and put Lucky on top of my dad's chest. Lucky licked my dad's face and woke him up. Boy, did we surprise him! Christian and I played with Lucky a lot that day. Lucky slept in my arms. How I loved that. What a special day that turned out to be.

Rachael Coassolo
Grade 5

The Day I Got My Dog

One day my grandma said to me, "I am going to get you a dog." We had been talking about it for a while. I wanted a special kind of dog, but there were none at the pet shop. My parents said I could get a dog. We already had two dogs.

The next day my grandma took me to her job. On my grandma's lunch break we went to the animal shelter. There were many cats and dogs. Finally we found the dogs. Then we were at the puppies.

There were no more puppies left. My grandma asked the manager, "Do you have any more puppies left?"

So the manager looked in the back and said, "No sorry."

Then she said to one of the workers, "Give that little girl that puppy."

The worker said, "I am holding it for someone else."

The manager said, "Too bad, this girl has been looking for a puppy all afternoon, give it to her."

So my grandma took the puppy to the viewing shelf to see if I wanted the puppy or not. I wanted her. She was only six weeks old. I thought of a name, Missiey. So Missiey had a tattoo on her stomach. Missiey was blonde, she had brown eyes she was six inches high and about six inches long. Then we went to the pet shop to get her stuff; like her cage, her leash, her collar, and her puppy food, also a bowl.

Sabrina Panetta
Grade 4

Zach Strikes Again!

What made me laugh was my dad's side of the family and I were in Orlando, Florida. On our way to MGM Studios we were talking about what we were going to do on our fabulous trip to MGM.

When we got to MGM, my 10-year-old cousin Zach was pulling my hair, and all of a sudden Zach saw this ice cream booth. He ran like a cheetah towards the ice cream booth. He saw someone's shoelace untied, and he just walks up to the girl, goes down on his knees, and starts tying her shoelace. After he finished tying the girl's shoelace he started running again. He looked at us to see if we were still there, and he runs into a pole!

My cousin Tyler and I were laughing so hard our faces got as red as an apple. Then Tyler said, "Let's go see if Zach is ok." Tyler and I went to go check on Zach and when we got there Zach had an enormous bump on his nose.

Tyler and I couldn't resist laughing. You don't usually see a big, pink bump on somebody's nose, so we helped Zach up and went back to where the family was.

I'll always remember the time when Zach strikes again!

Erin Ardin
Grade 4

The Legend of Zelda

The Legend of Zelda is the best swordsman game, because there is no blood when you hit the enemy. The enemy does not stay lying on the ground; they disappear. The Legend of Zelda is a game of knowledge. It has a lot of puzzles in the game. These puzzles are hard to solve for me, although some are easy.

The Legend of Zelda was created in Japan. I believe it is one of the best games they have created. I heard there would be a new Legend of Zelda game coming in March or April 2006. I think it will be the best Legend of Zelda. The new Legend of Zelda is called The Legend of Zelda: The Twilight Princess. There are many games. I think their games are very good, but this game may have better quality graphics than any other game they have created. The two Legend of Zelda games that I like the least are the first and second one.

I wish I could buy the other four games that I do not own. I might get them all soon because if you know me I am a Legend of Zelda girl. I even wish I could be a part of the Legend of Zelda game! I made up my own girl, named Zenya. I will always keep saying I may be a part of the game because I think I would do very well working at their company. I also began writing a story called "The Legend of Zelda: The New Sage." I really like the Legend of Zelda because it fits in my heart. I hope you might want to take a try at playing The Legend of Zelda.

Marianne Foote
Grade 4

The Hat

When I was ten years old I got a hat and I loved it. It said NY, which stands for New York, on the front and on the back it said Yankees. I love the Yankees because I like the players and how perfect they play. I wore it every minute of the day and I never took it off. Whenever I went, it went with me. At school I never wanted to take it off, but I had to.

When it was the end of the year the hat was really dingy. It was all scratched up and the stitches had come undone. When there was only 30 more days of 5th grade left it didn't say New York anymore, it was just a dirty hat. One day I forgot to bring my hat to school and I couldn't do my work. When I went home, my mom had thrown it out and bought me a new hat. Now I never think of the old hat. I don't wear the hat that much. I have the hat on my shelf. I only wear it when we go out some place. I hardly wear the hat so I gave it to my cousin who now wears it every day.

Jordan Rego
Grade 6

My Dogs and Family

My dog's name is Bella. She is cute and funny. I just got Bella for Christmas. My other dog's name is Copper. He does all kinds of tricks. My mom and dad's name is Susan and Ellis Smeal. I have three brothers and two sisters. Their names are Poke, Chuck, Devin, April, and Billy Joe.

I live with my gram. Her name is Jennete, she hates that name. We call her Nam. Nam is funny. My dad drives a truck. My mom stays home and watches me and Devin. My mom likes to take me to basketball. Devin wants to play basketball. He can't because he did not get the paper in on time.

Dakota Smeal
Grade 4

A Road to Follow

Henry David Thoreau once said, "*Go confidently in the direction of your dreams! Live the life you've imagined. As you simplify your life, the laws of the universe will be simpler.*" Following my dream is important to me because I've imagined it since I was a little kid. It inspired me to get up and get moving! The first moment I dreamed of becoming a vet was a while ago. If you want, follow through with your dreams. Following your dreams is also important to me because if I believe in it enough, I will make it happen. The first step for me is getting into a good school. A good school will give me the education I need. Second, is for me to find a person or professor to help me follow my dream. Good help is a good education. Third, is to become what I want. Becoming what I want will make my dream come true and myself happy! Following your dream will help you to follow many more things in life.

Hannah Witten
Grade 6

Dancing Through Life

On one of the final days of fourth grade, our teacher, Mrs. Loveless, shared a beautiful song called "I Hope You Dance" by Lee Ann Womack. At first, we were confused about why she was teaching us a new song at the very end of the year, but by the time she finished playing it, we understood. I believe this song teaches some important laws of life.

The lyrics offer encouragement by telling us that to succeed in life we should be loving, "give faith a fighting chance," and partake in every opportunity to experience life and give joy to others.

The song reminds us to be reverent of God's gifts. It tells us to have what we need yet strive to do better in life. We should be thankful for every day we're given and not take time on Earth for granted. We're reminded to love one another — as this is the best way to find love for ourselves. We should be humble and "small" in light of everything around us — including other people, animals and our environment. The song reminds us that even when it seems everything's falling apart, we should keep trying. Finally, we're told to "give faith a fighting chance" and not give up on ourselves and others.

Simply, we should "dance" and thrive. When we have the chance to do something good for ourselves, others or our world — we should not just sit it out. We should dance!

Theodore Caputi
Grade 5

What Makes People Unique

What makes people unique? It is their clothes, their fashion sense, their likes or dislikes, or maybe it is even their character? There are so many factors to being unique. With all the people in this world, you are probably wondering how some people stand out more than others do.

Some people believe it is how they act or behave. People who are unique stand out in a crowd. People who are loud and outgoing can attract people by just being themselves. Quiet people attract attention by saying the right things that people around them want to hear.

There is an old saying, "The clothes make the man." Some people may dress a little different but that is part of what makes them unique. Peoples fashion sense makes a statement.

Abilities also make people unique. When people use their abilities in a positive way, people remember them. Think of the last nice thing someone has done to you. You remember that person.

You can tell if someone is unique just by looking at them, or talking to them for 5 minutes. We're all unique in our own special way.

Mike Crawford
Grade 6

Atlantis

When I went to Atlantis with my whole family for my grandparents' anniversary it was awesome. I went out to the beaches, I went to really nice restaurants and my family went on wild rides too. The best part was…well actually there were two best parts of my vacation. There was getting a versace shirt and spending time with my family especially my older cousin B.

Let me give you a little information about Atlantis. It's in the Bahamas. The whole entire place went underwater. Enough about Atlantis back to the vacation. Like I said the hotel we stayed in was the Coral Towers. It was beautiful. It had awesome views and landscaping. There were ten people in my family and we all got separated but in close rooms. In the first area where I stayed we saw a giant slide and it's really tall too! My grandparents were in the next room and the other room was for my two cousins.

The first adventure we did was going to really nice pools with big slides. My cousin Jeffery who's seventeen went down that big slide I was telling you about. My dad and uncle went down it too. I was going to go down there but then I kind of chickened out. There was another slide called the serplant slide. That was my favorite. I went down it with my cousin B. I also went to really nice restaurants like Carmine's, Seafire and the beaches were really nice too.

Samantha Klaus
Grade 6

Why My Mom Is Special

My mom is kind. She is a wonderful person because she gives me things. She is the most wonderful person in my life. My mom makes me proud.

My mom is a very special person to me. She always takes care of me. When I go home she always has a smile and I think that's a good mother. She buys me a lot of things if I am good. She tells me that I'm very special to her. My mom is a good cook. She gives me a lot of gifts. On Christmas my mom is a very good mom. She gives gifts to her friends on holidays or birthdays, or when they come out of the hospital.

My mom helps me clean my room. When I clean my room, she sometimes lets me go out with my friends. She is a happy person and if you get to know her then you'll know that she is a happy person. You should taste her best cake and flan because it tastes good. Every time I tell her if she can bring something to me she does, and that is a great mother.

My mom is a great person. She is the most wonderful person in my life. She loves me and I love her. She makes me a good meal and that is very generous. She washes my clothes so that I can look nice to go to school. I love her.

Israel Rivera
Grade 6

Best Coach Ever

Have you ever had a teacher or coach, and when you met them everything clicked? I had one coach like that. Her name is Danielle Kenealy, she teaches gymnastics. The moment I met her I knew she was going to be the best coach I was ever going to have. Danielle has taught me more than half of the things I have learned in gymnastics. She has helped almost everybody above the level she teaches.

She has a special way of getting you to do tricks. I had so many fears of doing tricks and she helped me accomplish all of them. Some things that she helped me get over my fear of are: jumping to the high bar, round-off back handspring, and an arial. Her way of getting you to do things isn't making you work nonstop or yelling at you like some coaches do; she is quiet, peaceful, and funny. The way she can get you to do things is through her eyes. Those eyes of hers are like magic. They tell you what to do which makes it so she doesn't have to speak. Ask anyone in the gym what Danielle has taught them and they'll be able to name at least two things.

Danielle works nonstop and is dedicated to her work. She goes to Sudbury Gymnastics Center every day of the week and she also goes to school. If you ever meet Danielle you'll think she's the best coach ever, too!!!

Rebecca Jette
Grade 6

The Birthday

The invitations were out and we were headed to my grandma's house. That's where we have all our parties. When we got there I stationed myself in front of the television. My younger brother, Holden, walked in my grandma's room, he saw something move so he went over to see it. What he saw was a guinea pig that I asked my mom to get me two months earlier. Zachary, my cousin, whispered, "Holden what are you doing in here? Don't tell Shane what you saw okay?"

Holden replied, "Okay." He came out with a smirk and walked down the stairs. Now my friends Christian, Perry, Evan and my relatives were all here. We played games like musical chairs and drop a clothespin in the opening of a gallon of water.

My mom yelled, "Presents." I bolted for the old screen house. I opened all the presents, then I asked, "Where's mom's present?" She signaled Danny my oldest brother to get the surprise gift, which he had to go upstairs for. He came back and put it in front of me. What I saw was a cute, fluffy guinea pig, but she was only fluffy because she was scared. Her dark chocolate brown fur was melted together with the white fur. One half of her head was tannish brown like a graham cracker. So Christian said, "You should name her S'mores," because she had all the colors of a s'mores. When the party was over another story began.

Shane McCallister
Grade 6

The Revenge of the Hornets

The day began as any other Saturday would. I was kind of bored. Then my dad showed me something that he had in his drawer, a GPS, something I was really interested in. I tried it out and found that it worked.

My mom remembered a game she had read about in the newspaper called "Geocaching." People hid things and posted the coordinates online. Then other people would go and find the objects.

We found out about a cache in Sands Point Preserve. We drove out there, parked the car, turned on the GPS and entered the woods to search by foot. We eventually got right around the spot and looked inside a hollowed out tree. We didn't find anything.

On our way back, we passed a hole in a tree. Hornets attacked us, stinging my dad six times, me four times, and my mom only once. She was lucky. We got lost while running from the hornets and had to take an alternate route that was about a mile long. We finally found our car and drove home.

My dad applied Cortisone cream to the stings. It took a few days, but we all fully recovered. Our family has come to a mutual agreement never to walk off the trail without first putting on bug spray. Maybe someday, we'll get a chance to return and find the cache.

Jonathan Masci
Grade 6

Why I Like Basketball

I played basketball ever since I was 5, I was bad back then but now I got a jump shot. I think no one can stop me when I'm at the three point line because once the ball leaves my hands it's over. I know it's going right through the net. I've beat my older brother and he is 18 years old, but the only reason I beat him he said was because he smokes and it slows him down and he can't keep up with me.

I want to become a basketball player because I want to be able to play in the NBA. I love basketball, and they practice every day. They live in mansions and other nice big houses, they also have everything Lamboes, Cadillacs, and other nice cars, and every video game ever made, Xbox 360, Xbox, PS2, PSP, Gamecube, flat screen TV; come on please, 2 million dollars a year, and you get paid from playing your favorite hobby.

If I go to the NBA I want to be on the 76ers because I would want to play with the All Star on the 76ers, Allen Iverson. He is my favorite basketball player and I think it would be awesome if I can play basketball with Allen Iverson.

I want to go to college, take 2 years there, and then go to the NBA because I at least want to graduate and go to college. That's what I why I want to be a basketball player.

Thomas Wild
Grade 6

One of My Greatest Friends and Teachers

Some of the most important people in my life are my teachers. From tying my shoes, to counting by fives, from learning to add to learning to divide, all of these I learned from my past teacher, Jackie Schmidt. She was one of my greatest inspirations. Jackie and I had a special bond. She taught me for three years. By the third year, she and I were the greatest of friends. At the end of kindergarten when I moved, we missed each other very much. I would call her when I became bored, and she would call me. Near the end of first grade I finished the first Harry Potter book. The first person I told was Jackie.

Eventually it was discovered that she had cancer in her left leg. For a while she was doing extremely well, but then it became worse. Before long, her leg was amputated. Her cancer only got worse. A few weeks ago, she died.

When my parents told me I felt a burning within. I felt as if I couldn't breathe as my tears poured down. My mom and I went to the funeral home. The pictures made me recognize how beautiful she was. As I walked to the coffin, tears poured down my cheeks. I knew then that when I grew up, I would help to solve cancer once and for all.

Andrew Levin
Grade 5

3 Important Things To Me

There are many things important to me. My family, my dogs, and baseball are important to me. There are many reasons that they are, and I will tell you why in the next paragraph.

My family is important to me. I am in a family of 5 children. I have 2 brothers and 2 sisters. I am the 2nd youngest. My brother Andrew might work with me on baseball, and Josh is always around to be a playmate. Sometimes he is around too much. Amy and Laura do many things. My parents keep me straight. They also do many more things for me. I love my family.

Our animals are important to me. We have four dogs, and their names are Ralph, Cookie, Chrissy, and Bud. They love on you. My dogs are very playful. You could also call them watch dogs. I love my dogs very much.

Last, but not least, baseball is important to me. Baseball is my favorite sport. Every spring and maybe fall I play. If it is possible I would love to go pro. In baseball the most exciting things are the dreams you always have. Some people dream of being at bat in game seven of the World Series with two outs, and two strikes and a runner on second. The pitcher throws a 99 MPH fast ball. You are down by one run. Then, all of a sudden, you blast one. You are World champs. Baseball is the best!

I told you that my family, baseball, and my dogs are important to me. What about you?

Ben Pittman
Grade 5

Cornelia Funke

Cornelia Funke was born in 1958, in Dorsten, Germany. When she was a child, she dreamed of becoming an astronaut, until she realized military training was involved. At age eighteen, she left central Germany and moved to the northern city of Hamburg. In Hamburg, she graduated from the University of Hamburg with a degree in educational theory. After school, she worked as a social worker for three years.

Following a postgraduate course in book illustration at the Hamburg State College of Design, she worked as a designer of board games and as an illustrator of children books. She was disappointed in some of the stories because of how they were told.

Cornelia wanted to create "magical worlds and fabulous creatures" and was inspired to write stories for young adult readers. While she was a social worker, she heard stories that started her imagination.

At age 35, she realized her true love of storytelling and became a full-time writer. Before she writes a story, she does research. After that, she writes down the plot for the first 20 chapters. Then, after about six months she writes her first sentence.

Cornelia has written over 40 books. Four of those books are novels and two have been made into movies. She has won several awards including the Zurich Children's Book Award (2000) and the Children's Book Award from Vienna House of Literature (2001).

Cornelia Funke now lives in Los Angeles, CA with her husband Rolf (45), their daughter Anna (14), and their son, Ben (9).

Katherine M. Muise
Grade 5

Derek Jeter

Derek Jeter is a shortstop for the New York Yankees. He is a great player not only as a batter, but as a fielder. As a batter Jeter hit .314 in his first season as a Yankee. He also was voted the American League Rookie of the Year, and also a member of the world champion Yankees. They won the World Series three times in Jeter's first four years. In his first season he hit ten home runs, which is great for a rookie straight out of high school. The reason I like Derek Jeter is because I also dream of one day playing for the Yankees, and I also dream of being picked straight out of high school.

He is also the reason I started playing baseball. Derek Jeter also showed me how to work hard, because in his first game he struck out twice, but he did not quit. He kept on practicing and once he became the best player on the team, the New York Yankees drafted him. Derek Jeter is one of the best shortstops to ever play baseball and I aim to do the same thing.

Jay'Cwan Staples
Grade 5

A Rockin' Rush

Everybody has a special place to them, a place where they can unwind and relax, like a secret retreat where they can forget all their worries. For me, that one magnificent place is Walt Disney World in Florida. To me, that place is more than just an amusement park; it's a place where magic is real. It's a place where fun and fantasy meet adrenaline and excitement, all contained in four theme parks. Each is unique in its own beautiful way, with that same Disney touch. One extraordinary time made my last vacation all worthwhile…

My heart was pounding. It wouldn't be long before I would face the ultimate rush in Disney World. I was about to ride the Rockin' Roller Coaster, the most stomach-wrenching of all Disney rides. I watched in anxiety as I heard the screams of riders launching into the darkness. I forced myself to swallow as I stepped into the next car. I took one last glance at the road sign, saying, "Traffic jammed…NOT!"

Boom! The coaster shot forward, like a bullet on wheels. My eyes were sealed shut as I felt myself swirl upside-down three times. My screeches pierced the air like a knife until the ride jerked to a complete halt.

I lumbered out of the car, noticing my legs had morphed into spaghetti. I collected all my thoughts on that incredible flashing moment I had just braved. An immense grin the size of Florida appeared as I knew after that experience, I'd NEVER forget it.

Alexandra Golway
Grade 6

Diwali

One holiday the Asian Indians celebrate is Diwali. Diwali is the festival of lights. On this day it is a joy, they have lots of fun. It is celebrated all around India. It has meant to bring light to every house.

There is a reason why Diwali is celebrated. Long ago there lived a prince named Ram in India. He was sent to the forest for fourteen years. So he, his wife Sita, and his brother, Luxman went to the forest. But soon the evil Ravan found out that they were staying there, so he made a plan to kidnap the wife and he did. So Ram and Luxman tried to save Lady Sita. So they built a bridge to Sri Lanka with their monkey army. At Sri Lanka, Hanuman, the monkey god, sees Sita and tells her that Ram is here. In the end, Ram destroys Ravan and saves all the prisoners. Then Ram's family go back to where they belong.

In India on Diwali the people do a lot of things. They light their houses with lights, they light the firecrackers, and they go on rides such as the merry-go-round or the Ferris wheel. The people eat a lot of sweets.

Rutuja Ajgaonkar
Grade 6

Trombone

Two years ago in fourth grade, we had a school assembly. I didn't think it was that big of a deal. We were going to see what instruments we could play in the school band. There were flutes, clarinets, drums, and a few other instruments. Most of my friends chose the drums, but I decided I would play the trombone. The trombone looks hard to play, but it is fairly easy, aside from memorizing all the positions on the slide. My first music teacher was Mr. Diedrick. Mr. D. was very kind and faithful to us. When I first started playing, I was not very good and thought of giving up. But, as time went by, I started getting better.

In fifth grade, I got a new music teacher, Mr. Cordell. He helps me a lot, especially because he plays the trombone, too. He went to a music school where he mastered the trombone. Mr. C. always believes in me and never loses faith in me or my friends. Sometimes when I play a wrong note, Mr. Cordell will play his trombone so I can match my note with Mr. C.'s note.

Just a little while ago, Mr. Cordell entered me into the Regional Band. That is where very talented musicians go to practice, and at the end, we do a concert. I have much to learn, but with help from my friends, teachers, and loving parents, I will be a very talented trombonist.

Patrick Keefe
Grade 6

Seasons

Living here in New Jersey, I experience many different seasons. Winter is usually snowy and cold. Spring is often rainy and mild. Summer is usually boiling hot and sunny. And fall has big leaf piles and chilly winds.

My favorite season is winter. I love playing outside in the frosty snow. It's thrilling to fly down a hill on a sled, dodge snowballs thrown by my friends and go cross-country skiing. And when I'm almost frozen, it's great to go inside to a warm fire and tasty hot chocolate. I like the winter!

No wait, I like spring too! I love how the outdoors seem to wake up in spring — flowers bloom, birds sing and small green leaves sprout. And, my birthday, which I LOVE celebrating, is in spring! I like spring a lot!

Oh yeah, I like summer too! It's so much fun to go to the pool and jump off the springy diving board. And going to the beach, building sand castles and riding waves are summer highlights. Summer is a great season!

And, there's fall too! In the fall I love to jump in the crunchy leaf piles and bike in the park. It's wonderful to go hiking and listen to the sound of boots on small pebbles and look up at the leaves — hot red, fiery orange and bright yellow. Fall is a beautiful season!

I guess I don't have a favorite season. Each season has its highlights and is special in unique ways. I enjoy them all!

Eliana Tyler
Grade 4

A Walk on the Beach

My feet sunk into the damp sand. The ocean's foam licked my feet. With every step, the water splashed me. My loose hair blew with the wind. My eyes were fixed on the ocean.

What was left of the sun lit the ocean in oranges and yellows. The clouds you could still see were glowing pink. I always thought the sun setting into the waves was the most majestic sight. Maybe that's the reason why I favored this time of night for a walk on the beach.

My nose was filled with the scent of salt water. My ears took in every sound of the waves. While staring at the ocean, I dipped my feet into it.

The sun was hardly there at all, the sky was darker, now I could see some of the moon. The icy air was stronger now, the water was cooler than it had been before, it reminded me of stepping into snow. Yet it cooled me off. I looked back at it.

The ocean somehow talks to me, shares its secrets with me. It teaches me lessons on life. In the ocean there are no walls that hold it back, nothing can lock it up, or keep it contained. It's free, not letting any walls build up around it, nothing's stopping it. That's how you have to be, you have to have no limits. Nothing should stop you in life, you can't let anything get in your way. Like the ocean, nothing can hold me back.

Sarah Wolfe
Grade 6

Baseball Memories

We were playing baseball. I was a pitcher and Gary and Ivan were batters. Gary was the first batter, and Ivan was the second. When Ivan wanted to bat again, he did. Gary did not back up when I pitched, and he got hit in the head. He screamed and fell to the ground; Ivan got him up. I went to tell my mom, and when she came outside, I freaked-out. Mom took Gary over to our store to clean him up. He had blood everywhere, and he kept crying out. We tried to clean him up the best we could before taking him to the hospital.

Mom and my brother left me by myself when they went to the hospital. Later, I got scared because it was 1:00 am, and they were still not home. I finally called my dad, who was at camp, to come home so I would not be home by myself. I couldn't wait for him to get home!

I called my mom and told her Dad was coming home, and she said Gary needed 20 stitches. My brother did not go to school for a week. Then, when he went back to school, he fell to the floor, dizzy. He needed to spend some more time at home to recover.

It's not fair that a game could bring such problems!

Brittany Heubel
Grade 5

Playing in an Orchestra

It's very difficult to play an instrument in an orchestra. Watching the conductor is the most important thing to do. The conductor sets the speed of the song and signals sections to start playing at the right time. If you don't watch the conductor, you could play at the wrong time or play faster than everyone else.

The second most important goal is to display bow awareness. This requirement is important only if you play a string instrument because you need a bow to do it. Bow awareness means that you watch everyone else's bow to make sure yours is in the same area and moving in the same direction. This is very important because you want to look good in your concert. If you didn't have bow awareness in a concert, bows would be going all over the place, and the performance would not look very professional.

The third most important step is to watch the concert master or mistress's body signals. Watching the concert master or mistress is like watching the conductor. The concert master is the violinist that sits in the first chair. This person gives body signals by nodding her head, waving her instrument, or making a loud breathing noise. These signals indicate when the violin section should start playing. That's why you need to watch the signals in order to contribute to the performance.

If you play in an orchestra, you must follow these steps for a great performance.

Emily Symes
Grade 6

All About Me

My name is Hanna Sheppard, and I'm eleven years old. I'm in 6th grade, and I go to Bellport Middle School. I have a brother and a sister. My brother is two years younger than me and his name is Peter. My sister is two years older than me and her name is Molly. I'm the middle child.

Other people in my family are my dad, my mom, my au pair (nanny), and a dog. My dog is a Hungarian dog. Her name is Violet and she is a vizsla. She is a medium-sized dog.

My dad is the best, he works hard and takes care of us. My dad works in Islip, NY at the Mac Arthur airport. He is a supervisor for air traffic controllers. He is the boss of a group of people and his job is very stressful.

My mom is nice and fun to be with. I talk to my mom on the phone all the time and sometimes visit her at the mall (where she works). I went to see her yesterday (February 13, 2006). My mom works in a salon and spa.

My au pair's name is Gisa. She is really nice. She is from Germany and she is nineteen.

Well, that's all about me and my family.

Hanna Sheppard
Grade 6

Rushing to Grow Up

Why do young girls rush to grow up? This is something that puzzles me as I am starting my adolescence. Realizing why young girls rush to grow up is an experience I am going through and one I can relate to. It is hard for me to see my older sisters have more privileges than me. Sometimes I wish I could do some of the things they can, one example of growing up fast. A lot of girls my age feel the need to wear make-up, have boyfriends, go out late, dress provocatively, and do things that they shouldn't be doing yet.

Make-up, boyfriends, going out late, and dressing provocatively are just a few examples of why young girls rush to grow up. Middle school girls feel the need to wear make-up to impress other people such as boys. I am also tempted to do these things because I see other students doing this. Taking time to hang out with your friends is way more important than having a boyfriend. Why should you have a boyfriend to keep you busy? With your friends you can go to parties, play sports, and just hang out with your friends. Some students when going out late dress provocatively. Everyone loves impressing other people.

Seeing peers do this makes me want to do it even more, but I think all of this should stop. Everyone should just be themselves, have fun, and just enjoy everything around them.

Deanna Picciano
Grade 6

The Greatest Gift of All

Love is the greatest gift one could give. Love is an ecstasy greater than happiness or excitement. It comes in various different forms and ways, but despite the differences, love always gives comfort. Love is the greatest gift of all because it brings you happiness, we are able to live with each other through it, and we are able to learn from it.

Love brings a joy no one can explain. It's a joy that is greater beyond its limits. It gives you an amazing feeling in your heart. When you are loved, you feel like you're on top of the world. Love gives you an ecstasy like no other.

Love enables us to exist with each other. Without love, the world would be complete chaos. Love from others gives us the motivation and encouragement to move on even in the darkest of times. Through love, all the hatred in the world can be ceased. Love can bring the tranquil life back into humankind.

We are able to learn from love. Love teaches us that violence is not the answer. Love defines other virtues. It defines understanding, patience, and loyalty. Love teaches all of us these things, and through it, we can end war.

Love is a great emotion shared by all. It comes from the heart and never fades. It puts a smile on your face, and it puts joy in your heart. Love is truly the greatest gift anyone could give.

Jessica Uy
Grade 6

Trust

Trust is the most important gift that you could give someone. Trust cannot be wrapped; it is just given. Trust is extremely important because without trust, the world would be chaotic. I give a lot of trust to my friends and family. I give my trust to my parents in many ways. One is when I get my report card. I always show them even if I get bad grades. Also, I don't lie to them. If I fail in a game, I am not embarrassed to tell them. I give trust to my friends by keeping secrets. They can tell me something that I won't tell anyone. Just like my parents, I don't lie to my friends either. If I trust my friends and they trust me, then I know that they're my friends. In addition, I try to give trust to my sister, and she tries to give trust to me. Other people try to give trust to people they don't know, too. When a carpenter builds a house, the people paying the carpenter must trust the carpenter to make the walls sturdy and to make sure there are no leaks in the roof. Therefore, trust is the most special gift that can't be wrapped in a box.

William DeCesare
Grade 6

The Benefits of Being President of the United States

Have you ever wondered what it's like to be president of the United States?

Being the president of the United States is an exciting, yet very demanding job. To qualify, you must be a natural born citizen of the United States and be at least thirty-five years old. That's just the beginning; you also have to live in the United States for at least fourteen years. Amongst your many responsibilities, as president there are the roles of: Chief Executive, Head of State, Commander-In-Chief, Chief Diplomat, Legislative Leader, Party Leader, and National Leader.

As president you also have many luxuries. You get to live at the White House in Washington D.C. for a four-year term with 132 room surrounded by 18 acres of parkland. Everything you need can be found without ever having to leave the White House. Imagine having your doctor, dentist, and barber shop right in your house. If the voters think you did a great job, you could serve another four years. Just think, you'll have your own personal transportation with bodyguards to protect you. Government transportation is the safest way to travel whether by car, limousine, train, helicopter, or airplane. The president travels on Air Force One, which is like being at home in the air. These are only some of the benefits of being the president of the United States.

Imagine being president and having your face on a coin or dollar bill.

Emily Lubach
Grade 4

My Gift

If I could give one person one gift, I would give my grandma one more year to live. I would do this not to get praised but because she died when I was only 6-years-old. Now I am 12 and there are 7 grandchildren she never got a chance to meet. I also would give her this gift because she had cancer, and I really do not think it was her time to die. I was the closest grandchild to her. I went to her house 2 times a week.

My grandma was a very dedicated person. She put 200 percent into everything she did whether it was working, volunteering, helping her children or grandchildren, or studying. Grandma worked very hard. After she raised six children she worked part-time as a secretary for her church. At night she went to Brooklyn College. It took her a number of years, but she finally graduated. She was so well liked at Brooklyn College; she got a job working in the School of Psychology.

It must have been very difficult for her to work and go to school, but she was very dedicated to her goal of graduating from college. She even managed to watch me a few days during the week. She always took time to play with me and read to me. I remember she would even take me to Pathmark to go food shopping, and she managed to make a regular errand seem like so much fun!

Siobhan O'Donnell
Grade 6

Football

Playing football and being on a team are two of my favorite activities. I love the intensity and roughness, but the best part about it is my teammates, and how good we play when we come together as a team. Football is the only sport where your team must really work together. In football everyone on the team has to play their hardest and depend on each other. If you run the ball and everyone doesn't try their hardest to block, then the run will be unsuccessful.

My favorite position is running back, and on defense, middle linebacker. It is the best feeling when I score a touchdown and everyone cheers. It feels like all the practice and hard work has finally paid off. When I play middle linebacker, it is really intense. Tackling is challenging, but fun. You always try to hit powerfully, but you don't ever want to get hurt or hurt the opponent.

If the game is close and I get the ball, I try to work my hardest. I know everyone is depending on me. However, when that happens I know the coach and the team trust and believe in me. Even if I am so tired that I can barely stand, I find the strength to make one last play, my best.

Football is one of my favorite sports. I can't wait to go to middle school and high school where it gets even more competitive and exciting.

Alessandro Troia
Grade 6

The Aim

I stood on the field terrified. The football was coming towards me! My hands open, I'm looking all around, my teammates all surrounded. My stomach dropped. What was I going to do? My face was red like a red burning pepper. I had to do it.

I got that brown diamond-shaped ball. I was going to go for it. I had 2 minutes to run the field. The goal seemed miles away. My team was depending on me. My head shook from side to side, my eyes only seeing the goal. People jumping to knock me down. My throat thirsty like a fish wanting to go back in the water. My legs wanting to give up, sweat down my face dripping on my shirt. I threw the ball swirling in the air depending on it to make the touchdown to win. I couldn't feel my feet. I felt like I was in the air feeling like I'm the football.

That football swirling in the air, my eye looking straight on the football. That football wasn't going to give up, just like me. I wouldn't give up. I wanted to prove to my friends I'm as tough as them. My heart pounding like a ball bouncing on and off the wall. I could hear the ball sizzling in the air and my heart felt like it stopped. When that ball made the touchdown my stomach dropped, like a brick off a building. I proved to myself. My arm is tough.

Nizama Omanovic
Grade 5

Air Force

The Air Force is a good career because these servicemen fight for freedom, help people in need and risk their lives for others. They also develop friendships and are rewarded for their service.

Helping others is second nature to the Air Force. They helped others in need by bringing food to the victims of Hurricane Katrina. They helped in the 9/11 tragedy. They checked the planes to make sure that our lives were safe.

My dad, an Air Force aircraft fueler, fought in the war. He got a lot of awards for combat missions and protecting important things. He also had a M16 for guarding a president. He lost friends in combat, some even in friendly fire. It is very sad to hear that.

My grandfather was also in the Air Force. My dad and grandfather were in the service together and they both loved it, their career in the Air Force. "I really like the F-16 aircraft, and how it is faster than the speed of sound, so when it flies by it is quiet, and then it's really loud, sometimes it hurts your ears when they come," my dad said. "He would go back in a heartbeat."

Losing lives, fighting for your freedom, risking their lives for strangers, enduring through boot camp with other servicemen, and building friendships are some reasons to consider a career in the Air Force.

Christopher Kuczinski
Grade 6

The Greatest Gift of All

The greatest gift of all is life. Life is the greatest gift because it allows you to do so many things, you experience so many feelings, and you meet so many new obstacles that change your life forever.

One reason that life is the greatest gift is because it allows you to do so many things. You can do whatever with your life, and nothing can hold you back because your life is your personal property.

Another reason is that you experience so many new feelings. With feelings, you can know when to trust someone, and when to stay away. Love, trust, anger, sadness, happiness, sickness, sleepiness, and confusion are some examples of feelings.

The third reason is because you will face so many obstacles that will change your life. Some people don't realize that they themselves make their own good and bad opportunities. Someone that is not doing so well in school has the opportunity to study or to fail. A drug user has two choices, to go to rehab, or to die of the drug's side effects. Remember that not all choices are good.

Life is the greatest gift of all because it gives you the "power" to be different and it is yours only.

Kathryn Bradley
Grade 6

Family

My most important thing in my life is my family. Because they are the most beautiful thing I have. They are everything for me. My mom shows me a lot of different things; like being responsible, honest and friendly. To treat people the same way I like to be treated and to take responsibility for my mistakes. My dad shows me to study, he always talks about being someone important in the future. To always stay in school, to be careful choosing my friends, to stay out of trouble. I love my dad for all the good advice he always gives me.

My sister is very important to me. She's always looking out for me. She baby-sits me. She helps me to do my homework, studies with me, and also shows me games and plays with me. My grandma is important to me because she is who taught my dad what he now teaches me and she is who makes my dad the wonderful person he is today. She also talks and reads me the bible, takes me to church and makes me laugh with her stories. That's why my family is the most important thing I have in my life. I think the family should be important for everybody. They are a gift God gives us. For this reason we need to respect them, love them, and take care of every member of them, so God can bless us every day of our lives.

Ashley Ferreira
Grade 4

Polamalu vs Bettis

Hi, I'm Ashley, and I'm going to tell you about the differences and likings about two football players. Their names are Troy Polamalu and Jerome Bettis.

Troy Polamalu and Jerome Bettis both have a lot of differences between each other and I'm going to tell you what they are. Did you know that Jerome Bettis is a running back and Troy Polamalu is a strong safety? Well, they are. Also, Jerome Bettis is on offense. Troy's on defense. Defense is where the other team has the ball. Offense is where we have the ball. Also, Jerome is retiring, Troy is not. Troy can make interceptions, Bettis cannot. Those are the differences for them.

Now I will tell you how they are alike in some ways. Did you know that they both can make touchdowns? Well, they both can. Troy and Jerome are both very nice, tough, and very fast. Polamalu tackles people, but Jerome can, too. They have very important jobs to do. They both play for the Pittsburgh Steelers. With the help of their teammates we won the Super Bowl. Also, as we all should know, Pittsburgh is in Pennsylvania. Also, both of them work in the Heinz Field Stadium. Those are some of the ways they are alike.

I love Troy and Jerome they are both cool football players. They are alike and different in many ways. They both do a great job at playing. Those are some of the reasons why I like them.

Ashley Niznik
Grade 6

Special Place

One day I looked in one of my closets and noticed that it was filled with junk. Two days later when I was in trouble and had to stay in my room for the rest of the night, I had an idea.

I decided since my closet was long but not very wide, it was a great place for a hiding spot. So that day I stacked up all the junk in the front of the closet and emptied out the back. This gave the illusion that it was filled to the brim. To get into the closet where there was a wall of junk, I had a bag as a door. The bag allowed me to pull it away without the other items collapsing so I could get in. The bag entrance was small but I managed to crawl in. I went in the closet almost every day and soon I had a radio, books, light, a Gameboy, pillows and a blanket.

It was one sad, rainy day. I came home and I rushed to my closet to do my homework in there. As I opened the door to my special place, I stood in horror to see that the stacked junk had collapsed. I quickly sprung into action to try to retrieve the items that I put in the closet. Minutes later I had found everything except for the light.

I never built the special place again but I plan to rebuild it.

Christian Salvaterra
Grade 6

The Black Marlin vs Gary Hall

Hi, my name is Emily. I'm a sixth grade student at WA Middle School. When I got this assignment I thought, "Not another boring essay!" It turned out, though, to be one of my favorites. Read on and find out why!

While researching, and comparing the Black Marlin (the world's fastest fish) and Gary Hall Jr. (America's fastest man in the water) I discovered that they have many similarities, but also many differences.

Gary, a three time Olympian, swam the 50m freestyle in 21.76 seconds or about 2.3 meters per second. The Black Marlin swims 36.1 meters per second, more than 15 times faster than Gary.

This is where my essay gets interesting. I discovered that the marlin can grow to 4.48 meters and can weigh up to 700 kilograms. While trying to find Gary's height and weight information so I could compare the two, I came across his official website. This information wasn't available; however, I noticed a phone number at the bottom of the page for further information about Gary. So I dialed the number. A lady answered, but she didn't know the answer either and asked me to hold. A man answered and I then asked him the same question. To my surprise, the man replied, "This is Gary!" I was so excited! The answer, though, was that he is 6'6" tall and weighs 215 pounds.

As a swimmer myself, this was an awesome moment for me and something I'll never forget.

Emily Pia
Grade 6

The Gift of Love

If I had to choose one thing to give to my mother it would be the gift of love. My mother has always been there for me when I was sick or feeling down in the dumps. She has always loved me and that is what I would give back to her. Love is something that cannot be wrapped up, it is an action that can be made to show someone how much you appreciate them. My mother has given me love a lot of times and probably does not realize how much I love her back. This is a little something everyone needs in life so they know someone is loving and caring toward them. I love my mother very much so if I had to choose, I would give her love. Some people are homeless and poor and have no one to love but themselves and no one loving and caring to them. It is very sad to picture a lonely person having no one who loves them. From this you can see how much people need this gift. When you receive the gift of love, you will remember that moment for years to come because it is always special. You can see why I have chosen this gift to give because that person will always remember the moment when love came into their life.

Kelly Smestad
Grade 6

My Dog Named Maddie

What I think is important to me is my dog named Maddie. She is important to me because she's my special little puppy dog. Her breed is a Rottweiler German Shepherd mix. My family got her when she was two years old, in the year of 2000.

Every morning it is my job to feed Maddie. Every day after I get home, I give her a doggy biscuit. When I get home from school, she is always laying on the front porch until I get close. Then she will run to me and jump and dance with happiness. When I'm done with my homework, I get a few doggy cookies, and we both play outside.

During the nights, she sometimes comes downstairs, jumps on my bed, and sleeps with me. She wakes me up when she gets up at around 5:30 in the morning. When Maddie is on my bed, she warms up my feet.

Maddie is a lot more than just a dog to me. She comforts me when I am down and gives me about a million kisses an hour. Sometimes she is a bad girl and chews things up. Most times after she does that, everyone gets very mad at her and she follows me to my room where she cries.

If Maddie ever got trapped in a fire, I would risk my life to save her. If she died, I wouldn't be able to stop crying. I wouldn't want a dog for a replacement.

Katlynne Georgiana
Grade 5

A Gift I Can Give — A Prayer

I would like to give this gift to the victims of Hurricane Katrina; I would like to pray for them. They have gone through so much, they deserve a gift. I will pray for them because most of them have lost their families. Anyone can give money, food and clothes but I think that the greatest gift of all is knowing that someone is praying for you and cares about you. It just seemed like no one cared about them because it took so long to get help to the victims. FEMA (Federal Emergency Management Agency) was slow to respond and didn't know what to do first. FEMA was very disorganized and did not have good leadership. Many families split up. Government trucks came to take people to safety but there were too many people. So, mothers gave their children to be sent to higher ground and eventually they were reunited. The elderly and the handicapped were too weak to survive. They died because they were too old to brave the fierce elements. Many families have been relocated to different states; this is very stressful on parents. Thousands of people are in unfamiliar surroundings and need new jobs. Their children are in new schools. They don't have any school supplies or any backpacks. The victims of Hurricane Katrina really, really need a prayer. I am the one to do it!

Matt Geiselmann
Grade 6

Why It Is Good to Have a Pet

I think it is very good to have a pet because they can keep you company when you are alone. They also can make you feel better when you are sad.

I also think cats, dogs, parrots, and hamsters are the best kinds of pets because snakes, lizards, frogs, or tarantulas cannot cuddle with you or walk around the house with you. Another reason why it is good to have a pet is that you really start to love them once you have one, and it feels good to have a pet to love. Most of the time if you love your pet and are very nice to it, they will love you back. When we have company over they want to see our cat. You can have a friend that is your own pet. That may sound strange, but it is true. I love my kitten so much that the first thing I do when I get home from school is go see my precious kitten Socks. When I get home from school my kitten is so happy to see me. He purrs and purrs and purrs and will not stop! Just the way that he looks at me shows that he loves me.

Some people say that their pet is their most prized possession! They must really love their animal. I hope my essay has encouraged you to see the importance of having a pet. It does not matter what kind of pet you get; but if you do not have one, get one soon!

Brittany Humphreys
Grade 5

Long Distance Running

I am writing an essay on a long distance run between an ostrich and an Olympic champion, Gabriela Szabo. Gabriela holds a record of a 5000 meter run. She completed this in 14 minutes and 30 seconds. An ostrich can run 5000 meters in 6 minutes and 15 seconds. They are both great runners.

An ostrich is an animal that lives in Australia. They are flightless birds and since they can't fly, they run, sprint and walk to get around. When an ostrich is fully grown, it develops one of the most advanced immune systems known to mankind, which keep it healthy and moving. They are extremely resourceful and can keep speeds of 50 kilometers per hour for half an hour. Ostrich also have large, flexible, flat feet that help them run.

As you know, Gabriela Szabo holds the world record for the 5000 meter jump. She also did very well in some other competitions too. In the Olympics, she placed third for the 1500 meter jump. She has been participating in the Olympics for a while. She has participated in track and field, races, and jumps.

In this essay, I compared Olympic medalist Gabriela Szabo to an ostrich. I told you that an ostrich can run 5000 meters in 6 minutes and 15 seconds. Then I told you that Gabriela can run 5000 meters in 14 minutes and 30 seconds. So that means that the long distance run championship between the two is the ostrich. That is my essay about comparison.

Samantha Shepherd
Grade 6

A Special Gift

Most gifts that you buy can make a person happy. But some gifts can make people feel very special, a gift without a price tag. A special kind of gift that I can give like that is a hug to my grandma. Especially because of her age, she would absolutely love it. I've never seen her so happy as when I give her a gift, but she knows that I did it for her, which is the best out of all things. I'm my grandma's grandson, and she would appreciate anything that I give her, no matter what it is. Since my grandma sometimes leaves for a few weeks, it's nice to show how much I care. When I give her my gift, it makes me feel good because she doesn't get special presents often. I also feel good because I know it makes her feel good as well. When gifts are given, it is mostly something that people sometimes want. My grandma never asks for one, but I know that a hug would help a lot. If she had asked for one, it wouldn't be as special. A special kind of gift is something that comes from the heart and is special, no matter what anyone thinks, or in however form it's given. I think that these kinds of gifts should be given more often.

Bryan Somaiah
Grade 6

How Does Believing Help You?

"I can't do this!" That's what most people say when they are frustrated or annoyed with something they're trying to do. Whining and complaining won't get you anywhere. All you have to do is relax and say, boldly and with confidence, "I can do this." Believing in yourself will make whatever you're trying to do much easier.

Believing will also help you succeed in any life task that you are given. It will also make you want to persevere and rise to the challenge! No hero has ever completed something without believing in himself. You don't have to just believe in yourself in school. Do it on the soccer field or when you're playing games on the computer. Believing will help you challenge yourself to new levels and broaden horizons. It might also make you more creative and make you step outside of the box. You achieve goals that you never thought you could!

You can also be a good friend and believe in your peers. Believing in others shows that you care about them and what they do. This will also encourage them to believe in you.

Wow! Would you have ever thought that all this can be accomplished when you just believed that you could? It isn't always about knowing all the time, sometimes you just have to believe.

Alyson Hayden
Grade 6

My Best Friend Max

I had a dog named Max, he was a German shepherd. Max was very big and strong and he would always keep me from harm. Me and Max would always go to the park. We would play tag and of course Max would always win. Max and me loved each other very much. I had to take Max with me everywhere because I never wanted to be apart. I would never let anyone harm him, Max was like the baby brother I never had.

I first got Max at a police shelter. I knew he was the one for me as soon as I laid eyes on him. It was the happiest day of my life. When I brought Max home he looked like he was scared, so I went over and gave him a kiss and a hug. After a couple of days he got used to us, so I took Max on our first walk together. When we were walking down the street, I saw a man coming near me. He was about to touch me but Max bit him in the legs. I started to run, and Max was right beside me 100 percent.

It was my last day in Egypt and we were going to the airport. As soon as we were driving around Max started barking, turns out he was just excited about all the places along the way. It took us about two hours and a half to go there, but I am surprised Max didn't have to go to the bathroom. When we went to the bathroom, I turned around and Max was gone. I looked everywhere, and I put up flyers but nothing worked. It was the last day I ever saw Max again.

Nermin Moustafa
Grade 5

Ryan Miller #30

Imagine being Ryan Miller with a twenty-one and eleven record on the Buffalo Sabers as the starting goal tender. Ryan Miller spends a lot of time practicing. That is why he is a good goalie.

Ryan Miller was born in East Lansing, Michigan on July 17, 1980. While growing up, he loved playing hockey. He also enjoyed baseball; he was a catcher. When he caught, it taught him to play low in goal.

When he went to high school, he was the best goalie in the district. When he went to the Amateur Hockey League, he received an award for winning the most games in a season. Before coming to the Sabers, he played for the Rochester Americks.

When he was with the Americks, he had 21 wins, 8 losses and 1 shutout. Now he is with the Buffalo Sabers and he has played 35 games. His record is 21 wins, 12 losses, one tie, and one shutout.

The Buffalo Sabers drafted him in 1999. Now he is the starting goalie for them. He broke his thumb earlier in the year and was unable to play. Since he has been back, he has had 5 wins and 2 losses.

Ryan Miller is very talented and is one of the best goalies in the NHL. He has an outstanding record. This year he may make the U.S. Olympic team.

Peter Chopra
Grade 4

About Harriet Tubman

Have you ever heard of a slave called Harriet Tubman? Well, I have. In this essay, I will discuss who she was. I will also discuss the things that she accomplished. Harriet Tubman was a woman of courage.

To begin with, Harriet was born a slave. She made up her mind that she would not die a slave. When Harriet was a slave, her childhood was much more than just play. She started to work when she was just five years old. She was hired out to a nearby plantation to care for the owner's baby. When she was just six, she learned to weave and make clothes. As a young teen, she worked in the fields of corn, potatoes, and tobacco. Harriet was strong. She was really good at her job.

Soon after, Harriet got directions to the house of a woman who would help on the first part of her journey. Harriet did not know this person. Could it be a trap? It was certainly not a trap! The woman told Harriet to hide in a waiting wagon. The kind woman was part of the Underground Railroad. The railroad wasn't a real railroad. It was a network of people and routes on land and water. They helped people like slaves escape.

Finally, Harriet was a famous and respected American. The former slave risked her life many times to help other people become free. She also served her country during the Civil War as a spy and scout. In her later years, she opened her home to people in need.

Baiyinah Lewis
Grade 5

Fantastic Family Fun

Do you have a good family? Does your family help you when you need help? Families are essential because they play games with you, help you, and teach you new things. The members of my family have a good bond because we love each other.

My family loves to play games. My sister and I love to play Mario Party 7 and Crash Tag Team Racing together. Every Christmas at my pap and grandma's house, my whole family plays L C R (Left, Right, Center). We love competing with each other.

My family is great because they help me out. My dad helps me with my homework. My Grandma Emily plays Rummy 500 every so often, we love to play together, and she also teaches me new techniques.

We love to teach each other. I taught my mom Rummy 500 when I was at my grandma's house. If I need help with my homework, someone helps me. My sister and my brother taught my cousins L C R.

Families are very important because they play with you, help you, and teach you new things. Start having fun with your family, maybe even start a family fun night.

Joe McCann
Grade 6

A True American Hero

"Imagination is more important than knowledge," was a famous phrase by Albert Einstein. He won many prizes, made inventions, and was a genius. Also, he had theories that proved scientists wrong.

Besides being a genius, he won many awards. One prize that he won was the Nobel Prize in 1921. In 1921 he was elected Fellow of the Royal Society. During 1925 he was awarded the Royal Society Copley Medal. A generous deed he did was dedicating his brain for scientists to study.

Albert Einstein made inventions and theories that helped us with science today. An invention that he made, called the atomic bomb, helped end World War II. Also, he helped develop the television. His theories of space helped us understand that space is nothing. The theory of relativity ($E = mc2$) is his most famous theory. He made this theory when he was 26 years old.

"I know not what weapons World War III will be fought with, but World War IV will be fought with sticks and stones." We can all agree that he was a genius, and that he changed the world. His life was dedicated to science. This shows that he is a true American hero.

Sandy Scott
Grade 6

Having Fun with Horses

Have you ever ridden a horse before? Have you heard the sound of hooves under you or the feel of the wind rushing through your hair? These are some things which you feel and hear during your ride on a horse. Riding horses in vast pastures and pulling carriages is not something many children get to do on a family vacation to their grandparents.

Riding horses is what I do on vacations at my grandparents. When I am riding it makes me feel like a cowgirl. It makes me feel like a cowgirl because they often rode horses to get around on the farm. I also feel very responsible because I know that I am in control of the horse and if something goes wrong I will most likely be blamed for it.

I ride in a great big pasture near their house. The pasture is so big and so empty that it makes me feel free. The open space seems endless. My spirit soars. In the open field were flowers, bright green grass, and other horses.

My favorite thing to do is to pull the carriages with the horses. I like to imagine the old days when they had no cars, just wagons. I enjoy getting to sit by my family and friends.

In conclusion, the imaginative play and the freedom I feel when riding horses are experiences of a lifetime. Riding horses is a fun family affair. Everyone should try it at least once.

Megan Jarrell
Grade 6

Charles Adams

Have you ever wondered who invented chewing and bubble gum? I know who did. His name is Charles Adams and he is from New York.

After the Spanish-American War ended in 1848, the Spanish general Santa Anna chewed chicle, the dried sap of the sapodilla tree. While Santa Anna was in New York, he gave some of the chicle to Charles Adams. Charles was an inventor. Adams tried to make several items out of the chicle but failed. Finally, he did what the Mexicans had been doing for years — he put a wad of the chicle in his mouth and chewed it. Then he got the idea of adding flavor to it. He did just that. Gum caught on quickly with Americans and it became very popular. He made the first machine to make chewing gum. Next he made a machine to make the gum into rectangles which was easier to wrap. Later he started, owned, and managed his own factory. Then he became very rich. Throughout the process he was patient and he persevered. He didn't get frustrated and he never quit trying.

I think gum is important because so many people use it. It is said that the average American chews at least 200 sticks of gum a year! When you have bubble gum it is fun to blow bubbles. Even now doctors still say that it is bad for your health.

Kids should learn about him because they might have to write an essay about inventors someday and this one was quite interesting.

Luke LeSuer
Grade 4

My Dog "Lucky"

The most important thing to me is my dog, Lucky. She is important to me because about two days after I got her, I almost lost her. Let me tell you the story…it all started when a dog that lived on my farm had a litter of eleven puppies! From the day my brother and I discovered the puppies and their mother, we took the mother food every afternoon. When the puppies were old enough to separate from their mother, my mom called the county to pick them up. Then about two weeks later, my brother and I were playing outside when we decided to go in and there on our front porch we discovered a puppy. I immediately recognized her as one of the puppies from the litter. So my brother and I begged my mom to keep it and she finally said "yes." From that day on, we took her into our home and cared for her and loved her.

Then about two days later, we noticed she wasn't herself so we took her to the vet. She stayed there for four days because she had a life threatening disease. Those four days were probably the scariest days that I've ever gone through because I loved her so much. When she got home, we still hadn't named her so we decided to name her Lucky. Today she is still with me and is the dog I've always known.

Sarah Hammond
Grade 6

Expressing Myself Through Dance

I am naturally a shy person at first, but when you get to know me, I am actually very outgoing. I like to express myself in many different ways. My favorite way is through dance.

In dance sometimes the instructor choreographs a piece for you. In a group, everyone is supposed to look the same. But since every individual interprets the piece in their own way, every step you take expresses the inner you.

In my life, I've had three important dance teachers. My Hillside dance teacher, Mrs. Kriftner, teaches mostly jazz, my ballet teacher, Tomomi, really makes you stretch, and my favorite dance instructor, Maya. Maya really lets you express yourself in many different ways. She says, "Dancing with other people doesn't mean you have to look like zombies, all the same. You have to make my dance, your dance."

I like it when people choreograph for me, but creating my own dance provides a chance to express my feelings. That's another thing I like about Maya. She takes suggestions from the 9, 10, and 11 year olds in her class.

I love to dance, I have been dancing since I was 4 or 5 years old. I look forward to the years ahead so I can continue expressing myself through *dance*.

Amelia Dunnell
Grade 5

My Trip to Las Vegas

My trip to Las Vegas was very exciting! First we went on the plane for 5 hours. The flight seemed even longer in the plane because you have to sit the whole time, and the food is not the best. When we got to our hotel we were amazed! In the hotel in every room there was a huge window! When we looked out of the window we saw the back of the hotel, a view of animals, pools, tennis courts, basketball courts, ponds, and many palm trees!

In Las Vegas, there is a long road called the Strip. While we walked on the Strip we saw people and buildings on it. We saw a variety of amazing shows at casinos and entertainment sites! My favorite part was a pirate show at Treasure Island. The show was about a pirate ship run by girls, in battle with pirate ship run by guys. They fought with explosions and bombs! At a water show, fountains shot streams of water. At a volcano show, a big pile of rocks sent forth different colored steam.

All the food was just about the same as here, but more expensive. There were lots of people selling hot dogs and different things on the streets too. If you ever get a chance to visit L.V. I would suggest that you go! If you do get a chance to go, stay a while, because of all the wonderful sites and events to do.

Allison Boncella
Grade 5

The Beatles

In the 1960's there was a band called The Beatles. The people in the band were John Lennon, Paul McCartney, George Harrison, and Richard Starr who is known as Ringo. John Lennon played the rhythm guitar, Paul McCartney played the bass guitar, George Harrison played the lead guitar, and Ringo played the drums.

In 1967 a man by the name of Brian Epstein became the Beatles' manager. The Beatles soon became a big hit around Liverpool. Soon, they were a big hit all over England. They even played for the Queen. The Beatles sold over one million records and soon brought their music to America. Two of their albums were *Abbey Road* and *Rubber Soul*. The group became the most popular singing group in the world.

In 1970, the Beatles split up. They each wanted to try doing their own music. Paul's band soon became Wings, and George and Ringo recorded their music and played at concerts. Sadly in 1980 John Lennon was killed.

Today it is very easy to listen to the Beatles' music because it is on compact discs, tapes, and the radio. The legend of the Beatles still lives today.

Kevin Faulk
Grade 5

Amelia Earhart

Do you have a nickname? Mine is Amelia, after Amelia Earhart. I look up to her because of what she has accomplished for women. Amelia Earhart became the first woman to cross the Atlantic Ocean by air. From a young age, she decided what she wanted to do.

Amelia Earhart believed that she could do whatever she set her mind to. Amelia proved that women can do the same things men can do. When Amelia was twenty-four years old she had her first flying lesson, and bought her first airplane. She named her plane the Canary. In 1928, Amelia was the first woman to pilot across the Atlantic Ocean. In 1932, she again flew across the Atlantic Ocean, but this time it was a solo flight.

As Amelia got older, she became more adventurous and determined. In 1935, Amelia made two historical trips. On June 1, 1937, Amelia and her navigator, Fred Noonan, left to fly around the world. On July 3, 1937, Amelia's plane disappeared over the Pacific Ocean. She was never heard from again. She never got to complete her destiny.

Amelia knew the trip was dangerous, but she had courage to try it anyway. Amelia Earhart is still known as the "First Lady of the Air." Amelia Earhart is my role model. When I grow up, I want to be like her. I do not want to be afraid to try new things and I want to have the courage to follow my dreams.

Jenalee Jenkin
Grade 4

Cajun Music

"Laissez les bon temps rouler!" Do you know what that means? It is the unofficial Cajun motto, and in Cajun French, it means "Let the good times roll!"

Cajun culture is like no other, and if you ever hear Cajun music, you'll never forget it. Cajun music is played in the bayous and prairies of Louisiana by the descendants of early French settlers. It is traditional music that can be spirited, sad, or sweet.

Cajun music is a way for the Cajuns to tell stories of their ancestors. Long ago the Acadians (later shortened to Cajuns) were French subjects in Nova Scotia, Canada. In 1713, Great Britain acquired their country. The Acadians wanted to stay loyal to their French homeland, but the British ordered them to give up their Catholic religion and pay homage to the English Queen. The Acadians refused and the entire Acadian population, over 10,000 people, were loaded onto prison boats and sent to British colonies. Hundreds died enroute, but those who lived settled in what is now southwest Louisiana. They began new lives rooted in old traditions, including music.

Today Cajun families gather together after a long day of work and sing "complaintes" which are story songs of their French heritage. They also sing lullabies, children's songs, and party songs. Their music is an important part of festivals such as the famous yearly Mardi Gras. With their music, Cajuns sing, dance, and celebrate life — they forget sadness and they "Let the good times roll!"

Mary Plum
Grade 6

Gymnastics

Gymnastics is an open range of activity. In gymnastics, there are activities, wardrobe, and stunts.

First, you need to have the correct wardrobe. You need to wear a leotard. A leotard is like a one-piece bathing suit. Also, you must pull your hair in a bun or a ponytail. Sometimes, you can wear tights and ballerina shoes.

Second of all, there are a lot of different stunts. You can do cartwheels and flips. Also, you can do rolls and bridges. You also can do teapots and round offs. Teapots are when you put your knees on your elbows when your head is on the ground. A round off is like a cartwheel but you land on both feet. Bridges are when you put your hands on the floor and you lift up. There are so many different stunts I can't name them all.

Third, there are four activities. There are: beam, vault, parallel bars, and floor exercises. I like the beam the best because; I think it is the easiest!

In conclusion, in gymnastics you do activities, stunts, and wardrobe I feel that gymnastics is fun because you get to do a lot of stuff. I love gymnastics so much!

Chloe Miller
Grade 5

Picture Smart

I can express my feelings of happiness by drawing and using art. Drawing bunnies and characters I make is how I express myself. The two characters I love to draw are Butterscotch and Scotch Tape. Sewing and knitting is another way I express my feelings. You can express yourself too if you use…ART!!!

When I use art, I feel like I'm actually in my work. I draw bunnies because they are my favorite animals. Drawing them in a certain way makes me feel good inside. Sewing and knitting is something else I really enjoy. My friend and I already sewed 1 shirt, 1 pair of socks, 1 pair of arm socks, and 2 pairs of shorts. Currently I am knitting a pink fluffy scarf. My friend and I sew with a lot of color because our store name will be "Abstract Fashions." I am very artistic.

Being picture smart lets you really feel confident. Any time I use art and get frustrated with my work, I always try to calm down and concentrate. Normally, my grandma helps me with my work. My grandma actually showed me how to draw, sew, and knit. She still helps me enhance my work today. She gives me sewing lessons, too. That's where she sits me down and lets me use her sewing machine. Sometimes, she sits down and draws with me. Being picture smart is an honor.

Dominique Kelly
Grade 4

Dinner with Rocky Bleier

If I could have dinner with anyone in the world, it would be former Pittsburgh Steelers runningback Rocky Bleier. This is because he is just about the toughest person I know of. Also, even when he was in great pain or was partially disabled, he still kept going.

When he first came to the NFL, he was not a star and was not expected to be one. One season Rocky was playing with the Steelers when he was drafted into the army. While serving in Vietnam, he got half of his foot blown off. I would ask him about how painful it was to have this happen to him.

Doctors said he was 30% disabled and may never walk again. When he returned from the war, Art Rooney, owner of the Steelers at that time, was just being nice to him and letting him use the facilities. Rocky could barely walk. The Steelers and all other NFL teams never expected him to come back and play. Three or four seasons later, Rocky returned to the NFL and ran for over 1,000 yards. I think it would be interesting to ask what kept him going and how he kept his spirits up. This is why I would pick Rocky Bleier to have dinner with me.

As you can see, Rocky Bleier was not just a hero in sports, he was also a hero in war.

Bryan Murphy
Grade 6

Terrell Owens

Was Terrell Owens the only reason Eagles had a rough season in 2005?

Terrell Owens was not the only reason the Eagles had a bad season in 2005, because the Eagles wide receiver Todd Pinkston got injured in the Super Bowl and was out for the next season. Their tackler Tra Thomas got injured and was out for the season, and corner back Lito Sheppard was out for the season, and center Hank Fraly was out for the season.

Most substitutions for the injured people were not so good like the sub for Donnavan McNabb was not so good, his name was Mike McMahon. None of the subs were good. The defense was worse because it was rookies in for the injured people. The defense was a major problem this year. The Eagles gave up 357 points, one of the biggest amounts in the history of the Eagles.

Bret Farve from the Green Bay Packers wanted to switch to the Eagles but coach Andy Reid said he did not need him to go to the Super Bowl, so the team got worse and worse. But people said the Eagles would have been better with Bret Farve. That's the reason why Terrell Owens was not the only reason the Eagles had a bad season.

Omar Jackson
Grade 4

Football: An American Tradition

American football, which is known in America and Canada just as football, can trace its roots prior to the 19th century. However, the modern forms of football we see today emerged in the 1800's. At this time football became popular in the United States because students in elite schools and universities started playing games. The rules have evolved over the years into what we now know as traditional American football.

Football is a competitive team sport where the object of the game is to advance the football towards the other team's end zone to score points. Getting the ball into the end zone can happen several different ways. You can run the ball, throw the ball, or hand the ball off to your teammate and let him run. You can also kick the ball through the goal posts. The team with the most points wins the game.

In America there is professional, college, and amateur and youth teams. The only professional football league in the U.S.A. is the National Football League. College football is also very popular and a big part of the culture of small-town America. Youth and amateur teams are played recreationally throughout the United States. All of these organized teams are almost always played by men and boys.

American football has turned into a major sport since its beginning in the 1800's. It attracts fans of all ages including men and women and now is a very important part of the American culture and society.

Andy Madore
Grade 6

Cats

Cats are mammals. That means that they are warm-blooded and give birth to their young. Cats are carnivores. They have powerful bodies, sharp claws, and pointy teeth. They usually eat fish and meat, but if they're starving they eat fish.

A cat has about 250 bones in its body. Its front legs are shorter than its back legs. Its heart beats about two times as fast a human's and it breaths four times as fast. Cats don't chew, they just swallow in chunks.

Cats use their paws to catch prey. Their claws can go in and out (they retract.) The cheetah is the only cat that keeps its claws out. Cats also use claws to climb trees.

Cats are normally controlled and graceful, but without warning they can explode with energy. Cats are great jumpers. Most cats leap better than run, except the cheetah.

Cats use smell to recognize each other. Different friends have different scents. They also groom each other. Fur is the cat's best feature. Wildcats have two layers of fur. Others, like the sphynx, are bald except for their tail. It can be burned easily.

People say, "Cats always land on their feet" and, "cats have nine lives" because they have good balance. First, the inner ear senses when it falls. Next the upper body turns, then the lower body turns. Catnip relaxes cats, and makes them roll over. In the night, cats' pupils get bigger. In the light, they get smaller.

Now you know a lot about cats.

Rebecca Mercuro
Grade 5

He Would Have Loved That Golden Heart

If I could give something that I cannot buy to someone I would have given my grandpa a golden heart. I would give him a golden heart that would never stop beating. My grandpa would really appreciate this because he would never have wanted his heart to stop. He would also like this because he had a family and didn't want to leave them. He had three sons who all loved him. He had a wife who loved him with her life. My grandpa told great stories that I loved and used to drive me places that no one else would take me. I have many great memories with him and he had many memories with me. He used to love my hair a lot. I will always remember when he used to come over. Out of the seven hundred channels he would go to the cowboy channel that he got on his thirteen channels. If he had a golden heart he could enjoy it even more. I think that a lot of people deserve a golden heart but I would pick him out of anyone to have a golden heart. All humans I think should have golden hearts because no one wants their heart to stop. If people's hearts never stopped beating there would be more inventions and more diseases cured.

Ian Callahan
Grade 6

Family

If I didn't have my family I wouldn't have been able to survive. My family is most important to me. I love my mom and dad in my family. My sisters and brother too. I love spending time with my family.

I love my mom. I love her because she always loves me no matter what I do. Also, she cares about my education and always makes me study when I have a test. She always tells me what not to do and that really helps me make decisions. She is the most important person 'cause I spend time with her.

Also, I care about my dad as much. He loves me very much and he'll do anything if something happens to me. He always gives me money and he gives me how much I need. My dad is the most supportive person from my family.

I love my brother and sisters as much. My sisters sometimes take me out to eat when I'm getting bored. My sisters help me solve my problems. My brother is kind he doesn't annoy me. My life is so much fun 'cause of my brother and sisters.

My family is very special to me. The people I love most in the world are my mom, dad, brother, and sisters. My life would be incomplete without them.

Shaheera Kazmi
Grade 6

How Dancing Has Changed My Life

Dancing has taught me to be stronger in my dedication and discipline. I have to be on time every class. That is really hard for me because I'm late all the time. I have to practice dance to get better. I am not just going to get better by going to one class a week which is what I thought at first. I am going to have to work, but I love to dance so it's worth it. Dancing is one of the hardest things I've ever done. However, it's also one of the most rewarding.

My dance teacher Miss Linda has helped me excel in ballet so much. She's taught me how ballet can make my physically stronger. Dancing really helps you to be healthier because it is great exercise. When you leave dance class you're tired, sore, and burning hot. Your legs are shaking but, as my wonderful teacher Miss Linda says, "that means you've worked hard."

Dancing not only helps you to become physically stronger but stronger emotionally too. The way it helps me is, when I feel frustrated, I just dance. At times like that, I just take out my frustration in the dancing. I've found when I do that my dancing seems to be better because of how hard I'm concentrating. Dancing can also help you emotionally because it makes you feel strong and proud to be who you are. Dancing has made a great impact on my life.

Annie Lowenthal
Grade 5

Never Judge a Dog by Its Fur

Everyone has heard that popular saying "Never judge a book by its cover," but…no one ever heard "Never judge a dog by its fur." Dogs are very popular and almost everyone in the world has one, but not everyone likes them. If you are a dog lover, like me, you know about dogs, and how much you love them. If you want a dog you don't just have to settle for one kind. You can get a Husky, a Pekingese, a German Shepherd, a Dachshund, a Black Lab, a Golden Retriever, a Lhasa Apso, a Shiba Inu, a Pekepoo, a Beagle, a Basset Hound, a Collie or just a plain mixed breed dog. That is just to name a few.

You can adopt a dog from a pound too. If you have a dog, you have a lot of responsibility. You have to feed and bathe them and make sure they get exercise. If you get a chance, you should adopt a dog. You might even save their life. I adopted a dog and I'm glad I did. It's good to have a dog. When we got our dog from the pound, he looked very skinny and scraggly. We thought he was ugly at first. We gave him food and love and made him part of our family. Now he is as pretty as can be. So, if you get a dog that looks sick, give them love and they will look better.

Kaitlyn Mecannic
Grade 6

Overcoming Death

Everyone loses a loved one some point in life. Death is something you may experience multiple times. I lost my grandmother a while back, so I know how you feel. Remember, it's perfectly normal and healthy to grieve. How often do you think people die? The truth is, someone dies every sixteen seconds. If you felt alone, now you know you're definitely not!

Dying is the way of life, it makes the world go around. If every human lived forever we may be the only species left, because we'd overpopulate. This means bye pets or any other animal that meant something to you. This is because there are so many hunters already, think about past hunters. How many hunters are still alive? Enough already, I'll tell you that!

Never forget about your loved ones, they'll always be with you in your heart. Someday you'll be with them in heaven, in paradise. People die often, but people are born just as often. Whoever died is in a better place. Dying may be cruel, but perhaps their soul is now the next person born. What's the cruelest fate? I'd say cancer, because it chooses you, and there really isn't a cure.

Everyone dies. We'll all be in heaven together with our friends and family. People die because of others' carelessness. Cancer is fatal, but never let the victims give up. There's always hope. Nobody should ever give up. Help the victims stay hopeful so more people don't grieve.

Amber Kell
Grade 5

My Family and I

One bright and sunny day, July 11, 1995, a cute little baby named Taylor Morgan Storey (and of course that was me) was born into a family with three other little girls. Later, when I was six my mom had another baby girl, and that made five girls in my family. I know what you are thinking, no boys! Except for my dad, it is all girls. Of course you could count our dog, Jake and our cat, Reggie. They are both boys. Then we also have four fish who may be boys or girls. We do not know!

My whole family likes music and sports. You may think we have a full house, and yes, it is full and a little noisy, but it is also a lot of fun.

We live in a medium-sized house with five bedrooms and a huge yard. Since we are the youngest, I have to share a room with my younger sister, but someday my mom says I will get my own room.

Our house is in the country and we enjoy hiking the trails around where we live. In the summer we like to go for rides on dirt roads in the back of my dad's truck. Sometimes we camp out in our backyard. It can be fun to live in the country.

My aunt lives in the city. I think I like the city better than the country though, but I can live with it a few more years.

Taylor Morgan Storey
Grade 5

My Special Place

My special place is in my house. It is in my library where my TV is and all of the books are around me.

This is my favorite place to be because when I do my homework there, I feel more comfortable. I also have a lot of books to help me with any questions I have for anything I'm doing. I have my dictionary there. If I need to look up a word, I can look it up because it is right there.

I love coming in and getting comfortable on my big, comfy chair which is green, by the way, my second favorite color after pink. I also love watching TV in the library because it soothes me, but only on the weekends. I pay more attention to my work during the week. I love having the phone right next to me because I don't have to use any muscles or energy to get it. This was especially true this past week when the phone was ringing off the hook. Friends and relatives wanted to know why I was in the hospital.

I also sleep in my library. In my library I either take a nap or sleep at night. What I do is get in my big green chair and then I put my blanket over me. I only do this when it's nice and warm.

My library is a quiet and peaceful place. That is why I love it.

Yelena Zangas
Grade 6

My Amazing Grandma

My grandma's a wonderful person. She's loving and fun, and much more. I really love her and I am going to tell you a little about my grandma.

My grandma is loving. She's loving because she always comforts me. She comforts me when I am sad. She's loving because she never likes to see us sad and if we are sad she always makes us feel better. She's also loving because she is always kind to others. My grandma never argues with someone. She also never argues with my brother or me. Another reason she is loving is that she always takes me places with her.

My grandma is fun. She's wild when we play games. It's fun when we play games because she is the one who makes it fun. Whenever I play with my grandma I have a crazy time. If you played with my grandma you would have fun too. My grandma and me love to play Candy Land. She usually wins. I don't know why I always lose. Only once have I won a game with my grandma and it was hard.

My grandma is loving, giving, and fun. I really miss my grandma because she is in Bosnia and I have not seen her for a long time. My grandma sends me pictures of my aunt, uncle, and herself.

Amina Habibovic
Grade 5

Jazz

What does jazz mean? Jazz is about freedom. Jazz is a form of musical communication. Everybody knows it and everybody enjoys it. It celebrates life. When it first started it was made by slaves. They were aliens in a new world. They expressed their sorrow, their happiness, and all their emotions through music. They hollered or made rhythms with household tools. Since everywhere they went a white watched them, they created a code. Jazz was their code. Through the music, they communicated to each other. In jazz, people just don't play music they live in their music and that's what makes it great. One musician who heard an old man banging his dish in a sad rhythm understands that the man had had a bad day. Some play a merry jig that makes you want to dance because they are happy. In jazz, you don't follow any order you played what you felt and what you did. It helped African Americans feel at home and not so alien anymore. Without jazz, they will have nothing to bring their hopes up. Jazz also means music. All kinds of music up, down, low key, high key, Trumpet, Trombone it meant everything to music. It was the very foundation of American music from Hip Hop — slow, it meant every thing to American music. Even though Jazz was created by Africans, they didn't sing it at home.

Abdii Kassa
Grade 5

How Kids Juggle Play and School

You might think kids are having fun at school, but did you know that kids get 90% of their stress from their school work? So they need to play at home to balance school and play.

Kids go to school for about eight hours a day, and still have homework that takes about an hour or two. Think of it this way: we usually get home at 2:56, and it takes one or two hours to do homework. At night we have to take a shower, and that takes about 20 min. That leaves only about three hours of play, and sometimes parents make us read, so that's another 20 min. So now you know that school outweighs play and kids need play to balance out their days. With all the wars going on, play literally heals our hearts, but in school (social studies) the more we learn, the more we fear. When we play, we just forget everything that worries us, and we don't feel insecure, we just feel happy because we're having fun. It's not boring having fun, but it is in school. How do you think I could write 250 words? I would not personally write all of those words. I would be outside playing even if it was winter. So now you know every kid's life.

Zachary Harmon
Grade 5

Doctor Kiess

Imagine somebody walking past security in an airport. He walks through the metal detector and it beeps. He has metal on him, but it's hidden. It may be a metal hip, or hip replacement.

When I grow up I want to be an orthopedic surgeon. I love the feeling of helping people; it makes me feel so proud about myself. I can only imagine how surgeons feel after the surgery, knowing that they've changed someone's life in a good way.

When I think of being an orthopedic surgeon, I think of my dad. He loves running. I watched him run two marathons. The first one was a great experience, but the second one he couldn't even finish. We were scared. The constant rubbing when he ran caused him to need a hip replacement. It has been about two months since he got it and now my dad barely even has a limp. He says that he is going to run another marathon and I'll be there watching him.

It must be genetic because my grandpa also had a hip replacement so we say my dad and grandpa are "hippies." Hopefully my dad will not have any limp in a few months either.

Helping people is what I love. Seeing how the doctors helped my dad inspired me. I intend to help people every day and achieve my dream. I am determined to help people in need no matter what.

Nicole Kiess
Grade 6

My Family

This is what my family means to me. I believe I have the greatest family in the world. I love my mom and dad so much. My cousins love me and cares about me. This is why they are my family.

I love my mom a lot. She loves me and takes care of me. She sees that I get a good education. She brought me into this world when I was born. She taught me to say my prayers. She let me enjoy my dance class. She takes me to the movies.

I love my dad and this is why he is important. He helps me with my homework. He bought me a computer and taught me how to use it. He taught me how to ride a bike. He works hard so I can have clothes for school. He always takes me to the football games. He started a bank account for me. This is why my dad is important to me.

My cousins love me and I love them. I spend a lot of time with my cousins. We all care about each other. We play games together. They are important and fun to grow up with. We go to church with each other. It's great to have a large family.

My mom, dad, and cousins are the only people I need. This is why my mom, dad, and cousins are very important to me. I love my family a lot and that's all that matters.

Candice Corbin
Grade 6

New Neighbor

My old neighbor was George. I just learned that he was moving. My new neighbors' names are Susan, Greg, Kyle, Robo, Dinky, and Autumn. When they came my mom became friends with Susan. Kyle was on my bus. I got to be Kyle's friend. Greg, every time I called, he said, "Wrong number." When I went to the house, Greg locked the door and said, "No one is home this is a recording." Then on the weekend I would go over and hope Greg was not at the door. We played video games, we played sports, and we rode our bikes. We also played in the snow. We also built snowmen.

I went over almost every day. We have a lot of things in common. We like the same kind of video games, and we like the same sport. We have a lot of fun. I mean a lot of fun. They are really nice. I joined basketball and he was on the same team. Now he is in wrestling. I'm not in wrestling because I don't like wrestling. These are the kind of video games we like: war, action, adventure, and war action. Next year he will be in 6th grade. Now I go over on Friday and sometimes on Saturday. I go over and watch some wrestling on Friday.

In good weather we walk his dogs. Dogs are sometimes hard to walk. Sage is hard to walk.

Justin Tripoli
Grade 4

Family

Family: a group of people who love and care for each other. My family is the most important thing to me. My family is always there for me; also my family loves me. My parents provide me with guidance. My family is very caring and special.

My family is always there for each other. When I'm sick; my family is always there for me. Like the last time I was sick my mom, dad, and brother all took care of me. Also, they always come to support me in my activities. I play a lot of sports, and no matter what they're always there. I support them too; whether it's sports, shopping, or cooking, we all pitch in and help. My family has always been there for each other.

My family loves me. My mom tucks me in every night. Every night she tucks me in and tells me she loves me. Furthermore, my dad loves helping me with soccer. He takes time to observe me. My brother helps me with my math homework. Sometimes I help him with his spelling. My family supports and helps each other.

They provide me with guidance. My parents teach me to have manners. They tell me to say please and thank you. In addition, my parents teach me to be respectful. They tell me to show others respect. Also they teach me to have morals. They teach me to tell the truth, do right, and help others. My parents have always guided me in the right direction.

My family is the most special thing to me. My family cares for me, cares about me, and shows me wisdom. I love my family.

Danielle Cifelli
Grade 6

Pets

There are many different kinds of pets. Three different types of pets are cats, dogs, and ferrets. Cats are good pets because cats like to play. Dogs are always there for you. They're man's best friend, and ferrets are always trying to cheer you up, and they never get enough love.

Cats are very curious and always want to know what you're doing. Cats eat cat food such as Friskies. Some cats drink warm milk, or just water. Most cats like to chase things. Cats like to chase bugs and birds. Cats are fun pets.

Secondly, dogs have always been man's best friend mostly because they're loyal. They like to hunt, similar to cats. They also like to fish, and love to go on walks. There are many different kinds of dogs, and they are wonderful pets.

Lastly, ferrets are great pets as well as cats and dogs. They're great companions. They're very cheerful, and always looking for lots of love. They like to go outside and just have fun. Ferrets are great pets.

There are many different kinds of pets. My favorites are cats, dogs, and ferrets, what're yours?

Casey Bills
Grade 5

Sports

I love playing sports. Sports are important to me in the world. I like to play basketball and football. I also love bowling. These are the three things I enjoy doing.

I love playing basketball. I love to run up and down the court. I love exercising for fun. I love shooting the ball; I like to get a lot more points for the team. I love the way we play as a team. I like to pass the ball around and take runs shooting. This is why I love playing basketball.

I like to play football. I like to play tackle with my friends. I like to make up all the rules. I love to run around in the street, at the park, and at my house in the backyard. This is what I like about football.

I enjoy bowling. I like to hear the crash of the bowling pins and the ball. I love…to roll the ball. I like racing my friends and cousins. This is what I enjoy with bowling.

I like to play basketball and football. I also enjoy bowling. Bowling is one of many favorite sports. These are all of my favorite sports.

Taylor Wilkins
Grade 6

My Cruise

The most awesome trip I have ever been on was a Royal Caribbean Cruise.

I had a blast; the ship had an arcade with more than 30 arcade games to play. I spent $40.00 just on the games. The ship also had six pools and nine hot tubs. I swam in all of them.

I also loved the basketball court; I played on it a lot. The ship also had a movie theater with a popcorn machine! The ship had a frozen yogurt machine so I could make yogurt cones. I loved it.

The mall in the center of the ship had everything a kid could want; I bought a silver bracelet.

The ice and roller blading rinks were awesome. I skated on them until the last day of the cruise.

I went to an adventure Ocean Kid's Club that went on all day and night until 1:30 am; this was awesome because I got to play Playstation 2, dodge ball, and we also got to play on the basketball and volleyball courts.

Every night my family would walk down to the main dining room for dinner. Once I had a really big lobster tail. There was a bunch of waiters and waitresses from different parts of the world, like China, Germany, Poland, Mexico, and Romania.

Our room was cool because it had a balcony. I could see the Caribbean Sea. My bed had to be pulled out each night by one of the stateroom attendants.

Now you understand why I thought that was my most exciting trip. My mom and my dad and I want to go on another Royal Caribbean Cruise, maybe to Alaska.

Kevin Nicholson
Grade 6

Should Kids Be Getting Homework?

Every day children like me ask ourselves why we get homework. Why should we? Kids don't think that it's fair. We learn for 180 days in school. Shouldn't we get a break? I know there is summer break, but don't forget summer reading and math packets. Sometimes teachers go overboard with homework. We don't have enough time to do it all.

Playing outside and doing sports keeps our bodies fit. If we have to do homework all the time, there is not enough time to play. We want to hang out with our friends after school and not have to do homework all night.

We learn in school, why do we have to learn at home too? Teachers say they give us homework to "practice" what was taught in class. Well, if we don't understand, we can ask for help. Only the bad kids should get homework as a punishment.

Teachers give way too much homework. How are we supposed to have time to do it all?
We have other things to do. For example: projects, studying, and homework from other classes or play sports. When teachers give us a lot of homework, they are making more work for themselves. Why would they want to do that?

The majority of kids say we are getting too much homework. What does that tell you? I mean we're only in middle school. Should we really be getting that much homework?

Melissa Carle
Grade 6

A Gift

A gift that is not wrapped or something that you can't buy can be the best gift of all! An intangible gift is very special because it comes from the heart. An intangible gift makes you really think, because you want it to be the perfect gift. The gift I would like to give is for my grandpa to walk again. My grandpa is very special to me. When I was about two-years-old he got cancer that left him paralyzed. He is now stuck in a hospital bed in his living room for the rest of his life. When I was younger he would always take me places, so if I give him this gift he can take my cousins and I to do fun things again. He also loved to travel so if he could walk again then he could travel to all the places he wanted to visit, but couldn't. My grandpa always asks my brother and I about our sports and when our next game is, so it would mean a lot to my brother, my grandpa, and I if he could come to one of our games. When I think of my grandpa I think of a miracle, because the doctor told us when he got the cancer he would have 3-6 months to live. That was ten years ago! Even though it is rather hard to give this gift to my grandpa, it is still nice to visualize him walking beside me.

Lauren Butterworth
Grade 6

The Pet of Tomorrow

Swoosh!!! Our car whisked down the slippery road on rainy July 13, 2001. Suddenly, the car slowed down and parked in front of an enormous brick building. I quickly slid open the damp door and jumped out of the vehicle. My family and I cautiously walked into the old structure. A worker happily greeted and led us into the back room.

There, before my eyes, were about 50 puppies just waiting to be adopted. After carefully examining some, I paused while looking at a shy and shaky Sheltie.

He had beautiful white, brown, and light brown fur. His shining black eyes stared into mine as I watched him.

We told the clerk that this was the one, and I showed him the trembling puppy. A surprised expression appeared upon his small face. But he said "O.K.," and off we went with proud looks on our faces.

That was the beginning of a friendship between my dog and me!

Bethany Anderson
Grade 4

My Hero

My hero is my brother. He sticks up for me whenever I need him to. There is only one special thing that separates us, that is the fact that he is African-American. People don't seem to understand that we are the same as any other brother and sister.

I always miss him when he goes on trips to places like Cincinnati and New York. When he is home we always play video games, and it's fun even though he always beats me. He always makes me laugh and smile no matter what mood I'm in. He always takes me to the movie theater and things like that.

My brother is my hero because he always finds time in his life for me. That is why my brother is MY HERO.

Paula Smith
Grade 5

My Role Model

Hi, my name is Felisha Freebern and I have a role model. My role model is Hannah Girard. She is funny, nice, and has a lot of friends, and one of them is me!!!

I have chosen Hannah as a role model because she is exciting, nice, uplifting, and really good at sports. She loves to play basketball, soccer, softball, and go swimming. Also, during the summer we play kickball.

She always seems to be in a good mood. I'm always happy when I am around her. Hannah has blonde hair and blue eyes, and loves to laugh. She is in Miss McLaughlin's class along with me and we are good friends.

Hannah is my friend, and my role model. After reading this, I'm sure you will understand how much fun we have!!

Felisha Freebern
Grade 5

Debate

A debate is going on in my family about getting a dog or not. It involves my mom and dad against my brother and me. We're for getting a pet, but my parents think the opposite. My brother and I are encouraging my parents that it will bring us closer as a family. We think it will teach us responsibility.

Having a puppy will bring my brother and I closer. We will be spending time together. We would take turns cleaning up after the puppy. Then we could play together with the puppy. You can sit around and watch us. We would end up being together more.

I think you would be teaching us a lot more responsibility. Since I'm older I could show my brother what responsibility is. He would learn that you have to put the puppy first, and then do what you want. Saving money for his food and toys teaches us also.

We know that taking care of a puppy is a lot of work. We are old enough and determined to take on this difficult job. It would be good for us. So please take the time and think it over. It would be a big job to take care of a puppy. My brother and I will take good care of the puppy. When the puppy gets older it will be harder for my brother and I to take care of it and feed it too.

Erin Rainey
Grade 5

Treat Our Earth Well

Have you ever been taking out the trash and noticed you have too many bags? The most reasonable response to this problem is that probably half of the trash in your bags should be in the recycling bin. Just think: all those recyclables that could be made into something else are going to the landfill, where they will never be used again. Most people throw away newspapers, but if you recycle them, you could be reading a brand new newspaper that was once your old newspaper.

Try using the three R's: reduce, reuse, recycle, and don't be the big W, waste! Most people know how to reuse and recycle, but reduce is a tough one. If you have cans; "squish" them so you can reduce the volume of your recyclables.

Littering, don't even get me started! Every time I walk out to the bus stop, there are at least two pieces of litter in our yard. It is one thing to litter in your own yard, but to litter on somebody else's, now that is just wrong.

When you need another sheet of paper, make sure that you have written on the front and the back of your paper. Remember, paper comes from trees, and trees are very important in our environment. I hope that my essay has made you think more of our planet. Treat our Earth well!

Alison Decker
Grade 5

My School

The name of my school is the Alfred Zimberg School. People also call it P.S.2. My school is very big. It has a lot of classrooms, a big gym, and a big courtyard. This school has a lot of records to its credit. The teachers here are nice and they help the kids do creative stuff. I like the school very much. The school's principal, assistant principal, and the teachers work very hard for the maintenance of discipline and good studies of the school.

The Alfred Zimberg School has a lot of opportunities for their students, even though this school is nearly a century old. The students still love this school and go to it. I know the school's principal is proud of himself for being the principal of such a great school. The children get a chance to win awards in events like the science fair, Halloween parties, and also some quizzes. There is going to be a laser light show in this school. I have been eagerly waiting for this show and to display my science project at the science fair. This school also has a lot of programs, like Hanac after school program, Saturday school to practice for the citywide tests, and also the clubs at 3:17 1/2 minutes.

This school has the perfect opportunity for me. This school also has a big library. It also has a computer lab with over 30 computers. I just love my school. It's the best school I've ever been to.

Amolbikram Singh
Grade 5

My Heroes

My heroes are my brother and sister. They are my heroes because they are nice to me. They care about me, and they are fun to play with. I can't always play with my mom or dad because they sometimes complain about their backs or the cold weather. If I play catch with them, they often quit before the game is done.

My brother and sister also help me with my homework. My sister helps me with my math; my brother can't help because he is too little. If I don't understand something, my sister helps me. I help my little brother with his homework. Sometimes my mom and dad help, but they don't always know what I have to do in math.

My brother and sister are nice to talk to. If I'm sad, I will talk to them. If I would have to pick my heroes, I would choose my brother and sister. If you have a brother or sister, you should talk to them.

The last reason why my brother and sister are my heroes is because if they were not here, I would have to do all the chores! If they were not here, I would be lonely. I'm glad that I have a brother and sister. Life would be very boring without them, my heroes.

Hunter Cook
Grade 6

Playing for the Love of the Game

One of my heroes is Gerry McNamara. He plays college basketball for Syracuse University. His position is point guard and he leads the team at the foul line. Gerry is known for his three pointers. Most of his fans refer to him as GMac.

Have you ever heard of or seen Gerry McNamara on ESPN? Well…if you have, you already know that he is an amazing basketball player. I play basketball and I try to get tips from him. Unfortunately, this is his final year at Syracuse because he's graduating. Gerry is my hero because he is an excellent player and is respected by tons of people. His determination and unselfishness also contribute to why he is my hero. For example, when Syracuse is losing, Gerry never gives up and plays his hardest. He demonstrates unselfishness when he gets his teammates involved. He also is one of the leaders for assists in college basketball. Gerry's former coach said that he could have easily scored 30 points a game, but he'd rather include everyone.

In conclusion, I believe Gerry is a wonderful role model for children today. He once said in an interview that he wanted to be remembered as a good person not just as a great player. His two goals were to win a national championship and to graduate from college. By the end of the year he will accomplish both. Gerry McNamara plays for the love of the game, not for fame. He will be remembered!!!

Nicole Campbell
Grade 6

Christopher Columbus, What Was He Trying to Prove?

Christopher Columbus was born in 1451 in Genoa, Italy. Genoa was on the water so growing up he probably spent a lot of time around the water. He was a dreamer. His dream was to sail to the East.

A lot of people think that Christopher Columbus was trying to prove the world was round. He knew this was true. Christopher Columbus was trying to find a short way to the Indies. He started to sail on August 3, 1492 with three ships, The *Santa Maria*, *The Pinta* and *The Niña*. He did not have motors on his ships. He had to use compasses and the stars to direct his ships. Christopher Columbus had to talk the men into continuing after three weeks. The men were afraid because no one had ever been out to sea that long.

He made several trips to America. On his fourth and final trip he took his 13 year old son Ferdinard. Ferdinard had a lot of friends to play with. Christopher Columbus liked to sail with young healthy boys instead of old men. He died May 20, 1506.

I think Christopher Columbus was brave. Many people probably thought he was crazy because of what he believed in. He believed he could prove them wrong and he did! I hope I can be like Christopher Columbus and be brave enough to stand up for what I believe in.

Matthew Hottle
Grade 4

I Will Never Stop Playing Soccer

Soccer is a good sport to get lots of exercise. Sometimes it is mostly running and kicking. If you want to play soccer you need good skills. You need to be able to score goals, get past all the defensive players, and especially, know a lot of tricks. People also need to have good sportsmanship. For example, be nice to other players, and if you lose the game, don't be mad.

Do you really like soccer? It's a hard sport. You need good pride, you need to like the sport, and practice every day. Sometimes you may fall, get hurt, or break something, but the sport is fun. There are four possible positions: offense, defense, middle field, and goalie. They are all hard to play. Some positions are harder than others.

If you want to be a good player, you need to make every practice and game so you are a part of the team. You should practice every day so you can get better. You should be very fast so that you can run the entire field. If you are slow, someone can take the ball from you. Soccer is one of the best sports in the world. When you play this sport it can help you to stay in shape.

Carlee Gonzalez
Grade 4

Kelly Clarkson

Kelly Clarkson is 23 years old, and was born on April 24, 1982 in Burkeson, Texas. Her favorite singer is Reba McEntire. Kelly graduated from Burkeson High School in 2000. Kelly originally wanted to be a marine biologist, but she changed her mind when she saw the movie, *Jaws*. Kelly worked at different jobs. She sang in shows at amusement parks. She also worked as a waitress and a drugstore clerk.

In 2002, Kelly moved to Los Angeles, California with one of her friends. She landed a tiny role on an episode of *Sabrina, the Teenage Witch*. Kelly moved back to Texas and her friend, Jessica Huggins, signed her up for an audition on *American Idol*. Kelly was one of 10,000 people to audition for *American Idol*. On September 4th, 2002 Kelly was voted the winner on *American Idol*.

Kelly has been nonstop since she won *American Idol*. Her first album, *Thankful*, opened at #1 in its first week, and has sold 2 million copies in the USA alone. Kelly has toured the world, filmed a movie, and has had 3 #1 hits with her first album. She was nominated for a Grammy with her first album, but did not win. Her 2nd album, *Breakaway*, was released on November 30th and has gone on to sell 4.7 million copies. Kelly Clarkson has won two Grammies for her 2nd album. "Since U Been Gone" won for best female pop vocal performance, and *Breakaway* won for best pop vocal album.

Paige Conroy
Grade 5

My Dog

Did you know that dogs are intelligent and helpful animals? My dog is exactly like this. My dog's name is Seathu. Seathu is a boy. Seathu's breed is a Labrador Retriever mixed with an unknown dog. Labrador Retrievers were first discovered in England. Seathu is an astonishing and adorable dog.

Seathu had three other brothers in the shelter. His three brothers had a glistening black coat with a white spot on their belly. Seathu also has a white spot on his belly, but he has a gleaming golden coat. I adopted Seathu from a shelter called Bide-A-Wee, which is located in New York. My dog is twenty pounds right now. He is four months old. Yes, he is still a puppy. Seathu has amazing qualities. He knows if you're sad, mad or any type of mood you are in. He can especially sense fear. Seathu has many fantastic qualities.

Seathu is a better dog and more affectionate dog because I got him from the shelter and didn't buy him. I think it is better to buy a dog from a shelter because it can reduce the amount of dogs dying and they would be more helpful and trustworthy, but this is my opinion. Others might feel the opposite. I believe a dog from a shelter is better than buying a dog.

Seathu is a great and humorous dog. Dogs are grand and are creatures that are amazing to mankind. Labrador Retrievers are magnificent dogs! Seathu is a stupendous dog!

Kevin George
Grade 6

For Horses' Sake

My name is Hali Hetz, and my favorite hobby is horseback riding. I love being in the saddle or even on the horse riding bareback, with no saddle at all. As long as I'm on or around horses, I'm OK.

My mother was pretty much addicted to horses when she was alive. I hardly knew my mom before she died, but by pictures, memory and the small barn in front of our old house, I know that horses were among her best friends. She passed away from cancer on April Fool's Day when I was two.

My mom tried to make a baby book for me, but there were mistakes hidden in it everywhere, at least two or three on every page because she was sick and slowly dying when she was making it. She was very creative and had brown curly hair just like me.

I remember riding one of mom's horses with her when I was a toddler, probably when I first became interested in horses. Before she died her horse had a baby, mom named her Mystique and gave her to me in memory of her. Mystique is a black thoroughbred and is about the same age as me, 10 years old. She is living near the border of New York, so I don't see her often. Mystique is both a horse and a good memory of my mother. I love her, for horses' sake.

Hali Hetz
Grade 5

Branches of Government

The branches of government are split into three parts. They are the Executive branch, the Judicial branch, and the Legislative branch. The three branches are different and do different work, but are equal in a way.

The Executive branch is very important. The President runs the Executive branch. It is also run by the Vice President and the cabinet.

The Judicial branch is also important. There are three important parts in the Judicial branch. They are the Supreme Court, the Federal Court, and the Court of Appeals. These courts are used to tell if you broke the law or owe money. There are many uses for courts.

The Legislative branch is also interesting and important. The Legislative branch is split into two parts, the Senate, and the House of Representatives.

There are many important facts about the three main branches. Did you know that the Executive branch can suggest laws and carry out laws? Did you also know that the Judicial branch decides the laws and whether laws have been broken? Did you know the Legislative branch makes the laws. All together the three branches work together as a team.

In conclusion, the three branches are very important. Although these branches are different, they are equally the same. That is called checks and balances. They are used to make sure the three branches are not over powering each other.

Stephanie VanNess
Grade 5

Pandas and Polar Bears

This is an essay on pandas and polar bears. I will tell you their comparisons and contrasts. This will be 4 paragraphs.

Pandas and polar bears both are actually bears. They wanted to have the panda a raccoon, but they saw it was a true bear. They both have white on them. Both of their heads are white. Polar bears and pandas are carnivores.

I'm telling you the contrast of the polar bear. The polar bear lives in Arctic Canada and in Alaska. They eat walruses and young seals. Polar bears are great swimmers. They have a waterproof coat. They can be found near the water or up on the tundra but that is not all the time. Polar bears are 7-11 feet long.

I'll tell you the contrast on pandas. They are up to 5-6 feet long. Pandas eat bamboo. They live in Central China and they live where there is bamboo and in the forest. Pandas are an endangered species. There are about 1,000 left. Panda's weight is 175-275.

That is my essay on pandas and polar bears. They have a lot in common. They mainly have a lot of differences. Pandas and polar bears are my favorite animals!!

Lindsey Bodiker
Grade 6

What Makes Me an Individual?

Being an individual means to be unique. It means to be different, being yourself, standing out, not always doing the same thing, and being special. Three ways I am an individual is that I have three sisters, we all take dance, and I broke my arm.

My three sisters are Haley, Michelle, and Rae. Rae is my little sister. I have to share a room with her. She always talks in bed. Michelle is older than me. We get along pretty well. Haley is my oldest sister. She sometimes gets on my nerves. Haley is fourteen, Michelle is twelve, Rae is eight.

My three sisters and I love to dance. My teachers are Miss Becky and Mrs. Angelique. We all take tap, ballet, and jazz. Haley and Michelle also take pointe. They are on an elite dance team too. I am going to try out next year.

Not many people break their arms, but I have. It hurt a lot. I am still not sure how I broke it. One day I went to dance class, there were about four or five people who had casts on! I was really surprised.

I am really lucky to have three sisters. They love and care for me like they did when I broke my arm. They also teach me new steps for dance and they help me learn them. It is great to have sisters who enjoy the same hobby as I do. I love my family.

Jillian Francis Wessel
Grade 5

My Cool Trip

One night I was talking to my friend down in North Carolina and she asked me if I wanted to go there to visit. I asked my mom and dad if I could go and they said yes. I told my friend and we were very happy. So I packed my clothes and stuff.

My mom or dad couldn't bring me so my friend Luke's mom and dad let me sleep over at their house until morning. We got up at 4:00 am because we wanted to get through the traffic and left at five. We drove a lot of miles and stopped at Cracker Barrel to eat dinner. After dinner we went to a hotel to stay until the morning. Then my friends from North Carolina came to pick me up and we went to their house.

When I walked into the house it was amazing and beautiful. There were 3 bathrooms, 3 bedrooms, and a nice bonus room with a 49" flat screen tv. Their dad has a new Silverado. They had an oval shaped pool with a shallow and deep part. I went in the deep part. We played every day except when they had to go to school. We went on bike trips, played Nintendo, walked to the bus stop and went to a place that I did not know. We did a lot of walking. My legs were in pain when we stopped. On the last day, I left at 4:00 am and went home.

Jason Higinson
Grade 4

Flute

Musical appreciation can turn people's hearts to God when their ears hear "joyful noises." Playing the flute is instrumental for me participating in this process. The first purpose I play is to relieve stress. The second motivation is that it has taught me that I am special. Finally, it is to bring people closer to God. Playing the flute has made a big impact in my life.

A great way to relieve stress and relax is listening to the flute's sound. I like to listen to the flute. When it goes through my ears it sounds peaceful and relaxing. It feels good to my soul.

The flute has taught me that I am special. In the orchestra, a flute is needed to keep all the high notes in the unique place where they should be. Learning how to play the flute has allowed me to make friends with people that have the same special interest.

Playing the flute can bring people to God. People love to hear music, and if they hear it they might be drawn in. People who are having a hard time might be able to listen to me play. For instance, if a person has cancer they might not be able to do much. In playing music they can listen and might seek their creator.

The flute has been a large influence in my life. Playing the flute relaxes me, helps me feel important, and glorifies God. Now, I am off to play more "joyful noises!"

Daniel Johnson
Grade 6

Kate and Me

I have a dog named Kate. She is black with a little bit of white on her nose. She is about ten years old. Kate used to belong to my next door neighbor, my Uncle Bill. She had to be chained up so she wouldn't run away. But when Uncle Bill died, I adopted her.

Now she lives inside the fence around my house. Sometimes she gets out of the fence, but I never know how. I can just call her name and she comes back and licks me on the face. But other times my brother has to pick her up and carry her back. I think that she gets out to search for Uncle Bill, but she never finds him. I miss Uncle Bill just as much as Kate does. Sometimes I think I know exactly how she feels.

When I leave for school she always kisses me, so I hug her and kiss her goodbye. When I walk away, I can hear her whining. Later when I come home, Kate barks and jumps up on me. When I play with her, she lays down and wants me to rub her belly or scratch her head. She loves it when I do that. Kate enjoys running around the yard and running up the bank. When she does that it makes me laugh a lot. I'm very happy that she is my dog. I love my dog, Kate, and she loves me, too!

Laura Kincer
Grade 4

A Big Surprise

One day I went to see my brother's soccer game with my mom. It was pretty boring, but I never guessed what was coming next. My dad was leaving work when he called my mom on her cell phone. Once she was done talking, I asked, "Mom, what were you talking about?" She said that Dad wasn't going to make it to the game. I didn't know why, but I didn't ask too many questions, I just sat and tried to enjoy myself.

Finally, the game ended. As we were getting into the car, I couldn't help wondering why Dad couldn't make it to the game. "What could he possibly be doing?" I had no idea what he was REALLY up to, but I had a better idea when we got home. I walked through the door, looking for Dad. When he wasn't there, I called Mom. She quickly replied, "He went to the pet store."

"Why would he go to the pet store?" I wondered. We only had one animal, a cat named Dixie, but we already brought her home.

As I was getting into bed, I heard a strange noise. Slowly, I got up and inched toward the sound. There, lying on the floor was a tiny, grey kitten. I picked her up, and carried her to my room. I named her Misty. And I have loved her ever since.

Melissa Schneider
Grade 6

Who I Look Up To

Do you have someone you look up to? Do you have any siblings? I have someone I look up to, and a sister. Actually my sister is the person I look up to. My sister's name is Natalie Michele Reid, and her birthday is January 10, 1988, and as you can see, she is 18 years old. Natalie is a senior at Notre Dame Prep High School. Next year she will be attending Yale University; she will also be playing lacrosse there.

My sister is the person I look up to because we have the same interests. She is smart, has a sense of humor, and is one of the nicest people you will ever meet. My sister and I have the same interests by having the same sense in style, and we love lacrosse. I also look up to my sister because I can count on her for advice, because she has already been in situations I am going through now. Another reason why I look up to her is because the school she goes to and the one she will attend for college are academically some of the best in the state, or country. One more reason why I look up to Natalie is because she is a good athlete.

My sister has had a huge impact on my life. I don't think I would be me without her. I'm glad I am blessed to have her by my side, especially when times get tough.

Caroline Reid
Grade 6

Buddy Trouble

My fat cat, Little Bud or as we call him Buddy, is just like a kid brother, but furrier. Don't get me wrong, my human brother is o.k., but since he is older, he just gets on my nerves.

Buddy talks a lot. Especially after he got new treats from my uncle. We can't get him to shut up! Buddy is a good cat. Except the one time he stood on the island in the kitchen. My dad walked out of the bathroom, and chased Buddy around the kitchen with a rolled up newspaper. Bud never did that again.

We were all packed for our vacation at my grandparents. I was worried about leaving Buddy home alone. It was going to be his first time without my family. I looked for him everywhere in my house, but I couldn't find him. I sat on the couch crying. When my brother asked me what was wrong I told him Buddy was missing. We heard a sound from the attic. We climbed the stairs to the attic. I slowly opened the door, hoping it wasn't a mouse. To our surprise it was Buddy. I was so ecstatic, that I forgot all about the whole trip. Buddy had snuck into the attic when my mom was taking out all the suitcases. After that, I was once again wishing I wouldn't have to leave Buddy alone.

Tia Limbeck
Grade 6

Boogie Boarding

I've had lots of fantastic memories in my life, but this was one of my favorites. It all started out at the beach, with a blue boogie board, and an excited little girl.

This was the exciting day I was going to boogie board for the first time. My benevolent parents bought me a miniature boogie board. I scrambled into the water and dived onto my sky blue buoyant boogie board. Waves splashed against my face, I wiped my hazel eyes and began to swim like a fish. My dad helped me to get a little farther. I was definitely scared at first but my dad convinced me it would be fun.

Soon as I was far enough into the deep glimmering ocean I pushed off like a rocket. Before my eyes was a colossal, blue wave and it was not feeble at all. "Casey, turn around!" my mom shouted. Without anticipating I turned around fast and for a second I felt like I was flying. "Splash" I was back on the water.

I felt like I was a motor boat zooming across the water. I could see the land slowly emerging. My mom and dad were waiting for me and yelling "Casey, that is great, Casey!" on the hot yellow sand. All of a sudden sand was scratching my sunburned legs. Shells were pinching my cold toes like small crabs. "How was it, Case?" Connor said. I exclaimed "GREAT!" I was extremely elated and wanted to do it again.

Casey Sweeney
Grade 4

Becoming the Best You Can Be

If you want to be all you can be in basketball, read this essay and you might become a basketball player in no time.

Basketball is a great sport. Remember, it is just a game. When you are against competition, don't get mad because they are winning and there is only one minute left. If they win, don't take your anger out on a locker door in the bathroom. Just be good about it because you will have another chance to try to beat them.

Basketball is not just a game. It is mostly about learning and having fun with your teammates. The basics are to try dribbling the ball and shooting the ball in the basket. Next you learn not to double dribble and travel. Double dribbling is when you dribble and stop, then dribble again.

A travel is when you stop dribbling and then move both feet. Then you have to learn the positions on the court. There are two guards in front, a point guard, and then you have your two people underneath the basket. Those are the positions on the court.

Now you know all the steps an positions in basketball. Now you can be a great basketball player. I hope you try the steps and learn how to play basketball.

Nakita Matthews
Grade 5

Mattie

In sixth grade, my teacher decided to introduce my class to a young man she thought was amazing. She showed us his work and told us his story.

His name was Mattie. Mattie Stepanek. Ever since he was born, Mattie suffered from Dysautonomic Mitochondrial Myopathy. His body didn't always function properly so he needed many tubes, extra oxygen, a power wheelchair and more. He lost three other siblings to the same life-threatening disease and his mother also suffers from it.

"I'm glad that no one else has to go through this," he said in a WB54, Baltimore, MD news profile.

Mattie was able to do many things despite his disability. He had a fantastic gift for writing and was able to touch the hearts of many through his NY Times best-selling Heartsongs poetry book series. His poetry is about everything you can imagine.

Mattie wanted to be remembered as a "Poet, Peacemaker and Philosopher who played." His philosophy was "Remember to play after every storm."

Mattie's great legacy ended June 22, 2004 at age thirteen. But his message is making an impact every day. I'm glad that I took the time to read Mattie's books and listen to his message. He's made a difference in my life, becoming a role model and changing my perspective. He has made me more aware and motivates me to follow his ideas of peace and love. So all I can say is, "Thanks Mattie."

Veronica Zoeckler
Grade 6

The Red Panda: An Endangered Species

Many people don't think about endangered species, so many people wouldn't know much about the red panda. The red panda, smaller than the giant panda, is an endangered species. Other names for the red panda are Wha and Poonya.

The red panda resembles a raccoon in size and appearance. It weighs 3-6 kg (7-13 lbs.) This marvelous creature is usually red on its upper surface and black underneath. Its face is white with black "tear" tracks under each eye. It has a long, furry tail with alternating light and dark rings. They are good tree climbers and spend most of their time in trees.

The red panda lives in the bamboo understory of cool mountain forests. It is found in a mountainous band from Nepal through northern India and Bhutan and into China, Laos, and northern Myanmar.

The red panda eats bamboo, berries, mushrooms, and bark. It will also eat birds, insects, and small rodents. One of the primary predators of the red panda is the snow leopard.

The red panda is rare and continues to disappear. It has already become extinct in 4 out of 7 Chinese provinces where it was previously found. The major threats to red pandas are loss and fragmentation of habitat due to deforestation. Overall, red pandas are magnificent creatures and people need to take care of them so they don't become extinct.

Sundus Razzaq
Grade 5

My Family

My family is important to me because they are always there for me no matter what. Although we disagree and fight sometimes, we love each other very much. When I am down my younger brothers and sisters come to cheer me up. When I need someone to talk to I can go to my older brothers and sisters and my parents, for I know they will understand.

My family can be very loud (especially me screaming), but when it comes to doing morning prayer on Sunday morning we quiet down. During prayer we say sorry to the ones we have offended. At the dinner table we all sit down to eat but first we pray, and then we start to eat and talk about how our day was. After dinner my dad goes right to the chore list and tells everybody their chores. Although I do not like to do my chores, I have to do them no matter what.

On Saturday morning my brothers, sisters and I wake up to watch cartoons, but when my dad wakes up we shut off the TV and clean up the house. Saturday night we go to church. When we get home we watch a movie or two then we go to sleep. That is why my family is so important to me.

Marta Suazo
Grade 4

What Tae Kwon Do Has Done for Me

Tae Kwon Do helped me have self-control. It has built my confidence over the years. It helped me move to the next belt levels by learning forms, combinations, sparring and other exercises that are required. Tae Kwon Do taught me how to be a leader and not a follower. You have to lead by setting the example. It teaches me how to be patient. It taught me how to build and make new friendships. Tae Kwon Do has taught me how to stay focused and pay attention to what I am learning. By taking Tae Kwon Do I have participated in several tournaments and won 1st and 2nd place trophies because I knew my material.

Tae Kwon Do helped me get stronger by working out and practicing on a daily basis. It teaches me how to control myself with my punches and kicks. It helped me learn how to concentrate. It helped make me a better performer with the different challenges I am faced with. It taught me how to be a role model for the other children and my little brother Quest. It teaches me how to be a team player. Tae Kwon Do has taught me how to be a winner and to always give my best. I will continue to do my best. Not only am I a straight A and honor roll student, I am a black belt.

Chance Anderson Albury
Grade 4

Losing Weight

The BMI of a person, or body mass index, may vary from person to person. You could be born with a large BMI, but I'm here to give you a few tips on how to lose weight. The most important rule of losing weight is your diet. If you have four to five snacks a day, cut that amount in half, but don't double the amount of food in the snacks that you are still eating. Once you feel comfortable with your snacks, cut it in half again until you have one to two snacks a day. To make your body healthier you should double the amount of vegetables you have in a day. A lot of losing weight has to do with food proportion.

The other important part for losing weight is doing activities. If you love to work out at the gym go ahead. A good method, at working out at the gym is to go once a week, and once you feel comfortable with this method, work out twice a week. If you are consistent with this you will be in great shape. If you don't really know what you like then I would say the best way to lose weight is to play a sport. Sports are really great because your coaches will make sure you are committed, and if you slack with the work you do, then you should try sports because to do a sport you have to be committed. One of the most important rules is not to try to lose weight too fast because you will get overloaded and will not be a good experience for you. Getting in shape is not a fast change. It takes time, effort, and practice. So, try really hard keep in shape and have fun!!!

Erica Blanchard
Grade 6

Darfur

A two-year-old girl helplessly searches for her mother. Little does she know, her mom is one of the many victims of the genocide in Darfur. Darfur is a region in western Sudan. Significant human right abuse, such as killing, torture, and looting of property, has occurred. Over 1.5 million refugees have been internally displaced and 200,000 refuges have sought asylum in Chad. The Arab forces, Jungaweed, have killed more than 70,000 people.

People against helping these refugees say that they do not want to enter the state's sovereignty. They know that a country has a right to rule itself and they don't want to interfere with that. People also think that we should simply send peacekeepers. The other side of this debate believes in interference. The main step to getting peace is taking down the government and rebels, and then giving relief to refugees. That way more people will not suffer. Lastly, the best thing to do would be to work with multinational forces to rebuild Sudan. We cannot send peacemakers now because ever since we sent them they have been a liability. They are not armed and cannot defend themselves.

We should break the state's sovereignty because if innocent people are being killed we have the right to stop it. People have the natural right to live and be happy. If people don't take action soon an entire race might be wiped out. We need to save Darfur!

Sanjana Salwi
Grade 6

The Art of Drawing

Have you ever had a really big project that no matter how long it took, made you feel really proud? Well, that's exactly what drawing feels like. When I have a pencil in my hand, and a great idea, I just put that idea on paper and transform it into a great drawing. You can draw anything that you like. I like drawing people, but you can draw animals, landscapes, still-lifes and much more. Drawing is a fun, relaxing hobby that is about you!

When you draw, it is easier if you have an object or a person to draw. It becomes much more realistic. I prefer to draw by using a real form, but occasionally, I draw from my imagination. You can choose whichever is easiest for you.

Having a professional work of art of a professional artist to guide you also helps. I took C.I. Art at my school, and I once took an art class out of school, and they both helped me become a better artist. Professional artwork helps because it shows you all different types of of techniques, like shading, blending, or adding light. You can go to an art museum to see artwork done by professionals like Monet or Van Gogh and compare the different techniques used by the two.

Art is fun and interesting, and I enjoy it a lot! I hope that under the influence of me, you will one day try drawing or another type of art like painting, or calligraphy.

Katie Charney
Grade 5

Where's the Music?

Have you ever turned on your radio and had to turn it off because of explicit language? If so, you're not alone. Music has really taken a turn for the worse since the 60's, 70's and 80's when music used to mean something.

Many contemporary artists have started a trend of rapping about women, money, and drugs. They also sing about problems between themselves and other rappers. I think this is stupid because it gives children a mindset of how rappers live, which is mostly a lie. Many rappers have not done most of the things they rap about.

With today's music, kids have become more violent and sexually active. There are more thugs and gangsters out there destroying their community. This must stop!

I think artists should try to better the songs for the community and stop trying to just sell records. It is not enough to go and tell kids to stay away from drugs and stay in school, then write a song about the complete opposite. Kids listen to rap music and believe every word. They want to be like the rappers they listen to. I, too, enjoy hip hop music and some rap songs, but I feel some songs are just too much. Rappers today should tone it down and think about who is listening to their songs. Society would be grateful.

Brianna Bazemore
Grade 6

Mrs. Best in the World

If you were to ask me who my favorite teacher is, it would take me less than a half of a second to say her name. Her name is really Mrs. Winkelstein, but the name that really describes her is, "Mrs. Best in the World."

She was my 2nd grade teacher. Mrs. Best in the World would take as long as you needed to get you to understand something. For example, one time I did not really understand something we were learning in math. Mrs. Best in the World spent her recess time trying to help us understand. For a week, we were writing math problems on the carpet with chalk. She also thought of fun ways to teach us things that were boring. To remember the states, we sang a song that had the states in alphabetical order. By the end of the year, everybody knew the song by heart. Also, when we read out loud from our reading anthology, if we finished reading a sentence perfectly with no mistakes, we got a piece of candy. It gave us a reason to want to read better.

I don't think that I'd be as good at reading or math as I am today if it was not for Mrs. Best in the World. By now, just by hearing very few of the cool things she does, you can understand why Mrs. Best in the World/Mrs. Winkelstein was my favorite teacher ever!

Ande Sabo
Grade 6

The Best Invention

Although the Romans took a lot of ideas from the Greeks they were some of the greatest builders of the time and great at many other things too. They even had their own architecture and learned how to make buildings with columns and arches. They improved the arch by making the dome.

Romans also made new building materials. One of the new materials was concrete, which they made by mixing lime and soil, that hardened when it dried. The Romans used concrete to build huge structures like the Coliseum.

To connect every part of their empire with Rome. Romans built miles and miles of road. The roads reached from one end of the empire to the other. The roads were built from 100 A.D. to 150 A.D. The Romans' roads were designed to last forever. They were made of heavy blocks, made from layers of crushed stone. Roman roads stopped being used around 110 years ago.

As the Roman Empire grew, the Latin language stretched to all parts of the empire. Latin is the basis for the languages of French, Spanish, Portuguese, and Romania. All of those languages are called the Romance languages. Even the German and English languages have some Latin words. Most of the Europeans used the original Latin Alphabet. The Greeks borrowed their alphabet from the Phoenicians. The Greek alphabet was then borrowed by the Romans.

Although most people in ancient Rome did not know how to read or write they accomplished all of these things.

Brandon Fafard
Grade 6

My Dog, Oscar

My dog, Oscar, is important to me because he is fun. My dog has very soft fur. Also, he really likes to eat. Finally, he is gentle.

My dog is fun. I get toys and throw them down the hallway, and he chases them. Most of the time, Oscar gets the toy and runs away from me. He doesn't like to play long though.

Oscar has very soft fur. His fur is shiny. He is cuddly because his fur is long and soft. When I pet him, his fur relaxes my hand.

Oscar really likes to eat. We give him a half of a cup of dog food twice a day. He begs for food a lot. In between his dog food meals, we give him a little bit of green beans and carrots.

My dog, Oscar, is really gentle. When we take him on walks, he doesn't run at all. He likes to lay down, and he does not run very long.

I appreciate playing with Oscar, and he likes playing with me. Oscar is my friend. When I'm bored, he is there to play with me. That's why Oscar is important to me.

Jessica Canonge
Grade 4

All About Me, Kimberly!

Hi! I am going to tell you all about me, Kimberly! I hope you enjoy my essay. Well, here I go!

My name is Kimberly Tran. I was born on November 24, 1995 in Boston, Massachusetts. I am 10 years old and I'm in 4th grade. My teacher's name is Mrs. Zaino. She's awesome!

I am a diligent worker. I don't mean to brag but I got straight A's on my report card last year in 3rd grade. My favorite subject is math because it is challenging but also fun.

I play soccer too. I've been playing since I was 8 years old. In the winter, I play indoor soccer because you know you can't play soccer in the snow. HA! HA! HA! Right now, my team is in 1st place. Can you believe it?!

The language that I speak is Vietnamese. I speak English too, but you probably already knew that! People think I'm Chinese but I always tell them I'm Vietnamese. They *still* don't listen!

Last but not least, I'm going to tell you one of my favorite hobbies. I dance. I dance to hip-hop and…mostly that's it! My other hobbies are playing soccer and collecting stickers. I know collecting stickers is weird but I think it's cool.

I hope you had a wonderful time reading "All About Me, Kimberly!"

Kimberly Tran
Grade 4

Sydney Language

Sydney waits as I enter the door, with butt stuck to the ground, and back straight up. Like I am the treat she gets when she waits for me, she tries to lick me furiously. I hang up my jacket and my backpack, as she springs on her hind legs trying to get high enough to get my face or knock me down from my knees. She leans back far and hits her head. It sounds like someone is trying to crack a rock on the ground. She shakes it off and gets back up. Trying to climb from the ground onto me like an ice climber, as I bend down to say hi, she succeeds. She licks me like she never wants me to leave.

When I sit with Sydney she is peaceful, has no worries, and stays perfectly still when I stroke her smooth red fur and try to move her to make her more comfortable, she remains in the position like a stuffed animal.

When Sydney wants me to run around or stroke her, she scratches my sock and tries to take it off as if saying, "Hey, over here, remember me, the cutie?" When no one pays attention to her, she amuses herself; swats a ball, chases after it, catches it and then the game begins again like a circular path with no ending.

The way she interacts with me is in her own language, Sydney language, but I understand every word she is saying.

Matt Downey
Grade 5

Can Pet Over-Population Be Prevented?

Did you know that every time a child is born in America, there are also 15 dogs and 45 cats born?

This problem is called over-population. Both dogs and cats are over-populated, meaning there are too many and not enough people to care for them. There is a way to help prevent over-population that is harmless and easy.

The way to prevent over-population is to spay or neuter your pets. To spay/neuter is to give your pet surgery, removing the reproductive organs. This prevents your pets from having babies.

There are many benefits of spaying/neutering your pet. These benefits are both physical and emotional, and may also be healthier for your pet.

"Fixed" pets will be less aggressive and more affectionate. There is also less chance of your pet being fat and lazy. Neutering reduces inappropriate urination and territorial issues.

Pets that are *not* spayed or neutered tend to roam, searching for a mate. If they travel on highways, they might get hit by a car. Animals also have less chance of becoming ill with cancer, which can cost a lot of money for treatment.

If fewer animals are born, more will have a good chance to find a home. They don't have to fight to live. Sometimes these "wild" dogs and cats carry diseases and can infect or attack other pets or people.

Pets give us unconditional love. We should love them back and do what is best for them. Everybody should spay or neuter their pet.

Patricia Edwards
Grade 6

My Summer Vacation

For my summer vacation we went to Pensacola Beach, Florida. As soon as we got there we went straight to the beach.

The second day everyone wanted to rest from our long drive, but my Pap and I decided to ride bikes around the villa. We rode clear to the next neighborhood where he used to live before Hurricane Ivan. Everything was destroyed, it was so sad. After all day riding we were ready to rest up for the next day of fun.

That morning we got up early to go to the beach before it got too hot. When we got there we rode jet skis, played on the beach, swam in the ocean and then had lunch. We went back home, relaxed for awhile then got ready to go back to the beach to watch a band and dance. Finally, around 11:00 we went to go to sleep.

The next day we were headed back home. Then that was the end of our trip.

Evelyn Dillie
Grade 5

Kind Words

I'm writing this essay so all of us can learn a lesson about kind words. Did you know that if someone is sad you can just say a kind word and their lives will brighten up right away?

Imagine you're a garbage collector collecting garbage at five o'clock in the morning. How would you feel if no one said "hello," "thank you," or "good morning?" In my opinion I would feel sad, doing such hard work and never hearing a kind word or two.

If you see someone collecting charity on a corner or in a subway, and you don't have a nickel or dime, at least give him/her a smile or kind word, like "good luck." Your kind words and facial expression will leave a lasting impression.

If you're shopping at the grocery, and your cashier is not in the best mood, why don't you say a kind word or two to cheer him/her up. It will probably work, because good moods can be contagious.

If we work on using kind words, then we'll see more happy faces in the streets. So, I'd like to send a message to anyone who reads this: please try to give at least five minutes of your time, saying "hello" to anyone you meet.

Tzivya Hadassa Beck
Grade 4

My Exciting Cruise to the Caribbean

My family and I went on our first cruise to the Caribbean in May of last year. The ship we cruised on was called the Voyager of the Seas. There were over three thousand people aboard. The ship is 1020 feet long and 138,000 gross tonnage. That's almost three football fields in length. As we were driving to the shipping dock we were able to see the ship off in the distance. I couldn't believe how big the ship was compared to the other ships in port. It was such a site to see.

When we boarded the ship I was so amazed how beautiful the ship was inside. As the ship left from Cape Liberty, NJ, we had a perfect view of the Statue of Liberty and the Empire State Building! That evening we sat down to a delicious dinner in a very grand dining room with a view of the sea. The next morning we all went to explore the ship. My family and I swam in the pool, relaxed and explored the ship until we came to our first port of call.

The first stop was Labadee, Hispaniola. We all relaxed on the beach that day and enjoyed a cookout. The island was so beautiful and the water was crystal blue. Some of the other ports of call were, Ocho Rios, Jamaica, George Town, Grand Cayman, and Grand Bahama Island, Bahamas.

We all had a great time on our cruise. We enjoyed wonderful food, spectacular shows, and even ice skating. The weather was fabulous and the ocean was so blue. I really had a great time and can't wait to go on another cruise.

Breanna Vosburg
Grade 6

Ring-Tailed Lemurs

Were you ever watching TV and see a furry animal with a longer tail than its body? Did you wonder what it was? If you did, the answer to your question is the Ring-Tailed Lemur. Ring-Tailed Lemurs and every other kind of lemur live on the island of Madagascar. They are very interesting creatures that have to live in a certain habitat and have a certain diet.

Ring-Tailed Lemurs are furry creatures that have very long tails which can be 14-22 inches in length, while their body is 12-18 inches in length! They have a very thick, grayish coat on their backs and a lighter grayish color on their stomachs. They weigh 5-8 pounds and often walk on all 4 feet but at times walk on only 2.

Ring-Tailed Lemurs live on the southwestern part of Madagascar and some neighboring islands. They live in mixed deciduous forest and gallery forest. They also live in the dry, bush forest. All lemur species are threatened by habitat loss.

Ring-Tailed Lemurs have to have a certain diet. In the wild this diet includes fruits (including figs and bananas), leafy vegetation and seed pods. Their diet is very different in zoos. In zoos their diet includes primate chow, fruits and vegetables.

Ring-Tailed Lemurs live 20-25 years but the longest living lemur lived to be 33 years old. Did you know that lemur means ghost in Latin and the scientific name for lemur is Lemur Catta?

In conclusion lemurs live an interesting life in the wild but sadly are endangered because of loss of their habitat.

Lura Mazurek
Grade 5

Dinner with a Musician

Jimi Hendrix went down in history for his unique guitar playing. He was born on November 27, 1942 and started playing guitar as a young boy. Jimi Hendrix began to write his own songs and he had his own band. He became so famous because he used guitar techniques such as feedback and distortion in ways that no one had ever thought of or done. He wrote many songs and was very passionate about guitar all of his life. Unfortunately, he died at the young age of twenty-eight.

If I could choose anyone famous to have dinner with I would choose Jimi Hendrix because I love to play guitar and I started it when I was young too. I also admire how unique his guitar playing was. I would ask him how much he would practice every day. I would also ask him if he ever got frustrated when he was trying to play a difficult part, and if he had any advice on how to stay motivated when it didn't sound just right. He has inspired me to keep playing guitar.

Lauren Bleyaert
Grade 6

Ballet vs Football

There are a lot of things that are alike and there are a lot of things that are different. This is called comparing and contrasting. I'm going to compare and contrast ballet and football.

I'm going to tell you four reasons why football and ballet are the same. In both you have to wear specific clothing. Girls and boys can both play football and both can do ballet. In both sports you have positions. You have to really concentrate in both of them.

Now I'm going to tell you four reasons why the two sports are different. They both wear different shoes. You have to wear padding in football. You have to throw a ball in football, you don't use a ball in ballet. In football you score points.

Ballet and football can be very different. Ballet and football can be a lot alike. In some ways they're different and some ways they're alike. So don't be surprised if your two topics are really different. Or, you might be surprised and they could be very similar.

Brittany Eakin
Grade 6

Technology and Communities

Could technology in America be hurting the development of close communities? A close community is important because if you know your neighbors, it develops trust, which means you can rely on a variety of people to help you if you have a problem.

In today's world do we talk too much on cell phones? If people would spend time together without cell phones constantly interrupting their conversations, then they could really get to know each other and develop close relationships. Maybe that's why kids have best friends and adults don't, because kids don't have constant interruptions.

People have become less patient because technology allows everything to happen right away. Cell phones, e-mails, faxes and digital cameras produce instant results. Commercials advertise the "quickest" services because Americans want everything immediately, so when we get in a situation where you may *have* to wait such as in traffic jams or grocery lines, people become impatient and rude.

Do we look at too much of our lives through a camera lens? A few photos are nice to document a vacation but it takes away from the enjoyment of the experience if you are constantly taking pictures. You end up looking at the vacation through a camera lens and not really living it.

Technology is important, but it can become overused, annoying and can prevent people from really listening and sharing with each other. Maybe limits on technology would make everyone slow down and get to know one another, which would create a closer community.

Laura Brillman
Grade 5

Early to Sleep and Early to Rise, Makes a Man Healthy, Wealthy, and Wise

Going to bed early and waking up early is important for humans for many reasons. First I would like to address that evolution ensures healthiness if you go to bed at sunset and wake at sunrise because we weren't supposed to invent the light bulb. Since the world was meant to function this way it would be much easier if we did.

Also recognize that many famous people have become successful through this sleeping habit. These people include Ben Franklin and Albert Einstein. Franklin, who said the quote above, always made sure he went to bed at sunset and in the summertime usually wouldn't go to bed any later than eight to eight-thirty. Sports players also often do this because sports are best in the daytime.

Lastly, studies show that people who use this pattern, are more active and friendly. This is thought to be because activity is best in daylight and friendship is often weary at night because people become irritable when they get tired. Most everything can be done more effectively, efficiently and thoughtfully in the daytime so we should go to bed and wake up earlier.

These reasons, evolution, fame, and happiness are only one more way to prove that the healthiest sleep pattern for a human is early to sleep and early to rise. So if currently it is after hours for you right now…go to bed!

Andrew Linzer
Grade 5

Who Is Important to Me

The first thing that is important is my family. They are important to me because they support me and they take good care of me. The other reason that my family is important is because we always spend time together and we always pray for everything. They are also important to me because I am always with them and anytime I need help they are always there to help me.

The next thing that is important to me is school. School is very important to me because I need education. I also need education because I need it to get somewhere in life. Another reason I need education is because when I get older I need to find a job and you have to have an education when you are looking for a job.

The other thing that is important to me is food. Food is important because I can't live without food because I can die. Food is also important because it makes you stronger.

Another thing that is important to me is sleep. Sleep is important because when I go to school I can't be tired. I can't have a good education if I go to school to sleep. Sleep is very important for everyone, because even older people who work need to sleep because of their jobs.

Cristal Munoz
Grade 4

When I Grow Up

When I grow up I want to be a scientist. I will start my own business. To start my own business I will build a building. Also I will hire nine people, and to hire them I will put an ad in the paper. When I work in this same building, I will discover a lot of things. I'll buy the equipment I use, like microscopes. I will also cure some sicknesses.

I will build a big building, with ten rooms in my yard. Then the nine people I have will each have two people in a room with them. Also, I will buy all my equipment that I will need. I will buy it over time.

Then, when I get better at using the equipment, I will cure sicknesses. Also, when I am a little better I will discover different things, like different gems, stones, and different types of germs.

That is what I want to be when I grow up. Also, what I will do when I work there.

Matthew Spirowski
Grade 5

Index